Handbook of Design Research Methods in Education

This *Handbook* presents the latest thinking and current examples of design research in education. Design-based research involves introducing innovations into real-world practices (as opposed to constrained laboratory contexts) and examining the impact of those designs on the learning process. Designed prototype applications (e.g., instructional methods, software or materials) and the research findings are then cycled back into the next iteration of the design innovation in order to build evidence of the particular theories being researched, and to positively impact practice and the diffusion of the innovation.

The *Handbook of Design Research Methods in Education*—the defining book for the field—fills a need in how to conduct design research by those doing so right now. The volume is organized in eight sections:

- Design Research and Its Argumentative Grammar
- Modeling Student Learning During Design Research
- Modeling Teacher Learning Using Design Research
- Modeling Stakeholder Commitments Using Design Research
- Reflecting on Design Research at the Project Level
- Reflecting on Design Research at the Program Level
- Extending Design Research Methodologically
- Tracking the Diffusion of Design Research

The chapters represent a broad array of interpretations and examples of how today's design researchers conceptualize this emergent methodology across areas as diverse as educational leadership, diffusion of innovations, complexity theory, and curriculum research. This volume is designed as a guide for doctoral students, early career researchers and cross-over researchers from fields outside of education interested in supporting innovation in educational settings through conducting design research.

Anthony E. Kelly is Professor of Educational Psychology, College of Education and Human Development at George Mason University, and former Program Officer at the U.S. National Science Foundation.

Richard A. Lesh is the Rudy Professor of Learning Sciences and Chair of Learning Sciences at Indiana University.

John Y. B enter for Advancement of Informal Science
Educatio

Handbook of Design Research Methods in Education

Innovations in Science, Technology, Engineering, and Mathematics Learning and Teaching

Edited by

Anthony E. Kelly
George Mason University

Richard A. Lesh
Indiana University

John Y. Baek
Center for Advancement of
Informal Science Education

Routledge
Taylor & Francis Group

NEW YORK AND LONDON

First published 2008
by Routledge
270 Madison Ave, New York, NY 10016

Simultaneously published in the UK
by Routledge
2 Park Square, Milton Park, Abingdon, Oxon OX14 4RN

Routledge is an imprint of the Taylor & Francis Group, an informa business

Typeset in Sabon by Swales & Willis Ltd, Exeter, Devon
Printed and bound in the United States of America on acid-free paper by
Sheridan Books, Inc.

Library of Congress Cataloging in Publication Data
Handbook of design research methods in education : innovations in science,
technology, engineering, and mathematics learning and teaching / edited by
Anthony E. Kelly, Richard A. Lesh, John Y. Baek.
   p. cm.
   Includes bibliographical references and index.
   1. Experimental design—Handbooks, manuals, etc. 2. Science—Study and
teaching—Statistical methods—Handbooks, manuals, etc. 3. Education—
Statistical methods—Handbooks, manuals, etc. I. Kelly, Anthony E. II. Lesh,
Richard A. III. Baek, John Y.
   QA279.H34 2008
   001.4'2—dc22
   2007052715

ISBN 10: 0–8058–6058–4 (hbk)
ISBN 10: 0–8058–6059–2 (pbk)
ISBN 10: 1–4106–1794–7 (ebk)

ISBN 13: 978–0–8058–6058–0 (hbk)
ISBN 13: 978–0–8058–6059–7 (pbk)
ISBN 13: 978–1–4106–1794–1 (ebk)

Contents

PART 9
Tracking the Diffusion of Design Research   509

Figures

Tables

Preface

This handbook describes an emerging methodology in education known as design research, whose goal is to synergize the study of learning and teaching at the intersection of design processes and research methods. Design processes are systematic, creative, dynamic, generative, and directed at solutions to real problems; whereas, research methods are systematized, rule-governed, tied to standards of evidence and warrant, and directed at establishing principles, theories, and laws. As the marriage of these approaches, design research holds great promise for promoting innovative educational solutions and discovering new knowledge in existing and engineered learning environments. Successful design research uses design processes, grounded in contexts of use, to inform and to be informed by the practice of research methods in order to develop principles, heuristics, models, and theories about design in learning and teaching settings.

Design research uses design processes to foster an open-ended, generative, and creative set of activities that bring into being innovations directed at challenges facing learners, teachers, administrators, and researchers. Innovations can include practices, products, artifacts, technologies, and general procedures that successfully empower and move a system closer to its own unfolding ideas of excellence (Kelly, 2003). Design processes can be enacted at each level of educational improvement from identifying problems and challenges, brain-storming potential solutions, developing prototypes, iteratively improving the prototypes, conducting confirmatory studies on local impact, to studying implementation at scale and documenting the process of the diffusion of innovations. Indeed, an entire program of design research activity can be considered the object of study in design research (Bannan-Ritland, 2003); for example, see Clements, Roschelle, Tatar and Kaput, and Martinez Peterson, Bodner, Coulson, Vuong, Earl, and Shaw (all this volume).

Within the larger design process, design researchers attempt to discover how students, teachers, administrators and researchers learn through the process of investigating the iteratively engineered environments in which people function. Design researchers are interventionist-observers. They draw upon existing and emerging models of learning and (often) the affordances of new technologies to perturb learning and teaching so as to document, measure, and theorize about the way the participants in the learning environment respond. Design researchers come from a variety of backgrounds: instructional design; learning sciences; neuroscience; statistics; science, mathematics, and technology education research; educational leadership; and curriculum development (e.g., Design-Based Research Collective, 2003).

We hope that this handbook will inspire many researchers to consider the marriage of the divergent character of design processes with the convergent constraints of basic and applied educational research as the fertile ground for exploring solutions to and the reconceptualization of education at all levels.

The goal of this handbook is to use examples of design research (at the student, teacher, administrator, researcher, and methodologist levels) to guide interested researchers as they consider adopting some of these emerging methods in their work.

Methodologically, many authors have begun the important work of moving design research from a focus on model formulation to model estimation and validation (Sloane & Gorard, 2003). They have begun to outline an argumentative grammar for design research so that the model of argumentation that undergirds design research can be drawn separately from the particulars of each design research study (Kelly, 2004). The authors reflect on the design choices they make, dynamically, during their work, the logic of the methods and procedures used, as well as the impact and the consequences of these choices.

For the purposes of this book, design research is inclusive of terms like design-based research, design experiments, or design studies in education. Three special issues in top educational research on design research were published within months of each other: *Educational Researcher* (Kelly, 2003), *The Journal of the Learning Sciences* (Barab & Squire, 2004), and *Educational Psychologist* (Sandoval & Bell, 2004). In addition, a Dutch volume on educational design research has appeared (van den Akker et al., 2006). We hope that the current book serves to grow the foundation for this exciting progress in educational research and development.

Support from this book came primarily from a US National Science Foundation-supported project aimed at clarifying the nature of principles that govern the effective use of design processes in framing and guiding research around educational innovations and improvement (Kelly & Lesh, 2001; NSF-DRL: 0107008). This volume extends the work from a prior NSF grant, the results of which were published in *The Handbook of Research Design in Mathematics and Science Education* (Kelly & Lesh, 2000). The current project supported a series of mini-conferences (three in Santa Fe, one in San Diego, and one in Fairfax, VA, at George Mason University), in which leading thinkers in education, engineering, and business contributed a variety of perspectives on the topic of design research.

In Part 1, Introduction, the chapter by Kelly, Baek, Lesh, and Bannan-Ritland was written based on an analysis of the chapters in the book. It explores some of the identified themes of the book. In some cases, authors of chapters supplied abstracts. We often found that we could not improve on their words, and in some cases we have reproduced verbatim extracts. We are grateful for the clarity of their prose.

In Part 2, Design Research and its Argumentative Grammar, the authors reflect on design research at a general level in order to explicate some of the principles and practices that provide the growing foundation for design research in education as a methodology.

In Part 3, Modeling Student Learning During Design Research, the authors illustrate design research studies that place a strong emphasis on how modeling how students think and learn can guide the processes of design, redesign, and knowledge claims.

In Part 4, Modeling Teacher Learning Using Design Research, the authors illustrate design research studies that center on how modeling how teachers think and learn can enable new approaches to teacher professional development.

In Part 5, Modeling Stakeholder Commitments Using Design Research, the authors show how design research methods may be used to model the multi-stakeholder and multilevel resource issues in play during actual decision making in organizations.

In Part 6, Reflecting on Design Research at the Project Level, the authors show how critical stock-taking during and at the end of a design research project can highlight design decisions that can deepen the systematic inquiry into design processes, and add to the lessons learned.

In Part 7, Reflecting on Design Research at the Program Level, the authors explain insights from extended design research programs that have lasted many years and that have experienced much change over the course of multiple cycles of design and redesign.

In Part 8, Extending Design Research Methodologically, the authors go outside of current design research practice to find frameworks from other research methods that might provide models to better estimate the effects of iterative design research on learning.

In Part 9, Tracking the Diffusion of Design Research, the authors view design research itself as an innovation and describe how its growth and development would be considered an object of study in the diffusion of innovations literature.

References

Bannan-Ritland, B. (2003). The role of design in research: The integrative learning design framework. *Educational Researcher*, *32*(1), 21–24.

Barab, S. & Squire, K. (eds) (2004). Design-based research: Clarifying the terms [Special issue]. *Journal of the Learning Sciences*, *13*(1).

Design-Based Research Collective (2003). Design based research: An emerging paradigm for educational inquiry. *Educational Researcher*, *32*(1), 5–8.

Kelly, A. E. (ed.) (2003). The role of design in educational research [Special issue]. *Educational Researcher*, *32*(1).

Kelly, A. E. (2004). Design research in education: Yes, but is it methodological? *Journal of the Learning Sciences*, *13*, 115–128.

Kelly, A. E. & Lesh, R. A. (eds) (2000). *Handbook of research design in mathematics and science education*. Mahwah, NJ: Lawrence Erlbaum Associates.

Kelly, A. E. & Lesh, R. A. (2001). NSF-DRL: 0107008.

Sandoval, W. A. & Bell, P. (eds) (2004). Design-based research methods for studying learning in context [Special issue]. *Educational Psychologist*, *39*(4).

Sloane, F. C. & Gorard, S. (2003). Exploring modeling aspects of design experiments. *Educational Researcher*, *32*(1), 29–31.

van den Akker, J., Gravemeijer, K., McKenney, S. & Nieveen, M. (eds) (2006). *Educational design research*. London: Routledge.

Acknowledgments

This book was prepared with support from the National Science Foundation to Anthony E. Kelly and Richard A. Lesh (NSF-DRL: 0107008). The opinions expressed in these chapters are those of the authors and do not necessarily reflect the opinions of the National Science Foundation.

The editors are grateful to Audrey Pendergast, who served as the professional copyeditor. Christina Blue provided additional editorial assistance.

Eamonn Kelly and Richard Lesh offer their sincere appreciation to each of the following conference participants for their far-reaching and thoughtful contributions, and their warm collegiality:

Santa Fe I, December 2001: Bob Anderson, Brenda Bannan-Ritland, Sasha Barab, Philip Bell, Sandra Berry, Peter Bryant, Lupita Carmona, Kefyn Catley, Woodie Flowers, Shane Gallagher, Stephen Gorard, Michael Helfrich, James O'Kelly, Leah Kelly, Catherine Lewis, Joanne Lobato, James Middleton, Bruce McCandliss, Patrick O'Neill, Dan Reed, Donald Saari, Richard Shavelson, Barry Sloane, Susan Stucky, Curtis Tatsuoka, Chris Taylor, and Raul Zaritsky.

Santa Fe II, March 2002: Bob Anderson, Brenda Bannan-Ritland, Sasha Barab, Brigid Baron, Philip Bell, Sandra Berry, Peter Bryant, Lupita Carmona, Kefyn Catley, Paul Cobb, Jere Confrey, Shane Gallagher, Stephen Gorard, Mindy Kalchman, James Kelly, Ashling Leavy, Richard Lehrer, Catherine Lewis, Joanne Lobato, Michael Matthews, Bruce McCandliss, James Middleton, John Nash, Priscilla Norton, James O'Kelly, Patrick O'Neill, Roy Pea, Everett Rogers, Leona Schauble, Barry Sloane, Emma Smith, Curtis Tatsuoka, Chris Taylor, Patrick White, and Raul Zaritsky.

Santa Fe III, January 2003: Bob Anderson, Brenda Bannan-Ritland, Peter Beck, David Brazer, John Cherniavsky, Paul Cobb, Bruce Colletti, Peter Engstrom, Ellen Goldberg, Manuel Gomez, Tom Gruber, Vicky Inge, Jim Kaput, Robin Kellar, Catherine Lewis, Joseph Maxwell, Peter Mulhall, Nancy Robert, Nora Sabelli, David Skyrme, Curtis Tatsuoka, Chris Thorn, Etienne Wenger, Raul Zaritsky and Judi Zawojewski.

San Diego, September 2003: Brenda Bannan-Ritland, Lupita Carmona, Paul Cobb, Allan Collins, Jim Dietz, Barry Fishman, Shane Gallagher, Dan Hickey, Joanne Lobato, and Raul Zaritsky.

George Mason, September 2004: Brenda Bannan-Ritland, John Baek, David Carraher, Douglas Clements, James Dearing, Jim Dietz, Margaret Eisenhart, Shane Gallagher,

Eric Hamilton, Margret Hjalmarson, David Kaplan, Mani Le Vasan, Joanne Lobato, Ridzuan Bin Abdul Rahim, Chris Rasmussen, Barry Sloane, and Raul Zaritsky.

Most especially, the editors would like to thank the reknowned philosopher, Stephen Toulmin, for taking the time to sit down for an individual interview to discuss the logic of argumentation, August 2002, in Los Angeles.

Part 1

Introduction

1 Enabling Innovations in Education and Systematizing their Impact

Anthony E. Kelly
George Mason University

John Y. Baek
Center for Advancement of Informal Science Education

Richard A. Lesh
Indiana University

Brenda Bannan-Ritland
George Mason University

Introduction

Design research in education is directed at developing, testing, implementing, and diffusing innovative practices to move the socially constructed forms of teaching and learning from malfunction to function or from function to excellence (Kelly, 2003). In this way, the open character of design together with the self-imposed constraints of research are placed in service of the growing demands of society for citizens and knowledge workers who can add to and take advantage of emerging technologies and the explosion in scientific knowledge.

Although some policy-makers view the need for improved human capital as primarily a vehicle for supporting national competitiveness (Committee on Science, Engineering, and Public Policy, 2007; Domestic Policy Council, 2006), we view the development of talent among learners and productivity among teachers as a universal good, in concert with a motto attributed to President John F. Kennedy that, "a rising tide raises all boats." For this reason and because learning challenges are global, this book draws on both US and international contributions.

The preface of this book describes the burgeoning growth in scientific knowledge and the growing complexity of science as a practice, globally. How should educational researchers respond to these challenges so as to reengineer models of schooling that are little changed since the Industrial Revolution?

A central question for educational research is how to design interventions that move beyond describing "what is?" or confirming "what works?" to designing "what strategy or intervention might work better?"—especially in content domains with little prior research (Cobb et al., 2003). Or, more expansively, "what systemic reengineering of learning environments might work better to teach students and teachers to respond to the opportunities rapidly unfolding in modern science?"

Modern educational interventions must respond to new scientific knowledge emerging from technology-infused, internet-intensive, highly social, networked science. Given the pace of change, many educational researchers find inadequate guidance and theorizing from psychology or cognitive science or from the findings about the effectiveness of prior (but perhaps dated) interventions (e.g., Brown, 1992). As

McCandliss et al. (2003) argue, a collaborative dialogue among methods is needed that yields both internally and externally valid findings. And, we would add, a dialogue that responds to local resource demands and capabilities, including human creative capital.

We believe that the hybrid methodology now known as educational design research, which was initiated in education research circles in the early 1990s (e.g., Brown, 1992; Kelly, 2003) offers significant promise in this regard. Design research is characterized in this book, but other sources should be consulted for a more complete treatment (e.g., van den Akker Gravemeijer et al., 2006; Barab & Squire, 2004; Kelly, 2003, 2004, 2007). In this chapter, we wish to explicate design research by: (a) comparing its commitments to those of more traditional approaches, and (b) by illuminating the research themes across the chapters in this volume.

Commissive Spaces in Research Practice

First, we contrast the *commissive spaces* of more systematized research approaches to that of the newer design research methodology. Commissive spaces describe the background commitments, rules, and shared implicit and explicit values held by members of a community that permit and undergird the conversations and actions that define that community (Design-Based Research EPSS, 2006; Kelly, 2006).

To illustrate the commissive space of traditional research, examine the orientation for framing of educational research that was outlined by the National Research Council:

> To simplify matters, the committee recognized that a great number of education research questions fall into three (interrelated) types: description—What is happening? cause—Is there a systematic effect? and process or mechanism—Why or how is it happening?
>
> (2002: 99)

The commissive space within which these questions are posed and answered assumes (for those editors, at least) commitments to evidence, warrant, and methods that privilege the stance of the researcher-as-observer of some more-or-less remote phenomenon. The goal of answering these questions is to advance a field of knowledge by adding reliable observations, facts, principles, or descriptions of mechanisms to an existing and growing body of laws, regularities and mechanisms. The methods for achieving that goal (particularly for "causal" questions) include those such as randomized clinical trials, which value commitments to: (a) an a priori alignment with theory (if available), (b) rigorous elimination of competing explanations via random assignment to condition, (c) the identification and implementation of a known and describable "treatment" implemented with some desirable "fidelity," and (d) commitments to standardized (i.e., pre-existing) measures of achievement (see also, Coalition for Evidence-Based Policy, 2003). The immediate audience for such research findings is peer researchers, and to the extent that the research is "applied," the audience may extend to various interpreters, implementers, or users of the research, including policy-makers or practitioners.

Actors in this commissive space favor: (a) a convergence of observation, methods, and metrics with a priori stances, (b) a tendency not to pursue what appear to be tangential or emergent phenomena, (c) a proclivity to devalue context, and (d) a commitment to valuing the researcher's assumed objective stance over the subjective stance of the "subjects."

By contrast, while the design research commissive space shares many of the commitments of more traditional approaches, design researchers foreground the fluid, empathetic, dynamic, environment-responsive, future-oriented and solution-focused nature of design. Design researchers often recruit the creativity of students, teachers or policy-makers not only in prototyping solutions, but also in enacting and implementing the innovation, and in documenting the constraints, complexities, and trade-offs that mold the behavior of innovative solutions in contexts for learning. By observing and participating in the struggles of the design, and the implementation or diffusion of an innovation, design researchers may learn not only how to improve an innovation, but also how to conduct just-in-time theory generation and testing within the context of design processes and in the service of the learning and teaching of content.

Indeed, design researchers posit that more than a single theory may be required to describe, explain or predict the success or failure of an innovation (e.g., Lesh & Hjalmarson, this volume). On the other hand, in some cases, theoretical or modeling work will fail to provide an adequate account of the success or failure of an innovation, and the designer and users will "satisfice" and "work with" procedures and products that appear to be advancing shared goals even in the absence of final understanding (e.g., Bannan-Ritland & Baek, this volume; Barab, Baek, Schatz, Scheckler, & Moore, this volume). Such a result is often the case in medical practice in which drugs or other therapies have successful outcomes for which mechanistic explanations are currently unavailable. Moreover, innovations are sometimes suggested and revised on the basis of poorly articulated theoretical groundings, championed nonetheless by powerful stakeholders (e.g., Bannan-Ritland & Baek, this volume; Brazer & Keller, this volume).

Design researchers also embrace, in some form, the traditional instructional design ADDIE tradition (Analysis, Design, Development, Implementation, and Evaluation). However, they move beyond instructional design as craft knowledge toward understanding the know-how/know-why of the design (e.g., Clements, this volume). Since design researchers are co-designing the environments they are studying, they can gain insight into who might best deploy solutions or be likely to adopt them in practice (e.g., Ejersbo, Engelhardt, Frølunde, Hanghøj, Magnussen, & Misfeldt, this volume). They may also dynamically articulate what systemic and contextual resources are present or lacking (e.g., Cobb & Gravemeijer, this volume). It should be noted, however, that the principles of ADDIE still hold significant value for design researchers (see Barab et al., this volume). Moreover, the ADDIE model, itself, has become more complex over time (Clark, 2007).

Thus, design research inhabits and defines a commissive space of novelty tempered by research evidence that unfolds over multiple cycles within a study or across a program of studies (Bannan-Ritland, 2003), drawing, sometimes opportunistically from— and organistically adding to—many sources of information and knowledge. Design research attempts to: (a) help design innovations, (b) explain their effectiveness or ineffectiveness, theoretically, and (c) re-engineer them where possible, while adding to the science of design itself (e.g., Bannan-Ritland & Baek, this volume; Barab et al., this volume; Cobb & Gravemeijer, this volume; Kali, this volume; Martinez et al., this volume; Roschelle, Tatar, & Kaput, this volume). Design research strives to mine the massive "information loss" that can occur when interventions are designed "off-line" and applied with little revision, and with little attention to the causes of failure or success. Within this larger frame of design processes, design research draws, when appropriate, from the strengths of other research traditions, and multiple approaches to assessment.

Larger Framing for Design Research Studies

We want to stress that design research methods are a work in progress and are not advocated as a panacea for promoting and developing educational innovations. As has been stressed from early work in this field (e.g., Bannan-Ritland, 2003; Clements, this volume), design research methods make sense at some points in a larger developmental process but not at others.

The Integrative Learning Design Framework (ILDF: Bannan-Ritland, 2003; Bannan-Ritland & Baek, this volume) provides one overarching structure within which to position design problems, selected methods, and design moves in the design research process. By acknowledging the fluid, dynamic, evolving nature of design in design research and the many layers of decisions and judgments required in design (cf. Brazer & Keller, this volume), the ILDF encourages design researchers to consider other factors beyond theoretical conjectures. The generation and refinement of theory, the selection of research questions, methods, and design features become integrated with pragmatic processes of design (see also, Barab et al., this volume).

As a second example, Clements (this volume) describes the Curriculum Research Framework (CRF), which consists of ten phases of the development research process that warrant claiming that a curriculum is based on research. While Clement sees a role for design studies, he recognizes that other research and development strategies are necessary to meet the goals of a complete curriculum research and development program. As has been noted, elsewhere (e.g., Kelly, 2003, 2004, 2006), design studies are unable to control many variables in complex settings; rarely analyze in full the large amount of data collected before the next cycle of revision, enactment, and analysis takes place; and may value different data from the perspectives of different participants. As a result the paths and products may be arbitrary to an extent and generalization may be difficult.

Clements argues that randomized trial experimental designs provide some of what design studies cannot. In addition, he notes that the use of phases in the a priori foundations and learning model categories of the CRF provide useful constraints and theoretical groundings for design experiments. Conversely, design experiments, as well as other methods such as teaching experiments and classroom-based teaching experiments, can help accomplish what randomized trials cannot (Kelly & Lesh, 2000). These methods include conceptual and relational, or semantic, analyses, and are theoretically grounded. They allow researchers to build models of learning and of teaching interactions. Ultimately, as Clement elucidates, because it includes a coherent complement of methods, the CRF has built-in checks and balances that address the limitations of each method, with concentration on the learning model especially useful for maintaining theoretical and scientific foci.

As a third example, for Middleton et al. (this volume) design research is analogous to engineering design. Among the necessary conditions for calling aspects of product development "design research" are the provision of a coherent model with an explicit chain of reasoning connecting the features of the innovation and the social and cognitive systems they purport to affect, and the development of methods and generation of evidence that have the potential to replicate and transport across studies and implementation settings. The design cycle for Middleton et al. draws on Bannan-Ritland (2003), and is presented as having seven distinct stages, beginning at conceptualization of the problem to be addressed and extending to market and revision of an actual product. These stages consist of: (a) grounded models, (b) development of artifact, (c) feasibility studies, (d) prototyping and trialing, (e) field study, (f) definitive test, and

(g) dissemination and impact. This is an augmentation of the "what works model" as applied to education in that it explicitly marks feasibility, prototyping, and field studies as distinct stages, showing that each contributes significantly to both the development of an hypothesized innovation, and to the education theory which is being built and tested.

Factors in Current Design Research in Educational Innovations

In the prior section we described how the commisive space that design research occupies differs from traditional research approaches. In this section we continue to explore the commissive space by highlighting what we consider to be the important themes in the current design research reported by the contributing authors. In providing this commentary of the work, we intend to illuminate some underlying factors that are necessary for designing and researching educational innovations. The core idea that provides the most resonance in the design research literature is the idea of iteration, the capacity and knowledge to modify the intervention when it appears not to work or could be improved. We have outlined below some of the bases on which design researchers decide to launch an iteration of some innovation. Some design researchers use a theoretical base, some use insights from measurement or instrumentation, others use input from team members or stakeholders and review combinations of these sources.

Iteration and Assessment

Assessment is a critical problem for design researchers since modeling learning during re-design cycles defines the approach: whether learning by students (e.g., Lobato, this volume; Cobb & Gravemeijer, this volume; Rasmussen & Stephan, this volume), teachers (Bannan-Ritland, this volume; Zawojewski, Chamberlin, Hjalmarson, & Lewis, this volume), policy-makers (Brazer & Keller, this volume), or researchers (e.g., Bannan-Ritland & Baek, this volume; Lesh, Kelly, & Yoon, this volume).

In design research as currently practiced, assessment is not directed at some summative sense of learning, though a summative measure of student learning would be central to later attempts at confirmatory studies, i.e. to show local impact (Bannan-Ritland, 2003). That being said, Hake (this volume)—arguing that physics education research is a genre of design research—uses gain scores in pre-post testing to validate his process model of causality (Maxwell, 2004). For him, assessment acts as a guide for improving the teaching and learning of physics, in a broad programmatic sense.

Design research also differs from formative assessment with regard to the student's knowledge end state and how feedback loops are enacted. Formative assessment is the gathering of data relative to some predetermined fixed point, providing feedback that informs the students and teacher of their current knowledge state in relation to some end state (see Black & Williams, 1998). In design research, assessment may be used formatively in order to dynamically determine progress toward mastery of disciplinary knowledge (e.g., Cobb & Gravemeijer, this volume) or to guide the design of a prototype and to inform its iterative re-design as necessary or both. In fact, sensitivity to assessment practices themselves may inform changes to the act of assessment itself (e.g., Lobato, this volume; Lesh et al., this volume). Ultimately, design researchers are challenging the assumptions about learning, teaching, and knowing that underlie available assessment techniques, not only in terms of the psychometric assumptions (like item response theory), but also the function of assessment itself within and across the stages of design research (see Sloane & Kelly, this volume).

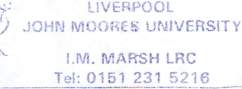

Assessment and Theory Building

Within design research circles, there is a debate about the status of theory generation and the centrality of theorizing in the design process (e.g., see Bannan-Ritland & Baek, this volume; Barab et al., this volume; Design-Based Research Collaborative, 2003; Middleton, Gorard, Taylor, & Bannan-Ritland, this volume). Theory acts in two different ways in design research: the theory of learning that is assumed by the researcher, and generation of theory through the process of design. Where do the theories used in design research projects come from? Though design researchers see the world through participant eyes, they are informed by relevant theory, pragmatically selecting the most relevant at the time. Theories may draw from studies of cognition, perception, motivation, neuropsychological function, interpersonal communication, or, more generally, from principles of social organization.

Decision points are not always informed by learner assessment. Pragmatic, political, and participatory factors can influence the decision to iterate. Being responsive to externalities, these factors emerge within a design context that is "ready" to listen and address them directly into the design (e.g., Wolf & Le Vasan, this volume).

Assessment and Teaching Experiments

To the extent that the assessments of learning-in-progress are explicit and rigorous and tied to disciplinary knowledge, they can also inform local instructional theory building (Cobb & Gravemeijer, this volume). The approach known as teaching experiments, particularly in mathematics education, have been documented elsewhere (e.g., Steffe & Thompson, 2000). More recently, teaching experiments have been reconceptualized within the more general framework of design research (Cobb & Gravemeijer, this volume; Cobb et al., 2003).

Cobb and Gravemeijer's chapter differentiates among three phases of a design experiment: (a) preparing for the experiment, (b) experimenting in the classroom to support students' learning, and (c) conducting retrospective analyses. The initial preparation phase is crucial to the success of the experiment and can be extensive, especially when there is little prior research on which to build. Key issues that need to be addressed in this phase include clarifying instructional goals by identify the central ideas in a particular domain and documenting the instructional starting points both by drawing on the relevant literature and by conducting initial assessments as part of the pilot work. In addition, it is essential to delineate an envisioned learning trajectory that consists of conjectures about both a learning process that culminates with the prospective instructional goals and the specific means of supporting that learning process. As they illustrate, the primary objective in the second phase of experimenting in the classroom is not to demonstrate that the envisioned learning trajectory works but to improve the envisioned trajectory by testing and revising conjectures about both the prospective learning process and the specific means of supporting it. This conjecture-testing process depends crucially both on the kinds of data that are collected in the course of an experiment, and on the adequacy of the analytic framework that is used to document both students' learning, and the evolution of the classroom learning environment. The intent of retrospective analyses conducted during the third phase of an experiment is to contribute to the development of a domain-specific instructional theory by documenting both a substantiated learning trajectory and the demonstrated means of supporting students' learning along that trajectory. This theoretical goal gives rise to a number of methodological challenges, not the least of which is to differentiate between aspects of the classroom learning environment that are necessary and those that are merely contingent in supporting student learning. The additional methodological issues that the authors consider include the trustworthiness, repeatability, and generalizability of the findings.

Assessment and Variation Theory

In this book, there are some attempts to tie assessment practices to some larger theory. For example, Holmqvist, Gustavsson, and Wernberg (this volume) show how student performance on brief, objective tests tied directly to a narrow set of concepts can guide the redesign of instruction, guided by *variation theory*, which grows from perceptual psychology (Gibson, 1986) and Bransford and Schwartz's (1999) *Preparation for Future Learning* framework. According to variation theory, learning occurs as a function of how attention is selectively drawn to critical aspects of the object of learning by the student. Teachers, as a function of their competence, may direct attention toward critical aspects (e.g., by using contrasting cases) or away from critical aspects and toward irrelevant aspects, sometimes to the students' detriment. For example, to learn the definition of the size of angles, the student should focus on the amount of *rotation* between the two rays defining the angle, rather than on the *length* of the rays themselves. A study guided by variation theory would, for example, examine both the teaching and the student learning of angles in order to determine if by selective attention or teacher (mis)direction whether the student was focusing on critical, irrelevant, or inaccurate aspects of the definition of an angle. Micro-analyses of classroom activities and of test-item performance would identify any misgeneralizations in response to teaching episodes, which would guide the re-design of instructional strategy or content (e.g., designing a lesson that showed that angle size was not dependent on the length of rays).

Assessment and Transfer

The chapter by Lobato examines design cycles in educational settings from the perspective of transfer of learning. In the traditional view, a learner is assumed to learn from one task, and apply (or "transfer") the insight to a second task that is similar (from the researcher's perspective, at least). The study of transfer of learning is described in detail in this chapter, in which the author outlines the major competing views (including Bransford and Schwartz's). According to Lobato's (2003) own view (that of actor-oriented transfer), the judgment of the "similarity" of the tasks must take into account the interpretations of both tasks by the learner, which may (from the traditional researcher's perspective) be viewed as non-normative or lead to incorrect performance.

As the actor-oriented perspective has matured, Lobato has tackled the notion of "mechanism" or more accurately how the generalization of learning experiences is brought about as a socially-situated phenomenon. She and her research team are investigating how the ways in which students generalize their learning experiences are related conceptually to the particular mathematical regularities that students come to notice in mathematics classrooms when multiple sources of information compete for their attention. The "focusing interactions" framework that they have developed allows them to document the social organization of this "noticing" behavior and coordinate it with psychological processes. The significance of this work for mathematics education researchers and teachers is found in the demonstration that the durable concepts that students generalize from instruction are influenced, not simply by the macro-level actions often recommended by reforms (e.g., use of collaborative groups, inquiry-oriented materials, or manipulatives) but also by many subtle micro-features of instruction that come into play as different mathematical foci emerge in classrooms.

Lobato's chapter raises important questions for educational practice in general, particularly questions of construct validity in the design of assessments of learning, both proximal and distal. Like Minstrell (e.g., Minstrell, 1992; van Zee & Minstrell, 1997), Lobato challenges educational researchers to consider the partial understanding of learners (given the learner's perspective and level of expertise) as part of a foundation upon which later learning may be built. Lobato's work raises questions not just about similarity of assessment tasks, but argues for a more forgiving scoring rubric, closer to Minstrell's "facets of understanding" model (see also the work of diSessa and colleagues: Cobb et al., 2003; diSessa, 1993; diSessa & Cobb, 2004).

Lobato's model also implicates features of instruction in the learner's (mis)conceptions about topics. Teachers may inadvertently draw attention to irrelevant features of the task or mislead learners by misconstruing central conceptual aspects during a lesson. Lobato terms this occurrence a "focusing phenomenon," which she describes in her chapter. The reader may wish to compare Lobato's treatment of focusing phenomena with the Holmqvist et al.'s (this volume) use of "variance theory" to inform re-design of lessons in their work.

IMPLICATIONS FOR DESIGN RESEARCH

Lobato's work has a number of implications for design research (which she began to spell out in Lobato, 2003). Her work challenges "humble theory" building in design research to identify which of the views of transfer of learning is assumed to be dominant during the design process. Each model of transfer has different implications for who has the privileged position in designing the artifact and on whose knowledge base to decide when it is time to revise the design. More generally, the design of the assessments both formative *and* summative should similarly reflect a commitment to a model of transfer, since design research strives to support not just achievement, but also learning to learn in new contexts.

Thus, Lobato's work has implications not only for early stage, prototyping, or discovery research, it also has implications for the design of assessments during more definitive testing (e.g., using randomized clinical trials) or later during diffusion stages of research (e.g., Bannan-Ritland, 2003).

Assessment and a Theory of Change

One goal of the design researcher is to build instructional artifacts that improve student learning. Sloane and Kelly (this volume) stress the importance of specifying a theory of learning (i.e., one based on changes in what a learner masters), rather than on a theory of achievement, which reduces learning to the attainment of an assumed terminal point. They encourage the use of models that can capture changes in learning over time that are qualitative, non-linear, or non-additive. They highlight some of the definitional features of change implicit in education research to guide design researchers as they move to quantify student growth over time. They note that the challenges posed to design researchers in modeling change afflict, equally, the modeling of change even by those with mastery of current statistical modeling formalisms.

Assessment and Learning to Learn

Given the emphasis on design processes in design research, some authors champion approaches to assessment that place the task of design squarely on the learners, be they students (e.g., Lesh et al., this volume; Roschelle et al., this volume) or teachers (e.g., Bannan-Ritland, this volume; Zawojewski et al., this volume). Lesh and his colleagues (e.g., Lesh & Lamon, 1992; Lesh et al. 2000) have argued for decades that assessment should fold back on the learner the responsibility for documenting growth toward and the construction of a solution. Thus, Lesh advocates the use of model-eliciting (or thought-revealing) problems, where the "answer" is a model or blue-print for solving a class of problems, not a single number. In Lesh et al. (this volume), the authors show how a similar approach to assessment can work in a multitiered fashion so that students' growth in modeling provides data for teachers' growth in modeling of student learning, which, in turn, provides data for researchers' growth in modeling both teacher and student learning.

The goal of design research in Lesh's model is to engage the participants in a study (including the researchers) in ongoing reflexive cycles of design and re-design, so that while there is an end-in-view for the study (and for learning), the constitution of that end-in-view and how progress toward constructing and measuring it is co-determined, primarily, by the learner. Stated differently, Lesh views assessment itself as a dynamic object of study and a primary driver within design research studies.

Assessment and Codifying Innovation or Efficiency

Schwartz, Chang, and Martin (this volume) are interested in the development of instrumentation as an effective way to help move design research from the construction of new possibilities to openness to tests of causality and generality. Their argument is that the creativity behind an innovation can be expressed via instrumentation, which then exists after the design research to support efforts at efficiency in implementation (on this point, see Martinez et al., this volume; Roschelle et al., this volume).

Similar to the approach suggested by Lesh and his colleagues, Schwartz et al. describe design research studies in which high school students are expected to invent a way to measure variability. They show that this demand for innovation later helps the students to learn efficient canonical solutions. For researchers, they demonstrate how developing a novel double-transfer instrument enabled the measurement of an important type of learning that conventional measures miss. By working on instrumentation, the researchers equip themselves with the tools necessary to replicate the experiment and measure their progress.

Finally, Schwartz et al. discuss the need for warrants of innovation by distinguishing between innovating knowledge and innovating practice. Both are goals of design studies, but individual instances of research often emphasize one or the other. One warrant for both types of innovation is based on the reconciliation of inconsistencies: a thing is recognizably new and innovative when it resolves a previous contradiction in knowledge or in social practices. This warrant relates to the idea of praxis, where a theory is proven by becoming a reality. They believe praxis is a highly relevant way of warranting educational research that seeks to create new ways for students to learn.

Both Schwartz and Lesh and their colleagues are concerned with developing in students the capacity to learn-to-learn, i.e. to learn to respond to challenges from outside the learning system. As our technological society continues to change and advance, new challenges and emergent phenomena will be the rule. Students should be adequately prepared to face the chaos and complexity of the world rather than shy away from it (e.g., Saari, this volume). The transformative goals of learning and education are set in design research: not to teach reading, but to build readers; not to teach mathematics, but to build mathematicians. Metaphorically, learning how to be a good traveler is as important as learning how to reach and enjoy Paris.

Assessment, Argument, and Collective Activity

One of the challenges facing design researchers is how to assess collective activity in a large group in order to determine if there is "general understanding" of some concept. As we have seen, many researchers view learning at the level of the individual. Recently, some researchers have begun to posit the argument that if classroom discourse appears to indicate that some new construct has become generally accepted in the group, then it can be taken "as-if-shared" by every member in the group, but without independent confirmation by the researcher at the member level.

Rasmussen and Stephan (this volume) developed a three-phase methodological approach for documenting the collective activity of a classroom community. Most interesting, they place the concept of collective activity on a strong footing by basing their method on the systematic use of Toulmin's argumentation scheme over extended classroom lessons. Toulmin's basic model of argumentation describes the structure and function of an argument in terms of four parts: the data, the claim, the warrant, and the backing. They developed the following two criteria for determining when mathematical ideas function as if shared: (a) when the backings and/or warrants for an argumentation no longer appear in students' explanations (i.e., they become implied rather than stated or called for explicitly, no member of the community challenges the argumentation, and/or if the argumentation is contested and the student's challenge is rejected), and (b) when any of the four parts of an argument shifts position (i.e., function) within subsequent arguments and is unchallenged (or, if contested, challenges are rejected). The usefulness of the methodology is two-fold. First, it offers an empirically grounded basis for design researchers to revise instructional environments and curricular interventions. Second, it offers an innovative way to compare the quality of students' learning opportunities across different enactments of the same intervention. They illustrate the methodology with an example from a first-grade class learning to measure and from a university course in differential equations. They conclude the chapter by discussing issues of the generalizability and the trustworthiness of the methodology.

Documentation

Documentation is the archiving and indexing of artifacts of the design research process that serves as a way of gathering evidence of the effects of design changes, and serves to inform re-design if changes to a prototype prove ineffective. The process of documentation embraces yet exceeds the function of assessment. Bannan-Ritland and Baek (this volume) identify the importance of documenting theoretical, opportunistic, political, and practical decisions. Documentation of the progress of design can not only make explicit the influence of factors that support and constrain effective practice, but may also serve as the basis for adding to a science of design (see also, Kali, this volume).

In their chapter, Barab et al., using a design narrative methodology, illuminate the challenges of designing a web-based community, the Inquiry Learning Forum (ILF). They highlight the design challenges and successes and advance some theoretical assertions in hopes that others may more fruitfully carry out their own design work. A challenging part of doing educational research on design-based interventions is to characterize the complexity, fragility, messiness, and eventual solidity of the design. All too often, designers simply report the ready-made structures, thereby obscuring or "black-boxing" the trajectories through which design decisions are made. This is problematic in that much of the theory generation process necessary to move from design work to design-based research occurs through an examination of these situated processes. Therefore, in helping others to determine the local utility of the derived theoretical assertions, a core goal of this chapter is to lay open and problematize the completed design in a way that provides insight into the "making of" the design. This process involves not simply sharing the designed artifact, but providing rich descriptions of context, guiding and emerging theory, design features of the intervention, and the impact of these features on participation and learning. The characterization of the ILF is intended to have both local resonance with the data as well as more global significance.

Multitiered Models for Teacher Professional Development

The chapter by Zawojewski, Chamberlin, Hjalmarson, and Lewis explores the use of multitiered design studies to support mathematics teachers' professional development while producing generalizable theory about the interpretive systems teachers use to teach. They describe the design of educational objects (e.g., an algebra lesson, a student problem-solving approach sheet) that support professional development while making explicit the interpretive systems of the teachers, professional development facilitators, and teacher education researchers who use them. Two examples of multitiered design studies are examined. In the first example, "student thinking sheets," teachers use, analyze, and re-design problem-solving approach description sheets that capture students' thinking about complex mathematical problems. In the second example, "lesson study," teachers design, teach, analyze, re-design, and re-teach a lesson designed to help students identify and mathematically express a pattern.

In both examples, a designed artifact simultaneously supports professional development while making teachers' and professional development designers' interpretive systems visible for study. Teachers examine classroom situations and their own interpretive systems, and researchers and professional development designers examine teachers' interpretive systems (as well as their own) in order to derive principles for professional development that may be transportable to other contexts. An auditable trail of artifacts from the professional development work is the primary data source, allowing researchers to focus on the actual performance of the professional work. The design study approach is argued to be well suited to situations in which participants are expected to grow and improve in different ways, rather than necessarily converge toward a particular standard. Further, the approach is argued to be well suited to situations in which teachers address problems that they themselves have chosen. The notion of design study is proposed as a means to embrace such diversity in systems where changes in one part of the system can reverberate throughout the system (e.g., teacher change leads to change in the professional development provider perspective, leads to change in the professional development materials and implementation, which influences students' learning, which impacts teachers' development, etc.).

Statistical and Other Modeling Formalisms

Along with theory building, design researchers also build instructional artifacts to support student learning. In the practice of design research, many students and teachers participate in multiple forms or iterates of the designed artifact or emerging practice, making it difficult to know which version of the artifact, or changed practice, caused the observed change or learning on the part of the participants. In their chapter, Sloane, Helding, and Kelly explore the possibilities for between-student modeling over time to work around the lack of a naturally occurring counterfactual in these emerging research designs, with the goal to improve the quality of warranted claims in design research.

Learning occurs in nested data settings: students in classrooms, or learning groups, or classrooms in schools, for example. These "nestings" create problems in conceptualization, design, and analysis. While much design research is qualitative in nature, Sloane (this volume) describe how quantitative researchers have begun to deal with nested data structures and the complexities of building theory and drawing inferences when data have this nested structure. In this chapter, the hierarchical linear model (HLM) is described and is shown to provide a conceptual and statistical mechanism for investigating simultaneously how phenomena at different organizational levels interact with each other.

Two themes in design research include the paths taken and not taken during the design process (Bannan-Ritland & Baek, this volume), and the relationship of parts to the whole intervention process that embrace but extend beyond the idea of nesting described in Sloane (this volume). In his chapter on modeling complexity, Saari (this volume) explores some of the potential applications of fractals, chaos theory, and other formalisms on understanding systems that cannot be accounted for with simple cause-and-effect descriptions. Both this chapter and the one by Hjalmarson and Lesh argue that perturbing a system, and predicting outcomes and measuring them is not neatly linear. Indeed, when the intervention becomes a part of and influences the system, the selection of a good control condition becomes difficult.

Tools to Build a Design Research Community

In addition to efforts to build a community of design researchers, such as exemplified by this book and the one by van den Akker et al. (2006), Kali's chapter proposes a mechanism (the Design Principles Database) to enable researchers to systematically add their design principles to a database of other lessons learned. The Design Principles Database encourages community building, in which researchers build on each others' knowledge of design, articulated as principles for design, to create new designs. Researchers explore the application of these principles in new contexts and bring their findings back to the network. In this manner, knowledge about design grows in the community, and design principles are debated, refined, or warranted with additional, field-based evidence.

Technological Affordances

Much is made of the affordances of technologies, with often extravagant claims about how each new technology will revolutionize education. Zaritsky's chapter discusses how affordances or features (in this case of DVDs) that might impress a developer may not influence learning as expected. Additionally, media grammars (cinematic techniques) were utilized in his project, but often went unnoticed by users. Zaritsky argues that small focus groups of prospective users of technology are highly informative about the likely impact of technologies and should be used more widely. In short, Zaritsky stresses the importance of confirmation of impact of technologies rather than enthusiastic presumption. In this way, we are reminded of the crucial step of the deployment, or implementation, of the design, as stressed by Ejersbo, Engelhardt, Frølunde, Hanghøj, Magnussen, and Misfeldt (this volume) in their osmotic model of design research.

Scaling and Diffusion

Scaling research looks at how innovations move from small to larger implementations, while being actively promoted by some external source. Diffusion research looks at how innovations are adopted, adapted, revised, or rejected as part of a social process among some identified community, often without direct external promotion (Rogers, 2003).

Brazer and Keller (this volume) provide a model to underscore how multiple stake-holders with different objectives support decision-making regarding innovations that are often at odds with and do not support the goals or desires of the innovators. Prioritizing the needs of different stakeholders in the system is often a political process, and can lead to retrograde consequences from the innovator's point of view.

Wolf and Le Vasan (this volume) argue that schools are not uniform organizations. Some may be fertile ground for adopting an innovative practice; others, for a variety of reasons (e.g., lack of administrative support, the press of academic testing) are not. They show that in doing design research in Singapore, it matters that a school, and its organizational climate, provide conditions for the innovation to survive among teachers. The authors provide an instrument that may be used to gauge the "readiness" of a school to be successfully involved in a design research project.

The chapter by Ejersbo et al. introduces an "osmotic" model to underscore the inter-play between designing and reflecting on theory. By the use of three examples, the authors demonstrate (as others do in this book) that actual design research projects are more complex and nuanced than simple descriptions might suggest. Of course, this remark applies equally to any research method, even stylized methods such as randomized field trials (e.g., National Research Council, 2004).

Drawing on a unique record of building toward the scaling of an innovation, Roschelle, Tatar, and Kaput (this volume) point out that neither traditional program evaluation research nor design research are adequate to the task of understanding how to bring an innovation to scale. Part of the problem is that there may be no prior adequate measure of success or that success may be defined differently in different settings.

The authors describe the research trajectory of *SimCalc*, an innovation that supports learning the mathematics of change and variation, as occurring in six phases, each moving successively closer towards a scaled project. The phases fit either into the con-text of design or the context of implementation. Most strikingly, they point out that over-specifying an innovation can restrict its adaptability, and consonant with Rogers (2003) they show that an adoptable vision cannot be too radically different from existing practice within the community of potential adopters.

Another unique long-term project that illustrates recursive cycles of development, intervention, and re-design of the intervention was conducted by the MIND Institute for a project called M + M (Math + Music) during the academic years 1998 through 2004 (Martinez, Peterson, Bodner, Coulson, Vuong, Hv, Earl and Shaw, this volume). The keyboard component was designed to teach basic musical concepts and skills necessary for playing the piano. Independently and in groups, students learned a reper-toire of progressively more difficult songs. STAR (spatial-temporal animated reasoning) software was designed to develop skill in transforming mental images to enhance spatial-temporal abilities and understanding of mathematics concepts. The transformations involve symmetry operations applied to two-dimensional figures. Other computer-based games challenged children to apply their spatial-temporal skills to solve mathematics problems in particular, problems involving fractions, proportions, and symmetries. The data show that a spatial-temporal approach to learning key mathematical concepts, allied with music instruction, can produce gains in proficiency with mathematics concepts and skills among children who are academically at-risk. Using a largely non-verbal approach to teaching mathematics concepts, the M + M intervention produced an overall benefit on mathematics achievement for participating second graders in comparison to control group students.

The cumulative findings of this multi-year research project imply that a large segment of students, perhaps most, could benefit from an approach to learning mathematics that appropriates spatial-temporal reasoning along with music training. The use of spatial-temporal reasoning and representations might hold special promise for English language learners because of its relative de-emphasis of language. The M + M project was not a static intervention, but instead evolved through feedback over the course of its implementation. In aggregate, the M + M project demonstrates the viability of the design research approach to educational interventions for advancing students' learning and the theories on which effective interventions are based.

Conclusions

We have attempted, by use of the device of the "commissive space" and this cross-cutting review of themes, to position existing and emerging discussions on research methodology in a climate of engagement and discussion. While we value critiques of all methods, we eschew criticisms that can only lead to sterile debate and provincialism. A review of the chapters in this book will illuminate the proposition that the scientific study of interventions in complex educational contexts remains in its infancy, but that visible progress is underway. We hope that the reader will find useful the highlighting of cross-cutting themes that differ from the nine-part structure of the book. In particular, we see the importance that assessment plays in guiding iteration in design research cycles. We also described: (a) the role of documentation in illuminating theory, (b) the availability of statistical models that match the messiness of design research projects, (c) the progression of knowledge as a design research field through use of database tools, (d) the testing of affordances as an integral part of design research, and (e) the issues of scaling and diffusion that impact how design research is implemented at higher levels of organization. What remains is the pleasure of reading the individual chapters of the many authors who responded to the general challenge: how may the processes of design and research intersect and cross-pollinate to advance education?

References

Bannan-Ritland, B. (2003). The role of design in research: The integrative learning design framework. *Educational Researcher*, *32*(1), 21–24.

Barab, S. A. & Squire, K. (eds) (2004). Design-based research: Clarifying the terms [Special issue]. *Journal of the Learning Sciences*, *13*(1).

Black, P. & Williams, D. (1998). Assessment and classroom learning. *Assessment in Education*, *5*, 7–74.

Bransford, J. & Schwartz, D. (1999). Rethinking transfer: A simple proposal with multiple implications. *Review of Research in Education*, *24*, 61–100.

Brown, A. L. (1992). Design experiments: Theoretical and methodological challenges in creating complex interventions in classroom settings. *Journal of the Learning Sciences, 2,* 141–178.

Clark, D. (2007). *Instructional systems design concept map,* at http://www.nwlink.com/~donclark/hrd/ahold/isd.html.

Coalition for Evidence-Based Policy (2003). *Identifying and implementing educational practices supported by rigorous evidence: A user friendly guide.* Washington, DC: US Department of Education, at: http://www.ed.gov/rschstat/research/pubs/rigorousevid/guide_pg5.html.

Cobb, P., Confrey, J., diSessa, A., Lehrer, R. & Schauble, L. (2003). Design experiments in educational research. *Educational Researcher, 32,* 9–13.

Cobb, P., McClain, K. & Gravemeijer, K. (2003). Learning about statistical covariation. *Cognition and Instruction, 21,* 1–78.

Committee on Science, Engineering, and Public Policy (2007). *Rising above the gathering storm: Energizing and employing America for a brighter economic future.* Washington, DC: National Academies Press.

Design-Based Research Collective (2003). Design-based research: An emerging paradigm for educational inquiry. *Educational Researcher, 32*(1), 5–8.

Design-Based Research EPSS (2006). *Interviews with design-based research experts,* at: http://projects.coe.uga.edu/dbr/expertinterview.htm.

diSessa, A. A. (1993). Toward an epistemology of physics. *Cognition and Instruction, 10,* 105–225.

diSessa, A. A. & Cobb, P. (2004). Ontological innovation and the role of theory in design experiments. *Journal of the Learning Sciences, 13,* 77–103.

Domestic Policy Council (2006). *American competitiveness initiative: Leading the world in innovation,* at: http://www.whitehouse.gov/stateoftheunion/2006/aci/aci06-booklet.pdf.

Gibson, J. J. (1986). *The ecological approach to visual perception.* Hillsdale, NJ: Lawrence Erlbaum Associates.

Kelly, A. E. (2003). Research as design: The role of design in educational research. *Educational Researcher, 32*(1), 3–4.

Kelly, A. E. (2004). Design research in education: Yes, but is it methodological? *Journal of the Learning Sciences, 13,* 115–128.

Kelly, A. E. (2006). Quality criteria for design research: Evidence and commitments. In J. van den Akker, K. Gravemeijer, S. McKenney & N. Nieveen (eds), *Educational design research* (pp. 166–184). London: Routledge.

Kelly, A. E. & Lesh, R. A. (eds) (2000). *Handbook of research design in mathematics and science education.* Mahwah, NJ: Lawrence Erlbaum Associates.

Lesh, R. A. & Lamon, S. J. (1992). *Assessment of authentic performance in school mathematics.* Washington, DC: AAAS.

Lesh, R. A., Hoover, M., Hole, B., Kelly, A. & Post, T. (2000). Principles for developing thought-revealing activities for students and teachers. In A. E. Kelly & R. A. Lesh (eds), *Handbook of research design for mathematics and science education* (pp. 591–646). Mahwah, NJ: Lawrence Erlbaum Associates.

Lobato, J. (2003). How design experiments can inform a rethinking of transfer and vice versa. *Educational Researcher, 32,* 17–20.

Maxwell, J. A. (2004). Causal explanation, qualitative research, and scientific inquiry in education. *Educational Researcher, 2,* 3–11.

McCandliss, B. D., Kalchman, M. & Bryant, P. (2003). Design experiments and laboratory approaches to learning: Steps toward collaborative exchange. *Educational Researcher, 32*(1), 14–16.

Minstrell, J. (1992). Facets of students' knowledge and relevant instruction. In R. Duit, F. Goldberg & H. Niedderer (eds), *Research in physics learning: Theoretical issues and empirical studies* (pp. 110–128). Kiel, Germany: Institut für die Pädgogik der Naturwissenschaften.

National Research Council (2002). *Scientific research in education* (R. J. Shavelson & L. Towne, eds). Washington, DC: National Academy Press.

National Research Council. (2004). *Implementing randomized field trials in education: Report of a workshop* (L. Towne & M. Hilton, eds). Washington, DC: National Academies Press.

Rogers, E. M. (2003). *Diffusion of innovations* (5th ed.). New York: Free Press.

Steffe, L. P. & Thompson, P. W. (2000). Teaching experiment methodology: Underlying principles and essential elements. In A. E. Kelly & R. A. Lesh (eds), *Handbook of research design in mathematics and science education* (pp. 267–306). Mahwah, NJ: Lawrence Erlbaum Associates.

van den Akker, J., Gravemeijer, K., McKenney, S. & Nieveen, M. (eds) (2006). *Educational design research*. London: Routledge.

van Zee, E. & Minstrell, J. (1997). Using questioning to guide student thinking. *Journal of the Learning Sciences*, 6, 227–269.

Part 2

Design Research and its Argumentative Grammar

2 The "Compleat" Design Experiment[1]
From Soup to Nuts

James Middleton
Arizona State University

Stephen Gorard
University of York

Chris Taylor
Cardiff University

Brenda Bannan-Ritland
George Mason University

Introduction

In this chapter, we articulate a methodology for design experiments and situate it within the larger cycle of design in educational settings, beginning with the initial conceptualization of design problems to the dissemination of educational products; hence, the impetus for the second part of our title: From Soup to Nuts. The term *design* is used by a variety of fields, ranging from art to engineering. In education, the type of research associated with the development of curricular products, intervention strategies, or software tools has been designated "design research" (e.g., Brown, 1992; Collins, 1992). In recent years, the number of investigators associating their work with this genre has become more prevalent in the literature and the focus of special issues in prominent journals about education, among them *Educational Researcher* (Kelly, 2003) and *Journal of the Learning Sciences* (Barab and Squire, 2004). This chapter contributes to the collective attempt of the field of education to clarify further methods of and perspectives on design research. Evidenced by the diversity of views incorporated in this book, ranging from product development to children as designers, it is clear that design research is a complex endeavor.

To begin our contribution to the conversation, we employ the theory of design from the engineering sciences as a useful analogy. Education research has been associated previously with an engineering process (as opposed to the sciences) by a number of prominent researchers (e.g., Cobb et al., 2003; Confrey, 2003). These research programs warrant revisiting the metaphors and analogies used to guide their work in design research. To a certain degree, a large portion of mainstream education research *is* engineering if what we mean by engineering is to design products and systems that solve problems of import to society.

This chapter describes the concept of design from an engineering perspective, touching on the distinction between design and artifact. The meat of the chapter (following the soup to nuts reference) presents a cyclic model of the overall design process and provides a detailed analysis of design experimentation and the role it assumes in the comprehensive cycle. Finally, we present an extended example of a program of research that conforms to our notion of design experimentation.

What is Design?

In the field of engineering, design is considered the essence of the profession. Engineers design. That is what they do. The emphasis of the word in this context is two-fold—relating to design as the practices of engineering, and designs, the intellectual products that those practices engender. As such, in the grammar that we are attempting to articulate, design functions as both a verb and a noun.

Design (the verb) is the creative process by which designer(s), considering a problem in their field of expertise, generate a hypothetical solution to that problem. Design (the noun) constitutes that general hypothetical solution, often embodied in material form (e.g., a blue-print or a physical model).

Design activity consists of a subtle but complex interaction between the designer and contextual constraints and is accomplished by proposing the *form* of an artifact, system, or process, which in turn drives its *behavior*, which in turn can be compared with its desired *function*. Because artifact, system, or process is cumbersome when repeated throughout a text, we will use henceforth the general term *system* to denote the ostensible outcome of a design except where a specific example is given. Both the form (proposed and at some point realized) and the desired function are hypothetical entities that are linked by a theoretical *model* (see Figure 2.1). In mechanical engineering, this model is called the *function structure*. The behavior of the system constitutes observable data. Therefore, the degree to which an artifact's behavior embodies its function can be considered a partial index of both: (a) the quality of the design, and (b) the degree to which the form of the system produced or served as a conduit for the behavior (Shooter et al., 2000). The iterative, design-and-test cycle that engineers use is critical for the transformation of both the form of the system and of its (intended) function to conform to the pragmatic demands of utility and market.

If education research were merely the development of teaching tools and techniques, or the progressive empirical movement of students' achievement toward the meeting of *standards*, there might be little or no emphasis on determining the adequacy and veracity of particular educational designs across contexts. The design cycle would consist of an entirely self-contained system, begun when a problem is encountered and finished when a product is refined to the extent that it solves a pragmatic problem and meets market demands. To a great extent, this approach epitomizes some product design cycles and traditional instructional systems design perspectives, at least in their implementation (Dick & Carey, 1990). Alternatively, many product development processes do incorporate significant testing throughout a systematic process of design and development (Urlich & Eppinger, 2000), and instructional design processes do support

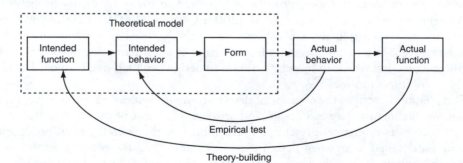

Figure 2.1 General Model of Design Research.

conducting evaluation of learner preferences, behaviors, organizational results, and return on investment in designed training or education systems (Kirkpatrick, 1998). However, in many cases, the focus of the design process is primarily on the development of an instructional innovation (e.g., software or an interactive multimedia system), and the design is rarely evaluated beyond learner preferences and surface-level reactions to the innovation (Tessmer & Wedman, 1995).

More current perspectives on the intersection of design research and instructional systems design attempt to extend the traditional systematic approach to emphasize further learning processes, data collection, and diffusion processes across a program of research that can inform the adequacy, veracity, and viability of the instructional strategies and the theoretical rationale embodied by a design (see Bannan-Ritland, 2003, for example). The distinction between the traditional instructional design process, product development, and design research, then, lies in the overt emphasis on *programmatic generation, development, and testing of a theory* of learning, instruction, or human factors as it relates specifically to design research (cf., Shavelson et al., 2003). This shift in emphasis is even more crucial given the perspective that much of the research related to instructional systems design as well as educational research in general has been criticized for the subjects' limited exposure to treatment materials, a lack of longitudinal analyses, and inadequate theory-building (Reeves, 2000).

For design to constitute design research generally, or a design experiment in particular, it must conform to standards of scholarship usually recognized by the scientific and educational communities as necessary conditions for programmatic study (Shavelson & Towne, 2002). Among these necessary conditions are the provision of a coherent and an explicit chain of reasoning, the attempt to yield findings that replicate and transport across studies, and the disclosure of methods and analyses for critique by the broader community (Gorard, 2002a). Although the structure of a complex instructional tool may be considered an embodiment of a local theory, unless that structure is made explicit and the propositional framework upon which the design rests laid bare, it does not constitute a *test* of that theory and therefore contributes little to the broader body of disciplined knowledge about teaching, learning, or human factors.

This is not to say that local theories are neither important nor transformative in a broader sense. In the iterative process of design and test, a design can be transformed to enact a chosen function better, but it also can change the way in which the initial problem is perceived, or it can generate as yet unseen problems such that new functions become possible. For example, the invention of Bakelite (phenol formaldehyde) in the early twentieth century was initiated by the need to coat bowling alleys with a hard, lacquer-like surface. Once the initial problem was solved, the designed properties of Bakelite afforded *transportation* to other problems of the day such as the mass production of billiard balls (before the invention of Bakelite, billiard balls had been manufactured by carving ivory on a lathe).

In part, due to its transportability across critical problems of the late industrial age, Bakelite became a common material for the production of everyday household products such as containers, picture frames, and heat-resistant handles for cookware. Theoretically, it stimulated the most pervasive material revolution of the twentieth century: the development of complex polymers such as polyethylene and nylon-plastics. We use the word *transportation* here as opposed to *generalization* or *transfer* to refer to the efficacy that a design provides beyond its initial conditions of development. We consider generalization to be a probabilistic argument (i.e., generalizability) as opposed to *transportation* as a fit between design and function. On the other hand, transfer is a psychological construct relating to the degree to which something learned in one context can be performed in a different context. *Transportation*, as we are defining it, relates to the physical or applicational movement of a thing, a design, to a new applicational context (even if the details of the design have to be altered somewhat to fit the parameters of the new context).[2]

In education, also, there have been advances that have afforded widespread adoption and adaptation, leading to a similar revolution. The invention of the intelligence test and associated aptitude and achievement instruments has generated both new specialties in statistics (e.g., item response theory and multidimensional scaling) and intricate procedures for the adaptation of test theory to the assessment of attitudes, beliefs, and other indirect survey methods (e.g., the Likert scale and multiple-choice formats). It also has sparked a new political landscape focused on accountability in education—in essence, changing the very goals of education by changing the markers by which society gauges educational outcomes.[3]

Both of these examples illustrate the fact that a design is *not* an ostensible product. Rather, each of these designs can be thought of as the *theory* that specifies the parameters of an ostensible product and explicates the necessary and sufficient conditions under which a product (if it embodies the design) can be implemented successfully—in other words, its form, function, and behavior (Horowitz & Maimon, 1997).

For a design to become an actual thing (e.g., a structure, material, or program), it must go through cycles of modeling and testing, which may alter the *original* conceptual entity based on empirical evidence of how each successive *enacted* design performs under conditions of use. This distinction between a design and a product is crucial to our argument. To synthesize our notion of design with our earlier discussion of product design and instructional systems design, we see the development of an educational product or a software program as a substage in a larger set of coordinated theoretical activity. Imagine how a psychologist might create a series of tasks that uncover ways in which a student thinks about missing addend problems in arithmetic to test a model of how children process the semantics of story problems (see Carpenter & Moser, 1982). Similarly, an instructional designer might create a series of tasks or set of tools that, if enacted, would test a model of how children move through a hypothetical terrain that embodies the complexities of story problems. In both cases, the design of the tasks embodies a larger theory of cognition or situated learning. The tasks themselves (and the software or multimedia environment in which they are embedded) are tools that both uncover important information that helps build the theory (for instance, finding that children solve missing addend problems through counting up from the first addend before counting up from the larger) and that tests the theory (i.e., showing where the model of the development of arithmetic knowledge breaks down or where it is downright wrong). Lastly, the tasks and the environments embodying the theory eventually become enacted as plausible solutions to problems of education.

As in engineering, education design can be thought of as this process of generating plausible solutions to problems of teaching and learning that can be turned into ostensible products whose form enables particular behaviors, which in turn can be compared to the desired function (see Figure 2.1). However, just as in engineering, there are sources of variation that make the larger process of design problematic in moving from initial concept to product with appropriate fidelity and adaptation. These sources of variation have immense impact on the coherence of the methods of design research and on the subsequent claims that can be made about the theoretical implications of a data set.

Design Theory and Sources of Variation

All current theories of design assume a temporal process flowing roughly from conceptualization to realization. In this process, the flow of information moves downstream through various channels (i.e., departments, people with divergent expertise, design team members, different interested parties, target audience members, etc.) as a product is refined continually for market. However, design theories differ in the number of concurrent channels through which the design activity may flow and in whether information may flow back uphill in larger cycles. We synthesize these ideas later in our description of the Compleat Design Cycle into a general descriptive model that may serve the education community as first principles.

A point of fact: information flow between and among designers varies both upstream and downstream in the design process, as do materials and local conditions. As will be seen later on, a number of the conditions that have a potentially fatal impact on the enactment of a design are out of the control of the designer and, instead, are contingent upon the political and situational features of a potential application, including the decisions made by the technician building the designed product. Other conditions are under the control of the designer, but they can have a fatal impact if the design process involves a large team, or if the flow of information downstream from the conceptual designers to the manufacturers is inconsistent or prevented. In a similar manner, if the conditions under which the manufacture of the design is to be accomplished are not known by the upstream personnel, the parameterization of the design may not be realizable. For example, many technology-based design products are constrained severely by the designer's limited understanding of the capabilities of the software creation tools and the programmer's lack of knowledge of learning theory, thereby limiting potential interaction between these individuals and the possible flow of information both upstream and downstream. Under concurrent engineering methods (Ullman, 1992), whereby designers in all areas of product development work simultaneously, the distributed activity, by its very nature, is untenable without clear channels of information flow. The National Academy of Engineering (2004: 7) promotes an elegant definition of engineering (and other design fields by association) as being "design under constraint."

Related to the idea of conducting design under constraints, one of the newest innovations in design theory is the idea of generating a range of satisfactory design parameters in upstream phases of design activity. By specifying the tolerances of deviation in function, a conceptual designer provides a wider range of possible local adaptations to the downstream designers (Kalsi et al., 2001). These approaches have revolutionized manufacturing by enabling local producers to use cheaper, more readily available materials or procedures that get the job done (e.g., a *satisficing threshold*), as opposed to conforming to overly rigid standards that might push the cost of production beyond a reasonable limit. In addition, they have fostered the design of products with diverse functions that use interoperable components (Dahmus et al., 2001).

In education, our analogous situation might be the development of modular curriculum materials (e.g., *Connected Mathematics*, Lappan et al., 2002; *Mathematics in Context*, Romberg, 2000). The designs of these curricula are flexible, allowing school districts and teachers to modify the order in which booklets are used and to choose, from among alternatives, the tasks and tools that enable them to accomplish the desired function of the curriculum. This analogy breaks down in the extent that the curriculum designers both understood and made explicit at the outset the range of parameters that could be altered and still ensure the fidelity of the product. Moreover, the channels of communication of the design parameters from upstream (the curriculum developers) to downstream (the teachers and students) seem to be applied differentially across implementation sites as the market for these materials gets broader and reliance on publishing houses to support the professional development of teachers grows stronger. It is still not standard practice for teachers and school staff to be factored into product design from the outset (for alternative depictions of interactive social science, see Gibbons, 2000; Stokes, 1997).

What Makes Design Rigorous?

In education, it is often easier to make changes in learning or instruction than to gather information about what made those changes happen. This is the crucial difference between the design aspects and the scientific aspects of design research. Syllogistically, if design in education is about engineering particular forms of learning and instruction and if experimentation is about generating knowledge about those forms and subjecting that knowledge to empirical verification, then *the theoretical model underlying particular designs must be made explicit and programmatic* for any program of study to be termed a *design experiment*.[4] Moreover, methods of model testing and revision must be generated that do test the *comprehensiveness, accuracy, and utility* of the theoretical model. These additional requirements are fundamental and also promote an approach to educational innovation that is coherent, logical, and disciplined on the one hand, but also pragmatic. In the classical view of design, products are seen to evolve through a *continuous comparison* of the design state and the desired function. This is possible only when the parameters of the function are capable of being specified beforehand (Ullman, 1992). In relatively simple, robust implementations of education research, this kind of parameterization may be possible.[5]

The other, more modern, view of design tackles parameterization differently. Indeed, it has to primarily because the problems it attempts to solve involve too many variables to specify beforehand. Instead, a design problem is seen as the successive development and application of constraints that narrow down the subset of all possible product designs until only one remains (Ullman, 1992). This emergent solution should not be taken in any sense for an ultimate answer to the problem it attempts to solve. Despite these efforts, even the finest of designed architectural objects may fail ultimately (even the greatest bridges collapse eventually), and, at some point in the process, a decision will need to be made based on cost or other external constraints. After all, it is a fair question for policy-makers and interested parties to ask whether the enactment of an innovation is worth the material and human costs given the relatively small effect sizes (say, less than 0.25 standard deviation units) generally reported in education studies. However, should these considerations endure, the winning design holds a "good enoughness" in its behavior relevant to its desired function to justify its implementation and holds a cost relative to its benefit that makes implementation tenable. It is likely that most education problems are of this type—constrained by pragmatic and fiscal considerations in addition to those of scientific merit (Shavelson & Towne, 2002).

This is not to say that the classical design sequence is neither useful nor important in education research; it is and, in fact, is often used to develop solutions to small subsets of a larger design project. However, the economic and societal necessity for continuous improvement in education dictates that researchers and reformers engage in the design of tools, environments, and systems without knowing beforehand either: (a) all of the relevant parameters that impact their eventual success, or (b) the universe of potential designs from which their final design will emerge. It is likely that, in some instances, the reformer may not be completely clear what the real problem is for which he or she is designing solutions. Cobb et al. (2003) refer to this as the "humble" nature of design experiments.

In attempting to articulate the design process as it applies to education research and development, we adopt this latter view. Our model is not prescriptive because our collective wisdom is limited to our own areas of scientific expertise, and we do not purport to know (let alone understand) many of the potential problems of education. As both researchers and designers, we present our model as descriptive, articulating the larger process and intersections of research and design of which design experiments, or design studies, are but a part. The role that experimentation plays in the design cycle ensures that the rigor and disciplined nature of the empirical facets of design, testing, and theory building are built in and not considered merely in the summative portion of project evaluation. In this manner also, design research aligns with the engineering (manufacturing) concept of continuous improvement (Bisgaard, 1997), which makes heavy use of iterative design cycles to generate pragmatic solutions with attention to time urgency. Our model may be useful for and applicable to the development and marketing of educational innovations by others who share our concern for the impact and rigor of scientific work.

The Compleat Design Cycle

The "classic" research model or cyclic research sequence promoted by advocates of scientific research, in education typically comprises four phases (see Figure 2.2). The first phase often (although not always) establishes the research problem or pedagogic issue that is to be addressed in the design of a particular artifact or intervention. In scientific terms, the aim is to produce a researchable hypothesis or question and a grounded theoretical model from which to develop an artifact that can be tested. This is commonly based upon a systematic approach, involving a review of the relevant literature and knowledge base, drawing upon existing theoretical developments and perhaps a desk-based analysis of existing data sets (both quantitative and qualitative). As the extent of our knowledge and understanding increases, much greater attention is being paid to the importance of these systematic approaches in identifying the pedagogic issue. Therefore, the review of existing literature has to become more systematic, and the availability of relatively large-scale secondary data sets means that a greater preliminary understanding of the problem can be ascertained before the research hypothesis or problem is finalized. However, this is not to ignore other, more nonsystematic inputs into this phase of the scientific research sequence, such as our own personal biographies, experiences, ideologies, and perhaps even serendipity. These types of inputs into developing the research hypothesis and a grounded theoretical framework are equally valuable and important to the initial phases (which might be the primordial "soup" from which clarity emerges).

Once a clear and researchable hypothesis has been established and the relevant grounded models identified, the second phase—to develop a testable artifact or intervention—can begin. This is often the most creative phase of the research sequence, where pedagogic experience can be of immense value. For scientific inquiry to continue, the resulting artifact and/or design of instructional sequences have to be testable against some predetermined criteria, such as pupil assessment, speed of delivery, pupil satisfaction, etc. Whatever educational criteria are chosen, the third phase of the scientific research sequence is to undertake a trial or intervention that will be able to isolate the systematic effects and begin to identify associated causal relationships. For a definitive

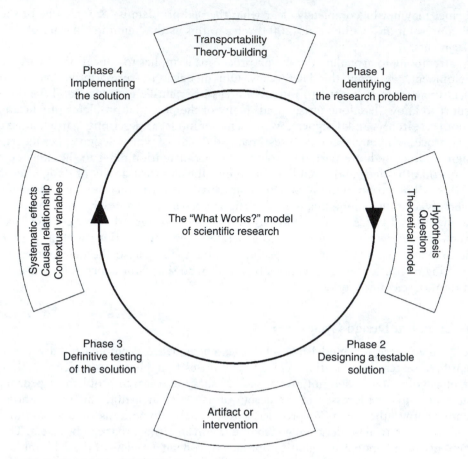

Figure 2.2 Basic Model of Scientific Research in Education.

test, this trial would need an intervention and a control group, and, ideally, the groups or individuals would be allocated randomly. Such a randomized control trial would produce results indicating whether the artifact was more effective than an alternative or existing pedagogic practice. In some experimental research designs, it also may be possible to identify relevant contextual variables in this phase. These could provide useful information for the next phase of the research process.

The last phase of the classic scientific research model would be to take the results of the definitive trial and disseminate the findings to the rest of the teaching and learning community. This would show how effectively the artifact worked, providing practitioners and/or policy-makers with the necessary information to decide whether to implement the new system. However, this phase of the research sequence also should ensure that the artifact is *transportable* to other contexts or situations. It also should ensure that the *new* knowledge and understanding generated throughout the research sequence can contribute to *further* theoretical developments. So not only is the aim of the last phase to implement a "successful" system or pedagogic instrument more widely, but also it should be to develop a greater understanding of the original research problem or pedagogic issue, such that when the first phase of the research sequence resumes, the grounded theoretical models can be advanced.

In clinical medicine, as well as in education, the randomized controlled trial (RCT) is established as the best way of identifying the relative impact of alternative interventions on predetermined outcomes (Shadish et al., 2002). The salience of this research design is largely because of the random allocation of participants to the alternative treatments, such that any difference in outcomes between the groups is due either to chance, which can be quantified, or to the difference in treatment. The RCT is applied most easily to the measurement of the efficacy of simple, well-defined interventions, such as a defined course of drug treatment, when delivered in an ideal research setting. Such four-phase studies are clearly useful in a range of other fields also and, perhaps especially, education (Torgerson & Torgerson, 2001), but they can be almost completely atheoretical in nature. For *simple* intervention studies, where we are concerned only with what works and not why, this lack of theory is not a problem, but it does limit the transportability of the results. Without an explanatory principle, it is not clear to what extent a successful intervention would be effective in a different context or for a different educational setting. And without in-depth data drawn from the same study, it is not clear what can be learned from an unsuccessful intervention (other than that it does not work). But, by themselves, descriptive approaches to research, drawn from ethnographic and narrative genres, can provide considerable and rich detail about the processes of learning and can generate ideas about the improvement of learning. Yet, essentially passive approaches such as these cannot answer the probabilistic question of whether a suggested improvement works. For this, we have traditionally used the four-phase model (Figure 2.2).

The United Kingdom's Medical Research Council (Medical Research Council, 2000) suggests that for more complex health education interventions, trials are most likely to be successful if they are based on sound theoretical concepts and involve *both* qualitative observation and quantitative testing (Campbell et al., 2000). Although many good quality RCTs have been undertaken in medicine and elsewhere, many of them generally have evaluated simple, almost naïve interventions, delivered in homeopathic doses, and inevitably have produced disappointing results. They have been less successful in identifying drug treatment interactions and other more complex clinical questions. On the other hand, several, high-quality, complex interventions generally have not been evaluated rigorously, and their effectiveness has not been demonstrated unequivocally.

Traditionally, trials have required that the interventions being tested are standardized and delivered uniformly to all participants. However, because educational interventions are so dependent on the quality of delivery, the value of trials predicated on "ideal" conditions can be limited. For example, some education interventions have been found to work well in efficacy trials when delivered by enthusiastic teachers with ample curriculum time. Yet, when implemented in practice, they have not been found to be effective, and the researchers have not known why necessarily (Nutbeam et al., 1993). Therefore, it is better to take a pragmatic approach, with the intervention delivered in the trial in a lifelike way. This approach sacrifices standardization for realism and means that the natural variability in delivery that occurs between practitioners must be recorded and monitored by in-depth means, perhaps by video-recording, as well as by more traditional outcome measures. This is not to imply that video-recording and analysis are simple tasks; in fact, educational researchers have called attention to the inherent problems and difficulties of this particular form of theoretical data collection (Hall, 2000). However, video data have the potential to complement and inform RCTs. In summary, the "trial design ensures that an unbiased estimate of the average effect of the intervention is obtained, while the qualitative research provides useful further information on the external factors that support or attenuate this effect" (Moore, 2002: 5).

There is no doubt that it is easier to conduct RCTs of simple interventions. However, there is little value in compromising the likely effectiveness of the intervention by simplifying it merely to make it more amenable to evaluation in a trial. Indeed, RCTs are expensive both in monetary terms and, more particularly, in terms of their demands on research subjects and researchers. Hence, it is morally dubious to conduct a fully fledged trial until one is confident that the intervention is likely to be effective. Therefore, before conducting a RCT to demonstrate an intervention's effectiveness, three earlier phases of investigation should have been completed. In effect, these three additional phases constitute what we term the *design experiment* (Figure 2.3). Meanwhile, the first two phases of the "what works?" model of educational research in essence remain the same (i.e., identifying the research problem and designing a testable solution).

The first new phase would involve the initial design of the intervention based on current theoretical understanding, ensuring that the intervention was grounded in theory and an explicit interpretation of the causal mechanism that it intended to promulgate. Furthermore, the transition between the second phase (the design of the artifact or intervention) and the (new) third phase (the feasibility study) would involve primarily qualitative methods in the formative evaluation of the intervention, using interviews, focus groups, observation, and case studies to identify how the intervention is working, barriers and facilitators to its implementation, and how it might be improved. Moving from the design to the feasibility stages might draw heavily on design and research processes in other fields such as product design and market research (Urlich & Eppinger, 2000). These more "explanatory" routes of inquiry complement powerfully the earlier use of secondary data analysis in identifying the research problem (Phase One).[6]

In the third (new) phase (or the beginning of our design experiment), the intervention should be sufficiently well developed to be tested in a feasibility study, where it can be implemented in full and tested for acceptability by both the providers (health professionals, teachers, etc.) and the target audience (patients, pupils, etc.). The feasibility study is also an opportunity to test trial procedures, such as the definition of the alternative treatment, which may be the usual care, the control, or an alternative intervention, and to pilot and test outcome measures. It also may be used to provide a tentative estimate of the intervention effect, which then can be used to plan the size of the (main) (or definitive?) trial. The results of the feasibility study (Phase Three) will help to decide

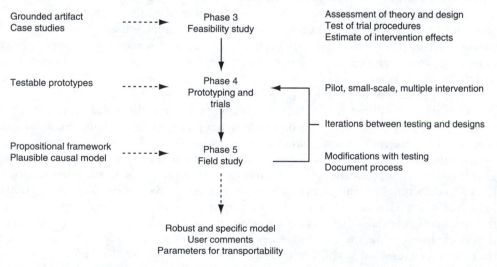

Figure 2.3 Three "New" Phases in the Design Experiment—Phases 3 to 5 of the Compleat Research Process.

whether the intervention should proceed to the next phase (teaching experiments) or whether it is necessary to return to the initial phases of identifying the research problem and developing the theoretical framework on which the intervention is based originally. Given the pragmatic and fiscal constraints of all scientific research discussed earlier, the results of the feasibility study may suggest that the entire research process should end.

The following fourth phase (prototyping and trials) begins a process of iteration between the testing and further modification of the intervention. Parallel to this is the potential to iterate the process between the laboratory (or other controlled environments) and the classroom (or real-life environments) (Brown, 1992). These iterative processes continue into the fifth phase (field study). However, Phase Four is characterized by piloting small-scale, multiple prototypes of the intervention. As the iterations between testing and further design become more sophisticated and the iterations between laboratory and classroom settings become more robust, advances are made in the intervention's propositional framework and in outlining its plausible causal models. It is at this point that the research sequence enters the fifth phase (the field study), where it is implemented in full and tested for acceptability by both the providers (health professionals, teachers, etc.) and the target audience (patients, pupils, etc.). The field study is also an opportunity to test trial procedures, such as the definition of the alternative approaches, which may be the usual care, traditional instruction, the control, or an alternative intervention, and to pilot and test outcome measures. It, too, may be used to provide a tentative estimate of the intervention effect, which then can be used to plan the size of the main trial. The iterative process may continue, but the design of the instructional sequences becomes stronger, leading eventually to a robust model that aids the implementation of the artifact in many contexts. It is at this point that the documentation and recording of the process for implementing the artifact should be more systematic, because this develops the parameters for further transportability.

Once a series of "satisficing" objectives has been met, the compleat research process is ready to move on to the sixth phase, the definitive trial or evaluation. This phase is no different from the third phase of the original scientific model of educational research outlined earlier. However, the addition of three new phases to the research sequence ensures that the artifact or design to be tested should be effective. It also means that there is now a design of instructional sequences to aid the artifact's transportability. Figure 2.4 shows the compleat research sequence with all seven phases combined. These additions to the simple scientific model of educational research are illustrated now in a real example of a mathematics design experiment.

An Extended Example From Mathematics Education

In this example, we analyze a current project, organized around the tenets we have established for design research, which has progressed far enough through the above phases to be a practical example. Note that, as a case, it specifies many of the necessary conditions for design experiments to be considered worthy contributions to the larger field of teaching and learning research. The case does not embody all possible, or probably all *sufficient*, conditions to be applicable generally to any study labeled *design experiment*. A broader survey of the current state of the art in the field is necessary to provide that background and that is beyond the scope of this chapter. As our case progresses through subsequent phases of the design cycle, we first provide the theoretical and methodological considerations that the researchers encountered and then follow them up with specific examples from practice.

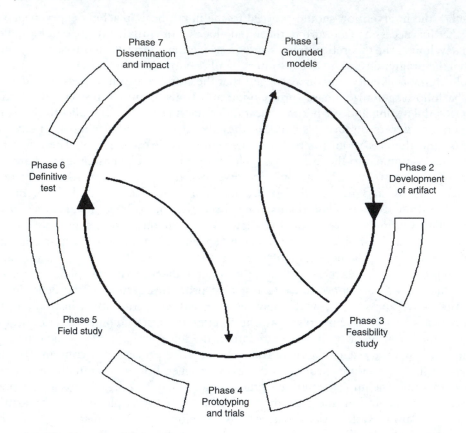

Figure 2.4 The Compleat Design Cycle.

Design Experiments: Phases Three through Six

For design to be iterative, progressive, and disciplined, a method of empirical analysis of the intended function → form → behavior proposition must exist and drive both the smaller iterative design cycles and the larger test of the overall theory under investigation. Usually, when a proposition (e.g., a hypothesis) is put to an empirical test, the general qualities of that portion of a line of inquiry is termed an experiment. Most experiments involve actual manipulation of the conditions that impact the parameters of the proposition, such that evidence is created that would either: (a) falsify the proposition by showing that the given conditions do not influence subsequent actions in the manner that the theory would suggest, or (b) provide confirmatory evidence that the proposition is functional for a given set of conditions. As stated earlier, design experiments, by which we mean the kind envisioned by Brown (1992), Collins (1992), and articulated more fully by Cobb et al. (2003), are a subprocess in the larger cycle of design. In particular, we see them as the articulation of Phases Three through Six in the model we present.

To illustrate the role of design experiments in this larger context, we describe a program of study embarked upon by one of the principal authors of this manuscript. In brief, this ongoing program attempts to create a theory of children's development of understanding of quotients, within the larger structure of rational numbers and arithmetic operations (see the Rational Number Project publications, e.g. Behr et al., 1992;

Kieren, 1976, 1993). Moreover, pertaining to broader sociocultural theory, this research attempts to generate methods to describe specifically how individual cognition contributes to the collective understanding of groups of individuals in instructional settings (de Silva-Lamberg & Middleton, 2002). We describe here the considerations for the feasibility of this program of research (Phase Three); the prototyping of tasks, trials, and the development of an initial plausible model of development through intensive individual teaching experiments (Phase Four); and the refinement of that model to be sufficiently explanatory so that it could be used as a hypothetical structure for the design and testing of instructional sequences (Phase Five).

Phase Three: Establishing the Feasibility of the Research Program

Assuming that there is some theoretical justification for a design to be created, an additional consideration for educational scholars is whether the social capital of their work warrants the perturbation of students' educational experiences; namely, the relatively intrusive process of interviewing, video-taping, and more formal testing that might be interwoven over an extended period of time in the conduct of a study. Also, the nesting of any individual study within the larger program of research, particularly if the theory or model under examination is longitudinal in nature, must be justified. In the Children's Understanding of Quotients project (CHUQ) (de Silva, 2001; Middleton et al., 2001; Toluk, 1999; Toluk & Middleton, 2001), we examined the curricular offerings in mathematics for middle-grade students and found that there was no systematic treatment of fractions as quotients, nor any integration of the instruction on division as an arithmetic operation, with the theory of fractions as rational numbers. Fractions were treated almost exclusively as part—whole quantities, and division was treated almost exclusively (but particularly so in the early portion of the middle grades) as resulting in whole numbers with remainder or decimal quantities. This established a curricular warrant, because the ability to understand fractions as numbers, or that quotients represent a division relationship (i.e., a multiplicative inverse), is critical for proportional reasoning and further understanding of algebraic fractions in general and rational expressions in particular—both central concepts of elementary algebra.

However, the negotiation of eight weeks of intense work with individual children and another five weeks with teachers and their classrooms for this portion of the program required the investigators to negotiate time, prerequisite experiences, and the involvement of the teacher and to establish a reasonably firm assurance of the benefits of participation in such a demanding set of procedures. This meant that the researchers had to develop a close relationship with the teacher, school, and school district, with the promise of long-term collaboration (i.e., beyond the study at hand and even beyond the overall program of research; see Middleton et al., 2002 for a description of the relationship of the author with this particular system).

The initial strategy of starting with individual interviews and building to the classroom study had two advantages. Theoretically, it allowed the researchers to articulate their model more precisely, providing initial examples and vignettes to help the classroom teacher understand the model of development they had created (see Figure 2.3). Pragmatically, it provided a means of withdrawing from the project for the teacher, school, and school district should the model prove untenable or inarticulate in the initial phases with individual children.

Lastly, the researchers had to articulate the initial theoretical justification for the study in terms that were both understandable and rigorous to social scientists (to pass the Human Subjects Institutional Review) and versed in the language and values of the teacher, school, and school district. For proper informed consent to be made, there needed to be acceptance, conceptually and politically, by all the interested parties. That justification took the following form:

- Instruction on fractions consists almost entirely of part—whole treatment. Instruction on division consists almost entirely of whole numbers with remainder treatment. At no time in the elementary or middle grades are these two strands of instruction connected explicitly and their conceptual unity articulated.

We know this because we have analyzed both the larger national research literature and the particular curriculum and materials your teachers use.

- Having a connected understanding of fractions as division is critical for the success of your children.

We know this because so much of their future algebra experiences will use this knowledge.

Again, we have analyzed both the national data and the curricular experiences of your children.

- Together (researchers, teacher, school, and school district), we can generate a model of the development of children's understanding of quotients, use that model to create instructional sequences to teach in the real conditions of schools, and test and refine those sequences so that they can be transported across classrooms to maximize the benefit for all your students.

Here, the researchers negotiated the roles of the researchers, students, teacher, school, and school district, and articulated the individual study → classroom study structure.

This justification is a proposition—a hypothesis—stated in the form that design researchers often use: articulating a real problem that exists, a method of solution to that problem, and engaging the implementing community (i.e., the *downstream* designers and technicians) in the design process.

Phase Four: Prototyping, Trials, and Multiple Interventions

Following the establishment of the warrant, the articulation of the hypothetical structure to be investigated is critical for a design experiment to be truly an *experiment*. In particular, the researcher must pay attention to not only what is happening (i.e., the description), but also why it is happening (i.e., the causal model), and how it is happening (i.e., the cause-and-effect mechanism) (Gorard, 2002b; Shadish et al., 2002; Shavelson et al., 2003). In most design research, including our own (lest we point fingers), scholars have focused primarily on the descriptive portion of the data. The narrative of a child confronting fractions as division is compelling and useful as a case that can be compared and contrasted to other cases and used in professional development to illustrate certain processes of development. However, without the causal model articulating *why the child is thinking the way he or she does*, given the prompt and their particular learning history, the practitioner has little efficient information about how to impact thinking in ways that are mathematically sound. Moreover, without an articulated mechanism to effect appropriate learning (i.e., teaching methods, tools, and sequences), a practitioner's subsequent course of action is left to a "best guess" kind of strategy, as opposed to coherent and consistent designed experiences. This need underscores the requirement for iterative cycles of test and revision in the design process at the prototyping phases to provide *both* the full complexity of a compelling case and the theoretical model by which the case can be understood as a case *of something* (Shulman, 1986).

The late Ann Brown (1992) presented her own view on design experimentation as moving progressively from working with children in laboratory settings to more complex and naturalistic interventions. Her characterization of design experiments does not distinguish between the power of the laboratory or the classroom as settings for the generation of theoretical knowledge. Instead, she promotes each as providing a different lens on how children learn and on what systems and strategies can be envisioned to promote quality learning. In particular, her presentation evokes a dual-method approach whereby laboratory research assists in the building of detailed models of learning, upon which instructional models can be based. The laboratory also can provide details of individual thinking and learning that the larger context of the classroom cannot (see also McCandliss et al., 2003). The classroom, for its part, provides the practical setting and the complexity that the laboratory cannot emulate properly. Any compleat design experiment must take the instructional setting and epistemological basis for the study into account when designing the methods of product design, data collection, and analysis.

As presented in Phase Three, the researchers developed a general strategy for coming to understand children's thinking about quotients. In Phase Four, the details of designing a method for researching children's thinking and creating an initial plausible model were undertaken. The researchers could have begun with prototypical problems in small-group or classroom settings, or they could have used larger data sets and survey instrumentation for the empirical data upon which a plausible model of development was generated. Because the project is rooted in a psychological tradition and builds upon a body of research that makes heavy use of teaching experiment methods, a modification of microgenetic interview techniques (see Steffe & Thompson, 2000), it was deemed appropriate to build from that methodological base. This decision is a critical one, we think. As stated earlier, no design is any ultimate answer to the problem it attempts to solve, but the epistemological basis upon which a design is built will determine its form and function. In this case, the interest of the researchers was to understand children's thinking at the individual level and then build classroom sequences upon that basis. Others would be more interested in the nature of classroom discourse related to quotients and build their theory and instructional sequences on that basis. It is unlikely that both approaches would yield the same solution design. The coherence of theory to methodology, therefore, is of fundamental importance in the evaluation of design experiments and is critical to explicate for any future scholar or practitioner who attempts to replicate or implement the findings of a design study.

Following this example, in the CHUQ project, the researchers conducted four parallel individual teaching experiments that lasted approximately 16 sessions per child (two per week for eight weeks). The purpose of this initial research was to study fifth graders' conceptualizations of the quotient under instructional conditions that expressly required them to confront and connect the isomorphisms inherent in thinking about fractions and in thinking about division. Specifically, the experimenters focused on the transitional understandings that children construct as they move from the division of whole numbers to the depiction of fractions as the quotient of division situations.

Baseline interviews were conducted with standard problems relating to fractions and division to give the experimenter information on the initial understandings and skills. From this information, the experimenter designed initial problems with two basic strategies in mind:

1   To provide isomorphic problems in close contiguity, one that promotes *fractional* interpretations, the other that promotes *whole number division* interpretations. A sample problem is shown in Figure 2.5(a).
2   To bridge the two conceptual strands by presenting fair sharing problems with partitionable remainders, then focus on the remainders. See Figure 2.5(b) for an example of this strategy.

By presenting problems that were isomorphic, but that had potentially fractional versus divisional interpretations, the authors attempted to confront the children with the notion that the process of partitioning quantities was the same conceptually. By focusing on the remainder in a division problem, the experimenters attempted to confront the children with division and fractions in the same problem—that is, that fractions were the result of division.

As the children constructed new schemes as new information was provided, the experimenter would devise additional problems to test whether children had developed

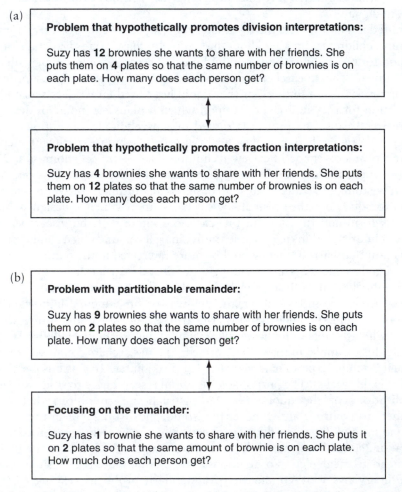

Figure 2.5 Standard Fractions and Division Problems Given During Baseline Interviews.

a different understanding and, if so, provide a description of that understanding. At the end of the data collection portion of the study, the authors had four parallel cases. The commonalities among the cases were analyzed and incorporated in the development of a first model—a plausible model—of children's development of understanding of the quotient construct. At this point, the model was primarily descriptive, tracing the new schemes that the children had constructed to deal with successively more difficult depictions of fractions, division, and their confluence. As the research program moved to the larger scale design and implementation study in a classroom, it served as a causal model, addressing the trajectory along which the children were assumed to develop (e.g., a hypothetical learning trajectory; Cobb et al., 1997), and positing the key transitional conceptualizations the children needed to develop and positing the kinds of instructional strategies that would facilitate those transitions. At this point, it became both design specifications for a sequence of instruction and a hypothesis that could be tested empirically under the naturalistic conditions of classroom life.

Phase Five: Modification and Testing

As empirical evidence for a design grows, so does the complexity of the problem(s) it can address. Initial prototypes are likely to be flawed, both in their conceptualization and in their implementation. Coordinating the theoretical conceptualization and implementation (i.e., contextual) parameters as a design moves downstream in the process is by no means an easy task. For example, in the CHUQ project, a plausible model of the development of children's understanding of quotient—telegraphic, simplistic, narrow in applicability—needed to be transformed into a sequence of instructional tasks that would move a whole class of children to a higher level of understanding. Where does one begin?

The CHUQ researchers began by using the story problems, tasks, and sequences of conversations—data they had gleaned from the significant amount of transcriptions generated in the teaching experiments. Many of their first attempts were inadequate at best, but the advantage of an iterative longitudinal design is that one gets better as one goes along (this actually came as a surprise). The project was influenced heavily by the classroom design studies described by Cobb et al. (1997), where they shared in some detail the theory of classroom teaching and learning as emergent phenomena and subsequently designed a program of research both to teach place value and to research students' collective understandings (see also Cobb et al., 2003). Moreover, as the project moved from a model of individual development to an implementation situated in a real classroom, it had to expand its research base to include instructional theories. In our case, because it had a consistent epistemological worldview with the emergent perspective, the model of anchored instruction was employed to structure the initial curricular sequence of tasks and to situate classroom discourse in a common colloquial understanding: fair sharing through planning a party. It was assumed that as children encountered successively more formal and conceptually difficult notions of fractions as quotients, the party context would enable the teacher to identify and challenge their informal understanding better and also would serve as a source of problems for group discourse.

A lesson or sequence of instruction is a window into the long-term goals of a project. It is not merely a product, or an episode, but an enacted hypothesis about the nature of children's understanding and how that plays out across an important mathematical or scientific concept. As an ostensible product, the instructional unit developed by CHUQ consisted of a workbook with sets of story problems, tasks, and thought questions (see above) that built on the original research into children's thinking. It was structured to build conceptual linkages between children's understandings of fractions and their understandings of division in the ways that the plausible model derived from the empirical evidence would predict. The unit began with a complex video anchor (e.g., Cognition and Technology Group at Vanderbilt, 1992) that exposed children to issues of unit and partitioning (e.g., a case of soda in the United States consists of 24 cans; a case then is partitionable into 24 (1) cans, 4 (6) cans, 2 (12) cans, etc.). In the process of planning a party for a large group of children, the notions of division, fractions, and remainders are encountered inevitably, and these notions are dependent upon the concepts of unit and partitioning. So, to summarize, the content of the unit: (a) embodied critical theoretical considerations from the research on rational numbers in general, (b) structured them based on the specific empirical evidence generated in the teaching experiments conducted earlier in the research program, (c) situated the sequences in a format that embodied the theory of teaching exemplified by anchored instruction, and (d) embedded the perspective on knowledge development in classroom settings in the emergent perspective from a sociocultural tradition. What then, of all of these things, do you test?

We admit that one cannot test all of these design considerations in a single study. For the purposes that the CHUQ researchers set out to accomplish with the teacher, school, and school district, the immediate test had to address the adequacy and veracity of the plausible model. Not only were these the simplest to test conceptually, but also they were the *only* considerations that could be tested given that they were the only real hypotheses of the lot. The first, third, and fourth considerations were assumptions upon which the instructional unit was based and, as such, were a backdrop through which the plausible model could be situated and tested under conditions of use. The researchers could have used a different set of assumptions to test the plausible model, and they may have seen different results. However, because all of the considerations were developed so that they held common assumptions about what constitutes knowledge, how teachers and students interact in the classroom discourse, and the roles of tasks and tools in facilitating knowledge, they represented one of a finite number of *coherent* configurations of perspectives at appropriate levels of detail and focus (Cobb et al., 2003). It is not that research uses a configuration of perspectives that is at issue from critics of the state of the art in design experimentation, but the mutuality of those perspectives and whether they each contribute at the appropriate level and scope to a coherent epistemological argument (Shavelson et al., 2003).

Following the initial drafting of the instructional sequence, the researchers (including the classroom teacher) developed conjectures—mini hypotheses—about how children would approach the tasks presented and what kinds of tools the teacher would use to build upon their reactions. They did this for the entire sequence, knowing full well it was likely that a large portion of the tasks would change either in order or in form as the study progressed. When the classroom instruction commenced, the researchers recorded whole-class conversations through a digital video camera, followed target students in a small group through their dialogue and individual seatwork with a second camera, and recorded all instances of all 24 children's scribblings, journal entries, physical models, and other inscriptions with digital photographs for the five full weeks of the study. All the digital data had a coordinated time stamp so that the exact moment when a conjecture, drawing, or other exteriorized piece of evidence of thinking was generated, could be placed at its proper moment in the overall discourse.

The results of this study indicated that the practices of the classroom moved *more or less* along the hypothetical trajectory established by the plausible model and instantiated through the instructional unit. However, there were some fundamental differences in how the classroom as a collective progressed as opposed to the individual children in the study. In particular, the need to establish norms for representing fractions and division was more critical in the whole-class application. Also, the children in the classroom study had more difficulty seeing nested sets of units in fractions and had been socialized into seeing "improper" fractions as just that—improper. A huge watershed occurred when students saw improper fractions as division and as numbers greater than one without converting to the whole number plus a fraction less than one notation. Lastly, although children in whole and small groups appeared to understand and be able to deal with the concept of division as a number (e.g., a quotient as a fraction), many were not able to do so on their own. Much of these differences can be attributed to the difference between the conditions of individual teaching experiments and whole class instruction, but some (particularly the last) cannot. All indications are that the original model developed from studies of individual children is generally sound and is a useful structure with which to organize sequences of instruction. However, the ways in which the researchers originally characterized children's understanding of division as number has to be reconceptualized and retested.

Additional benefits of situating studies of learning within a larger design experiment include the ability to generate new knowledge about several aspects of learning and instruction simultaneously. For example, although the use of coordinated time stamps on digital video and still photographs allowed the project to trace individual development within the larger complexity of the classroom, it also shed light on the ways in which inscriptions are used as media for communication and, more precisely, generate models of how information is propagated and how individuals contribute to a collective knowledge structure (Lamberg & Middleton, 2003). These data are helping the researchers articulate the emergent perspective on classroom discourse more carefully and are helping them generate a disciplined method for modeling classroom discourse from both the individual and the collective lenses simultaneously.

Phases Six and Seven: What Next?

If we go back to the beginning of this chapter and examine the general model of design research depicted in Figure 2.1, we see an endless cycle of theory-building, designing, and testing. The CHUQ project, as described here, exemplifies this academic side of design research. It has generated both a useful and verifiable theoretical model, developed that model into an embodiment with the form of an instructional sequence, and tested that model against conditions of use. At its current state, it is, in the lexicon of the mathematical community, an existence proof. We know that children can think about quotients in these ways under these conditions, and that, given the expertise of the researchers, the theoretical model can be transported from the individual interview to the classroom setting. At some point, however, the project has to disseminate some ostensible products that will be of use beyond the relatively small scale of the design test bed. Here is where issues of scope and scale loom eminently. We envision two avenues for definitive trials of the theory: first, by examining the qualities of students' understanding of quotients following instruction using the instructional sequence or analogous materials developed; second, by examining the impact, if any, that such instruction has on the larger domain of rational numbers that currently constitutes the bulk of the US mathematics curricula in the middle grades.[7]

The first class of definitive trials would involve a nomothetic approach, using randomized or carefully stratified samples, with relatively large numbers of students.

Controlling for variation in the consistency of instruction and students' prior experiences, the researchers will be able to determine the relative impact on students' learning statistically through computation of effect sizes (reference) and repeated measures analyses. Pragmatically, this kind of trial gives an estimation of the immediate impact of an innovation in curriculum and instruction. However, not all impact is assessable in the short term. By nature, education is both cumulative and transformative (cognitively, both assimilative and accommodative). The consistency of experiences over several years of mathematics instruction also will determine the quality of students' learning. These considerations predicate that other conceptualizations of rational numbers be considered simultaneously with that of the quotient.

The second class of definitive trials, assessing the impact of quotient understanding on the larger domain of rational numbers, is more difficult to assess. It may be that, viewed as a whole, focusing on one important subset of the rational numbers domain is insufficient for any long-term change to occur (e.g., any gains found in a short-term study are nullified by the overall impact of the curriculum that is taught for several years). Alternatively, it may be that quotients (fractions as division)—because they have both conceptual utility and operational applicability across the other conceptualizations of rational numbers—have a catalytic effect on long-term fluency. We do not know. Without some type of evaluative study in the form of a set of clinical trials or other nomothetic technique, we may never know.

Eventually, the unit designed for research may make it to market (Phase Seven). It is unlikely, however, that it will have much of an impact, in terms of scope and scale, because it is not attached to any large set of published curricular materials. In the literature on the diffusion of innovations, a determination of whether a clever design will become widely adopted by users is its *observability*; that is, the degree to which the results of the innovation are visible to potential users (Rogers, 1995). The curriculum adoption process in the United States is big business, with a small number of large publishing houses competing for huge profits. The development and marketing of coherent sets of materials and associated teaching tools virtually preclude the wide-scale adoption of our five-week, instructional sequence designed for 11-year-olds. Moreover, although the authors of this chapter strive to disseminate their work more broadly, the accepted venues for the communication of research in the university community—journal articles and other, expository-framed text—do not appeal to the masses of teachers we are hoping to reach.

Recently, however, the education research community *has* had a venue for wide-scale impact: working with publishing houses as partners for reform. With the assistance of the US National Science Foundation, several sets of curricular materials have been developed, based on (at the time) the latest research on learning, teaching, and technology. By and large, the authors of these curricula were researchers who had contributed to the body of work, but they certainly were not experts in all of the areas of cognition, instruction, and social psychology that they needed to incorporate into their materials development projects.

Nevertheless, the qualities of these curricula are fundamentally different from the materials that constituted the bulk of the published texts when they were published, and there is some large-scale evidence of their effectiveness under most conditions of schooling (Confrey & Stohl, 2004; Webb et al., 2001). In at least one of these projects much of the processes we are calling design research was employed with good measure (Romberg, 2000). Some projects are in the process of revision. Should the collective argument promoted by the authors of this chapter prove useful, we hope that our framework will serve these revision projects as principles for designs that will lead to more theoretically defensible products with even greater pragmatic value.

Conclusions

Throughout this chapter, we have emphasized the articulation of theory, method, and pragmatic considerations in the design cycle overall and in design experiments in particular. The examples we have provided illustrate both the conceptual and instrumental advantages of such an articulation, but also the tensions that arise when assumptions about theory, learning, policy, and social contexts are not coherent or do not reflect the conditions of the design process. These tensions are countermanded somewhat through the iterative structure of design whereby unanticipated difficulties can be dealt with expeditiously. However, this does not negate the imperative for careful consideration of epistemological coherence at the outset. In the cases we cited, success was predicated to a great extent upon the coherence of the theory and the attention to areas where the empirical evidence at different levels of cognitive or social complexity complemented each other and therefore could be merged into a comprehensive hypothesis about the impact of a design. This rigorous attention to complexity has not been a hallmark of education research in general.

Often, education problems are stated in terms of yes or no questions, that is: "*Does* a certain approach work or not?" The all-or-nothing nature of such questions yields outcomes of research, including theory, that take the form of particular prescriptions or nothing at all. A shift to research questions and associated methods that ask: "*Why* might a certain approach work?" (e.g., curricular sequences, social environments, human–computer interfaces, state-level policies) leads to the generation of potentially transportable models of teaching, learning, or policy that, in turn, facilitate the creation of products that embody these models (e.g., a shift to the creation of workable systems). Concurrently, attention to questions of "*How* a certain approach might work" can provide the theoretical basis for the *mechanisms* of innovation, their instantiation, and their adaptation. The use of both individual (i.e., laboratory) and group (i.e., field) studies allows the scholar to develop first plausible models of thinking and the kinds of tasks that facilitate that thinking, then to test those models subsequently to ascertain the mechanisms that make them transportable to analogous situations.

We offer the concept of transportation as an alternative to the traditional notions of generalizability and transfer. Transportation has many of the inductive features embodied by statistical and theoretical generalization, but it also carries the communicative and responsive features of analogical generalization (cf., Smaling, 2003). As such, it is complementary to both kinds of generalization but stands on its own, describing very different kinds of phenomena. In particular, transportation is concerned with the diffusion of innovation both broadly (i.e., scope) and situationally (i.e., value-added). Moreover, the term refers explicitly to designed systems as opposed to habits or mental constructs or population characteristics. After all, unlike these constructs, when a design is transported from one situation to another, like a good book, it can be shared, with corresponding benefits for all parties.

Concerning the diffusion of innovation, the issue of "research-to-practice" should not be problematic, if the research *is* practice. Even when the classroom teacher is not a member of the research team (as was the case in the CHUQ individual teaching experiments), the system of teacher/researcher to students' interaction exhibited a remarkable self-similarity; that is, the ways in which problems were presented, students' thinking was recorded, and hypotheses were conjectured and tested were remarkably similar both in the individual teaching experiment conditions and in the whole-class conditions (but with added complexity). Lesh and Kelly's (2000) description of multitiered teaching experiments has an analogous self-similarity, although their projects deal with the professional development of teachers related to the teachers' own understanding of students' thinking. Recent commentary on issues related to teachers' professional development may provide the additional directions needed to address the critical importance of teachers' learning and adoption of design research innovations (see Borko, 2004). A question for scholars who pursue design research in using laboratory and classroom settings might be: "To what extent do the differing conditions of the research project need to reflect a common methodology?" At present, this is unanswered, but our best guess is that the closer the methods are between the laboratory and the classroom, the more transportable the initial plausible model to be enacted will be.

This issue, then, changes the generalizability argument radically to one of scale and transportability; that is, "Are people able to take the key design aspects of the innovation and transport them to their own contexts in some useful fashion?" and "What aspects of the innovation are applicable to large numbers, where delivery, institutional context, and culture vary radically from those under which the innovation was designed?" It seems likely that these questions would require the development of design specifications that state in a clear way what the parameters are for transportability and scale and by what measures they can be assessed (Sloane & Gorard, 2003). In particular, we are intrigued by the discussion of the perceived relative advantage of an innovation provided by Rogers (1995), as well as the more current perspectives on this issue of Zaritsky et al. (2003). Some market research concerning the characteristics of educational innovations that are perceived as relative advantages over existing situations—with appropriate compatibility and complexity for successful adoption to occur—would be an excellent step in the direction of continuous educational improvement.

We have taken care to demonstrate that design experiments are valuable methodological additions to the standard procedures that already include randomized controlled trials and other traditional experimental studies, as well as descriptive studies from narrative and ethnographic traditions. The methods we describe assume a refreshingly uncomplicated combination of both qualitative and quantitative approaches that capitalize on their mutual strengths without sacrificing their mutual rigor. Each approach can be seen as necessary to the process of design, and neither can be seen as sufficient alone. Others have pointed out the complementary nature of methods and how they constitute lenses by which complex educational systems can be understood better (e.g., Behrens & Smith, 1996; Jaeger, 1997). We have attempted to add to this discussion by situating design research in this centrist position.

Perhaps the most important contribution we could provide is a set of references of good examples upon which to model design studies. After all, most of us learn by emulating others. The sources we have cited continue to inspire our own work, and each of those projects embodies high levels of rigor, openness to critique, and practicality. We think that the fears of the critics of design research would be assuaged somewhat if they examined the painstaking detail to which our examples have gone to ensure that their claims are warranted and that such claims have broader applicability to the education community.

The bulk of this chapter was devoted to the articulation of a model that would provide two contributions to the field by commenting on the theoretical considerations to be taken into account and by providing an extended example to illustrate the complexities of doing so. The first contribution was to establish a model that researchers who are interested in design can use to help them plan and build research programs. We emphasize programs because the model is written at the program level and not at the project level. This highlights the issues of time and complexity (and money) that often keep design projects from leading to systematic and programmatic theory. Second, our model is provided as a first step in the establishment of standards by which design research can be evaluated. Different types of research and development can be mapped onto this model with fidelity, and the scholar outside the science and mathematics education fields, which represent the bulk of the research we have reviewed, can see his or her place in the larger genre of theory and methods.

Acknowledgments

The research reported in this chapter was supported in part by grants from the United States National Science Foundation, the United States Department of Education, and the United Kingdom's Economic and Social Research Council. The opinions expressed are solely those of the authors and do not reflect the opinions of the United States National Science Foundation, the United States Department of Education, or the United Kingdom's Economic and Social Research Council. All of the authors contributed equally to this chapter.

Notes

1 The archaic use of "compleat" in the title hearkens back to a classic text on angling by Izaak Walton, "The Compleat Angler, or the Contemplative Man's Recreation," originally published in 1653. Modern editions of the book are available.

2 See also the concept of *transferability* (Guba & Lincoln, 1989; Lincoln & Guba, 1985; Smaling, 2003), which is analogous to our use of *transportation*, but because the roots of the terms are identical, more easily confused with *transfer*.

3 The extent to which these consequences of design transportation are intended or even beneficial is beyond the scope of this chapter. Needless to say, because design research is, to a large extent, social engineering, the ethical and moral consequences of design creation and adoption must be considered critically.

4 Of course, the implicit assumption here is that there *may* be studies labeled *design experiments* that may not be design experiments according to this definition.

5 This approach to combining methods has been termed the *new* political arithmetic (Gorard, with Taylor, 2004).

6 We assume that the reader is familiar with the methods of establishing a theoretical warrant for the conduct of education research, so we do not treat it here. Suffice it to say that the authors did their literature review and found a significant gap in the knowledge base on rational number learning, right where the quotient should be located.

7 Although a number of mathematical strands are emphasized in both the standards and textbooks, rational numbers is a domain that transcends these boundaries, appearing in number, algebraic, geometric, and statistical contexts ubiquitously. It has been named a watershed domain in the field of mathematics (Kieren, 1976).

References

Bannan-Ritland, B. (2003). The role of design in research: The integrative learning design framework. *Educational Researcher*, 32(1), 21–24.

Barab, S. & Squire, K. (eds) (2004). Design-based research: Clarifying the terms [Special issue]. *Journal of the Learning Sciences*, 13(1).

Behr, M. J., Harel, G., Post, T. R. & Lesh, R. (1992). Rational number, ratio and proportion. In D. Grouws (ed.), *Handbook of research on mathematics teaching and learning* (pp. 296–333). New York: Macmillan.

Behrens, J. T. & Smith, M. L. (1996). Data and data analysis. In D. C. Berliner & R. C. Calfee (eds), *Handbook of educational psychology* (pp. 945–989). New York: Simon & Schuster Macmillan.

Bisgaard, S. (1997). *The role of scientific problem solving and statistics in quality improvement: Some perspectives* (Report No. 158). University of Wisconsin-Madison: Center for Quality and Productivity Improvement.

Borko, H. (2004). Professional development and teacher learning: Mapping the terrain. *Educational Researcher, 33*(8), 3–15.

Brown, A. L. (1992). Design experiments: Theoretical and methodological challenges in creating complex interventions in classroom settings. *Journal of the Learning Sciences, 2*, 141–178.

Campbell, M., Fitzpatrick, R., Haines, A., Kinmouth, A. L., Sandercock, P., Spiegelhalter, P. et al. (2000). Framework for design and evaluation of complex interventions to improve health. *British Medical Journal, 321*, 694–696.

Carpenter, T. P. & Moser, J. M. (1982). *Addition and subtraction: A cognitive perspective.* Hillsdale, NJ: Lawrence Erlbaum Associates.

Cobb, P., Confrey, J., diSessa, A., Lehrer, R. & Schauble, L. (2003). Design in educational research. *Educational Researcher, 32*(1), 9–13.

Cobb, P., Gravemeijer, K., Yackel, E., McClain, K. & Whitenack, J. (1997). Symbolizing and mathematizing: The emergence of chains of signification in one first-grade classroom. In D. Kirshner & J. A. Whitson (eds), *Situated cognition theory: Social, semiotic, and neurological perspectives* (pp. 151–233). Mahwah, NJ: Lawrence Erlbaum Associates.

Cognition and Technology Group at Vanderbilt (1992). The Jasper experiment: An exploration of issues in learning and instructional design. *Educational Technology Research and Development, 40*, 65–80.

Collins, A. (1992). Toward a design science of education. In E. Scanlon & T. O'Shea (eds), *New directions in educational technology* (pp. 15–22). New York: Springer-Verlag.

Confrey, J. (2003). Scientific research in mathematics education: Answering the challenge and challenging the answer. Paper presented at the Research Presession annual meeting of the National Council of Teachers of Mathematics, San Antonio, TX, April.

Confrey, J. & Stohl, V. (2004). *On evaluating curricular effectiveness: Judging the quality of K–12 mathematics evaluations.* National Research Council Committee for a Review of the Evaluation Data on the Effectiveness of NSF-Supported and Commercially Generated Mathematics Curriculum Materials. Washington, DC: National Research Council.

Dahmus, J. B., Gonzalez-Zugasti, J. P. & Otto, K. N. (2001). Modular product architecture. *Design Studies, 22*, 409–424.

de Silva, T. (2001). Quotient construct, inscriptional practices and instructional design. *Dissertation Abstracts International, 62*(06), 2014. (UMI No. 3016016).

de Silva-Lamberg, T. & Middleton, J. A. (2002). Inscriptional practices as indices of emergent understanding of the quotient. Paper presented at the annual meeting of the American Educational Research Association, New Orleans, LA, April.

Dick, W. & Carey, L. (1990). *The systematic design of instruction* (3rd ed.). New York: Harper Collins.

Gibbons, M. (2000). Mode 2 society and the emergence of context-sensitive science. *Science and Public Policy, 27*, 159–163.

Gorard, S. (2002a). Fostering scepticism: The importance of warranting claims. *Evaluation and Research in Education, 16*, 136–149.

Gorard, S. (2002b). The role of causal models in education as a social science. *Evaluation and Research in Education, 16*, 51–65.

Gorard, S., with Taylor, C. (2004). *Combining methods in educational and social research.* London: Open University Press.

Guba, E. G. & Lincoln, Y. S. (1989). *Fourth generation evaluation.* Beverly Hills, CA: Sage.

Hall, R. (2000). Videorecording as data. In A. E. Kelly & R. A. Lesh (eds), *Handbook of research design in mathematics and science education* (pp. 647–663) Mahwah, NJ: Lawrence Erlbaum Associates.

Horowitz, R. & Maimon, O. (1997). Creative design methodology and the SIT method. *Proceedings of the ASME International Design Engineering Technical Conferences*, New York: American Society of Mechanical Engineers.

Jaeger, R. M. (ed.) (1997). *Complementary methods for research in education*. Washington, DC: American Educational Research Association.

Kalsi, M., Hacker, K. & Lewis, K. (2001). A comprehensive robust design approach for decision tradeoffs in complex systems design. *Journal of Mechanical Design, 123*, 1–10.

Kelly, A. E. (ed.) (2003). The role of design in educational research [Special Issue]. *Educational Researcher, 32*(1).

Kieren, T. E. (1976). On the mathematical, cognitive, and instructional foundations of rational numbers. In R. Lesh (ed.), *Number and measurement* (pp. 101–144). Columbus, OH: Ohio State University, Educational Resources Information Center.

Kieren, T. E. (1993). Rational and fractional numbers: From quotient fields to recursive understanding. In T. Carpenter, E. Fennema & T. Romberg (eds), *Rational numbers: An integration of research* (pp. 49–84). Mahwah, NJ: Lawrence Erlbaum Associates.

Kirkpatrick, D. L. (1998). *Evaluating training programs: The four levels*. San Francisco, CA: Berrett-Koehler.

Lamberg, T. d. S. & Middleton, J. A. (2003). Anchored instruction, an environment for integrating formal and symbolic knowledge in fractions: A case of instructional design. Paper presented at the Annual Meeting of the American Educational Research Association, Chicago, IL, April.

Lappan, G., Fey, J., Fitzgerald, W., Friel, S. & Phillips, E. (2002). *Connected Mathematics*. Boston, MA: Prentice Hall.

Lesh, R. A. & Kelly, A. E. (2000). Multi-tiered teaching experiments. In A. E. Kelly & R. A. Lesh (eds), *Handbook of research design in mathematics and science education* (pp. 197–230). Mahwah, NJ: Lawrence Erlbaum Associates.

Lincoln, Y. S. & Guba, E. G. (1985). *Naturalistic inquiry*. Beverly Hills, CA: Sage.

McCandliss, B. D., Kalchman, M. & Bryant, P. (2003). Design experiments and laboratory approaches to learning: Steps toward collaborative exchange. *Educational Researcher, 32*(1), 14–16.

Medical Research Council (2000). *A framework for development and evaluation of RCTs for complex interventions to improve health*. London: Medical Research Council.

Middleton, J. A., de Silva, T., Toluk, Z. & Mitchell, W. (2001). The emergence of quotient understandings in a fifth-grade classroom: A classroom teaching experiment. In R. S. Speiser & C. Maher (eds), *Proceedings of the 28th Annual Meeting of the North American Chapter of the International Group for the Psychology of Mathematics Education*. Snowbird, UT: Education Resources Information Center.

Middleton, J. A., Sawada, D., Judson, E., Bloom, I. & Turley, J. (2002). Relationships build reform: Developing partnerships for research in teacher education. In L. English (ed.), *Handbook of international research in mathematics education* (pp. 409–431). Mahwah, NJ: Lawrence Erlbaum Associates.

Moore, L. (2002). Lessons from using randomised trials in health promotion. *Building Research Capacity, 1*, 4–5.

National Academy of Engineering (2004). *The engineer of 2020: Visions of engineering in the new century*. Washington, DC: National Academies Press.

Nutbeam, D., Macaskill, P., Smith, C., Simpson, J. M. & Catford, J. (1993). Evaluation of two school smoking programmes under normal classroom conditions. *British Medical Journal, 306*, 102–107.

Reeves, T. C. (2000). Enhancing the worth of instructional technology research through "design experiments" and other development research strategies. Paper presented at the annual meeting of the American Educational Research Association, New Orleans, LA, April.

Rogers, E. M. (1995). *Diffusion of innovations* (4th ed.). New York: Free Press.

Romberg, T. A. (ed.) (2000). *A blueprint for maths in context: A connected curriculum for grades 5–8*. Chicago, ILL: Encyclopaedia Britannica Educational Corporation.

Shadish, W. R., Cook, T. D. & Campbell, D.T. (2002). *Experimental and quasi-experimental designs for generalized causal inference*. New York: Houghton Mifflin.

Shavelson, R. J. & Towne, L. (2002). *Scientific research in education*. Washington, DC: National Academy Press.

Shavelson, R. J., Phillips, D. C., Towne, L. & Feuer, M. J. (2003). On the science of education design studies. *Educational Researcher, 32*(1), 25–28.

Shooter, S. B., Keirouz, W. T., Szykman, S. & Fenves, S. (2000). A model for information flow in design. *Proceedings of the ASME International Design Engineering Technical Conferences*. New York: American Society of Mechanical Engineers.

Shulman, L. S. (1986). Those who understand: Knowledge growth in teaching. *Educational Researcher, 15*(2), 4–14.

Sloane, F. C. & Gorard, S. (2003). Exploring modeling aspects of design experiments. *Educational Researcher, 32*(1), 29–31.

Smaling, A. (2003). Inductive, analogical, and communicative generalization. *International Journal of Qualitative Methods, 2*(1).

Steffe, L. P. & Thompson, P. W. (2000). Teaching experiment methodology: Underlying principles and essential elements. In A. E. Kelly & R. A. Lesh (eds), *Handbook of research design in mathematics and science education* (pp. 267–306). Mahwah, NJ: Lawrence Erlbaum Associates.

Stokes, D. (1997). *Pasteur's quadrant: Basic science and technological innovation*. Washington, DC: Brookings Institution Press.

Tessmer, M. & Wedman, J. (1995). Context-sensitive instructional design models: A response to design research, studies and criticism. *Performance Improvement Quarterly, 8*, 38–54.

Toluk, Z. (1999). Children's conceptualizations of the quotient subconstruct of rational numbers. *Dissertation Abstracts International, 60*(11), 3944. (UMI No. 9949182).

Toluk, Z. & Middleton, J. A. (2001). The development of children's understanding of quotient: A teaching experiment. In M. van den Heuvel-Panhuizen (ed.), *Proceedings of the 25th annual meeting of the International Group for the Psychology of Mathematics Education* (pp. 265–272). Utrecht, The Netherlands: Hogrefe.

Torgerson, C. & Torgerson, D. (2001). The need for randomised controlled trials in educational research. *British Journal of Educational Studies, 49*, 316–328.

Ullman, D. G. (1992). *The mechanical design process*. New York: McGraw-Hill.

Urlich, K. T. & Eppinger, S. D. (2000). *Product design and development*. Boston: Irwin McGraw-Hill.

Webb, N. L., Romberg, T. A. & Shafer, M. C. (2001). Variations in student performance. Paper presented at the meeting of the American Educational Research Association, Seattle, WA, April.

Zaritsky, R., Kelly, A. E., Flowers, W., Rogers, E. & O'Neill, P. (2003). Clinical design sciences: A view from sister design efforts. *Educational Researcher, 32*(1), 32–34.

3 Instrumentation and Innovation in Design Experiments

Taking the Turn Towards Efficiency

Daniel L. Schwartz, Jammie Chang, and Lee Martin
Stanford University

Introduction

A design experiment is a form of interventionist research that creates and evaluates novel conditions for learning. The desired outcomes include new possibilities for educational practice and new insights on the process of learning. Design experiments differ from most educational research because they do not study what exists; they study what could be.

Methods for determining "what could be" are underdeveloped. A science of novel intervention needs both practical methods for doing productive research *and* logical methods for evaluating research. Some authors propose that intervention research should adopt product design methodologies that include iterative cycles of mid-stream modification, retrospective sense-making, case studies, and human sensibilities (e.g., Collins et al., 2004). These methods are good for making products, but they are not ideal for producing generalizable causal knowledge. Others propose that intervention research should resemble classic experiments that emphasize random assignment, dispassionate analysis, and hypothesis testing (e.g., Shavelson et al., 2003). These approaches are good for creating generalizable knowledge, but they are not practical for early stages of innovation.

These methodological camps are often set apart as opposites, and at best, some researchers imagine that they can bridge the gap by jumping from observational design methodologies to large-scale clinical trials. As we discuss below, this jump is rarely optimal. We find it more productive to re-characterize the methods in a larger learning space that arose from an analysis of the ways people generalize learning to new contexts (Schwartz et al., 2005). The learning space has two axes (Figure 3.1(a)). The horizontal axis represents processes and outcomes associated with efficiency. The vertical axis represents innovation. We say much more about these dimensions of learning. For now, Figure 3.1(b) shows the learning space adapted to science.

Design methodologies are high on the innovation dimension, but low on efficiency: their goal is often discovery and the creation of novel practices, but they are poor at developing efficient tests and descriptions of causal hypotheses about learning. Clinical trials are high on the efficiency dimension, but low on innovation: they test hypotheses about which intervention causes superior learning, but they require sample sizes that are too costly for vetting every innovative idea. Good science needs a balance of innovation and efficiency. In the upper-right corner, we position the ultimate goal of science—the cumulative growth of knowledge—which requires innovation and efficiency.

Given the space of innovation and efficiency, the question is not which methodology is right. The question is how to promote movement through the space. The arrow in the

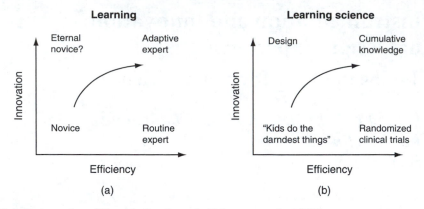

Figure 3.1 Trajectories of Knowledge Growth (Schwartz et al., 2005).

figure reflects our proposal that an optimal trajectory first accelerates along the innovation dimension and then turns towards efficiency. Science would hardly advance if people merely tested and refined their pre-existing hypotheses. However, innovation-oriented research needs to include provisions for a turn to efficiency, lest the field get mired in isolated innovations without prospect of accumulation.

Our research attempts to facilitate this movement through the design of innovative research instruments. Though we design technologies, classroom structures, lesson plans, and the like, we think of these primarily in terms of instrumentation. Most of our lab discussions involve creating, evaluating, and calibrating instruments. We are not alone—instrumentation is central to all science. We asked a physicist how much of his research involves conducting experiments. He responded that 95 per cent of his time is spent on instrumentation (Jose Mestre, 2004, personal communication), by which he meant both the design and calibration of apparatus to precipitate effects and the methods to measure those effects. In our experience, the ability that differentiates novices from domain experts in science is the ability to determine the right instruments for the task.

Designing instruments provides a bridge between innovative design and efficient experimentation. In our work, we expend great effort testing the innovative value of our instruments through *assessment experiments*. In the primary example below, we argue that current instruments to promote and measure learning often miss people's *preparation for future learning* (Bransford & Schwartz, 1999). To make this argument, we innovated both the apparatus that prepared students to learn and the measures that evaluated this preparation. This work did not involve isolating or proving causality. Rather, we wanted to show that our instruments reveal something that others do not. At the same time, these instruments, which generated and measured a phenomenon, equip us for subsequent efficiency research that can address issues of causality and generality.

We divide the chapter into four sections. In the first section, we develop the case for considering learning and science in terms of innovation and efficiency. In the second section, we argue that instrumentation can encourage both innovation and efficiency in learning and science. In the third section, we show how instrumentation research can support both student learning and science through a trajectory of innovation that turns towards efficiency. In the final section, we turn to the problem of knowledge warrants in design experiments. Efficient science has a number of formal techniques for warranting claims of knowledge progress (e.g., p-values, control conditions). Can design experiments be evaluated by warrants of progress in *innovation* before these innovations are mature enough to stand the tests of efficient science? We distinguish innovations in knowledge from innovations in practice, and our solution highlights the belief that criteria of efficient science depend on predicting future regularities, whereas criteria of innovation depend on reconciling past irregularities.

The Case for the Efficiency and Innovation Space

Learning

Figure 3.1(a) shows the hypothesized learning space. When people are high on the efficiency dimension, they can rapidly retrieve and accurately apply appropriate knowledge and skills to complete a routine task or solve a familiar problem. Typically, learning scientists use measures of speed, accuracy, and consistency to capture efficiency. Everyday examples of efficiency include people who have a lot of experience with certain types of tasks and problems; for example, doctors who have frequently performed a specific surgery or skilled typists. Efficiency is important in all domains. As a field, we have learned a great deal about how to accelerate development along the efficiency axis through properly organized and situated practice (Bransford et al., 1999).

While efficiency works well when people operate in constant environments, there are perils to efficiency. Experimental studies show that efficiency can produce "functionally fixed" behaviors where people perseverate on previously efficient schemas instead of letting go to see new alternatives (Luchins, 1942). For example, nine-year-old children trying to learn about fractions often count pieces by using efficient, whole number counting schemas, which interferes with their abilities to interpret the pieces as parts of wholes (Martin & Schwartz, 2005). Hatano and Inagaki (1986) discuss "routine experts" who become increasingly efficient at solving familiar problems, but who do not engage with new problems and situations.

Innovation involves creating new skills and concepts, often as a way to adapt to new situations. As a field, we know less about innovation. Relevant psychological variables, like creativity, are often considered general traits or skills. Efforts to cultivate creativity typically involve brainstorming techniques. "Content-lite" approaches like these are not ideal, because meaningful innovation requires integration with an extensive body of efficient knowledge. Ericsson et al. (1993), for example, found that original intellectual contributions to a field occur after people spend ten years developing the requisite domain expertise.

Ideally, the goal of education is to position people in the upper-right corner of Figure 3.1(a). People often think of innovation and efficiency as incompatible (e.g., discovery learning versus "back to basics"). However, the possibility of balancing efficiency and innovation is highlighted by Hatano and Inagaki's (1986) notion of adaptive experts who have a wealth of efficient knowledge but are also able to adapt to situations that require innovation. Efficiency in some processes (decoding written words) frees attention for other things (reading for meaning). If people have solved aspects of a complex problem before, this helps make sub-problems routine, freeing them to concentrate on other aspects of the situation that may require innovation. At the same time, it is important to resist practiced responses to situations that do not call for them. A major challenge for the learning sciences is to understand how to balance efficiency and innovation in learning.

Design research can contribute by developing interventions that strike the right balance of innovation and efficiency experiences and that place students on a trajectory towards adaptive expertise. This research should also create ways to determine whether students are on that trajectory, and this requires more than borrowing standard off-the-shelf measures of efficiency. Efficiency measures can misdiagnose the value of an innovative experience. For example, Schwartz and Bransford (1998) asked college students to innovate representations of data taken from classic studies of memory. Other students wrote a summary of a parallel chapter. On a subsequent true–false test—a standard test of efficient factual recall—the summarize students did better than the innovate students. However, a new type of measure revealed the value of the innovative experiences. Students from both conditions heard a common lecture that reviewed the studies and their implications for human behavior. A week later, the students had to predict the results of a new, but relevant, experiment. The innovation students produced twice as many correct predictions with no increase in wrong predictions—they had been prepared to learn from the lecture and adapt what they learned to predict the results of the new experiment. The benefit of the innovative experiences was missed by the standard efficiency-oriented assessment, but it was captured by a measure that looked at students' subsequent abilities to learn. As a field, it is important to develop ways to measure the benefits of innovative experiences, lest these experiences look useless on standard tests of efficiency.

Science

We can export the learning space to scientific inquiry without too much damage. Efficiency research nails down the regularities identified by prior work. It involves applying, refining, or testing prior beliefs. One example would be the human genome project; the techniques of gene sequencing were already established and finishing was a matter of time. Another example occurs when well-delineated hypotheses create testable predictions, and at their finest, can create a "Galilean experiment" that adjudicates between two theories (Medawar, 1979).

As with learning, there are scientific perils to an efficiency-only approach. Recent political developments in educational research push for large clinical studies to determine which models of instruction are the most effective. As the Design-Based Research Collective (2003: 6) noted, "the use of randomized trials may hinder innovation studies by prematurely judging the efficacy of an intervention." The political push for clinical trials may promote the use of efficient experimental methods to make choices between sub-optimal alternatives. Moreover, good research designs may be compromised by inappropriate measures, such as evaluating students' efficiency in school tasks rather than their potential for future learning and decision making beyond school. Raudenbush (2005: 29) states the concern clearly, "Indeed, one might argue that a failure to attend systematically to this process of creating good outcome measures is the Achilles heel of evaluation research on instructional innovation."

Innovations in science take many forms. One form involves explanation; for example, a theory for why children find division harder than multiplication. Another form involves the discovery of a new phenomenon like X-rays. In contrast to efficiency research, innovative science does not necessarily depend on generalization or causal identification. A single case is often sufficient to challenge a long-standing theory. The invention of the telescope led to the discovery of lunar imperfections, which undermined the prevailing theory of heavenly perfection (Kuhn, 1957).

There are also perils to innovation-only research. In the context of design experiments, Brown (1992: 171) writes, "It is not sufficient to argue that a reasonable endpoint is an existence proof, although this is indeed an important first step." One peril is that because the work is about innovation, it often needs to let go of current theories. This can create a tower of innovation babble with little short-term hope of cumulative knowledge. A second peril is that if innovations must stand on their own, with limited support from prior theory, the research is difficult and runs a high risk of failure. DiSessa and Cobb (2004), for example, argue that a preeminent goal of design experiments is to create new theories. This may be a fine goal for brilliant researchers at the top of their game, but for the rest of us, it is a recipe for heart-felt platitudes.

Innovation-only and efficiency-only approaches are not sufficient for the types of progress needed to improve education. The ultimate goal of research is to contribute to a growing body of knowledge that comprises tested "truths" but adapts to new findings and historical times. The challenge for design experiments is to find a way to balance the goal of innovation with the need for subsequent efficiency. We propose that a focus on instrumentation can help achieve this balance.

Instrumentation for Promoting Innovation and Efficiency

If it were possible to quantify contributions to the advancement of science, instrumentation would compete well. New instruments open territories that scientists quickly populate. One only needs to look at the effects of fMRI on psychology. Interestingly, instrumental innovations are often independent of specific research methodologies. Video-taping, for example, can be used in clinical, experimental, and cultural applications. Sometimes we wonder if debates over research methods are missing the action. The most highly cited authors, at least in psychology, are those who make new instruments for research. Here, we describe examples of how instrumentation research supports innovation and the subsequent turn to efficiency. We begin with science, and then develop the parallel for individual learning.

Science

Innovation in Instrumentation

New instruments often foster scientific innovation by enabling scientists to see what they could not see before; cell stains, telescopes, and the habituation paradigm are just three examples. They exemplify the first half of the instrument equation—the "apparatus" that makes phenomena observable. Passive apparatus (cameras) and emissive apparatus (radar) are staples of the natural sciences. In the behavioral sciences, researchers often use perturbing apparatus that trigger processes to make their features more visible. For example, psychologists can use an "apparatus" of word stimuli to trigger people's thoughts and see how they affect memory.

Design experiments, because they are interventions, can also be recast as a "perturbing" apparatus. Cobb et al. (2003: 9) state, "Prototypically, design experiments entail both 'engineering' particular forms of learning and systematically studying those forms of learning. . . ." When design researchers devise novel lessons, technologies, or social practices, they are designing a new apparatus for perturbing the environment to reveal processes of learning.

The second half of the instrument equation is the development of measurement. Measurement converts observations into precise communicable information. Though measurement reduces the totality of a phenomenon, the gains in precision can aid innovation. Precise measures can pick up aberrations from the expected. Astronomers in the early 1800s found that the measured positions of Uranus did not match its predicted orbit. This anomaly led to the hypothesis and eventual discovery of an eighth planet, Neptune. Galileo had seen Neptune through his telescope, but he observed it as a star. The precision of measurement, and not pure observation, led to discovery.

Taking the Turn Toward Efficiency

Instruments that were once innovative may subsequently support efficient progress in science. Piaget created instruments to evaluate children's cognitive function (e.g., Piaget & Inhelder, 1975). The instruments themselves could be disseminated and evaluated independently of Piaget (e.g., cross-cultural applications). Instruments can be "handed off." This allowed the research community to take a turn from an innovative but singular set of studies to a more efficient mode of research that refined the instruments and addressed what causes change in the measurements (and whether Piaget was correct).

The measurement component of instrumentation also permits other people to determine if they are "seeing" the same thing. Measurements can be quantitative, for example the time to complete a task. Measurements can also be qualitative, for example a set of observational criteria for the presence of a phenomenon. If researchers want, they can convert qualitative measurements into a quantitative form by recording the frequency or intensity of an observation. The benefit of quantification is that it permits researchers to use the substantial structural apparatus provided by mathematics to draw inferences. However, quantification is not a prerequisite of measurement, and oftentimes it is a mistake to force a set of observations into a particular mathematical model (e.g., a linear model).

A challenge for innovation research is that "the decision to employ a particular piece of apparatus and to use it in a particular way carries an assumption that only certain sorts of circumstances will arise" (Kuhn, 1970: 59). Some researchers reject the idea of using measures because they worry the measures will foreclose the possibility of detecting the unanticipated. Consequently, many rely on narratives rather than discrete measures to create inter-subjectivity. An extreme position, like that of Eisner (2001), argues that a research report should help the reader *experience* what the researchers saw, including their epiphanies and failures. Unlike some traditionalists (Shavelson et al., 2003), we do not have a strong opinion about narrative. We do not know of any evidence one way or another that determines whether narrative yields precise agreement between the researcher and the audience.

Personally, we report discrete process and outcome measures in scientific papers. This does not mean that we are not highly attentive to occurrences that elude our measures. (We are present throughout our studies, we video-tape, and we collect artifacts.) It is naïve to assume that researchers who use measures are not also keen on discovering processes and outcomes they never imagined. For example, when we design a new paper-and-pencil assessment, we exhaustively code every response looking for interesting patterns. In the studies below, each instrument averaged seven different categories of response. We would love to report all the responses and patterns that we find. However, like all scientific authors, we decide which of the patterns will be most compelling and economical to report—this is often a simple percent correct, but not always.

Implications for Design Experiments

A place for substantial improvement in design research involves the use of measurement. Design research is quite good at developing techniques for the apparatus half of the equation—innovative instruments that precipitate effects. However, most design research has not finished the equation by developing innovative measures suited to those effects. This lack of measure is surprising. It is very important to note that, unlike ethnographers, design researchers are orchestrating "what could be" rather than observing what already exists. Therefore, they must have some goal in mind. Ideally, this goal would be specific enough that it is possible to begin precisely measuring its attainment.

One hope of design research seems to be that the instructional apparatus will jump from the quadrant of high-innovation and low-efficiency in Figure 3.1(b) to the quadrant of cumulative knowledge, perhaps through large-scale clinical trials involving random assignment and standard achievement measures. Most standardized tests of achievement and intelligence, however, are created to rank people and not to precisely reveal the component knowledge and processes responsible for an answer. Without working on measures that are tightly matched to the perturbing intervention, the research will yield claims like, "Our intervention was *significantly better* than standard practice." Though good at satisfying evidence-based educational policy, we fear the vagueness of the measure will not contribute to the cumulative growth of scientific knowledge. For example, when the social climate changes what it means to "do better," these studies will become irrelevant instead of leaving documentation of exactly what learning a particular design yields or how to improve it. Creating measures that are tightly coupled to an apparatus of change can better facilitate a productive turn to efficiency.

Learning

To us, it is clear that instrumentation can support innovation and the turn to efficiency in science. The idea that working on instrumentation can also propel individual learning is less obvious. Measurement, in particular, often conjures images of students mechanically using rulers. This is an efficiency-only take on measurement that presupposes the techniques and outcome categories already exist in the mind of the learner. The innovation side of measurement is not so banal, though it has been overlooked in the research literature. The standard cognitive study of scientific reasoning emphasizes methodological thinking over measures. People receive a set of well-defined input and output variables (the instruments), and their task is to design unconfounded experiments to discover the relations (Chen & Klahr, 1999; Kuhn et al., 1992). Our experience with hundreds of adults has been that it is not the ability to reason within an experimental design that is the difficult part of scientific thinking. Novices quickly learn about confounds, though they sometimes forget to use this knowledge efficiently, or find it tedious. The more difficult challenge is found in developing measures suited to a specific situation. By the same token, asking novices to attempt to innovate measurements can be an excellent source of domain learning. Creating measurements encourages specificity in understanding. For example, asking students to measure how well people learn from a reading passage can help them develop more differentiated knowledge of what it means to learn, such as whether it is more appropriate to measure free recall, recognition, comprehension, inference, or transfer.

Another benefit is that measurement can indicate places that require innovation. As a rather grand example, we consider Plato's learning paradox. This paradox raises doubts about whether people can innovate new knowledge, and accepting the paradox leads to an efficiency view of learning that emphasizes the refinement of prior knowledge (e.g., innate concepts, language modules, phenomenological primitives, and so forth). Through the dialog of the *Meno*, Plato (1961) formulates two components of the paradox:

> But how will you look for something when you don't in the least know what it is? How on earth are you going to set up something you don't know as the object of your search? To put it another way, even if you come right up against it, how will you know that what you have found is the thing you didn't know?
>
> (80.d)

The first half of the paradox asks how people can look for knowledge if they do not already know what they are looking for. Plato's solution is that incommensurables alert people to the need for innovation. The term incommensurable refers to the situation where multiple elements cannot be measured within the same rational system. For example, if we try to determine whether an Olympic weightlifter broke the world record by more than a long jumper did, we cannot use weight to measure distance or distance to measure weight—the performances are incommensurable. Thus, a failure in the measurement system lets one know where to look for new knowledge. It causes the disequilibrium that begins the search for resolution.

The second half of the paradox asks how people can recognize whether they have found knowledge if they do not already know it. The solution is that people know they have found new knowledge when the incommensurables can be explained within the same system. In the case of weightlifting and long jump performances, one makes them commensurable by using standardized scores. People know they have learned something new because it is possible to relate what they could not previously. We return to the example of standardized scores below, but for our present purposes, it is noteworthy that Plato resolves the learning paradox by offering measurement as a premiere example of an innovation in learning.

In our work teaching children statistics, we capitalize on the potential of measurement for propelling learning. An example from the materials we use to teach variability can help demonstrate the point. Each grid in Figure 3.2 shows the result of a test using a different baseball-pitching machine. The black circles represent where a pitch landed; the X is the target. Students receive the innovation task of developing a formula or procedure that computes a reliability index for each machine. The reliability index can help shoppers decide which machine they would like to purchase.

The pitching grids were designed to help students develop more differentiated and structured knowledge. By highlighting key quantitative distinctions, the contrasting grids alert learners to the properties that their measurements need to handle. For example, most students initially misinterpret variability as a lack of accuracy. The pitching grids specifically include an example where all the pitches are extremely close together, yet they are far from the target. This helps the students notice that variability and lack of accuracy should be distinguished.

By asking students to innovate a single measure by which to compare the machines (the reliability index), this task also promotes a more structured understanding of variability, because the students' formula must accommodate the various dimensions along which the grids differ. For example, the grids use different sample sizes. Many students begin by summing the distances of the pitches from the target, but they quickly realize that grids with more pitches will tend to get higher variability scores, even if the pitches are close to the target. A simple summation measure makes samples of different size incommensurable. The need to handle sample size becomes a structural element of students' understanding of variability.

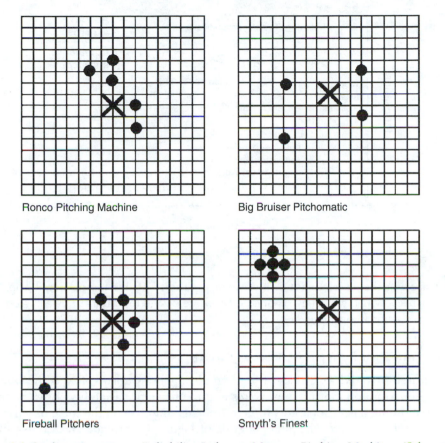

Ronco Pitching Machine

Big Bruiser Pitchomatic

Fireball Pitchers

Smyth's Finest

Figure 3.2 Students Innovate a Reliability Index to Measure Pitching Machines (Schwartz & Martin, 2004).

We do not expect students to innovate the conventional measurement. Instead, our assumption is that the innovation activities prepare the students to understand efficient expert solutions more deeply. For example, when they hear the standard solution for finding variability, they will appreciate how dividing by "*n*" elegantly solves the problem of comparing samples of different sizes (by taking the average of the deviations from the mean). In accordance with our learning space, we have students accelerate on the innovation dimension first, before they take the turn to efficiency. An emphasis on instrumentation, in this case measurement, can facilitate this trajectory. An alternative would be to just tell the students how to compute variance at the outset. We believe this yields efficiency, but it does not create a trajectory towards adaptive expertise. The following section tests this belief.

A Double Demonstration of the Innovation—Efficiency Space

Figure 3.3 summarizes our claims so far. We believe that both scientific progress and individual learning benefit from accelerating first on the innovation dimension before taking a turn to efficiency, and we propose that this trajectory is particularly well-supported by an effort to develop instrumentation. To make our claims more concrete, we provide an example of this double-trajectory in a study we did with ninth-graders. Notably, none of the research we describe is about proving causes. Instead, it is about

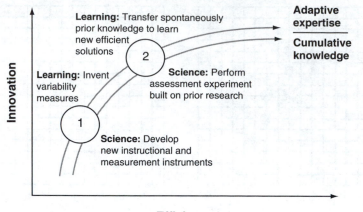

Figure 3.3 Taking the Turn in Learning and Science.

demonstrating the discriminant and ecological validity of our instructional apparatus and measures, which we believe is one place where design research can excel in contributing to scientific knowledge.

DEMONSTRATION 1: HIGH ON INNOVATION, LOW ON EFFICIENCY

This research involved six classes of ninth-grade algebra students. It was the students' first introduction to innovating measures and the topic of variability. It was our first effort at building a new apparatus to help students innovate on the topic of variability and to detect the effects. The pitching-grids of Figure 3.2 provide an example of one instructional apparatus. We provide an example of an innovative measure below. A complete description of the full set of instruments and results may be found in Schwartz and Martin (2004).

Students spent a few hours innovating their own ways to measure variability in a variety of tasks. Students worked in groups, and there were class discussions about the invented solutions. Students never invented a canonical solution, and the teacher did not present one during the innovation phase. The task was an innovation task rather than a "discovery" task, because we did not expect students to "find" the canonical solution. Instead, we expected the innovation activities to prepare the students to learn the canonical solution when it was presented. At the end of the innovation activities, the teacher gave a five-minute lecture on the mean deviation (an efficient way to measure variability) and students practiced for another ten minutes. The question was whether students' innovation activities would prepare them to learn the efficient solution, and whether we could measure any special benefits of the innovation activity.

All six classes received the same instruction. Putting classes into control conditions was premature. Still, there are ways to make scientific progress. We included techniques, such as benchmarking our instruments, to support plausible inferences on whether we (and the students) were on a good trajectory. By plausible inference, we mean the evidence confirms our expectations. This is a much weaker warrant than the standard of falsification in efficient science, and these kinds of designs cannot guarantee that there were not other sources of influence. However, in early stages of research methods that do not involve falsification designs can be a valuable source of preliminary evidence. We have conducted many design experiments where the results did not support plausible inference, leaving us to decide whether there was a problem with our instruments or whether our guiding ideas were wrong. Deciding whether to try again is a problem faced by all researchers. Instrumentation cannot guarantee successful innovation—nothing can. Therefore, we usually minimize the risk by conducting small studies first, and then pursue the most promising results.

The most important of our techniques for achieving plausible inference is to use "targeted measurement." We tune our measures to specific features of our intervention. For example, as part of our assessment, we used a number of off-the-shelf techniques for measuring efficiency, such as asking students to compute variability and to solve word problems. Students improved from 5 percent at pretest to 86 percent at post-test. A year later without any intervening review, they were still at 57 percent. This measure indicated that the students had learned the efficient solution, which is very important, but we thought it missed the unique benefits of the innovation activities. We needed to invent new measures that targeted the novel benefits of our instruction.

We included a large number of targeted measures specifically addressing our expectation that students' innovation activities would help them subsequently understand why a statistical procedure takes the form it does. For example, we expected the pitching grid activity to help students notice that their reliability index needed to handle the different sample sizes across the grids. By noticing the challenge of different sample sizes and working to resolve it, students would be prepared to appreciate how variability measures handle issues of sample size. To test our expectation, we developed a "symbolic insight" measurement. Students receive a formula and have to explain one of its symbolic operations; for example, "Why does this variability formula divide by 'n'?" As a comparison, we also created symbolic insight questions about another formula they had learned recently but not through our innovation-to-efficiency curriculum. We exhaustively coded the different types of answers and found a number of interesting patterns (see Schwartz and Martin, 2004). Table 3.1 simplifies the data by using an aggregated measure of symbolic insight. The students did better with the variability formula than other formulas they had been taught in other ways, and they showed greater gains than a benchmark of college students who had taken a full semester of college statistics. This leaves us with the plausible inference that our intervention helped students develop symbolic insight, and that this insight is not a common outcome of other forms of instruction.

Without a control group, we cannot go beyond the plausible inference that the innovation component of the lessons prepared students to learn the variability formula so well from the brief lecture. Being early on the innovation curve, the time was not right for efficient tests of causal hypotheses. However, the study equipped us with the instrumentation to find out.

Table 3.1 Percentage of Students who Successfully Explained why a Formula Uses a Given Operation

Formula	Ninth graders (%)		College statistics (%)	
	Pretest	Post-test	None	One
Why does $\Sigma(X - \mathrm{x})/n$ divide by n?	6	63	0	12
Why does m = $y_2 - y_1/x_2 - x_1$ subtract x_1?	10	14	11	29

DEMONSTRATION 2: TAKING THE TURN

The second demonstration involves the same students after two weeks of innovating statistical measures and subsequently hearing efficient solutions. The students were further along the curve in their statistical knowledge, and they were able to take a turn towards adaptive expertise. The second demonstration also shows how our research was able to take the turn to efficiency through the use of an assessment experiment. To better explicate the design and purpose of the experiment, we provide some background.

The experiment arose from a concern that most current assessments of knowledge use sequestered problem solving (Bransford & Schwartz, 1999). Like members of a jury, students are shielded from contaminating sources of information that might help them learn during the test. It appears that this assessment paradigm has created a self-reinforcing loop where educators use efficiency-driven methods of procedural and mnemonic instruction that improve student efficiency on sequestered tests. However, we suppose that a goal of secondary instruction is to put students on a trajectory towards adaptive expertise so they can continue to learn and make decisions on their own. Like many others, we fear that measures of the wrong outcomes drive instruction the wrong way. In prior work, we had shown that preparation for future learning (PFL) assessments, which directly examine students' abilities to learn, are a viable alternative to sequestered assessments, and they better reveal the strengths and limitations of different forms of instruction in college-level psychology (Schwartz & Bransford, 1998). However, one series of studies with one demographic profile using one content area is insufficient. Moreover, in those studies, students were directly told what they were supposed to learn. Ideally, good instruction can help students learn in the future without explicit directives. Thus, with the current assessment experiment, we wanted to continue work on PFL measurements using a new age group, a new topic, and a new format that determined whether students spontaneously took advantage of a potential learning resource.

The assessment experiment crossed the apparatus of instruction with the method of measurement. The topic of instruction was normalizing data. We first describe the two instructional conditions shown at the top of Figure 3.4. Students received raw data that required them to compare individuals from different distributions to see who did better. For example, the students had to decide if Bill broke the high-jump world record more

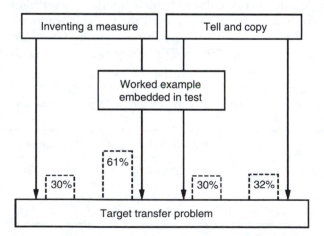

Figure 3.4 Design of Assessment Experiment and Results (Schwartz & Martin, 2004).

than Joe broke the weightlifting record (given data of the top jumps and lifts that year). Three randomly selected classes were assigned to the invention condition. These students had to innovate their own way to solve this problem. There were neither class presentations nor feedback, which helped isolate the value of innovation from other features in the larger design experiment. The other three classes received the tell-and-copy treatment. These students were taught an efficient visual procedure, which they copied using the data sets.

The second factor involved the method of measurement and whether students received an embedded learning resource in their post-test, several days later. In Figure 3.4, this is shown by whether arrows go through the middle box. The resource was a worked example that showed how to compute standardized scores (see Appendix). The example showed how Cheryl determined if she was better at the high dive or low dive. The students had to follow the example to determine if Jack was better at high jump or javelin. Half of the students from each condition received this worked example as part of their post-test and nearly everyone followed it correctly. The question was whether students followed their usual efficiency-oriented practice of treating the example as something to just copy, or whether they adapted to learn what the problem had to offer. To detect spontaneous learning, there was a target transfer problem later in everybody's post-test (see Appendix). It involved a different context and format, and its solution depended on using standardized scores as in the worked example. The worked example and the target transfer problem created a novel *double-transfer assessment* of preparation for future learning; students needed to "transfer in" to learn from the worked example and they needed to "transfer out" from the worked example to solve the target transfer problem.

Figure 3.4 shows the percent of students who solved the target transfer problem. Students who had innovated their own methods for normalizing data learned the efficient solution from the embedded worked example and spontaneously transferred this learning to solve a novel problem, more so than students who had been told and had practiced a specific visual technique for normalizing data. This difference shows the effectiveness of innovation activities in helping students take the turn towards adaptive expertise. Students in the innovation condition who did not receive an embedded resource were probably still better prepared to take the turn than the tell-and-copy students, but they had no opportunity to demonstrate that readiness and looked the same. Thus, the PFL measure demonstrated discriminant validity, because it detected a difference that was missed when there was no embedded learning resource. This example also shows how PFL assessments can be sensitive measures of levels of understanding that we care about but that can be missed by sequestered measures of efficient problem solving.

There are two points to make with this example. One point is that student learning can advance on a curve that first accelerates along innovation and then turns to efficiency. The value of innovation activities for student learning seems obvious in retrospect, but there is a great deal of confusion in this area (see Schwartz & Martin, 2004). We hope these studies are a useful demonstration of the hidden value of innovation for subsequent efficiency.

The second point is that instrumentation can help innovative research take the turn to efficiency. For example, in the study above, we taught the classes ourselves. We then gave our instruments to classroom teachers who implemented the study the following year with seven new classes. Results indicated a very high degree of replication.

Good instrumentation research does not have to depend on causal claims, and good instrumentation does not have to inhibit the innovative spirit of design experiments.

Nowhere in this work did we isolate specific causal ingredients, and we were able to leverage our instrumentation with little cost to the design experiment itself. This instrumentation focus permitted us to make cumulative and replicable progress without cutting the research into expensive experimental designs that are efficient in terms of causal proof but inefficient in terms of resources.

Warrants of Innovation

If anything unifies the literature on design experiments, it appears to be the goal of useful innovation. Until now we have skirted a fundamental question—what is an innovation? How can a researcher or funding agency decide if there is productive movement on the innovation dimension? It would be useful to have some grounds for identifying and evaluating design innovations, especially if that is what design researchers claim to do! The goal here is not a set of practical guides to innovation (e.g., instrumentation) or practical criteria of innovation. There are already a number of practical criteria for judging innovation. For example, the legal system judges whether an innovation deserves a patent based on categories including novelty, non-obviousness, and utility. Historically, however, there was so much variability in legal opinion that it was necessary to make a single federal court to handle patent cases. Ideally, we can find a logic for evaluating innovation that is more stable than pragmatic agreement.

Our goal here is to provide a "sacrificial first draft" for a discussion of warrants for scientific innovation. We think this is important because design researchers can best justify their work in terms of innovation. If so, it is important to be clear about one's grounds for making an innovation warrant. The significance of being clear comes from the story of a university job talk. The candidate described a few heroic teachers who had teamed together to innovate a successful program in an environment of indifference and poverty. This candidate was making an innovation argument by showing that what people implicitly thought was impossible, actually could exist. The faculty in the audience, however, challenged the work. The candidate made a mistake and started to defend causal claims about why the program succeeded. This single case could never crisply defend causal claims. The defense came off as speculation and craft knowledge. We wish the candidate had said, "Those are great questions, and the value of my single data point is to show that these are important questions precisely because our theories should, but cannot, explain it. Here are some of the instruments I developed to help us move forward. . . ." As in all things, knowing the logic of one's claims can only help.

As we began thinking about the problem of evaluating innovations, we realized that we, and perhaps others, had confounded two distinct forms of innovation—innovating new knowledge and innovating material change. Producing new knowledge about learning is different from producing a new artifact or social practice, though they are both important innovations. The difference between innovating knowledge and material change can be captured by two possible stances on the value of design research that we label "scientific" and "substantive." Innovations in scientific design involve discovery and theory, whereas substantive innovations involve actual changes to the circumstances of learning. We begin by drawing the distinction between the two, and then we describe one warrant for innovation that has logical force for both types of design research.

Scientific and Substantive Design

Scientific design proposes that design methodologies are the best way to develop innovative knowledge in educational research. The assumption is that there are truths about the world that need to be uncovered. DiSessa and Cobb (2004), for example, propose that a significant goal of design research is "ontological innovation"—the invention of new scientific "categories that do useful work in generating, selecting among, and assessing design alternatives" (p. 78). The goal is to uncover categories of phenomena that support explanation. We suppose these authors actually meant "epistemic innovation," because ontology refers to what exists and epistemology refers to knowledge of what exists. These authors appeared to be defending design methodologies on the grounds that they make new knowledge and not on the grounds that they make new realities (though they may have held that belief as well).

In contrast, substantive design holds that the goal of a design experiment is to improve education per se (as opposed to just improve knowledge of education). The goal is to make changes to the world, and design is the shortest distance from idea to change. Cobb et al. (2003: 10) state that one purpose of design experiments ". . . is to investigate the possibilities for educational improvement by bringing about new forms of learning in order to study them." These authors appear to advocate the creation of new forms of learning, but they justify the endeavor from a scientific design stance. A pure substantive position does not justify its efforts in terms of developing scientific knowledge. Some of the best technology innovators appear to adopt a strong substantive position. They create stunningly innovative technologies to support learning. They are less committed to accounts of why or whether these technologies promote learning. This seems a useful way to make progress, though it is important to appreciate that the goal of educational design research is not technological innovation per se, but rather innovation in learning practices. Thus, pointing to an innovative technology is less compelling than pointing to an innovative learning practice it creates.

Substantive design is appropriate to intervention research because it holds that research can change reality rather than just study it. G. H. Mead captures the quixotic implication:

> In society, we are the forces that are being investigated, and if we advance beyond the mere description of the phenomena of the social world to the attempt at reform, we seem to involve the possibility of changing what at the same time we assume to be necessarily fixed.
>
> (1899: 370)

The idea that design can innovate new forces and facts by which the world operates is inconceivable in domains like physics. But human affairs take place in a social world, and the laws that regulate social behavior have their own organization which is consistent with, but under-determined by, physical and biological laws. Therefore it may be possible to change the social world by design (e.g., Searle, 1995; Simon, 1996). Freire (1970) refers to this as the dialectic of objective and subjective experience. For example, a capitalist economy has a different set of forces than a communist one. At some reductionist level, people in capitalist and communist societies are built from the same fundamental material laws, but at the level of subjective experience and the objective analysis of that experience, they operate according to different rules. Karl Marx's theory built on the possibility of changing the forces that regulate our lives. As he wrote, there were no full-blown communist states. His theory could only be true to the extent that it could change reality to fit itself. This is the notion of praxis, where the proof of a theory is in the change it creates (Cook, 1994). Praxis is highly relevant to claims that a new plan for classroom organization will change what students learn, and it provides an interesting way to warrant a substantive design innovation.

A Warrant for Innovation

Developing warrants for useful innovation is important, lest the mechanisms for evaluating innovative work reduce to consumerism. Toulmin (1972) provides a useful list of types of conceptual change in science: (a) extension of current procedures to fresh phenomena, (b) improvement in techniques for dealing with familiar phenomena, (c) intra-disciplinary integration of techniques, (d) inter-disciplinary integration of techniques, and (e) resolution of conflicts between scientific and extra-scientific ideas. These can be recast into warrants for innovation. Take (a), for instance—an instrument can be considered an innovation if it permits us to observe a fresh phenomenon. Unlike efficient science that gains warrants through reliable prediction of the future, each of the resulting innovation warrants would depend on showing some advance over the past.

Toulmin's first two categories suggest that one method of warranting an innovation is to show that what has been innovated was previously absent. This works well for scientific design, because there is a documented canon of knowledge one can exhaustively search to demonstrate prior absence. However, demonstrating absence is problematic for substantive design in the social sciences. A design may create a seemingly novel social practice, but then it may turn out there is a tribe in a remote location that already engages in those practices.

Toulmin's latter three conditions, which emphasize integration, suggest a warrant that can work for both scientific and substantive design. The warrant is the reconciliation of inconsistencies, and returns us to Plato's resolution of Meno's learning paradox. A warrant for innovation depends on finding an incommensurability or contradiction and then reconciling the horns of the dilemma in a synthesis. The synthesis is an innovation by definition, because it resolves what extant knowledge systems could not. For learning, one example comes from the students who tried to relate high-jumping and weightlifting scores. They could not measure distance in terms of weight, or weight in terms of distance. The innovation they were struggling towards was a way to normalize data so they could compare unlike measures. For them, the solution of standardized scores was an innovation on logical grounds, because it reconciles within one structure what their prior knowledge of absolute magnitudes could never do. Similarly, in science, a powerful logical warrant for knowledge innovation exists when the innovation provides a way to put previously incompatible evidence or theory in the same rational structure. Galileo was a master at generating evidence that contradicted the theories of the day, and then presenting his alternative that was able to synthesize all the evidence within one framework.

The reconciliation warrant for innovation can also work for substantive design. In this case, it involves the reconciliation of contradictory forces rather than contradictory knowledge. The physical world does not contain any contradictions (nature might contradict our theories, but it cannot contradict itself), but, in the social world of goals and means, contradictions are possible. In remote Alaskan villages, for example, schools attempt to improve village life by preparing native students for jobs that require *leaving* the village for the city. A substantive design that removed this contradiction would have a strong warrant for innovation through praxis.

To achieve this warrant in substantive design, it is necessary to first identify an inconsistency. This is a needs assessment, but one with logical force. Saying that children have confused identities is a weak needs assessment compared to one that identifies the contradictory forces that lead to confused identities. Engeström (1999) takes this needs assessment approach, for example, by identifying contradictions in social organizations (e.g., the elderly health care system), and then creating innovations that resolve those contradictions (e.g., postal workers check elderly on their rounds). We find his methodology compelling because it illuminates the contradiction and shows how the innovation attempts to reconcile this contradiction, whether or not it works.

In our research, we identified a contradiction that we tried to reconcile. Most educators want their students to be on a trajectory to adaptive expertise so they can continue to learn and make their own choices as citizens. At the same time, educators try to promote this goal by implementing efficiency-only curricula and assessments, which we believe unwittingly contradicts the goal of adaptive expertise. We tried to resolve this contradiction by innovating a knowledge framework that puts innovation and efficiency together rather than as opposites, and we innovated a pedagogy in which innovation and efficiency practices can co-exist and put learners on a trajectory towards adaptive expertise. Ultimately, we believe our substantive design efforts fell short. The failure was not in the study's outcome; we showed that efficiency measures can miss the value of innovative experiences where PFL measures do not. Rather, the failure was in proving the contradiction: perhaps efficiency-only training does lead to adaptive expertise in the long run and there is no contradiction. We hope that our instrumentation focus will enable us to generate subsequent research to determine whether, or when, we are correct.

Conclusions

We want to make design experiments a more productive scientific endeavor. Innovating in educational settings is largely intractable by standards of efficient science; it is too costly to use the sample sizes and control conditions needed to test every idea of what could be. At the same time, just trying out different ideas is not adequate either. We have been frustrated by the design experiment debate because it has reified methodological positions as incommensurable, while ignoring those things that are most important to working scientists. Though discussions of method and theory are very important, empirical scientists in most fields spend their time working on instrumentation. We proposed that it might be profitable to position design experiments in a larger space of innovation and efficiency. The question is, what features might be added to design research to ensure it maximizes the chances for innovation while also setting the stage for more standard tests of scientific value?

We argued that a focus on instruments that both precipitate and measure effects has historically been effective at supporting innovation and the turn to efficiency. There is a repertoire of ideas for evaluating instrumentation that do not depend on identifying causality or generality (e.g., discriminant validity). We also provided an empirical demonstration where innovating measures led to impressive learning gains for students, and hopefully demonstrated the potential of PFL measures for advancing learning science.

In the last part of the chapter, we initiated a discussion around the logic of justification rather than the practical process of innovation. There can be no logical method for guaranteeing discovery or innovation (Phillips & Burbules, 2000; Popper, 1968), but we thought it might be possible to work towards a logic for warrants of innovation.

We think it is important for the design experiment community to create compelling standards for evaluating its success at innovation. We have found that people often try to use efficiency arguments that cannot succeed, or they provide no warrants at all. We tried to clarify two arguments for the value of design innovations—scientific innovations that involve knowledge and substantive innovations that involve change. We think the substantive design position is particularly relevant to design researchers, but its logic of justification has not been sufficiently explored.

We argued that a logical warrant for innovation is the resolution of incommensurables. (Not surprisingly, this is also the type of innovation we asked students to pursue in reconciling contrasting cases.) This warrant helps draw a strong distinction between the logic of efficiency and innovation. Whereas criteria of efficiency depend on predicting future regularities, the criteria of innovation depend on reconciling past irregularities. Reconciling past irregularities requires planned design, but the causal components of the plan are not being put to the test. What is being put to the test is whether the irregularity is necessary or whether it can be resolved.

We find the two goals of design research—discover knowledge versus plan change—equally compelling. It is an empirical question whether designing our way to a better educational system is more effective than first developing scientific knowledge and then engineering change from established "laws." We do not believe these approaches are incompatible, and in fact, we suspect that both are needed. This consideration led, in part, to our proposal that design experiments would be well-served by explicitly engaging in instrumental innovation that paves the way for efficient scientific methods, while also providing the apparatus for creating and recreating the qualities of what could be.

References

Bransford, J. D. & Schwartz, D. L. (1999). Rethinking transfer: A simple proposal with multiple implications. *Review of Research in Education, 24,* 61–100.

Bransford, J. D., Brown, A. L. & Cocking, R. R. (1999). *How people learn: Brain, mind, experience, and school.* Washington, DC: National Academy Press.

Brown, A. L. (1992). Design experiments: Theoretical and methodological challenges in creating complex interventions in classroom settings. *Journal of the Learning Sciences, 2,* 141–178.

Chen, Z. & Klahr, D. (1999). All other things being equal: Acquisition and transfer of the control of variables strategy. *Child Development, 70,* 1098–1120.

Cobb, P., Confrey, J., diSessa, A., Lehrer, R. & Schauble, L. (2003). Design experiments in educational research. *Educational Researcher, 32*(1), 9–13.

Collins, A., Joseph, D. & Bielaczyc, K. (2004). Design research: Theoretical and methodological issues. *Journal of the Learning Sciences, 13,* 15–42.

Cook, T. E. (1994). *Criteria of social scientific knowledge: Interpretation, prediction, praxis.* Lanham, MD: Rowman & Littlefield.

Design-Based Research Collective (2003). Design-based research: An emerging paradigm for educational inquiry. *Educational Researcher, 32*(1), 5–8.

diSessa, A. A. and Cobb, P. (2004). Ontological innovation and the role of theory in design experiments. *Journal of the Learning Sciences, 13,* 77–103.

Eisner, E. W. (2001). Concerns and aspirations for qualitative research in the new millennium. *Qualitative Research, 1,* 135–145.

Engeström, Y. (1999). Activity theory in individual and social transformation. In Y. Engeström, R. Miettinen & R.-L. Punamäki (eds), *Perspectives on activity theory* (pp. 19–38). Cambridge: Cambridge University Press.

Ericsson, K. A., Krampe, R. T. & Tesch-Römer, C. (1993). The role of deliberate practice in the acquisition of expert performance. *Psychological Review, 100,* 363–406.

Freire, P. (1970). *Pedagogy of the oppressed*. New York: Herder & Herder.

Hatano, G. & Inagaki, K. (1986). Two courses of expertise. In H. Stevenson, H. Azuma & K. Hakuta (eds), *Child development and education in Japan* (pp. 262–272). New York: W. H. Freeman.

Kuhn, T. S. (1957). *The Copernican revolution: Planetary astronomy in the development of western thought*. Cambridge, MA: Harvard University Press.

Kuhn, T. S. (1970). *The structure of scientific revolutions* (2nd ed.). Chicago: University of Chicago Press.

Kuhn, D., Schauble, L. & Garcia-Mila, M. (1992). Cross-domain development of scientific reasoning. *Cognition and Instruction*, *9*, 285–327.

Luchins, A. S. (1942). Mechanization in problem-solving: The effect of Einstellung. *Psychological Monographs*, *54*(6).

Martin, T. & Schwartz, D. L. (2005). Physically distributed learning: Adapting and reinterpreting physical environments in the development of the fraction concept. *Cognitive Science*, *29*, 587–625.

Mead, G. H. (1899). The working hypothesis in social reform. *American Journal of Sociology*, *5*, 369–371.

Medawar, P. B. (1979). *Advice to a Young Scientist*. New York: Harper and Row.

Phillips, D. C. & Burbules, N. C. (2000). *Postpositivism and educational research*. Lanham, MD: Rowman & Littlefield Publishers.

Piaget, J. & Inhelder, B. (1975). *The origin of the idea of chance in children* (translated by L. Leake, Jr., P. Burrell & H. D. Fischbein). New York: Norton.

Plato (1961). *Collected dialogs of Plato including the letters* (E. Hamilton & H. Cairns, eds). Princeton: Princeton University Press.

Popper, K. R. (1968). *The logic of scientific discovery*. New York: Harper and Row.

Raudenbush, S. W. (2005). Learning from attempts to improve schooling: The contribution of methodological diversity. *Educational Researcher*, *34*(5), 25–31.

Schwartz, D. L. & Bransford, J. D. (1998) A time for telling. *Cognition & Instruction*, *16*, 475–522.

Schwartz, D. L. & Martin, T. (2004). Inventing to prepare for learning: The hidden efficiency of original student production in statistics instruction. *Cognition & Instruction*, *22*, 129–184.

Schwartz, D. L., Bransford, J. D. & Sears, D. A. (2005). Efficiency and innovation in transfer. In J. Mestre (ed.), *Transfer of learning from a modern multidisciplinary perspective* (pp.1–52). Greenwich, CT: Information Age Publishing.

Searle, J. R. (1995). *The construction of social reality*. New York: Free Press.

Shavelson, R. J., Phillips, D. C., Towne, L. & Feuer, M. J. (2003) On the science of education design studies. *Educational Researcher*, *32*(1), 25–28.

Simon, H. A. (1996). *The sciences of the artificial* (3rd ed.). Cambridge: MIT Press.

Toulmin, S. E. (1972). *Human understanding*. Princeton: Princeton University Press.

Appendix

Double-Transfer Assessment Items (Schwartz & Martin, 2004)

Worked Example Resource Problem Randomly Placed in Half the Post-Tests

A standardized score helps us compare different things. For example, in a swim meet, Cheryl's best high dive score was an 8.3 and her best low dive was a 6.4. She wants to know if she did better at the high dive or the low dive. To find this out, we can look at the scores of the other divers and calculate a standardized score.

	High dive	Low dive
Cheryl	8.3	6.4
Julie	6.3	7.9
Celina	5.8	8.8
Rose	9	5.1
Sarah	7.2	4.3
Jessica	2.5	2.2
Eva	9.6	9.6
Lisa	8	6.1
Teniqua	7.1	5.3
Aisha	3.2	3.4

To calculate a standardized score, we find the average and the mean deviation of the scores. The average tells us what the typical score is, and the mean deviation tells us how much the scores varied across the divers. Here are the average and mean deviation values:

	High dive	Low dive
Average	2.0	25.0
Mean deviation	0.1	6.0

The formula for finding Cheryl's standardized score is her score minus the average, divided by the mean deviation. We can write:

$$\frac{\text{Cheryl's score} - \text{average}}{\text{mean deviation}} \quad OR \quad \frac{X - \text{mean of x}}{\text{mean dev x}}$$

To calculate a standardized score for Cheryl's high dive of 8.3, we plug in the values:

$$\frac{(8.3 - 6.7)}{1.8} = 0.85$$

Here is the calculation that finds the standardized score for Cheryl's low dive of 6.4:

$$\frac{(6.4 - 5.9)}{1.9} = 0.26$$

Cheryl did better on the high dive because she got a higher standardized score for the high dive than the low dive.

Cheryl told Jack about standardized scores. Jack competes in the decathlon. He wants to know if he did better at the high jump or the javelin throw in his last meet. He jumped 2.2 meters high and he threw the javelin 31 meters. For all the athletes at the meet, here are the averages and mean deviations:

	High jump	*Javelin*
Average	6.7	5.9
Mean deviation	1.8	1.9

Calculate standardized scores for Jack's high jump and javelin and decide which he did better at.

Example of a Target Transfer Problem in the Post-Test

Susan and Robin are arguing about who did better on their final exam last period. They are in different classes, and they took different tests. Susan got an 88 on Mrs. Protoplasm's biology final exam. In her class, the mean score was a 74 and the average deviation was 12 points. The average deviation indicates how close all the students were to the average. Robin earned an 82 on Mr. Melody's music exam. In that class, the mean score was a 76 and the average deviation was 4 points. Both classes had 100 students. Who do you think scored closer to the top of her class, Susan or Robin? Use math to help back up your opinion.

4   Experimenting to Support and Understand Learning Processes

Paul Cobb
Vanderbilt University

Koeno Gravemeijer
Freudenthal Institute

Introduction

In this chapter, we describe an approach to design research[1] that we have refined while conducting a series of design research projects in mathematics education over a ten-year period. Our intent in doing so is to highlight a number of issues that we believe it is essential to consider when conducting a design experiment regardless of the specific approach followed. For the purpose of this chapter, we define design research as a family of methodological approaches in which instructional design and research are interdependent.[2] On the one hand, the design of learning environments serves as the context for research, and, on the other hand, ongoing and retrospective analyses are conducted in order to inform the improvement of the design. This type of research involves attempting to support the development of particular forms of learning and studying the learning that occurs in these designed settings. The learning of interest might be that of individual students who interact one-on-one with a researcher in a series of teaching sessions (Cobb & Steffe, 1983; Steffe & Thompson, 2000), a group of students in a classroom (Cobb, 2000a; Confrey & Lachance, 2000; Gravemeijer, 1994b), preservice teachers in a university course (Simon, 2000), or practicing teachers who collaborate with researchers as members of a professional teaching community (Kazemi & Franke, 2004; Stein et al., 1998). In each of these cases, design research enables us to investigate simultaneously both the process of learning and the means by which it is supported and organized. As we will argue later in the chapter, the potential contributions of the methodology become particularly apparent when the current research base is thin and provides only limited guidance for the design of learning environments.

We focus specifically on design experiments in classrooms in which a research team assumes responsibility for a group of students' learning both because they are the most common type of design research and because most of our work has involved experiments in classrooms. However, the methodological issues on which we focus can be extended to experiments that attempt to support the learning of individual students and of preservice and practicing teachers. We introduce these issues by discussing the three phases of conducting a design experiment: preparing for the experiment, experimenting to support learning, and conducting retrospective analyses of the data generated during the course of the experiment. To ground the discussion, we draw on two classroom design experiments that focused on statistical data analysis as illustrative cases. The first experiment was conducted in a seventh-grade classroom and involved the analysis of univariate data: the second experiment conducted with some of the same students the following school year was focused on the analysis of bivariate data.

Preparing for the Experiment

The preparation phase for an experiment encompasses a range of issues that include clarifying the instructional goals to which the experiment aims and documenting the instructional starting points. Against this background, the immediate challenge is to delineate an envisioned learning trajectory that consists of conjectures about both a learning process that culminates with the prospective instructional goals and the specific means of supporting that learning process.[3] Finally, the preparation phase also involves placing the planned experiment in a broader theoretical context by framing it as a case of a broader class of phenomena.

Clarifying the Instructional Goals

In our view, it is critical to scrutinize the current instructional goals in the mathematical domain of interest when preparing for a design experiment (Cobb, 2001; Gravemeijer, 1994a; Lehrer & Lesh, 2003). It is important to acknowledge that these goals have become institutionalized in the curriculum over an extended period of time and are the product of history, tradition, and assessment practices. Rather than accepting them unquestioned, we attempt to problematize the particular mathematical problem under consideration from a disciplinary perspective by identifying the central organizing ideas. As an illustration, the current goals for statistics instruction at the middle-school level typically consist of a relatively long list of separate topics such as mean, mode, and median, and conventions for drawing different types of graphs (e.g., histograms, box plots). The extensive literature review that we conducted when preparing for the seventh-grade design experiment revealed that there was a lack of consensus on what the central ideas of middle-school statistics should be (McGatha, 2000). However, by both synthesizing this literature and examining what statistical data analysis entails, we came to the conclusion that the notion of distribution plays a central role and could serve as an overarching idea in statistics instruction from elementary school through college. From this perspective, notions like "center," "skewness," "spread," and "relative frequency" become ways of characterizing how the data are distributed, rather than separate topics or concepts that are to be mastered in isolation from each other. Further, various types of statistical graphs come to the fore as different ways of organizing data in order to detect relevant patterns and trends.

This illustration emphasizes that our intent when conducting a design experiment is not merely to develop more effective instructional approaches for addressing traditional instructional goals but also to influence what the goals could be by demonstrating what is possible for students' mathematical learning. Consequently, the approach that we take to design research is interventionist in character. In the case of statistics, part of our agenda was to influence what the instructional goals might be by demonstrating what is possible for students' learning of statistics.

Documenting the Instructional Starting Points

The intent in documenting the instructional starting points is to identify both the aspects of students' current reasoning on which the designer might build and the initial instructional challenges involved in doing so. However, it is important to stress that we view ourselves not as documenting the level of reasoning that is typical of students of a particular age but as documenting the consequences of their prior instructional histories. The existing research literature can be useful, particularly interview studies conducted from a psychological perspective, because they can give insights into what students typically learn in a particular mathematical domain in the context of standard instruction. Also, it is often necessary to conduct additional assessments when preparing for an experiment because the tasks used in many of the existing studies reflect the way in which the domain is institutionalized in school. Because such assessments involve the development of novel tasks, video-recorded interviews and whole-class performance assessments prove initially to be more effective than written instruments and can lead to the development of such instruments (Desimone & Le Floch, 2004).

In preparing for the two design experiments in teaching statistics, we relied primarily on whole-class performance assessments conducted with two, intact, seventh-grade classes.[4] In conducting these assessments, the research team member who served as the teacher did not attempt to support the students' learning but, instead, probed the students' reasoning in order to understand why they used particular approaches. The tasks required the students either to analyze data to inform a pragmatic decision or to develop a way of representing data that would be useful for a particular audience. The whole-class assessments revealed that, for most of the students, data analysis involved trying to remember what they were supposed to do with the numbers (Bright et al., 2003; Garfield, 1988; McGatha et al., 2002; Shaughnessey, 1992). This indicated that, for these students, data were not numbers plus context, to use Moore's (1997) pithy phrase. In other words, data were not measures of an attribute of a situation that was relevant for the problem or issue under investigation, and data analysis was not pertinent to gaining insights into that problem or issue. Instead, for these students, data were merely numerical values on which they either performed particular calculational procedures or graphed by following particular representational conventions. Therefore, our initial challenge in the design experiments was to support a change in what statistics meant for these students, so that they were analyzing data.

Delineating an Envisioned Learning Trajectory

When the instructional goals and starting points have been clarified, the next phase in preparing for a design experiment is to specify an envisioned or a hypothetical learning trajectory (Simon, 1995). In doing so, the research team formulates testable conjectures about both significant shifts in students' reasoning and the means of supporting and organizing these shifts. Typically, these means of support include those considered by materials developers such as instructional tasks and associated resources (e.g., physical and computer-based tools). We also believe that it is essential to envision how tasks and tools might be enacted in the classroom. Therefore, additional but frequently overlooked means of support include the nature of classroom norms and the nature of classroom discourse. For example, we know that the sociomathematical norm of what counts as an acceptable mathematical argument can differ radically from one classroom to another and that this can make a profound difference in the nature and the quality of students' mathematical learning even when the same tasks and resources are used (Hershkowitz & Schwarz, 1999; Lampert, 2001; McClain & Cobb, 2001; Simon & Blume, 1996; Voigt, 1996; Yackel & Cobb, 1996). The establishment of this and other norms, the ways in which tasks and tools are enacted in the classroom, and, indeed, the learning opportunities that arise for students depend crucially on the proactive role of the teacher. As a consequence, we do not view the instructional tasks and tools that we develop as supporting students' mathematical learning directly but, instead, consider the teacher to be a codesigner of the classroom's learning environment that constitutes the immediate social situation of their students' mathematical development. Given the central mediating role that we attribute to teachers, our immediate goal is to design tasks and tools that they can use as resources to support shifts in their students' reasoning.

In many domains, the research literature provides only limited guidance when formulating a hypothetical learning trajectory. When preparing for the statistics experiments, for example, we were able to identify only six relevant articles (Biehler & Steinbring, 1991; deLange et al., 1993; Hancock et al., 1992; Konold et al., 1997; Lehrer & Romberg, 1996; Wilensky, 1996). The types of articles that proved helpful focus on instructional goals that are at least partially compatible with those delineated for the planned experiment and report both the process of students' learning and the instructional settings, the tasks, and the tools that enabled or supported that learning. Given this limited research base, we considered the conjectures in our envisioned learning trajectory to be extremely speculative and anticipated that many of them would be refuted once we began experimenting in the classroom. The process of formulating the trajectory was nonetheless valuable in that it made it possible for us to improve our initial design by testing and revising the conjectures when we began experimenting in the classroom. Design research is therefore a bootstrapping methodology that is useful both when formulating and testing initial designs in domains where the current research base is thin and when adapting and improving already successful designs that are grounded in an established research base.

As an illustration, we focus on the first part of the envisioned trajectory that we formulated when preparing for the two experiments. As noted earlier, our initial challenge was to support a shift in the students' reasoning so that they were analyzing data rather than merely manipulating numbers or following graphical conventions. Because of time constraints, it was not feasible for the students to collect the data that they were to analyze. Nevertheless, we conjectured that it would be essential for them to experience the process of generating data for the purpose of answering a pragmatic question if the data were to mean measures rather than mere numbers for them (Bakker, 2004; Lehrer & Romberg, 1996; Roth, 1996). We further conjectured that this could be accomplished if the teacher introduced each instructional task by reviewing the data generation process with the students. In one of the first tasks, the students were to compare data on the life spans of two brands of batteries. First, the teacher clarified the significance of the issue that the students were to investigate by asking them if they used batteries; most of the students indicated that they did (e.g., in portable CD players, tape-recorders, and so forth). Next, the teacher delineated the relevant attributes of batteries that should be measured by asking the students what factors they consider when buying batteries (e.g., cost, life span). Then, the teacher shifted the discussion to issues of measurement by asking the students how it would be possible to determine which of two brands of batteries lasted longer (e.g., by putting a number of batteries of each brand in identical appliances such as flashlights or clocks). Against the background of this discussion, the teacher introduced the data that the students were to analyze inscribed in the first of three computer tools[5] that the students used over the course of the two design experiments, as shown in Figure 4.1. The life spans of ten batteries of two brands are each represented as a horizontal bar.

In designing this tool, we purposely chose situations that involved linearity (e.g., time) that would fit with this type of representation. We conjectured that this would enable the students to interpret the bars as signifying data values; thus they would use the options available on the computer tool to analyze data. Our conjectures about the means of supporting a shift in the students' reasoning proved to be well founded. There were clear indications that, within the first week of the first experiment, doing statistics came to involve analyzing data (Cobb, 1999; McClain et al., 2000).

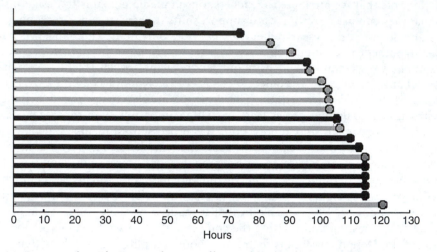

Figure 4.1 Data on the Life Spans of Two Different Brands of Batteries in the First Computer Tool.

Placing the Experiment in a Theoretical Context

Ethically, design research has a strong pragmatic orientation in that any experiment involves supporting the learning of a particular group of people. However, the intent is not to develop a rich ethnographic account of such learning. Instead, the overriding goal is to produce knowledge that will be useful in providing guidance to others as they attempt to support learning processes (Brown, 1992; Cobb et al., 2003b; Collins, 1992; Design-Based Research Collaborative, 2003; Edelson, 2002; Gravemeijer, 1994a). Therefore, when preparing for an experiment, it is critical to frame it explicitly as a paradigmatic case of broader phenomena. For example, we initially viewed the two statistics experiments as a case of supporting middle-school students' development of increasingly sophisticated forms of reasoning in a particular mathematical domain. This encompassed students learning about data generation (e.g., constructing representative samples, controlling extraneous variables) and developing and critiquing relatively sophisticated, data-based arguments (Cobb & Tzou, 2000; Cobb et al., 2003b). In addition, the experiments became a case in which a teacher became increasingly effective in supporting students' learning by building on their mathematical reasoning (McClain, 2002). They also became a case of the design and use of tools to support students' mathematical learning and, more generally, of semiotic processes in mathematical learning (Cobb, 2002; Gravemeijer, 1994b; Sfard, 2000b). Finally, we became aware during the experiments that the students were developing an interest in investigating real-world phenomena that they considered to be significant by analyzing data. As a consequence, it became a case of cultivating students' mathematical interests, an issue that is related directly to teachers' perennial concern about how they can motivate their students (Cobb & Hodge, 2002).[6]

These illustrations do not exhaust the possibilities, of course. For example, a classroom experiment might be framed as a case of negotiating general classroom norms or sociomathematical norms; of orchestrating productive, whole-class discussions; and of supporting equity in students' access to significant mathematical ideas. In addition, a series of experiments can be conducted and serve as the context for the development and refinement of interpretive frameworks that do useful work in generating, selecting, and assessing design alternatives. Examples of such frameworks developed by design researchers include the theory of metarepresentational competence (diSessa, 1992, 2002), the theory of quantitative reasoning (Thompson & Thompson, 1996), the theory of actor-oriented abstraction (Lobato, 2003), and the design theory of realistic mathematics education (Gravemeijer, 1994a, 1999; Treffers, 1987). Such frameworks can function both as a source of guidance for instructional design and as interpretive structures for making sense of what is happening in the complex setting in which a design experiment is conducted (diSessa & Cobb, 2004).

We will return to this issue of framing an experiment as a case of a more encompassing phenomenon when we discuss the third phase in a design experiment—conducting retrospective analyses of the data generated during the course of the experiment. For the present, it suffices to emphasize that such framings are critical if the findings are to be potentially generalizable.

Experimenting to Support Learning

In our view, only after the preparation work has been completed, the instructional endpoints have been specified, the starting points have been documented, a conjectured instructional theory has been formulated, and the experiment has been located in a broader context should a research team begin experimenting to support a group of participants' learning for an extended period of time. Because the term experiment may evoke associations with experimental or quasi-experimental research, it is important to clarify that the objective of the design experiment is not to demonstrate that the envisioned learning trajectory works. The primary goal is not even to assess whether it works; although the research team will do so, of course. Instead, when experimenting to support learning, the purpose is to improve the envisioned trajectory developed while preparing for the experiment by testing and revising conjectures about both the prospective learning process and the specific means of supporting it.

We begin our discussion of the process of experimenting to support learning by considering briefly the kinds of data that might be collected in the course of an experiment. Then, we address the need to explicate the frameworks used to interpret the participants' activity, their learning, and the evolution of the learning environment in which they are situated. Next, we focus on the tightly integrated cycles of design and analysis that characterize design research. Finally, we clarify one of the primary products of a series of design experiments: a domain-specific,[7] instructional theory.

Data Collection

Decisions about the types of data that need to be generated in the course of an experiment depend on the theoretical intent of the design experiment. These decisions are critical to the success of an experiment because when the researchers conduct retrospective analyses frequently, the data have to make it possible for them to address the broader theoretical issues of which the learning setting under investigation is a paradigmatic case. We will return to the issue of data generation when we discuss the argumentative grammar of design research that links data and analysis to final claims and assertions. For the present, we offer an illustration from the statistics design experiments. One of our broader goals in these experiments was to investigate the processes of supporting students' development of increasingly sophisticated forms of data-based reasoning. Therefore, we needed to document the shifts in the students' reasoning as well as the means by which these shifts were supported and organized in the classroom. To this end, we conducted individual pre- and post-interviews with the students, video-recorded all classroom sessions, made copies of all of the students' written work, and developed two independent sets of field notes. We also would have incorporated benchmark assessment items that focused on the central statistical idea of distribution had they been available. Generally, these data proved adequate for our purpose. However, in a prior experiment conducted in a first-grade classroom, we also investigated the relationship between the process of individual students' learning and what might be termed the mathematical learning of the classroom community, as assessed by the evolution of mathematical practices in the classroom. In that case, we also found it essential to video-record the performance of target students during the individual and small-group activities in the lessons.

Because design research is a relatively new methodology, researchers often find that they have to develop new data generation techniques or instruments (Cobb et al., 2003a; Confrey & Lachance, 2000; Design-Based Research Collaborative, 2003; Drijvers, 2003; Lehrer & Schauble, 2004; Lobato, 2003). As an illustration, we have noted that the statistics experiments became a case of cultivating students' mathematical interests. To investigate this issue, we had to document how the students understood both the general and the specifically mathematical obligations in the classroom and how they evaluated those obligations. A member of the research team conducted interviews with the students that focused on these concerns while the second of the two experiments was in progress. Although these interviews proved to be useful, our failure to conduct such interviews throughout the first experiment restricted the scope of our subsequent analyses. This example underscores the importance of thinking through the types of data that should be generated before experimenting in the classroom. Careful preparation of this type also ameliorates design researchers' tendency to squander limited resources assembling vast collections of data, most of which are never analyzed (Dede, 2004; Kelly, 2004).

As we have indicated, when experimenting to support learning, the overall goal is to improve the learning trajectory envisioned by testing and revising conjectures about both the prospective learning process and the specific means of supporting it. This process of testing and revising conjectures constitutes the learning process of the research team (Gravemeijer, 1994b). In our view, it is critical to document this process by audio-recording all research group meetings and by compiling a log of ongoing interpretations, conjectures, decisions, and so forth (Edelson, 2002). This log and the audio-recordings are useful when conducting retrospective analyses because they make it possible to reconstruct the rationales for particular decisions about a design.

Interpretive Frameworks

In the process of experimenting to support learning, the research team makes ongoing interpretations of both the participants' activity and the learning environment in which they are situated. These ongoing interpretations inform design and instructional decisions and thus shape the design effort profoundly. Unfortunately, design researchers often fail to articulate the key constructs of what they use when making these interpretations. This omission indicates strongly the status of design research as a fledgling methodology. Given the complexity and messiness of the settings in which design experiments typically are conducted, the ongoing interpretations are highly selective and involve implicit conjectures about the important aspects of the participants' activity, the learning environment, and the relation between them. In our view, it is essential that design researchers make explicit the conjectures, suppositions, and assumptions that ground their interpretations so that they can be subjected to public debate and scrutiny. As Kelly (2004) observes, reports of design experiments will be dismissed as anecdotal by critics if they fail to differentiate between what is necessary and what is contingent in a design. We will return to this distinction when we discuss the process of conducting retrospective analyses of the data generated in the course of an experiment. For the present, it suffices to note that researchers inevitably make implicit claims about what is necessary in the process of interpreting the evolving learning environment and the participants' developing activity.

The typical characterization of design research settings as complex and messy emphasizes further the importance of articulating, critiquing, and refining interpretive frameworks. These settings seem complex and messy because we have yet to develop adequate ways of understanding them and have difficulty in perceiving pattern and order. We have noted already that a series of experiments can develop and refine the interpretive frameworks that can guide the generation, selection, and assessment of design alternatives. For example, diSessa's (2002) theory of metarepresentational competence and Thompson's (1996) theory of quantitative reasoning both posit and account for previously unarticulated aspects of mathematical learning. In our own work in a series of classroom experiments, we attempted to develop an interpretive framework that enables us to account for students' mathematical learning as it occurs in the social situation of the classroom (Cobb & Yackel, 1996). Our intent in doing so was to begin to see some order in the complexity and messiness of the classroom.

The details of the framework that we proposed do not concern us here. However, it is worth emphasizing that the framework emerged over a period of several years while we attempted to understand specific events in the classrooms in which we worked. On the one hand, the framework grew out of our efforts to support students' mathematical learning. On the other hand, interpretations of classroom events organized in terms of the emerging framework fed back to inform the ongoing, instructional development effort. A central feature of this process is that the framework evolved in response to problems and issues encountered while experimenting to support learning. The frameworks proposed by the other researchers that we have referenced also were developed by means of a similar process. In each case, the proposed interpretive framework does not stand apart from the practice of experimenting to support learning but, instead, remains grounded in it. Therefore, each framework makes public a particular way of conceptualizing the learning process being supported. Furthermore, each one explicates suppositions and assumptions about what it is worth attempting to document when generating data. As a consequence, the frameworks guide the process of thinking through the types of data that should be generated.

Cycles of Design and Analysis

In focusing on the logistical issues involved in experimenting to support learning, we stress again that the overall goal is to test and improve the learning trajectory formulated during the preparation phase. Therefore, it is counterproductive at the outset to plan in finished form the means that might be used to support learning because, in all probability, they will be changed as the conjectures are revised. In the statistics experiments, for example, we outlined the types of instructional tasks that we anticipated using by developing the specific activities only a day or two in advance, as informed by our current conjectures. Therefore, each instructional task therefore embodied specific conjectures about the students' future learning at that particular point in the instructional sequence. As a part of the process of testing and revising these conjectures, we found it essential to have short debriefing meetings after each classroom session. In these meetings, members of the research team shared and debated their interpretations of events that had occurred in their classroom. When we reached consensus in our ongoing interpretations, we prepared for subsequent sessions by discussing our conjectures about possible developments in the students' reasoning. It was in the context of this discussion that we designed specific instructional tasks and considered other means of support (e.g., the renegotiation of specifically mathematical norms). We call these daily cycles of design and analysis "design minicycles."

Critics of design research have argued that this process of testing and revising conjectures based on single cases without controls is an inherent weakness of the methodology. Therefore, it is helpful to distinguish between two complementary treatments of causal explanation: the regularity type of causal description that is based on observed regularities across a number of cases and a process-oriented explanation "that sees causality as fundamentally referring to the actual causal mechanisms and processes that are involved in particular events and situations" (Maxwell, 2004: 4). Thus, process-oriented explanations are concerned with "the mechanisms through which and the conditions under which that causal relationship holds" (Shadish et al., 2002: 9, cited in Maxwell, 2004: 4). In contrast to the regularity conception of causality, in principle, viable explanations of this type can be discerned based on a single case (Maxwell, 2004), particularly if the research team is using a well-established, interpretive framework that has been honed during a series of prior experiments. When making ongoing interpretations and when conducting retrospective analyses, the intent is to develop explanations of this type that center on the relation between the learning processes and the means by which they are supported.

In addition to holding daily debriefing meetings during the statistics experiments, we found it valuable to have longer research team meetings each week in which we took stock of the continuous process of testing and revising conjectures in the classroom. In these meetings, we first clarified the overall goals of the design experiment in order to locate our ongoing work within the broader context of the entire experiment. Next, we outlined a revised learning trajectory for the entire experiment that took account of the adaptations we had made to the conjectures while experimenting in the classroom. It was only against the background of this broader discussion that we articulated possible learning goals and means of support for future classroom sessions. Our purpose in structuring the meetings in this way was to ensure that the relationship between the envisioned learning trajectory and the ongoing testing and revising of the conjectures was truly reflexive. On the one hand, the local design decisions that we made on a daily basis were guided by the envisioned learning trajectory. On the other hand, the envisioned learning trajectory evolved as a consequence of local interpretations and judgments that, ideally, should be grounded in a clearly articulated, interpretive framework.

In our view, organizing the research team's activity so that there is a reflexive relationship between local judgments and the entire perspective should be a basic tenet of design research. Simon (1995) addresses this issue when reporting a design experiment in which he served as the teacher and attempted to support the mathematical learning of a group of preservice teachers. He clarifies that he had a pedagogical agenda and thus a sense of direction at any point in the experiment, but that this agenda is subject to continual modification in the act of teaching. Simon likens this process to that of undertaking a long journey such as sailing around the world.

You may initially plan the whole journey or only part of it. You set out sailing according to your plan. However, you must constantly adjust because of the conditions that you encounter. You continue to acquire knowledge about sailing, about the current conditions, and about the areas that you wish to visit. You change your plans with respect to the order of your destinations. You modify the length and nature of your visits as a result of interactions with people along the way. You add destinations that prior to the trip were unknown to you. The path that you travel is your [actual] trajectory. The path that you anticipate at any point is your "hypothetical trajectory" (pp. 136–137).

As Simon emphasizes, this way of experimenting to support learning involves both a sense of purpose and an open-handed flexibility toward the participants' activity and learning. It also brings the learning of the research team to the fore. The deviation of the actual learning trajectory from the learning trajectory envisioned at the outset provides a general summative record of the research team's learning while experimenting to support the participants' learning.

Thus far, we have considered both design and analysis minicycles and the relation between these minicycles and the encompassing learning trajectory. Stepping back still further, an entire experiment can be viewed as a single cycle of design and analysis when it is located within a series of experiments. In this macrocycle, the envisioned learning trajectory formulated when preparing for an experiment is tested and revised while experimenting in the classroom and while conducting retrospective analyses, resulting in a revised learning trajectory that can serve as the basis for a subsequent experiment. In most cases, when conducting a series of experiments and enacting a sequence of design and analysis macrocycles, a primary goal is to develop a domain-specific, instructional theory.

Domain-Specific, Instructional Theories

The products of a series of design experiments typically include sequences of activities and associated resources for supporting a particular form of learning, together with a domain-specific, instructional theory that underpins the instructional sequences and constitutes its rationale. A domain-specific, instructional theory consists of a substantiated learning process that culminates with the achievement of significant learning goals as well as the demonstrated means of supporting that learning process. We call such theories domain-specific to emphasize that their scope is restricted to significant learning goals in a particular domain (e.g., students' development of sophisticated forms of reasoning in a specific mathematical or scientific domain, or mathematics or science teachers' development of particular forms of instructional practice in particular content domains). Elsewhere, theories of this type have been called humble theories to acknowledge their domain specificity (Cobb et al., 2003a).

A domain-specific, instructional theory is useful because it enables other researchers to customize the sequence of activities and resources produced during a series of experiments to the setting in which they are working. If the activities and resources were justified solely with traditional experimental data, other researchers would know only that they had proved effective elsewhere but would not have an understanding of the underlying rationale that would enable them to adapt them. In contrast, the justification provided by a domain-specific, instructional theory offers the possibility that other researchers will be able to adapt, test, and modify the activities and resources as they work in different settings. In doing so, they can contribute to both the improvement of the activities and the development of the domain-specific, instructional theory, thereby making the production of design-based knowledge a cumulative activity. As an example, Bakker (2004) carried out a series of classroom experiments that focused on statistics at the middle-school level in the course of which he tested, modified, and elaborated on the learning trajectory that had resulted from the two statistics design experiments we had conducted. Clearly, this process of building on and extending the findings of prior design experiments depends crucially on researchers distinguishing explicitly between what is necessary and what is contingent in their designs.

We conclude this discussion of experimenting to support learning by giving an overview of the learning trajectory that resulted from the two design experiments in statistics. In the context of the current discussion, this trajectory can be viewed as a prospective, domain-specific theory that could be elaborated in subsequent experiments, such as those conducted by Bakker (ibid.). Our intention in outlining this trajectory is to illustrate the level of specificity that we contend is essential when developing and revising designs for supporting learning. To make the presentation tractable, we focus on the three computer tools that the students used to analyze data with the understanding that they were but one of the means by which the students' learning was supported. Thus, we omit a discussion of both the classroom norms and the role of the teacher.[8] As background, we should clarify that the enactment of an instructional task often spanned two or more, 40-minute, classroom sessions and involved three phases: (a) a whole-class discussion of the data generation process, (b) an individual or a small-group activity in which the students typically worked at computers to analyze data, and (c) a whole-class discussion of the students' analyses.

In describing the first of the three computer tools (see Figure 4.1), we clarified its role in supporting an initial shift in the students' activity so that they were analyzing data. The students' use of this tool also proved to be necessary for a second reason. The inscription of data values as horizontal bars and the options of organizing data oriented the students to compare collections of data values in terms of how they are spread out and bunched up, a precursor to distribution. For example, the students dragged a vertical value bar along the axis either to partition data sets or to find the value of specific data points. In addition, they used another option on the tool to isolate a particular interval and compare the number of data points in each data set that were in that interval (see Figure 4.2).

Against this background, the teacher introduced the second computer tool in which data points were inscribed as dots in a line plot (see Figure 4.3). As can be seen by comparing Figures 4.2 and 4.3, the dots at the end of the bars in the first tool have been collapsed down onto the horizontal axis in the second tool. The teacher introduced this new way of inscribing data first by showing a data set inscribed as horizontal bars, then by removing the bars to leave only the dots, and finally by sliding the dots down onto the horizontal axis. As we had conjectured, the students were able to use the second computer tool to analyze data with little additional guidance, and it was apparent that the line plot inscription signified a set of data values rather than merely a collection of dots scattered along a line. However, this development cannot be explained solely by the teacher's careful introduction of the new tool. Instead, we also have to take account of a subtle but important aspect of the students' learning when they used the first tool. The crucial point to note is that, in using the options on the first tool to partition data sets and to isolate the data points within a particular interval, the students focused on the location of the dots at the end of the bars with respect to the horizontal axis. In other words, a necessary shift occurred as the students used the first tool. Originally, the individual data values were represented by the lengths of the bars. However, in using the tool, these values came to be signified by the endpoints of the bars. As a result of this development, when they were presented with the second tool, they could understand readily the teacher's explanation of collapsing the dots at the end of the bars down onto the axis.

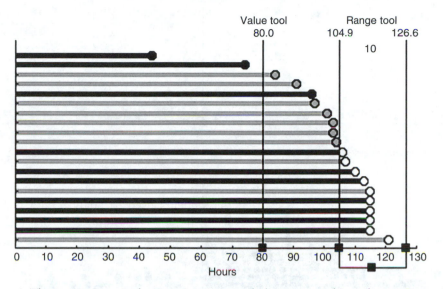

Figure 4.2 The Battery Data in the First Computer with the Options of Bounding an Interval and Partitioning at a Data Value Shown.

The data shown in Figure 4.2 come from a task in which the students used the second computer tool to compare the effectiveness of two treatments for AIDS patients. The task was to assess whether a new experimental protocol in which 46 people had enrolled was more successful in raising patients' T-cell counts than a standard protocol in which 186 people had enrolled. The options on this tool involved partitioning sets of up to 400 data values in various ways. For example, students could drag vertical bars along the axis in order to partition a data set into groups of points, groups with a specified interval width (i.e., a precursor of a histogram), and four groups that each contain the same number of data points (i.e., a precursor of a box plot). The students could use the second tool immediately because they had partitioned data sets routinely when they used the first tool. One of the more elementary analyses that the students produced involved partitioning the two data sets and the T-cell count of 550 (see Figure 4.4).

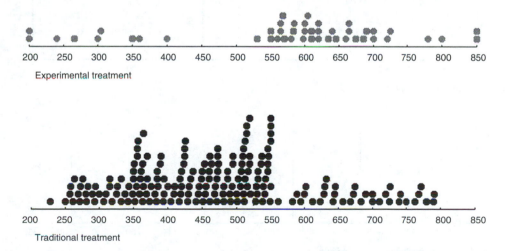

Figure 4.3 Data on the T-Cell Counts of Two Groups of AIDS Patients in the Second Computer Tool.

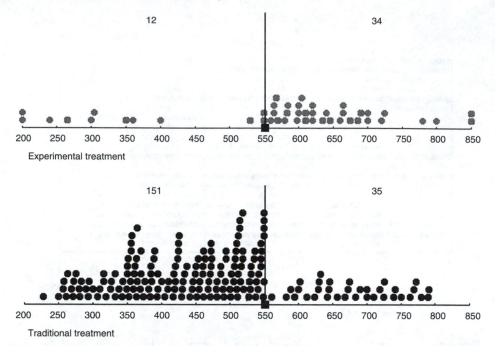

Figure 4.4 The AIDS Data Partitioned at the T-Cell Count of 550.

They concluded that the experimental treatment was more effective because the majority of these data were above 550, whereas the majority of the standard treatment data were below it. In contrast, the most sophisticated type of analysis involved partitioning both data sets into four groups, each of which contained 25 percent of the data, and hiding the dots that showed the location of each individual data value (see Figure 4.5).

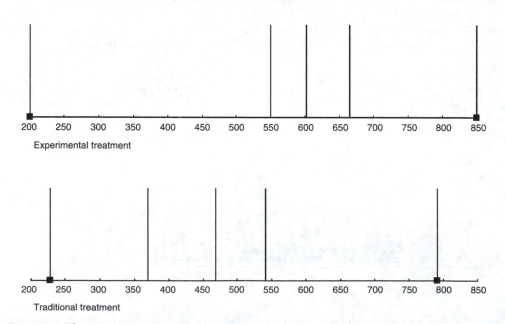

Figure 4.5 The AIDS Data Organized into Four Equal Groups with Data Hidden.

The students who produced this analysis argued that the experimental treatment was more effective because 75 percent of these data but only 25 percent of the standard treatment data are above the T-cell value of 550. In both solutions, the students compared the data sets in terms of how they were distributed by focusing on the proportion or relative frequency of the data points in particular intervals.

There was no regression in the sophistication of the analyses that the students produced between the end of the first experiment and the beginning of the second experiment despite the nine-month time lag. Further, within the first week of the second experiment, all the students were able to read the shape of a data set from a four-equal-groups display such as that shown in Figure 4.5 (i.e., they realized that the data were more bunched up or were distributed more densely when the bars were closer together and the interval was smaller). This development was necessary before the students could use the third computer tool productively to analyze bivariate data. In one instructional task, the students used the third tool to investigate possible inequities in the salaries of men and women who had the same number of years of education. Figure 4.6 shows the data for 300 women, 50 at each of the six education levels, inscribed in the third computer tool. It proved necessary to use displays of this type in which it was impossible to see all the data points because some of the dots were in the same location. One of the options on this tool allowed students to superimpose a frequency grid on the display and to hide the dots, as shown in Figure 4.7.

This option proved useful to the students because they could read how the data for each education level were distributed. For example, they could read how the salaries of the 50 women with 18 years of education were distributed from the last column of numbers in Figure 4.7 and noticed that they were skewed heavily toward the lower end of the range.

A second option on the tool allowed the students to partition the data at each of the six education levels into four groups, each of which contained the same number of

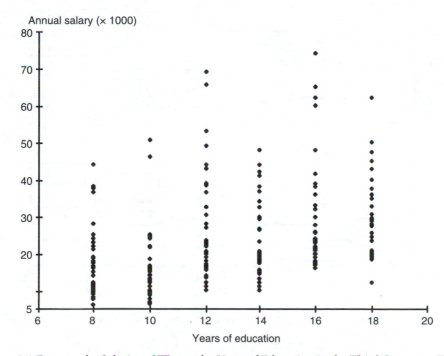

Figure 4.6 Data on the Salaries of Women by Years of Education in the Third Computer Tool.

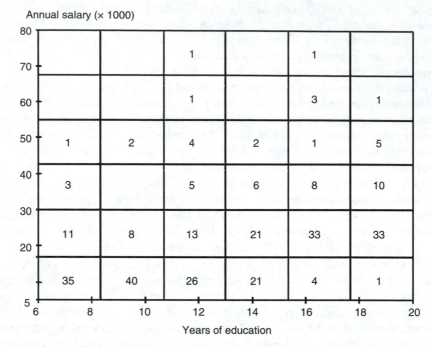

Figure 4.7 Salary and Education Data for Women Organized the Grids Option.

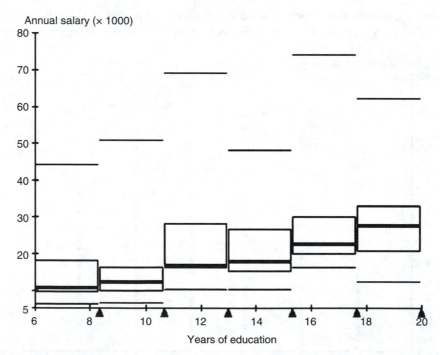

Figure 4.8 Salary and Education Data for Women Organized the Grids Option Four-Equal-Groups Option.

data points (see Figure 4.8). In essence, the four-equal-groups option on the second computer tool (see Figure 4.5) has been rotated 90 degrees and superimposed on each of the six "data stacks." As a consequence of their activity with the second tool, the students could read easily how the women's salaries at each of the six education levels were distributed. In particular, they could see again that although the women's salaries increased with their years of education, the salaries at each education level were skewed toward the lower end of the range. When compared with the men's salaries, the degree to which the women's salaries were skewed indicated a possible inequity.

In addition to illustrating the level of detail that we contend is necessary when formulating, testing, and revising instructional designs, this overview of the learning trajectory resulting from the two experiments exemplifies what it means to problematize a particular domain. Typically, scatter plots are viewed as two-dimensional inscriptions that show how two sets of measures covary in a relatively straightforward manner. However, proficient statistical analysts' imagery of covariation is no more two-dimensional than their imagery of univariate distributions is one-dimensional. This is clearer in the case of univariate data in that inscriptions such as line plots involve, for the proficient user, an additional second dimension that indicates relative frequency (see Figure 4.5). In the case of bivariate data, however, scatter plots do not provide such direct perceptual support for a third dimension corresponding to relative frequency. Instead, it appears that proficient analysts read this third dimension from the relative density of the data points. The third computer tool was designed to enable students to learn to read this missing dimension into scatterplots. This made it possible for them to analyze how bivariate data were distributed by investigating how the distribution of a set of measures (e.g., salary) changed as the second measure (e.g., years of education) increased.

Conducting Retrospective Analyses

Thus far, we have discussed the planning of a design experiment and the process of experimenting to support learning, which are central to design research. A further aspect of the methodology concerns the retrospective analyses that are conducted of the entire data set collected during the experiment. The ongoing analyses conducted while the experiment is in process usually relate directly to the goal of supporting the participants' learning. In contrast, retrospective analyses seek to place this learning and the means by which it was supported in a broader theoretical context by framing it as a paradigmatic case of a more encompassing phenomenon. As a consequence, the goals of the retrospective analyses depend on the theoretical intent of the design experiment. For easy explication, we assume that one of the primary goals of a design experiment is to contribute to the development of a domain-specific, instructional theory. The issues that we discuss concern the argumentative grammar of design research analyses and the trustworthiness, repeatability, and generalizability of the findings.

Argumentative Grammar

As Kelly (2004) observes, methodologies are underpinned by distinct schemes of argumentation that link data to analysis and to final claims and assertions. He uses the term *argumentative grammar* to refer to the scheme of argumentation that characterizes a particular methodology. As he clarifies, an argumentative grammar comprises "the logic that guides the use of a method and that supports reasoning about its data" (p. 118). He goes on to note that "the argumentative grammar of randomized field trials can be described *separately* from its instantiation in any given study so that the logic of a proposed study and its later claims can be criticized" (p. 118). This leads him to ask:

> Where is the separable structure [in design research] that justifies collecting certain data and under what conditions? What guides the reasoning with these data to make a plausible argument? Until we can be clear about their argumentative grammar, design studies in education lack a basis for warrant for their claims.
>
> (2004: 119)

Kelly pinpoints a weakness of design research that betrays its status as an emerging methodology. In the following paragraphs, we make an initial attempt to address this issue by restricting our focus to the development of domain-specific, instructional theories.

We begin by noting that design research differs from more established forms of research such as the randomized field trial in terms of the types of knowledge claims that the methodology aims to produce. In the case of a design experiment that concerns the development of a domain-specific, instructional theory, the goal is to develop an empirically grounded theory about both the process of students' learning in that domain and the means by which this learning can be supported. In developing such a theory, it is essential for researchers to explicate what they conceive of as competence in the domain, together with their conjectures about the process of its development. We have indicated the importance of expressing as problems the goals of the instructional sequence and can speak similarly of expressing as problems the process of learning mathematics. We find Freudenthal's (1973, 1983) analysis of mathematical learning to be valuable in this regard. Freudenthal argued that, in his view as a professional mathematician, mathematics is first and foremost an activity that he termed mathematizing and described as organizing subject matter (Freudenthal, 1971). Freudenthal's conception, as it has been elaborated in the domain-specific, instructional theory of realistic mathematics education (Gravemeijer, 1994b; Treffers, 1987), offers points of reference for assessing mathematical learning processes in particular domains.

As far as the goals of the instructional sequence are concerned, it is clearly essential to determine the particular forms of domain-specific reasoning that indicate the students' development of competence and to demonstrate that they would not have developed these forms of reasoning but for their participation in the design experiment. This obviously indicates the importance of using sound procedures for assessing the participants' reasoning, especially at the conclusion of the experiment. Assuming that such procedures have been employed, the logic of argumentation is typically straightforward if the domain under investigation was problematized while preparing the experiment. In such cases, researchers can draw on the literature to demonstrate that the documented forms of reasoning would not have emerged by themselves. In the statistics experiments, for example, there were no reports in the research literature of either middle- or high-school students reasoning about either univariate or bivariate data in the relatively sophisticated ways that we documented. In experiments where the problem in the domain has not been described, it is essential to conducted postexperiment comparison assessments with nonparticipants. A researcher who served as the project evaluator conducted assessment interviews with participating and nonparticipating students at the conclusion of the two statistics experiments, in the process documenting significant differences in the ways that the two groups of students reasoned about the data (Konold et al., 2005).

The demonstration that participants developed relatively sophisticated forms of reasoning is only the first element of an argumentative grammar for design research. To clarify the additional elements, we draw on Brown's seminal article on design research:

> The Hawthorne Effect, as presented in standard texts, refers to the fact that any intervention tends to have positive effects merely because of the attention of the experimental team to subjects' welfare. The infamous Hawthorne Effect has been dogging my tail for a long time. . . . Everywhere I go I can predict that someone will tell me that my results are just a Hawthorne Effect.
>
> (1992: 163)

Brown goes on to explain why she rejects such arguments:

> I have never taken the Hawthorne criticism of my work seriously because of the very specific nature of the improvements obtained [in participants' reasoning]. If I were creating a true Hawthorne Effect, I would not be able to predict which performance would improve. But in fact we can see a close coupling of the cognitive activities practiced and the improvements shown.
>
> (pp. 163–164)

Brown's observations further emphasize that the argumentative grammar of design research has to encompass the process by which the research team purposefully supported the participants' development of particular forms of reasoning and not others. This gives rise to two challenges.

The first challenge is to document the major shifts that occurred in the participants' reasoning in the course of the experiment. This requirement has obvious implications for the data collection procedures employed in that the goal is to document how each successive form of reasoning emerged as a reorganization of prior forms of reasoning. Explanations of this type are central to the argumentative grammar of design research in our view. Clearly, the use of an explicitly articulated, interpretive framework for understanding participants' learning is crucial when developing such explanations. As an illustration, in presenting the learning trajectory that resulted from the two statistics design experiments, we explained how the students' learning while using the first computer tool enabled them to use the second computer tool as soon as it was introduced. In particular, we described how, in using the first tool, the students learned to interpret the dots and the end of the bars as signifying data values. This analysis of the students' learning was oriented by a distributed view of cognition (Dörfler, 1993; Kaput, 1994; Meira, 1998; Pea, 1993), which enabled us to tease out how the students' use of the computer tools influenced the nature of their data analysis activity and thus their learning during the experiments. Elsewhere, we have described the interpretive framework that guided our analysis of the students' learning during these experiments (Cobb, 2000b).

The second challenge concerns the close coupling to which Brown (1992) refers between the process of the participants' learning and the means by which the emergence of successive forms of reasoning was supported and organized. This indicates the importance of being explicit about how the learning environment and its relationship to the participants' activity and learning are conceptualized. In experimental and quasi-experimental studies, for example, the learning environment is conceptualized typically as consisting of independent features that the investigator can manipulate and control directly. The implicit ontology is that of environmental settings made up of separate independent variables and of students composed of collections of dependent psychological attributes. Together, these two theoretical suppositions ground the investigations that seek to discern regularity types of causal relations between the manipulation of instructional conditions and the performance of a collective, statistically constructed subject. In our view, this conceptualization is highly appropriate when the goal is to produce a particular form of knowledge that concerns both the overall effectiveness of two or more instructional interventions and the conditions under which one is more effective than the other (cf. Slavin, 2004).

Design research aims to produce a different form of knowledge that involves creating and improving means of supporting learning and understanding how they work. In the context of this research enterprise, the conceptualization of the learning environment as composed of externally manipulable, independent variables proves inadequate. In the case of the two statistics experiments, for example, we noted that the means of support included both the classroom norms and the nature of the classroom discourse. Classroom norms and discourse cannot be manipulated directly by a researcher; instead, they are constituted jointly by the teacher and the students in the course of their ongoing interactions. As a second example, it is reasonable for the purposes of experimental studies to view the tools used in the classroom as components of the learning environment (cf. Shavelson et al., 2003). However, this conceptualization is inadequate for the purposes of design experiments because the same tools can be used very differently in different classrooms, and these differences can influence students' learning profoundly. When conducting a design experiment, it is essential not merely to document the presence or absence of particular tools, but also to understand how they are used. The ways in which tools are used are established jointly by the teacher and the students and depend on the tasks as they are realized in the classroom as well as on the classroom norms and discourse. For the purposes of design research, it is reasonable to conceptualize the classroom learning environment as an evolving ecology that does not exist independently of the teacher's and the students' activity but is constituted in the course of classroom interactions. The relationship between the learning environment so conceptualized and the students' activity is therefore one of reflexivity in that the students contribute to the constitution of the learning environment that both enables and constrains their learning.

Given this conceptualization, the second challenge involves specifying the aspects of the classroom learning ecology that are necessary, rather than contingent, in supporting the emergence of successive forms of reasoning. As an illustration, in discussing why the students who participated in the statistics experiments were able to use the second computer tool productively as soon as it was introduced, we identified their use of the first tool as a primary means of support. The way in which the students used the first tool depended on:

- The overall goal for doing statistics established in the classroom (i.e., to identify patterns in data that are relevant to the question or issue under investigation).
- The organization of classroom activities (e.g., talking through the data-generation process).
- The instructional tasks (e.g., comparing two data sets by analyzing data that students viewed as realistic for a purpose that they considered legitimate).
- The nature of the classroom discourse (e.g., engaging in discussion in which significant statistical issues emerge as topics of conversation).

This indicates that each of these aspects of the classroom learning ecology were also necessary in making it possible for the students to use the second computer tool productively.

In summary, the argumentative grammar for design research that we have outlined involves:

- Demonstrating that the participants would not have developed particular forms of reasoning but for their participation in the design experiment.
- Documenting how each successive form of reasoning emerged as a reorganization of prior forms of reasoning.
- Specifying the aspects of the learning ecology that were necessary, rather than contingent, in supporting the emergence of these successive forms of reasoning.

This argumentative grammar is grounded in what Maxwell (2004) terms process-oriented explanations, rather than the regularity type of causal descriptions. Taken together, the three components of this grammar specify how a particular form of learning that would not have occurred naturally was "engineered."

Trustworthiness

Trustworthiness is concerned with the reasonableness and justifiability of inferences and assertions that result from a retrospective analysis. This notion of trustworthiness acknowledges that a range of retrospective analyses might be made of a given data set for a variety of purposes. The issue is the credibility of an analysis. The most important considerations are the extent to which the analysis of the longitudinal data set generated during an experiment is systematic and is open to monitoring and critique by other researchers.

It is critical to analyze systematically the entire data set generated during a design experiment systematically while simultaneously documenting the grounds for particular inferences. Furthermore, all phases of the analysis should be documented, including the refining and refuting of inferences. Only then can final claims and assertions be justified by backtracking through the various levels of the analysis, if necessary to the original data. It is this documentation that provides an empirical grounding for the analysis. Further, it provides a means of differentiating systematic analyses, in which sample episodes are used to illustrate general assertions, from questionable analyses, in which a few, possibly atypical episodes are used to support unsubstantiated claims. Additional criteria that enhance the trustworthiness of an analysis include both the extent to which the analysis has been critiqued by independent researchers and the extent to which it derives from a prolonged engagement with participants (Taylor & Bogdan, 1984). Typically, this latter criterion is satisfied in the case of classroom design experiments and constitutes a strength of the methodology.

As an illustration, the data generated during the two statistics experiments included video-recorded pre- and postinterviews, video-recordings of all classroom sessions, copies of all of the students' written work, field notes, and audio-recordings of all research team meetings. The specific approach that we used to analyze these data is a variant of Glaser and Strauss' (1967) constant comparative method (see also Cobb and Whitenack, 1996). First, we worked through the data chronologically, episode by episode, at each point testing our current inferences against a subsequent episode. This first phase of the retrospective analysis produced a sequence of inferences and refutations that were tied to specific episodes. In the second phase of the analysis, this sequence of conjectures and refutations became the data. It was while "meta-analyzing" these episode-specific inferences, confirmations, and refutations that particular episodes came to be seen as pivotal. And they were pivotal in the context of the analysis because they allowed us to decide between two or more competing inferences. It was these episodes that we typically included in research reports.

In addition to analyzing the entire data set systematically, it is also important to explicate the criteria for using key constructs of the interpretive framework so that other researchers can monitor and critique the process of making inferences. This is a nontrivial task in our experience, in that it is one thing to use an explanatory construct while engaging in the activity of making sense of data and quite another to frame that sense-making activity as an object of reflection and tease out criteria that capture how a particular construct is being used. As an illustration, when characterizing the learning environment established in a particular classroom, one of the primary constructs that we use is a classroom norm. Generally, explicating the criteria for using this construct involves specifying the types of evidence used to determine that a norm has been established. A first, relatively robust type of evidence occurs when a particular way of reasoning or acting that initially requires a justification is used later to justify other ways of reasoning or acting (Stephan & Rasmussen, 2002). In such cases, the role of the way of reasoning or acting shifts from a claim that requires a warrant to a warrant that substantiates subsequent claims. This shift provides direct evidence that a particular way of reasoning or acting has become normative and beyond justification. A second, equally robust type of evidence is indicated by Sfard's (2000a) observation that normative ways of acting are not mere arbitrary conventions that can be modified at will. Instead, they are value-laden and are constituted in the classroom as legitimate or acceptable ways of acting. This observation indicates the importance of searching for instances where a student appears to violate a proposed classroom norm in order to check whether his or her activity is treated as legitimate or illegitimate by the teacher and other students. In the former case, it would be necessary to revise the conjecture, whereas, in the latter case, the observation that the student's activity was viewed as a breach of a norm provides evidence in support of the conjecture (cf. Cobb et al., 2001). Finally, a third and even more direct type of evidence occurs when the teacher and students talk explicitly about their respective obligations and expectations. Such exchanges typically occur when one or more members perceive that a norm has been violated.

In summary, retrospective analyses are trustworthy to the extent that:

- The method of analysis is systematic and involves refuting conjectures (Atkinson et al., 1988).
- The criteria for making claims are explicit, thus enabling other researchers to monitor the analyses.
- Final claims and assertions can be justified by backtracking through the various phases of the analysis, if necessary to the original data sources.
- The analyses have been critiqued by other researchers, some but not all of whom are familiar with the settings from which the data were collected.

Repeatability

Accounts of design researchers have sometimes emphasized that each learning setting is unique and have stressed the importance of developing "thick descriptions" of these settings. In doing so, they appear to eschew a concern for the repeatability of designs. In our view, it is critical that design researchers aim to develop designs or innovations that can be used to support learning productively in other settings. This view implies that, when conducting a retrospective analysis, one of the goals is to delineate the aspects of the learning process that potentially can be repeated in different settings. The argumentative grammar that we have outlined indicates the general form that the specification of the repeatable aspects of a design experiment might take:

- The development of particular culminating forms of reasoning.
- Successive shifts or reorganizations of reasoning that specify the process of development of the culminating form of reasoning.
- The aspects of the learning ecology that are necessary to support the emergence of these successive forms of reasoning.

It is important to clarify that a specification of this type does not imply that a design should be repeated by ensuring that it is realized in precisely the same way in different settings. Instead, the intent is to inform others as they customize the design to the settings in which they are working by differentiating between the necessary and the contingent aspects of the design. In the case of the two statistics design experiments, the characterization of repeatability as complete fidelity clashes with the view of teachers as professionals who adjust their plans continually on the basis of ongoing assessments of their students' mathematical reasoning (cf. Ball, 1993). However, the learning trajectory that resulted from the experiments can guide teachers as they use the instructional activities and computer tools as the basis for instruction. A detailed version of this trajectory specifies both successive reorganizations in students' statistical reasoning and the means that are necessary to support those reorganizations. This type of rationale offers the possibility that teachers who have reconstructed the learning trajectory in the context of their professional development will be able to differentiate between the necessary and the contingent aspects of the instructional sequence as they adapt and modify it in their classes.

Generalizability

In the context of design research, generalizability is related closely to repeatability and implies that others will be able to use the products of a design experiment to inform their efforts to support learning in other settings. We indicated the importance of generalizability when we emphasized the value of framing an experiment as a paradigmatic case of a broader class of phenomena. It is this framing of activities and events in the learning setting as exemplars or prototypes that gives rise to generalizability. However, this is not generalization by means of a representative sample that is based on the regularity type of causal descriptions. Instead, it is generalization by means of an explanatory framework that is based on process explanations of causality (Steffe & Thompson, 2000). Therefore, the achievement of this type of generalizability depends on the development of domain-specific, instructional theories whose structure corresponds to the argumentative grammar that we have outlined.

As a part of the process of constructing a robust, domain-specific, instructional theory, we have found it important to conduct follow-up trials with a range of participants in a variety of settings. These trials are not full-scale design experiments that aim to refine and improve the design but, instead, might involve customizing the design while working in a new setting. In the case of the statistics experiments, for example, we conducted follow-up trials in which we worked with middle-school students; at-risk high-school students; prospective elementary-school teachers; and practicing middle-school teachers. We were surprised by the extent to which we have been able to document regularities in the development of the participants' statistical reasoning across these various settings. In each trial, there was considerable diversity in how the participants reasoned at any time. However, we were able to predict the primary forms of reasoning in each group of participants at any point in each trial. This type of knowledge is useful because it enables teachers to anticipate their students' types of reasoning on which they can build in order to achieve their instructional agenda at each point in the instructional sequence.

Conclusions

In this chapter, we have discussed a range of methodological issues that arise when preparing for a design experiment, experimenting to support learning, and conducting retrospective analyses of the data generated in the course of the experiment. The preparation phase is crucial to the success of the experiment but can be extensive, especially when there is little prior research on which to build. Key issues that need to be addressed include clarifying instructional goals by identifying the central ideas in a particular domain and documenting the instructional starting points both by drawing on the relevant literature and by conducting initial assessments as a part of the pilot work. In addition, it is essential to delineate an envisioned learning trajectory that consists of conjectures about both a learning process that culminates with the prospective instructional goals and the specific means of supporting that learning process. Although some of these conjectures might be highly speculative, formulation of the learning trajectory envisioned enables the research team to engage in the process of testing and revising its initial design as soon as it begins experimenting to support learning. Finally, the preparation phase also involves locating the planned experiment in a broader theoretical context by framing it as a case of a broader class of phenomena, thereby indicating the level of generalizability to which the experiment aims.

We clarified that the objective during the second phase of experimenting to support learning is not to demonstrate that the envisioned learning trajectory works but to improve the trajectory by testing and revising conjectures about both the prospective learning process and the specific means of supporting it. We indicated the importance of thinking through the types of data that will make it possible for the researchers to address the theoretical issues identified at the outset when they conduct retrospective analyses. In addition, we noted that in the process of experimenting to support learning, the research team makes ongoing interpretations that shape the design effort profoundly. Therefore, it is essential that design researchers make explicit the suppositions and assumptions that ground these interpretations, in the process explicating how they differentiate between what is necessary and what is contingent in a design. We also drew on the work of Maxwell (2004) to clarify that the intent both when making ongoing interpretations while experimenting to support learning and when conducting retrospective analyses is to develop process-oriented explanations that, in principle, can be discerned on the basis of a single case. Finally, we focused on the tightly integrated cycles of design and analysis that characterize design research at the level of both minicycles that are enacted in the course of a single experiment and macrocycles that span a series of experiments. In doing so, we noted that one of the primary products of a series of design experiments is typically a domain-specific, instructional theory that consists of a substantiated learning process together with the demonstrated means of supporting that process.

In discussing the final phase of a design experiment, conducting retrospective analysis, we followed Kelly (2004) in observing that design research does not have a clearly articulated, argumentative grammar that can be specified separately from its instantiation in any given experiment. We made an initial attempt to address this pressing concern by outlining three components of such a grammar that corresponds to the structure of a domain-specific, instructional theory. Then, we considered the trustworthiness or credibility of retrospective analyses and emphasized the importance of analyzing systematically the large, longitudinal, data sets generated in the course of a design experiment so that the final claims and assertions can be justified by backtracking through the various levels of an analysis, if necessary to the original data. We also stressed the importance of explicating the criteria for using key constructs of the interpretive framework so that other researchers can monitor and critique the process of making inferences. Next, we discussed the issue of repeatability and argued that what must repeat across settings are a specified learning process and the means that have been identified as necessary to support that process. The final issue discussed was that of generalizability. We noted that the type of generalization that design research seeks is based on process explanations of causality and indicated the value of conducting follow-up trials with a range of participants in a variety of settings.

Acknowledgments

The analysis reported in this chapter was supported by the National Science Foundation under Grant No. REC 0231037. The opinions expressed do not reflect necessarily the views of the Foundation. The authors are grateful to Qing Zhao and Jana Visnovska for their constructive comments on a previous draft of the chapter.

Notes

1 In earlier publications, we used the term *developmental research* to denote this type of research. In this chapter, we use the terms *design research* and *design experiment* because they have become the more generally accepted terms.
2 The basic tenets of design research that serve to differentiate it from other methodologies have been discussed in some detail by Cobb et al. (2003) and the Design-Based Research Collaborative (2003).
3 The term *learning trajectory* can be used to describe either the rationale for a limited number of classrooms lessons or the rationale for an extended instructional sequence on a given topic. Here, we use the term in the latter sense.
4 The design experiments were conducted by Paul Cobb, Kay McClain, Koeno Gravemeijer, Jose Cortina, Lynn Hodge, Maggie McGatha, Beth Petty, Carla Richards, and Michelle Stephan. Erna Yackel and Cliff Konold served as long-term consultants.
5 The computer tools were developed by Koeno Gravemeijer, Paul Cobb, Michiel Doorman, and Janet Bowers.
6 Edelson and Joseph (2004) also have framed design experiments as cases in which to investigate the process of supporting the development of students' domain-specific interests.
7 The term *domain-specific*, as we use it in this context, refers to particular mathematical domains. This usage should be differentiated from Treffers' (1987) employment of the same term to refer to the domain of realistic mathematics education.
8 These aspects of the design are reported by Cobb (1999), Cobb et al. (2003), and McClain (2002).

References

Atkinson, P., Delamont, S. & Hammersley, M. (1988). Qualitative research traditions: A British response to Jacob. *Review of Educational Research*, *58*, 231–250.
Bakker, A. (2004). *Design research in statistics education: On symbolizing and computer tools*. Utrecht, The Netherlands: CD-ß Press.

Ball, D. L. (1993). With an eye on the mathematical horizon: Dilemmas of teaching elementary school mathematics. *Elementary School Journal, 93*, 373–397.

Biehler, R. & Steinbring, H. (1991). Entdeckende Satistik, Stenget-und-Blätter, Boxplots: Konzepte, Begründungen und Erfahrungen eines Unterrichtsversuches [Explorations in statistics, stem-and-leaf, boxplots: Concepts, justifications, and experience in a teaching experiment]. *Der Mathematikunterricht, 37*, 5–32.

Bright, G., Brewer, W., McClain, K. & Mooney, E. (2003). *Navigating through data analysis in grades six through eight.* Reston, VA: National Council of Teachers of Mathematics.

Brown, A. L. (1992). Design experiments: Theoretical and methodological challenges in creating complex interventions in classroom settings. *Journal of the Learning Sciences, 2*, 141–178.

Cobb, P. (1999). Individual and collective mathematical learning: The case of statistical data analysis. *Mathematical Thinking and Learning, 1*, 5–44.

Cobb, P. (2000a). Conducting teaching experiments in collaboration with teachers. In A. E. Kelly & R. A. Lesh (eds), *Handbook of research design in mathematics and science education* (pp. 307–334). Mahwah, NJ: Lawrence Erlbaum Associates.

Cobb, P. (2000b). The importance of a situated view of learning to the design of research and instruction. In J. Boaler (ed.), *Multiple perspectives on mathematics teaching and learning* (pp. 45–82). Stamford, CT: Ablex.

Cobb, P. (2001). Supporting the improvement of learning and teaching in social and institutional context. In S. Carver & D. Klahr (eds), *Cognition and instruction: Twenty-five years of progress* (pp. 455–478). Mahwah, NJ: Lawrence Erlbaum Associates.

Cobb, P. (2002). Reasoning with tools and inscriptions. *Journal of the Learning Sciences, 11*, 187–216.

Cobb, P. & Hodge, L. L. (2002). An initial contribution to the development of a design theory of mathematical interests: The case of statistical data analysis. Paper presented at the annual meeting of the American Educational Research Association, San Francisco, CA, April.

Cobb, P. & Steffe, L. P. (1983). The constructivist researcher as teacher and model builder. *Journal for Research in Mathematics Education, 14*, 83–94.

Cobb, P. & Tzou, C. (2000). Learning about data creation. Paper presented at the annual meeting of the American Educational Research Association, New Orleans, LA, April.

Cobb, P. & Whitenack, J. W. (1996). A method for conducting longitudinal analyses of classroom videorecordings and transcript. *Educational Studies in Mathematics, 30*, 213–228.

Cobb, P. & Yackel, E. (1996). Constructivist, emergent, and sociocultural perspectives in the context of developmental research. *Educational Psychologist, 31*, 175–190.

Cobb, P., Confrey, J., diSessa, A. A., Lehrer, R. & Schauble, L. (2003a). Design experiments in education research. *Educational Researcher, 32*(1), 9–13.

Cobb, P., McClain, K. & Gravemeijer, K. (2003b). Learning about statistical covariation. *Cognition and Instruction, 21*, 1–78.

Cobb, P., Stephan, M., McClain, K. & Gravemeijer, K. (2001). Participating in classroom mathematical practices. *Journal of the Learning Sciences, 10*, 113–164.

Collins, A. (1992). Toward a design science of education. In E. Scanon & T. O'Shey (eds), *New directions in educational technology* (pp. 15–22). New York: Springer.

Confrey, J. & Lachance, A. (2000). Transformative teaching experiments through conjecture-driven research design. In A. E. Kelly & R. A. Lesh (eds), *Handbook of research design in mathematics and science education* (pp. 231–266). Mahwah, NJ: Lawrence Erlbaum Associates.

Dede, C. (2004). If design-based research is the answer, what is the question? *Journal of the Learning Sciences, 13*, 105–114.

deLange, J., van Reeuwijk, M., Burrill, G. & Romberg, T. A. (1993). *Learning and testing mathematics in context. The case: data visualization.* Madison, WI: University of Wisconsin, National Center for Research in Mathematical Sciences Education.

Design-Based Research Collaborative (2003). Design-based research: An emerging paradigm for educational inquiry. *Educational Researcher, 32*(1), 5–8.

Desimone, L. & Le Floch, K. (2004). Are we asking the right questions? Using cognitive interviews to improve surveys in education research. *Educational Evaluation and Policy Analysis*, 26, 1–22.

diSessa, A. A. (1992). Images of learning. In E. d Corte, M. C. Linn, H. Mandl & L. Verschaffel (eds), *Computer-based learning environments and problem solving* (pp. 19–40). Berlin: Springer.

diSessa, A. A. (2002). Students' criteria for representational adequacy. In K. Gravemeijer, R. Lehrer, B. van Oers & L. Verschaffel (eds), *Symbolizing, modeling and tool use in mathematics education* (pp. 105–129). Dordrecht, The Netherlands: Kluwer.

diSessa, A. A. & Cobb, P. (2004). Ontological innovation and the role of theory in design experiments. *Journal of the Learning Sciences*, 13, 77–103.

Dörfler, W. (1993). Computer use and views of the mind. In C. Keitel & K. Ruthven (eds), *Learning from computers: Mathematics education and technology* (pp. 159–186). Berlin: Springer.

Drijvers, P. (2003). *Learning algebra in a computer algebra environment: Design research on the understanding of the concept of parameter* (dissertation). Utrecht, the Netherlands: CD-ß Press.

Edelson, D. C. (2002). Design research: What we learn when we engage in design. *Journal of the Learning Sciences*, 11, 105–121.

Edelson, D. C. & Joseph, D. (2004). The interest-driven design framework: Motivating learning through usefulness. Paper presented at the Sixth International Conference of the Learning Sciences, Santa Monica, CA, June.

Freudenthal, H. (1971). Geometry Between the Devil and the Deep Sea. *Educational Studies in Mathematics*, 3, 413–435.

Freudenthal, H. (1973). *Mathematics as an educational task*. Dordrecht, The Netherlands: Reidel.

Freudenthal, H. (1983). *Didactical phenomenology of mathematical structures*. Dordrecht, The Netherlands: Reidel.

Garfield, J. B. (1988). Obstacles to effective teaching of probability and statistics. Paper presented in the Research Presession at the annual meeting of the National Council of Teachers of Mathematics, Chicago, IL, April.

Glaser, B. G. & Strauss, A. L. (1967). *The discovery of grounded theory: Strategies for qualitative research*. New York: Aldine.

Gravemeijer, K. (1994a). *Developing realistic mathematics education*. Utrecht, The Netherlands: CD-ß Press.

Gravemeijer, K. (1994b). Educational development and developmental research. *Journal for Research in Mathematics Education*, 25, 443–471.

Gravemeijer, K. (1999). How emergent models may foster the constitution of formal mathematics. *Mathematical Thinking and Learning*, 1, 155–177.

Hancock, C., Kaput, J. J. & Goldsmith, L. T. (1992). Authentic inquiry with data: Critical barriers to classroom implementation. *Educational Psychologist*, 27, 337–364.

Hershkowitz, R. & Schwarz, B. (1999). The emergent perspective in rich learning environments: Some roles of tools and activities in the construction of sociomathematical norms. *Educational Studies in Mathematics*, 39, 149–166.

Kaput, J. J. (1994). The representational roles of technology in connecting mathematics with authentic experience. In R. Biehler, R. V. Scholz, R. Strasser & B. Winkelmann (Eds.), *Didactics of mathematics as a scientific discipline* (pp. 379–397). Dordrecht, The Netherlands: Kluwer.

Kazemi, E. & Franke, M. L. (2004). Teacher learning in mathematics: Using student work to promote collective inquiry. *Journal of Mathematics Teacher Education*, 7, 203–225.

Kelly, A. E. (2004). Design research in education: Yes, but is it methodological? *Journal of the Learning Sciences*, 13, 115–128.

Konold, C., Higgins, T., Russell, S. J. & Khalila, K. (2005). Data seen through different lenses. Unpublished manuscript, Scientific Reasoning Research Institute, University of Massachusetts at Amherst.

Konold, C., Pollatsek, A., Well, A. & Gagnon, A. (1997). Students' analyzing data: Research of critical barriers. In J. B. Garfield & G. Burrill (eds), *Research on the role of technology in teaching and learning statistics: Proceedings of the 1996 International Association for Statistics Education Roundtable Conference* (pp. 151–167). Voorburg, The Netherlands: International Statistics Institute.

Lampert, M. (2001). *Teaching problems and the problems of teaching*. New Haven, CT: Yale University Press.

Lehrer, R. & Lesh, R. (2003). Mathematical learning. In W. Reynolds & G. Miller (eds), *Comprehensive handbook of psychology*, Volume 7 (pp. 357–391). New York: Wiley.

Lehrer, R. & Romberg, T. (1996). Exploring children's data modeling. *Cognition and Instruction*, 14, 69–108.

Lehrer, R. & Schauble, L. (2004). Modeling natural variation through distribution. *American Educational Research Journal*, 41, 635–679.

Lobato, J. (2003). How design experiments can inform a rethinking of transfer and vice versa. *Educational Researcher*, 32(1), 17–20.

Maxwell, J. A. (2004). Causal explanation, qualitative research, and scientific inquiry in education. *Educational Researcher*, 33(2), 3–11.

McClain, K. (2002). Teacher's and students' understanding: The role of tool use in communication. *Journal of the Learning Sciences*, 11, 217–249.

McClain, K. & Cobb, P. (2001). The development of sociomathematical norms in one first-grade classroom. *Journal for Research in Mathematics Education*, 32, 234–266.

McClain, K., Cobb, P. & Gravemeijer, K. (2000). Supporting students' ways of reasoning about data. In M. Burke (ed.), *Learning mathematics for a new century (2001 Yearbook of the National Council of Teachers of Mathematics)* (pp. 174–187). Reston, VA: National Council of Teachers of Mathematics.

McGatha, M. (2000). Instructional design in the context of classroom-based research: Documenting the learning of a research team as it engaged in a mathematics design experiment. *Dissertation Abstracts International*, 61(03), 923. (UMI No. 9964905).

McGatha, M., Cobb, P. & McClain, K. (2002). An analysis of students' initial statistical understandings: Developing a conjectured learning trajectory. *Journal of Mathematical Behavior*, 16, 339–335.

Meira, L. (1998). Making sense of instructional devices: The emergence of transparency in mathematical activity. *Journal for Research in Mathematics Education*, 29, 121–142.

Moore, D. S. (1997). New pedagogy and new content: The case of statistics. *International Statistics Review*, 65, 123–165.

Pea, R. D. (1993). Practices of distributed intelligence and designs for education. In G. Salomon (ed.), *Distributed cognitions* (pp. 47–87). New York: Cambridge University Press.

Roth, W. M. (1996). Where is the context in contextual word problems? Mathematical practices and products in grade 8 students' answers to story problems. *Cognition and Instruction*, 14, 487–527.

Sfard, A. (2000a). On the reform movement and the limits of mathematical discourse. *Mathematical Thinking and Learning*, 2, 157–189.

Sfard, A. (2000b). Steering (dis)course between metaphors and rigor: Using focal analysis to investigate an emergence of mathematical objects. *Journal for Research in Mathematics Education*, 31, 296–327.

Shadish, W. R., Cook, T. D. & Campbell, D. T. (2002). *Experimental and quasi-experimental designs for generalized causal inference*. Boston, MA: Houghton Mifflin.

Shaughnessey, J. M. (1992). Research in probability and statistics: Reflections and directions. In D. A. Grouws (ed.), *Handbook of research on mathematics teaching and learning* (pp. 465–494). New York: Macmillan.

Shavelson, R. J., Phillips, D. C., Towne, L. & Feuer, M. J. (2003). On the science of educational design studies. *Educational Researcher*, 32(1), 25–28.

Simon, M. A. (1995). Reconstructing mathematics pedagogy from a constructivist perspective. *Journal for Research in Mathematics Education*, 26, 114–145.

Simon, M. A. (2000). Research on the development of mathematics teachers: The teacher development experiment. In A. E. Kelly & R. A. Lesh (eds), *Handbook of research design in mathematics and science education* (pp. 335–359). Mahwah, NJ: Lawrence Erlbaum Associates.

Simon, M. A. & Blume, G. W. (1996). Justification in the mathematics classroom: A study of prospective elementary teachers. *Journal of Mathematical Behavior*, *15*, 3–31.

Slavin, R. E. (2004). Educational research can and must address "what works" questions. *Educational Researcher*, *33*(1), 27–28.

Steffe, L. P. & Thompson, P. W. (2000). Teaching experiment methodology: Underlying principles and essential elements. In A.E. Kelly & R.A. Lesh (eds), *Handbook of research design in mathematics and science education* (pp. 267–307). Mahwah, NJ: Lawrence Erlbaum Associates.

Stein, M. K., Silver, E. A. & Smith, M. S. (1998). Mathematics reform and teacher development: A community of practice perspective. In J. G. Greeno & S. V. Goldman (eds), *Thinking practices in mathematics and science learning* (pp. 17–52). Mahwah, NJ: Lawrence Erlbaum Associates.

Stephan, M. & Rasmussen, C. (2002). Classroom mathematical practices in differential equations. *Journal of Mathematical Behavior*, *21*, 459–490.

Taylor, S. J. & Bogdan, R. (1984). *Introduction to qualitative research methods* (2nd ed.). New York: Wiley.

Thompson, A. G. & Thompson, P. W. (1996). Talking about rates conceptually, Part II: Mathematical knowledge for teaching. *Journal for Research in Mathematics Education*, *27*, 2–24.

Thompson, P. W. (1994). Images of rate and operational understanding of the fundamental theorem of calculus. *Educational Studies in Mathematics*, *26*, 229–274.

Thompson, P. W. (1996). Imagery and the development of mathematical reasoning. In L. P. Steffe, P. Nesher, P. Cobb, G. A. Goldin & B. Greer (eds), *Theories of mathematical learning* (pp. 267–285). Mahwah, NJ: Lawrence Erlbaum Associates.

Treffers, A. (1987). *Three dimensions: A model of goal and theory description in mathematics instruction—the Wiskobas project*. Dordrecht, The Netherlands: Reidel.

Voigt, J. (1996). Negotiation of mathematical meaning in classroom processes. In P. Nesher, L. P. Steffe, P. Cobb, G. A. Goldin & B. Greer (eds), *Theories of mathematical learning* (pp. 21–50). Hillsdale, NJ: Lawrence Erlbaum Associates.

Wilensky, U. (1996). Making sense of probability through paradox and programming: A case study in a connected mathematics framework. In Y. Kafai & M. Resnick (eds), *Constructivism in practice: Designing, thinking, and learning in a digital world* (pp. 269–296). Mahwah, NJ: Lawrence Erlbaum Associates.

Yackel, E. & Cobb, P. (1996). Sociomathematical norms, argumentation, and autonomy in mathematics. *Journal for Research in Mathematics Education*, *27*, 458–477.

5 Engineering and Design Research

Intersections for Education Research and Design

Margret A. Hjalmarson
George Mason University

Richard A. Lesh
Indiana University

Introduction

Design research as a methodological stance or a perspective on educational research has drawn on multiple methodologies and theoretical perspectives in education and other fields. In this chapter, we examine a process of research that draws on an engineering view of the process of design. Recent reports (e.g., "The Engineer of 2020" [National Academy of Engineering, 2004]) have described the process of engineering as both an applied science and a means for advancing technical and scientific knowledge. Engineering primarily involves the design and development of products that operate in systems. It includes the process of design as well as the tangible products of design. This interaction between process and product is the similarity between education and engineering that we point to in this chapter.

With each design that enters a system, new designs need to be engineered and old designs need to be refined. The tangible product is only the tip of the iceberg of the engineering process and its relevant results. Throughout the design of a product, plans, conceptual systems, and other intangible products are developed that inform the design of the next product. The intangible products formed during the design process are relevant because revision and extension in the system are inevitable. Consider, for example, designing a digital music player. The first player designed performs a function. When the product enters the system, the designers learn more about how clients use the product in different contexts (e.g., in the car, at work, at the gym), then they revise the product to meet users' needs more effectively. System integration occurs as the music player works with a stereo system or a computer. Products are seldom used in isolation from other products, and adaptability to changing conditions is needed with subsequent products. As a result, every product will have strengths and weaknesses that will need to be addressed in the next iteration of the design. Evaluation goes beyond identifying a "good" or "bad" product to investigating the circumstances and conditions under which a product is good or bad, useful or effective. Because designs change a system, flexibility and the potential for revision under changing conditions become important.

For education, the design could incorporate curricula, software, technological tools, and other innovations. The design is used in a system (or systems), users interact with the system, and new designs are developed in response to information about the last product and changes to the system. For example, curricula are used in classrooms, data about implementation are gathered in different contexts, standards and assessments may change, and the curricula need revision for continued implementation. Supplemental materials (e.g., assessments, teachers' professional development materials) are developed to aid the use of a curriculum. As a curriculum is used, teachers may learn more about their students and teaching and require new types of supplemental materials (e.g., technology, manipulatives). Students learn new information and think about mathematics in new ways that change their understanding of mathematics. The product influences the system and vice versa. The product (e.g., a curriculum) is entering a system where related products from previous iterations have been used already. Throughout this process, knowledge is gained about teaching, learning, and mathematics for the next iteration.

We draw parallels between design in engineering and the design of innovation in education in order to draw implications for research into education. The first parallel is that "engineering is about design under constraint" (National Academy of Engineering, 2004: 7). Constraints in engineering could be financial, material, technical, or political. Constraints also concern the ultimate users or consumers of a product. No one design will work under all constraints and conditions. Rather, engineering design is conducted in reasons, purposes, and conditions unique to a context. Users may not use a product as anticipated (with positive and negative consequences), may not share the engineers' understanding or interpretation of the situation, or may have expectations for a product not shared by the designers. To return to the curriculum example, teachers using a reform curriculum have used the materials in ways unanticipated and unintended by the original designers because the teachers have different expectations for mathematics teaching and learning than the designers (e.g., Middleton, 1999; Remillard, 2000). The lesson for curriculum designers is how to anticipate better teachers' use of the materials and to account for the possibility of unanticipated uses. In teaching and engineering, most decisions involve trade-offs among conflicting interests (e.g., time, money, and mandates from higher authorities). Accounting for the trade-offs often requires input from multiple disciplines and perspectives. Economics, science, materials, and technical knowledge from many fields are parts of the final design. In the education field, education, psychology, sociology, mathematics, and practical experience (among other perspectives) inform the use of a design.

Engineering Processes and Engineering Products

Although engineers share some common characteristics, it should be understood that engineering is an umbrella term that covers multiple disciplines. The Accreditation Board for Engineering and Technology lists more than 20 engineering disciplines; among them, long-standing fields (such as mechanical and civil) and more recent fields (such as bioengineering, environmental, and software). All of the fields require their own disciplinary knowledge, skills, and applications that build on and incorporate mathematical and scientific knowledge. Engineering impacts many aspects of daily life. Increasingly, engineering disciplines work across disciplinary boundaries to address design problems. As a result of the diversity of the disciplines and the applications, engineering encompasses the development of a diverse set of products and processes. Although many engineers are responsible for designing tangible products (e.g., electronics, cars, and bridges), another aspect of engineering is the design, development, and refinement of processes and procedures. For example, procedures are designed for the testing of mechanical parts such as pumps and valves that control water flowing through a power plant. The engineer is not designing a particular pump or valve. Rather, he or she develops procedures for testing and gathering data about pumps and valves (products that have been designed by other engineers).

The design of procedures applies to other engineering disciplines such as materials science, where engineers develop protocols for measuring qualitative characteristics quantitatively (e.g., the roughness of a surface or the degree of deformity in a material).

We have found that engineering and other design fields can provide useful ways of thinking about conceptual systems for teaching and design research. The first characteristic is that the process of design is product-driven. The design process occurs for a particular client in a particular situation with particular constraints and affordances. However, the design builds on prior knowledge and experience of design and results in information useful for future designs. The second characteristic of engineering work is that the design is intended to change the environment in which it is used (e.g., to solve a problem identified by the client). Often, this can be translated into a version of problem solving. For example, the design of a portable music player should allow people to take music anywhere. Once the player is available, the system responds with new needs (e.g., connecting it to existing stereo systems, integrating it with a computer, developing new methods for selling music online). When an educational innovation is introduced, the educational situation and context are similarly changed. New design problems may arise. For instance, if new types of tasks or technology are introduced into a class, new forms of assessment may be required, and instructors may want to assess new types of skills and abilities.

In addition to the challenges of carrying out research in a classroom system, there is a gap between the educational theories developed by researchers and teachers' needs for practical innovations that can be used with students. Essentially, educational practice requires objects to be designed while simultaneously developing and adjusting theories about learning and teaching. From an engineering perspective, this is akin to learning how theories about the properties and behaviors of materials are applied to designing new electronics like a digital music player. Designing new components of the player helps engineers learn about new materials and electronic systems. For education, teachers need curricular materials that are based on knowledge about how students learn mathematics. Researchers need to develop theories about teaching and learning to inform curricular materials. However, it is not enough merely to design one set of curricular materials. For example, when designing materials for a large, first-year engineering course, the use of design principles to develop materials provided grounding for the development of local materials. The principles could be shared with faculty at other institutions who had different local needs, but they could rely on the general design principles to develop high-quality materials.

In a recent curriculum project, statistic tasks were designed for an engineering course. When designing a statistical task, it was not enough to develop one statistics task. The designers also designed clones or twin tasks that employed the same fundamental statistics question in different contexts, and they modified the data sets in order to prevent cheating by students across the many years of the course. For the categorization of students' work, the same schema could be employed across tasks to understand students' statistical thinking even though the tasks were superficially different (Hjalmarson, 2004). It is important to know when, where, why, and for whom any educational innovation (e.g., a curriculum, software, or pedagogical methods) is useful and effective. In other words, a design research project should result in the development of a particular product as well as conceptual knowledge that can be used to design future products for other contexts. Hence, aspects of both the conceptual foundation and the design process should inform future work. The interaction between product and process is informed by the language of design.

Design as Verb and Noun

The language of design affords a different perspective on education research than other terminology. One advantage of the use of design terminology in relation to education research is the flexibility of the word itself. We use design as a verb in relationship to the process of design. We use design as a noun to refer to the object under development. Designs are designed. This flexibility in language underscores the ability of design research to document the development of a product over time by investigating simultaneously the usability of the product and the process for developing the product. The language flexibility also brings to the fore the idea that understanding the process of design is as important as understanding the object under design. Research about a design is more than only the final product. Design research is also an investigation into the process of design.

One risk with the language is that it may be unclear whether results pertain to the process or the product. In general, there will be results about both the process and the product. One reason is that a goal of design research is to improve the design process. The tangible product may represent only a part of the desired outcome. Another reason is that the product may be under constant revision and is more often the result of an ongoing, iterative, design revision process than the final result of one cycle of design. To return to the engineering metaphor, as engineers design a digital music player, they should learn about the particular device as well as the design process required for the design of other devices. Thinking about design as a process is conducive to thinking about teaching and learning processes. In a recent curriculum design project in engineering education, the design of new learning units for an engineering course was begun using principles for middle-school activities (Lesh et al., 2000), but it resulted in the development of modified principles for an engineering education context (Diefes-Dux et al., 2004; Moore & Diefes-Dux, 2004). Each design of an educational innovation should produce results for the object itself as well as for the process of design.

Characteristics of Design Research

Usually, designs in engineering and other design sciences are created for complex situations that contain a high number of variables and real-world constraints. Engineering, for example, requires interdisciplinary knowledge and the synthesis of information from many perspectives (e.g., environmental, financial, social, political, mathematical, or physical) (Grimson, 2002; John, 2000). For the digital music player example, engineers need to take into account mechanical, material, and economic considerations because different devices are designed for different purposes and different types of consumers. In addition, "design is a core feature of all engineering activity" (John, 2000: 217). Educational contexts involve a variety of complex interacting systems, and teachers make instructional decisions using a variety of theories (e.g., pedagogical or mathematical). When designing educational objects, multiple theories and methods are relevant in order to explain, predict, or make a decision. One motivation for drawing on many perspectives is the trade-off decisions inherent in the design context and process.

A trade-off decision occurs when variables impacting the design are in conflict. The designer must attempt to optimize and prioritize multiple variables and to justify decisions based on the priorities that have been set. There is room for compromise and the consideration of multiple variables, but sacrifices in one area are made for the benefit of other opportunities. For instance, for a digital music player, the designer should consider size, form, sound quality, and cost as trade-off considerations. A smaller device could be more expensive, but more desirable for consumers wanting to use the player while jogging. As a result, slightly modified devices are designed for different contexts of use (e.g., for a device to use in a car, size is not as critical as the amount of memory). In a parallel situation, teachers must make decisions based on the time available in a class or the varying abilities of the students in a class. The documentation of decisions about trade-offs aids the generation of theories about teaching and learning by providing information about when, how, where, and why an educational innovation is effective. Documentation also serves later design efforts by providing evidence about what was tried and why (whether attempts succeeded or failed), to inform future design. As in engineering, there are ethical, political, financial, and social constraints that force a designer (or an educator) to make decisions about trade-offs.

To make effective decisions about trade-offs in a design situation, fields that employ a design process use multiple theories and experiences in order to make decisions about designing. The designers' knowledge and experience come from different sources, both formal and informal. Designing a digital music player includes integrating electrical and computer engineering, materials for the case and the component chips, knowledge about people's music needs, and economics. To a certain extent, design also entails aesthetic form in light of the function of a device. A device needs to be visually appealing. At this point, design is the art of taking the knowledge available, integrating what is known about the context, and developing a product. For teachers, they must use their knowledge and experience about students, mathematical expertise, personal theories, and information about teaching in order to design a classroom environment that is conducive to learning. There is an aesthetic aspect because teachers consider the form and structure of what they do. Hence, the design of a learning environment is ultimately an integration of multiple theories and experiences. This integration of information from theory, experience, and practice is another parallel between classroom instruction and engineering design.

Iteration in Design

In a complex system, as modifications occur, the system may respond in unpredictable ways. Changes reverberate throughout the system. Iteration in this sense is a process of design, testing, and revision. An idea is expressed or externalized, then it is reviewed and tested. Modifications are made. The idea or innovation is tested in practice. A design is developed and the cycle continues. Iteration occurs naturally in the engineering design process even as students working in teams are learning about design (Hjalmarson et al., 2007).

Iteration is both a natural and a necessary part of design in education and engineering. Just as we encourage teachers to be reflective about their practice, so should designers be reflective about their design. However, reflection does not occur for the sake of reflection. Rather, reflection about design is an assessment or evaluation of the impacts and effectiveness of the design in meeting goals and objectives. Iteration moves in the direction of improvement and refinement, but it is also responsive to changing needs as innovations are introduced. Iteration means improving not only the design at hand, but also the context and system where the design is used.

The role of iteration relates to the use of cycles to describe the design process. The use of cycles highlights the continuous nature of the process, denoting that each phase is not meant to be the last and that design improvement depends on movement based on testing, knowledge development, and interaction between the design and the system where it is used. In the next section, we describe a design research cycle that moves between practice and needs while testing designs and developing improvements and modifications that are responsive to a changing system of use.

Design Research Cycle

We propose a four-phase design research cycle that incorporates the study of both the process of design and the products designed. As students go through cycles when generating solutions to modeling activities (Doerr & English, 2003), collaborators in design research also go through cycles of expression, testing, and revision of the final product. The cycles are guided continually by the end-in-view for the design research. For instance, one goal could be designing a product that would allow a teacher to understand students' solution processes for a complex, problem-solving activity (Hjalmarson, 2004). We examine explicitly the interaction between the conceptual foundations for the design of a product and the assessment of its use in a system.

The design research cycle encompasses four phases: the conceptual foundations, the design of the product, a system for its use, and a problematic situation. Each of the phases and the interactions between them are described in subsequent sections. The cycle can be entered at any of the phases and does not begin necessarily at any one phase or proceed necessarily in a linear fashion. Throughout the design research cycle, we emphasize that the endeavor includes characteristics of a design process (e.g., iteration, revision, and testing) and characteristics of a research process (e.g., hypotheses, data collection, description, and data analysis). Design does not occur exclusive of research or vice versa. Rather, design and research occur simultaneously and in parallel for the mutual benefit of both endeavors.

As an overview of the design cycle, we begin with the initial identification of a problem. A problematic situation is the origin of the design issue or the motivation for a product to be designed. A design is required and motivated by something problematic in the context. The problematic situation is the aspect of the context where a problem lies. The conceptual foundation is the knowledge, theory, experience, and conceptual systems that are brought to bear on the process of design. The conceptual foundation is what is known about the problematic situation, the context, the problem, and other relevant theories that inform the design process. The products designed are the tools, innovations, systems, or other designs developed to address the problematic situation, using the conceptual foundation. The system for use is the context and conditions where the products will be used. From the system for use, new problems arise once a design has been introduced. The cycle begins again to accommodate new problems with new conceptual foundations and new products for use in the system. As an example, consider the design of a curriculum for an engineering course. A curricular need is identified in a set of interests (i.e., the problematic situation) that are unmet by currently available materials and resources. Then, the models and principles for a curriculum are identified that might be helpful in the situation (i.e., the conceptual foundation). Next, curricular units are designed with input from multiple partners, consultants, instructors, and experts (i.e., the product design). Finally, the curricular units are tested in the classroom (i.e., the system for use). The cycle continues as new problems are identified.

There should be continuous movement around the cycle. There is also interaction and back-and-forth movement between the four phases of the design research cycle as the product is developed and the design process is documented. For instance, the process of designing the product may require a return to the conceptual foundation and then back to the problematic situation in order to ensure the fidelity of the design to the initial problem while addressing new problems that may arise throughout the process. This does not imply that the designers' interpretation and understanding of the initial situation remain unchanged throughout the process. Rather, as new information is gathered and the design proceeds, the designers should check the initial problem situation again. Throughout the system, documentation of the design process should be collected to inform future design and the constraints influencing the current iteration of the design.

Problematic Situations

Problematic situations motivate the design of a product. The problematic situation creates a need for a design. The problematic situation encompasses the constraints and affordances placed on the design, and it can play a number of roles in the design research cycle. For example, the problematic situation can be the initial starting point for a design. To illustrate, an engineering instructor determines that the current curriculum does not address the need for students to learn about technical writing and the process of engineering design. As a result, new types of activities are developed. The new activities can create new problematic situations (e.g., the need for new assessment strategies or training for teaching assistants).

The problematic situation relates to an objective (English & Lesh, 2003) because it is where the problem is identified and the client articulates goals for the design. The problematic situation is not isolated for the context and it interacts with other aspects of the system of use for the product. Throughout the design cycle, the designers should return to an examination of the problematic situation in order to identify whether the product is meeting the objective, if the new products need to be developed, if the problematic situation was changed by the design process, and to document how the needs of the situation have been addressed.

Conceptual Foundation

For design research, the conceptual foundation may draw from diverse knowledge bases, theories, conceptual systems, and experiences. Multiple theories are sensible when multiple variables impact a design. These variables are not used in isolation from one another. Rather, they are intertwined in complex ways. The existence of multiple variables creates trade-off decisions that are addressed by diverse areas of expertise and knowledge. Similarly, for the designers, multiple theories are used to design any one product or set of products. Design research seeks to make those theories more explicit through the products. However, design research requires more than making the theories explicit. The theories also should be tested in practice by the artifact. For example, although historical development in mathematics may be used to design a curriculum unit, the learner may not develop along the same lines as mathematical history. What may be sensible historically may not be a sensible route from the learner's perspective. The artifact tests the theoretical use of mathematical history as a basis for the design of a curriculum.

Teachers and decision-makers who confront real-life problems naturally use multiple theories when designing tools for their classrooms. They have to incorporate thinking from social theories, mathematical curricular materials, school or school district policies, pedagogical knowledge, and prior teaching experiences when designing a learning environment for their students. That learning environment includes how students are asked to interact with each other and the teacher (e.g., How do students collaborate in groups? How do students share their solution methods?). It also includes the mathematical topics and the approach to teaching those topics (e.g., How are the topics organized? How are the topics introduced and developed over time? What topics are important? What mathematical skills are important?). In order to answer teachers' questions about planning activities in their classrooms, assessing their students' learning, and making decisions about instruction, theories about teaching and learning mathematics need to incorporate these multiple theories and provide products useful in daily practice.

Product Design

The product designed is the object or innovation developed to meet the needs of the user, effect change in the problematic situation, and capitalize on the conceptual foundations relevant to the system. Our purpose in using an artifact or a product as the core of the research activity continues our emphasis on the design aspects of engineering where products are the center of research activity. In addition, different types of products (e.g., curricula) have been designed for many years; however, documentation of the process of design or the effectiveness of such products is somewhat limited. For example, *On Evaluating Curricular Effectiveness* (Confrey & Stohl, 2004) describes considerations for the evaluation of curricular materials and the types of evaluation that have been completed thus far. Curriculum design processes have lacked documentation to inform future design processes (Clements, 2002, this volume).

Product design generates externalized artifacts that reveal the thinking, interpretations, and assumptions of the designer. It also facilitates future revision. For instance, in modeling activities for students, students generate documentation about the model while they work on the tasks that can be analyzed to learn about their interpretations of mathematical situations (Carmona-Dominguez, 2004), mathematical knowledge, and the development of models (Doerr & English, 2003). The documentation makes knowledge and theories explicit to an observer. Research on teachers and teaching has focused on what teachers do in the classroom (e.g., their behaviors, methods of teaching, and use of a curriculum). However, differences in teaching may be more apparent when we examine what teachers see, rather than what they do, because classrooms are complex systems of interacting parts. As an example, we (as researchers) can see what teachers do in a classroom (e.g., they use manipulatives during a lesson about addition), but to investigate a teacher's understanding of manipulatives, it may be more important to understand how teachers see the classroom situation when they are using manipulatives for a mathematics lesson (Firestone et al., 2004; Schorr & Koellner-Clark, 2003). How does the teacher see the students using the manipulatives? What is the teachers' interpretation of the success of the lesson in advancing students' knowledge of addition? Information about how teachers see the situation may not be apparent in what they do with the manipulatives. In modeling activities, students generally produce a variety of mathematically rich responses. As a result of having new information about their students, the teacher's view of the students and how they learn mathematics may change. The task in design research with teachers is to ask them to design an artifact that reveals their thinking and expresses their theories about an experience in the classroom.[1]

In modeling activities for students (Lesh et al., 2000), a critical aspect of the activity for revealing students' thinking is that the activity should be model-eliciting. This means that the task should ask students to construct models that describe, explain, or predict in a specific situation for a particular client in a testable way. For example, an engineering, model-eliciting activity asked students to develop a model for measuring the size of aluminum crystals using digital images. Students had to determine a sampling method and a method for measuring irregularly shaped crystals (Diefes-Dux et al., 2006). Similar principles apply to design research studies involving teachers; namely, teachers should design artifacts that express their current ways of thinking about their students' learning in a testable format that can be revised based on the testing. For example, teachers can design products for their classrooms that can be tested then revised based on both their experience in classrooms and the many theories that may be relevant. Designers also develop products that are testable and that reveal the designers' thinking about a situation. Moreover, testing the products is inseparable from testing the theories that are included in the design of the product. The product and the conceptual foundation should improve and become more robust together. Although a designer may have a prior definition of what will be "good" in a situation, he or she should be open to the possibility that what is "good" in a situation may not be what is expected or what is predicted by the theories. Hence, not only do the artifacts change, but the theories are modified as well. Examples of theory revision based on results from stages in the design process include Gersten's (2005) examination of a social studies unit and Hoadley's (2004) discussion of a software design process.

System of Use

The system of use is where the design is tested. The system of use is related to the problematic situation because the problems may arise directly from the system of use. In turn, new problems may arise in the system of use that were not considered in the initial problematic situation. The system of use serves as the principle testing ground for the design. The goals of testing in design research are to advance knowledge about a theory and to develop an artifact that can be used in educational practice (Brown, 1992). The development process for the artifact both informs theory and is driven by theory. The development process is accomplished because the artifact is one representation of a theory, and both are tested and refined as the artifact is implemented in the classroom (Cobb et al., 2003; Edelson, 2002).

Products are tested in the intended context for use and with authentic users. Feedback from the users becomes available to revise the product. The goal in the testing is to document both the usability of the product as well as the modifications that may need to be made. Documentation of usability includes the potential users, the setting, prerequisites for use, and the purposes the product was intended to fulfill. Such documentation is important for the generation of theories because it provides evidence of the process of design. In addition, the purposes for products may change over time as new information is gathered from the setting, the needs of the users are re-evaluated, and the product is tested. Documentation also serves as a record of the theories that impacted the design process.

Because research into design seeks to bridge gaps between research and practice, the system of use is a critical component of the design of educational innovations. First, for design tasks involving teachers' expertise, the teacher should see a need for the design of the artifact. The need is an outgrowth of practice. Second, for authentic testing of a design, the teacher needs to understand the goal of the design. For example, a teacher designed scoring guides for the assessment of model-eliciting activities for students (Hjalmarson, 2004). The teacher initiated the design of the scoring guides. Hence, the task was personally meaningful for her. As a result of her meaningful involvement in the design of the product, she had a vested interest in testing the design and in understanding what was effective or not about the scoring guide.

Testing in the system of use provides a large part of the data-gathering for evaluating the design. Although other interviews and surveys may augment the data collection, information collected at the site while the design was being tested provides the foundation for the evaluation of the design and the theories underlying the design. Furthermore, clear documentation of the operation in practice provides a trail of information about the design process itself. As mentioned previously, design research provides findings about the design itself as well as the process of design. In terms of examining teachers' change, the design process can provide evidence of motivations for teachers to change and develop. The design process can illustrate how teachers' theories about how they teach mathematics change over time as well as the factors that are personally meaningful to them when designing a product for classroom use.

Testing in classrooms includes collaboration with teachers for feedback and input about a design. Teachers provide a connection to testing sites. Teachers provide an alternative perspective on the effectiveness of the design in meeting its objective. Sarama et al. (1998) describe a process of software design that included feedback from teachers and students that was sometimes in conflict. The teachers made assumptions about the students' interpretation of software that were not completely accurate. The researchers incorporated feedback from many participants and users in order to refine their product. In the process, they developed findings about ways to gather significant input from the teachers about the designs and to convey the purposes and intent of a design to the users. The products were tested in classrooms and refined based on the feedback received. The study included implications both for the design of the software and for the process of introducing it to teachers and using it in schools.

Designers and Other Participants in the Design Process

One aspect of design research involving multiple designers (usually researchers, teachers, and students) is that the eventual users of the artifact (often teachers and students) have input into the design. Teachers, in particular, can function as codesigners who bring expertise about students, classroom practice, and learning environments to the situation. The authors of other chapters in this book (e.g., Zawojewski, Chamberlin, Hjalmarson & Lewis; Bannan-Ritland) explore the practical aspects of a professional development design study with multiple tiers. What we propose here are more general guidelines for design research work with teachers. However, we advocate the collaborative aspects of multitiered teaching experiments. Hence, design research includes many constituents who are all engaged in the design of models (Lesh & Kelly, 2000; Schorr & Koellner-Clark, 2003). While students are designing mathematical models, teachers are designers of models that can be used to explain, predict, assess, encourage, and evaluate the students' models. While teachers are developing models, researchers are developing models of both the teachers' and the students' model design processes. Lesh, Kelly, and Yoon (this volume) and Lesh (2002) describe the interactions between multiple constituencies in more detail. Although this type of interaction between designers is complex and requires careful planning and monitoring, it generates results that contribute both to knowledge about teaching and learning as well as to products that can be used for the practice of teaching.

Individuals can play myriad roles in the design process. In the case of the teachers in Hjalmarson's (2004) study of middle-school teachers' design of assessment tools, each teacher played each role in the design process for his or her own tool—as client, expert, designer, and user. Each teacher identified a problem, used his or her own knowledge and experience about the situation, designed a product, and tested the product in his or her own classroom. In the case of an engineering curriculum design project, engineering education faculty were the clients. Engineering professors from different disciplines (e.g., materials engineering, nanotechnology) were enlisted as consultants for the content knowledge. Education and engineering graduate students worked as designers of the curriculum. Teaching assistants for the large, first-year, engineering course were the users and provided feedback about the curriculum that was used by the engineering education faculty to identify new problems (Diefes-Dux, 2005).

Methodological Concerns

As in any research study, there are methodological questions related to sampling, context, data collection, and data analysis. As Collins (1992, 1999) has emphasized repeatedly, design research is conducive to mixed-method research designs. As in any study, the methods should be selected based on the questions at hand. We reiterate the point that teachers can be collaborators in the type of design research cycles we have described here. Although different types of collaborators may have different types of responsibilities during the project for data collection and analysis, all of the collaborators are participants in the design of the final product and in the design of the methods used to evaluate the effectiveness of the final product at meeting its objective. Bannan-Ritland (2003) describes the interactions between individuals in a design research study where needs are assessed, existing theory is consulted, and theory is generated with product design.

A key point in design research is the selection of the objective to be studied by the designers. The objective should be chosen wisely so that the study results in a product that does what is required of it, but the goal does not depict the specific product. The goal should not limit the nature of the product too much. For example, in Chamberlin's (2002) study of middle-school teachers, she asked them to design a tool (i.e., a students' thinking sheet) for organizing the various mathematical methods that students employed to solve a complex, model-eliciting activity. The purpose was to understand the students' ways of thinking about the mathematical situation. The purpose was specific enough so that the teachers could design a tool to organize the students' solutions, but not so specific that there were a limited number of ways for the teachers to design the students' thinking sheets. Chamberlin then could examine the development in the teachers' interpretations of their students' work by examining their discussions with other teachers and the students' thinking sheets. The methods selected for the study were based on the objective and included sociological analysis of the teachers' interactions.

Collaborators in the design research project should be determined by its goal. If the goal is professional development for teachers, then researchers, facilitators, and teachers are possible collaborators (e.g., Zawojewski, Chamberlin, Hjalmarson & Lewis, this volume). As professional development projects expand, teachers who have been involved at many levels may become facilitators who help design learning experiences for other teachers or serve as teacher-leaders in their school. If the objective is the design of a software environment for teaching particular mathematics concepts, software designers, curriculum experts, teachers, and researchers can collaborate about the design of the software and the design of the classroom environment to support the software.

What Happens After the Design Research?

Design is a continuous process. Although the process has stopping points, we would be naïve to claim that a design is "finished." Refinements of a design occur in new contexts, grade levels, mathematics topics, or other teaching and learning situations. Refinements and modifications are made to the process of design in new contexts. In addition, a number of tools can accompany a design. For example, in designing curricular materials, there are typically needs for assessment tools, follow-up activities, observation tools, and additional curricular materials. Other directions could include investigation of the factors related to the process of design or the design of related tools. For instance, the principles used to design model-eliciting activities for middle-school students have been applied to the design of activities for first-year engineering students. Although the principles apply to activities in the engineering setting, the principles are interpreted differently for a first-year engineering class than for a middle-school mathematics class. The activities also are designed with the intent of introducing the practical work of engineering. The process of designing an activity includes refining the definition of what it means to do engineering and what it means to help students who have no engineering experience learn about what engineers do. Design studies also should cause designers to be more analytic about other parts of the curricula. For example, in the engineering project, as activities were designed for the first-year course, instructors of sophomore and junior-year courses were re-evaluating their curricula also. The principles for designing an activity were reinterpreted for the courses for more experienced engineering students. Activities were refined as the content became more complex and as activities were developed for specific content areas such as mechanical or materials engineering. The goal of a study that researches design is to have shareable products that can be disseminated to other learning environments. This may involve the scale-up of an innovation. As innovations are scaled up, new methods may be required as the objective changes from implementation in one classroom to implementation across many classrooms. These are only a few of the possible extensions of a design research project.

Conclusions

The parallels between engineering design and education design begin with the nature of the systems where the products of design are used. The systems are not fixed even if they are often stable. The systems require innovation, respond to innovation (e.g., a curriculum, a piece of technology), and are changed by innovation. As a consideration for design, if we think of classrooms as complex systems, then they are systems of complex interacting parts. When the parts interact and innovations are introduced, the systems change, requiring revision or addition to the innovation. When designs are introduced into the system, they should be designed with the potential and necessity for revision in mind. The design process also should account for the nature of the context of use for the design. Not all designs will work in all scenarios (e.g., instructional materials that are designed for different grade levels). Rather, designs likely will need to be modified for changing conditions, new contexts, and different classes of users. However, the design process and conceptual foundation for one product should inform the design of a revised product.

The design process involves cyclic movement between four areas: problematic situations, systems of use, conceptual foundations, and product design. The four stages correspond to movement between theory and practice, knowledge and experience, design and testing. Throughout the design process, an engineering process involving examination of the constraints of the situation and the needs of the client in light of the conceptual foundations and theory serves to advance knowledge. The final product is more like the nth iteration in a series of revisions than the last product that will ever be designed for a problem situation. Hence, the design research endeavor has results beyond the product itself. The results beyond the product include the principles guiding the design, the knowledge about the situation, and theories connected to the problem situation. This is akin to materials engineering adding to the development of theories about plastics and processes for measuring characteristics of plastics after designing a device. As an educational innovation, curricula designers should learn about curricula design processes, learning, and teaching as curricula are designed. Then, there are at least two products: the curricula and the design process.

Documentation of the design process informs the development of theory and future design. Documentation of the design process explains when, where, how, and for whom a design may be useful and the conditions and constraints under which the product was developed. Beyond the generalizability of the tangible product, the principles and theory behind the design may be more useful to consider in terms of generalizability. Although the product may not be usable under all conditions, the same principles can be used to design products for new conditions. For engineering design, the knowledge behind the design process serves future design efforts by examining what was effective and what was not. The knowledge and principles inform revisions in the complex system of use and the development of products for other contexts. The study results in knowledge about products and their design.

Note

1 See the chapter by Zawojewski, Chamberlin, Hjalmarson, and Lewis (this volume) for more details about teachers and artifact design.

References

Bannan-Ritland, B. (2003). The role of design in research: The Integrative Learning Design Framework. *Educational Researcher*, 32(1), 21–24.

Brown, A. (1992). Design experiments: Theoretical and methodological challenges in creating complex interventions in classroom settings. *Journal of the Learning Sciences*, 2, 141–178.

Carmona Dominguez, G. (2004). Designing an assessment tool to describe students' mathematical knowledge. *Dissertation Abstracts International*, 65(11A), 4137 (UMI No. 3154596).

Chamberlin, M. T. (2002). Teacher investigations of students' work: The evolution of teachers' social processes and interpretations of students' thinking. *Dissertation Abstracts International*, 64(09), 3248 (UMI No. 3104917).

Clements, D. H. (2002). Linking research and curriculum development. In L. D. English (ed.), *Handbook of International Research in Mathematics Education* (pp. 599–630). Mahwah, NJ: Lawrence Erlbaum Associates.

Cobb, P., Confrey, J., diSessa, A., Lehrer, R. & Schauble, L. (2003). Design experiments in educational research. *Educational Researcher*, 32, 9–13.

Collins, A. (1992). Toward a design science of education. In E. Scanlon & T. O'Shea (eds), *New directions in educational technology* (pp. 15–22). New York: Springer-Verlag.

Collins, A. (1999). The changing infrastructure of education research. In E. C. Lagemann & L. S. Shulman (eds), *Issues in education research: Problems and possibilities* (pp. 289–298). San Francisco: Jossey-Bass.

Confrey, J. & Stohl, V. (eds) (2004). On evaluating curricular effectiveness: Judging the quality of K-12 mathematics evaluations. Washington, DC: National Academies Press.

Diefes-Dux, H. (2005). Designing model-eliciting activities for first-year engineering students. Paper presented at the annual meeting of the American Educational Research Association, Montreal, Canada, April.

Diefes-Dux, H., Follman, D., Zawojewski, J., Capobianco, B. & Hjalmarson, M. (2004). Model eliciting activities: An in-class approach to improving persistence and retention of women in engineering. Paper presented at the annual conference of the American Society of Engineering Education, Salt Lake City, UT, June.

Diefes-Dux, H., Hjalmarson, M., Zawojewski, J. & Bowman, K. (2006). Quantifying aluminum crystal size. Part 1: The model-eliciting activity. *Journal for STEM Education*, 7(1&2), 51–63.

Doerr, H. M. & English, L. (2003). A modeling perspective on students' mathematical reasoning about data. *Journal for Research in Mathematics Education*, 34, 110–136.

Edelson, D. (2002). Design research: What we learn when we engage in design. *Journal of the Learning Sciences*, 11, 105–121.

English, L. & Lesh, R. (2003). Ends-in-view problems. In R. Lesh & H. M. Doerr (eds), *Beyond constructivism: Models and modeling perspectives on mathematics problem solving, learning and teaching* (pp. 297–316). Mahwah, NJ: Lawrence Erlbaum Associates.

Firestone, W. A., Schorr, R. Y. & Monfils, L. F. (2004). *The ambiguity of teaching to the test: Standards, assessment and educational reform*. Mahwah, NJ: Lawrence Erlbaum Associates.

Gersten, R. (2005). Behind the scenes of an intervention research study. *Learning Disabilities Research and Practice*, 20, 200–212.

Grimson, J. (2002). Re-engineering the curriculum for the 21st century. *European Journal of Engineering Education*, 21, 31–37.

Hjalmarson, M. A. (2004). Designing presentation tools: A window into mathematics teacher practice. *Dissertation Abstracts International*, 65(10), 3733 (UMI No. 3150775).

Hjalmarson, M. A., Cardella, M. & Wankat, P. C. (2007). Uncertainty and iteration in design tasks for engineering students. In R. A. Lesh, E. Hamilton & J. J. Kaput (eds), *Foundations for the future in mathematics education* (pp. 409–430). Mahwah, NJ: Lawrence Erlbaum Associates.

Hoadley, C. M. (2004). Methodological alignment in design-based research. *Educational Psychologist*, 39, 203–212.

John, V. (2000). Engineering education—finding the centre or "back to the future". *European Journal of Engineering Education*, 25, 215–225.

Lesh, R. (2002). Research design in mathematics education: Focusing on design experiments. In L. D. English (ed.), *Handbook of international research in mathematics education* (pp. 27–50). Mahwah, NJ: Lawrence Erlbaum Associates.

Lesh, R. A. & Kelly, A. E. (2000). Multitiered teaching experiments. In R. A. Lesh & A. E. Kelly (eds), *Handbook of research design in mathematics and science education* (pp. 197–230). Mahwah, NJ: Lawrence Erlbaum Associates.

Lesh, R. A., Hoover, M., Hole, B., Kelly, A. & Post, T. (2000). Principles for developing thought-revealing activities for students and teachers. In A. E. Kelly & R. A. Lesh (eds), *Handbook of research design for mathematics and science education* (pp. 591–646). Mahwah, NJ: Lawrence Erlbaum Associates.

Middleton, J. A. (1999). Curricular influences on the motivational beliefs and practice of two middle-school mathematics teachers: A follow-up study. *Journal for Research in Mathematics Education*, 30, 349–358.

Moore, T. & Diefes-Dux, H. (2004). Developing model-eliciting activities for undergraduate students based on advanced engineering content. Paper presented at the 34th American Society for Engineering Education/Institute of Electrical and Electronics Engineers—Frontiers in Education Conference, Savannah, GA, June.

National Academy of Engineering (2004). *The engineer of 2020: Visions of engineering in the new century*. Washington, DC: National Academies Press.

Remillard, J. T. (2000). Can curriculum materials support teachers' learning? Two fourth-grade teachers' use of a new mathematics text. *Elementary School Journal*, 100, 331–350.

Sarama, J., Clements, D. H. & Henry, J. J. (1998). Network of influences in an implementation of a mathematics curriculum innovation. *International Journal of Computers for Mathematical Learning, 3,* 113–148.

Schorr, R. & Koellner-Clark, K. (2003). Using a modeling approach to analyze the ways in which teachers consider new ways to teach mathematics. *Mathematical Thinking and Learning, 5,* 109–130.

6 Variation Theory

An Organizing Principle to Guide Design Research in Education

Mona Holmqvist, Laila Gustavsson,
and Anna Wernberg
Kristianstad University

Introduction

In this chapter, we present a study based upon a theory about learning that focuses equally on what teachers do and what students learn. We assume that what teachers do in an educational situation is crucial for what students learn at school. By concentrating on the enacted object of learning (what teachers do and what students experience), we try to capture what is needed for learning to take place. The enacted object of learning can be affected by what the teacher does or says, the student's own reflections, other students, or the learning materials. But what matters and what does not matter?

The project described in this chapter was carried out in cooperation with two groups of Swedish teachers in a nine-year, compulsory school (ages seven to 16). The point of departure was that the combination of what teachers do, how students learn, and theories about teaching and learning is crucial for attempts to improve education. The primary focus is on an object of learning as it is shaped in an educational situation, not on teaching methods. By applying a theory about learning (variation theory), which can be used by teachers both in planning instruction and in assessing students' learning outcomes, even more powerful educational situations can be developed. The method used is inspired both by lesson study (Lewis, 2002; Stigler & Hiebert, 1999; Yoshida, 1999) and by design study (Brown, 1992; Cobb et al., 2003; Kelly & Lesh, 2000). A fusion of these approaches, using variation theory, is called a learning study (Holmqvist, 2006; Marton, 2003), which seeks to build innovative learning environments and to conduct research into innovations in theory. It also tries to pool the valuable experience of teachers while continuing to emphasize an object of learning, instead of teaching methods.

The execution of the learning study is flexible, but a theory must be associated with the approach to the learning study. We have chosen to use a theory of variation, which focuses on the distinction between an intended object of learning (what the teachers are striving for), an enacted object of learning (what happens during the lesson and what it is possible to learn), and the lived object of learning (what the students learn). To make learning take place, a way of understanding an object can be defined in terms of the critical features that must be discerned and focused on simultaneously (Bransford et al., 1989). To find those critical aspects, microanalyses are conducted, which result in patterns of variation used by the teachers.

An individual must experience variation in order to be able to discern a particular feature. To develop a certain way of seeing something, the pattern of variation that they must experience has to be constituted. However, these patterns are often demonstrated unintentionally and unconsciously by the teachers, who are unaware of which critical aspects they offer the students and which they do not. The microanalyses are guided by variation theory, which makes the patterns visible to the teachers and provides the potential to predict forthcoming instruction. No matter which methods a teacher uses, he or she first has to examine what it takes to learn the desired learning object, then try to find the best method to reach that goal.

This chapter starts by highlighting the theoretical framework. Then, two examples are presented of how variation theory is used in two different learning study cycles.

The Theoretical Framework: Variation Theory

The theory of variation has its roots in phenomenography, which is a research specialization that was developed by researchers in the Department of Education at Göteburg University, Sweden in the 1970s (Marton et al., 1977). The object of this research—human experience—is shared by phenomenology, but phenomenology has a set of specific theories and methods that are shared only partly with phenomenography. The term *phenomenography* comes from the Greek words "phainemenon," which means "appearance," and "graphein," which means "description." Thus, phenomenography deals with descriptions of how things appear to us. Its goal is to describe qualitatively different ways of looking at, or experiencing, the same thing; variations in different ways of experiencing things are studied (Marton, 2003; Marton & Booth, 1997; Marton & Fai, 1999).

The purpose of this chapter is to describe different ways of seeing phenomena in order to plan successful learning situations. Although phenomenographic analysis can be used to describe students' previous knowledge, we needed to find which critical aspects of the learning object can be contrasted to this. One development of phenomenography is the ongoing building of a theory about learning, called the theory of variation (Holmqvist, 2004, 2006; Marton & Trigwell, 2000; Runesson, 1999). This theory is built upon research about discernment (Gibson, 1986; Rubin, 1915; Wertheimer, 1959), simultaneity, and variation (Bransford & Schwartz, 1999; Bransford et al., 1989; Schwartz & Bransford, 1998). Thus, instead of trying to find the right method to teach based on an expert view of how learning develops, variation theory examines different learning objectives in order to ascertain how learning develops in different ways connected to that objective. From this basis, the most powerful ways to teach can be proposed.

The question that institutionalized learning is faced with is: How can we prepare ourselves for the future when we do not know what the future holds? In other words, what are we to prepare for? How can we learn when we do not know what we have to learn?

In all phenomena, in every situation, certain aspects are discernible. If every aspect could be discerned and focused on at the same time by everyone, everything would be experienced in exactly the same way. However, only a limited number of aspects can be discerned and focused on simultaneously. The discerned aspects differ among different people, as pointed out nearly a century ago by Thorndike:

> All man's learning, and indeed all his behaviour, is *selective*. Man does not, in any useful sense of the words, ever absorb, or re-present, or mirror, or copy, a situation uniformly. He never acts like a *tabula rasa* on which external situations write each its entire contribution, or a sensitive plate which duplicates indiscriminately whatever it is exposed to, or a galvanometer which is deflected equally by each and every item of electrical force. Even when he seems most subservient to the external situation—most compelled to take all that it offers and do all that it suggests—it

appears that his sense organs have shut off important features of the situation from influencing him in any way comparable to that open to certain others, and that his original or acquired tendencies to neglect and attend have allotted only trivial power to some, and greatly magnified that of others.

(1914: 157)

Thus, we may experience the same situation differently. To experience means to discern something from a given context and relate it to this context or to another one. It also means discerning parts of what we experience and being able to relate the parts both to each other and to the whole (Carlgren & Marton, 2002; Wertheimer, 1959). Experience has both a structural and a referential aspect. To discern a structure, we must know its meaning; to know the meaning of something, we must discern its structure (Marton & Booth, 1997). In Figure 6.1, two geometric shapes can be seen, but they are not actually there; they are made up in the viewer's mind and are connected to his or her previous knowledge.

To discern something familiar to something you know already has been studied, especially by the Gestalt psychologists (Wertheimer, 1959). Criticism of the Gestalt psychologists' theories was founded in how meaningless figures become understandable by an illusion made up by the interpreters because of their previous knowledge but failed to explain a wholeness experienced in the nonsense figures. The study of learning and education might have something in common with understanding how nonsense figures are supposed to create a new wholeness for the one who experiences them. Gestalt psychologists' theories do not provide many answers about how learning develops in areas where the learner had few or no insights before.

In order for us to discern something, we have to focus on some aspects while not paying attention to others. To make it possible to focus on some aspects, they must be varied against an invariant background; that is, variation is necessary for discerning, and discerning is necessary for experiencing. The contrasts between what varies and what does not make a pattern of contrasts, which makes it possible to discern. Thorndike (1914: 14) wrote: ". . . man is originally attentive (1) to *sudden change and sharp contrasts . . .*", and Bransford and Schwartz (1999: 77) found that: "Data strongly supported the assumption that contrasting cases better prepared students for future learning." The contrasted aspects that can be focused on simultaneously make a pattern of the whole, which changes if the different aspects change. Bransford et al. (1989: 481–482) say: "a single stimulus has no meaning except in the context of

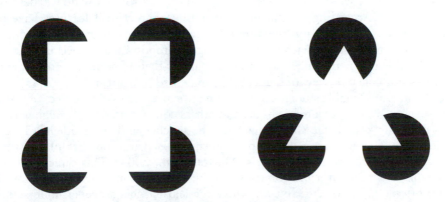

Figure 6.1 Geometric Shapes Suggested by Pre-existing Knowledge.

alternatives." If you describe a girl as short for her age, you have contrasted in your mind examples of other girls of the same age but different heights. Otherwise, you probably would not mention anything about her height.

Another example of the difference between people's numerous ways of experiencing depends on what aspects are being discerned and focused on simultaneously. Neuman (1987) gives an example of how the number nine refers to four different aspects at the same time: the quantity (nine items), the sequence (the ninth in a series), part–whole relationships ($9 = 7 + 2$), and the different unities that nine is composed of (nine 1s). These four aspects of nine are critical for a full understanding of the phenomenon. Thus, to experience the number nine fully means to be able to discern all four aspects and to be aware of all of them at the same time (Carlgren & Marton, 2002).

Schwartz and Bransford (1998: 504) found that "analyzing the contrasting cases provided students with the differentiated knowledge structures necessary to understand a subsequent explanation at a deep level." They also found that *telling* students about features was not as effective as *helping* them to discover them by using contrasted cases to guide their discovery of critical aspects (called significant features by them) and that deep understanding requires differential knowledge of empirical phenomena or theories as well as an understanding of their significance. When a learner has gained the ability to discern aspects of a phenomenon and can be simultaneously and focally aware of more aspects than before, this leads to a deeper understanding of phenomena through differentiation or enrichment, or the fusion of both.

To teach someone to experience in a new way requires building a structure of relevance and the architecture of variation. A structure of relevance means an awareness of a purpose, its demands, and information about where they will lead. To sum up, in a learning situation, there must be a structure of relevance and a variation to make it possible to discern critical aspects. The teacher must find the critical aspects of a phenomenon and the aspects of variation must be evoked. This variation can be presented by contrasted cases.

The alternatives needed to constitute a dimension of variation of the phenomenon's characteristics. Bransford and Schwartz (1999: 71) call this field of alternatives: ". . . a single stimulus is defined in the context of a 'field' of alternatives", and a field of alternatives can be " 'lived experience'. . . . These experiences can function as 'contrasting cases' . . . that help people notice features of their own culture that previously were unnoticed" (p. 85). One of the difficulties of teaching students subject matter that is familiar to the teacher includes the perception of how the students' understandings of the object of learning can differ from the teacher's views.

How do we know what dimensions of variation to look for? How do we identify the critical features? According to Marton et al. (2004), the critical features have to be found empirically, and they must be found for every specific object of learning. In this work, we assume that the teachers are playing an important role because "it seems highly probable that people need help thinking about their experiences and organizing them into some coherent view of the world" (Bransford & Schwartz, 1999: 85).

The teacher must enable students to focus on critical aspects of the object of learning. Some aspects must be presented as basic, and others concentrated on through variation. The basis is the knowledge shared by both the teacher and the students. To create a space of learning means to open up a dimension of variation that offers students new ways of discerning critical aspects (Marton et al., 2004). This dimension covers phenomena, but parts of a phenomenon can be separated into new dimensions as a kind of differentiation or enrichment, where the learner gets a deeper understanding. "Previous research on perceptual learning, for example, has shown that, if people discern distinctions within a domain, these distinctions can facilitate subsequent learning" (Schwartz & Bransford, 1998: 499).

The question is: What kind of variation gives students the most possibilities to learn? Schwartz and Bransford found that:

> In domains in which students have less prior experience, less complex contrasting cases may be more appropriate lest students get lost in the little contrasts. . . . The contrasts between the tools are less 'cluttered' compared to the contrasting cases of these studies. This makes it so students with limited algebra knowledge can still locate the important contrasts.

> (1998: 507)

Variation theory offers an opportunity to conduct microanalyses of the enacted object of learning (i.e., what happens in the lesson). The results of these microanalyses can be used to change very subtle details in the educational situation, which can result in different learning outcomes for students. This will be described later in this chapter, when results from two studies are presented.

The Methodological Framework: Learning Study

The approach used in the study discussed in this chapter is called the learning study method. It is a fusion of two methodological approaches: lesson study (Lewis, 2002; Lewis & Tsuchida, 1998; Stiegler & Hiebert, 1999) and design experiments (Brown, 1992; Cobb et al., 2003; Kelly & Lesh, 2000). Like a design experiment, a learning study seeks to understand the ecology of learning (Cobb et al., 2003). A learning study is an iterative process, designed in a cycle like the lesson study cycle. However, lesson study cycles do not grow necessarily from, or aim to develop, a scientific theory, which both design experiments and learning studies claim to do. A design experiment is also an iterative process, but it differs from the learning study in that the latter focuses on the classroom and the collaboration between teachers and researchers trying to study how a limited object of learning is learned. A design experiment can be used in several other settings, including the classroom, and can have other focuses than learning objects.

Another significant difference is the focus of the research project. In a design experiment, the researcher often owns this question, but, in a learning study, the teachers decide what the focus of the study will be. A shared goal of all three approaches is to improve the initial educational setting by revision based upon the analyses of the data that show the students' development. The most obvious differences between a design experiment and a lesson study are the focus on a theoretical framework and the tests in the design experiment, whereas the point of departure of a lesson study cycle is not necessarily a theory or the results of tests. A lesson study makes explicit certain methods for teaching; the students' learning process is important to the extent that it informs the teacher what aspects of the instruction are guiding learning through variation.

Examples of the stages of a learning study cycle (and the ones used in this chapter) are given below:

1   Critical aspects of the learning object are analyzed by studying the students' previously developed knowledge (readiness) through pretests (the lived object of learning, i.e. what the students have learned) combined with subject matter research from the literature.

2   The lesson plan is developed from the perspective of variation theory. In this study, the first lesson was implemented with student group 1.

3   The students were divided into three groups of equally mixed abilities. They were randomized by the teachers. The groups included students from three classes, divided into groups as shown in Figure 6.2.

4   The enacted object of learning in English Research Lesson One is analyzed, taking into consideration the outcome of the post-test and the analysis of the first lesson.

5   A revised lesson plan is created, in which it is attempted to understand better the students' readiness and to point out which kind of complexity in the varied critical aspects of the learning object may address the students' learning needs. The revised lesson is implemented with student group 2. The revised lesson is analyzed, taking into consideration the outcome of the post-test and contrasting the results with the outcome of English Research Lesson One.

6   The lesson plan is revised a second time. Again, attempts are made to understand better the students' readiness and to point out which kind of complexity in the varied critical aspects of the learning object may address the students' learning needs. The third variation of the lesson is implemented with student group 3. This lesson is analyzed, taking into account the outcome of the post-test and all prior analyses of the lesson.

7   A post-test is conducted.

8   The entire learning study cycle and its conclusions are documented.

Variation Theory in Practice

We have chosen two learning study cycles to describe the use of variation theory. In the first one, the subject was learning English as the second language; the second one was in literacy, with Swedish as the first language. Learning studies in mathematics and science and subjects related to those fields have been reported already (Lo & Pong, 2002; Marton & Morris, 2002). Most of the articles about learning studies describe learning situations at schools in Asia (Hong Kong), which may differ from school situations in Europe.

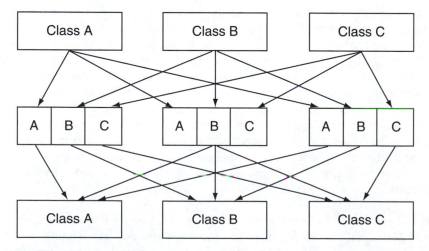

Figure 6.2 Selection Process Used to Make Up the Groups of Students who Participated in the Learning Study Cycles.

Learning Study Cycle in English as the Second Language

The first step in a learning study cycle is to choose an object of learning in cooperation with the teachers that focuses on a teacher-identified problem. In this study, the teachers chose the present tense—*am, are, is*—of the verb *to be*. The learning study described here is the second learning study cycle in a series of three such cycles carried out with the same group of teachers. The teachers had been introduced already to the theoretical framework used in the study (variation theory). All of the teachers ($N = 5$) participated in designing the learning study cycle and in planning the lessons. Three of them were chosen to teach one lesson each. For research purposes, the students ($N = 61$) were divided into three groups. The groups were constructed to be heterogeneous; that is, each group contained students with different levels of knowledge—high, middle, and low—who reflected normal classroom circumstances as much as possible.

Analyzing Critical Aspects of the Learning Object

Analysis of the critical aspects of the learning object takes as its point of departure the three central concepts of the theory: discernment, simultaneity, and variation. To begin, the teachers focused upon what the students had discerned already about how to use the verb *to be* in the present tense—*am, are, is*. To collect more precise data, the group decided to use different sources. These sources were: (a) written letters (which the students wrote as an answer to a letter to them from Holmqvist), (b) the teachers' experiences from previous teaching, (c) research findings, and (d) a scanning test whose design was based upon the results of the data from sources (a), (b), and (c).

To determine each student's ability, the teachers and researchers constructed a scanning test (see below), which gave the students the opportunity to show how they thought the Swedish word *är* (*am, are,* or *is*) should be translated into English. The students had not been told by the teacher which English words to use when they took the test. The test consisted of 11 items:

1 I _____ eleven years old.
2 My dog _____ at home.
3 My parents _____ at work.
4 Mary _____ my sister.
5 She _____ seven years old.
6 How old _____ you?
7 Sam _____ my friend.
8 He _____ ten years old.
9 Sam and Mary _____ at school.
10 Sam and I _____ best friends.
11 We _____ British.

The next step was to compare the test results with how the target words are used in the students' mother tongue. This analysis showed the differences that the students have not experienced in their mother tongue. There is only one word in Swedish—*är*—for *am, are,* and *is*. In other words, there is no variation in the Swedish language to indicate singular from plural or between first, second, and third person; the Swedish word *är* serves all these purposes. Therefore, in Swedish, students have not needed to focus on

Table 6.1 Comparison of the English and Swedish
Forms of the Present Tense of the Verb *To Be*

Personal pronouns		Verbs	
English	Swedish	English	Swedish
I	jag	am	är
you	du	are	är
he	han	is	är
she	hon	is	är
it	den, det	is	är
we	vi	are	är
you	ni	are	är
they	de	are	är

three different words (*am, are,* and *is*) and have to decide which is the right word to use. Thus, it has not been possible for them to develop this simultaneity when using their mother tongue because only one word is used in Swedish to express the three English words, as shown in Table 6.1.

The comparison in Table 6.1 shows that the information given by the present tense of *to be* in English (*am, are, is*) is more differentiated than the information that can be obtained from the Swedish word *är*. If the word *am* is used, it refers to the personal pronoun *I*; when the word *is* is used, it refers to *he, she,* or *it*. When the Swedish word *är* is used, it is not possible to get precise information. Therefore, the teachers studied first which knowledge the students might have because of their mother tongue by analyzing similarities and differences between Swedish and English. The skill that Swedish students have to master is when to use the word *am*, when to use the word *is*, and when to use the word *are* as a translation for the all-purpose Swedish word *är*.

The results of the scanning test were analyzed in categories that indicated the qualitative differences in discernment shown by the students (*N* = 61):

- No right answers: 10 students.
- *Är* is replaced by an incorrect word almost like the Swedish "er": 2 students.
- Discern one correct word, *are*: 23 students.
- Discern one correct word, *is*: 8 students.
- Discern at least two English words correctly: 18 students.

The last category is divided into subcategories depending on how well students are able to discern which of two or three English words to use instead of the Swedish word *är* (*n* = 18). At this level, it is possible to see which kind of simultaneity the students use, and if they are aware of the variation in a way that makes it possible for them to pick the correct word. The pattern of variation is shown by how the student is able to choose the correct form of *to be* in relation to different representations of personal pronouns or substantives (e.g., Billy *is*; Mary *is*; but Billy and Mary *are*). The students were judged on their knowledge of two different words (*is/are* or *am/are*); knowledge of all three words (*am, are,* and *is*); and knowledge of the difference between singular and plural (Billy and Mary *are*, my parents *are*).

From the analysis of the data collected, the critical aspects found at the beginning of the learning study cycle were the abilities to:

- Discern the three different words to use: am, are, and is.
- Connect the correct form of the verb to the personal pronouns (I am, you are, he is, she is, it is, we are, . . .).
- Know who or what *is* can be connected to: my mother (she) is, my cousin (he) is, my dog (it) is, the flower (it) is.
- Discern the difference between one or more (singular or plural) persons or objects when using are (Sam is and Mary is but Sam and Mary are, the flower is but the flowers are).
- Discern that the pronoun *you* can be both singular and plural.

The next step in the learning study cycle was to plan the first of the three research lessons. Although one of the teachers taught it, all of the members of the group participated in its design.

English Research Lesson One

The teacher started with a conversation whose purpose was to enable the students to distinguish between the three different words *am, are,* and *is.* Then, she focused on the plural form, contrasting it to the singular form. Next, she gave the students a sheet with some English text on it. They were supposed to search for the word *är* in English, working first in small groups and following that with a class discussion. The text was set up so that the students would have to make several distinctions, especially the difference between singular and plural. The text also was constructed so that it made apparent the patterns of variation. Previously, it had been found necessary for students to be able to recognize these aspects: (a) the three different words to use—*am, are,* and *is,* (b) the connection between the correct form of the verb and the personal pronouns, (c) to know who or what *is* can be connected to, (d) the difference between *one* or *more* (singular or plural) persons or objects when using *are,* and (e) that the pronoun *you* can be both singular and plural. The following sentences illustrate these aspects:

> My name *is* Bill. I *am* ten years old, and I live in England. I have a sister and a brother. *My sister is* six years old, and *my brother is* four years old. My *sister and brother are* sick today. My *mother is* at work, and my *father is* at home with my sister and brother today. Both my *parents are* 35 years old. We have got a dog. The dog's name *is* Tam. My sister has got two fishes. They *are* orange. We *are* British. [Italics by the authors]

Finally, the teacher and the students talked about the text and why the words *am, are,* and *is* change. After the lesson, the students took a post-test. The design of the post-test was almost the same as the pretest, except for a difference in the order in which the sentences were presented, as well as the names of the characters. The results showed improvements overall, especially in the singular form (he is, she is), but fewer in the plural form.

Analysis of the lesson showed that the teacher opened a space of learning that offered the students the opportunity to discern the three different words *am, are,* and *is.* However, the connections between the personal pronouns and the present forms of *to be* had not been presented simultaneously. Thus, the differences were still unclear to the students.

The differences between singular and plural were contrasted to each other, but not simultaneously in the first part of the lesson. The singular form was introduced first, then the plural form. When the students had to find the three English words that replace the single Swedish word *är* in an English text, the difference between those three words was discernible immediately. However, it did not seem to affect the learning outcome because the task appeared to be simple for the students.

The analysis suggested that the students found the three English words in the first part of the lesson. Because of this, they looked at the text as part of a whole, identifying the words that they had been introduced to previously in the lesson. One result of the analysis was to ask how to make it even clearer how to tell the difference between singular and plural.

English Research Lesson Two

The second lesson was planned to start at a more complex level than English Research Lesson One. The teacher used the same text as in Lesson One, but, this time, the students were not told which words to seek. This made the task more difficult for them. The theoretical principles, which suggest that the ability to discern different critical aspects simultaneously depends on the use of variation, were followed. By forcing the students to use the content of the text to discern the target words, they had the opportunity to see some patterns that indicate when the different words are used. The variations used in the text—my sister *is*, my brother *is*, but my sister and brother *are*—were assumed to make the pattern discernible.

The teacher started the lesson by asking the students to be detectives and search for the English equivalents of *är* words in the text. From the beginning, they were forced to think of the text as a whole unit, not knowing which words to look for. They had to understand the content of the text in order to find the words. After this part of the lesson, the teacher discussed the text and the words that the students had found. The next part of the lesson was similar to the first part of the first lesson, where the teacher had a conversation with the class. The conversation focused on sentences containing the words *am, are,* and *is*. The students had the possibility to discern both the singular and the plural forms simultaneously, and the teacher used an empty table on which she wrote in separate columns the sentences that the students gave her as examples that included *am, are,* or *is*, as shown in Table 6.2. The headings between parentheses were written after the sentences had been placed in the correct field by the teacher. The students and the teacher made the headings together, as a conclusion of the lesson.

The teacher made this table to help the students see patterns of how the different words are used. At the outset, when the teacher wrote the students' sentences on the table, it was impossible to distinguish when *am, are,* and *is* are used because the headings between parentheses were not written on the table at the beginning.

Table 6.2 Examples of Students' Sentences Containing *Am, Are,* and *Is* in English Research Lesson Two

Subject and verb	Student sentence example
I am.	I am a teacher.
You are.	You are a boy.
He/She/It is.	My name is Anna.
We are.	Sarah and I are friends.
You are.	You are students.
They are.	Your cousins are from England.

The teacher discussed the structure of the table after the students had stated their sentences; as noted above, the headings were written on the table at the end of this discussion. Although the students were able to discern the structure of the table spontaneously, which included the simultaneous presentation of the singular and plural forms, they had to think in steps in order to try to understand the pattern. For example, the teacher showed how the word *they* can be replaced with my sister and her friend or my parents and the word *she* with my sister or my grandmother. These were forms of "translations." Finally, the teacher focused on the word *you*, used in both the singular and the plural.

Like the first group of students, this group also took a post-test. Although two rather significant changes in the pattern of variation were made in the second lesson, the results were about the same as in the first lesson. The results still showed little improvement in the students' knowledge of the plural form. They also showed difficulties with the plural form when the plural is made by adding the letter *s*. The students were asked to connect *am*, *are*, and *is* to different persons or objects; the answers to questions in the test that were connected to examples in the lesson showed an improvement. But the students were not offered "Mary and Sam are" and "parents are" simultaneously with "they are." Instead, they "translated" "Sam and Mary" or "parents" into *they*, which decreased the variation and may be linked to the small improvement in the results of this test. The analysis also suggested that the text to students did not show explicitly the words that determine the correct form of the present tense of *to be* to use. By forcing the students to find the correct words by understanding the content of the story, it was assumed that they would discern the pattern. This should show a connection between the personal pronouns or the substantive and which form of the verb *to be* to use. However, the data do not support this conjecture.

English Research Lesson Three

The teacher began by asking the students to find sentences with the English equivalent (*am*, *are*, *is*) of the Swedish word *är* in them. The sentences were written in a table, as in English Research Lesson Two; however, the plural forms were not divided. In the table, the singular forms were divided into subgroups (*am*, *are*, *is*), but the plural form was left as one group (because *are* is always used when there is more than one person or object).

After this introduction, the teacher started a conversation that contrasted singular and plural forms simultaneously. She talked about "a girl *is* and a boy *is*, but a girl and a boy *are*." She also focused on the plural form shown by the letter *s* at the end of a substantive. Finally, she had the students concentrate on the words that determine that *am*, *are*, or *is* is the correct English usage, using the same text as in the previous lessons. However, the text was changed to make the students focus on the words that make these determinations by deleting all occurrences of *am*, *are*, and *is*. This differed from the previous lessons, in which the students only had to identify already discerned words in a written text (as in the first lesson). By understanding the text's content, they could find the words without reflecting on why the different forms appeared as they did. In English Research Lesson Three, they had to make a choice about which form to pick. In other words, they had to think about the words that determine the correct form. In fact, by deleting the word, the sought-after simultaneity was reached, although the students were forced to find some clues in order to decide which word to use. They got the insights that they could not focus only on the words *am*, *are*, and *is* and that more information was needed. This information can be gleaned from how the students had to think of the word that determines the use of *am*, *are*, or *is*. By focusing on two different kinds of words simultaneously, the students were able to see a pattern in how to use *am*, *are*, and *is*. This is the worksheet used in English Research Lesson Three:

1 My name _____ Bill.
2 I _____ ten years old, and I live in England.
3 My sister _____ six years old, and my brother _____ four years old.
4 My sister and brother _____ sick today.
5 My mother _____ at work, and my father _____ at home with my sister and brother today.
6 Both my parents _____ 35 years old.
7 We have got a dog. The dog's name _____ Tam.
8 My sister has got two fishes. They _____ orange.
9 Their names _____ Sim and Sam.
10 We _____ British.

Finally, the teacher and the class discussed the worksheet and why the words used were appropriate or inappropriate. Some of the results of English Research Lesson Three are worth mentioning. The students were told always to use *are* when talking about more than one person or object. This seemed to produce an improvement in the test results for the use of the plural form (with one exception). The teacher also asked the students to discern the plural form ending in *s*, as indicated by the following dialogue:

Teacher: How do we know it is many say, three friends? How can you see it? It is not just one friend; it is more friends.
Student: Friends.
Teacher: Friends, yes. What in "friends" says it is more than one?
Student: The letter *s*.

In the singular form, the need to divide them into subgroups was met. This was reflected in improved test scores. But by connecting *are* so strongly to the plural usage, the singular form of "you are" was difficult to discern. This appeared to account for a decreased score. The teacher tried to explain this, but it seems as if the focus on the "more than one" concept had been easier for the students to understand. This can be illustrated by analyzing the following excerpt of the Teacher from English Research Lesson Three:

Now, look at this. Here it says: "You are a teacher," but here it is: "You are boys." In the last phrase, you can see it is more than one boy. It is shown by *are* and *s*. But the first sentence says: "You are a teacher." When it is more than one word, it is you *are*, and you should choose *are*. *Du* [Swedish for you in the singular form in English] is the same as *ni* [Swedish for you in the plural form in English] in English.
(See Table 6.1 for the singular and plural forms of personal pronouns in English and Swedish.)

The test scores also showed a decrease in comprehension of the plural form for the phrase "Sam and I *are*" because the students believed strongly that *am* must always follow the personal pronoun *I*, as was emphasized in the lesson:

Teacher: In Swedish, we always use the same word, but, in English, we use *am*, *are*, or *is*. Now, we are going to find out when to use the first, the second, or the third word in English. Look at the first sentence: "I am a student." Which word is deciding the word *am*? Which word decides? What do you say, Sonny?

Student: I.

Teacher: It is I; after I, it is *am*. What do I mean?

Student: Jag [I in Swedish].

In spite of the errors, the development of the students' knowledge was greater in English Research Lesson Three than in the other two research lessons, as evidenced by the test scores, which are shown on Table 6.3.

Results of the Learning Study Cycle in English as the Second Language

Analysis of the enacted (what happened in the lesson) and lived (what the students learned) objects of learning made it possible to design changes in the educational situation that affected learning. Although the changes were subtle, they resulted in important differences in the students' learning outcomes. This learning study cycle is an example of how the use of a theory, combined with an iterative design, makes it possible to develop lessons that are associated with increased learning outcomes.

Table 6.4 shows the differences in what the students were offered in the three learning situations. The dimensions of variation and invariance differ. In English Research Lesson Three, the students had the possibility of discerning two dimensions of variation that were not offered to the students who participated in the first two lessons.

What conclusions can be drawn from this study? Can we assume that a worksheet with missing words to fill in is preferable to other kinds of worksheets? Such an assumption would be very misleading and is not the intention of variation theory. In fact, it would result in a loss of focus on the theoretical level and represent a step down to a methodological level, which we argued against initially. On the theoretical level, the focus is on what it takes to learn the learning object; based on this, the teacher chooses which method to use. If the focus had been on a methodological level, we might have

Table 6.3 The Lived Object of Learning Expressed as Percentages of Correct Answers in English Research Lessons One, Two, and Three

Subject and verb	Student Group 1			Student Group 2			Student Group 3		
	Pre (%)	Post (%)	Diff	Pre (%)	Post (%)	Diff	Pre (%)	Post (%)	Diff
I am.	15	45	+30	13	61	+48	12	85	+73
You are.	28	50	+22	50	74	+24	52	43	−9
She is.	35	75	+40	39	61	+22	38	81	+43
Mary is.	45	65	+20	43	78	+35	38	86	+48
He is.	38	55	+17	39	61	+22	33	86	+53
Sam is.	35	90	+55	43	70	+27	33	91	+58
My dog is.	25	40	+15	35	57	+22	33	91	+58
We are.	15	35	+20	39	57	+28	48	71	+23
Sam and Mary are.	15	40	+25	28	35	+7	43	86	+43
My parents are.	10	32	+22	28	26	−2	50	62	+12
Sam and I are.	15	28	+13	30	43	13	48	43	−5
Total	25	50	+25	35	57	22	39	75	+36

Table 6.4 The Enacted Object of Learning for the Three English Research Lessons

	Research Lesson One	Research Lesson Two	Research Lesson Three
Discern *am, are, is*	Conversation in which the students discern the different words one by one	The students find the different words in a text, followed by a conversation. All three words can be discerned simultaneously	The students create sentences in which the Swedish word *är* has to be mentioned. All three words can be discerned simultaneously
Discern the difference between singular and plural	Presentation of the singular form, followed by a presentation of the plural form. Sequenced design of the critical aspects—one by one instead of simultaneously	The students start with a text, in which the two forms are presented simultaneously	In a conversation led by the teacher, she uses examples in which the two forms are presented simultaneously
Discern the different forms of plural	Not discerned	Not discerned	More than one (by enumerating) and the plural *s* on the substantive were presented simultaneously to make the students discern the characteristics of plural in English – and by that understand the use of *are* in all plural forms
Discern what decides the form of the present tense of *to be* to use	Not discerned	Not discerned	By using a text in which the students have to fill in the correct form of *to be* in the present tense (*am, are, is*), the teacher makes the students focus on the words that determine the form to use

concluded that it is better to use worksheets with blanks to fill in. However, the theory is a tool to examine a learning object, to find the most appropriate way to present it, and not the means to find one single best method. This view is being developed still. A second learning study cycle in another subject is described next as a contrast.

Learning Study Cycle in Literacy with Swedish as the First Language

This study was carried out in the same way as the first one, but with another group of teachers and students from three different schools. Because of this, the students had to be kept together in their classes instead of being mixed as in Figure 6.2. The teachers decided that the object of learning was for the students to recognize the four ways that the Swedish *tj* sounds (similar to the initial sound in *child*, but without the initial *t* sound); it can be spelled *tj, k, kj,* or *ch*. The students' previous written texts suggested that they had limited mastery of the spelling of such words. The teachers constructed a test that also showed the students' uncertainty about spelling words with the *tj* sound. Analysis of the results of this test showed that the critical aspect was to focus upon the *second* letter in order to decide the correct way to spell *tj, k, kj,* or *ch*. By focusing simultaneously on words that involve the *tj* and *sj* sounds, the students were asked to discern the difference between these sounds. This also gave them the opportunity to learn something about the spelling. Otherwise, they could spell words with *sj* sounds (similar to the initial sound in *shop*) and spelled *sj, stj, sk,* or *skj* with *tj, k, kj,* or *ch* or vice versa, but they did not recognize the different sounds initially. The distinction in sound between the two groups of words also gave them some clues to the spelling.

Swedish Research Lesson Four

The first lesson started with the teacher asking the students to work in groups and locate as many words as they could containing the *tj* sound, which required them to listen very carefully in order to discern the difference between the *tj* and *sj* sounds. Afterwards, the teacher wrote all the *tj* words that the students had found in a jumble on the blackboard. The students had to find as many different kinds of spelling of the *tj* sound as they could. Then, the teacher asked if they could see some connections between the words that are spelled the same way. In the next part of the lesson, the teacher used the same kind of material as in the learning study cycle in English as the second language, introducing a written text in which the students had to find the words that included the *tj* sound. The text was in the form of a letter, which the teacher distributed, that involved variation by the use of different words, specifically words that contrasted the *tj* and *sj* sounds. Finally, the teacher put the letter on the blackboard, and, during a discussion, the students marked the *tj* sounds. They also connected them to the words they had found by themselves at the beginning of the lesson in order to find a pattern that would enable them to discern how to spell the words correctly. The scores on the learning outcome did increase, compared to the pretest. The teachers and researchers discussed whether it was advantageous or disadvantageous to the students' learning situation to focus upon the contrast between words that contained the *tj* and *sj* sounds; they decided to decrease the variation by focusing only on words that contained the *tj* sound.

Swedish Research Lesson Five

Swedish Research Lesson Five began in the same way as Swedish Research Lesson Four, with the teacher asking the students to work in groups to discover the different ways that the *tj* sound can be spelled. The students wrote their words in columns on the board. This resulted in four columns, with a few words in each column. After some discussion, some connections about how to spell the sound were found. The students got the same written letter as in Swedish Research Lesson Four, except that every *tj* sound was cut out of the text, like this: _uta; a line marked the place for the sound. The students had to fill in how they thought the sound would be spelled. After a class discussion, the lesson ended. After this lesson, there was a small increase in the scores on the post-test, but it was not as high as in Swedish Research Lesson Four. The analysis resulted in the assumption that the words presented on the board were too few, which did not offer the students a real chance to discern a pattern in how the words could be spelled. The teachers did not suggest contrasting words with the *sj* sound again. Instead, they suggested increasing the variation to stimulate the students to find more words with the *tj* sound. The number of words was decreased compared to Swedish Research Lesson Four, and the worksheet was changed as well. To find out which of the changes had an impact on the learning outcome, the teachers and researchers decided to keep the worksheet constant (with blanks), but they increased variation by using more words.

Swedish Research Lesson Six

The teacher started this lesson by distributing a pack of cards. The cards, which were given to each group of students, contained pictures illustrating different words spelled with the *tj* sound. The students were asked to sort the cards by the spelling of the *tj* sound. Afterwards, they had to say the words, and the teacher wrote them in columns on the board, depending on the spelling of the *tj* sound. Together, they discussed if connections could be seen between the words spelled the same way. The second part of this lesson was identical to the second part of Swedish Research Lesson Five, and the students got the same worksheet. The post-test showed an increase in the students' ability to spell the sound; however, it was about as limited as in the previous research lesson.

Results of the Learning Study Cycle in Literacy with Swedish as the First Language

The analyses suggested that the task given by the teacher in Swedish Research Lesson Four, to find as many words containing the *tj* sound as possible, explained the increased scores. The opportunity for learning was opened up in comparison to Swedish Research Lessons Five and Six, where the variation was limited. Furthermore, the students in Swedish Research Lesson Four had the opportunity to contrast the *tj* sound with the *sj* sound simultaneously by using the letter format. It was necessary for the students to search the entire text to see where they could find the *tj* sound. In Lessons Five and Six, the places for the *tj* sounds were left blank. The students only had to fill in the blanks, even if the teacher had told them to read the letter. They knew already which words they should look for, and there was no possibility of confusing the *tj* words with the *sj* words. By this decreased variation, the students did not face a challenge while looking for the words. They did not have to listen to the words to try to differentiate the correct sound from the incorrect sound. The meaning of the text in the letter was redundant because the words were identified already and marked by the blanks. Even if the students did not know which form of spelling to use, the choice was limited, and they did not have to listen to the words as carefully as the students in Swedish Research Lesson Four, who were offered more variation. The results of the spelling tests for the *tj* sound are shown in Table 6.5.

Table 6.5 The Percentages of Correct Answers in the Spelling Tests in Swedish Research Lessons Four, Five, and Six

Tj sound spelled as	Research Lesson Four			Research Lesson Five			Research Lesson Six		
	Pre (%)	Post* (%)	Post† (%)	Pre (%)	Post* (%)	Post† (%)	Pre (%)	Post* (%)	Post† (%)
k	64	80	86	65	85	83	77	85	88
tj	35	61	77	39	77	77	62	81	74
kj	5	29	71	12	88	62	2	78	67
Total	49	70	81	52	82	79	68	83	81

Note
* Post-test result immediately after the research lesson.
† Delayed post-test result four weeks after the research lesson.

Conclusions

The learning study cycle in English as the second language showed how a worksheet with blanks directed the students to examine the words in order to decide the correct form to use of the present tense of the verb *to be* (*am, are,* or *is*). A variation theory analysis suggested that the students' focus on single words (instead of the words in the text as a whole) made it hard for them to discern the pattern of use of the three different words. To recognize the usages in a text did not offer them a real challenge, especially when they had been introduced to the words already by the teacher. In English Research Lesson Two, the content showed a new group of students which words represented the forms to use of the present tense of *to be*. The content itself seemed to draw less attention to the words that determine the correct form to use. Not until blanks were inserted in the text did the students have to search for clues in the text to guide them to find the right form.

The learning study cycle in literacy with Swedish as the first language also included worksheets. The learning object was quite different, and use of the worksheet affected the learning outcome differently. In contrast to the learning study cycle in English as the second language, the best results in the learning study cycle in literacy were obtained when the worksheet did *not* include blanks, but why? The challenge in this study was to find the target words that included *tj* sounds by listening to them in a text. When blanks were put in the worksheet, the students did not have to listen any more because they could see which words were needed by the visual representation of the blanks. In other words, they could afford to stop listening to the sounds and look only at the differences between the two groups of words.

Similarly, the students in the learning study cycle in English as the second language had to focus on the text as a whole in order to find the words *am, are,* and *is*. This suggests that the focus on why the different representations appeared as they did was not discerned. Could the teachers in the learning study in literacy with Swedish as the first language have changed how they used the blanks to make another pattern of variation for the students to discern? If they had used blanks in the words containing both *sj* sounds and *tj* sounds, they had to think more carefully about the spelling because the words *(skj)uta* (shoot) and *(tj)uta* (scream) would look the same in a text with blanks. However, the distinction between the words is in the initial sounds, expressed in different ways to spell them. This means that the variation could be opened up to include two different groups of words, between which the students had to distinguish. However, too much variation does complicate the learners' ability to discern those aspects that are critical, and we think that the many different ways of spelling would have been too confusing. In the learning study cycle in literacy with Swedish as the first language, the learning object was to spell words that included the *tj* sound. If blanks had been used for this, variation theory suggests that the different ways to spell would be too many and complicate the students' possibilities to focus on how to spell the *tj* sound. First, the variation between two groups of words, differentiated by the *tj* and *sj* sounds, has to be focused. Second, the different ways of spelling those words differentiates between the two groups. To find the patterns in both of them would demand the discernment of many aspects. Thus, the variation might be too large, making it hard to see what varies and what is constant, and the pattern would be hard to discern.

Using a theory about learning to examine learning and education gives teachers increasingly precise knowledge about what matters in a learning situation and how to choose which aspects to change and which to keep constant. The two studies discussed in this chapter show small differences in the use of the method, which had important influences on the learning outcome. By using a theory in an iterative fashion, the teachers and researchers were able to try out different designs to see if one proved more powerful than the other. Analyses of the lived object of learning, shown in the students' learning outcomes, enabled the teachers and researchers to revise the plans for how the intended object of learning should be enacted with a new group of students. Different patterns of critical aspects, shown by different dimensions of variation, caused different learning outcomes. The knowledge the teachers gained by using this model at school developed their understanding of what it takes to learn an object of learning, which, in turn, enlarges the students' opportunities to learn. On the other hand, by documenting and analyzing the entire process in a learning study cycle (including the meetings with the teachers and the observations of how the teachers' and students' knowledge develops), the researchers were able to learn about the learning process. The questions that have to be asked in this kind of study are: What features of the learning task should be varied in order to support learning? Do these variations inform us about why, in the same learning environment, some students learn but others do not?

In this chapter, we showed how the use of variation theory can guide lesson design. In a learning study cycle, teachers can create a new lesson after the first and second research lessons. They have the opportunity to take into consideration the insights from the previous lessons to make an even more powerful way of creating knowledge with their students. Although each group of students participates in only one research lesson, the teachers have the opportunity to teach the same lesson three times to a new student group each time. This makes it possible for them to reflect upon three different designs and how each design affects the students' learning outcomes. The theoretical insights about learning and education can, and should, be shared both by the researchers and the teachers in order to make better learning circumstances for the learner. In the third research lesson with the students in group 3 in the learning study cycle in English as the second language, we found that the learning outcome increased in nearly all of the items except two (these were "Sarah and I *are*" and that *are* follows "you" in both the singular and plural), which was surprising. By analyzing the video sequences from this research lesson, we found the critical aspects that misled the students. Those were the ways that the teacher stressed the fact that, after I, *am* is always used, and *are* is always used when there is more than one object.

The design of this study, in which learning study was used as a method, gave researchers, teachers, and students increased knowledge about the learning object. The combination of a design experiment and a lesson study enables a learning study to be used to teach the same lesson to several different student groups (by giving the research lesson once to each student group) and to incorporate the results of one research lesson into the next one (by analyses of the test results and the data collected from the lesson itself). This makes it possible to improve the instruction and to study if the suggested improvements had the expected effects. Because pre-, post-, and delayed post-tests were used, it was possible for us to take into account the students' readiness for, and knowledge of, the learning object before, after, and four weeks after the research lessons. The very strong focus on how the students think, which is studied with the phenomenographic approach (Marton et al., 1977), makes the teachers concentrate more on the experiences that the students have than on those that they want them to have. This means that the instruction is modified more to take into account the students' points of view than it might be otherwise. The teachers' assumptions do not consider how the learning object is experienced by the students. When someone has performed a task already, it is like having read a detective novel already and then trying to forget who the killer was in order to be able to read the novel again and experience the original feelings of excitement and curiosity. When you have experienced the critical aspects of phenomena previously, it is impossible to understand what the phenomena would look like if you were not aware of one or two of their critical aspects.

Teachers often have an idea of what it takes to learn, but this idea emerges from the "expert" point of view. Sometimes, it is hard to tell what it takes to learn when you know the subject matter already. When you do not know the subject matter, it may be impossible to know what it takes to learn it. This paradox has to be dealt with in combination with the already learned and the going-to-be-learned perspectives. If the teacher's and the students' views of the learning object do not coincide, learning will not take place. Similarly, if we, as researchers, want teachers to use theories about learning, we have to recognize and acknowledge their thoughts and beliefs in order to know what it takes to learn how to use a theory in educational practice. The learning study is both a model, which can be used in teachers' in-service training, as well as a method used by researchers to capture the students' ways of seeing phenomena. In a learning study, teachers are introduced to a scientific theory about learning. The possibility for learning study to be used both as in-service training for teachers and by researchers is another facet that shows how lesson study and design experiment are combined into the learning study method. The manner in which teachers have to work in a learning study cycle forces them to focus on the intended object of learning in a theory about learning. The theory helps inform them how to vary their instruction in order to increase learning. To date, the three-fold aim to improve learning for students, teachers, and researchers has been fulfilled in the 18 learning study cycles that have been carried out in this research project.

Acknowledgments

In Sweden, the Research Council has started to strengthen praxis-related research at schools by establishing a Committee for Educational Science. The project mentioned in this chapter, called the Pedagogy of Learning, is one such activity financed by the Swedish Research Council.

We acknowledge the comments of Anthony Kelly, Ference Marton, and John Baek, which have been very valuable.

References

Bransford, J. & Schwartz, D. (1999). Rethinking transfer: A simple proposal with multiple implications. *Review of Research in Education*, 24, 61–100.

Bransford, J., Franks, J., Vye, N. & Sherwood, R. (1989). New approaches to instruction: Because wisdom can't be told. In S. Vosniadou & A. Ortony (eds), *Similarity and analogical reasoning* (pp. 470–497). Cambridge: Cambridge University Press.

Brown, A. L. (1992). Design experiments: Theoretical and methodological challenges in creating complex interventions in classroom settings. *Journal of the Learning Sciences*, 2, 141–178.

Carlgren, I. & Marton, F. (2002). *Lärare av imorgon* [Teachers of tomorrow]. Stockholm: Lärarförbundet.

Cobb, P., Confrey, J., diSessa, A., Lehrer, R. & Schauble, L. (2003). Design experiments in educational research. *Educational Researcher*, 32, 9–13.

Gibson, J. (1986). *The ecological approach to visual perception*. Hillsdale, NJ: Lawrence Erlbaum Associates.

Holmqvist, M. (ed.) (2004). *En främmande värld. Om lärande och autism* [A foreign world: About learning and autism]. Lund: Stucentlitteratur.

Holmqvist, M. (ed.) (2006). *Lärande i skolan. Learning study som skolutvecklingsmodell.* [Learning at school: Learning study as teacher in-service training]. Lund: Studentlitteratur.

Kelly, A. & Lesh, R. (eds) (2000). *Handbook of research design in mathematics and science education.* Mahwah, NJ: Lawrence Erlbaum Associates.

Lewis, C. (2002). *Lesson study: A handbook of teacher-led instructional change.* Philadelphia, PA: Research for Better Schools, Inc.

Lewis, C. & Tsuchida, I. (1998). A lesson is like a swiftly flowing river: How research lessons improve Japanese education. *American Educator, 22,* 12–17, 50–52.

Lo, M. L. & Pong, W. Y. (2002). *Catering for individual differences—building on variation. The first findings.* Hong Kong: INSTEP, Faculty of Education, University of Hong Kong.

Marton, F. (2003). Learning study—pedagogisk utveckling direkt i klassrummet. Forskning av denna världen—praxisnära forskning inom utbildningsvetenskap [Learning study—educational development in the classroom. Research of this world—educational research close to practice]. *Vetenskapsrådets Rapportserie, 2,* 41–45.

Marton, F. & Booth, S. (1997). *Learning and awareness.* Mahwah, NJ: Lawrence Erlbaum Associates.

Marton, F. & Fai, P. M. (1999). Two faces of variation. Paper presented at the 8th European Conference for Learning and Instruction, Göteborg University, Göteborg, Sweden, August. Available at: http://www.ped.gu.se/biorn/phgraph/civil/graphica/newph.html.

Marton, F. & Morris, P. (2002). *What matters? Discovering critical conditions of classroom learning.* Göteborg, Sweden: Acta Universitatis Gothoburgensis.

Marton, F. & Trigwell, K. (2000). Variatio est mater studiorum. *Higher Education Research & Development, 19,* 381–395.

Marton, F., Dahlgren, L-O., Svensson, L. & Säljö, R. (1977). *Inlärning och omvärldsuppfattning* [Learning and conceptions of reality]. Stockholm: Almqvist & Wiksell.

Marton, F., Tsui, A. B. & Chik, P. P. M. (2004). *Classroom discourse and the space of learning.* Mahwah, NJ: Lawrence Erlbaum Associates.

Neuman, D. (1987). *The origin of arithmetic skills: A phenomenographic approach.* Göteborg, Sweden: Acta Universitatis Gothoburgensis.

Rubin, E. (1915). *Synsoplevede figurer. Studier i psykologisk analyse* [Vision experienced figures: Studies in psychological analysis]. Copenhagen, Denmark: Nordiska Forlag.

Runesson, U. (1999). *Variationens pedagogik. Skilda sätt att behandla ett matematiskt innehåll* [The pedagogy of variation: Different ways to handle a mathematical content]. Göteborg, Sweden: Acta Universitatis Gothoburgensis.

Schwartz, D. & Bransford, J. (1998). A time for telling. *Cognition and Instruction, 16,* 475–522.

Stiegler, J. & Hiebert, J. (1999). *The teaching gap.* New York: Free Press.

Thorndike, E. (1914). *Educational psychology: Briefer course.* New York: Teachers College.

Wertheimer, M. (1959). *Productive thinking.* London: Harper & Row.

Yoshida, M. (1999). Lesson study: A case study of a Japanese approach to improving instruction through school-based teacher development. *Dissertation Abstracts International, 60*(11), 3895 (UMI No. 9951855).

7 Multitiered Design Experiments in Mathematics, Science, and Technology Education

Richard A. Lesh
Indiana University

Anthony E. Kelly
George Mason University

Caroline Yoon
University of Auckland

Introduction

This chapter describes an evolving new class of collaborative research methods called multitiered design experiments. After a brief introduction to the general concept of such studies, the chapter is divided into four sections. The first compares and contrasts the origins of the term design research in cognitive science versus mathematics and science education. The second describes how design research requires a reconceptualization of many traditional notions about researchers' roles, subjects, relevant theories, and the nature of results. The third gives a concrete example of a multitiered design experiment that investigated the development of knowledge for three interacting types of subjects—students, teachers, and experts who know about the kinds of mathematical knowledge needed for success beyond school. The fourth describes two common design flaws in design experiments; then, several quality assurance principles are described which should apply to the ways that such studies are conducted.

Origins of the Term Design Experiment in Mathematics and Science Education

In the cognitive sciences and learning sciences, the term design research generally is considered to have been introduced in two articles: Ann Brown's 1992 article in the *Journal of the Learning Sciences* about theoretical and methodological challenges in creating complex interventions in classroom settings and Alan Collins' 1992 article describing steps toward a design science of education in the volume *New Directions in Educational Technology*, edited by Scanlon and O'Shea. In each of these articles, the basic notions of design research were borrowed from design sciences such as architecture or engineering where many of the most important kinds of systems that need to be understood were created by humans and where there is a long history of intertwining theory development with artifact development. In Brown's case, design research methodologies were introduced explicitly to help increase the relevance of theory to practice—or, more precisely, to increase the relevance of cognitive science laboratory experiments to teaching, learning, and problem-solving activities in school classrooms. But, in Collins' case, the opposite influences also were apparent; that is, being a software developer as well as a theory developer (i.e., a researcher), Collins was aware that the best practices of the best practitioners often are more sophisticated and powerful than the best theories of the best theorists. Consequently, a key reason for Collins to adopt design research methods seems to have been to enable cognitive science researchers to benefit from the wisdom of practitioners.

In mathematics and science education, research methods that are coming to be called design experiments certainly were influenced by concerns similar to those that were emphasized by both Brown and Collins (Collins, 1992; Hawkins & Collins, 1992); but, other factors and concerns were perhaps even more significant (Lesh, 2002; Lesh & Kelly, 2000; Lesh & Lamon, 1994). For example, like Brown and Collins, the multi-tiered design experiments that are emphasized in this chapter were intended to reduce the gap between theory development and practice—often by involving teachers and other practitioners as co-researchers. Another goal was to increase the cumulativeness of research by focusing on coordinated sequences of studies that build on one another over longer periods of time. This latter characteristic is important because few realistic-ally complex problems in mathematics or science education are likely to be solved using only single isolated studies. Consequently, the kinds of multitiered design experiments that are emphasized in this chapter were developed explicitly to enable multiple researchers representing multiple practical and/or theoretical perspectives to work together at multiple sites over year-long periods.

Among mathematics and science educators, the origins of design research methods also were more gradual and less explicit than among cognitive scientists. For example, in the *Handbook of Research Design in Mathematics and Science Education* (Kelly & Lesh, 2000), many of the innovative research methods that were described as having been pioneered by mathematics and science educators could have used the language of design experiments to describe their work. One reason this was true surely was because, like Collins, most productive mathematics and science education researchers also function as curriculum developers, software developers, program developers, teacher developers, and/or student developers (i.e., teachers). In other words, most researchers in mathematics and science education also are practitioners in addition to being researchers. Therefore, they tend to be heavily engaged in design enterprises where knowledge development and artifact development interact. Consequently, it was natural for them to adopt general ways of working and thinking that were borrowed from the design sciences. Furthermore, because most productive mathematics and science education researchers received their early research training primarily in the natural sciences, more than in the cognitive or social sciences, they were accustomed to the culture of design and modeling research where: (a) models for describing complex systems are some of the most important products of research, (b) models are not true or false but instead are useful, not useful, or relatively useful (under some circumstances that need to be specified), (c) useful models of complex situations usually must draw on more than a single theoretical or practical perspective, and (d) useful models usually need to be developed using a series of iterative modeling cycles. In particular, they were familiar with laboratory experiences that involve modeling and measuring "things" that cannot be observed directly—and "things" whose nature may be changed signifi-cantly through the process of observation. Consequently, they were familiar with research whose goals involved investigating and measuring "objects"—ranging from neutrinos to gravitational fields—whose existences make little sense apart from the systems in which they are hypothesized to function.

In spite of the fact that mathematics and science educators tend to have natural affinities for design research methods, it was only in later documents, such as a chapter by one of the authors in the *Handbook of International Research in Mathematics*

Education (Lesh, 2002), that the language of design experiments began to be used to describe this work. In earlier work that involved the design of a complex artifact and iterative cycles of development, mathematics and science educators tended to describe their work using the language of teaching experiments (Cobb, 2000; Kelly & Lesh, 2000; Simon, 2000; Steffe & Thompson, 2000; Verschaffel et. al., 1999), clinical interviews (Clement, 2000; Lesh et al., 2000), action research (Confrey, 2000), participant observation studies (Ball, 2000), iterative video-tape analyses (Lesh & Lehrer, 2000), or projects in which curriculum development, software development, program development, or teacher development played central roles (Clements & Battista, 2000; Cline & Mandinach, 2000; Doerr & Lesh, 2002; Koellner-Clark & Lesh, 2003; Schorr & Lesh, 2003). One reason why such language was used was because the preceding methods evolved out of Piaget's biology-inspired theories of cognitive development (Lesh, 2002) or out of Soviet-style teaching experiments (Kilpatrick et al., 1969), more than out of laboratory experiments associated with computer-inspired, information-processing theories in cognitive science. Thus, compared with notions of design research that prevail in the cognitive sciences and learning sciences, mathematics and science educators tend to think of such methods and models in ways that are far more organic and less rooted in machine metaphors (or computer metaphors) for characterizing the conceptual systems used by students, teachers, or researchers (Lesh & Doerr, 2003).

Finally, in mathematics and science education research, the nature of design research was influenced strongly by the fact that many of the most important subjects that we seek to understand involve systems that are complex, dynamic, interacting, and continually adapting. For example, such systems often involve many levels and types of interacting agents that have partly conflicting goals; and, they also often involve feedback loops, second-order effects, and emergent properties of the systems as a whole that are not derived merely from properties of the parts of the systems. Consequently, these systems generally cannot be characterized using only a list of simple input–output rules or simple declarative statements. As a result, in mathematics and science education, the most important products of design research seldom are reducible to simple hypotheses that are tested or to simple questions that are answered. Instead, the products of design research often are models, or related conceptual tools, which are not true or false but whose success is determined by criteria such as usefulness (in a specified situation), shareability (with others), and reusability (in other situations) (Lesh, 2002). In other words, appropriate quality assurance procedures are similar to those used in the design sciences—ranging from architecture to aeronautical engineering—where: (a) researchers and developers are comfortable with demands for a high level of accountability, (b) development usually involves both design and experimentation, (c) development usually draws on more than one theoretical perspective, (d) research teams typically involve people with diverse practical or theoretical perspectives, and (e) rigorous cycles of testing and revision generate auditable trails of documentation that contribute to the development of both knowledge and complex artifacts (which may range from spacecraft to biological ecosystems).

An Introduction to Multitiered Design Experiments

In addition to the characteristics of design research that were emphasized in the preceding section, the kind of design experiments that we wish to emphasize here often involve multiple tiers because they were created explicitly to investigate the interacting development of several levels or types of subjects (students, teachers, researchers, and developers) each of whom can be understood only incompletely, from the authors' perspectives, if the development of the others is not taken into account. For example, in a typical multitiered design experiment: (a) students develop models for making sense of a problem-solving situation (which was designed by teachers and/or researchers), (b) teachers develop models for making sense of students' modeling activities, and (c) researchers develop models for making sense of the interactions among teachers' and students' modeling activities.

The authors' multitiered investigations involve design because they often investigate the nature of subjects' ways of thinking by engaging them in activities that entail the parallel and interactive development of two distinct, but closely related, types of products:

1   Complex artifacts (or tools) that are needed for a specific purpose that lies (to some extent) outside the prejudices imposed by specific theories. Therefore, the assessment of success is not determined completely by the theories that are used to produce the relevant artifacts.
2   Underlying conceptual systems (e.g., theories or models) that are embodied in the relevant artifacts (or tools). Therefore, when the artifacts (or tools) are tested and revised, the underlying conceptual systems also are tested and revised.

Finally, the kind of multitiered design investigations that we emphasize tend to involve experimentation because the development of both the artifacts and the underlying conceptual systems usually involves a series of iterative cycles of testing and revision. Consequently, each temporary "product" tends to be the nth step in a continuing series. This is especially true in mathematics and science education because many of the "subjects" that we seek to understand involve systems that are partly products of human creativity (or design) and because as soon as we develop better understandings of such systems, this understanding is used to change them. As a result, inferences about the ultimate directions for development tend to emerge from trends that become apparent in auditable trails of documentation that are generated across time—not from fragments of information collected at any given moment. In fact, the kind of multitiered design experiments that we use sometimes have been characterized as longitudinal development studies in mathematically enriched learning environments (Kelly & Lesh, 2000).

The Nature of Researchers, Subjects, Results, and Relevant Theories Found in Multitiered Design Experiments in Mathematics and Science Education

In some ways, the kinds of systems that need to be understood in mathematics and science education are even more complex than many of the physical systems found in the physical sciences. For example, the developing conceptual systems of both teachers and students are complex in their own right but their development involves even more complexity because they interact. Consequently, such complexity often creates the need to reconceptualize traditional notions and assumptions about researchers' roles, subjects, the nature of results, and theories used to explain results. These topics are expanded below.

Researchers

Instead of emphasizing only the one-way transmission of research into practice (or practice into research), multitiered design experiments in mathematics and science education often emphasize bidirectional interactions and feedback loops that involve many levels and types of participants (students, teachers, researchers, curricula designers, policy-makers). Furthermore, many participants may play more than a single role (e.g., participant-observers, researcher-developers, teacher-researchers), and a given participant's roles often range from identifying and formulating problems to be addressed, to gathering, filtering, and organizing information that is most relevant, to interpreting results, to other key roles in the research process.

Subjects

Most of the subjects that need to be understood are (or involve) complex adaptive systems (Casti, 1994; Hmelo et al., 2000; Holland, 1995)—not necessarily in the strict mathematical sense[1]—but at least in the general sense that these systems are dynamic, interacting, self-regulating, and adapting continually. Furthermore, among those systems that are most important for mathematics and science educators to investigate, many do not occur naturally (as givens in nature) but, instead, are products of human construction. Also, many cannot be isolated because their entire nature tends to change if they are separated from the systems in which they function; many of their most important characteristics cannot be observed directly but can be known only indirectly through their effects on other agents or events; and most participate in "communities of practice" (meta-agents), where interactions involving agents and meta-agents also are significant. Two examples are given below to describe subjects when design experiments are useful:[2]

1   The primary subjects may be programs of instruction. In large systems that characterize complex programs of instruction, the hearts of important subsystems often are the conceptual systems that various agents use to create productive teaching, learning, or problem-solving experiences. Complexities arise not only because "within-agent" (conceptual) systems are complex, but also because of "among-agent" (interaction) systems where: (a) multiple agents have conflicting agendas, (b) trade-offs need to be considered among factors such as costs and quality, (c) feedback loops lead to second-order effects that outweigh first-order effects, and (d) emergent characteristics of the system as a whole cannot be derived from characteristics of the individual agents within the systems. The behaviors of such systems may be inherently unpredictable in the sense that exceedingly small differences between two systems often result in radically different outcomes because of resonances associated with patterns of interaction. Similarly, when they are observed, or when information is generated about them, changes often are induced that make researchers (and assessments) integral parts of the systems being investigated or measured.

2   The primary subjects may be students' or teachers' conceptual systems; and, instead of focusing on only procedural capabilities (e.g., "What kinds of computations are students proficient at doing?" or "What behaviors characterize effective teaching?"), relevant research may focus on conceptual capabilities (e.g., "What kind of situations can students describe mathematically so that available computational skills can be used?"). But, when students or teachers develop an interpretation of a situation, their interpretation abilities tend to change; and, this is especially likely to happen if the interpretations are embodied in sharable and reuseable tools (Lesh & Doerr, 2003). So, tasks that are used to observe students' interpretation abilities also tend to induce changes in these interpretation abilities; and again, researchers tend to become integral parts of the systems being investigated.

The second of the preceding examples illustrates why simple-minded aptitude treatment interaction studies did not work—especially for cases that involved interpretation abilities. The prediction was that when a person with attributes (a,b,c, ... n) encountered a treatment with characteristics (α,β,χ, ... η) then the result would be (X,Y, Z)—or more simply, when A goes in, X comes out. Such simplistic input–output models might work nicely for systems that involve no interacting agents and no feedback loops; but, they have not proven to work well for complex adaptive systems whose most essential characteristics are that they cannot be modeled adequately using nothing more than simple input–output rules.

For similar reasons, simple input–output models are not likely to be useful for describing the kind of complex adaptive systems that characterize most successful programs of instruction. For such programs, the action tends to be in the interaction, in feedback loops, and in adaptability; and, the kind of functions that need to be monitored and manipulated tend to be dynamic and systemic—not static, rigid, and piecemeal.

Implications

When researchers design something, the underlying design (or conceptualization) often is one of the most important parts of the product that is produced because adaptability depends heavily on the quality and clarity of these underlying design principles.

Similarly, when researchers construct something, the underlying constructs (or concepts and conceptual systems) often are among the most important parts of the products that are produced. Or, when researchers model something, the underlying conceptual model may be among the most important parts of the result that is produced. Consequently, in all such cases, relevant research typically must include knowledge development as well as artifact development; and, in research that involves complex adaptive systems, useful results seldom can be expected to be reducible to lists of tested hypotheses or answered questions. For example, some of the most important pieces of knowledge that need to be produced tend to be models (or other types of conceptual tools) for constructing, describing, or explaining complex systems.

For the preceding kinds of reasons, for the kinds of design research that are emphasized in mathematics and science education, it is important to distinguish between: (a) model-developing studies and model-testing studies, (b) hypothesis-generating studies and hypothesis-testing studies, and (c) studies aimed at identifying productive questions that should be investigated versus those that are aimed at answering questions that practitioners (such as policy-makers) already consider to be priorities. For example, it may do little good to use sophisticated control group procedures and highly objective pre- and post-test designs to show that "it works" (for a given instructional program or curriculum innovation), if it is not clear what "it" is and what "works" means. And, this is especially true in cases where it is clear that nothing works unless relevant agents make it work.

An analogy can be made with the world of cooking. For example, does a recipe in a cookbook work? For whom? For what purposes? Under what conditions? Probably, if any recipe could claim the prize for working best (without regard to the preferences of the customers, the competencies of the cook, the quality of the ingredients and equipment, the weather, or the climate), it would be the recipe for *Toll House* chocolate chip cookies. Yet, if several mathematicians are given the same cookie recipe to follow at home, the results are sure to be several considerably different products. Conversely, if several superb cooks make *Toll House* chocolate chip cookies, they are sure to modify the recipe to suit their own preferences, the characteristics of their resources and cooking environments, and the preferences of the people who are expected to eat the cookies. In fact, malleability, not rigidity, tends to be one of the most important hallmarks of a great recipe. In other words, a good recipe, like a good instructional activity or instructional program, usually needs to be shareable and reusable; it also should be easy to modify to fit a variety of teachers, students, and circumstances. Of course, cooking becomes much less algorithmic when it involves varying degrees of fresh fruit, vegetables, meat, herbs, and so on. Tasting and adjusting become as important as following the rules.

The results of multitiered design experiments often are conceptual tools that have some of the same characteristics as tools such as chainsaws, airplanes, automobiles, or cookbooks. There is no such thing as the best saw, plane, car, or cookbook. Each is designed for specific purposes, for specific people who will use them, for specific conditions, and under certain constraints (such as those that involve costs and available materials). Tools with different profiles of characteristics may be most useful for different purposes, people, preferences, and circumstances; to make judgments about usefulness, trade-offs often need to be considered that involve conflicting factors such as costs and quality. Likewise, every subject (or system) that is studied in multitiered design experiments has a complex profile of characteristics; no profile is "good" in all situations. In fact, successful subjects tend to be those who can manipulate their own profiles to fit changing circumstances, not those who adopt a single, fixed, and rigid profile. Partly for these reasons, useful assessment results generally need to look more like the information that is given in consumer guidebooks (for purchasing automobiles or other commodities) or in reports monitoring the progress of complex businesses (which typically use a variety of benchmarks, indicators, metrics, and other devices for tracking progress toward the goals specified in strategic plans).

A second way in which the results of multitiered design experiments are similar to tools such as saws, airplanes, cars, and cookbooks is that they tend to induce significant changes in the situations where they are intended to be used; in other words, their existence usually leads to new problems, new opportunities, and new purposes for similar tools in the future. Therefore, the existence of new tools generally leads to the need for even newer tools. This is why it is important to realize that results in the form of conceptual tools are not final but are really the nth step of an ongoing process.

Relevant Theories

In fields such as engineering, or in other mature design sciences that are heavy users of mathematics, science, and technology, experienced researchers consistently emphasize that realistically complex problems usually cannot be solved by relying on only a single theory, a single discipline, or a single textbook topic area. Why? Woody Flowers, one of the creators of the Massachusetts Institute of Technology's famous undergraduate robotics design laboratories, answers this question in a recent personal communication when he noted: "The primary characteristic of a design project is that you always have conflicting goals (e.g., quality and costs) and too few resources (e.g., time and money). Trade-offs need to be considered, and compromises need to be made." Similarly, in education, a classroom teaching decision that seems to involve only issues of cognitive science at first may turn into a classroom management issue, which turns into an administrative policy issue, and so on. As Dewey and other pragmatists argued long ago, in realistically complex decision making, what is needed is a framework capable of integrating ways of thinking from multiple points of view (Dewey, 1938, 1981).

Contrary to the naïve wishes of those who hope to use design research as a methodology for translating (a single) theory into practice, and contrary to the naïve claims of those who insist that each research project should be based on (a single) theory, design research in realistically complex settings should be expected to be multidisciplinary, multiaudience and multistakeholder.

With the preceding perspectives in mind, it is unrealistic to expect one-to-one correspondences between research projects and solved problems. It is at best a half-truth to claim that research projects should answer questions that are priorities for practitioners (such as teachers or policy-makers) (Lesh, 2002). To generate useful solutions for realistically complex problems, it is more reasonable to expect a two-step process in which: (a) research should inform theory (or coherent bodies of knowledge), and (b) theory should inform practice. Yet, even this conception of the relationship of theory to practice is overly simplistic. This is because few realistically complex problems are likely to be resolved by drawing on only a single theory. So, the kind of knowledge that can be expected to be most useful may be models which explicitly integrate ideas drawn from multiple practical and theoretical perspectives.

In model-development research, cumulativeness (shareability, reusability, modifiability) is a primary factor to emphasize in order to increase the quality of research. This is why useful research should be expected to design for shareability, reusability, and modifiability—rather than simply testing for these characteristics. It also is why emerging new research designs in mathematics and science education often emphasize collaborations over extended periods of time, at multiple sites, with multiple interacting subjects, and with investigators representing a variety of practical or theoretical perspectives. Finally, it is why coordinated clusters of studies need to be designed to study interactions among: (a) student development, (b) teacher development, (c) the development of relevant learning communities, and (d) the development of productive materials, tools, and programs for instruction and assessment. In the next section, a concrete example is given of a multitiered design experiment that studied three such levels of complex systems.

An Example of a Multitiered Design Experiment: *Case Studies for Kids*

During the last decades leading into the twenty-first century, tectonic-like shifts have occurred in traditional disciplines and new hyphenated fields of study have emerged, creating a demand for new kinds of abilities and expertise. The kinds of employees who are most sought-after in job interviews tend to be those who are proficient at mathematizing (or making sense of) complex systems, those who are capable of adapting rapidly to continually changing conceptual tools, and those who are able to work productively and communicate effectively in diverse teams of specialists working in complex multistage projects (Lesh et al., 2006). Furthermore, the kinds of mathematical conceptualization and communication abilities that are needed often involve more visualization abilities and multimedia representational fluency and less traditional computation.

At Purdue University's Center for Twenty-first Century Conceptual Tools (TCCT), multitiered design experiments have been used to investigate such questions as: What is the precise nature of these new types of problem-solving situations? What new understandings and abilities are needed, even in traditional topic areas such as calculus, geometry, or statistics? How do these understandings develop? What can be done to facilitate their development? This section describes three levels of one multitiered design experiment that involved the development and implementation of *Case Studies for*

Kids, a set of problem-solving activities for middle-school students that are simulations of real-life situations where mathematical thinking is useful beyond school in a technology-based age of information (Lesh et al., 2002). For each tier, the reasons are described for which it was found useful to adopt design experiment methodologies and how the design process resulted in multiple revisions and testing.

Tier One: Developing the Knowledge and Abilities of Researchers and/or Developers

A major goal of the TCCT Center was to investigate the nature of the most important understandings and abilities in mathematics, science, language, and literacy that are most significant in order to provide foundations for success beyond school in a technology-based age of information (Lesh et al., 2003). In other words, the TCCT Center investigated how the 3Rs (Reading, wRiting, and aRithmetic) may need to be reconceptualized to meet the demands of the new millennium.

Early research on such questions typically involved either interviewing experts or observing problem-solvers in real-life problem-solving, or decision-making, situations (Lesh et al., 2006), often with the aid of video-tapes. One shortcoming of such research has been that choices about *where* to observe (in grocery stores? engineering firms? internet cafés?), *who* to observe (farmers? cooks? shoppers? computer programmers? baseball fans?), *when* to observe (only when they are calculating with numbers?), and *what* to count as mathematical or scientific thinking (on video-tapes or naturalistic observations) inevitably exposed preconceived notions about what it means to think mathematically or scientifically and about the nature of real-life situations in which mathematical or scientific thinking is useful.

A second way to enlist the opinions of experts has been more pragmatic and seems to focus on development more than research. For example, in 1989, the *Curriculum and Evaluation Standards for School Mathematics*, published by the National Council of Teachers of Mathematics, ignited a "decade of the standards" in which professional and public organizations in virtually every curricular area generated similar statements of instructional goals at the local, state, or federal levels. Most of these standards documents were developed by school people and academics, and the overriding concerns focused on making incremental improvements in the traditional curricula. Parents, policy-makers, business leaders, and other community leaders seldom were involved; such questions as what is needed for success beyond school seldom were treated as priorities. When it came to implementation, many schools formed blue-ribbon panels of local teachers to convert national standards to local versions that would not be viewed as top-down impositions and to write new test items or performance assessment activities that were aligned with these "local" standards. More often than not, school districts merely adopted existing standardized tests, which claimed to be aligned with their standards, and applied pressure on teachers to teach to these tests by promoting accountability.

Research conducted at the TCCT Center acknowledged that the knowledge of experts is crucial if the 3Rs are to be reconceptualized. But how can this knowledge be used in ways that challenge preconceived notions of mathematical thinking and real-life situations and do not lead to top-down attempts to reform curricula, resulting in standardized testing of superficial abilities? The authors chose to adopt a design experiment approach, enlisting teams of evolving experts (e.g., teachers, parents, policy-makers, mathematics and science education researchers, and professors in future-oriented fields that are heavy users of mathematics, science, and technology) as co-investigators and co-designers of *Case Studies for Kids* (Lesh & Doerr, 2002). Each of the evolving experts is recognized as having important views that should be considered. Yet, the methodology also recognizes that different experts often hold conflicting views; none has exclusive insights about the truth, and all of them tend to evolve significantly when they go through a series of iterative, testing-and-revising cycles that mold and shape the final conclusions that are reached.

The evolving experts work in teams of three to five people to express their current ways of thinking about what is needed for success beyond school in forms that must be tested and revised repeatedly based on formative feedback and consensus-building (Lesh, 2002). They are given certain design specifications that provide "ends-in-view" for the kinds of tasks they were challenged to produce. These design specifications require the teams to consider: (a) the nature of real-life, problem-solving situations in which mathematical thinking is needed for success, (b) the nature of deeper and higher-order understandings and abilities that contribute to success in such situations, and (c) how to identify a broader range of students whose extraordinary abilities and achievements are apparent in real-life, problem-solving situations, even though their performance has been unimpressive in past situations involving traditional textbooks, tests, and teaching (Lesh & Lamon, 1994). Tasks that fail to be useful for these purposes are rejected or revised, no matter how appealing they may seem in other ways.

Thus, in TCCT's ongoing evolving expert studies, the design processes that are used are similar to those that applied scientists use to design bridges, automobiles, ecosystems, and other complex systems. This approach recognizes that respecting the views of teachers, parents, professors, researchers, and other experts does not mean that any of their views should be accepted passively. Furthermore, it encourages participants to go beyond preconceived ways of thinking without presupposing that the nature of the improvements is known in advance.

Tier Two: Developing the Knowledge and Abilities of Teachers

In the book, *Beyond Constructivism: Models and Modeling Perspectives on Mathematics Problem Solving, Learning, and Teaching* (Lesh & Doerr, 2003), many of the research studies that are reported investigated the nature of teachers' developing knowledge and abilities (Doerr & Lesh, 2003; Koellner-Clark & Lesh, 2003; Schorr & Koellner-Clark, 2003; Schorr & Lesh, 2003) as well as interactions between teachers' development and students' development. Most of these teacher-level studies used research methods that satisfy the criteria described in the first sections of this chapter. In other words, they could have been called teacher-level design experiments because teachers repeatedly expressed their current ways of thinking in the form of complex conceptual tools that they designed, tested, and revised many times in order to meet specific teaching needs, and the tools were designed to be shareable (with others) and reusable (in a variety of situations).

Various concerns led to the previous investigations. First, many of the authors in the models and modeling book (Lesh & Doerr, 2003) have contributed significantly to the large and impressive research base that has developed about the nature of students' developing mathematical knowledge and abilities in such topic areas as early algebra, rational numbers, and proportional reasoning. Although a great deal is known about the development of students' understandings and abilities in these content areas, relatively little is known about the nature of teacher-level knowledge and abilities in them. For example, it certainly is clear that teacher-level understandings of ratios and proportions should involve more than student-level understandings. But what is the nature of these additional, deeper, or higher-order understandings? In addition to understanding how relevant concepts develop logically (e.g., how can the concepts be defined logically?), teachers also probably need to understand how they develop psychologically (e.g., what representational systems contribute to their meanings in the minds of typical children?), historically (e.g., what issues led to their development in the history of science?), instructionally (e.g., what prerequisites exist in alternative curricular materials that are available?), and pragmatically (e.g., for what purposes, and in conjunction with what other ideas, are the ideas useful in real-life, problem-solving situations?). Also, what else should be involved in the understandings and abilities of outstanding teachers? How do these understandings and abilities develop? What kinds of experiences promote their development? Further, how can deeper and higher-order achievements be assessed or documented?

A second type of concern that led to the models and modeling book's teacher-level studies was related to the fact that it does very little good for evolving experts to provide curricular materials such as the *Case Studies for Kids* described in the previous section unless teachers are able to recognize and make use of the thinking that their students exhibit. For example, even if student-level tasks are designed so that students reveal a broad range of mathematical understandings and abilities, there is no guarantee that teachers will recognize these achievements. Teachers who are skillful at guiding students toward teachers' ways of thinking are not necessarily skillful at recognizing students' ways of thinking. Teachers who can do things right do not do the right things at the right time, necessarily. Clearly, teaching expertise entails seeing at least as much as doing. But what is the nature of productive ways of thinking in situations such as: (a) analyzing complex pieces of work that students produce and giving them feedback about their strengths, weaknesses, and ways to improve, (b) observing processes and roles that are productive as students work on complex projects and giving them feedback on ways to improve their future performance, or (c) generating a concise summary of students' alternative ways of thinking as they are reflected in oral reports describing the results of their work?

A third concern that influenced the teacher-level research in the models and modeling book (Lesh & Doerr, 2003) focused on the assessment of teachers' knowledge and abilities. Teaching expertise does not appear to be reducible to a checklist of skills, and such checklists do not appear to improve significantly by adding lists of vague dispositions and performances. Nonetheless, many attempts to assess teaching expertise have supplemented what can be documented using short-answer tests by requiring teachers to produce portfolios that contain artifacts that are intended to document complex understandings and abilities. Many of these portfolios are similar to personal diaries, even though it is well known that teachers who talk articulately are not necessarily the same as those who produce results (Schorr & Lesh, 2003). Consequently, video-tapes often are used to show actual teaching episodes. However, almost anybody is able to perform capably in a few situations. Therefore, specific video-taped episodes seldom yield persuasive evidence about general capabilities, and doing something right in one situation, is quite different from doing the right things in a variety of situations.

As a result, in the teacher-level research that is reported in the models and modeling book, teachers' ways of thinking were investigated as they worked collaboratively to design shareable, reusable, thought-revealing tools for implementing *Case Studies for Kids* tasks in the classroom. This design process often generated auditable trails of documentation that revealed important characteristics of teachers' developing knowledge and abilities. In these cases, the design specifications required teachers to use formative feedback and consensus-building to make judgments about directions for development that are increasingly "better" without feeling that they must converge toward a naïve conception of "best." One of the most effective ways that researchers have found to promote teachers' development is to help them become wiser about the nature of their students' ways of thinking about the major themes in the topic areas they are trying to teach (e.g., Carpenter et al., 1989). Furthermore, by focusing on the design of conceptual tools that deal with classroom decision-making issues, teachers' everyday teaching experiences can be turned into learning experiences. Such design tasks can provide the basis for effective types of on-the-job, classroom-based, teacher development activities; byproducts of these learning activities also produce documentation that reveals the nature of the understandings and abilities that develop. In particular, these byproducts include theory-based and experience-tested prototypes for materials, programs, and procedures to emphasize the following goals:

- Early democratic access to powerful conceptual tools (constructs, conceptual systems, capability amplifiers) that enable all students to achieve extraordinary results in simulations of real-life, problem-solving situations that are typical of those in which mathematical and scientific thinking is needed (after their school years) in the twenty-first century.
- Experiences in which students (who may be either adults or children, in or out of school) both develop and document deeper and higher-order understandings related to complex achievements that seldom are assessed on brief, easy-to-score, standardized tests.
- Ways to identify a broader range of students whose exceptional abilities and achievements often have not been apparent in settings involving traditional tests, textbooks, and teaching by recognizing the importance of a broader array of the knowledge and abilities needed for success in future-oriented fields ranging from agriculture to business to engineering to medicine and to other fields that are becoming increasingly heavy users of mathematics, science, and technology.

Tier Three: Developing the Knowledge and Abilities of Students

Two of the biggest concerns that led to the use of design research methods in studying the development of students' knowledge and abilities were: (a) how to elicit and document the complex kinds of thinking that occur when students work on complex, problem-solving activities that require them to develop powerful conceptual systems, not traditional procedural kinds of answers, and (b) how to ensure that the development of the conceptual systems being elicited from the students is not guided by a teacher's or textbook's conception of what is "right"?

Much of the authors' research done on students' thinking has been on students working in groups of three to four, on *Case Studies for Kids* activities, which were designed to address these questions (Lesh & Zawojewski, 2006). In a very real sense, students working on these activities are conducting their own design experiments in which they are designing a mathematical model to explain a meaningful situation by quantifying, dimensioning, coordinating, systematizing, or (in general) mathematizing objects, relations, operations, transformations, patterns, regularities, or other systemic characteristics of learning or problem-solving situations. Over the course of the problem-solving session, their mathematical model goes through multiple design cycles as the students notice more relevant information about their problem and re-organize their model.

Two principles for developing *Case Studies for Kids* ensure that students' models go through multiple design cycles, without the teacher or the textbook guiding them directly (Lesh et al., 2000). The self-evaluation principle requires that activities have built into them ways for students to assess realistically the quality of their own modes of thinking, without predetermining what their final solution should look like. For example, in the quilt problem (see Appendix), students know that they have finished it when their quilt templates produce a quilt built to scale where all the pieces fit together, but they are not told what form their solution should take. Consequently, students working on these activities are able to develop their ways of thinking into powerful constructs and conceptual systems without being told which path to take.

The model documentation principle demands that the activities provide realistic conditions under which students are required to express and document their thinking in forms that are reusable, shareable, and modifiable. Instead of statements asking students to explain their solution, which often are added onto many word problems as an afterthought, these activities provide a realistic "client" who asks for a general solution to a specific problem, where the process is the product. For example, in the quilt problem, students are asked to describe how to make the templates for the pieces of a quilt, not only for the quilt pictured, but also for quilts of any design. Therefore, their final answer is a documentation of their problem-solving process.

The results of the preceding kind of problem-solving experiences show that, when students work on a series of such problems over the course of a semester, the power and the range of usefulness of their underlying ways of thinking tend to increase significantly. This is because every time they design a new, thought-revealing tool, they are extending and revising the underlying ways of thinking that the tools embody. As a result, the development of the tools involves significant forms of learning, and, as learning occurs, the tools produce auditable trails of documentation that reveal important information about the constructs and conceptual systems that the students are developing. Hence, the activities contribute to both learning and assessment. Furthermore, a broader range of students working on these tasks naturally emerges as having extraordinary potential (Zawojewski et al., in press). Many of these students whose abilities were unrecognized previously come from populations that are highly under-represented in fields that emphasize mathematics, science, and technology.

Investigating the Interacting Development of the Three Tiers Involving Students, Teachers, Researchers, Developers, and Others

One advantage of using the kind of thought-revealing design activities that are described in the preceding examples is that thought-revealing activities for students often provide ideal contexts for equally thought-revealing activities for teachers, researchers, curricula developers, and other kinds of evolving experts. For example, in Purdue University's TCCT Center, emphasis has been placed on multitiered design experiments in which three interacting levels (and three interacting types) of problem-solvers are engaged in semester-long sequences of experiences in which: (a) students may design shareable, reusable, conceptual tools to meet the needs of clients who are described in *Case Studies for Kids* that focus on understandings and abilities that are typical of those that may be needed for success beyond school in a technology-based age of information, (b) teachers may design shareable, reusable, conceptual tools for assisting, analyzing, and assessing students' work in *Case Studies for Kids*, and (c) researchers, developers, and other evolving experts may develop shareable, reusable, conceptual tools for assisting, analyzing, and assessing both teachers' and students' work in *Case Studies for Kids*. In other words, students develop models for making sense of mathematical, problem-solving situations; teachers develop models for making sense of students' models and modeling activities; and researchers develop models for making sense of both teachers' and students' models and modeling activities. Therefore, it is possible for researchers to investigate the interacting development of students, teachers, curricular materials, and programs.

Principles for Preventing the Typical Design Flaws that Occur in Multitiered Design Experiments

This chapter concludes by addressing a question of research quality: When the subjects being investigated are so complex, how can one ensure that both the designs and the underlying conceptual systems are being developed scientifically at each level of a multitiered design experiment? In answering this question, it is important to note that, in many ways, the goal of science is to go beyond common sense toward *un*common sense (based on inferred systems, patterns, and relationships beneath the surface of things). Therefore, design processes need to include ways to tease out and test foundation-level assumptions that seem like common sense. Failure to do so is often the source of serious design flaws. In particular, two of the most common design flaws occur in the following types of design experiments:

1   Practice-driven design experiments, in which the primary goal is to develop a complex artifact (or conceptual tool) that needs precise specific design specifications (situations and purposes) that exist apart from any given theory or theories. For example, in mathematics or science education, relevant artifacts or conceptual tools may involve software development, instructional materials development, assessment materials development, or the development of programs for learning, assessment, or problem-solving. In these cases, design flaws occur sometimes when the design processes involve little more than merely unprincipled tinkering; that is, where practical problems are solved, but no attempt is made to generate knowledge or information that is shareable or reusable beyond the immediate situation.

2   Theory-driven design experiments, in which the primary goal is to revise, refine, or extend a theory or way of thinking about teaching, learning, or problem-solving. In these circumstances, the most significant design flaws occur because the design processes never allow underlying ways of thinking to be tested (with the possibility of rejection) because they never consider seriously alternatives to the current ways of thinking. Theory-driven design can degenerate into little more than ideology-driven flights of fancy, where Karl Popper's (1963) principle of falsifiability is never allowed to occur. According to Popper, the main difference between a scientific theory and an ideology is whether there are possibilities for current ways of thinking to be rejected or alternative ways of thinking to be adopted. In design experiments, there are two main ways in which the possibility of rejection is avoided. First, some studies are designed so that the only kinds of evidence and arguments that are allowed into consideration are those that the theory sanctions; tunnel vision often takes over so that basic ways of thinking are never really challenged. Second, some studies are designed so that the responses to failures never involve more than tinkering with (or endlessly embellishing) basic ways of thinking, rather than considering alternatives.

The authors have found it useful to consider four design principles in order to prevent these design flaws from occurring and to facilitate scientific development. These principles were developed so that they apply similarly to each level of a multitiered design experiment: students, teachers, curricula developers, program developers, software developers, and other types of researchers, developers, or practitioners. When implemented, these principles ensure that, at each level, the design in question involves developing an underlying conceptual system that is testable, shareable, reusable, generalizable, and can add to the body of research knowledge in the field.

The Externalization Principle or Documentation Principle

Conceptual systems that are being investigated should be expressed in the form of artifacts or tools that can be examined by both researchers and other relevant participants. Thus, the task of designing such artifacts tends to be a thought-revealing activity (Lesh et al., 2000). In this sense, the artifact embodies the conceptual system(s) that were used to produce it because important components of the underlying conceptual systems are apparent in the artifacts themselves.

This is necessary because, in the process of designing complex artifacts and conceptual tools, participants often externalize their current ways of thinking in forms that reveal the constructs and conceptual systems that are employed. This is what is meant by saying that the products are embodiments of the relevant conceptual systems. This tends to be true especially if the products are conceptual technologies in the sense that they include not only procedures for doing something but also conceptual systems for describing and explaining the situations in which the artifacts or conceptual tools are intended to be useful. That is, the objectives for which these tools are developed often focus on interpretation, description, explanation, or sense-making more than on data processing (which presupposes that the data have been interpreted meaningfully already).

The Construct Assessment Principle

Design specifications (or goals) should be specified that provide criteria that can be used to test and revise trial artifacts and conceptual tools (as well as underlying ways of thinking) by weeding out products that are unacceptable or less useful than others.

The design specifications should function as Dewey-style "ends-in-view" (Zawokewski et al., 2003). That is, they should provide criteria so that formative feedback and consensus-building can be used to refine thinking in ways that are progressively "better" based on judgments that can be made by the participants themselves. In particular, the "ends-in-view" should enable the participants to make their own judgments about the need to go beyond their first primitive ways of thinking and the relative strengths and weaknesses of the alternative ways of thinking that emerge during the design process. In addition to emphasizing power and usefulness in specified situations, productive goals also should require participants to develop constructs and conceptual systems that are: (a) powerful (to meet the needs of the client in the specific situation at hand), (b) shareable, (c) reusable, and (d) transportable. In other words, both the tools and the underlying ways of thinking should be shareable and generalizable.

The Multiple Design Cycle Principle or Knowledge Accumulation Principle

Design processes should be used in which the participants understand clearly that a series of iterative design cycles probably will be needed in order to produce results that are sufficiently powerful and useful. Furthermore, they also should understand that any current state is always merely one in a continuing series.

If design processes involve a series of iterative development, testing, and revision cycles and if intermediate results are expressed in forms that can be examined by outside observers as well as by the participants themselves, then auditable trails of documentation are generated automatically. This documentation should reveal important characteristics of the developments that occur. That is to say, the design processes should contribute to learning and to the documentation and assessment of learning.

The Diversity and Triangulation Principle

Design processes should promote interactions among participants who have diverse perspectives; they also should involve iterative consensus building to ensure that the knowledge, tools, and artifacts generated will be shareable and reusable, and so that knowledge accumulates in ways that build iteratively on what was learned during past experiences and previous design cycles.

In general, to develop complex artifacts and tools, it is productive for participants to work in small groups consisting of three to five individuals who have diverse understandings, abilities, experiences, and agendas. By working in such groups, communities of relevant constructs tend to emerge in which the participants need to communicate their current ways of thinking in forms that are accessible to others. Once diverse ways of thinking emerge, selection processes should include not only feedback based on how the tools and artifacts work according to the objectives that were specified, but also according to feedback based on peer review. In this way, consensus-building processes involve triangulation that is based on multiple perspectives and interpretations. Thus, the collective constructs that develop are designed to be shareable among members of the group and in ways that enable knowledge to accumulate.

Notes

1 In mathematics, complexity theory deals mainly with systems in which the agents within the systems obey relatively simple condition-action rules; so it is the interactions among the agents that lead to complexity. In mathematics education, however, even the agents are (or involve) complex systems. So, compared with the kinds of complex systems that are emphasized in mathematics, those that occur in mathematics education are deeply complex. If several layers of agents are involved (much like letters within words, words within phrases, phrases within sentences, sentences within paragraphs, paragraphs within chapters, etc.), the agents at each layer have properties associated with complex systems.

2 In each of the examples, it is important to distinguish between the generalizations about the agents themselves and generalizations about the conceptual systems that the agents use. For example, generalizations about students themselves (e.g., this student is a gifted student, or a concrete operational thinker, or a creative thinker) are quite different from generalizations about the nature and development of students' concepts and conceptual systems. Whereas cognitive science focuses on generalizations about the nature of learners or learning, mathematics and science educators tend to focus on generalizations about the nature of ideas and problem-solving situations, in what might be called experimental genetic epistemology (Piaget, 1970).

References

Ball, D. L. (2000). Working on the inside: Using one's own practice as a site for studying teaching and learning. In A. E. Kelly & R. A. Lesh (eds), *Handbook of research design in mathematics and science education* (pp. 365–402). Mahwah, NJ: Lawrence Erlbaum Associates.

Brown, A. L. (1992). Design experiments: Theoretical and methodological challenges in creating complex interventions in classroom settings. *Journal of the Learning Sciences*, 2, 141–178.

Carpenter, T., Fennema, E., Peterson, P., Chiang, C. & Loef, M. (1989). Using knowledge of children's mathematics thinking in classroom teaching: An experimental study. *American Educational Research Journal*, 26, 499–532.

Casti, J. L. (1994). *Complexification: Explaining a paradoxical world through the science of surprise*. New York: HarperCollins.

Clement, J. (2000). Analysis of clinical interviews: Foundations and model viability. In A. E. Kelly & R. A. Lesh (eds), *Handbook of research design in mathematics and science education* (pp. 547–589). Mahwah, NJ: Lawrence Erlbaum Associates.

Clements, D. H. & Battista, M. T. (2000). Designing effective software. In A. E. Kelly & R. A. Lesh (eds), *Handbook of research design in mathematics and science education* (pp. 761–776). Mahwah, NJ: Lawrence Erlbaum Associates.

Cline, H. F. & Mandinach, E. B. (2000). The corruption of a research design: A case study of a curriculum innovation project. In A. E. Kelly & R. A. Lesh (eds), *Handbook of research design in mathematics and science education* (pp. 169–189). Mahwah, NJ: Lawrence Erlbaum Associates.

Cobb, P. (2000). Conducting teaching experiments in collaboration with teachers. In A. E. Kelly & R. A. Lesh (eds), *Handbook of research design in mathematics and science education* (pp. 307–333). Mahwah, NJ: Lawrence Erlbaum Associates.

Collins, A. (1992). Toward a design science of education. In E. Scanlon & T. O'Shea (eds), *New directions in educational technology* (pp. 15–22). New York: Springer-Verlag.

Confrey, J. (2000). Improving research and systemic reform toward equity and quality. In A. E. Kelly & R. A. Lesh (eds), *Handbook of research design in mathematics and science education* (pp. 87–111). Mahwah, NJ: Lawrence Erlbaum Associates.

Dewey, J. (1938). *Experience and education*. New York: Collier.

Dewey, J. (1981). Experience and nature. In J. A. Boyston (ed.), *John Dewey: The later works, 1925–1953*, Volume 1. Carbondale: Southern Illinois University Press (original work published 1925).

Doerr, H. & Lesh, R. A. (2003). A modeling perspective on teacher development. In R. A. Lesh & H. Doerr (eds), *Beyond constructivism: Models and modeling perspectives on mathematics problem solving, learning, and teaching* (pp. 125–139). Mahwah, NJ: Lawrence Erlbaum Associates.

English, L. (ed.) (2002). *Handbook of international research in mathematics education*. Hillsdale, NJ: Lawrence Erlbaum Associates.

Hawkins, J. & Collins, A. (1992). Design-experiments for infusing technology into learning. *Educational Technology*, 32, 63–67.

Hmelo, C. E., Holton, D. L. & Kolodner, J. L. (2000). Designing to learn about complex systems. *Journal of the Learning Sciences*, 9, 247–298.

Holland, J. H. (1995). *Hidden order: How adaptation builds complexity*. New York: Addison-Wesley.

Kelly, A. E. & Lesh, R. A. (eds) (2000). *Handbook of research design in mathematics and science education*. Mahwah, NJ: Lawrence Erlbaum Associates.

Kilpatrick, J., Wirszup I., Begle, E. & Wilson, J. (1969). *Soviet studies in the psychology of learning and teaching mathematics*. Stanford, CA: School Mathematics Study Group.

Koellner-Clark, K. & Lesh, R. A. (2003). A modeling approach to describe the teacher knowledge. In R. A. Lesh & H. Doerr (eds), *Beyond constructivism: Models and modeling perspectives on mathematics problem solving, learning, and teaching* (pp. 159–173). Mahwah, NJ: Lawrence Erlbaum Associates.

Lesh, R. A. (2002). Research design in mathematics education: Focusing on design experiments. In L. English (ed.), *Handbook of international research in mathematics education* (pp. 27–50). Hillsdale, NJ: Lawrence Erlbaum Associates.

Lesh, R. A. & Doerr, H. (2003). *Beyond constructivism: Models and modeling perspectives on mathematics problem solving, learning, and teaching.* Mahwah, NJ: Lawrence Erlbaum Associates.

Lesh, R. A. & Kelly, A. E. (2000). Multitiered teaching experiments. In A. E. Kelly & R. A. Lesh (eds), *Handbook of research design in mathematics and science education* (pp. 197–230). Mahwah, NJ: Lawrence Erlbaum Associates.

Lesh, R. A. & Lamon, S. (eds). (1994). *Assessment of authentic performance in school mathematics.* Hillsdale, NJ: Lawrence Erlbaum Associates.

Lesh, R. A. & Lehrer, R. (2000). Iterative refinement cycles for videotape analyses of conceptual change. In A. E. Kelly & R. A. Lesh (eds), *Handbook of research design in mathematics and science education* (pp. 665–708). Mahwah, NJ: Lawrence Erlbaum Associates.

Lesh, R. A. & Zawojewski, J. S. (2006). *Problem solving and modeling: The second handbook of research on mathematics teaching and learning.* Reston, VA: National Council of Teachers of Mathematics.

Lesh, R. A., Hamilton, E. & Kaput, J. (eds) (2006). *Models and modeling as foundations for the future in mathematics education.* Hillsdale, NJ: Lawrence Erlbaum Associates.

Lesh, R. A., Hoover, M., Hole, B., Kelly, A. E. & Post, T. (2000). Principles for developing thought-revealing activities for students and teachers. In A. E. Kelly & R. A. Lesh (eds), *Handbook of research design in mathematics and science education* (pp. 591–645). Mahwah, NJ: Lawrence Erlbaum Associates.

Lesh, R. A., Zawojewski, J. S. & Carmona, G. (2003). What mathematical abilities are needed for success beyond school in a technology-based age of information? In R. A. Lesh & H. Doerr (eds), *Beyond constructivism: Models and modeling perspectives on mathematics problem solving, learning, and teaching* (pp. 205–222). Mahwah, NJ: Lawrence Erlbaum Associates.

National Council of Teachers of Mathematics (1989). *Curriculum and Evaluation Standards for School Mathematics.* Reston, VA: National Council of Teachers of Mathematics.

Piaget, J. (1970). *Genetic epistemology.* New York: W. W. Norton.

Popper, K. R. (1963). *Conjectures and refutations: The growth of scientific knowledge.* London: Routledge.

Schorr, R. & Koellner-Clark, K. (2003). Using a modeling approach to analyze the ways in which teachers consider new ways to teach mathematics. *Mathematical Thinking and Learning*, 5, 191–210.

Schorr, R. & Lesh, R. A. (2003). A modeling approach for providing teacher development. In R. A. Lesh & H. Doerr (eds), *Beyond constructivism: Models and modeling perspectives on mathematics problem solving, learning, and teaching* (pp. 141–157). Mahwah, NJ: Lawrence Erlbaum Associates.

Simon, M. A. (2000). Research on the development of mathematics teachers: The teacher development experiment. In A. E. Kelly & R. A. Lesh (eds), *Handbook of research design in mathematics and science education* (pp. 335–359). Mahwah, NJ: Lawrence Erlbaum Associates.

Steffe, L. P. & Thompson, P. W. (2000). Teaching experiment methodology: Underlying principles and essential elements. In A. E. Kelly & R. A. Lesh (eds), *Handbook of research design in mathematics and science education* (pp. 267–306). Mahwah, NJ: Lawrence Erlbaum Associates.

Verschaffel, L., De Corte, E., Lasure, S., Van Vaerenbergh, G., Bogaerts, H. & Ratinckx, E. (1999). Learning to solve mathematical application problems: A design experiment with fifth graders. *Mathematical Thinking and Learning*, 1, 195–229.

Zawojewski, J. S., Diefes-Dux, H. & Bowman, K. (eds) (in press). *Models and modeling in engineering education: Designing experiences for all students.* Rotterdam: Sense Publications.

Zawojewski, J. S., Lesh, R. & English, L. D. (2003). A models and modeling perspective on the role of small group learning. In R. A. Lesh & H. Doerr (eds), *Beyond constructivism: Models and modeling perspectives on Mathematics problem solving, learning and teaching* (pp. 337–358). Mahwah, NJ: Lawrence Erlbaum Associates.

8 Balancing Product Design and Theoretical Insights

Lisser R. Ejersbo, Robin Engelhardt,
Lisbeth Frølunde, Thorkild Hanghøj,
Rikke Magnussen, and Morten Misfeldt
Learning Lab Denmark, University of Aarhus

Introduction

Design research has been described ideally as a process of continuous cycles of design, enactment, analysis, and redesign (Design-Based Research Collective, 2003), where the design experiments entail both "engineering" particular forms of learning as well as studying systematically those forms of learning in the context defined by the means of supporting them (Cobb et al., 2003). In practice, though, this research process can be unbalanced and end up with an emphasis on either the design process or theory development. In a professional production environment, there typically will be a strong focus on finishing a product and not necessarily on generating theoretical insights. In academic projects, the focus will be on what new knowledge the project can provide and not necessarily on whether a product is produced and deployed.

The newly established Center for Learning Games at Learning Lab Denmark grew out of a wish to find new approaches to education research in an increasingly complex social context: in Europe, this context is sometimes referred to as a "Mode 2 society."[1] Using problem-oriented design experiments has proved valuable here. A Mode 2 society is characterized as having heterogeneous criteria and demands on research, emerging from sources outside academia (Gibbons et al., 1994; Nowotny et al., 2001). Thus, it is radically different from a classical "Mode 1 society," where research questions are solved within well-established disciplines, mainly with internal criteria of quality. Our aim at Learning Lab Denmark is to create methodologies that satisfy these heterogeneous criteria on research by generating new theories about learning, to develop innovative products, and to communicate and support their possible application in practice. We also consider these methodologies relevant for creating organizational changes. These changes always have two objectives: to improve the conditions for learning and to study the changed system. Thus, the purpose of studying the new learning situations goes beyond improving a given product or method. It is equally important to study the social setting that is changing because of the introduction of the new products or learning processes.

Using design experiments as a methodological tool for education research has several advantages. Designing an artifact can act as a source for finding relevant research topics and help to organize the complexity in education research. Also, empirical knowledge about learning is always highly contextualized. Extracting more or less generalizable knowledge from such contextualized phenomena requires conscious choices and value judgments. In an effort to give the reader an overview of the process of doing research projects within these methodological concepts, we have generated an "osmotic model" (see Figure 8.1), which shows the give-and-take between designing artifacts and developing theoretical insights. The left circle mimics the traditional way of doing education

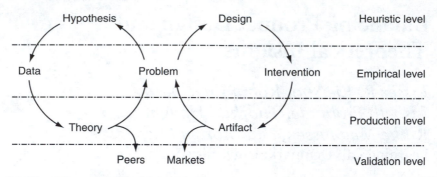

Figure 8.1 The "Osmotic" Model, which Represents our Current Understanding of How to Balance Artifact and Theory Generation in a Design Research Paradigm.

research, where the main "customers" are the peers. The right circle mimics a normal production cycle, but with a much stronger involvement of user feedback. Ideally, a design research project moves in synchronous circular movements, starting from the center and going in both directions. However, this synchronicity rarely happens in practice. Finally, we present three cases as examples of projects conducted at Learning Lab Denmark, demonstrating that real-life research projects can seem like a far cry from the ideals of how to conduct problem-oriented design research.

Case Study One, Mathematical Writing, is an example of a research process that focuses more on the theory-generating part of the process and less on the designing part. The case exemplifies a typical problem in new scientific fields. There are few examples of technological solutions where initial theory generation is crucial in order to to be able to do theoretically informed designs of a prototype. Case Study Two is an example of the opposite approach. This case concerns the development of the learning game *Homicide* and how the procedure ended up with a strong focus on the design process and less on the generation of theory, partly because of the demand for developing professional technology for school education.[2] In the last case study, Redesigning Mathematics In-Service Education, we describe a research process that has changed from an ethnographic study of teachers' practice to a design research process where new means of in-service education are designed. These three cases illustrate how the constraints of various organizational, financial, technical, political, or pedagogical factors make it more or less impossible to implement an ideal or "perfect" research project that maintains a good balance between the processes of product design and theory generation.

Developing Models

For the purposes of discussing and maintaining a balance between product and theory generation, a researcher can try to visualize an idealized work flow for a research project. In a problem-oriented approach, the typical starting point is a problem area or the theme that a "problem owner" wants to study and have solved. It also could be called an area of opportunity. Ideally, the problem is investigated by a cross-disciplinary research team, who will collect data in collaboration with the problem owners. The group of researchers might be assembled for the course of the research project only because each new study requires a research team possessing a new combination of competencies (Gibbons et al., 1994). A problem or "opportunity-oriented" approach is not defined normally by a well-established theory within a given paradigm, where a hypothesis can be verified or rejected through empirical investigations and existing theories can be refined. Rather, an opportunity-oriented approach can use design as a way of finding new approaches and solutions. A design experiment is seen as an iterative process by which better designs can be created. The knowledge production is related to the iterative cycle of design, interventions, and redesign, where value creation is related not only to the application of knowledge but also to the production of knowledge, whereas internal and external communication of knowledge can be qualified by the continuous input of users.

In order to have a model that addresses the push and pull of the work flow in projects, we have developed the "osmotic" model shown in Figure 8.1. This model refers to the process of osmosis because there is an inherent fluctuation between concentrating on designing and reflecting on theory. The osmotic model is not an instruction manual for doing proper research, but merely a simplification for navigating between various aspects of the research process. The arrows are meant to show that there is flow—a dynamic osmotic force. The arrows are not indicators of a sequence or a chronology; rather, they represent phases of a research process that seem to be necessary for the maturity of a design research project. The point of departure is at the center or the "problem"; the optimal research process should be understood as performing iterative and synchronous circle movements in both directions. The word "artifact" should not be understood necessarily as a material object like an abacus or a game; it could be learning strategies, organizational changes, or other intangible process descriptions, which serve as curricular objectives or inspirations for prototypes.

To explain this very idealized and macroscopic model for conducting research, we break down the model into four steps or phases: (a) from problem to design and from problem to hypothesis, (b) from design to intervention and from hypothesis to data, (c) from intervention to artifact and from data to theory, and (d) from artifact to markets and from theory to peers.

From Problem to Design and from Problem to Hypothesis

Going from a problem at hand to a hypothesis or a design entails making a move from the empirical level to the heuristic level, probably the most exciting but also the most difficult part of doing research. A prerequisite is that the researcher has a fairly good knowledge of existing theories about the theme. It also helps to have a sound scientific intuition when making a new hypothesis (a prototheory) about how the particular problem could be confronted and possibly solved. In order to make this move, a researcher should be able to induce a solution; for example, a change of practice. This requires a working knowledge of existing theories, existing artifacts, and design intuition.

From Design to Intervention and from Hypothesis to Data

It is on this level that design research has a great deal to contribute. Design research implies that the move from design to intervention is never linear; rather, it is a circular iterative process. There can be infinite loops of designing, intervening and redesigning. So, like Ptolemy, we ought to draw small epicircles into the figure, between "design" and "intervention" and between "hypothesis" and "data," in order to acknowledge this fact.

From Intervention to Artifacts and from Data to Theory

Single-classroom interventions and follow-up qualitative research are the prime activities for design researchers at universities. But, in order to maintain the goal of infusing learning communities with new tools and new ideas, we need to create innovative instructional designs that are readily translatable and adaptable to many contexts. An aspect of this need is preparing the artifact for diverse contexts and not settling for localized prototypes. It is an important goal, and it presents some serious challenges, even obstacles.

From Artifacts to Markets and from Theories to Peers

To ensure successful interventions in education practice, researchers should consider deployment just as important as theory and artifact development. However, there is cause for skepticism. The history of education reform shows us that very little of lasting effect has been produced by education design experiments to date (Williamson, 2003). Some people argue that successful interventions are nothing but a Hawthorne effect (Brown, 1992), that they are too particular and narrow in scope and impact, and that not much can be done to create permanent positive change in classroom teaching and learning. In addition, international studies show it is unlikely that learning will improve markedly by introducing new technologies and media in the classroom without changing the dynamics of teaching and learning (Orgainization for Economic Cooperation and Development, 2004; Venezky & Davis, 2002) and without including out-of-school activities in order to create inspirational, formal, learning environments (Kozma, 2003).

In addition to the dynamics in Figure 8.1, four conceptual levels are identified. These levels are: the heuristic level, the empirical level, the production level, and the validation level. The heuristic level relates to hypothesis and prototype design, where common sense rules, and intuitions and creative processes are mixed and used in order to increase the probability of finding a good candidate for further inquiry. It involves brainstorming processes, mental experiments of advantages and disadvantages, trial-and-error, and lateral thinking. By contrast, the empirical level tries to systematize what can be known and what is unknown through well-established scientific operands of experiments, observations, verification, falsification, and so on. The production level involves competencies such as organizing, framing, planning, synthesizing, and sometimes delegating work. Last, but not least, the validation level is less in the hands of a researcher than of the people or mechanisms that are used for authentication and dissemination.

Some final comments on the osmotic model. We are proposing that one way to contribute to education reform in the future is to be extremely conscious about creating marketable products that are disseminated to the proper audiences. In this way, we can extend academic validation through peers by external evaluation and selection through users and markets. Thus, evaluation has three facets: peers, markets, and user feedback. "Markets" should not be misunderstood as "mass markets". Markets should be understood as the many different recipients, target groups, and interested parties of the artifacts in question. These interested parties might be relevant people who have never heard of your artifact, but who might profit from your design efforts. Thus, in order to ensure successful interventions in educational practice, deployment should be seen as being equal in importance to development theory and artifacts.

The Ideal Research Project Versus the Real-Life Challenges

As mentioned before, there may be situations where a design solution is too far removed from the problem at hand. Some fundamental research problems might not yet be suitable for design experiments. Such a situation is described in Case Study One. Also, the time needed to do iterative research work is often lacking. Design research takes time because of the need to conduct research on learning in context and to develop learning materials in an iterative and collaborative process. Sufficient time for development is a persistent problem because of the nature of academic funding for blocks of time or stipends, such as for doctoral dissertations or grants.

Realistically, even though researchers succeed in creating marketable artifacts, there are other salient issues in schools, such as lack of teacher training, digital infrastructure, and continuous technical support, that present challenges. The learning context as a whole—meaning the sociocultural and political ecology and the cultural aspects (including gender)—is often neglected or downplayed when considering the deployment and adaptation of new curricular initiatives and artifacts. The later stages of design artifact and teaching practice involving dissemination and diffusion are gaining attention in design research. For example, the Integrative Learning Design Framework (ILDF) devised by Brenda Bannan-Ritland provides an overview of the development and design process, drawing from traditions of instructional design, product design, user-centered design, traditional educational research, and web-enabled protodiffusion. Notably, Bannan-Ritland integrates sociological perspectives on the diffusion of innovations to market (Rogers, 2003; Zaritsky et al., 2003).

Case Studies: Design-Based Research and Mode 2 in Practice

In the following three case studies, we describe some of our experiences with the methodological dilemmas that we try to balance, along with the challenges that we have faced in practice.

Case Study One: Mathematical Writing

The genesis of this project was to question how technology can support mathematical writing, similar to the way that prose writing is supported by word processors. Computers are becoming the widest used medium for written communication. It seems as if everything, from personal communications and school reports to research articles, is developed and presented using a computer now. This is a development with many advantages. As an example, consider how the global internet supports the development of online learning communities and improves the infrastructure for distributed collaboration. Yet, these advantages are dependent mainly on written communication. Word processors allow for other kinds of writing processes than previous technologies, which may be due to the printed appearance of text and the minimal effort involved in restructuring and revising text.

Several attempts to take advantage of the potentials of digital writing in connection with mathematics, especially mathematics education, seem to be unsuccessful (e.g., Guzdial et al., 2002). This observation motivated the mathematical writing project. Understanding how technology might be able to support mathematical writing can be considered a very challenging design problem. Our review of the literature (and our design intuition) indicates that the ideal tool for writing mathematics has not been made yet, although many candidates have been proposed.

So, instead of starting this project by developing a theoretically informed design of a prototype, it seemed necessary to understand more fully what people do when they "write mathematics." In order to study people in context, we turned to the ethnographic approaches used in the areas of workplace studies and computer-supported collaborative work. Here, pragmatic versions of ethnography have proved effective for understanding the problems with existing designs and generating new designs. The ethnographic grounding works well in capturing the complexity of, for instance, collaborative working situations. Figure 8.2 shows the progression of the research, the rationale behind the ethnographic approach, and how it relates to theory and design.

In this approach, the start of the research is a problem or an interesting practice. Then, this practice is observed and described empirically, with attention to the phenomena related to the problem and to keeping a very open hypothesis. These observations should lead to a theoretical description of practice, showing problematic or interesting areas and should provide us with new insights. Design is the expected outcome of the research activity, in the sense that the promise of such research in the long run is a new or an improved artifact that facilitates the practice in question. Figure 8.2 shows this evolution from research, from theory generation to design artifact.

Initial observations about using a computer for mathematical writing were that the existing technology is unsatisfactory and that it is not obvious what to do to improve it. This led us to a methodological approach that is mainly ethnographic. The research focused on what different types of people do when they work with mathematics; that is, how they write, what media they use, what kinds of representations are central, and how they collaborate. Two investigations were done: one with professional mathematics researchers about their various writing processes (Misfeldt, 2004b, 2005b) and one with undergraduate students about their collaborative writing (Misfeldt, 2005a).

The first investigation was based on interviews with mathematics researchers, and consisted of 11 semistructured interviews. During the interviews, the mathematics researchers explained the purposes that writing has for them, both in their individual work process and in their collaborative work processes. The investigation indicated that writing is very important to these researchers in almost all phases of their work. They use writing to clarify early ideas about a problem, using pen and paper in a way that supports thinking. Then, as an idea has to be developed further, writing and doing calculations are crucial. Furthermore, writing is central in collaboration and for saving ideas. Mathematics researchers tend to use pen and paper for calculations in order to support thinking. For many of these researchers, computers become part of the writing process at a very late stage.

The second investigation was a field study of undergraduate students' collaborative work in connection with completing an assignment. This investigation was based on several data sources. We followed two groups of students, having weekly contact with them and doing video observations of seven of their group meetings. Furthermore, each of the students kept a detailed diary log during one week of work with their assignment.

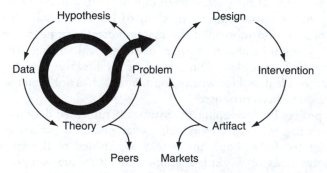

Figure 8.2 The Ethnographic Approach Taken in the Mathematical Writing Project.

The investigation showed that there is a complex interplay between the use of writing as a personal tool, an ostensive tool, and a product in collaborative writing activities on mathematics.

The results of the two investigations are discussed using a semiotic framework (Misfeldt, 2004a). This framework allowed us to examine the structure of interaction between people and between people and media on the same level. Our field work led to theory-building about how different types of semiotic mathematical representations relate differently to existing writing technology. It seems that for the linear types of mathematical notation, such as algebraic formulas, there is a potential for using the oral register (the way formulas are spoken aloud) as a design heuristic. This heuristic is well known from the way that the Windows-based computer systems handle Japanese character (iconographic) writing. It seems sensible to copy that interaction for developing new formula editors.

We hope that our results contribute to developing principles for the design of a new writing technology. Using the way that formulas are spoken aloud as a design heuristic is not the usual way of designing mathematical writing tools, and it counters most of the existing and new designs. The more diagrammatic or two-dimensional the notation gets, the less meaningful the connection becomes. Hence, other interaction forms are needed. It appears that face-to-face interaction about mathematics draws on several media and that the role of these media changes rapidly between being social and individual. These results are not well suited as a starting point for the design of digital technology, but they could point to developing design principles for working environments and for the organization of collaborative projects.

Case Study Two: Designing the Learning Game Homicide

This project was initiated in 2003 at Learning Lab Denmark and was not set up initially as a design-based research project, but with a Mode 2 approach. The project was an experiment in bringing innovative learning materials to markets; that is, the focus was on deploying new learning materials to schools for further research and development. The artifact is an information technology-supported, role-playing game called Homicide, in which students play forensic experts solving a murder case (Magnussen & Jessen, 2004). In a week-long investigation, students analyze clues, such as fingerprints and blood found at crime scenes, using both theoretical and hands-on, practical methods. The investigations are conducted both in the virtual game space and in the physical space in the schools' laboratories. The game is a mixed-media supported game, with the main part of the interaction and problem-solving taking place in the social space in the classroom and not as computer–student interactions. The computer serves as a knowledge base that students can consult for such information as criminal investigation handbooks with procedures and scientific background materials, data from crime scenes, video interrogations of suspects, document support, forensic reports, etc. Thus, this game-based learning environment was designed to develop science competencies through simulation of a real-life learning situation.

The goal was to explore the possibilities for developing a learning game that would support working with the scientific method, using a scientific process of inquiry, and still be an exciting game to play. The aspiration was to make a playful, humorous, yet fairly low-budget learning game. We intended the game to be used in schools for integrating different subjects. Aspects of crime stories and real-life, crime laboratory genres from television series were combined with computer games and traditions of "learning by doing" through role-playing and simulation methods.

The development team consisted of a core of people functioning as designers, writers, developers, and researchers. A common feature was that all of the participants had some type of academic theoretical approach to game development as well as a practical, media production background. The team included others as needed: actors, consulting teachers, and specialized education researchers.

The development project had four phases. The first phase was the theoretical founding and conceptualization. The team started with a knowledge-gathering phase, studying the content of the game (forensic techniques) and researching situated learning theory, activity theory, literary theories, and role-playing theories in order to conceptualize the learning structure of the game. In the second phase, the team developed and produced a pen-and-paper version of *Homicide*, which was alpha-tested and generated results on the players' use of roles and their level of science learning content. The researcher was an integrated part of this process, working primarily with the science learning content. Phase Three was the final stage of the game development period and led to the production of a beta version of the game, which went through several iterations (related to two interventions in schools) before the game design was finalized. The game designers, researchers, and teachers worked together on integrating science learning elements and game elements in the final product. Phase Four included dissemination, teachers' education, and proposals for future studies of the game as a learning environment. The approach taken in designing *Homicide* is shown in Figure 8.3.

In the two studies of *Homicide* in action, we saw that the game's learning environment supported working with the process of inquiry and that it was motivating and engaging for students. In the first interventions with the game in school, the social learning in the game-based learning environment has proved highly interesting also. In the observations of the play intervention, we saw not only how the students handled large amounts of data to establish theories, but also how they redesigned the game tools independently in an effort to establish a coherent hypothesis. These tools became increasingly more sophisticated during the week-long play intervention, which seems to indicate that the students not only used individual skills, but also that they operated on a methodological metalevel where tools and methods are evaluated and adjusted to meet the challenges of the game. A theoretical description of this type of simulated, situated, game-based learning space is relevant because we have little knowledge yet about what types of learning processes take place in these kinds of learning spaces, what makes a design effective, and how to adapt findings to other settings. Future, long-term observations and design-based research studies of players playing *Homicide* are needed to gain an understanding of both the theoretical and the learning aspects.

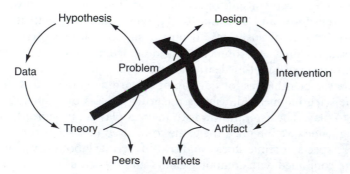

Figure 8.3 The Product Design Approach Taken in the *Homicide* Project.

The project's focus was on the development of the game. The initial design concept was theory-driven, but the process as a whole lacked deeper analysis in relation to redesign and theory-building. This problem may be rooted in the balancing of the roles of the developers and the researchers, and this issue may be endemic to design research projects, especially large development projects like *Homicide*. A team needs to find a common language and cultivate respect for the contributions of each member of the team, yet accept certain limitations on the level of engagement in all aspects. The question here is whether the developers and the researchers in larger development projects should have equal focal points in the research and development outcome of the project or whether they should have separate processes? For example, it may not be possible for researchers to understand and integrate fully the theory that is the focus point of the material produced without being an integrated part of the development process. The designer will not be able to make theory-driven designs without being an integrated part of the research, but there might be processes that are meaningless to other parts. When the game is working well, it might be meaningless to the developer to keep changing elements to get a deeper understanding of the learning processes that the game facilitates. On the other hand, the researcher might find it meaningless to keep adjusting technical details that are unimportant to the research focus. Therefore, one solution could be that the researchers and the designers should consider having certain separate processes.

In regard to changing existing practice, since 2004, the development and research team has been in demand at conferences and the like and has been showcased for the originality of its approach to designing curricular materials and for introducing a new breed of learning materials. Thus, the *Homicide* game itself does indeed seem to inform educational policies and practice in schools, creating demands for teachers' training and provoking debates about such issues as curriculum design, cross-disciplinarity, and students' decreasing interest in learning science.

Case Study Three: Redesigning Mathematics In-Service Education

The goal of this research project was to investigate a narrowly focused curriculum initiative, mediated by an in-service course for mathematics teachers in a traditional Mode 1 type of study. In-service education is the most commonly used way to implement new curriculum initiatives, yet little is known in Denmark about how it influences classroom practice. The initial research questions were: How clearly were the intentions in the initiative delivered in the in-service course and in the classrooms? What was the effect of the teachers' in-service course on the subject, which was open problem-solving in mathematics?

The background for this project was a new type of oral mathematics examination after grade nine in the lower secondary schools, which became compulsory in Denmark in 1997. According to the governmental curriculum requirements, the examination tasks had to be formulated as practical problems of an open character. This new type of examination led to an in-service course, "Preparing for Mathematics Exams," offered to mathematics teachers in 1996. These in-service courses were run by pedagogical consultants, but the courses were offered only when enough participants enrolled.

However, there was no concomitant plan for researching how open problem-solving might have positive or negative effects in the classroom. In 2002, a doctoral dissertation research project at Learning Lab Denmark made it possible to start studying the effects of an in-service course on open mathematics problem-solving; namely, how did the in-service course influence teachers to change their practice?

The doctoral researcher started by reviewing curriculum theories and then collected data about the content of the in-service course and the teachers' subsequent teaching practice. The research question was: To what extent can teaching mathematics with open practical problems be learned in an in-service course by the participating mathematics teachers?

The methodological approach was qualitative, with investigations of teachers' practice through ethnographically inspired fieldwork and in-depth interviews. The research methods included semistructured interviews (Kvale, 2001; Patton, 2002), video-tapes (Pirie et al., 2001; Powell et al., 2003), diaries produced by the teachers, and materials produced by teachers and students. One of the early research findings was that the in-service course did influence the teachers in using open mathematics problems in the classroom, but, at the same time, using open problems creates a situation of paradigmatic and authoritative flux where continuous immediate decisions have to be made by the teacher. Many of the teacher's decisions are "uncertain" in the sense that they are made on the spot and in response to local conditions. One of the significant elements of working with open problem-solving is that students ask questions or suggest solutions, for which the teacher cannot always be prepared. Therefore, the teacher has to listen carefully to the student and find quick and suitable responses. The teacher has to concentrate on: What does the student mean? What is the context? What is a good response for this particular student, etc.? However, what typically happens is that the teacher does not listen carefully enough and gives automatic responses, as other research confirms (Jarvis, 1999; Skott, 2000).

Listening and responding become crucial skills when using open problem-solving in the classrooms. The teacher has to listen in another way because open problem-solving can go in so many directions. It seems that teachers stay with their old discourse habits of knowing the answers to all of the questions. Indeed, the new context requires new types of leadership and development of the skill to listen in another way, along with the ability to ask powerful questions and give clear responses.

As the researcher reflected on the early findings, another question appeared: Why does the teacher listen and respond so poorly when students solve open, practical, mathematics problems? With this more narrow focus, the project moved into a design research approach, where part of the focus was on redesigning the in-service course with design experiments, developing instructional activities, and conducting analyses of the processes of the students' and teachers' learning and the means by which that learning is supported and organized (Cobb, 2001; diSessa & Cobb, 2004). This approach is shown in Figure 8.4. The project started out with a specific "artifact"— the existing in-service course. This course is being redesigned on the basis of the ethnographic data and theoretical refinements obtained.

The shift into the design research framework gave the study a boost because it made clear to the researcher how to ground the redesign of the curriculum. Based on the interpretation of the research data, the evaluations made by the teachers, combined with material on the stated goals and visions for the mathematics, the redesign of the course explored how to engage the teachers in "reflective cooperation." The theoretical framework under development was about the similarities and the differences in the school classroom and in the in-service course classroom.

The results of the study show that the teachers took with them back to their classrooms what they had learned at the in-service course. However, the researcher observed that none of the classroom communication came near a kind of "reflective discourse" organized through communication about the open problem-solving. What was the reason for that? How could the in-service course be prepared differently to meet those

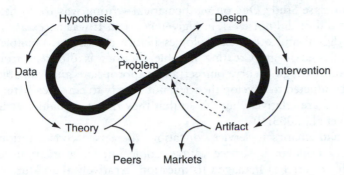

Figure 8.4 The Methodological Path Taken in the Teachers' In-Service Education Project Using Open Problem Solving in Mathematics.

needs (needs that the teachers maybe were not aware of)? The new method entailed asking the teachers to keep diaries of the communications in their classrooms and doing self-observation and reflection about their teaching practice in more focused ways. The redesign contained reflective cooperation, which was done by arranging a situation where the teachers could experience their own listening and response activities.

One of the theoretical frameworks used was Leron and Hazzan's *The Virtual Monologue* (1997), a game whose purpose is to imagine a virtual inner monologue in the communicating persons (Ejersbo, 2005; Ejersbo & Leron, 2005). The crucial point of The Virtual Monologue is to get the teachers to be aware of their habits and to recognize the importance of changing together as a group and on the individual level when they are back alone in their classrooms. It is hoped that this insight will enable the teacher to become aware of his or her ways of listening and responding and, consequently, develop the necessary skills and competencies.

The research project started as a Mode 1 project, influenced by Mode 2 requirements, but it changed in the middle into a design research project. That was possible because the in-service courses continued in a cycle, with a course each year. One of the difficulties was balancing the different roles between being a consultant and being a researcher. The course was redesigned, grounded on the theoretical frameworks from the research. On the one hand, the participating teachers were satisfied still; on the other hand, the redesigned courses were evaluated immediately after the course by the participating teachers only, without any classroom studies. The old courses were very popular too, and a remaining question is how much the new course influences the subsequent mathematics teaching and why. An iterative process can go on.

Discussion

The evidence from the three case studies shows that there is no straightforward way to plan and carry out a design research project. There are many possibilities and many caveats and there are no stable methodological paradigms or theoretical recipes by which to proceed. Therefore, as a researcher, one has to be pragmatic about the choices at hand and concede that it may be impossible to do everything at once. Sometimes, it will be unimaginable to do intervention trials; at other times, it will be impossible to deploy an artifact. Sometimes, it may be best to use some heuristics; at other times, applying field studies is sensible if the situation cannot be supported by the designs available.

The approach chosen in Case Study One on mathematical writing was to do field work in order to see what did or did not work in a given context. It was necessary to observe how people use digital and other technologies before creating a "humble" hypothesis and concrete design ideas. Creating humble theories is different from attempting to make a grand or high theory, but certainly appropriate and valuable: "Design experiments are conducted to develop theories, not merely to empirically tune 'what works.' These theories are relatively humble in that they target domain-specific learning processes" (Cobb et al., 2003: 9).

In Case Study Three, mathematics in-service education, these two considerations merge nicely. Being a very popular, in-service course, some impact is guaranteed. Nevertheless, the research project has managed to question iteratively the nature of this impact and to feed back the knowledge to a revised version of the course, maintaining a large impact. The question is still to explain in a researchable way why the new designs work and to suggest to which new circumstances they could be adapted. The crucial point in Case Study Three is to keep the balance between developing the course in response to the market condition or the research condition.

In Case Study Two, *Homicide*, the focus was on the development part of the process, where intuitions and practical experiences were more dominant in the designing of a new type of learning material than theoretical knowledge. It is difficult to say anything definite about what the right balance is between theoretical findings, heuristics, and empirical analysis because it is highly dependent on the context, but it should be something that developers and researchers pay attention to throughout the whole process. Also, in this case study we struggled with the richness of the data embedded in the final design of the game. In the beginning, we were tempted to create a broad, all-encompassing theory on why and how a learning game works. "Beyond just creating designs that are effective and that can sometimes be affected by 'tinkering to perfection,' a design theory explains why designs work and suggests how they may be adapted to new circumstances" (Cobb et al., 2003: 9). However, the need to restrict the research questions became clear quickly. The grand questions were broken down into an analysis of details, single parameters, certain context aspects, or a specific hypothesis. Case Study Two illustrates an osmotic pressure, where the concentration of energy was so much on the development of a new type of learning material at the beginning; now, the pull is toward developing the theoretical insights.

There are also lessons to be learned by the design research community. It is not enough to have some nice prototypes that work in some small selected contexts (Barab & Squire, 2004). The production of deployable artifacts is crucial for creating a lasting impact on learning communities, although deployment can be seen as a problem for maintaining an iterative design process. The question of why cognitively oriented, technological innovations have not become widespread has been addressed by Fishman and colleagues (2004), who state that a key reason for the limited impact is that most design-based research does not address explicitly systemic issues of usability, scalability, and sustainability. We agree. Perhaps, popular notions of "demo or die" should be complemented with "demo and deploy" or "meet the market." We would add criteria of communication and deployment of scientific ideas and artifacts. These criteria can have positive consequences for design-related research. First and foremost, there is the consequence that the design involved in the research process should be disseminated at some point to some kind of open market, even though this could mean stopping the iterative design process temporarily. The second consequence is to communicate to relevant interested parties throughout the entire research process. Research communication should be more than research reports that appear only in specialized journals years after the project is finished.

Conclusions

In this chapter, we have described some of the central methodological considerations in our attempt to make a practice-oriented approach to education research. We have developed an "osmotic" model in order to describe how it is possible to balance the dynamics of a research process. Using this model, we presented three of our research projects and evaluated how they match our ideal of doing education research. The picture that emerges from these three case studies shows that it is hard to achieve our ideal, mainly because it is impossible to address all the aspects involved in the model with full intensity simultaneously. Our advice is that researchers need to select a suitable methodological approach, guided by a combination of analysis and heuristics about the problem, as well as pragmatic concerns about resources, partners, and so on.

We hope to contribute to the development of methodologies in design research. On our side, there are some continuing problems in the choice of approaches, and much work lies ahead in trying to align the work done with the ideals. We understand research contexts as potential, collaborative, idea and theory generators that reach beyond intervention or improving theoretical accounts of teaching and learning. We believe that research results and prototypes should be aimed at different communications areas and that innovative thinking is an issue to consider methodologically. Finally, we think that a wider pragmatic diffusion of pedagogical and didactic innovation in scalable, replicable, and sustainable form is imperative in order to avoid narrow research projects that never reach maturity.

Acknowledgments

The project is supported by the Danish Ministry of Education's ITMF (Public School Information Technology and Media) fund.

Notes

1 Science, Technology and Learning Group at Learning Lab Denmark, Danish University of Education website: http://www.lld.dk/.
2 Learning Lab Denmark *Homicide* project website: http://www.drabssag.dk/.

References

Bannan-Ritland, B. (2003). The role of design in research: The integrative learning design framework. *Educational Researcher, 32*(1), 21–24.

Barab, S. A. & Squire, K. D. (2004). Design-based research: Putting our stake in the ground. *Journal of the Learning Sciences, 13*, 1–14.

Brown, A. L. (1992). Design experiments: Theoretical and methodological challenges in creating complex interventions in classroom settings. *Journal of the Learning Sciences, 2*, 141–178.

Cobb, P. (2001). Supporting the improvement of learning and teaching in social and institutional context. In S. M. Carver & D. Klahr (eds), *Cognition and instruction: Twenty-five years of progress* (pp. 455–478). Mawah, NJ: Lawrence Erlbaum Associates.

Cobb, P., Confrey, J., diSessa, A., Lehrer, R. & Schauble, L. (2003). Design experiments in educational research. *Educational Researcher, 32*(1), 9–13.

Design-Based Research Collective (2003). Design-based research: An emerging paradigm for educational inquiry. *Educational Researcher, 32*(1), 5–8.

diSessa, A. A. & Cobb, P. (2004). Ontological innovation and the role of theory in design experiments. *Journal of the Learning Sciences, 13*, 77–103.

Ejersbo, L. R. (2005). Virtual monologue as a reflection tool—a way to use theory in practice. Paper presented at the 15th study congress of the International Commission on Mathematical Instruction, Águas de Lindóias, Brazil, May.

Ejersbo, L. R. & Leron, U. (2005). The didactical transposition of didactical ideas: The case of the virtual monologue. Paper presented at the fourth congress of the European Society for Research in Mathematics Education, Sant Feliu de Guíxols, Spain, February.

Fishman, B., Marx, R. W., Blumenfeld, P., Krajcik, J. & Soloway, E. (2004). Creating a framework for research on systemic technology innovations. *Journal of the Learning Sciences, 13*, 43–76.

Gibbons, M., Limoges, C., Nowotny, H., Schwartzman, S., Scott, P. & Trow, M. (1994). *The new production of knowledge: The dynamics of science and research in contemporary societies.* London: Sage.

Guzdial, M., Lodovice, P., Realf, M., Morley, T. & Carroll, K. (2002). When collaboration doesn't work. Paper presented at the fifth International Conference of the Learning Sciences, Seattle, WA, October.

Jarvis, P. (1999). *The practitioner-researcher. Developing theory from practice.* San Francisco, CA: Jossey-Bass.

Kozma, R. B. (ed.) (2003). *Technology, innovation and educational change—A global perspective.* Eugene, OR: International Society for Educational Technology.

Kvale, S. (2001). *InterView, an introduction to qualitative research interviews* (2nd ed.). Copenhagen, Denmark: Hans Reitzels Forlag.

Leron, U. & Hazzan, O. (1997). The world according to Johnny: A coping perspective in mathematics education. *Educational Studies in Mathematics, 32*, 265–292.

Magnussen, R. & Jessen, C. (2004). *Research report, Homicide.* Copenhagen, Denmark: Learning Lab Denmark.

Misfeldt, M. (2004a). Computers as media for mathematical writing: A model for semiotic analysis. Paper presented at the International Commission on Mathematical Instruction, Copenhagen, Denmark, July.

Misfeldt, M. (2004b). Mathematicians writing: Tensions between personal thinking and distributed collaboration. Paper presented at the Coop, the sixth International Conference on the Design of Cooperative Systems, Nice, France, May.

Misfeldt, M. (2005a). Conversations in undergraduate students' collaborative work. Paper presented at the fourth congress of the European Society for Research in Mathematics Education, Sant Feliu de Guíxols, Spain, February.

Misfeldt, M. (2005b). Media in mathematical writing. *For the Learning of Mathematics, 25*(2), 36–42.

Nowotny, H., Scott, P. & Gibbons, M. (2001). *Re-thinking science: Knowledge and the public in an age of uncertainty.* London: Polity Press.

Organization for Economic Cooperation and Development (2004). *Completing the foundation for lifelong learning: An OECD survey of upper secondary schools,* at: http://www1.oecd.org/publications/e-book/9604011E.pdf.

Patton, M. Q. (2002). *Qualitative research and evaluation methods.* London: Sage.

Pirie, S. I. B., Borgen, K., Manu, S. S., Jenner, D., Thom, J. & Martin, L. C. (2001). Theory, video and mathematical understanding: An examination of what different theoretical perspectives can offer. In R. Speiser, C. A. Maher & C. N. Walter (eds), *Proceedings of the 23rd annual meeting of the North American chapter of the International Group for the Psychology of Education* (pp. 343–380). Columbus, OH: ERIC Clearinghouse of Science, Mathematics, and Environmental Education (ERIC Document Reportduction Service No. ED476613).

Powell, A. B., Franscisco, J. M. & Maher, C. A. (2003). An analytical model for studying the development of learners' mathematical ideas and reasoning using videotape data. *Journal of Mathematical Behavior, 22*, 405–435.

Rogers, E. M. (2003). *Diffusion of innovations* (5th ed.). New York: Free Press.

Skott, J., (2000). The images and practice of mathematics teachers. Unpublished doctoral dissertation, Royal Danish School of Educational Studies.

Venezky, R. & Davis, C. (2002). *Quo vademus? The transformation of schooling in a networked world*. Paris: Organization for Economic Cooperation and Development/Centre for Educational Research and Innovation.

Williamson, B. (2003). *The participation of children in the design of new technology: A discussion paper*, at: http://www.nestafuturelab.org/research/discuss/01discuss01.htm.

Zaritsky, R., Kelly, A. E., Flowers, W., Rogers, E. & O'Neill, P. (2003). Clinical design sciences: A view from sister design efforts. *Educational Researcher, 32*(1), 32–35.

Part 3

Modeling Student Learning During Design Research

9   Research Methods for Alternative Approaches to Transfer

Implications for Design Experiments

Joanne Lobato
San Diego State University

Introduction

> Prevailing theories and methods of measuring transfer work well for studying full-blown expertise, but they represent too blunt an instrument for studying the smaller changes in learning that lead to the development of expertise. New theories and measures of transfer are required.
>
> (Bransford & Schwartz, 1999: 24)

A central and enduring goal of education is to provide learning experiences that are useful beyond the specific conditions of initial learning. Issues of the generalization of learning are particularly important in design experiments. For example, in design experiments, researchers typically use a complex artifact (often a computer software tool) and then are interested in how learners' interactions with the artifact will influence their attempts to solve problems without the artifact. Furthermore, the generation of these creative and innovative artifacts is often aimed at helping students to develop robust understandings that will generalize to decision making and problem solving outside the classroom. Finally, information about the specific ways in which students are generalizing what they have learned in local iteration (x) of a design experiment can inform the action of redesign as the design experiment progresses to iteration (x + 1).

However, researchers' progress in understanding and supporting the generalization of learning has been limited because of methodological and theoretical problems with the transfer construct. Numerous critiques of transfer (Beach, 1999; Carraher & Schliemann, 2002; Greeno, 1997; Lave, 1988; Packer, 2001) have contributed to a growing acknowledgment that "there is little agreement in the scholarly community about the nature of transfer, the extent to which it occurs, and the nature of its underlying mechanisms" (Barnett & Ceci, 2002: 612).

Theoretical Perspectives on the Transfer of Learning and Design Experiments in Education

In a previous paper, I argued that the theoretical assumptions underlying a researcher's model of transfer affect how a design experiment in education evolves (Lobato, 2003). For example, whether one takes what MacKay (1969) calls an observer's (expert's) or an actor's (learner's) perspective toward transfer affects information that is available to researchers as they make design decisions. Specifically, in the classical transfer approach, transfer is said to occur when subjects perform correctly on tasks that are structurally similar to initial learning tasks from an expert's point of view. (By the classical transfer approach, I refer to the common elements theories that have dominated the twentieth century, from Thorndike's [1906] emphasis on identical elements in the physical environment to the mainstream cognitive accounts of identical or overlapping mental schemes [e.g., Anderson et al., 1995].)

The classical approach underestimates the amount of generalization of learning that occurs, in part because generalizations that result in incorrect performance are not counted as evidence of transfer. Moreover, transfer experiments typically reveal whether or not transfer occurs and do not tend to identify the specific generalizations that students form, especially when those generalizations are non-normative or result in incorrect performance. As a result, attempts to revise the curriculum without the benefit of data regarding the many and specific ways in which students have generalized their learning experiences may lead to a decision to align the instruction more closely with the transfer tasks. This can lead to gains on transfer measures due to a training effect rather than to significant shifts in the nature of students' generalization of learning (details are provided in Lobato, 2003).

In contrast, researchers operating from an actor-oriented transfer perspective (Lobato, 2003, 2007; Lobato & Siebert, 2002) seek to understand the processes by which people generalize their learning experiences, regardless of whether the personal relations of similarity that people form across situations lead to correct performance. Although mathematical correctness should not be ignored or de-emphasized as an instructional goal, limiting the definition of generalization to that of correct formal descriptions supports fewer insights into what students themselves construe as general (Ellis, under review). More importantly, the actor-oriented approach provides a way to link individual students' generalizations to the features of instructional environments that afford these generalizations (Lobato et al., 2003). Additionally, these relationships are articulated with sufficient detail to inform revisions in curriculum materials and pedagogical approaches during iterative cycles of instructional design (Lobato, 2003). In sum, one's theoretical assumptions regarding the transfer of learning (e.g., whether the observer's or the actor's perspective is privileged) affect how a design experiment evolves.

Transfer Methods and Design Experiments

In this chapter, I extend the argument that transfer theories can influence design decisions by attending to the research methods employed in various transfer perspectives. Classical models of transfer rely on experimental methods for measuring transfer, whereas the actor-oriented transfer approach relies upon ethnographic methods. These different methodological approaches affect the nature of the information that one can obtain and consequently affect design decisions. Furthermore, several alternative approaches to transfer have emerged in recent years, yet little has been written comparing the approaches, especially in terms of the methods employed. In Part One of this chapter, I articulate the methodological approach of five transfer perspectives—the classical approach, the actor-oriented approach, and three other alternative perspectives—by arguing that transfer methods and transfer theories are related reflexively. For example, I demonstrate how the methods used in a transfer perspective reflect theoretical assumptions about the studies underlying phenomena measured by transfer, and, in turn, how the nature of one's research questions about transfer is related to the type of methods utilized.

Once the foundations have been laid for articulating the general methodological approach of various transfer perspectives and the relationship of these methodological approaches to theoretical assumptions about transfer, I turn to the development of specific transfer methods. Although the methods used in the classical transfer approach are well established, the methods used to document most of the alternative transfer perspectives are emerging. In Part Two, I present two specific techniques that evolved in the course of our efforts to document actor-oriented transfer in a variety of mathematics education studies: (a) a method for identifying instances of actor-oriented transfer in classroom settings, and (b) a method for capturing the socially situated nature of actor-oriented transfer.

Purpose

This chapter has two purposes: (a) to demonstrate the reflexive relationship between transfer theory and methods by contrasting the general methodological approaches and accompanying theoretical assumptions of five transfer perspectives, and (b) to present two specific methods that have emerged during our efforts to develop an alternative approach to the transfer of learning. I then use the arguments from both parts of the chapter to reflect on the implications for design experiments. The chapter concludes with a brief discussion of how actor-oriented transfer might be combined with other transfer approaches at different stages in a multistage model of design research.

Part One: Relationships Between Theory and Methods in Transfer Models

In Part One, I argue that the relationship between the research methods employed to measure transfer and the theoretical assumptions regarding transfer is reflexive. I demonstrate how research methods influence the definition of transfer within a transfer perspective, and, reflexively, how a shift in one's definition of transfer influences the methods one employs to measure transfer. I then illustrate how reflexive relationships also exist between research methods and other dimensions of transfer models.

The relationships between theory and methods will be explicated by comparing and contrasting five theoretical perspectives on transfer. Although the main focus is between the classical transfer model and the actor-oriented transfer perspective, three additional alternative transfer perspectives will be discussed: transfer as preparation for future learning (Bransford & Schwartz, 1999; Schwartz & Martin, 2004; Schwartz et al., 2005), the affordance and constraints approach (Greeno, 1997; Greeno et al., 1993, 1996), and transfer as consequential transitions (Beach, 1999, 2003). The purpose of comparing perspectives is not to pit one against another in order to arrive at a "best" view. Rather, it is to illustrate how one's theoretical and methodological approach to transfer affects both the amount and the nature of the transfer that one sees. As a result of describing what is gained and lost by adopting a particular perspective, we can advance later the argument that different transfer perspectives are useful for different stages of a multistage design experiment (see the Discussion section for details).

How Research Methods Influence Transfer Definitions

In a classical approach, transfer is defined as the application of knowledge learned in one situation to another situation (National Research Council, 2000). From the actor-oriented perspective, transfer is defined as the generalization of learning, which also can be understood as the influence of a learner's prior activities on his or her activity in novel situations (Lobato, 2003, 2007). These definitions seem similar until one looks more closely at the methods employed in each approach. In fact, there are instances in which researchers operating from a classical perspective describe transfer as the influence of prior learning experiences on attempts to solve problems in new situations (e.g., see Marini & Genereux, 1995; Reed et al., 1974). However, in this section, I argue that researchers from a classical transfer perspective treat transfer methodologically as the formation of particular, highly valued generalizations, rather than as the generalization of learning more broadly, and that this difference is significant.

Researchers operating from a classical transfer model typically present subjects with a sequence of tasks. The subjects are taught a solution, response, or principle in an initial learning task (Task A). Then, the subjects perform a transfer task (Task B). Tasks A and B share some structural features (e.g., a common solution strategy) but have different surface forms (e.g., different contexts for word problems). The performance of the experimental group is compared with that of a control group, which receives no practice on Task A, but starts directly with Task B. If the performance of the experimental group on Task B is better than that of the control group, there is positive transfer from Task A to Task B; if it is worse, there is negative transfer. A variety of formulas have been used historically to calculate the amount of transfer, but the simplest is Gagné's raw score formula, which is the difference between the score of the experimental group and the control group on transfer Task B.

When performance improves, the researcher using a classical transfer approach infers that the subjects have generalized some aspect of the learning experience to the transfer tasks. Researchers typically predetermine "what" will transfer, rather than making the "what" an object of investigation. Even when researchers do identify the particular knowledge that has transferred (e.g., the particular mappings that people construct between base and target solutions and problems), they typically rely on models of expert performance (e.g., see Gentner, 1989) and that knowledge is examined only for subjects who have performed correctly on the transfer tasks.

In contrast, evidence for transfer from an actor-oriented perspective is found by scrutinizing a given activity for any indication of influence from previous activities and by examining how people construe situations as similar using ethnographic methods, rather than relying upon statistical measures based on improved performance. As a result, the actor-oriented transfer perspective responds to diSessa and Wagner's (2005) position that transfer theories should describe knowledge, not merely successful or unsuccessful performance.

Operating from an actor-oriented view of transfer can result in the gathering of significantly different information about students' generalizing processes than is possible from the classical transfer perspective. For example, as part of a design experiment aimed at helping high-school algebra students develop conceptual understanding of slope and linear functions, Lobato (1996) performed two contrasting analyses—from classical and actor-oriented transfer perspectives—on the same set of data. Using classical transfer measures, the level of transfer was poor (40 percent to a playground slide task and 33 percent to a roof task), despite high performance on tasks encountered in the experimental curriculum, such as finding the slope of staircases (87 percent correct) and lines (80 percent correct). The results for the larger population of 139 students were similar to the results for the 15 students in the interview sample.

On the other hand, every interview participant demonstrated evidence of transfer from the actor-oriented perspective. A typical response to a transfer task is provided in Figure 9.1. Jarek recalled correctly the slope formula as "rise divided by run" but selected incorrectly the length of the platform as the run. In the actor-oriented transfer perspective, the general analytic approach for establishing evidence of transfer is to look for relations of similarity that learners construct between transfer and learning

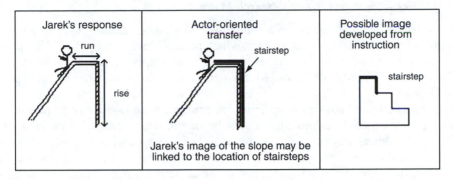

Figure 9.1 Relation of Similarity Inferred from the Work of One Student.

situations. The first step in this process is to examine the nature of the instructional experiences in order to see how they could be influencing the learner's perception of the new situation. In this case, the instructional activities related to slope had been dominated by explorations of real staircases, a computer microworld with dynamic staircases, and the use of mathematical "stairs" to determine the slope of a line and other objects. With this in mind, the data were re-analyzed by looking for ways in which these experiences with staircases may have influenced the students' comprehension of the transfer situations. Specifically, Jarek's work on the slide task is consistent with a "stairstep" relation of similarity. Jarek's choices for rise and run suggest that he was looking for a stairstep in the slide setting (e.g., something that appears to have visually-connected "up" and "over" components and affords climbing in an imagined state of affairs), which he found on the right side of the slide apparatus (see Figure 9.1). The platform as the run may have held particular appeal for Jarek because it is the only "tread" or "over" affordance present in the diagram. (A correct run, on the other hand, needs to be constructed with the use of an auxiliary line.)

In sum, according to the classical measure of transfer, the students in the study showed little evidence of generalizing their learning experiences. In contrast, the analysis from the actor-oriented perspective illuminated how each of the learners generalized their learning experiences by showing how the new situations were connected with the thinker's conception of previous situations even though the relations of similarity were unexpected and nonstandard.

In light of the contrasting methodological treatments of transfer, the definitional differences between the two approaches become more apparent. In the classical approach, transfer is characterized more accurately as the application from one setting to another of a predetermined set of knowledge from the researcher's or expert's point of view. In the actor-oriented perspective, transfer is treated broadly as the influence of a learner's prior activities on his or her activity in novel situations, which entails any ways in which learning generalizes (as opposed to that learning being restricted to the initial context of learning). The actor-oriented transfer approach has focused primarily on the process of "similarity-making," but, in some accounts, we have analyzed also the roles of discerning differences (Lobato et al., 2005) and modifying situations (Lobato & Siebert, 2002). The most striking difference between the two transfer approaches is the acceptance in the actor-oriented perspective of students' idiosyncratic and even (mathematically) incorrect relations of similarity as evidence of transfer. In short, in the actor-oriented approach, transfer is taken to be the generalization of learning, whereas, in the classical approach, transfer is the formation of particular, highly valued generalizations.

How Transfer Definitions Affect Research Methods

Just as research methods result in a refinement of transfer definitions, the particular definition of transfer determines, in part, which methods are appropriate. This point is illustrated briefly with the affordances and constraints approach to transfer (Greeno, 1997; Greeno & The Middle School Mathematics through Application Project Groups, 1998; Greeno et. al., 1993, 1996).

The affordances and constraints perspective emerged in response to critiques that the classical transfer model accounts inadequately for the structuring of material artifacts or the sociocultural environment (Laboratory of Comparative Human Cognition, 1983; Lave, 1988; Pea, 1989; Rogoff & Gardner, 1984). Greeno et al. (1993) redefined transfer as the extent to which participating in an activity in one situation influences one's ability to participate in another activity in a different situation. Transfer is not an invariant property of the individual but, rather, an ability to interact with things and people in various ways. By redefining transfer in this manner, Greeno et al. were seeking to remove it from the sole domain of the cognitive structures of the individual and distribute it across people, artifacts, and situations.

As a result, new methodological tools were needed to account for transfer as an interaction between agents and material resources. Greeno et al. (1993) provided general analytical tools in the form of affordances and constraints. They argued that for transfer to be possible, there must be some affordances (the support for particular activities created by relevant properties of the things and materials in the situation) and/or constraints (regularities) in the learning situation that are invariant under the transformation that changes the learning situation into the transfer situation and that the learner must become attuned to these invariants. The extended examples provided by Greeno et al. illustrate the methodological approach of combining an analysis of affordances and constraints in particular situations with an ethnographic account of people's activity in those situations. Other researchers have developed additional methodological tools that are consistent with the affordances/constraints approach to transfer (Hickey & Pellegrino, 2005; Hickey et al., 2003). In sum, by creating a definition of transfer that is compatible with a situated view of knowing, different methodological tools needed to be developed, thus illustrating how transfer theory can influence research methods.

Relationships Among Methods and Other Dimensions of Transfer Theory

A model of the transfer of learning involves much more than its definition. Other dimensions are equally important, such as the type of research questions that can be investigated productively by operating within a particular perspective, the nature and location of the transfer processes, assumptions about the transfer tasks, conceptions of abstraction, and so on. In this section, I examine the relationships between research methods and two of these dimensions—the research questions and the location of transfer processes.

How the Nature of the Research Question is Related to the Methods

I examine how research questions are related to research methods by comparing the ethnographic methods employed in the actor-oriented transfer perspective with the experimental methods used in the preparation for future learning approach (Bransford & Schwartz, 1999; Schwartz & Martin, 2004; Schwartz et al., 2005).

The preparation for future learning approach responds to the critique that the classical transfer approach ignores the real-world conditions that people can often exploit, such as soliciting help from colleagues, seeking additional learning resources, and having opportunities to obtain feedback. Classical tests of transfer involve what Bransford and Schwartz (1999) call "sequestered problem solving," meaning that students work in environments where they have no "contaminating" information sources other than what they have learned previously. In contrast, the preparation for future learning approach examines how various instructional treatments prepare students to benefit from a learning opportunity.

The preparation for future learning approach demonstrates how the usefulness of prior knowledge may not be apparent to students until they are given the opportunity to learn new information. For example, Schwartz and Bransford (1998) compared how two instructional interventions prepared students for future learning. In the "invent a method" treatment, students analyzed simplified data sets from classic memory experiments and invented their own graphs to show what they discovered. In the "summarize" treatment, students wrote a summary of a chapter on the same memory experiments. Students in the invention treatment performed poorly on transfer tasks. Interestingly, when students in both conditions received a learning resource in the form of a follow-up lecture, the results reversed themselves. On a subsequent transfer assessment, the "invention" students made twice as many correct predictions about a novel experiment as the "summarize" students. The researchers could attribute the gains to the invention treatment preparing the students to learn from the lecture, because one group of invention students did not hear the lecture and performed poorly on the transfer assessment.

The general methodological approach used in the preparation for future learning perspective can be summarized as follows. Students are assigned one of two instructional treatments. Half of the students from both treatments are given access to a common learning resource such as a lecture or a sample worked problem embedded in an assessment, followed by a request to solve a transfer problem. The other half from both treatments are asked to solve the transfer problem directly without access to the learning resource. The researchers call this a double-transfer paradigm because students need to "transfer in" what they learned from the instructional method to learn from the resource, and they need to "transfer out" what they learned from the resource to solve the target problem (Schwartz & Martin, 2004; Schwartz et al., 2005).

The experimental methods used in the preparation for future learning approach are well suited for exploring the research question: "What conditions facilitate transfer?" Specifically, researchers can compare performance on the transfer assessment to determine which method of instruction prepares students better to benefit from the learning opportunity, and they can determine whether the inclusion of the learning resource changes the performance on the transfer tasks (Schwartz & Martin, 2004). They also can investigate how different habits of mind and dispositions facilitate or constrain the transfer of learning (Bransford & Schwartz, 1999).

In contrast, the ethnographic methods used in an actor-oriented transfer approach are best suited for exploring the ways in which learners construct relations of similarity across situations. The research questions in an actor-oriented transfer study are not: "Was transfer obtained?" or "What conditions produce transfer?" but, rather, "What are the images by which learners construct two situations as similar?" and "How does the environment structure the production of similarity?"

The latter questions can also be addressed from a preparation for future learning perspective if other methods are used. For example, Bransford and Schwartz (1999) cite a study by Burgess and Lin (1998), in which fifth-graders and college students were asked to create a statewide recovery plan to protect bald eagles from the threat of extinction. Each group was asked to generate questions that they would like to have answered to help them learn more about recovery plans for the eagles. By using qualitative methods to examine the nature of the questions, the researchers ascertained major differences between the children and the college students, which appeared to be related to the students' prior experiences. Because the Burgess and Lin study provided information about how each group construed the eagle situation as similar to past experiences, the study is consistent with an actor-oriented perspective. It is also consistent with the theoretical assumptions of the preparation for future learning approach because transfer occurred during a learning activity but not during sequestered problem-solving.

Although the use of qualitative methods is a part of what makes the Burgess and Lin study compatible with an actor-oriented perspective, the primary distinguishing feature of the actor-oriented approach is the effort to relinquish normative notions of what counts as transfer and immerse oneself in the learner's world instead. Because experimental methods rely on measures of improved performance to identify transfer and upon expert models, they tend to miss instances of generalizing that are captured in the actor-oriented perspective.

One could argue that the nonstandard or mathematically incorrect relations of similarity that are identified in an actor-oriented approach are captured in experimental methods also through the construct of negative transfer (National Research Council, 2000). However, there are important differences between actor-oriented transfer and negative transfer. Negative transfer is a behavioral construct (i.e., it is identified when performance is diminished as a result of prior experiences), whereas actor-oriented transfer represents a process of constructing relationships among situations. More importantly, negative transfer connotes interference. In contrast, the actor-oriented approach follows Smith et al. (1993) in conceiving of the construction of relationships of similarity that result in incorrect, unsophisticated, or non-normative performance as being potentially important building blocks for later competence, rather than something to be avoided. Being able to analyze what transfers, rather than treating transfer as a desirable performance outcome, can have positive benefits for design experiments. For example, one can identify levels of increasingly sophisticated actor-oriented transfer, which is powerful for design studies because moving up levels of sophistication may be linked with successive iterations in the design cycle (Lobato, 2003).

How the Location and Nature of Transfer Processes are Related to One's Unit of Analysis

In classical accounts of transfer in mainstream cognitive science, transfer measures a psychological phenomenon. People construct symbolic representations of an initial learning situation and of a transfer situation. Transfer occurs if these two representations are identical, if they overlap, or if a mapping can be constructed that relates features of the two representations (Anderson et al., 1995; Reed, 1993; Sternberg & Frensch, 1993). Critics maintain that these mechanisms dissociate cognition from its contexts and do not account for the structuring resources of socially-situated activity (Gruber et al., 1996; Lave, 1988). In response, Beach's (1999, 2003) consequential transitions perspective and the actor-oriented approach conceive of transfer as being distributed across mental, material, social, and cultural planes. However, the particular unit of analysis that one chooses affects which aspects of the distributed phenomenon are foregrounded in an investigation. This notion is explored briefly by comparing the units of analysis in the consequential transitions and actor-oriented perspectives.

In Beach's (1999) reconceptualization, transfer is not taken as the reproduction of something that has been acquired elsewhere; rather, it is conceived as a transition involving the transformation of knowledge, skill, and identity across multiple forms of social organization. Transitions involve a notion of progress for the learner and are understood best as a developmental process. Because these transitions involve a change in identity—a sense of self, social position, or becoming someone new—they are consequential. Consequential transitions (transfer) are not changes in the individual or in the social context but, rather, are changes in their relationship. Examples of consequential transitions include high school students taking part-time work in fast food restaurants, industrial machinists trained on mechanical machines learning to use computerized numerical control machines, and Nepali high-school students becoming shopkeepers (Beach, 1995; Beach & Vyas, 1998; Hungwe, 1999; Hungwe & Beach, 1995).

To analyze transfer as consequential transitions, Beach (1999) utilizes a developmental "coupling" (in the sense used by Varela et al., 1991) as a unit of analysis. A developmental coupling encompasses aspects of both changing individuals and changing social activity. The coupling itself is the primary unit of analysis, rather than the individual or the activity. The coupling is developmental in that one assumes that individuals move across space, time, and changing social activities, rather than being situated in an unchanging context. This coupled unit reflects the fact that both the person and the social context contribute to a consequential transition and are linked reflexively.

In the actor-oriented transfer perspective, many "players" are involved in generalizing activities: individuals who create personal connections across activities, material resources that enable certain actions and connections while constraining others, people who are oriented toward helping individuals see particular similarities or who focus learners' attention on particular regularities and away from others, and the practices in which activities takes place. Rather than using a coupled unit, the actor-oriented approach coordinates analyses at the individual and social levels (in the spirit of Cobb and Yackel, 1996). First, interview data are analyzed in order to identify the ways in which individuals generalize their learning experiences. Second, aspects of social structuring are identified in the analysis of classroom data. These aspects can include language (which encodes a culture's theory of the connections among situations, objects, and ideas), artifacts, and actions by more knowledgeable others. Finally the two analyses are coordinated. Details of this method are provided later in this chapter.

By choosing different units of analysis, the consequential transitions and the actor-oriented approaches highlight different aspects of the generalizing process. By investigating changing forms of social organization (e.g., transitions between school to work), Beach (1999) identifies elements that have been missing from other analyses (including actor-oriented transfer accounts), such as how leading activities, the power structure, and social status play a role in transfer. Although Beach includes an examination of individual behavior, such as the use of a variety of arithmetic strategies, he has not focused on psychological processes. In contrast, the actor-oriented approach is useful for identifying individuals' generalizations (including the particular relations of similarity that people construct as their mathematical strategies evolve) and for demonstrating how individuals' generalizations are constrained by sociocultural practices (specifically by features of instructional environments).

Part Two: Specific Methods Used in the Actor-Oriented Transfer Approach

In Part Two, I present two specific techniques that evolved in the course of our efforts to document actor-oriented transfer in a variety of mathematics education studies. Although these methods are informed broadly by the constant comparative method and interpretive techniques used in grounded theory (Glaser & Strauss, 1967; Strauss & Corbin, 1990), the specific techniques have evolved in the course of our efforts to document actor-oriented transfer in various studies. Previous reports (Lobato, 1996, 2003; Lobato & Siebert, 2002; Lobato et al., 2003) placed in the foreground the development of an alternative perspective on the transfer of learning while the methods remained in the background. By contrast, this chapter foregrounds the methods, while backgrounding the content-specific details that appear in earlier reports.

Method One: How to Establish Evidence of the Transfer of Learning in a Design Experiment from an Actor-Oriented Transfer Perspective

In this section, I describe a specific method used to provide evidence for the transfer of learning from an actor-oriented perspective, in the context of a design experiment. Although it is not the only method compatible with the actor-oriented transfer approach (see Ellis [2004, under review] for the identification of generalizing activity during classroom discourse rather than during interviews), it serves as a prototypical example of how we establish relations of similarity from the actor's perspective.

Structure of the Claims

In general, a case for the existence of the transfer of learning from an actor-oriented perspective in the context of a design experiment is made by providing evidence for the following claims:

- There was significant change in the student's conceptualization and performance on the transfer tasks from pre- to postinterviews.
- The student's performance on the other pre-interview tasks and during the early curriculum activities of the design experiment demonstrates limited knowledge of key conceptual components of the transfer tasks.
- A plausible relationship of similarity can be established between the student's reasoning on the transfer tasks in the postinterview and in some activity during the design experiment.
- A case can be made that the changed reasoning on the transfer tasks is not due entirely to spontaneous construction, but, rather, can be linked to what the student learned during the design experiment.

Each of these four elements is articulated using data reported in Lobato and Siebert (2002). The data were drawn from a design experiment that consisted of 30 hours of instruction during the summer in a university computer laboratory with nine high-school students, taught using an inquiry-based approach (Lobato & Thanheiser, 2000, 2002). A major goal of the design experiment was to help the students develop an understanding of slope as a ratio that measures some attribute (such as speed, steepness, sweetness, or density). This is what Simon and Blume (1994) call a "ratio-as-measure." First, I describe the task design for the students' interviews, then turn to the four claims comprising an argument for an instance of transfer from the actor-oriented perspective.

Design of the Transfer Tasks

The design of an actor-oriented transfer study typically includes the use of the same set of transfer tasks in semistructured interviews (Bernard, 1988; Ginsburg, 1997) conducted before and after the design experiment. Task creation begins as it would in the classical transfer approach by generating tasks that, from our perspective as experts, share structural features with activities from the design experiment but differ across surface features. See Figure 9.2 for the interview tasks used in the Lobato and Siebert (2002) study. These tasks were conceived by the researchers as affording opportunities to use the ideas about ratio-as-measures developed in the instruction in the novel context of a wheelchair ramp situation. Once the tasks have been designed, the observer's perspective is set aside and the approach to the tasks differs from the classical transfer approach in three ways.

First, in the classical transfer approach, the researcher uses the transfer tasks to see

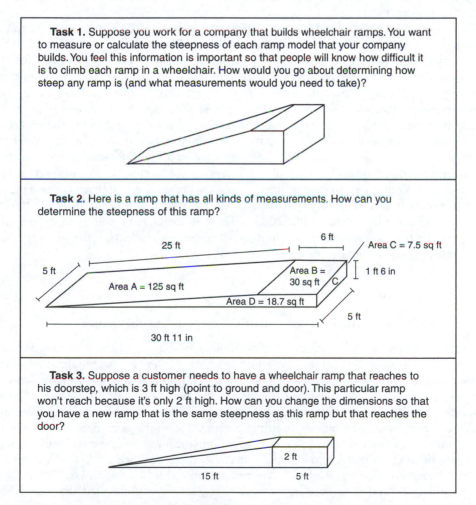

Figure 9.2 Transfer Tasks Used in Interviews.

whether the learner perceives a particular predetermined similarity. This restricts the researcher to an investigation of the psychological conditions under which an individual perceives this predetermined similarity. As a result, researchers operating from the classical transfer perspective often learn more about the theorist's construction of similarity than the learner's (Pea, 1989). In the actor-oriented perspective, the tasks are used as settings in which to explore students' often idiosyncratic ways of connecting learning and transfer situations.

Second, the central organizing metaphor for the classical transfer paradigm has been that of "applying knowledge," which suggests a static process in which the "transferor" reproduces existing relations between fixed tasks (Beach, 1999). However, in the actor-oriented transfer approach, the metaphor of production replaces that of application and transfer is conceived of as a dynamic process. In fact, the Lobato and Siebert (2002) paper provides an instance in which a student reconstructs and changes the transfer situation until it becomes similar to something he knows (see also Bransford & Schwartz, 1999; Carraher & Schliemann, 2002; Rebello et al., 2005). In this sense, the interviews conducted in the actor-oriented transfer approach collapse the "transfer in"/ "transfer out" distinction made in the preparation for future learning approach because the transfer interviews are treated as settings in which change, modification, adaptation, and learning can occur also.

Finally, at the heart of the classical transfer approach is an assumption that the initial learning and transfer situations share a similar level of complexity (for students). In the actor-oriented approach, this assumption is made for the researchers but not for the students. For example, several studies have demonstrated that a surface feature for an expert may present a structural complexity for students (Lobato, 2007; Lobato & Thanheiser, 2000, 2002; Olive & Lobato, in press). Consequently, follow-up questions in the interviews make students' conceptualization of transfer situations the object of inspection. For example, as a follow-up to Task 1 (Figure 9.2), students were asked how increasing or decreasing the length of the base or the length of the platform would affect the steepness of the ramp. To probe their conceptions of steepness, students were asked if the ramp was the same steepness throughout or whether it was steeper in some places than in others (which is surprisingly difficult for many high-school students to differentiate, as indicated in Lobato et al. [2005]). These questions allowed us to explore the complexities that accompany the attribute of steepness for students, rather than treating steepness as a surface feature of the transfer task.

Establishing the Four Claims

1. CHANGES EXIST IN THE STUDENT'S CONCEPTUALIZATION OF THE TRANSFER TASKS

In the study reported by Lobato and Siebert (2002), both researchers worked separately to infer analytic categories of the case study student's (Terry's) conceptualization of the wheelchair ramp situation from the transcripts of the pre- and postinterviews (Glaser & Strauss, 1967; Miles & Huberman, 1994; Strauss & Corbin, 1990). Because Terry's responses to the transfer tasks were complex and not understood easily, we revised our conjectures repeatedly by making multiple passes through the same data set. We sorted out troublesome cases through a process of argumentation, seeking confirming as well as disconfirming evidence, and revising our conjectures until we settled on a common set of inferred conceptions (Cobb & Whitenack, 1996; McClain & Cobb, 2001).

The most striking difference in the way that Terry comprehended the wheelchair ramp situation before and after instruction is described briefly. Analysis of all of Terry's work on the wheelchair ramp tasks led to several inferential claims: (a) height dominated Terry's image of steepness, (b) height had greater status than length, and (c) length was dependent upon height. We reported only claims for which relatively strong evidence existed; that is, when there were multiple utterances in different parts of the interview supporting the conception or when the participant offered the idea independently (as opposed to answering a question from the interviewer with a "yes" or "no" response).

For example, evidence that Terry did not conceive of length independently of height was gathered in part from the drawing he produced in response to a follow-up question to Task 1 (Figure 9.2). The interviewer asked Terry what would happen to the steepness of the ramp if the length of the base were shortened. Rather than shortening the length of the base directly, Terry fixed the leftmost tip of the ramp and moved the rightmost vertical portion of the ramp to the left until it was lined up with the spot in the diagram indicated by a dashed line (see Figure 9.3). This allowed him to use his better-developed understanding of the effect of changing the height to reason that he had made the ramp "taller and steeper." Because the length of the base of the new ramp was shorter now, decreasing the length of the base indeed had resulted in a steeper ramp. It is important to note that rather than reasoning directly about the length, Terry reasoned about the effect of changing the height and treated length as dependent upon changes in height.

We conjectured that the lack of independence of height and length in his conceptions affected negatively Terry's ability to conceive of height and length in a proportional relationship (which is necessary in order to understand slope as a ratio of height to length). In the third wheelchair ramp task (Task 3 in Figure 9.2), the interviewer asked Terry to construct a new ramp 50 percent higher than the ramp in the figure but with the same steepness. Terry had great difficulty with this question. Initially, he suggested decreasing the length from 15 ft to 10 ft, so that the height of 2 ft would increase. When the interviewer reminded Terry that the goal of the task was to create a ramp that was taller than, but just as steep as, the original ramp, Terry was stumped.

After instruction, Terry appeared to conceive of height and length independently of each other. When the interviewer returned to the proportion problem that had eluded Terry before instruction (Task 3, Figure 9.2), Terry not only solved the problem correctly, but also solved a much more difficult follow-up task; namely, to predict the height of the ramp if the length were increased from 15 ft to 16 ft. To solve this problem, Terry appeared to have created a different image of the ramp than he exhibited in the pre-interview. In this new image, Terry was able to vary height and length independently of each other. In Terry's words:

> Mmm [pause], all right, like you could pull up this [the height] a little bit [draws a 1/4 inch vertical segment extending up from the point where the incline meets the platform (see Figure 9.4)]. Like, you could lift this, but then you should make this

Figure 9.3 Author's Representation of Terry's Method for Decreasing the Length of the Base of the Wheelchair Ramp.

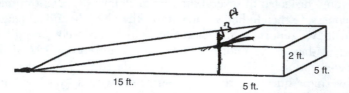

Figure 9.4 Terry's Drawing for Finding the Amount by which he Needs to Extend the Height of the Wheelchair Ramp in Order to Keep its Steepness the Same when the Length is Extended by 1 foot.

longer [draws a horizontal line segment extending left from the tip of the ramp]. So, you just add on both parts so it evens out.

Terry manipulated the length and height independently of each other. To determine the height, Terry divided 2 by 15, explaining that he was trying to determine how much height he needed for one foot of length. He correctly interpreted his quotient of 0.13 as "how high it has to be [for] one foot [of length]. So you can just make this [points to the height] point 13 feet taller." Terry's explanation indicates that he formed a ratio between height and length and interpreted the ratio appropriately for the ramp situation.

2. STUDENT HAS LIMITED KNOWLEDGE OF RELEVANT CONTENT ENTERING THE
DESIGN EXPERIMENT

In order to establish that Terry's ability to form a ratio between height and length in the postinterview resulted from the formation of a relation of similarity with an idea from the design experiment, it was important to rule out that Terry entered the design experiment with this knowledge. As a result, we looked for evidence of Terry's ability to reason proportionally before and during the design experiment. At the outset of the design experiment, Terry demonstrated many difficulties with ratio reasoning, including reasoning additively and consistently misinterpreting quotients (see Lobato and Siebert, [2002] for details). Furthermore, in the early activities of the design experiment, Terry reasoned additively rather than multiplicatively and this persisted for much of the instructional unit.

3. A RELATION OF SIMILARITY CAN BE IDENTIFIED

Evidence for actor-oriented transfer is gathered by examining a given activity for any indication of influence from previous activities. Specifically, we made several passes through the transcripts of the instructional sessions in order to identify examples of Terry's reasoning with ratios in a manner similar to that of the postinterview. It is certainly easier for the researcher if a student states explicitly how one situation is like another situation (e.g., if Terry had proclaimed, "Oh, the wheelchair situation is just like the speed situation"). However, an account of transfer should allow for the construction of relations of similarity to be unarticulated by students. Thus, establishing students' personal connections across experiences often involves gathering evidence to create a plausible inferential case.

Near the end of the design experiment (session eight of ten sessions), Terry demonstrated sophisticated proportional reasoning quite similar to that which he demonstrated in the postinterview. This occurred during an exploration of the ratio of distance to time as a measure of speed. The students had been working with the speed simulation software *MathWorlds* (Roschelle & Kaput, 1996).[1] Specifically, they were shown a character who walked 10 cm in 4 s (at a constant rate) and were asked to enter different time and distance values for a second character to make it walk at the same speed as the first character. Terry's reasoning was nonproportional at the outset of the activity but advanced dramatically during the three-hour instructional sequence. In the relevant episode, Terry explained to the whole class why walking 10 cm in 4 s was the same speed as walking 2.5 cm in 1 s.

In both the speed and the wheelchair ramp situations, Terry appeared to form a ratio as a composed unit (Lamon, 1995). In the speed situation, he created a "10 cm in 4" unit (referred to here more succinctly as a 10:4 unit). In the wheelchair ramp situation, he created a "15 ft of length to 2 ft of height" unit (or 15:2). In both situations, Terry provided explanations in which he attended to the conservation of the attribute measured by the ratio (namely, speed and steepness). In both situations, Terry appeared to partition the composed unit to create a unit ratio. In the speed situation, he partitioned the 10:4 unit into four equal parts. In the wheelchair ramp situation, he partitioned the 15:2 unit into two equal parts.

Additionally, in both situations, Terry appeared to connect the arithmetic operations of division and multiplication correctly with the quantitative operations of partitioning and iterating, respectively. In the speed situation, he partitioned the 10:4 segment into four equal parts and said that 2.5 could be found either by calculating $10 \div 4$ or finding one-fourth of 10. In the ramp situation, he appeared to partition the 15:2 unit into two equal parts and calculated $15 \div 2$ to obtain 7.5, which he interpreted correctly as 7.5 ft of length for 1 ft of height. In the ramp situation, he iterated the 7.5:1 unit 3 times (by multiplying each quantity by 3) to arrive at a length and height of 22.5 ft and 3 ft, respectively. In the speed situation, he talked about the 2.5:1 unit as going into the 10:4 unit four times. In sum, Terry appeared to create a set of relations of similarity between the speed and the ramp situations.

4. THE STUDENT'S REASONING IS NOT ENTIRELY SPONTANEOUS

Finally, we need to consider that Terry's proportional reasoning in the wheelchair ramp situation might have been a spontaneous construction, one that was unconnected to his experiences in the design experiment. The mathematics education literature on proportional reasoning suggests strongly that Terry's reasoning in the postinterview is unlikely to be a spontaneous construction. Research indicates that the task of creating a ramp with the same steepness when the length was increased from 15 ft to 16 ft is particularly difficult for students, given that 15 and 16 are relatively prime (Harel & Behr, 1989; Kaput & Maxwell-West, 1994; Lamon, 1994). This suggests that Terry's demonstration of sophisticated proportional reasoning on this task likely was rooted in prior experiences involving proportional reasoning, rather than a spontaneous construction. Furthermore, Terry's dramatic change from the pre- to postinterview suggests strongly that the design experiment influenced his reasoning, especially because he entered the study exhibiting very limited proportional reasoning. Additionally, our ability to locate specific relations of similarity between Terry's explanation for the speed and wheelchair ramp tasks suggests that Terry's work in the postinterview was not a spontaneous construction.

Method Two: Coordinating Social and Individual Levels of Generalizing Activity in the Actor-Oriented Transfer Approach

The method used in the actor-oriented approach presented above highlights the role of the learner's agency in the generalization of learning. I turn now to methods for linking conceptually individual generalizations with social aspects of generalizing activity. The idiosyncratic forms of transfer often identified through the use of the actor-oriented transfer perspective may seem arbitrary or random at first, especially when considering generalizations that result in incorrect mathematical performance (such as Jarek's work shown in Figure 9.1). However, our work on the construct of focusing phenomena is demonstrating a basis by which actor-oriented transfer is constrained (Ellis & Lobato, 2004; Lobato, 2003, 2005; Lobato & Ellis, 2002a, 2002b; Lobato et al., 2003).

Focusing phenomena are features of classroom environments that regularly direct students' attention toward certain (mathematical) properties or patterns when a variety of features compete for students' attention. Focusing phenomena emerge not only through the instructor's actions but also through mathematical language, features of the curricular materials, and the use of artifacts. This notion has allowed us to account for the ways in which features of social environments influence what students attend to mathematically, which, in turn, becomes a central basis from which students generalize their learning experiences (Lobato et al., 2003). Rather than studying the occurrence of transfer as a function of controlling external conditions, as is typically the case in transfer studies (de Corte, 1999; Gentner et al., 2003), the construct of focusing phenomena affords the study of transfer as a constrained, socially situated phenomenon.

In this section, I describe the specific method used to coordinate social and individual aspects of generalizing activity from the actor-oriented transfer perspective. The details of our original focusing phenomena study are reported in Lobato et al. (2003). The results of the study are backgrounded in this section and the method is foregrounded. The method draws upon the constant comparative method of grounded theory (e.g., Strauss & Corbin, 1990) and extends the approach presented in Method One above by accounting for the ways in which instances of actor-oriented transfer are afforded and constrained by features of classroom environments. The data described briefly in this section are drawn from a study situated in a reform-oriented, high-school, introductory algebra class that emphasized the use of real-world situations. The study consisted of two sets of video-taped individual interviews of a subset of better performing students and video-taped classroom instruction of 15 90-minute lessons on slope and linear functions.

Phase One: Analysis of Individual Generalizations

The design of the individual component of the study is similar to that described above in Method One. Thus, it is discussed briefly here, highlighting only the unique features of the design and presenting the data necessary to make sense of the later analysis of the classroom data. Purposive sampling (Patton, 1990) was used to select seven (of 36) students to participate in semistructured interviews (Bernard, 1988; Ginsburg, 1997). Because we were interested in the generalization of learning, it was important to select interview participants who were poised to learn from the instruction (so that there would be something to generalize). Therefore, all interview participants were identified by the classroom teacher as students who were prepared for the curriculum, based on the criteria of average to high mathematics grades, willingness to participate in classroom discussions, and discipline in completing homework assignments.

Interview tasks were designed to include what, from our perspective as content experts, represented near and far transfer tasks. It is important to note that it was not our intent to evaluate the curriculum or to assess all the aspects of learning, which is one way in which we distinguish our studies of transfer from studies of learning. We heed Barnett and Ceci's (2005) warning that assessments may be misleading if they merely measure children's ability to reproduce specified procedures in the classroom without assessing the transfer of broader principles to novel problems. By giving students problems that they have not seen in their instruction, we gain a better picture both of what has been learned and of how learning experiences influence students' comprehension of new settings.

Once the interviews had been conducted, we set aside our expert assumptions and used the actor-oriented transfer perspective to look for any evidence of the influence of the instruction on students' reasoning patterns, rather than predetermining what would count as transfer. It was striking that all of the students who were able to write an equation for a given line or table wrote "$y = \Box \pm \Box x$" (rather than the more standard $y = mx + b$) and referred to the value in the first box as the "starting point" and the value in the second box as "what it goes up by." The students appeared to have generalized a linear equation as "y equals the 'starting point' plus 'what it goes up by' x," which was unusual and clearly tied to the language and inscriptions used in class.

Analysis of the interpretations that students held for the value of the second box in $y = \Box \pm \Box x$ (which is the m or slope value) proceeded through the use of open coding (Strauss, 1987), a process used to infer categories of meaning. Two members of the research team developed analytic categories independently and coded the transcripts from Interview One. We sorted out troublesome cases through a process of argumentation and settled on a common set of categories. We tested for the validity of the categories by reviewing the transcripts for Interview One, seeking confirming as well as disconfirming evidence. We then applied the categories to the data from Interview Two and made appropriate modifications to the categories.

The analysis revealed three different meanings for m: (a) a difference in y values, (b) a difference in x values, and (c) the scale of the x axis (a particularly troubling conception because the nature of the function is not dependent upon the value chosen for the scale of either axis). In each case, the students appeared to have conceived of m incorrectly as a difference and generalized this understanding to the novel interview tasks, rather than interpreting m correctly as a ratio of the change in values of the dependent variable for each one-unit change in the corresponding independent variable. From a classical transfer approach, we would have concluded that there was a massive failure to transfer. However, the actor-oriented perspective revealed distinct and compelling evidence that the students were generalizing, albeit in ways that resulted in incorrect mathematical performance, on the basis of features of the classroom instruction. In response, we conducted a detailed analysis of the data video-taped in the classroom in order to understand how the instructional environment supported these unintended generalizations.

Phase Two: Analysis of Features of the Instructional Environment

Our primary goal was to understand how the instructional environment might have supported the development of the students' generalizations of m as a difference, rather than as a ratio. One method for coordinating psychological and sociocultural accounts of learning is Cobb and Yackel's (1996) Emergent Perspective, in which collective units of analysis are used to identify emergent mathematical practices, social norms, and socio-mathematical norms and then coordinated with psychological analyses of individuals' conceptions, general beliefs, and mathematical beliefs (e.g., see Stephan et al., 2003). Because our goals were more constrained, namely, to make sense of generalizing activity rather than all of the learning, we used individuals' generalizations (as inferred from the interviews) as our starting point, then sought to explain how the instructional environment (unwittingly) supported each of the three categories of meaning for *m*.

The classroom analysis drew generally upon the constant comparative method used in the development of grounded theory (Glaser & Strauss, 1967; Strauss & Corbin, 1990), which involves constantly comparing data as they are analyzed against the conjectures generated thus far in the data analysis and revising the conjectures accordingly (Cobb & Whitenack, 1996; McClain & Cobb, 2001). In addition to being compared against conjectures, incidents of the participants' activity in the classroom are compared against one another. This gives rise to general themes or patterns and leads to an ongoing iterative refinement of the broad theoretical categories developed from the data (Cobb et al., 2001).

More specifically, we started by investigating one of the most striking and ubiquitous elements of the interviews, namely, the use of the phrase "goes up by" to refer to the *m* value in a linear equation. We coded each classroom transcript for every instance of the "goes up by" language. Open coding (Strauss, 1987) was used to identify and name five meanings for "goes up by": (a) the change in *y* values of the function per one-unit change in *x* values (what the line goes up by), (b) the change in *y* values of the function (what the *y*s go up by), (c) the change in *x* values of the function (what the *x*s go up by), (d) the scale of the *x* axis (what the *x*s go up by), and (e) the scale of the *y* axis (what the *y*s go up by). Only the first is a mathematically correct meaning for slope (which was used by the teacher); the other interpretations represent differences (and were used repeatedly by the students). Because of the ambiguity of the language, the students were able to engage in discussions in which the teacher may have thought the students were using "goes up by" to refer to a ratio, whereas, in actuality, they often used it to refer to a difference (for details, see Lobato et al., 2003).

Additionally, we compiled all of the class episodes in which slope was discussed formally or informally. For each of the three types of meaning for *m*, we assembled the relevant classroom episodes. For example, over half of the interview participants had referred incorrectly to the *m* value as the scale of the *x* axis. We then located every instance of reference to the scale of the *x* axis in class. These instances clustered around the use of the graphing calculator. Next, we applied open coding to all of the relevant graphing calculator episodes in order to identify the ways in which the use of the calculator may have focused attention on the scale of the *x* axis.

As instructional categories emerged, such as the "goes up by" language or the particular ways in which the graphing calculators were used, we employed axial coding (Strauss, 1987) to identify conceptual relationships between instructional categories and categories for the meaning of *m*. As a result, the central theoretical construct of focusing phenomena emerged and informed further passes through the data.

We continued with this process until we had created a plausible set of conceptual connections between classroom events and each of the three meanings for *m* demonstrated in the interviews (see Figure 9.5). Analysis of the classroom data revealed four focusing phenomena: (a) the ambiguous "goes up by" language, (b) the use of uniformly ordered data tables, (c) the ways in which graphing calculators were used, and (d) an emphasis on uncoordinated sequences and differences. The details provided in Lobato et al. (2003) demonstrate how the focusing phenomena regularly directed students' attention to various differences—Δy, Δx, and the scale of the *x* axis—rather than to the coordination of two quantities.

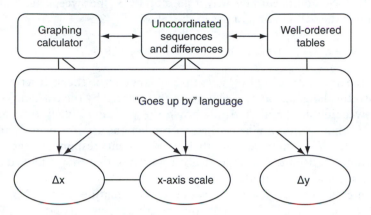

Figure 9.5 Focusing Phenomena and their Relationships to One Another and to Students' Generalizations.

Figure 9.5 illustrates what Strauss and Corbin (1994) call "theory" in the grounded theory approach, namely the "plausible relationships proposed among concepts and sets of concepts" (p. 278). As seen in Figure 9.5, these four categories interact and affect one another. In particular, the "goes up by" language occurred throughout the entire instructional unit and served to facilitate the attention on differences within each of the other three focusing phenomena.

To demonstrate how two focusing phenomena work together, consider an example in which both the use of well-ordered tables and the "goes up by" language appear to draw students' attention to slope as the difference in *y* values, rather than as a ratio between *y* and *x* values. The curricular unit on linear functions opened with a lesson that had many features desirable in reform-oriented classrooms. Students collected data to investigate the relationship between the distance of an overhead projector from a wall and the enlargement factor between real and projected images. Messy, real-world data were used, rather than "canned" data. Students were actively involved, and the teacher tried to use informal language that appeared to be meaningful to the students. While the data were being recorded in a table (see Table 9.1), the teacher invited the students to look for patterns, as indicated in the following excerpt from the transcript:

Ms. R: What does that 10.3 tell us, then?
Student: It goes up by 3.

Table 9.1 Data Collected by Students Showing the Enlargement Factor of an Overhead Projector Placed Varying Distances from the Wall

Distance of the projector from the wall (in meters)	Enlargement factor
1	2.2
2	4.8
3	7.8
4	10.3
5	
6	

Ms. R: It goes up by 3? So you mean, this way it goes up by 3 [she sweeps her hand vertically down the column of *y* values in the table]?

Student: Yeah.

Ms. R: That looks like a good pattern. Approximately 3? Very good.

This excerpt includes the first instance of the "goes up by" language in the instructional unit. The students used this language first, which was appropriated by the teacher. The teacher gestured by sweeping her hand vertically down the *y* column, likely focusing additional attention on the *y* values. When asked to predict the enlargement factor when the projector was 5 m and 6 m from the wall, several students responded that the enlargement factors would be 13 and 16, respectively, suggesting that they attended to the difference between successive *y* values.

After the data were collected, the teacher introduced the equation $y = \square \pm \square x$ to express the relationship shown in the table. To obtain the value for the second box (i.e., the *m* or slope value), the teacher explicitly directed the students to focus on the change in *y* values by asking: "So if we took one of the measurements that we have right now, how would we get to the next number? Would you add exactly 2 or exactly 3?" The students suggested finding the average of the change in *y* values, which is 2.7. The teacher summarized the meaning of 2.7 by stating: "To get to the next number, you add approximately 2.7, so 2.7 is how much you do to one number to get to the next number." In order to produce an equation (in this case, $y = 0 + 2.7x$ or $y = 2.7x$), the teacher instructed the students to "remember what is the starting value and what you are doing to get to the next value." Thus, she directed the students' attention to the change in *y* values, rather than to the dependency relationship between the corresponding *x* and *y* values. It was possible to do this and generate a correct equation because the data were uniformly ordered, with the change in *x* values (Δx) equal to 1. In these cases, the change in *y* values resulted in the correct slope value.

However, the influence of beginning the unit with a uniformly ordered table in which $\Delta x = 1$ was seen throughout the unit. Every time a table was used in which $\Delta x \neq 1$ (all the tables used in the unit were uniformly ordered), many students associated *m* with the difference in *y* values. A typical example occurred during the warm-up activity for Day 10. Students worked individually to find the rate of change of a function depicted in tabular form. The values in the *x* column were 0, 3, 6, and 9, and the corresponding *y* values were 20, 32, 44, and 56. During the class discussion of the problem, the teacher guided a student through the process of calculating the rate of change, reminding him to divide his response of 12 by the change in *x* values. She noted the widespread response from students that the slope of the function was the change in *y* values: "A lot of people put 12 as their slope. You're right that it is going up by 12 when *x* goes up by 3, but we want to know what it goes up by if *x* is only going up by 1." Although the teacher was able to use the "goes up by" language to coordinate the change in y values with the change in *x* values in a uniformly ordered table, many students appear to have focused on the slope as the difference in *y* values.

Discussion: Implications of the Use of Alternative Transfer Perspectives and Methods in Design Experiments

In considering the implications for design experiments, it is tempting to address only the implications of adopting an actor-oriented transfer perspective because that is the approach I have been developing. However, this plays inadvertently into the "linear march of progress" (see Cobb, 2005) by conceiving of an alternative transfer perspective as overcoming the limitations of the classical approach and thus replacing it. In contrast, Cobb points to a different metaphor for comparing theoretical perspectives, namely, that of "co-existence and conflict." In keeping with this latter metaphor, I claim that there is no one best approach to conceive of the transfer of learning. Instead, there are points of tension and compatibility among the various emergent models of such transfer, and trade-offs that each approach makes, given the purposes for which each perspective was developed.

Consider for a moment the trade-offs made by using ethnographic methods (in the actor-oriented transfer perspective) and experimental methods (in the preparation for future learning perspective). These two transfer models are compared because they utilize different methods but are both well suited to classroom studies. By using experimental methods, the preparation for future learning approach capitalizes on the logic of stochastic causality to make causal claims about the effectiveness of particular preparatory activities on students' ability to perform on transfer tasks (Schwartz & Martin, 2004). As a trade-off, the amount of generalization of learning that is captured is underestimated because of reliance on an observer's perspective, despite the fact that the preparation for future learning approach captures more instances of generalizing than the classical transfer approach does. Additionally, experimental methods are better suited to answer "is there" questions (i.e., Is there a systematic effect?) than "why or how" questions (i.e., How is the instructional environment influencing the ways in which individuals construe novel situations?) (Maxwell, 2004).

In contrast, the grounded theory methods used in the actor-oriented perspective allow researchers to posit new conceptual constructs, explore conceptual connections between instructional features of environments and individuals' generalizations, and capture a broad range of generalizing activity by detecting the influence of prior learning experiences on activities in novel settings. The trade-off is the small scale of the work, the associated difficulties in generalizing researchers' claims and accounting for selection bias, and the emphasis on model formation, rather than validation (Sloane & Gorard, 2003).

A Multistage Approach to Design Experiments

Rather than choosing a single transfer perspective, researchers could select one that is appropriate for the stage in which they are operating in a multistage model of design research. Researchers from the fields of engineering and product design typically have conceived of design research as entailing multiple stages of cyclic research and design (Kelly, 2003). Bannan-Ritland (2003) brings a multistage design model from engineering to education research by positing four stages: (a) informed exploration (involving needs analysis, brain-storming, and the development of an initial prototype), (b) enactment (cycles of intervention, design, and redesign on a small scale), (c) local impact (a cycle of formative evaluation, revision, implementation, and summative evaluation to establish internal validity), and (d) broader impact (studies of implementation, adaptation, and diffusion with summative evaluation to establish external validity). The first two stages fit roughly into what some scholars have called the context of discovery and the last two fit into the context of verification (Holton, 1998). In the context of discovery, exploratory studies are conducted that lead typically to the generation of hypotheses, concepts, categories, and models; in the context of verification, theory-driven, systematic experimentation is conducted in an effort to achieve model estimation or model validation (Kelly, 2004; Sloane & Gorard, 2003).

Stage-Appropriate Use of Transfer Models

Discovery Stages

The actor-oriented transfer perspective is well suited for the initial stages of design research for three reasons. First, the actor-oriented transfer perspective provides a way to examine the processes employed by novices in the generalization of learning, thus responding to the opening epigraph for this chapter. If one considers that the classical transfer approach investigates only highly valued, expert generalizations, then it is not surprising to find overwhelming evidence in the literature for the lack of transfer of learning because we know that novices do not make the same set of connections as experts.

Second, the actor-oriented approach provides a way to use information gained through the investigation of students' generalizations (including incorrect and non-normative generalizations) to inform revisions in curricular materials and pedagogical approaches during iterative cycles of instructional design. For example, in our focusing phenomena study (Lobato et al., 2003), we identified relationships among instructional features, what students attended to mathematically, and their accompanying generalizations, with sufficient detail to suggest principled ways in which we could make design responses. Preliminary findings of two subsequent revisions of the instructional approach suggest that: (a) by regularly directing students' attention to the coordination of covarying quantities, they are more likely to generalize slope as a ratio, and (b) it is possible to identify a nuanced and differentiated view of levels of transfer (Ellis & Lobato, 2004; Lobato, 2005; Lobato & Ellis, 2002c). Identifying levels of increasing sophistication in non-normative or incorrect displays of the transfer of learning is related to Minstrell's (2001) articulation of facets of students' understanding of physics. In Minstrell's approach, one can identify a particular facet as indicative of more complex and sophisticated understanding than another facet, even when both facets represent incorrect or non-normative reasoning. Similarly, one can identify levels of actor-oriented transfer, which is powerful for design studies because moving up levels of sophistication may be linked with successive iterations in the design cycle.

Third, through the notion of focusing phenomena, the actor-oriented transfer perspective can link conceptually features of instructional environments with students' reasoning patterns and performance. The notion of focusing phenomena addresses the need for examining the conceptual links and processes by which some events influence other events (which Maxwell [2004] calls process causation and Miles and Huberman [1994] call local causality). This is how Shadish et al., prominent proponents of experimental research, distinguish between causal description and causal explanation:

> The unique strength of experimentation is in describing the consequences attributable to deliberately varying a treatment. We call this *causal description*. In contrast, experiments do less well in clarifying the mechanisms through which and the conditions under which that causal relationship holds—what we call *causal explanation*.
>
> (2002: 9)

Our work with focusing phenomena in an actor-oriented transfer perspective has afforded an investigation of causal explanations and of "how and why" questions in the initial stages of design research, leaving causal description and "what works" questions for the verification stages.

Verification Stages

I have argued that, in the early stages of design research, it is important to dissociate from normative or correct performance as a criterion for transfer in order to permit an investigation of how students' generalizations (whether correct or not) are afforded and constrained by specific instructional practices. However, by the time the design study moves to the definitive trial stage, the design innovation should be working well enough to support productive, actor-oriented transfer for students, in which case transfer perspectives based on expert models could be used. For example, the classical transfer approach may work well for studying mature understanding in Bannan-Ritland's (2003) final stage of design research (the "broader impact" phase). The avoidance of sequestered problem-solving and the inclusion of measures to assess learning readiness make the preparation for future learning perspective (Bransford & Schwartz, 1999) an attractive model for studies conducted at the "local impact" stage of design research.

By using experimental methods, the preparation for future learning approach allows researchers to make claims about systematic effects regarding the effectiveness of preparatory and learning activities on students' performance on novel tasks. At some point, instructional innovations that have been revised based on information gathered from the actor-oriented transfer approach should be validated experimentally, which could be accomplished by using the preparation for future learning approach. Furthermore, the design used in the preparation for future learning approach to compare several instructional approaches allows researchers to test their conclusions against plausible alternative interpretations.

Remaining Challenges

When using different methods for different stages of design research, a central challenge remains of how to conduct the various studies so that they are connected conceptually and can inform each other. Without such a connection, researchers could demonstrate significant effects of instructional treatments but still be unable to explain why a particular approach works. Resolving this dilemma is beyond the scope of this chapter. However, I conclude by suggesting that the resolution involves two important areas of work—assessment and the design of studies that can bridge the discovery and verification stages. With respect to assessment, more sophisticated techniques for assessing non-normative instances of transfer need to be designed in a form that can be used on a large scale (e.g., online or by using paper-and-pencil tests with multiple-choice items) in the verification stages of a design experiment. With respect to bridging the discovery and verification stages, it is important to note that the independent variable in many experimental designs is the instructional approach. In contrast, the independent variable in our focusing phenomena studies is an interaction between teachers' actions, other instructional features, and the mathematical saliency of particular features for students. Thus, in order to move from small-scale ethnographic work to large-scale experimentation, it is important to conduct bridging studies in which this interactional variable changes while other factors, such as students' entering knowledge of key concepts, are controlled.

Conclusions

Although the methods used in the classical transfer approach are well established, the methods used in most of the alternative transfer perspectives are emerging. Therefore, one goal of this chapter was to present two specific methods that emerged during efforts to document the transfer of learning from an actor-oriented perspective in a variety of mathematics education studies. One method is used to identify instances of actor-oriented transfer in classroom settings; the second method is used to coordinate social and individual aspects of generalizing activity.

However, it is important that research methods are not presented as isolated techniques. Thus, the second major goal of the chapter was to demonstrate the relationships between transfer theory and research methods. By comparing five theoretical perspectives on transfer, I illustrated how a close examination of the particular research methods refine the definition of transfer used in a given perspective, and, reflexively, how a shift in one's definition of transfer influences the methods that one employs to measure such transfer. Similarly, the use of experimental versus ethnographic methods to identify instances of transfer affects the nature of the research questions that one can pose related to the generalization of learning. Finally, the theoretical assumptions that one makes about whether transfer is a psychological or a distributed phenomenon affect the unit of analysis that one takes methodologically.

By conceiving of the methods used to measure transfer as a function of the theoretical assumptions that one makes, we were able to explore the points of tension and compatibility among various models of transfer. As a result of describing what is gained and lost by adopting a particular perspective, it is possible to transcend pitting one perspective against another and, instead, to see the selection of a transfer perspective and its accompanying methods as dependent upon its appropriateness for the stage in which one is operating in a multistage model of design research.

Acknowledgments

The research described in this chapter is supported by the National Science Foundation under Grant REC-9733942. One of the design experiments was conducted in a computer laboratory funded by the National Science Foundation under Grant DUE-9751212. The views expressed do not reflect official positions of the Foundation.

I offer my gratitude to Anthony E. Kelly, John Baek, and Christina De Simone for their thoughtful feedback on an earlier draft of this paper.

Note

1 A special *MathWorlds* script was designed by Jeremy Roschelle and Janet Bowers for the Generalization of Learning project, in which students could control the starting position, distance, and time of characters who traveled across the screen.

References

Anderson, J. R., Corbett, A. T., Koedinger, K. & Pelletier, R. (1995). Cognitive tutors: Lessons learned. *Journal of the learning sciences, 4*, 167–207.

Bannan-Ritland, B. (2003). The role of design in research: The integrative learning design framework. *Educational Researcher, 32*, 21–24.

Barnett, S. & Ceci, S. J. (2002). When and where do we apply what we learn? A taxonomy for far transfer. *Psychological Bulletin, 128*(4) 612–637.

Barnett, S. & Ceci, S. J. (2005). Assessing whether learning transfers beyond the classroom. In J. P. Mestre (ed.), *Transfer of learning from a modern multidisciplinary perspective* (pp. 295–312). Greenwich, CT: Information Age Publishing.

Beach, K. D. (1995). Activity as a mediator of sociocultural change and individual development: The case of school—work transition in Nepal. *Mind, Culture, and Activity*, 2, 285–302.

Beach, K. D. (1999). Consequential transitions: A sociocultural expedition beyond transfer in education. In A. Iran-Nejad & P. D. Pearson (eds), *Review of research in education*, Volume 24 (pp. 101–140). Washington, DC: American Educational Research Association.

Beach, K. D. (2003). Consequential transitions: A developmental view of knowledge propagation through social organizations. In T. Tuomi-Gröhn & Y. Engeström (eds), *Between school and work: New perspectives on transfer and boundary-crossing* (pp. 39–62). Oxford: Elsevier.

Beach, K. D. & Vyas, S. (1998). Light pickles and heavy mustard: Horizontal development among students negotiating how to learn in a production activity. Paper presented at the Fourth International Conference on Cultural Psychology and Activity Theory, Aarhus, Denmark, June.

Bernard, H. E. (1988). *Research methods in cultural anthropology*. Beverly Hills, CA: Sage.

Bransford, J. D. & Schwartz, D. L. (1999). Rethinking transfer: A simple proposal with multiple implications. In A. Iran-Nejad & P. D. Pearson (eds), *Review of research in education*, Volume 24 (pp. 61–100). Washington, DC: American Educational Research Association.

Burgess, K. & Lin, X. (1998). Study of adaptive and non-adaptive expertise. Unpublished manuscript, Vanderbilt University, Nashville, TN.

Carraher, D. & Schliemann, A. D. (2002). The transfer dilemma. *Journal of the Learning Sciences*, 11, 1–24.

Cobb, P. (2005). Introduction of abstraction theme. Presentation at a meeting funded by the National Science Foundation: An international working conference: Addressing the transfer dilemma, San Diego, CA, January.

Cobb, P. & Whitenack, J. (1996). A method for conducting longitudinal analyses of classroom videorecordings and transcripts. *Educational Studies in Mathematics*, 30, 213–228.

Cobb, P. & Yackel, E. (1996). Constructivist, emergent, and sociocultural perspectives in the context of developmental research. *Educational Psychologist*, 31, 175–190.

Cobb, P., Stephan, M., McClain, K. & Gravemeijer, K. (2001). Participating in classroom mathematical practices. *Journal for the Learning Sciences*, 10(1&2), 113–163.

de Corte, E. (1999). On the road to transfer: An introduction. *International Journal of Educational Research*, 31, 555–559.

diSessa, A. & Wagner, J. (2005). What coordination has to say about transfer. In J. P. Mestre (ed.), *Transfer of learning from a modern multidisciplinary perspective* (pp. 121–154). Greenwich, CT: Information Age Publishing.

Ellis, A. B. (2004). Relationships between generalizing and justifying: Students' reasoning with linear functions (doctoral dissertation, University of California, San Diego and San Diego State University). *Dissertation Abstracts International*, 65(06), 2127 (UMI No. 3137248).

Ellis, A. B. (under review). *A taxonomy for categorizing generalizations: Generalizing actions and reflection generalizations*.

Ellis, A. B. & Lobato, J. (2004). Using the construct of "focusing phenomena" to explore links between attentional processes and "transfer" in mathematics classrooms. In J. Lobato (chair), Attentional processes, salience, and "transfer" of learning: Perspectives from neuroscience, cognitive science, and mathematics education. Symposium conducted at the annual meeting of the American Educational Research Association, San Diego, CA, April.

Gentner, D. (1989). The mechanisms of analogical learning. In S. Vosniadou & A. Ortony (eds), *Similarity and analogical reasoning* (pp. 199–241). Cambridge: Cambridge University Press.

Gentner, D., Loewenstein, J. & Thompson, L. (2003). Learning and transfer. *Journal of Educational Psychology*, 95, 393–408.

Ginsburg, H. P. (1997). *Entering the child's mind: The clinical interview in psychological research and practice*. Cambridge: Cambridge University Press.

Glaser, B. G. & Strauss, A. L. (1967). *The discovery of grounded theory: Strategies for qualitative research*. Hawthorne, NY: Aldine.

Greeno, J. G. (1997). Response: On claims that answer the wrong questions. *Educational Researcher*, 26, 5–17.

Greeno, J. G. & The Middle School Mathematics through Application Project Group (1998). The situativity of knowing, learning, and research. *American Psychologist, 53*(1), 5–26.

Greeno, J. G., Collins, A. M. & Resnick, L. (1996). Cognition and learning. In D. Berliner & R. Calfee (eds), *Handbook of educational psychology* (pp. 15–46). New York: Macmillan.

Greeno, J. G., Smith, D. R. & Moore, J. L. (1993). Transfer of situated learning. In D. K. Detterman & R. J. Sternberg (eds), *Transfer on trial: Intelligence, cognition, and instruction* (pp. 99–167). Norwood, NJ: Ablex.

Gruber, H., Law, L., Mandl, H. & Renkl, A. (1996). Situated learning and transfer. In P. Reimann & H. Spada (eds), *Learning in humans and machines: Towards an interdisciplinary learning science*. Oxford: Pergamon.

Harel, G. & Behr, M. (1989). Structure and hierarchy of missing value proportion problems and their representation. *Journal of Mathematical Behavior, 8*, 77–119.

Hickey, D. T. & Pellegrino, J. W. (2005). Theory, level, and function: Three dimensions for understanding transfer and student assessment. In J. P. Mestre (ed.), *Transfer of learning from a modern multidisciplinary perspective* (pp. 251–294). Greenwich, CT: Information Age Publishing.

Hickey, D. T., Kindfield, A. C. H., Horwitz, P. & Christie, M. A. (2003). Integrating curriculum, instruction, assessment, and evaluation in a technology-supported genetics environment. *American Educational Research Journal, 40*, 495–538.

Holton, G. (1998). *The scientific imagination*. Cambridge, MA: Harvard University Press.

Hungwe, K. N. (1999). Becoming a machinist in a changing industry. *Dissertation Abstracts International, 61*(05), 1741 (UMI No. 9971926).

Hungwe, K. & Beach, K. (1995). Learning to become a machinist in a technologically changing industry. Poster session on *Learning and development through work* presented at the annual meeting of the American Educational Research Association, San Francisco, CA, April.

Kaput, J. J. & Maxwell-West, M. (1994). Missing-value proportional reasoning problems: Factors affecting informal reasoning patterns. In G. Harel & J. Confrey (eds), *The development of multiplicative reasoning in the learning of mathematics* (pp. 235–287). Albany, NY: State University of New York Press.

Kelly, A. E. (2003). Research as design: The role of design in educational research. *Educational Researcher, 32*, 3–4.

Kelly, A. E. (2004). Design research in education: Yes, but is it methodological? *Journal of the Learning Sciences, 13*, 115–128.

Laboratory of Comparative Human Cognition (1983). Culture and cognitive development. In P. H. Mussen (ed.), *Handbook of child psychology: Vol. 1. History, theory, and methods* (pp. 295–356). New York: Wiley.

Lamon, S. J. (1994). Ratio and proportion: Cognitive foundations in unitizing and norming. In G. Harel & J. Confrey (eds), *The development of multiplicative reasoning in the learning of mathematics* (pp. 89–120). Albany, NY: State University of New York Press.

Lamon, S. J. (1995). Ratio and proportion: Elementary didactical phenomenology. In J. T. Sowder & B. P. Schappelle (eds), *Providing a foundation for teaching mathematics in the middle grades* (pp. 167–198). Albany, NY: State University of New York Press.

Lave, J. (1988). *Cognition in practice: Mind, mathematics, and culture in everyday life*. Cambridge: Cambridge University Press.

Lobato, J. (1996). Transfer reconceived: How "sameness" is produced in mathematical activity (doctoral dissertation, University of California, Berkeley, 1996). *Dissertation Abstracts International, 58*(02), 406 (UMI No. 9723086).

Lobato, J. (2003). How design experiments can inform a rethinking of transfer and vice versa. *Educational Researcher, 32*, 17–20.

Lobato, J. (2005). Attention-focusing and the "transfer" of learning. In J. Emanuelsson & M. F. Pang (chairs), *Contrasting different perspectives on the object of learners' attention*. An invited symposium of the Special Interest Group on Phenomenography and Variation Theory conducted at the 11th Biennial Conference of the European Association for Research on Learning and Instruction (EARLI), Nicosia, Cyprus, August.

Lobato, J. (2007). How rethinking assumptions about the "transfer" of learning can inform research, instructional practices, and assessment. In C. Rasmussen & M. Carlson (eds), *Making the connection: Research and teaching in undergraduate mathematics*. Washington, DC: Mathematical Association of America.

Lobato, J. & Ellis, A. B. (2002a). An analysis of the teacher's role in supporting students' connections between realistic situations and conventional symbol systems. *Mathematics Education Research Journal, 14,* 99–120.

Lobato, J. & Ellis, A. B. (2002b). The focusing effect of technology: Implications for teacher education. *Journal of Technology and Teacher Education, 10,* 297–314.

Lobato, J. & Ellis, A. B. (2002c). Paradox or possibility: The generalization of situated reasoning. Paper presented at the annual meeting of the American Educational Research Association, New Orleans, LA, April.

Lobato, J. & Siebert, D. (2002). Quantitative reasoning in a reconceived view of transfer. *Journal of Mathematical Behavior, 21,* 87–116.

Lobato, J. & Thanheiser, E. (2000). Using technology to promote and examine students' construction of ratio-as-measure. In M. L. Fernández (ed.), *Proceedings of the twenty-second annual meeting of the North American Chapter of the International Group for the Psychology of Mathematics Education*, Volume 2 (pp. 371–377). Columbus, OH: ERIC (ERIC Document No. ED446945).

Lobato, J. & Thanheiser, E. (2002). Developing understanding of ratio as measure as a foundation for slope. In B. Litwiller (ed.), *Making sense of fractions, ratios, and proportions: 2002 Yearbook* (pp. 162–175). Reston, VA: National Council of Teachers of Mathematics.

Lobato, J., Clarke, D. & Ellis, A. (2005). Initiating and eliciting in teaching: A reformulation of telling. *Journal for Research in Mathematics Education, 36,* 101–136.

Lobato, J., Ellis, A. B. & Muñoz, R. (2003). How "focusing phenomena" in the instructional environment afford students' generalizations. *Mathematical Thinking and Learning, 5,* 1–36.

MacKay, D. (1969). *Information, mechanism, and meaning.* Cambridge, MA: MIT Press.

Marini, A. & Genereux, R. (1995). The challenge of teaching for transfer. In A. McKeough, J. Lupart & A. Marini (eds), *Teaching for transfer: Fostering generalization in learning* (pp. 1–20). Mahwah, NJ: Lawrence Erlbaum Associates.

Maxwell, J. (2004). Causal explanation, qualitative research, and scientific inquiry in education. *Educational Researcher, 33,* 3–11.

McClain, K. & Cobb, P. (2001). The development of sociomathematical norms in one first-grade classroom. *Journal for Research in Mathematics Education, 32,* 234–266.

Miles, M. B. & Huberman, A. M. (1994). *Qualitative data analysis* (2nd ed.). Thousand Oaks, CA: Sage.

Minstrell, J. (2001). Facets of students' thinking: Designing to cross the gap from research to standards-based practice. In K. Crowley, C. Schunn & T. Okada (eds), *Designing for science: Implications from everyday, classroom, and professional settings* (pp. 415–444). Mahwah, NJ: Lawrence Erlbaum Associates.

National Research Council, Committee on Developments in the Science of Learning (2000). Learning and transfer. In J. D. Bransford, A. L. Brown & R. R. Cocking (eds), *How people learn: Brain, mind, experience, and school* (pp. 51–78). Washington, DC: National Academy Press.

Olive, J. & Lobato, J. (in press). Research on technology and the development of understanding of rational number. In K. Heid & G. Blume (eds), *Research on technology and the teaching and learning of mathematics*. Greenwich, CT: Information Age Publishing.

Packer, M. (2001). The problem of transfer, and the sociocultural critique of schooling. *Journal of the Learning Sciences, 10*(4), 493–514.

Patton, M. Q. (1990). *Qualitative evaluation and research methods* (2nd ed.). Newbury Park, CA: Sage.

Pea, R. (1989). *Socializing the knowledge transfer problems* (Report No. IRL89–0009). Palo Alto, CA: Institute for Research on Learning.

Rebello, S., Zollman, D., Albaugh, A. R., Engelhardt, P. B., Gray, K. E., Hrepic, Z., et al. (2005).

Dynamic transfer: A perspective from physics education research. In J. Mestre (ed.), *Transfer of learning from a modern multidisciplinary perspective* (pp. 217–250). Greenwich, CT: Information Age Publishing.

Reed, S. K. (1993). A schema-based theory of transfer. In D. K. Detterman & R. J. Sternberg (eds), *Transfer on trial: Intelligence, cognition, and instruction* (pp. 39–67). Norwood, NJ: Ablex.

Reed, S. K., Ernst, G. W. & Banerji, R. (1974). The role of analogy in transfer between similar problem states. *Cognitive Psychology, 6,* 436–450.

Rogoff, B. & Gardner, W. (1984). Adult guidance of cognitive development. In B. Rogoff & J. Lave (eds), *Everyday cognition: Its development in social context* (pp. 95–116). Cambridge, MA: Harvard University Press.

Roschelle, J. & Kaput, J. (1996). SimCalc MathWorlds for the mathematics of change. *Communications of the ACM, 39,* 97–99.

Schwartz, D. L. & Bransford, J. D. (1998). A time for telling. *Cognition and Instruction, 16,* 475–522.

Schwartz, D. L. & Martin, T. (2004). Inventing to prepare for future learning: The hidden efficiency of encouraging original student production in statistics instruction. *Cognition and Instruction, 22,* 129–184.

Schwartz, D. L., Bransford, J. D. & Sears, D. (2005). Efficiency and innovation in transfer. In J. P. Mestre (ed.), *Transfer of learning from a modern multidisciplinary perspective* (pp. 1–52). Greenwich, CT: Information Age Publishing.

Shadish, W. R., Cook, T. D. & Campbell, D. T. (2002). *Experimental and quasi-experimental designs for generalized causal inference.* Boston: Houghton Mifflin.

Simon, M. A. & Blume, G. W. (1994). Mathematical modeling as a component of understanding ratio-as-measure: A study of prospective elementary teachers. *Journal of Mathematical Behavior, 13,* 183–197.

Sloane, F. C. & Gorard, S. (2003). Exploring modeling aspects of design experiments. *Educational Researcher, 32,* 29–31.

Smith, J. P., diSessa, A. & Roschelle, J. (1993). Misconceptions reconceived: A constructivist analysis of knowledge in transition. *Journal of the Learning Sciences, 3,* 115–163.

Stephan, M., Cobb, P. & Gravemeijer, K. (2003). Coordinating social and psychological analyses: Learning as participation in mathematical practices. In M. Stephan, J. Bowers & P. Cobb (eds), *Supporting students' development of measuring conceptions: Analyzing students' learning in social context* (*Journal for Research in Mathematics Education* Monograph No. 12, pp. 67–102). Reston, VA: National Council of Teachers of Mathematics.

Sternberg, R. J. & Frensch, P. A. (1993). Mechanisms of transfer. In D. K. Detterman & R. J. Sternberg (eds), *Transfer on trial: Intelligence, cognition, and instruction* (pp. 25–38). Norwood, NJ: Ablex.

Strauss, A. L. (1987). *Qualitative analysis for social scientists.* Cambridge: Cambridge University Press.

Strauss, A. L. & Corbin, C. (1990). *Basics of qualitative research: Grounded theory procedures and techniques.* Newbury Park, CA: Sage.

Strauss, A. L. & Corbin, J. M. (1994). Grounded theory methodology: An overview. In N. K. Denzin & Y. S. Lincoln (eds), *Handbook of qualitative research* (pp. 273–285). London: Sage.

Thorndike, E. L. (1906). *Principles of teaching.* New York: Seiler.

Varela, F. J., Thompson, E. & Rosch, E. (1991). *The embodied mind: Cognitive science and human experience.* Cambridge, MA: MIT Press.

10 A Methodology for Documenting Collective Activity

Chris Rasmussen
San Diego State University

Michelle Stephan
University of Central Florida

Introduction

Mathematics and science education has witnessed an increase in the number of design research studies in which researchers spend extended amounts of time in classrooms implementing and investigating interventions to support students' conceptual growth (Kelly & Lesh, 2000; Suter & Frechtling, 2000). One issue of theoretical and pragmatic concern that has emerged from design research is documentation of the normative or collective ways of reasoning that develop as learners engage in mathematical or scientific activity. The purpose of this chapter is to explicate a methodology for documenting learners' collective activity. Although methodologies for documenting the learning of individuals are well established in the mathematics and science education fields, methodologies for detailing the intellectual activities of classroom cultures are less so. Therefore, we maintain a focus in this chapter on a methodology for documenting collective activity, an important endeavor in its own right.

We define collective activity as the normative ways of reasoning of a classroom community. We stress that collective activity is a social phenomenon in which mathematical or scientific ideas become established in a classroom community through patterns of interaction. To give an analogy, consider a couple, let us call them Sam and Pat, that, as a pair or dyad, are characterized aptly as argumentative. All of us know couples whom we would describe as having a particular characteristic: "Oh, the Smiths, they're a fun couple, or the Robinsons are argumentative." In other words, being argumentative is a quality of the pair. However, we might say that, as individuals, neither Pat nor Sam is particularly argumentative. Being argumentative is a characteristic of the collective activity of the couple (or, in this case, dyadic activity) and is not necessarily a characteristic of each individual. Similarly, the collective activity of a mathematics class refers to the normative ways of reasoning that develop as learners solve problems, explain their thinking, represent their ideas, etc. These normative ways of reasoning that can be used to describe the mathematical or scientific activity of, say, Mr. Jackson's class may or may not be appropriate descriptions of the characteristics of each individual student in the class. This last point is critical to our notion of collective activity because it offers a view of the social context of the classroom that affords students *opportunities* for conceptual growth without necessarily being deterministic.

The issue of collective activity is one that resonates with a variety of social theories, among them activity theory (Davydov & Radzikhovskii, 1985; Leont'ev, 1981), sociocultural theory (Lerman, 1996; Moschkovich, 2004; van Oers, 1996), and socioconstructivist theory (Bauersfeld et al., 1988; Cobb, 2000; Simon, 2000; Yackel, 1997). These social theories of learning offer analytical lenses for viewing and explaining the complexities of learning in classrooms; however, detailed methods for documenting collective activity under the guidance of these theoretical orientations are underdeveloped.

Rigorous qualitative methodologies are needed to document the collective activity of a class over extended periods of time. We address this need by first detailing the theoretical orientation that can serve as the basis for such an analysis. Then, we describe Toulmin's (1969) model of argumentation, which serves as an analytic tool in the methodology. Next, we outline a three-phase, methodological approach for documenting the collective activity of a classroom community and highlight two criteria using Toulmin's scheme for determining when ideas begin to function "as if shared." Our use of the phrase "as-if-shared" is intended to emphasize that normative ways of reasoning in a community function *as if* everyone shares this way of reasoning. However, there is individual variation within collective activity.[1] The usefulness of a methodology that examines collective activity, rather than individual variation, within a group's normative ways of reasoning is two-fold. First, it offers an empirically grounded basis for design researchers to revise instructional environments and curricular interventions (cf., Brown & Campione, 1994). Second, it is a mechanism for comparing the quality of students' learning opportunities across different enactments of the same intervention. Then, we illustrate the two criteria using Toulmin's scheme with an example from a first-grade class learning to measure and from a university course in differential equations. These two content areas are chosen in order to increase the likelihood that the methodology we describe is accessible to a wide range of readers and applicable across content domains. We conclude by discussing issues of the generalizability and trustworthiness of the methodology.

Theoretical Orientation

A research methodology expresses both the methods used in analysis and the theoretical orientation that underpins such methods because the particular methods one chooses are influenced by the theoretical lens one is using to view the results of an investigation (Moschkovich & Brenner, 2000; Skemp, 1982). For example, if a researcher or teacher desires to create a model of how individuals construct rate of change concepts, then a cognitive theory that views learning as primarily a mental construction of accommodations and assimilations might be most useful. On the other hand, if a researcher or teacher is attempting to analyze the activity of a community of learners, social theories can be more useful.

One particular lens that has been helpful for analyzing students' learning in social contexts is that of symbolic interactionism (Blumer, 1969), which treats interaction among people as central to the creation of meaning. From this perspective, learning refers to the conceptual shifts that occur as a person participates in and contributes to the meaning that is negotiated in a series of interactions with other individuals. Such a view is consistent with theories of argumentation that define an argument as a social event in which individuals engage in genuine argumentation (Krummheuer, 1995). Genuine argumentation occurs when the persons involved engage in a back-and-forth flow of contributions (often in verbal, gestural, and symbolic forms), in which each person interprets actively the meaning of another's statement and adjusts his or her response based upon the meaning they infer. Often, these adjustments and interpretive actions are at the implicit level of students' awareness. Moreover, genuine argumentation requires a social situation in which participants explain and justify their thinking routinely. Such a social situation does not happen by accident; it requires the proactive role of a knowledgeable teacher.

Social theories, such as symbolic interactionism, that treat meaning as created in interactions among individuals serve as the theoretical underpinnings of the methodology we describe in this chapter. Also at the foundation of our methodology are those social theories that place prominence on the roles that tools and gestures play in mathematical development. Our methodology takes as primary the notion that learning is created in argumentations when individuals engage language, tools, symbols, and gestures (cf. Meira, 1998; McNeill, 1992; Nemirovsky & Monk, 2000; Rasmussen et al., 2004). This view is consistent with distributed theories of intelligence in which learning is said to be distributed across tools and symbols (Pea, 1993).

With this theoretical basis, we now turn explicitly to our central analytic tool, Toulmin's argumentation scheme. Because collective activity refers to the negotiated normative ways of reasoning that evolve as learners engage in genuine argumentation, we use argumentations that occur in public discourse (i.e., discussions that can be heard by all participants, usually whole-class discussions) as our unit of analysis. Next, we explain Toulmin's (1969) model of argumentation and how it can be used to document when particular mathematical ideas begin to function as if they were shared.

Toulmin's Argumentation Scheme

In his seminal work, Toulmin (1969) created a model to describe the structure and function of certain parts of an individual's argument. Figure 10.1 illustrates that, for Toulmin, the core of an argument consists of three parts: the data, the claim, and the warrant.

In any argumentation, the speaker makes a claim and presents evidence or data to support that claim. Typically, the data consist of facts or procedures that lead to the conclusion that is made. For example, imagine a fourth-grade class that has been asked to find the area of a 4 × 7 rectangle. During a discussion, Jason makes a *claim* that the answer is 28. When pushed by the teacher to say more about how he got his answer, Jason says, "I just multiplied the length times the width." In terms of Toulmin's scheme, Jason has made a *claim* of 28 and given evidence (*data*) in the form of his method for obtaining his answer. Although his explanation is clear to us, other students may not

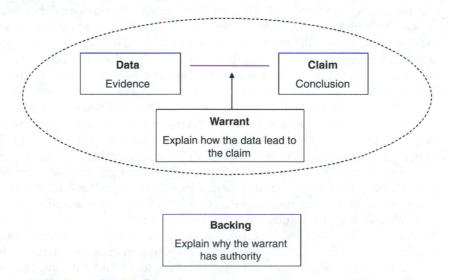

Figure 10.1 Toulmin's Model of Argumentation.

understand what Jason's statement "multiply length times width" has to do with obtaining 28 as the answer. In fact, a student (or the teacher) may challenge Jason to clarify how his evidence relates to his conclusion, so Jason must present some kind of bridge between the data and the conclusion. When this type of challenge is made and a presenter provides more clarification that connects the data to the conclusion, the presenter is providing a *warrant,* or a connector between the two.

Often, the content of a warrant is algorithmic (Forman et al., 1998) in that the presenter states more precisely the procedures that led to the claim. In our fourth-grade example, Jason might provide the following warrant: "Because you multiply length times width to find area, I just said 4 × 7 and that's 28." A student may see now how Jason went from data to claim with such an explanation but not understand or agree with the content of the warrant used: "I see where you get 28 now, but *why* do you multiply 4 by 7 to get 28?" The mathematical authority (or validity) of the argument can be challenged, and the presenter must provide a backing to justify why the warrant, and therefore the core of the argument, is valid. Then, Jason might provide a backing by drawing unit squares inside the rectangle and saying, "You see, you have 4 rows of 7 squares. That's why you can multiply 4 by 7 to get the answer."

Documenting Argumentation

In general, documenting the structure and function of students' argumentations is facilitated by the following rules of thumb. Claims are the easiest type of contribution to identify in an argumentation and consist of either an answer to a problem or a mathematical statement for which the student may need to provide further clarification. Data are less easy to document but usually involve the method or mathematical relationships that lead to the conclusion. Most times, warrants remain implied by the speaker and are elaborations that connect or show the implications of the data to the conclusion. Finally, a backing is identified typically by answering the question: "Why should I accept your argument (the core) as being sound mathematically?" Backings, therefore, function to give validity to the argumentation.

Documenting ongoing collective argumentation is much more difficult than we have portrayed in the example above. Normally, classroom conversations do not occur in the clean crisp manner we have used to illustrate Toulmin's (1969) model. Often, many claims are made simultaneously, such as when students get different answers for the same problem. In such cases, the researchers must record the data, warrants, and backings, if any, that students give as each claim is being justified and which claims are rejected in the classroom. Sometimes, the class seems to agree on one answer (claim) but may offer different warrants and backings as support. This situation occurs frequently in classes in which open-ended problem-solving is used because teachers encourage a variety of solution processes. To use our 4″ × 7″ rectangle example again, the class may agree that the conclusion is 28 square inches and the students may use the same data (e.g., a drawing of the rectangle cut into 4 rows of 7″ unit squares), yet several different warrants might emerge in their arguments. For example, a student may say that he or she used the picture to count all the squares one by one and got 28 (W1). A different warrant that ties the data or inscription to the conclusion may be that a student added 4 seven times (W2), added 7 four times (W3), or merely multiplied 4 by 7 (W4). We have seen at least six different warrants (and two backings) in support of the same conclusion. Analyzing the collective argumentations that emerge in classrooms and shift in quality over time can shed sight on the mathematical ideas and learning that gain currency within that community. In the next section, we describe more specifically the general, three-phase approach we have developed for documenting collective activity in classrooms—an approach that capitalizes on analyzing the collective argumentations that evolve over time.

The Three-Phase Approach to Documenting Collective Activity

To document the collective activity of a classroom community we developed a three-phase approach. Classroom teaching experiments are a form of design research in which the goals include investigating and developing effective means to support student learning of particular content (Cobb et al., 2003). Previous reports (Rasmussen et al., 2004; Stephan & Rasmussen, 2002; Stephan et al., 2003) placed the collective mathematical learning in the foreground, whereas the method itself remained in the background. The goal of this chapter is to offer a broader theoretical account by foregrounding the method itself and backgrounding all the content-specific details that appear in earlier reports. We encourage the reader to refer to these earlier reports for more information on the collective activity of the various classroom communities that we have studied. This approach evolved in the course of our efforts to document the collective activity in different classroom teaching experiments.

Phase One

In our classroom teaching experiments, we gather data from multiple sources: video-recordings of each classroom session, video-taped interviews with students, field notes from multiple researchers, reflective journals (from the teacher and/or researchers), and students' work. With such a vast amount of data to organize, we start Phase One by creating transcripts of every whole-class discussion from all the class periods under consideration. Then, we watch video-recordings of every whole-class discussion and note each time a claim is made by a student or the teacher. Next, we use Toulmin's (1969) model to create an argumentation scheme for each claim that was made. This is a time-intensive process that yields an "argumentation log" across whole-class discussions for several weeks. In our differential equations experiment, we found anywhere from two to seven different conclusions being made and/or debated in any one class period. The argumentation log orders all of the argumentation schemes sequentially.

For reliability purposes, a team of at least two researchers is needed to draw up an argumentation scheme (or a sample thereof) and then to verify and/or refute the argumentation scheme for each instance of a claim or a conclusion. We come to agreement on the argumentation scheme by presenting and defending our identification of the argumentation elements (i.e., the data, conclusion, warrant, and backing) to each other. In general, paying particular attention to the *function* that various contributions make is critical for identifying properly the elements of each argumentation. For example, is the student's contribution functioning to provide a bridge between the data and the conclusion? If so, we would label it as a warrant. In the fourth-grade example, we pointed to several rules of thumb for identifying these elements.

Phase Two

The second phase of the analysis involves taking the argumentation log as data itself and looking across all the class sessions to see what mathematical ideas expressed in the arguments become part of the group's normative ways of reasoning. We developed these two criteria for when mathematical ideas function as if shared:

1   When the backings and/or warrants for an argumentation no longer appear in students' explanations (i.e., they become implied rather than stated or called for explicitly, no member of the community challenges the argumentation, and/or if the argumentation is contested and the student's challenge is rejected), we consider that the mathematical idea expressed in the core of the argument stands as self-evident.
2   When any of the four parts of an argument (the data, warrant, claim, or backing) shifts position (i.e., function) within subsequent arguments and is unchallenged (or, if contested, challenges are rejected), the mathematical idea functions as if it were shared. For example, when students use a previously justified claim as unchallenged justification (the data, warrant, or backing) for future arguments, we would conclude that the mathematical idea expressed in the claim has become a part of the group's normative ways of reasoning.[2]

We then make a "mathematical ideas" chart for each day that includes three columns: (a) a column for the ideas that now function as if shared, (b) a column of the mathematical ideas that were discussed and that we want to keep an eye on to see if they function subsequently as if they were shared, and (c) a third column of additional comments, both practical and theoretical, or connections to related strands of literature. For example, a page out of our charts from the differential equations teaching experiment for this second phase of analysis looked like Table 10.1.

Table 10.1 is only one page out of a series of daily charts that took the argumentation logs for each day as data and summarized the days on which we observed certain mathematical ideas moving from the "keep-an-eye-on" column to the "as-if-shared" column. As we create these charts, we look at previous days' charts to see which ideas in the second and third columns move to the first or second column in the current day's argumentation schemes (from right to left). This is consistent with Glaser and Strauss' (1967) constant comparison method in which we look for regularities in students' argumentations one class period at a time. We make conjectures about argumentations in which ideas function as if they were shared and look for further evidence (or refutations) of these conjectures in subsequent class periods.

Table 10.1 A Page of the Mathematical Ideas Charts

Ideas that function as-if-shared	Ideas to keep-an-eye-on	Additional comments
The slopes are the same horizontally for autonomous differential equations (shifts from conclusion to data)	The graphs are merely horizontal shifts of one another for autonomous differential equations	The rate of change is based on an equation, not on a real-world setting; relate basis of claims to RME heuristics
No real-world backing is given	Using the rate of change equation as data to show that slopes are invariant	Making predictions about solutions functions as if it is a shared goal (sociomathematical norm?)
		Isomorphism between graphic and analytic techniques

Note
RME = Realistic Mathematics Education.

Phase Three

In the third phase of the analysis, we take the pages of charts from Phase Two, list the ideas from the "as-if-shared" column, and organize them around common mathematical activities. For example, in the differential equations teaching experiment, we took our list of mathematical ideas and organized several of them under the general activity of predicting individual solution functions. Hence, the third phase of the analysis involved taking the list of as-if-shared mathematical ideas and organizing them according to the general mathematical activity in which the students were engaged when these ideas emerged and became established.

We define this level of general mathematical activity as a *classroom mathematical practice*. This definition of a classroom mathematical practice is different from earlier definitions put forth by Cobb and Yackel (1996), which are restricted to one mathematical idea. In our methodological approach, a classroom mathematical practice is a collection of as-if-shared ideas that are integral to the development of a more general mathematical activity. For example, in the differential equations teaching experiment, the fifth classroom mathematical practice, which we called "Creating and organizing collections of solution functions," entailed the following four normative ways of reasoning:

1   The graphs of solution functions do not touch or cross each other (at least for the equations studied thus far).
2   Two graphs of solution functions are horizontal shifts of each other for autonomous differential equations.
3   Solution functions can be organized with different inscriptions.
4   The phase line signifies the result of structuring a space of solution functions.

Moreover, the collection of classroom mathematical practices is different from the typical scope and sequence for a course in two ways. First, classroom mathematical practices, unlike a typical scope and sequence, can be established in a non-sequential time fashion. In a previous analysis that documented the constitution of classroom mathematical practices in a first-grade mathematics class (Stephan et al., 2003), the various practices proceeded in a more or less sequential fashion: the initiation and constitution of the first practice preceded the initiation and constitution of the second practice in time, etc. In our experience, a linear temporal development of classroom mathematical practices is not always the case. The second way in which classroom mathematical practices differ from a typical scope and sequence is that classroom mathematical practices can emerge in a non-sequential structure. On some occasions, we characterized some as-if-shared ideas as parts of more than one practice. This suggests that the practices themselves can have structural overlap, rather than a timing overlap of when the practices are initiated and constituted (Stephan & Rasmussen, 2002).

Now that we have described the general, three-phase approach to documenting the evolution of classroom mathematical practices, we will use examples from two different classroom teaching experiments to illustrate the two criteria that we developed for documenting the researcher's belief that an idea is taken as-if-shared.

Criterion One: The Dropping Off of Warrants and Backings

Consider an example from a first-grade classroom discussion on linear measurement to help illustrate the first criterion for determining when an idea becomes part of a group's normative ways of reasoning. This example is significantly more difficult to interpret than the fourth-grade example because there will be a number of individuals contributing to the emerging argumentation rather than only one student. During small group work, students had been asked to measure the length of items with their feet. The teacher noticed that the students had two different ways of counting their paces, as pictured in Figure 10.2; some students counted "one" as they began stepping (see Figure 10.2(a)), and others counted "two" as they began stepping (see Figure 10.2(b)). The teacher's mathematical goal was to support the students' interpreting the purpose of their measuring activity as one of covering space. Therefore, she organized a follow-up, whole-class discussion in which the students could contrast these two methods of measuring.

In the transcript below, Sandra explains her method of measuring and Alice contrasts Sandra's method with her own.

Sandra: Well, I started right here and went 1 [she starts counting as in Figure 10.2(a)], 2, 3, 4, 5, 6, 7, 8 [the teacher stops her].

Teacher: Were people looking at how she did it? Did you see how she started? Who thinks they started a different way? Or did everybody start like Sandra did? Alice, did you start a different way or the way she did it?

Alice: Well, when I started, I counted right here [she counts as in Figure 10.2(b)], 1, 2, 3.

Teacher: Why is that different . . . [from what Sandra did]?

Alice: She put her foot right here [she places it next to the rug] and went 1 [she counts like Sandra], 2, 3, 4, 5.

Teacher: How many people understand that Alice says that what she did and what Sandra did was different?

In analyzing the preceding episode using Toulmin's (1969) model of argumentation, we notice that Sandra first presented the data that led to her conclusion (of eight paces). The data consisted of her method of starting at a particular spot on the rug and counting 1 with the next step, 2, 3, 4, and so on until the teacher stopped her. In this portion of Sandra's argumentation, her warrant was not explicitly present. Later, the teacher will ask questions and provide visual supports that lead the students to articulate the warrant for Sandra's argumentation more explicitly. The teacher asked if other students started differently from how Sandra began. Alice presented different data and a conclusion: "Well, when I started, I counted right here. 1, 2, 3." Her conclusion was three paces, and her evidence for her conclusion consisted of displaying her method of measuring in front of the class.

When the teacher asked whether other students in the class understood the difference in the methods, many students expressed confusion. The problem in understanding the

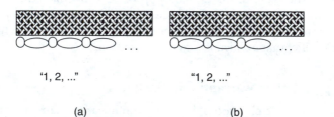

"1, 2, ..."   "1, 2, ..."

(a)   (b)

Figure 10.2 Two Methods of Counting as Students Paced the Length of a Rug.

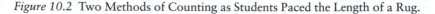

difference between the methods lies in the difficulty of distinguishing which paces were or were not being counted. As soon as the students lift his or her foot, the record of their pace disappears. Therefore, after the students had paced three or four paces, it was difficult for: (a) the demonstrating student to communicate what "1" referred to and, (b) the other students to see what the demonstrator meant by the first pace. The teacher then asked questions to support a discussion where the warrants (i.e., more information connecting a student's method to his or her answer) would become more explicit. The teacher asked a student, Melanie, to measure the rug while she placed a piece of masking tape at the beginning and end of each pace. In the dialogue below, we will see that the record of pacing preserved by the masking tape contributed to the teacher's agenda of making the difference between the two methods explicit. In Toulmin's terms, the warrants were articulated.

Melanie: Sandra didn't count this one [she puts her foot in the first taped space]; she just put it down and *then* she started counting 1, 2. She didn't count this one, though [she points to the space between the first two pieces of tape].

Teacher: So she would count 1, 2 [she refers to the first three spaces because the first space is not being counted by Sandra]. How would Alice count those?

Melanie: Alice counted them 1, 2, 3.

Teacher: So, for Alice, there's 1, 2, 3 there, and, for Sandra, there's 1, 2.

Melanie: Because Alice counted this one [she points to the first taped space] and Sandra didn't, but if Sandra . . . [had] counted it, Alice would have counted three, and Sandra would have too. But Sandra didn't count this one, so Sandra has one less than her.

In this portion of the dialogue, Melanie used the record of paces to communicate clearly the difference between the methods, why Sandra counted the first three spaces as two, and why Alice counted them as three. This instance is an example of how a student's explanation serves the function of making explicit how each student's method (way of starting to count) related to the two conclusions they were drawing (i.e., three paces or two); in Toulmin's (1969) terms, the warrants for each claim were made explicit. The record of paces played a crucial role in supporting the emergence of warrants that could be interpreted readily by the students who were having difficulty understanding the previous explanations.

Thus far, the core of the collective emerging argumentation looks like Figure 10.3. Notice that the warrants and the data are very similar in their content. Toulmin (1969) explains that it is not the *content* of what is said that necessarily characterizes statements as warrants, but rather the *function* that the statements serve. Initially, explaining one's

---

The core	
Data 1 and 2:	Two different methods of measuring, i.e., counting feet in particular ways.
Claims 1 and 2:	Two different resulting measures.
Warrants 1 and 2:	Counting with the *placement* of the first foot as "1" (Figure 10.2(a)) versus counting the *placement* of the first foot as "2" (Figure 10.2(b)). The arguments are supported by the masking tape record.

Figure 10.3 The Core of the Collective Emerging Argumentation.

method of measuring served merely as data for the claims (i.e., the resulting measure) that each student made. However, when challenged by the teacher to articulate the *difference* between the two methods more explicitly, the students explained their procedures again, with the intention of making the difference in the methods more explicit. Their explanations served the function of detailing how the resulting measures (their claims) related to the method they used (the data).

It is important to note that, although the teacher and the students had tried to make their interpretations more clear, the focus of the discussion had concerned only *how* the students counted their paces when they measured and the different results that their methods obtained. Yet, the teacher's intention was to lead a discussion in which measuring became an activity of covering space. In the next part of the dialogue, the teacher pushed the mathematical agenda (that of measuring becoming about covering space) by asking a pivotal question:

Teacher: What do you think about those two different ways—Sandra, Alice, or anybody else? Does it matter? Or can we do it either way? Hilary?

Hilary: You can do it Alice's way or you can do it Sandra's way.

Teacher: And it won't make any difference?

Hilary: Yeah, well, they're different. But it won't make any difference because they're still measuring but just a different way and they're still using their feet. Sandra's leaving the first one out and starting with the second one, but Alice does the second one and Sandra's just calling it the first.

Phil: She's 15 [he is referring to the total number of feet Sandra counted when she paced]. Alice went to the end of the carpet [he means the beginning of the carpet]. Sandra started after the carpet. Hers is lesser 'cause there's lesser more carpet. Alice started here and there's more carpet. It's the same way, but she's ending up with a lesser number than everybody else.

Alex: She's [Sandra's] missing one right there. She's missing this one right here [he points to the first taped space]. She's going one but this should be one cause you're missing a foot so it would be shorter. Since you leave a spot, it's gonna be a little bit less carpet.

The question that the teacher posed: "Does it matter?" raised the level of the discussion from talking about which paces the students counted to whether it made a difference which method was used. Such questions served the function of eliciting, according to Toulmin (1969), the backing for the core of the emerging argumentation. The teacher's question prompted the students to verify which method they believed was valid for their purposes. As seen by the explanations above, several students argued that, if one measured as Sandra did, part of the rug would not have been counted (i.e., they would have missed a spot). Critical to this emerging discussion is the fact that the students used the record of pacing to support their interpretations by pointing to the tape on the rug as they referred to the space they counted as "one." In this way, reasoning with tools was an integral part of the collective meaning that emerged during this discussion.

Eliciting backings is crucial for supporting the evolution of increasingly sophisticated mathematical ideas. If the preceding discussion had remained at the level of warrants, any method of measuring would have been acceptable. However, the teacher and the students negotiated what counted as an acceptable measuring interpretation by providing backings for the emerging argumentation. As it happened, backings involving not missing any space were judged as acceptable in this class, and the group's collective goal of measuring was to cover amounts of space as determined by the length of the item.

After these discussions, the students explained their measuring in whole-class discussions by counting with the method shown in Figure 10.2(b). Further, they no longer made their warrants explicit or provided backings to justify why they measured that way and none of them objected or challenged anyone's interpretation any further. As noted earlier, when warrants become implicit and there is no longer a need to provide backings in public discourse, we claim that a mathematical idea (i.e., measuring is an activity of covering space) functions as if shared. This constitutes the first criterion for documenting when a particular mathematical idea can be characterized as a collective activity:

- *Criterion One:* When the backings and/or warrants for an argumentation no longer appear in students' explanations (i.e., they become implied rather than being stated explicitly or called for), no member of the community challenges the argumentation, and/or if the argumentation is contested and the student's challenge is rejected, we consider that the mathematical idea expressed in the core of the argument stands as self-evident.

This criterion is consistent with the one developed by Yackel (1997), in which she contends that mathematical practices are established when students no longer need to provide the supports (i.e., warrants and backings) for their conclusions. When we attempted to use this criterion to analyze the collective activity of the students in the differential equations teaching experiment, we found that it was useful, but insufficient, for our analysis. The students in the differential equations class used backings infrequently to support their arguments; therefore, we often were unable to use the first criterion to analyze their learning.[3] This constraint enabled us to develop a new criterion for documenting when mathematical ideas become a part of a group's collective activity. In the next section, we use examples of students' argumentations in the differential equations design experiment to describe this new criterion.

Criterion Two: The Shifting Function of Argumentation Elements

The example we use to illustrate the second criterion for documenting collective activity occurred during a 15-week classroom teaching experiment in an introductory course in differential equations that was taught from a reform-oriented approach (see also Rasmussen et al., 2004, 2005; Stephan & Rasmussen, 2002). According to our mathematical ideas charts from Phase Two (see the sample given in Table 10.1), the idea that the slopes at a certain population (P) value remain constant across time (t) for autonomous differential equations[4] first emerged as a topic of argumentation in the second class period. However, from the discourse below, we see that no backings were provided by the students to support why two slopes at the same P value across time should be the same, and the teacher did not push for one in this case. The problem that the students had solved involved trying to estimate the number of rabbits predicted by the rate of change equation $dP/dt = 3P$ at half-year increments and quarter-year increments. The students had argued that the solution function starting with an initial population of ten rabbits would be an exponential curve, and the teacher drew the graph shown in Figure 10.4 on the board.

The teacher then asked the students what the graph of the solution would look like if they started with an initial population of 20 rabbits instead of ten. In the following discussion, the students began to think about the structure of the space of solution functions by relating the slope on one solution curve (with the initial condition of 10) to the slope on the curve with the initial condition of 20.

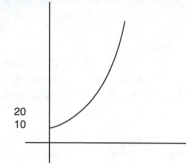

Figure 10.4 The Teacher's Graph of the Fate of the Rabbit Population Starting with Ten
  Rabbits.

Teacher: What if you start at 20?
Andy: It would increase quicker. There's more rabbits so you would start off, they'd
   have more babies, it'd just go faster like further [*sic*] up on the 10 curve.
Rick: If you just look at the graph you have already, when you're at 20, it's already
   a steep increase.
Teacher: So, at 20, you already have a steep increase over here [she points to where P
   is 20 on the 10 curve].
Rick: It's just the same thing.
Teacher: So this kind of increase here might be more like a similar increase here. This
   rate of change [she marks a slope line on the 10 curve] is similar to the
   rate of change here [she marks the same slope line at P = 20 and t = 0] (see
   Figure 10.5).

Using Toulmin's (1969) model of argumentation, Andy's claim was that "it"
increases quicker. The data for his conclusion were that there were more rabbits (20,
not 10), so the population here would have more babies. He then went on to make
a more complex conclusion; namely, that "it'd just go faster, like further [sic] up on
the 10 curve." Rick expanded on Andy's argument by claiming that the slope or rate
of change is just the same at t = 0, P = 20, as it is on the 10 curve at the same P = 20
height. The data and warrant for this emerging argument were coconstructed by
Rick and the teacher when Rick explained that one can "just look at the graph . . ."
and the teacher pointed to the graph on the board as Rick explained the method.

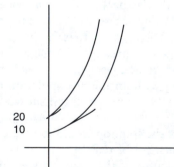

Figure 10.5 The Teacher's Sketch of the Relation Between the Slopes on Two Solution
  Curves.

At this point, neither the teacher nor the students challenged the legitimacy of this argument; that is, why it should be self-evident that the slopes at the same P value will be the same across time. Therefore, because no backing was provided during this argumentation and it was the first instance that such an argument was given, we cannot claim that the *invariance of slopes across time* functioned as if shared at this point, the second class session of the semester. Rather, we continued to look at the mathematical ideas charts to see if this idea, which we had placed in the "keep-an-eye-on" column, emerged again from the students and if backings or challenges to the argument were present. The most we can claim in this episode is that the students were beginning to create and organize a slope field[5] by finding patterns in the slopes of the solutions.

The idea that slopes remain invariant across time re-emerged on the fourth day of class as the students filled out a slope field for the differential equation $dP/dt = 3P(1 - P/100)$. During the whole-class discussion of this problem, the teacher asked John to share his group's insights. John came to the front of the classroom and said that his group discussed that the slopes would be the same all the way across the t axis for any particular P value. To support his claim that they would, John drew on an argument from previous class periods in which they had discussed the solutions to the equation $dP/dt = 3P$. In terms of Toulmin's (1969) model, we see that a prior argument (for $dP/dt = 3P$) served as the warrant for the second part of John's argument for the equation $dP/dt = 3P(1 - P/100)$:

John: We were kind of thinking about it for awhile and . . . I looked back at our original question, what we were doing like even before the rabbits, when we had dP/dt was just equal to 3P and we were just trying to . . . we had the 10, we had the 30 and 50, and we were just going with 3P and we had no cap [he draws the axes and indicates 10, 30, and 50]. . . . When we discussed it in class, we said that the 10, the rate of change, is going to be very slow if we just started off with ten rabbits [he draws the solution function corresponding to the initial condition of 10, similar to that shown in Figure 10.4]. And we said that the rate of change immediately is going to be increasing a lot more when we start off at 30 [he draws in the solution function corresponding to the initial condition of 30]. When we look back on it, when we started at time, when we started at ten rabbits [he points to a population of 10 at time zero on his drawing], and we got to, say, the three years or whatever that it went by and we finally got to 30 rabbits [he draws in a slope mark at population 30 on the solution corresponding to the initial condition of 10], even though we started off with 30 rabbits over here [he gestures to the slope at the initial condition of 30], it had the same slope as that 10 did at time like two years. So I applied this or our whole group applied this to our problem now.

In this part of the argument, John made a claim that "the slopes are the same." For this argument, John's evidence to support his claim involved describing that the rate of change at 10 is slow and the rate of change at 30 is faster, and he drew a graph on the board to inscribe these ideas. The warrant for how the evidence relates to his claim that the slopes will be the same all the way across was that if you go along the 10 curve until you get to the point where P = 30, you can draw in the slope and notice that it is the same as the slope where P = 30 on the 30 curve (empirically-based reasoning). Rather than give a backing for this argument, John proceeded with the remainder of his argument for $dP/dt = 3P(1 - P/100)$ as if he took it for granted that the other students agreed with his findings:

John: That they're initially going to start off and have a little different slopes but they're all going to be, kinda, when it reaches a certain point, they're all going to have the same slope at certain numbers. When 15, when they finally get to 30, that's going to have the same slope as 30 starting off at time zero. So we kinda all decided that all the slopes are going to be the same.

According to Toulmin's (1969) model of argumentation, the structure of John's argument can be summarized as shown in Figure 10.6. John provided no backing for why anyone should believe that this argument holds true. As a matter of fact, no backing was provided for the prior argument about why the slopes should be the same for a given P for the equation $dP/dt = 3P$, especially because this invariance does not hold for all equations. However, another student, Jen, summarized his contribution by stating:

Jen: "So, basically, he's saying that the rate of change is only dependent on the number of rabbits, not the time."

In order to assess whether the students accepted this contribution, the teacher asked then if they agreed with Jen's comment. They argued that the slopes would be invariant horizontally because the rate of change equation does not have a variable t on the right-hand side of the equation; if you "replace the P with a t on the right-hand side," the slopes would be the same vertically. Therefore, another way in which the students justified John and Jen's conclusions was by using the rate of change equation to make predictions about the invariance of slopes. Another student took the argument to a higher level by saying:

Andy: Another thing we found out that like since all the graphs' slopes are the same, it's just like you're sliding this whole graph over one. Like going over here, toward 15 [he gestures to grab the curve for the initial population just above 0], it's like the exact same thing. If you slide it over one more time, you get the 30 graph; another time, you get the 45. So if you know the graph,

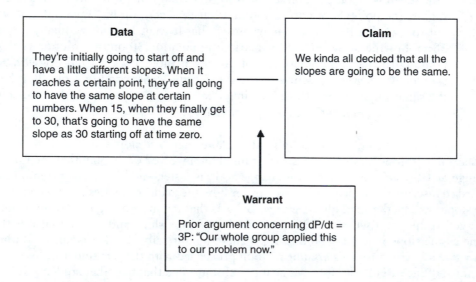

Figure 10.6 John's Argument for the Invariance of Slopes.

you can kinda predict what happened in the past, a little bit before your time zero because the graph is the same for all of them. You just pop it back for whatever your time interval was between the different 15 and 30 populations.

Teacher: So let's put the shifting of the graph left and right out as a conjecture.

In the examples above, we see evidence that the notion that slopes would remain invariant across time for autonomous differential equations functioned as if shared. This evidence comes from analyzing the argumentation structures, both John's and Andy's contributions, as well as how their arguments were dealt with by the community. The *claim* that Andy made above built on John's conclusion that the slopes were invariant. Andy used the previous conclusion of invariant slopes as data to conclude something new; one could merely slide the whole graph left or right. Here, we see an example of a case where the conclusion that was debated previously now functioned as the data for a more sophisticated conclusion (see Figure 10.7).

Therefore, according to our second criterion for documenting collective activity (restated below), the notion that slopes are invariant across time for autonomous differential equations functioned here as if it were shared.

- *Criterion Two:* When any of the four parts of an argument (the data, warrant, claim, or backing) shift position (i.e., function) in subsequent arguments and are unchallenged (or, if contested, the challenges are rejected), the mathematical idea functions as if it were shared by the classroom community. For example, when students use a previously justified claim as an unchallenged justification (the data, warrant, or backing) for future arguments, we conclude that the mathematical idea expressed in the claim becomes a part of the group's normative ways of reasoning.

As the measurement and differential equations examples illustrate, analyzing the structure and function of students' argumentations is interpretive in that the researcher must infer the intentions of the speaker(s) as they make contributions in the flow of the conversation. Therefore, for the methodology to be strong and credible, safeguards must be in place in order to ensure the trustworthiness of the analytic process. We discuss issues of trustworthiness as well as generalizability in the next section.

Generalizability and Trustworthiness of the Methodology

Of central concern about any methodology are issues related to the generalizability and trustworthiness of the approach. Generalizability in teaching experiments (and in

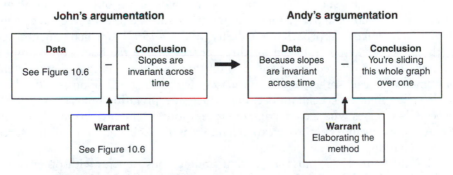

Figure 10.7 A Shift from Conclusion to Data.

design research more generally), as emphasized by Steffe and Thompson (2000), is an issue about the *usefulness* of the products from these interventions in settings other than the one in which they were built. The initial setting in which we developed the methodology for documenting collective activity was a first-grade, elementary school class. Our attempts to analyze the measurement practices in this class led us to invent a methodology that draws on argumentation theory. The first incarnation of the methodology involved the creation of the first criterion in which warrants and backings drop out of students' arguments. Our efforts to use this criterion in a new classroom teaching experiment—differential equations—proved fruitful in that (a) we learned that our methodology was useful for understanding the collective activity of a different group of students and a different mathematical domain, and (b) we were able to refine the methodology by creating criterion two. Thus, we found that the methodology was useful in more than one context (i.e., it was generalizable), and, in turn, we used the new context to strengthen the methodology. Although the methodology to date is relatively rigorous and stable, it is, of course, open to further revision as researchers use it in their own contexts.

We view these instances of testing and revising in other contexts not as negating the generalizability of the methodology, rather as strengthening it. Because of these diverse settings, we argue that our methodology would be effective for documenting collective activity in almost any mathematics course in which there is genuine argumentation. We conjecture that the methodology also would be useful in science classes when there is genuine argumentation. We do not think, however, that the methodology we describe would be useful in classroom environments where there is no genuine argumentation (e.g., a classroom in which the teacher dominates the discourse).

Another type of usefulness of the methodology extends to the instructional innovators involved in the original design research study. In particular, it has been our experience that analyses of classroom mathematical practices provide new inspirations for revising and refining the instructional theories underpinning the intervention (e.g., see Yackel et al., 2003). Classroom mathematical practices provide an account of the quality of the mathematical experience of the community, as well as of the processes (i.e., argumentation, tools, gestures, etc.) that support their emergence. In addition, Cobb (2003) argues that a classroom mathematical practice analysis describes the evolution of the mathematical content as experienced and created by the participants. Thus, the documentation of the collective activity can ultimately impact teachers and students not involved in the original intervention but who benefit from the research-based, instructional interventions. The benefit is seen as teachers attempt to adapt the instructional theory, comprised primarily of documented mathematical practices, to create their own instructional environments that are commensurable with the initial classes.

We turn next to the issue of the reliability or trustworthiness of the methodology for documenting collective activity. Our method is made reliable by the fact that we employed an interactive approach to reliability (Blumer, 1969) in which two, and sometimes three, researchers conducted all three phases of the method. For example, in Phase One, we each created argumentation schemes and then compared and defended our schemes with each other, ending ultimately with an agreed-upon set of schemes. Multiple viewpoints are crucial for deciding which interpretation holds the most viability, especially in cases where conflicting interpretations are involved (Lincoln & Guba, 1985). A complementary approach to reliability is to seek quantitative measures of interrater reliability.

Lincoln and Guba (1985) also argue that finding consistencies with other research strengthens reliability. Our methodology grew out of the work of other researchers who were seeking to establish methods for documenting the social contexts of classrooms (Cobb & Yackel, 1996). We also drew on Yackel (1997), Krummheuer (1995), and Toulmin (1969) to create our criteria for documenting collective activity and found overlap in our methodology with the work of Forman et al. (1998). We argue that trustworthiness is strengthened in our methodology by prolonged engagement with the subjects (from several weeks to the entire semester), multiple observations (analyzing every whole-class argumentation in every class period), triangulation of sources (videos, artifacts, field notes, interviews, etc.), and member checking (the teacher was one of the researchers involved in the analysis in the differential equations study).

Finally, we take a step back and examine the methodology as a legitimate way of assessing students' learning. In this chapter, we used Toulmin's (1969) model to analyze the arguments that students create during mathematics class. Mislevy (2003) argues that Toulmin's scheme can be used in a broader way—namely, to judge the effectiveness of an educational researcher's methodology for assessing learning. Therefore, we employ Toulmin's scheme at a metalevel to examine the three-phase method for assessing collective learning in order to determine the legitimacy of our means of assessment. As shown in Figure 10.8, Toulmin's scheme of data, claim, warrant, and backing is used to structure the argument that the method itself makes.

The data for the method are the argumentation log from Phase One and the patterns that emerge from Phase Two of the analysis. The claim or conclusion is the collective activity; that is, all the as-if-shared ways of reasoning. The warrant, the logic that allows us to make these claims from the data, is the two criteria for determining when particular ideas begin to function as if shared. In other words, these two criteria function as the license we use to go from our raw argumentation data to our conclusions about what ideas functioned as if shared in the classroom. Finally, we see three types of backing that validate the core of the method. At a theoretical level, knowing is inseparable from

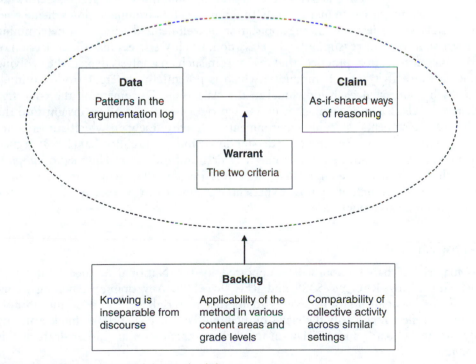

Figure 10.8 The Structure of the Methodology.

discourse, and, therefore, argumentations are a valid way of discerning learning. This theoretical position is well developed by, among others, Toulmin (1969), Wittgenstein (1958), and, more recently, Sfard and Kieran (2001). A second backing for the core of the method is the fact that the method has been useful in a variety of content and grade level domains. A third backing, one that is emerging still for us, is the comparability of collective activity across several instantiations of the same instructional intervention with different teachers.

The analysis of the structure of the method for documenting collective activity provides what Kelly (2004) refers to as the "argumentative grammar" for the method. Kelly explains that

> an argumentative grammar is the logic that guides the use of a method and that supports reasoning about its data. It supplies the logos (reason, rationale) in the methodology (method + logos) and is the basis for the warrant for the claims that arise.
>
> (2004: 118)

Thus, the structure detailed in Figure 10.8 begins to move the three-phase approach from method to methodology. Design research studies have the potential to offer the field new research methods. These new research methods, such as the one we developed in this chapter, will increase their currency when accompanied by an argumentative grammar.

Conclusions

In the previous sections, we outlined a three-phase, methodological approach for documenting the collective activity of a classroom community of learners. Central to the methodology are a systematic use of Toulmin's (1969) argumentation scheme over extended classroom lessons and the application of well-defined criteria for determining the normative ways of reasoning at the classroom level. We stress that the collection of classroom mathematical practices that result from such an analysis depicts the evolving mathematical activity of a community, which is potentially different from the intellectual achievement of each individual in the classroom. Documenting the collective activity of a classroom is significant in its own right because it offers insight into the quality of the students' learning environment, an environment in which students are active agents in the construction of understandings. Indeed, Freudenthal (1973) argued that mathematics should be a human activity first and foremost. The methodological approach that we developed in this chapter offers a way to document mathematics as a human activity—an activity whose experiential richness can be traced systematically through genuine argumentation.

Acknowledgments

This material is based upon work supported by the National Science Foundation under Grant Nos. REC 9875388 and REC 9814898. Any opinions, findings, conclusions, or recommendations expressed in this material are those of the authors and do not reflect necessarily the views of the Foundation. The authors thank Anthony Kelly, Joanne Lobato, and Juli Dixon for their comments on an earlier draft of this chapter.

Notes

1 In conversations, individuals negotiate meaning through an exchange of words until, at some point, they come to a mutual agreement about the meaning of an idea. When an agreement is struck (most often implicitly) among individuals so that the conversation can progress, we say that it is *as if* the individuals share the idea. We do not make the stronger claim that the individuals share the idea, but that they act as if they share the idea in order to proceed with a different or more elaborate argument. Other researchers have used the term "taken-as-shared" to refer to this phenomenon.

2 In practice, the most difficult contributions to categorize are the distinctions between warrants and backings. In our experience to date, distinguishing between these two, although difficult, is not critical in order to use this methodology. The two criteria that we developed for deciding when an idea functions as if shared tend not to necessitate distinguishing between the warrants and the backings. The first criterion involves the supporting statements (the warrants and backings) dropping out of students' argumentations. Because they both drop out, it is not crucial to have made the distinction between the two. For the second criterion, we have seen conclusions typically shift function in subsequent argumentations and serve as data for more elaborate support (warrants and backings). We have not seen warrants or backings shift function in subsequent argumentations, and, therefore, the distinction between the two is not paramount. We are exploring ways in which making the distinction between warrants and backings can have implications for the methodology.

3 The fact that backings appeared infrequently in students' argumentations is consistent with Toulmin's (1969) theory in which he states that backings often are not required to continue an argumentation. A person does not have the time to give the backing for every argument he or she makes. If backings were required, a conclusion might never be reached.

4 An autonomous differential equation is one that does not depend explicitly on the independent variable, usually time. For example, $dP/dt = 2P - 1$ is an autonomous differential equation, whereas $dP/dt = 2P + t$ is not. In general, an autonomous differential equation has the form $dP/dt = f(P)$. Moreover, because autonomous differential equations do not depend explicitly on time, the slopes of solutions to such equations in the t–P plane are invariant along the t axis. For example, the slope of the function $P(t) = 20e^{3t}$ at any particular P value is the same as the slope of the graph of the function $P(t) = 10e^{3t}$ at that same P value. As a consequence, the graph of the functions $P(t) = 10e^{3t}$ and $P(t) = 20e^{3t}$ is horizontal shifts of each other along the t axis. The reader may recall that, unlike algebraic equations that have numbers as solutions, solutions to a differential equation are functions. For example, the function $P(t) = 10e^{3t}$ is a solution to the differential equation $dP/dt = 3P$ because the derivative of $P(t)$ is $3*10e^{3t}$, which is the same as $3*P(t)$; that is, the function $P(t) = 10e^{3t}$ satisfies the equation $dP/dt = 3P$. Similarly, the function $P(t) = 20e^{3t}$ is a solution to $dP/dt = 3P$. In general, $P(t) = ke^{3t}$ is a solution to $dP/dt = 3P$ for any real number k.

5 A slope field for a differential equation $dy/dt = f(t,y)$ is plotted by selecting evenly-spaced points $t_1, t_2, \ldots, t_m$ along the t axis and a collection of evenly-spaced points $y_1, y_2, \ldots, y_n$ along the y axis; at each point (t_i, y_j), a small line with a slope $f(t_i, y_j)$ is drawn. Slope fields offer a way of sketching graphs of solutions to differential equations, even when the analytic form of the solutions is unknown or unobtainable.

References

Bauersfeld, H., Krummheuer, G. & Voigt, J. (1988). Interactional theory of learning and teaching mathematics and related microethnographical studies. In H.-G. Steiner & A. Vermandel (eds), *Foundations and methodology of the discipline of mathematics education* (pp. 174–188). Antwerp, Belgium: Proceedings of the Theory of Mathematics Education Conference.

Blumer, H. (1969). *Symbolic interactionism: Perspectives and method*. Englewood Cliffs, NJ: Prentice Hall.

Brown, A. & Campione, J. C. (1994). Guided discovery in a community of learners. In K. McGilly (ed.), *Classroom lessons: Integrating cognitive theory and classroom practice* (pp. 229–270). Cambridge, MA: MIT Press.

Cobb, P. (2000). Conducting teaching experiments in collaboration with teachers. In A. E. Kelly

& R. A. Lesh (eds), *Handbook of research design in mathematics and science education* (pp. 307–334). Mahwah, NJ: Lawrence Erlbaum Associates.

Cobb, P. (2003). Investigating students' reasoning about linear measurement as a paradigm case of design research. In M. Stephan, J. Bowers, P. Cobb & K. Gravemeijer (eds), *Supporting students' development of measuring concepts: Analyzing students' learning in social context* (*Journal for Research in Mathematics Education*, Monograph No. 12, pp. 1–16). Reston, VA: National Council of Teachers of Mathematics.

Cobb, P. & Yackel, E. (1996). Constructivist, emergent, and sociocultural perspectives in the context of developmental research. *Educational Psychologist*, *31*, 175–190.

Cobb, P., Confrey, J., diSessa, A., Lehrer, R. & Schauble, L. (2003). Design experiments in educational research. *Educational Researcher*, *32*(1), 9–13.

Davydov, V. & Radzikhovskii, L. (1985). Vygotsky's theory and the activity-oriented approach in psychology. In J. Wertsch (ed.), *Culture, communication, and cognition: Vygotskian perspectives* (pp. 35–65). New York: Cambridge University Press.

Forman, E., Larreamendy-Joerns, J., Stein, M. & Brown, C. (1998). "You're going to want to find out which and prove it." Collective argument in a mathematics classroom. *Learning & Instruction*, *8*, 527–548.

Freudenthal, H. (1973). *Mathematics as an educational task*. Dordrecht, The Netherlands: Reidel.

Glaser, B. G. & Strauss, A. L. (1967). *The discovery of grounded theory: Strategies for qualitative research*. New York: Aldine.

Kelly, A. E. (2004). Design research in education: Yes, but is it methodological? *Journal of the Learning Sciences*, *13*, 115–128.

Kelly, A. E. & Lesh, R. A. (eds) (2000). *Handbook of research design in mathematics and science education*. Mahwah, NJ: Lawrence Erlbaum Associates.

Krummheuer, G. (1995). The ethnography of argumentation. In P. Cobb & H. Bauersfeld (eds), *The emergence of mathematical meaning: Interaction in classroom cultures*. Hillsdale, NJ: Lawrence Erlbaum Associates.

Leont'ev, A. N. (1981). *Problems of the development of mind*. Moscow: Progress Publishers.

Lerman, S. (1996). Intersubjectivity in mathematics learning: A challenge to the radical constructivist paradigm? *Journal for Research in Mathematics Education*, *27*, 133–168.

Lincoln, Y. & Guba, E. (1985). *Naturalistic inquiry*. Beverly Hills, CA: Sage.

McNeill, D. (1992). *Hand and mind: What gestures reveal about thought*. Chicago: University of Chicago Press.

Meira, L. (1998). Making sense of instructional devices: The emergence of transparency in mathematical activity. *Journal for Research in Mathematics Education*, *29*, 121–142.

Mislevy, R. J. (2003). Substance and structure in assessment arguments. *Law, Probability and Risk*, *2*, 237–258.

Moschkovich, J. (2004). Appropriating mathematical practices: A case study of learning to use and explore functions through interaction with a tutor. *Educational Studies in Mathematics*, *55*, 49–80.

Moschkovich, J. & Brenner, M. (2000). Integrating a naturalistic paradigm into research on mathematics and science cognition and learning. In A. E. Kelly & R. A. Lesh (eds), *Handbook of research design in mathematics and science education* (pp. 457–487). Mahwah, NJ: Lawrence Erlbaum Associates.

Nemirovsky, R. C. & Monk, S. (2000). If you look at it the other way. . . . In P. Cobb, E. Yackel & K. McClain (eds), *Symbolizing, communicating, and mathematizing: Perspectives on discourse, tools, and instructional design* (pp. 177–221). Mahwah, NJ: Lawrence Erlbaum Associates.

Pea, R. D. (1993). Practices of distributed intelligence and designs for education. In G. Solomon (ed.), *Distributed cognition* (pp. 47–87). New York: Cambridge University Press.

Rasmussen, C., Stephan, M. & Allen, K. (2004). Classroom mathematical practices and gesturing. *Journal of Mathematical Behavior*, *23*, 301–323.

Rasmussen, C., Zandieh, M., King, K. & Teppo, A. (2005). Advancing mathematical activity: A view of advanced mathematical thinking. *Mathematical Thinking and Learning*, *7*, 51–73.

Sfard, A. & Kieran, C. (2001). Cognition as communication; Rethinking learning-by-talking through multi-faceted analysis of students' mathematical interactions. *Mind, Culture, and Activity, 8,* 42–76.

Simon, M. A. (2000). Research on the development of mathematics teachers: The teacher development experiment. In A. E. Kelly & R. A. Lesh (eds), *Handbook of research design in mathematics and science education* (pp. 335–359). Mahwah, NJ: Lawrence Erlbaum Associates.

Skemp, R. R. (1982). Theories and methodologies. In T. P. Carpenter, J. M. Moser & T. A. Romberg (eds), *Addition and subtraction: A cognitive perspective.* Hillsdale, NJ: Lawrence Erlbaum Associates.

Steffe, L. & Thompson, P. (2000). Teaching experiment methodology: Underlying principles and essential elements. In A. E. Kelly & R. A. Lesh (eds), *Handbook of research design in mathematics and science education* (pp. 267–306). Mahwah, NJ: Lawrence Erlbaum Associates.

Stephan, M. & Rasmussen, C. (2002). Classroom mathematical practices in differential equations. *Journal of Mathematical Behavior, 21,* 459–490.

Stephan, M., Cobb, P. & Gravemeijer, K. (2003). Coordinating social and individual analyses: Learning as participation in mathematical practices. In M. Stephan, J. Bowers, P. Cobb & K. Gravemeijer (eds), *Supporting students' development of measuring concepts: Analyzing students' learning in social context* (*Journal for Research in Mathematics Education*, Monograph No. 12, pp. 67–102). Reston, VA: National Council of Teachers of Mathematics.

Suter, L. E. & Frechtling, J. (2000). *Guiding principles for mathematics and science education research methods: Report of a workshop.* Arlington, VA: National Science Foundation, at: http://www.nsf.gov/pubs/2000/nsf00113/nsf00113.html.

Toulmin, S. (1969). *The uses of argument.* Cambridge: Cambridge University Press.

van Oers, B. (1996). Learning mathematics as meaningful activity. In P. Nesher, L. Steffe, P. Cobb, G. Goldin & B. Greer (eds), *Theories of mathematical learning.* Hillsdale, NJ: Lawrence Erlbaum Associates.

Wittgenstein, L. (1958). *Philosophical investigations* (G. E. M. Anscombe, Trans.). Englewood Cliffs, NJ: Prentice Hall.

Yackel, E. (1997). Explanation as an interactive accomplishment: A case study of one second-grade mathematics classroom. Paper presented at the annual meeting of the American Educational Research Association, Chicago, April.

Yackel, E., Stephan, M., Rasmussen, C. & Underwood, D. (2003). Didactising: Continuing the work of Leen Streefland. *Educational Studies in Mathematics, 54,* 101–126.

Part 4

Modeling Teacher Learning Using Design Research

11 Developing Design Studies in Mathematics Education Professional Development

Studying Teachers' Interpretive Systems

Judith Zawojewski
Illinois Institute of Technology

Michelle Chamberlin
University of Northern Colorado

Margret A. Hjalmarson
George Mason University

Catherine Lewis
Mills College

Introduction

Design research has been used to investigate students' mathematical development and to design more effective learning environments, with the twin purposes of designing and studying the impact of educational innovations (e.g., Brown, 1992; Design-Based Research Collective, 2003; Verschaffel et al., 1999). For example, Brown (1992) proposed using design experiments in classes in order to investigate the design of learning communities and to advance methods for carrying out research about learning within the complexity of the actual classroom situation. This research resulted both in the development of theory about learning and in improved innovations for helping students learn. Recent calls for more rigorous scientific research in education and more connections between research and classroom practice (e.g., National Research Council, 2002) extend to research on mathematics teaching practice. We propose the extension of design research to teachers' learning and development in order to understand both how teachers develop in their practice and how to design environments and situations to encourage the development of that practice.

The purpose of this chapter is to propose how design study may be used for conducting research on teachers' growth in the context of long-term, professional development, with two assumptions being made: that teachers will grow in ways that cannot be predicted always and that teachers' growth will take place in complex situations. The first assumption is in contrast to professional development organized around a particular model of teaching to which teachers aspire, and in which predetermined characteristics and behaviors can be identified and measured. Research methodologies are needed for professional development experiences where participants are not expected to converge toward a particular standard, yet teachers grow and improve as a result of participating in the professional development experience. Teachers' growth is often unpredictable because they use their own interpretive systems to function in daily prac-tice. In doing so, they draw on multiple theories and models: cognitive learning theory, economic models, political models, etc. Even so, Doerr and Lesh (2003) suggested that the knowledge base and expertise of teachers can develop in ways that can be seen as continually better, even without a particular end point in mind. The challenge is to design studies of professional development that characterize the ways in which teachers develop and how their growth can be documented.

The second assumption—that teachers' growth takes place in complex situations—is based on the notion that professional development experiences should address the problems that teachers want to solve. The situations that teachers face are complex and involve trade-offs among many factors, such as the learning goals for the students, the costs of implementing desired programs and methods of instruction, and negotiations between the teachers' goals and the goals of the various interested parties (e.g., parents, the school district's statement of standards). Experts in the field, such as Lieberman (1996) and Putnam and Borko (1997), support the notion that professional develop-ment should be relevant to local needs. Ball and Cohen (1999), Darling-Hammond and Ball (1998), the National Council of Teachers of Mathematics (2001), and Putnam and Borko (2000) recommend that the planned experiences should engage teachers in work that is related directly to their classroom practice; others (Darling-Hammond & McLaughlin, 1995; Guskey, 1995; Hawley & Valli, 1999; Loucks-Horsley et al., 1987) suggest that the professional development experience needs to provide reasons for teachers to share their ways of thinking about their own practice with peers and to participate in the development of a community of practice. This collection of recommendations paints a picture of professional development as existing in complex dynamic systems where the system influences the nature of the professional develop-ment and the professional development influences the nature of the system. Consider, at the classroom level, that as a teacher interprets students' thinking, the teacher's actions toward the students change; the students change in response to the teacher's altered expressions and expectations; and the cycle repeats as the teacher again interprets stu-dents' thinking and modifies his or her thinking about the students. Consider also, at the school level, that when a teacher explains new insights about students to the princi-pal, the principal changes his or her ways of conversing with parents; the principal's expressed perceptions prompt changes in how parents interact with their children; stu-dents' classroom behavior and performance change as a result of parental influence; and the cycle repeats as the teacher again modifies his or her thinking about the students. Speck and Knipe (2001: 217) say that professional development facilitators must "view professional development practices in the context of the larger system with the inter-connectedness of all the parts and the continuous flow of change." The notion of design study provides a means to think about research methods that can embrace and capital-ize on dynamic and complex school situations, rather than thinking about how to control those same factors.

In 1992, Brown described the need to develop research methodologies that acknow-ledge that change in one part of the system may perturb the whole system. In addition to Brown, Collins (1992) introduced the concept of design experiment to the field of education, and other researchers, such as Cobb et al. (2003), the Design-Based Research Collective (2003), and Hawkins and Collins (1992), have carried on Brown's recommendations, explaining that design experiments provide an avenue for studying learning within the complexity of interacting educational systems. In these lines of research, the term design experiment is used to indicate that a tangible product (e.g., for Cobb et al. [2003], a trajectory of student learning) is being designed by the research team and developed over a series of trials, through systematic data collection and analysis.

The notion of design experiment draws on the scholarly work of engineers in which their design process involves expressing, testing, and revising functional objects, procedures, and theory. Unlike engineering research, educational research in professional development must deal with multiple interacting layers of designers: teachers design educational tools (e.g., lesson plans, questioning techniques, rubrics for interpreting students' work) for their own practice; facilitators design professional development sessions based on what they have learned from previous sessions; researchers design theories for professional development that can guide similar experiences in different contexts with different teachers, which in turn impact the facilitator's immediate professional development plans. Thus, aspects of the multitiered teaching experiments described by Lesh and Kelly (1997) are important for capturing the realities of the multiple constituencies involved in professional development in educational settings, the problems identified by teachers, and the inability to predict always the ways in which teachers grow.

This chapter focuses on and fleshes out the teacher development tier of the Lesh and Kelly (1997, 2000) multitiered teaching experiment model. The first section describes the characteristics of multitiered professional development experiences that provide opportunities to conduct design study research for investigating changes in teachers' interpretive systems. Then, two illustrative cases of professional development (lesson study and students' thinking sheets) are described and serve as examples for points we make in subsequent sections. The section after them characterizes teachers' interpretive systems for teaching and learning and how professional development is designed to prompt changes in their interpretive systems. The final section addresses practical aspects of constructing a multitiered professional development design study.

The Nature of Multitiered Professional Development Design Studies

Professional development experiences that are planned explicitly as design studies have distinctive characteristics: teachers are engaged in the development of artifacts that reveal aspects of their own thinking; teachers are engaged in testing and revising the artifact; and teachers are asked to describe and document the guiding principles they have used while revising the artifact. When teachers produce educational objects for use in their own practice, they have the opportunity to examine their own thinking because their artifacts are an external representation of their own interpretive systems. Testing and revision take place when small groups of teachers negotiate the development of the artifact, when the educational object is field-tested in the classroom, and when classroom data are reported to and discussed among peers. Peer interaction provides important opportunities for teachers to express, test, and revise their artifact *and* their ways of thinking about teaching and learning as related to the artifact. When teachers are asked to be explicit about the principles that guide their decisions about artifact revisions, they externalize general aspects of their interpretive systems. The principles and guidelines that teachers express are revealed to themselves, their peers, the facilitator, and the researcher of the professional development experience. The facilitator and the researcher proceed through a similar process of testing and revising their plans for, and theories about, professional development. Hence, the design study is multitiered as teachers examine classroom situations and their own interpretive systems, and researchers and facilitators examine teachers' interpretive systems as well as their own and derive principles for professional development that may be transportable to other contexts. In order to ensure transportability to other situations, Middleton, Gorard, Taylor, and Bannan-Ritland and Hjalmarson and Lesh in their chapters in this volume describe a model for design research that moves between the proposed or intended function of the design and its actual implementation in the classroom. The two professional development cases described in this section—lesson study and students' thinking sheets—illustrate the assumptions underlying design study, the methodological considerations for this type of research, and the characteristics of professional development situations planned as design studies.

Lesh and Kelly (2000) describe multitiered teaching experiments that involve three interacting tiers (researchers, teachers, and students) represented hierarchically in a diagram—Figure 11.1. The design study perspective for teachers' professional development described in this chapter draws on their multitiered model but adds a facilitator tier that is responsible for designing the professional development experience for teachers and that focuses more on the collaboration between the tiers. In particular, the diagram in Figure 11.1(a) shows the iterative design cycles involved in the design process and the diagram in Figure 11.1 shows how the teachers, researchers, and facilitators are collaborators in the design of educational objects. Figure 11.1(b) suggests a more interactive and collaborative process than the hierarchical process (hence, their use of the term *tier*) described by Lesh and Kelly. Students are put in the center because all of the constituents are concerned with students' thinking in some way (even if it is through a different constituent—e.g., a researcher through teachers' interpretations) and all of the tiers are trying to cause change and improvement to students' thinking (even if it is through a different tier—e.g., improving students' learning by improving teaching). Each tier receives feedback from and influences the development of the other two constituents.

Aspects of design study, as defined above, happen naturally in the classroom on a daily basis. Teachers are designing constantly products for classroom instruction, such as a curricular unit, a plan for implementing small group work, a daily lesson plan, or a rubric to communicate to students what is valued in their work. Teachers engage in the experimentation process as they implement the product they have designed, gather information about its effectiveness, and revise the product on the spot or revise it for future use. The difference in professional development design studies is that teachers

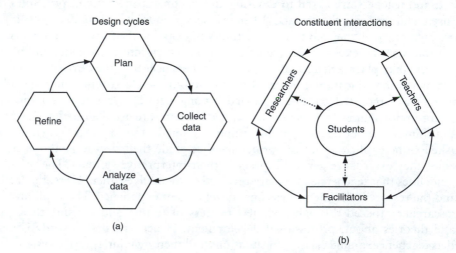

Figure 11.1 Design Study Situated in Context.

externalize their thinking explicitly through the educational objects they design, then they make their theories explicit by describing and explaining their principles (e.g., how the educational object worked, under what conditions, and why). The challenge to facilitators of professional development is to design experiences for participants that address the problems important to teachers and also prompt cycles of teachers expressing, testing, and revising their educational objects. The researcher works hand in hand with the facilitator in the design of the professional development experience while expressing, testing, and revising his or her theory of professional development. In this chapter, this type of professional development research is termed *design study*, which conveys a sense of designing and studying at the same time and in multiple dimensions.

Examples of Multitiered Design Studies for Professional Development

Next, we describe two examples of studies that can be characterized as multitiered design studies.[1] Both the lesson study and the students' thinking sheet examples were carried out in the complex setting of classroom practice and set about investigating teachers' thinking through the designing of an educational object. In the case of the lesson study, the object under design was an algebra lesson; in the students' thinking sheet example, the object was a tool for representing students' mathematical thinking on model-eliciting activities. The two studies are used in subsequent sections to illustrate some of the considerations and decisions that need to be made when conducting a multitiered design study for teachers' professional development.

Lesson Study

Lesson study has long been the major form of professional development chosen by Japanese teachers and is credited with the transformation of Japanese elementary mathematics and science instruction over the past several decades (Lewis, 2002a, 2002b; Lewis & Tsuchida, 1997, 1998; Stigler & Hiebert, 1999; Yoshida, 1999). Lesson study has been initiated by educators at a number of sites in the United States (Lewis, 2002a, 2002b).[2] The brief lesson study case described here is drawn from a school district in the western United States where teachers founded and led a lesson study effort based on English-language descriptions of Japanese models (Lewis, 2002b; Stigler & Hiebert, 1999; Yoshida, 1999), as well as collaboration with Japanese practitioners. The case focuses on the six teacher-members of a lesson study group who worked together during a summer workshop. The workshop was designed to immerse interested teachers in the study of both algebra and lesson study and was part of a larger, teacher-led effort in the school district to improve mathematics instruction and to build lesson study as an effective means of professional development. In the context of a recent state mandate for all grade-eight students to take algebra, the workshop engaged teachers in identifying and building the elementary mathematics experiences that would lay a foundation for success in algebra.[3] The summer experience generally followed Japanese protocols for lesson study that were introduced by local teacher-leaders and by Japanese educators who had participated in local research lessons during several, prior, multiday workshops.[4]

Lesson study begins by having teachers consider their long-term goals for students and then design collaboratively one or more "research lessons" to bring these goals to life (Lewis, 2002b). The goals serve as an "end in view"[5] to keep in mind as the teachers engage in design cycles of teaching and revising the lesson. They observe and collect carefully data on student learning and development during implementation of the lessons and use these data to refine their instructional approach. In some cases, participants reteach a revised version of the research lesson (Lewis, 2002a, 2002b; Yoshida, 1999). In this lesson study case, after studying the state mathematics standards, the adopted textbook, other mathematics curriculum resources, and solving and discussing algebra problems, the small group of teachers decided to focus the lesson study on students' capacity to recognize and extend patterns—a key, algebra-related theme in the state mathematics standards. The teachers planned a research lesson designed to promote students' capacity to recognize, extend, and express patterns mathematically, using the pattern-extension activity in Appendix A. This began an iterative design cycle in which members of the lesson study group taught the lesson a total of three times (twice during the summer workshop and once during the following fall). On each occasion one member taught the lesson and the other group members observed and collected the data that would be used to reflect on and revise the lesson.

The iterative process of expressing, testing, and revising an educational object (the research lesson) was the focus of the lesson study sessions. For example, after the first teaching (and observing) of the lesson, the teachers revised the lesson by (a) eliminating a worksheet that (teachers hypothesized) had spoon-fed the pattern to students, (b) asking students to organize the data from the problem and write about it, and (c) asking students to share their counting methods with the class (based on evidence from the first lesson that these counting methods revealed ways of thinking about the problem). The teachers teaching the research lesson a third time made additional modifications (e.g., adding a requirement that the groups come to consensus about the pattern).

Students' Thinking Sheets

The students' thinking sheets workshop series was a professional development experience initiated in a midsized midwestern town in the United States in response to a strategic plan developed by the school community. The school's long-term plan included a commitment to increase emphasis on problem-solving in both the teachers' professional development and in the school curriculum. Teachers working collaboratively with a professional development facilitator and researcher developed a program for an initial group of volunteer teachers. The plan was for the teachers to implement a series of five problems with students and to design for each problem a students' thinking sheet that would illustrate different mathematical approaches taken typically by students. The goal was to use the teacher-developed students' thinking sheets in the development of a teacher's handbook for their colleagues to use the following year as they began to incorporate problem solving into their classes. The particular problems used are called *model-eliciting activities* (Lesh et al., 2000) because the problems were designed to have students create and articulate a mathematical procedure, explanation, or description (i.e., a model) as a solution to the problem. (See Appendix B for a sample problem.) Students prepared their final product so that it could be presented to the client described in the problem statement and to meet the client's well-specified need. Therefore, the students' solutions revealed their thinking to the teachers, providing opportunities for the teachers to analyze their students' mathematical approaches. The book edited by Lesh and Doerr (2003) provided the theoretical foundation for the design of the professional development study.

Seven teachers volunteered to attend the workshops, positioning them to be facilitators for their peers in the subsequent academic year. There were five cycles of professional development, each of which involved the teachers in: (a) completing the problem,

(b) implementing the problem with students, (c) examining the students' work to identify mathematical approaches, (d) presenting an individually produced draft of a students' thinking sheet to colleagues, and (e) developing a group consensus, students' thinking sheet for the problem. This group of teachers decided to include in each student thinking sheet excerpts from students' actual work, details about mathematical understandings and abilities associated with each way of thinking, and an evaluation of how effective each approach could be in meeting the needs of the client. Appendix C includes a sample students' thinking sheet for the Departing-On-Time task illustrated in Appendix B.

Teachers' Interpretive Systems

The lesson study and the students' thinking sheet professional development experiences each have an implicit assumption that engaging teachers in the collaborative development of educational artifacts and in cycles of testing and revising the artifact will lead them to grow professionally. What does it mean to say that teachers grow professionally? In both illustrations, teachers used their own conceptual systems to make instructional decisions, interpret students' thinking, design curriculum for students (and peers), analyze their own experiences and data, etc. The conceptual systems that teachers use for their educational practice can be called *interpretive* systems for teaching and learning mathematics. These systems are complex and cannot be defined precisely, but they are to a large extent mathematical (Koellner-Clark & Lesh, 2003). Teachers need to interpret students' mathematical thinking even when students do not use conventional terminology or symbolism, which requires that the teachers' understanding of the mathematics be profound (Ma, 1999); that is, teachers have to understand mathematics not only as a discipline but also through students' perspectives and through the perspective of systems of teaching and learning. Teachers' interpretive systems cannot be "seen," are difficult to describe, are multidimensional and not labeled readily, yet they can be considered the most important target for professional growth. An important goal for the researcher in professional development is to find ways to reveal aspects of teachers' interpretive systems and how those systems are changing. Lesh and Clarke (2000) have described educational researchers' search for evidence of teachers' interpretive systems as similar to physicists searching for evidence of neutrinos, which are particles of matter that cannot be seen. Although, with current technology, the particles themselves cannot be found, physicists are able to provide evidence of their existence by using a theoretical framework and setting up experiments that leave a trail of documentation of these particles. Both the lesson study and the students' thinking sheet cases produced trails of documentation of changes in teachers' interpretive systems. Then, the documentation could be analyzed by the researcher and the facilitator for the generation of theory related to teachers' development, as well as for planning future sessions.

The lesson study case illustrates how change in teachers' interpretive systems can be detected, in particular when examining the iterations of the written lesson plans created by the group of teachers and the conversations captured on video-tape that the teachers had concerning revisions to the lesson. In this case, at the first teaching of the lesson, students were given a worksheet that used the pattern problem in Appendix A and included a two-column table, with one column for the number of tables and one column for the number of seats, to be filled in by the students. All 22 students completed the sheet correctly, showing that the number of seats was always two more than the number of tables, but when asked to write about patterns in the problem, only five students mentioned the plus-two pattern (i.e., that there were always two more seats than the number of tables). The plus-two rule was verbalized several times in the classwide discussion. However, when asked at the end of the lesson to represent this rule as an equation, few students could explain the connection between the plus-two pattern and the problem. In the postlesson symposium, the teacher recalled:

> At the very end, when I was trying to get them to say the number of tables plus two equals the number of seats, there was a lot of confusion. It's easy for them to just go plus two, plus two, and they sort of lose the whole picture of what the plus two is representing.

Teacher 5 noticed the same problem:

> I could see that students were able to fill out the worksheets quickly but never really saw any indication of what does that mean they know . . . they could add plus two to the numbers, but that work didn't necessarily show the kids understand the pattern.

As they replanned the lesson later that day, the teachers revisited what was revealed in their lesson about students' understanding:

Teacher 3: You tried the equation thing and . . .
Teacher 1: It flopped.
Teacher 3: It was too much for them.
Teacher 1: But actually I'm really glad I tried it because I think it's really clear to all of us that we were not where we thought we were. If I hadn't done that, I might have thought they'd gotten it.

Building on Teacher 1's analysis that "Our worksheet set it up for them, spoon-fed them," the group decided to eliminate the worksheet, give each student a particular number of tables to calculate, and have him or her organize the data and find a pattern that would help to solve the problem. Although some members felt discomfort initially about eliminating the worksheet (because the lesson would be taught again just two days later), they agreed eventually that, in the messy work of organizing the data, students might see better the connection between the problem and the plus-two pattern. This lesson redesign suggests that the teachers were thinking in new ways about what it means for students to "understand" a pattern (i.e., more than merely filling out a worksheet correctly) and about how the challenge of organizing data, rather than merely filling in a pre-organized worksheet, might build such understanding.

The lesson study case also provides evidence that interactions with fellow teachers, as well as data from students, led to changes in thinking, which also influenced how the lesson was revised. Teacher Five reported during the postlesson colloquium that by watching how the students counted the seats, she had learned something about how they thought about the problem:

> I noticed kids counting the seats different ways, and this was a kind of a big aha for me . . .. When I've done the problem myself, I've always counted [shows counting around the edge], and it didn't occur to me that there was another way of counting it . . .. But [student name] had laid out 20 triangles . . . and she was counting [demonstrates counting top and bottom alternately, followed by the ends], and then it looked totally different to me; I could see there are 10 triangles on top, 10 on

bottom, and a seat on either end. Now, I was seeing the pattern a different way. Up until then, I had always seen it as you're taking away a seat and adding these two, taking away a seat and adding these two (shows adding a triangle and subtracting the side that is joined). I was seeing a pattern from somebody else's perspective. That's why I thought it might be helpful to have kids talking about how they're counting it. How are you seeing the seats, and the numbers, and the increases, and where does that come from? So, I think definitely having the kids use the manipulatives is important, and watching how they use them is going to tell us a lot about how did they see the pattern.

(Teacher 5)

As a result of this observation, the group decided to redesign the lesson in order to have students share their counting methods. When reflecting at the end of the workshop on what they had learned from revising and reteaching the lesson, Teacher 1 recalled that when the suggestion was made to have students share their counting methods, she could not understand why this would be helpful but decided to go along with it. However, when students shared their counting methods during the second teaching of the lesson, she could see the geometric reason for the plus-two pattern (that each non-end triangular table contributes one seat and the two end triangular tables each contribute two seats). In this situation, not only were the teachers producing a trail of documentation in their research lessons, but also they were creating opportunities for their students to produce a trail of documentation about how they were counting. Incorporating opportunities for teachers to reflect on the changes they have made helps them to identify and document their own growth. The resulting documentation can be used to form a compelling case that can be reported to external audiences describing changes in teachers' own interpretive systems.

Aspects of teachers' interpretive systems for teaching and learning can be documented by planning professional development experiences that require the externalization of teachers' thinking through the design and creation of educational objects that are subjected to testing and revision. When such documentation is available, the professional development facilitator and the researcher can use the information gleaned from the artifacts and observations of teachers' interactions to gain some understanding of teachers' evolving interpretive systems and to plan subsequent experiences based on what has been learned about the teachers. In addition, at the end of the professional development experience, the teachers have high-quality educational resources for their classes. In the case of the lesson study, the teachers had well-constructed lessons. In the students' thinking sheets example, the teachers had a handbook that could be used the next year and shared with other teachers. Most important is the teachers' opportunity to examine and reflect on the evidence of their own interpretive systems, which pushes the professional development system further. Professional development experiences that are designed to include teachers' documentation of the principles underlying their decisions for revisions can provide an even more complete picture of teachers' interpretive systems and the changes in those systems. If the goal is to study teachers' interpretive systems as teachers develop, then professional development experiences need to be designed to make teachers' interpretive systems grow and to trace those changes. Developing a program of professional development goes hand in hand with creating a design study of that professional development experience.

Creating a Multitiered Design Study

Creating a multitiered design study requires that the researcher and the facilitator work together to plan activities that will provide simultaneously opportunities for teachers to grow and for them to document their growth. The research questions need to be complementary to a clearly articulated end in view, which keeps the orientation of the professional development on track, addressing teachers' problems while providing flexibility in the activities planned. Data, or documentation, may be obtained from multiple sources and is elicited as part of the professional development process. Each participant in the professional development experience analyzes data from his or her perspective, leading to multiple conclusions and implications of the research. Different aspects of formulating a design study are addressed in the following four sections:

- What are the research questions?
- What is the nature of the data?
- How are the data collected?
- How are the data analyzed?

What Are the Research Questions?

The researcher is interested in studying the teachers' data for patterns to inform theory, principles, or frameworks that can be shared with mathematics educators in the field. By focusing on the mechanisms that prompt the development of teachers' interpretive systems, the information gathered for the study has the potential to inform others in professional development about ways to devise cycles of teachers expressing, testing, reflecting, and revising. Cobb et al. (2003) emphasize the importance of clarifying the theoretical intent before each cycle of experimentation. In the lesson study and the students' thinking sheet examples the design principle they held in common was: mechanisms that prompt teachers to express, test, and revise their interpretive systems should be incorporated into the teachers' experience. The assumption underlying this principle is that as teachers express, test, and revise their educational object, their interpretive systems for learning and teaching will grow and change. Further, aspects of the changes are often evident in the iterative designs of the objects and available for the teachers' self-assessment and for the researcher to trace aspects of the teachers' development. The mechanism used to enact this principle in the lesson study and the students' thinking sheet examples was to have teachers design an educational object relevant to their practice (i.e., the algebra lesson, the students' thinking sheet). The research questions were: How do these mechanisms work? Why? Understanding how the mechanisms work helps to reduce the amount of design necessary for transporting the theory to new contexts.

What Is the Nature of the Data?

Because one cannot presume to know what is in another's mind, investigating the interpretive systems of others is based necessarily on external representations: the spoken word, the written word, diagrams, actions, etc. Many professional development studies involve the use of surveys and self-reporting by individuals in which they testify about their own growth. However, these types of data have long been suspect in the social sciences research methodology literature (Cohen, 1990; Spillane & Zeuli, 1999). Other professional development studies use pre- and post-tests of teachers' knowledge.

The use of tests as evidence of teachers' growth presumes that what is tested represents and captures the most important aspects of teachers' knowledge development, that teachers' knowledge growth will converge on the content that is tested, and that what is tested will translate into classroom practice. A different kind of data is performance-based data or documentation that comes from what teachers actually *do* as they engage in practical work. These types of data have a high degree of face validity and have the potential to provide compelling evidence about how different teachers grow in different ways.

Performance-based data that have the potential to reveal teachers' thinking can be gathered from activities designed to reveal teachers' thinking. Chamberlin (2004) has proposed principles for developing effective, thought-revealing activities for teachers. She characterizes the desired activities as the design of classroom tools or resources that reveal teachers' thinking as they engage in an iterative process of expressing, testing, and revising their creation. This design process results in thought-revealing products created by teachers that can be assessed by themselves, their peers, the facilitator, and the researcher. The lesson study case involved three points of written, performance-based data obtained from the series of revised lessons written by the teachers. Although the problem to be solved by the students remained the same over the three lesson revisions, the tasks given to the students were redesigned repeatedly in response to the data collected during the lessons. The final lesson produced by the teachers showed how they designed the activity to reveal the students' thinking at various points during the lesson. The teachers obtained an initial round of data when the class discussed the solution to a problem for a small number of tables. Then, working with partners and using pattern blocks, the students were asked to solve the problem for some larger numbers, resulting in written records of the students' data on the handout. Finally, the class was to discuss the patterns that the partners saw, providing another round of information to the teachers. Another task was given at the end of the lesson in which the students were asked, as a class, to write an equation that would express a mathematical rule relating the number of triangles to the number of seats. The equation that students chose revealed how they mathematized the relationship between the number of triangles and the number of seats. These data sources provided the primary information that the teachers used to revise the lesson, and the facilitator and the researcher gained performance-based data from the teachers.

How Are the Data Collected?

Similar to the process of data collection described by the Design-Based Research Collective (2003), the collection of performance-based data in professional development design studies faces issues of complexity. Lesh and Kelly (2000) focused on the interactions among various tiers involved in teaching studies. In particular, they emphasized the role of the facilitator/researcher in *planning* for ways to document the thinking of all the constituencies: the students, the teachers, and the facilitator/researcher. The data collected in a design study can be considered a trail of documentation, rather than a series of static data points over time. Figure 11.2 illustrates the products designed by different constituencies in the students' thinking sheet case. For example, in the students' thinking sheet workshops, the activities given to students were model-eliciting, meaning that the activities were crafted carefully, using the design principles described by Lesh et al. (2000) to require students to reveal their thinking in their final products.[6] The products created by students serve as the primary sources of information about the groups' mathematical thinking, which typically prompt teachers to reflect on the

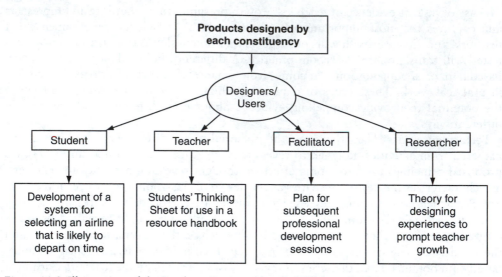

Figure 11.2 Illustration of the Products Designed by the Different Constituencies.

relationship between how their students are using mathematical knowledge and how the teacher is planning for instruction (Chamberlin, 2002). In the students' thinking sheet case, the thought-revealing activity for teachers was to develop the students' thinking sheets. The teachers needed to interpret the students' responses and categorize common approaches that students took in their final products. A trail of documentation was produced by planning for cycles of teachers expressing their individual ideas about students' approaches, testing their ideas with peers during the workshop session, and revising their ideas as the group of teachers converged on a consensus students' thinking sheet. In Chamberlin's study, teachers' reflections were captured by video-taping, transcribing, and analyzing the conversations among teachers that took place during the session.

The construction of a design study should plan not only for the teachers' documentation, but also for the documentation of teachers' analysis of their own reflections. In the lesson study case, each research lesson was preceded by a presentation by the teachers of the principles that governed their lesson design and redesign. For example, before the research lesson, group members made a presentation to outside observers in order to explain the changes in the lesson, the reason for each change, and what they had learned from the experience of revising and reteaching the lesson. The teachers justified their decision to eliminate the worksheet by citing evidence from the first lesson that students did not understand the pattern fully despite filling out the worksheet correctly. For the students' thinking sheet, the teachers might have been asked to write a final chapter in the handbook that would provide principles or frameworks for their peers to use in identifying students' approaches to model-eliciting activities. Planning for cycles of expressing, testing, and revising those principles would provide not only a trail of documentation of the teachers' metacognitive development, but also the teachers themselves would have been engaged in the analysis process.

How Are the Data Analyzed?

Data analysis methods need to be aligned with the nature of the research questions posed (Shavelson et al., 2003). Although the two illustrations in this chapter involve the qualitative analysis of data, different types of research questions may draw on various types of qualitative and quantitative analyses, in part depending on the phase of the research in the complete design cycle described in Middleton, Gorard, Taylor, and Bannan-Ritland (this volume). Data analysis in multitiered design studies at these particular phases involve the:

- Teachers analyzing their students' data for the purpose of designing an educational tool or resource.
- Teachers analyzing data about their own interpretive systems for the purpose of developing principles or frameworks for designing the educational object.
- Facilitator interpreting the teachers' analyses for the purpose of planning further professional development experiences.
- Researcher analyzing data about his or her own interpretive systems concerning the teachers' teaching and learning for the purpose of revising and refining their theories, frameworks, and mechanisms for professional development.

Just as complexity is assumed in professional development research, so it is assumed to exist in the analysis of the data. Figure 11.3 illustrates the process of analysis embedded in the process of designing an educational object, a professional development session, or a theory. It should be kept in mind that this is happening for each constituent in the design study, from the teachers through the researcher. Teachers analyze the students' data because it not only facilitates their professional development,

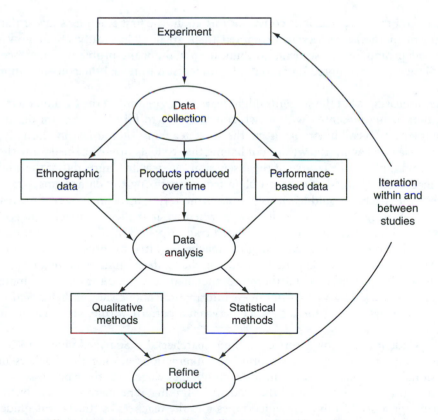

Figure 11.3 Different Options Available for Collecting and Analyzing Data.

but also it prompts them to express aspects of their own interpretive systems. The educational objects produced by the teachers (e.g., the lessons) provide primary evidence of changes in their thinking over the course of the professional development experience.

The facilitator/researcher in the lesson study analyzed performance-based data (i.e., video-tapes of the teachers' planning meetings, lessons, and postlesson symposia). The goals were to document the teachers' thinking over time for use in planning subsequent sessions and to understand the teachers' developing of interpretive systems. For example, during the symposium following the first lesson, one lesson study team member commented:

> Our worksheet set it up for them, spoon-fed them. . . . One of the things we're going to be talking about later is: Was the worksheet helpful in focusing their thinking, or did it close off that aspect and not give us the feedback about where the students were starting from?

Another team member added:

> I could see that students were able to fill out the worksheets quickly but never really saw any indication of what does that mean they know . . . they could add plus two to the numbers, but that work didn't necessarily show the kids understand the pattern. Since we'll have an opportunity to reteach it, we're thinking about . . . how to revise it so we can see more of the students' thinking in the lesson.

These data from the teachers' conversations about the first teaching suggest that the mechanism of the lesson design prompted them to think critically about how their lesson was prompting the students to think deeply about the problem. The process of lesson design also prompted them to modify the lesson to reveal the students' thinking better.

After discussing what the students might learn from organizing the data on their own, rather than being presented with a two-column table to fill out, the team decided to eliminate the two-column table from the next teaching of the lesson. Initially, the teachers disagreed about the wisdom of having the students organize the data without a two-column table. In the course of the discussion, the teachers agreed that the students might learn something about the problem from organizing the data themselves, or at least that the teachers could learn something from trying it this new way. One teacher said, "It's exciting to see what will happen when we make this change. I guess that's what you call lesson study." Thus, the video transcripts revealed further confirmation that, over the course of their planning, the teachers crafted progressively a lesson that they perceived was more adequate for building the students' understanding of patterns than the one in the textbook. Furthermore, they had developed the students' materials to go with the lesson and had obtained information about the mathematical issues related to the lesson (e.g., the difference between a pattern, a rule, an equation, and a formula).

In the students' thinking sheets case, the researcher also analyzed video-taped data. She video-taped each session to capture the interactions among the teachers in the professional development session in order to obtain evidence of their processes of posing and testing interpretations of the students' thinking. The method of analyzing the transcripts produced from these video-tapes and the teachers' artifacts was guided by the *grounded theory* approach of Strauss and Corbin (1998). Two different trails of documentation (using both written and video-taped data) could be examined: the intermediate and final products over the course of a problem and the form of the students' thinking sheets over the course of the five problem-based cycles.

The researcher found that the production of the students' thinking sheets led the teachers to engage in *mini-inquiries*, occasions during which the teachers inquired into why their students thought about the associated, model-eliciting activities as they did or the teachers inquired into the underlying mathematical complexities associated with the model-eliciting activities. During these mini-inquiries, the teachers met some of the challenges of attending to students' thinking that are described in the reform documents, including looking for sense in their students' thinking (Chamberlin, 2005). For example, during the Departing On-Time (Appendix B) discussion, the teachers saw an evolution in the students' thinking. They reported that students often initially computed values for total minutes late or average minutes late, decided that the results were too close to use to rank the airlines, and therefore moved on to another strategy either as a tiebreaker or as a new way to approach the problem (e.g., the frequency of on-time departures).

At other times, the teachers' discussions did not result in such inquiries, leading to the need to revise for a subsequent study the locally developed professional development mechanism (i.e., the students' thinking sheets developed by the teachers). Specifically, through further analysis, the researcher recognized three adaptations to the production of the students' thinking sheets that may have led the teachers to express, test, and revise their interpretive systems more frequently. First, the facilitator should strive to establish more specific norms for the development of the students' thinking sheets. According to Ball and Cohen (1999), to take on a stance of inquiry, teachers need to develop collective social norms, such as avoiding leaps to definitive conclusions, presenting interpretations as conjectures, and relying upon evidence and critical methods of reasoning for making conclusions. Second, in order to enhance the teachers' ability to examine the students' ways of thinking, the facilitator should ensure that every teacher has a copy of the students' thinking sheets that each teacher designed individually. This would enable the teachers to examine more critically the other teachers' descriptions of their students' thinking (i.e., by being able to refer directly to the other teachers' interpretations of the students' work). Finally, as mentioned previously, the facilitator and the researcher should ask the teachers to produce a final chapter for the teachers' handbook that would help the teachers express, test, and revise their principles for implementing model-eliciting activities and for developing students' thinking sheets.

Summary

Guided by the professional development design principle that teachers should be engaged in experiences that result in expressing, testing, and revising their interpretive systems, the researcher and the facilitator in each professional development case designed mechanisms to enact this principle. As a result of testing these mechanisms, trails of documentation were revealed about a teacher's development and were used to revise the mechanisms further. The lesson study experience designed for this particular context was built upon the established literature in the field and, as such, was being field-tested in a new context, similar to Phase Five of the complete design cycle described in the chapter by Middleton, Gorard, Taylor, and Bannan-Ritland in this volume. The students' thinking sheet example, on the other hand, was in the initial stages of having a mechanism designed for it, which was expected to lead to further rounds of revision. Thus, in the latter example, one sees how the express-test-and-revise process applies to the development of mechanisms for local contexts and hints at how design experiments move from prototype and trial (Middleton et al.) to a field study.

Some Practical Considerations

During a design experiment, in some ways, the teacher and the researcher function more as co-researchers than as researcher and participant (Design-Based Research Connective, 2003; Lesh, 2002); that is also the case for the teachers, facilitators, and researchers in design studies for professional development. Each is involved in the research and development of an educational object, each is testing and analyzing data in order to refine the object under design, and each is reflecting on his or her own interpretive systems. Clearly, the students and their teachers are two different constituencies, but although the facilitator and the researcher have different purposes, much of their work is collaborative and closely related. Thus, it is possible to design a study in which the researcher and the facilitator are one and the same person. In fact, in the students' thinking sheets case, the facilitator and the researcher were the same person. The facilitator/researcher sought outside support to keep track of her different roles, to keep the purposes distinct yet in harmony, to discuss the possibilities for future sessions based on information gathered, and to keep the end-in-view in mind. Although it is challenging to take on both roles simultaneously, it is possible, especially in a small-scale study. Further, it is possible for an individual to conduct a series of studies over time, keeping both roles and building a program of research that can lead to transportable theories and frameworks for designing the particular type of professional development. Another way to approach creating and implementing a design study for professional development would be to use a team-based model, in which the facilitator and the researcher are two individuals (or teams). In the lesson study case, the teacher-leaders researched the process actively (e.g., documenting each iteration of the lesson and asking the group members to report on what they learned from lesson changes), but outside researchers assisted with additional elements of the process (e.g., video-taping, transcribing discussions, and developing a flowchart to describe changes in the lesson). The advantage is the opportunity to have multiple perspectives involved in the design of the professional development and of the theory, principles, or frameworks being developed for the field. Continual opportunities for the facilitator and the researcher to express, test, and revise their ideas are important for all the tiers in the design study.

Design studies in professional development require that multiple goals and purposes be kept in mind simultaneously. The teachers' problem to be solved is always in the forefront, as the end-in-view, and the product to be designed at each level needs to be thought revealing in order to prompt growth to take place (through cycles of express, test, and revise) and to provide documentation of the conceptual or interpretive systems of the constituency. Given that the professional development process is flexible and responsive to the changing conditions of the school environment, organizational tools are needed to facilitate the planning, implementation, documentation, and analysis processes. Table 11.1 is a chart intended to help a facilitator and a researcher begin planning a design study and represents an initial externalization of the authors' theory of how to create a design study for professional development.

Table 11.1 An Initial Planning Chart for a Design Study

Tier (participant level)	What is the end in view for the overall program of research?		
	Product to be designed	*Nature of the thought-revealing activity*	*Research and design process*
Student	What product is the student being asked to design?	How does the student's product reveal his or her thinking?	What is the purpose, or need, that the student is addressing by designing the product? How will the motivation to assess and revise the design be built into the classroom experience?
Teacher	What educational object will the teachers design? How will it help them advance toward the end in view?	How will the educational object reveal and document the teachers' thinking?	How will the students' data motivate the teachers' assessment and revision of the educational object under design?
Facilitator	What is the professional development experience being designed by the facilitator?	How will the facilitator document the changes and rationales for the changes in the planned professional development experience?	How will the facilitator use information gathered at the professional development sessions to reflect on and revise plans for the subsequent professional development sessions?
Researcher	What theory, principles, or framework is the researcher designing?	How will the researcher document the changes and rationales for the changes in the theory, principles, or framework being designed?	How will the researcher use information gathered at the professional development sessions to reflect on and revise the theory, principles, or framework under design?

Conclusions

The purpose of this chapter has been to propose a way of approaching research in professional development in situations where the nature of teachers' growth cannot be predicted always and where the professional development takes place in the complex context of schools. The proposed form of the design study for professional development is based on gathering information from what teachers *do* in preparing for instruction rather than from what they say *about* instruction. Designing the professional development experience around teachers' needs and around teachers' designs of educational objects or resources can work to enhance the professional development experience and, simultaneously, to provide documentation of the teachers' interpretive systems for learning and teaching. Planning the experience in a way that motivates teachers to go through cycles of expressing, testing, and revising the educational object they are designing leads to trails of documentation that can be used as evidence of change in teachers' interpretive systems. Engaging teachers in the process of reflecting on and analyzing evidence of their own interpretive systems not only enhances their professional development experience, but also provides the facilitator and the researcher with better insights into teachers' ways of thinking and their interpretive systems. The facilitator and the researcher, like the teacher, also are designing educational theories about which they reflect and produce a trail of documentation. The facilitator is designing the professional development experience and the researcher is designing the theory, principles, or frameworks that can be shared with and used by other researchers or educators interested in professional development in mathematics.

Rather than trying to control the factors of complexity associated with school-based, professional development, the proposed approach to design study is intended to embrace the complexity and the dynamic nature of the system in which teachers learn and grow. In addition, the professional development should feel more collaborative in nature. Fishman et al. (2004) describe a model for technology innovation that encourages explicitly collaboration between partners in an educational innovation. For professional development, we have described a model that encompasses the teachers' perspective in an end in view and the needs of the local school situation. However, the model also provides for the development of principles that are transportable to other situations in the sense that Middleton et al. (in this volume) describe. Thus, design experiments for professional development as we have conceptualized them are one way to think about what might be next for investigating teachers' interpretive systems and the development of those systems over time.

Acknowledgments

This material is based upon work supported by the National Science Foundation under Grant No. 0207259. Any opinions, findings, conclusions, or recommendations expressed in this material are those of the authors and do not reflect necessarily the views of the Foundation.

Notes

1 The studies described here seem to fall into the design experiment phases (three, four, and five) of the complete design cycle for a program of research described by Middleton, Gorard, Taylor, and Bannan-Ritland in another chapter in this book. It is conceivable that each study could become part of a larger program of research that would complete the seven phases described by them.
2 See the on-line database of lesson study groups at: www.tc.columbia.edu/lessonstudy/lsgroups.html
3 They received an honorarium for their attendance.
4 A group of 26 teachers initiated a lesson study in the autumn of 2000. By mid-2002, 87 teachers in the school district had joined lesson study groups voluntarily. For the protocols, see Lewis, 2002b; http://www.ger.com; http://www.tc.columbia.edu/lessonstudy.
5 English and Lesh (2003) used the term *end in view* to describe the final goal of a task in which the solution process is likely to be characterized by cycles of formulating the problem, modeling the problem, and revising the problem's interpretation and the model. In other words, the solution process mirrors a complex system that changes over time as the problem is being solved.
6 The illustrative, model-eliciting activity in Appendix B is typical, in that it begins with an article or a story that provides background in the contextual information and then uses "readiness questions" to review the context and address prerequisite skills. Finally, the model-eliciting product (i.e., model) should serve.
7 When the students completed this activity, they had access to computers. Thus, they performed their calculations by hand on paper and then used the word-processing capabilities of the computers to type their letters. The excerpts here are from their typed letters.

References

Ball, D. L. & Cohen, D. K. (1999). Developing practice, developing practitioners: Toward a practice-based theory of professional education. In L. Darling-Hammond & G. Sykes (eds), *Teaching as the learning profession: Handbook of policy and practice* (pp. 3–32). San Francisco, CA: Jossey-Bass.

Brown, A. (1992). Design experiments: Theoretical and methodological challenges in creating complex interventions in classroom settings. *Journal of the Learning Sciences*, 2, 141–178.

Chamberlin, M. T. (2002). Teacher investigations of students' work: The evolution of teachers' social processes and interpretations of students' thinking. *Dissertation Abstracts International*, 64(09), 3248 (UMI No. 3104917).

Chamberlin, M. T. (2004). Design principles for teacher investigations of student work. *Mathematics Teacher Education and Development*, 6, 61–72.

Chamberlin, M. T. (2005). Teachers' discussions of students' thinking: Meeting the challenge of attending to students' thinking. *Journal of Mathematics Teacher Education*, 8, 141–170.

Cobb, P., Confrey, J., diSessa, A., Lehrer, R. & Schauble, L. (2003). Design experiments in educational research. *Educational Researcher*, 32(1), 9–13.

Cohen, D. K. (1990). A revolution in one classroom: The case of Mrs. Oublier. *Educational Evaluation and Policy Analysis*, 12, 311–329.

Collins, A. (1992). Toward a design science of education. In E. Scanlon & T. O'Shea (eds), *New directions in educational technology* (pp. 15–22). New York: Springer-Verlag.

Darling-Hammond, L. & Ball, D. L. (1998). *Teaching for high standards: What policymakers need to know and be able to do.* Center for Policy Research in Education Joint Report Series (ERIC Document Reproduction Service No. ED426491).

Darling-Hammond, L. & McLaughlin, M. W. (1995). Policies that support professional development in an era of reform. *Phi Delta Kappan*, 76, 597–604.

Design-Based Research Collective (2003). Design-based research: An emerging paradigm for educational inquiry. *Educational Researcher*, 32(1), 5–8.

Doerr, H. M. & Lesh, R. A. (2003). A modeling perspective on teacher development. In R. A. Lesh & H. M. Doerr (eds), *Beyond constructivism: A models and modeling perspective on mathematics problem solving, learning and teaching* (pp. 125–140). Mahwah, NJ: Lawrence Erlbaum Associates.

English, L. & Lesh, R. (2003). Ends-in-view problems. In R. A. Lesh & H. M. Doerr (eds), *Beyond constructivism: A models and modeling perspective on mathematics problem solving, learning and teaching* (pp. 297–316). Mahwah, NJ: Lawrence Erlbaum Associates.

Fishman, B., Mars, R. W., Blumenfeld, P., Krajcik, J. & Soloway, E. (2004). Creating a framework for research on systemic technology innovations. *Journal of the Learning Sciences*, 13, 43–77.

Guskey, T. R. (1995). Professional development in education: In search of the optimal mix. In T. R. Guskey & M. Huberman (eds), *Professional development in education: New paradigms and practices* (pp. 114–131). New York: Teachers College Press.

Hawkins, J. & Collins, A. (1992). Design-experiments for infusing technology into learning. *Educational Technology*, 32, 63–67.

Hawley, W. D. & Valli, L. (1999). The essentials of effective professional development: A new consensus. In L. Darling-Hammond & G. Sykes (eds), *Teaching as the learning profession: Handbook of policy and practice* (pp. 127–150). San Francisco, CA: Jossey-Bass.

Koellner-Clark, K. & Lesh, R. (2003). A modeling approach to describe teacher knowledge. In R. A. Lesh & H. M. Doerr (eds), *Beyond constructivism: A models and modeling perspective on mathematics teaching, learning and problem solving* (pp. 159–174). Mahwah, NJ: Lawrence Erlbaum Associates.

Lesh, R. (2002). Research design in mathematics education: Focusing on design experiments. In L. English (ed.), *International handbook of research in mathematics education* (pp. 27–50). Mahwah, NJ: Lawrence Erlbaum Associates.

Lesh, R. & Clarke, D. (2000). Formulating operational definitions of desired outcomes of instruction in mathematics and science education. In A. Kelly & R. Lesh (eds), *Handbook of research design in mathematics and science education* (pp. 113–150). Mahwah, NJ: Lawrence Erlbaum Associates.

Lesh, R. & Doerr, H. M. (2003). *Beyond constructivism: A models and modeling perspective on mathematics teaching, learning and problem solving.* Mahwah, NJ: Lawrence Erlbaum Associates.

Lesh, R. & Kelly, A. E. (1997). Teachers' evolving conceptions of one-to-one tutoring: A three-tiered teaching experiment. *Journal for Research in Mathematics Education, 28,* 398–430.

Lesh, R. & Kelly, A. E. (2000). Multi-tiered teaching experiments. In A. Kelly & R. Lesh (eds), *Handbook of research in mathematics and science education* (pp. 197–230). Mahwah, NJ: Lawrence Erlbaum Associates.

Lesh, R., Hoover, M., Hole, B., Kelly, A. & Post, T. (2000). Principles for developing thought-revealing activities for students and teachers. In A. Kelly & R. Lesh (eds), *Handbook of research design in mathematics and science education* (pp. 591–646). Mahwah, NJ: Lawrence Erlbaum Associates.

Lewis, C. (2002a). Does lesson study have a future in the United States? *Nagoya Journal of Education and Human Development, 1,* 1–23.

Lewis, C. (2002b). *Lesson study: A handbook for teacher-led improvement of practice.* Philadelphia, PA: Research for Better Schools.

Lewis, C. & Tsuchida, I. (1997). Planned educational change in Japan: The shift to student-centered elementary science. *Journal of Education Policy, 12,* 313–331.

Lewis, C. & Tsuchida, I. (1998). A lesson is like a swiftly flowing river: Research lessons and the improvement of Japanese education. *American Educator, 22*(4), 12–17, 50–52.

Lieberman, A. (1996). Practices that support teacher development: Transforming conceptions of professional learning. In M. W. McLaughlin & I. Oberman (eds), *Teacher learning: New policies, new practices* (pp. 185–210). New York: Teachers College Press.

Loucks-Horsley, S., Harding, C. K., Arbuckle, M. A., Murray, L. B., Dubea, C. & Williams, M. K. (1987). *Continuing to learn: A guidebook for teacher development.* Andover, MA: Regional Laboratory for Educational Improvement of the Northeast and Islands.

Ma, L. (1999). *Knowing and teaching elementary mathematics.* Mahwah, NJ: Lawrence Erlbaum Associates.

National Council of Teachers of Mathematics (2001). *Practice-based professional development for teachers of mathematics.* Reston, VA: National Council of Teachers of Mathematics.

National Research Council, Committee on Scientific Principles for Education Research (2002). *Scientific research in education.* Washington, DC: National Academy Press.

Putnam, R. T. & Borko, H. (1997). Teacher learning: Implications of new views of cognition. In B. J. Biddle, T. L. Good & I. Goodson (eds), *International handbook of teachers and teaching* (pp. 1223–1296). Dordrecht, The Netherlands: Kluwer.

Putnam, R. T. & Borko, H. (2000). What do new views of knowledge and thinking have to say about research on teacher learning? *Educational Researcher, 29*(1), 4–15.

Shavelson, R. J., Phillips, D. C., Towne, L. & Feuer, M. J. (2003). On the science of educational design studies. *Educational Researcher, 32*(1), 25–28.

Speck, M. & Knipe, C. (2001). *Why can't we get it right? Professional development in our schools.* Thousand Oaks, CA: Sage.

Spillane, J. P. & Zeuli, J. S. (1999). Reform and teaching: Exploring patterns of practice in the context of national and state mathematics reforms. *Educational Evaluation and Policy Analysis, 21,* 1–27.

Stigler, J. W. & Hiebert, J. (1999). *The teaching gap: Best ideas from the world's teachers for improving education in the classroom.* New York: Summit.

Strauss, A. & Corbin, J. (1998). *Basics of qualitative research: Techniques and procedures for developing grounded theory.* Thousand Oaks, CA: Sage.

Verschaffel, L., DeCorte, E., Lasure, S., Van Vaerenbergh, G., Bogaerts, H. & Ratinckx, E.

(1999). Learning to solve mathematical application problems: A design experiment with fifth graders. *Mathematical Thinking and Learning*, 1, 195–229.

Yoshida, M. (1999). Lesson study: A case study of a Japanese approach to improving instruction through school-based teacher development. *Dissertation Abstracts International*, 60(11), 3895 (UMI No. 9951855).

Appendix A

Lesson Study Table Task

We have a long skinny room and triangle tables that we need to arrange in a row with their edges touching, as shown. Assuming each side can hold one seat, how many seats will 1 table, 2 tables, 3 tables hold? Is there a pattern that helps you figure out how many seats 10 tables will hold?

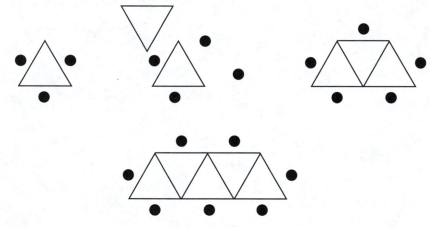

Figure 11.A1

Appendix B

A Model-Eliciting Activity

Newspaper Article: The Challenges of Flying

Chicago, Illinois—With 180,000 people flying in and out of O'Hare International Airport in Chicago each day, nearly 70 million people per year, O'Hare is one of the busiest airports in the world. Being this busy has advantages for passengers. For instance, if one's flight is canceled, one has a very good chance of finding another flight. Also, O'Hare has flights to virtually every other airport in the world.

However, along with these advantages come some disadvantages for passengers. It can be difficult to get to one's gate, to park one's car, to pick up one's baggage, and to check in when you have to compete with thousands of other people each day. Despite these disadvantages, people keep coming back to the airport and passengers have even rated the airport as their favorite airport in the world (on an internet survey). On the survey, passengers provided numerous reasons for their like of O'Hare airport. A popular reason was that all of the airlines at O'Hare try to stay on schedule. Staying on schedule is very important because one or two little disturbances can offset the entire airport schedule.

Travelers typically have three main concerns when flying to their destination. First and foremost, they are concerned with safety. When asked, most passengers say that they would not mind being a few minutes late to ensure that they arrive at their destination safely and without incident. After safety, the passengers' second most common concern is whether the flight takes off and arrives on time. Third, they want their baggage to be shipped to the correct destination and to arrive on time also.

O'Hare does a fantastic job of making sure the planes arrive and leave on time; however, many things can impact this timing. Those who travel regularly can make a calculated guess about whether their flights will arrive on time. This timing is contingent on several factors.

First, the origin of the flight impacts the plane's chance of arriving on time. For example, planes rarely leave late from San Diego, California due to San Diego's great weather, but they frequently leave San Francisco late due to weather conditions such as fog. Veteran travelers often try to avoid flights that leave San Francisco to come to O'Hare. Second, the on-time arrival is based on the flight's destination. For example, sometimes, a destination takes a plane into a very busy airport that may be too small for the amount of daily air traffic. In this case, a gate may not be ready always for the plane to pull up to and unload the passengers. Thus, the plane will have to wait. Similarly, an understaffed maintenance department may impact the company's ability to fix planes on a timely basis. Third, the on-time arrival may be dependent on the company. Some airlines are known for being on time consistently, whereas other airlines are known for not being on time.

For some travelers, arriving on time is not an

issue because they are not in a hurry. For example, a family flying from Pittsburgh to Orlando in order to visit Disney World may not be too concerned if they arrive 15 to 30 minutes late. However, business travelers may miss important meetings if their flights arrive late.

Readiness Questions

1   Where is one of the busiest airports in the world?
2   What do you believe might be another busy airport?
3   Why would arriving on time be important to some travelers and not as important to other travelers?
4   List one thing cited in the article that may cause a plane to be late.
5   Can you think of other reasons for a plane to be late that are not mentioned in the article?

Problem Statement

Information

In June, Ridgewood High School's Spanish club is going on a study abroad trip to Venezuela, and they have hired your class to help them select which airline to fly. Last year the Spanish club had a miserable experience when traveling to Barcelona. Their connecting flight to Reykjavik, Iceland was late, so they missed their next flight to Barcelona. The entire class had to stay overnight in the airport.

This year the class has decided to take a more systematic approach to choosing an airline. So far, the class has identified five airlines with economical fares that fly from O'Hare Airport to Venezuela, but they are still in the process of identifying more airlines that fly to Venezuela. Most of the flights have a connecting flight in Mexico City. They are hoping to find the airline that has the smallest chance of departing late from O'Hare so that they are less likely to arrive late in Mexico City. They don't want to miss their one connecting flight to Venezuela this year!

In Table 11.B1, you will find information about departure times for flights on the five airlines that the Spanish Club has identified thus far. The departure times are for flights leaving from O'Hare Airport and scheduled to arrive in Mexico City. Rank the five airlines in terms of most likely to be on time to least likely to be on time for departing from O'Hare Airport. As you rank the airlines, keep track of your process. Describe your process in a letter to the Spanish Club so that they may use a similar process to rank the additional airlines they may identify at a later time.

Table 11.B1 Number of Minutes Late for Flights Departing from O'Hare Airport

Sky Voyage Airline	Central American Airlines	Mexico Express	Sudamerica Internacional	Southeast Airline
5	15	9	0	0
0	9	5	25	5
20	4	5	0	0
5	0	5	9	9
0	0	125	0	40
6	14	10	0	0
0	20	5	4	5
0	15	10	0	25
15	16	0	35	10
0	0	4	0	30
0	0	10	0	12
7	15	10	10	0
0	10	10	5	0
5	10	9	55	10
40	25	7	0	9
4	5	12	0	5
0	20	5	0	0
0	15	0	17	27
0	11	10	5	11
0	12	7	0	0
3	0	13	65	30
60	5	0	5	5
5	0	0	0	0
0	30	10	0	4
7	4	5	2	40
0	5	4	0	0
0	10	6	0	15
123	10	5	75	0
0	25	7	0	6
5	4	5	0	9

Appendix C

	Description of the Strategy
Strategy 1	Total or Average Number of Minutes Late: Students may find the total number of minutes late for each airline. Then, some students will continue to find the average number of minutes late per day for each airline. They then order the airlines from lowest to highest to rank the airlines from most likely to depart on time to least likely to depart on time.

Total Number of Minutes Late:

> We found this information out by adding all the minutes for every airline in the month of June. In this case the airline with the smallest sum was the best.

Average Number of Minutes Late:

> We have been looking over various airlines' flight times from the month of June in 1999. We added up the total amount of minutes they were late and divided it by 30 to find the average amount of minutes a particular airline was late per day.

Strategy 2	Counting the Number of On-Time Flights: Students may count the number of times that each airline is on time; that is, count the number of zeros for each airline. Then, they may find either the ratio of flights on time per the 30 flights for each airline or they may find the percentage of on-time flights for each airline. They then order the airlines from highest to lowest to rank the airlines from most likely to depart on time to least likely to depart on time.

Counting the Number of On-Time Flights:

> We found our answer by counting how many times the airlines were on time. We picked one that was on time the most.

Strategy 3	Redefining Late:

Students may recognize that departing anywhere between one and twenty minutes late will still allow a passenger to catch a connecting flight. Therefore, they may redefine late as occurring when a flight departs more than 20 minutes late. Then, they may incorporate this new definition for lateness into Strategy 1 or Strategy 2. For example, similar to Strategy 1, they may find the average number of minutes that flights are late when they are late. Similar to Strategy 2, they may count the number of times that each airline departs later than 20 minutes.

Counting the Number of Flights Departing Less than 5 Minutes Late:

> If you are wanting to know the probability of the airlines being late, you must find the ratio. We did this by not counting 5 minutes and under as being late. Sky Voyage Airline's ratio of being late, for instance, is 22/30, 22 being the times the airlines is not late and 30 being the amount of days. We found that Sky Voyage and Sudamerica Internacional are tied for first and Southeast Airlines somewhat behind at 15/30, so half the time it is late. Central American Airlines is late 2/5 of the time, coming in last place. We hope this helps you and thanks for asking us for the job.

	Mathematics in the Strategy	*Meeting the Needs of the Client*
Strategy 1	Adding the total number of minutes for each airline. Finding the average by dividing the total number of minutes for each airline by 30. Comparing and ordering the averages or total minutes to rank the airlines. Students often rounded their averages to the nearest tenth of a decimal point.	This strategy would be easy for the Spanish Club to implement. However, it is not very effective for the Spanish Club. More specifically, one or two very late departures on the part of an airline will be equal to a large number of minimally late departures on the part of another airline. Also, the differences between the averages are only a matter of seconds, not a good measure for ranking the airlines.
Strategy 2	Adding the number of times that an airline left on time. Finding the ratio of on-time departures to total departures (30). Dividing the number of times on time by 30 for each airline, then multiplying by 100 to find the percentage of on-time departures for each airline. Comparing and ordering the ratios or percentages to rank the airlines.	This strategy is also fairly easy for the Spanish Club to implement. It is more effective than Strategy 1, but the strategy does not take into account that departing up to 20 minutes late may still be acceptable for catching a connecting flight.
Strategy 3	Determining an acceptable range for departure times. The same mathematics as Strategy 1 or 2 depending on which approach is used.	This strategy is a little bit more difficult for the Spanish Club to implement. It depends on identifying an acceptable range for departures and requires associated computations. However, this strategy proves more effective than Strategy 1 or 2. It takes into account that departing up to 20 minutes late may be acceptable for catching a connecting flight.

12 Teacher Design Research

An Emerging Paradigm for Teachers' Professional Development

Brenda Bannan-Ritland
George Mason University

Introduction

This chapter presents a new approach to teachers' professional development called Teacher Design Research (TDR), whose goal is to promote the growth of teachers as adaptive experts. The premise of the TDR approach is that the involvement of teachers in long-term cycles of design research (Kelly, 2003, 2004) may have the potential to promote profound learning of content, encourage their adaptive expertise in the classroom, and prompt them to rethink their beliefs and practices.

TDR challenges teachers to undertake research activities in their classrooms by designing and testing instructional material prototypes (including software) and participating in novel teaching procedures involving other teachers (working in teams with a research team) engaged in multiple cycles of data collection about their students' learning. The failures or successes of such designed activities to promote students' learning can prompt teachers to reconsider their core teaching ideas, beliefs, and competencies. Thus, the instructional aspects of TDR come not from outside experts, but, rather, from the teachers' cognitive dissonance experiences as designers in design cycles.

Teachers' perspectives and practical knowledge of adapting classroom practices are paramount. As researchers learn about applied teaching approaches and as teachers as designers wrestle collaboratively with their individual and collective interpretations and practices, they naturally explicate and reformulate their understanding of teaching and learning issues. Teacher design research then becomes a context of inquiry that meaningfully provokes teachers to restructure their core ideas, beliefs, and practices. The shared and collaborative nature of TDR can work toward establishing the mutual trust in problem solving and the theory-building that is needed to go beyond local contexts and practices in the social processes and to support diffusion of innovations. The tenets, characteristics, and an illustrative example of TDR supported with qualitative data are described in detail below.

Design Framework

Collinson (1996) characterized teachers' professional development as typically involving:

- In-service workshops that emphasize private individual activity.
- Brief single sessions that offer often unrelated topics.
- Reliance on an external "expert" presenter.
- An expectation of passive teacher-listeners.
- An emphasis on skill development.

Similarly, Sparks (1995) described teachers' professional development as an atheoretical activity where quick visible results are expected and where the emphasis is on "training" teachers outside the context of the classroom. Teachers' professional development activities seem to focus primarily on their expressed needs rather than on explicit linkages to expectations about students' learning (Sparks & Loucks-Horsley, 1989). Although teachers' professional development efforts in educational reform are ubiquitous, their value has been questionable (Borko, 2004).

Some theorists argue that the goal of professional development for teachers is to help them grow as "adaptive experts," which requires "moving beyond existing routines and often requires people to rethink key ideas, practices, and even values in order to change what they are doing" (Hammerness et al., 2005a: 361). Developing adaptive expertise among teachers means that they go beyond their existing routines to reconceptualize their practice in order to address both efficiency and innovation in their teaching (Schwartz et al., 2005).

In this section the six tenets of Teacher Design Research as a design framework are discussed.

Teacher Design Research Should be Directed Toward an Instructional Challenge that Evidences Significant Conceptual Complexity

The investment of time and resources required for TDR should not be applied to the teaching of straightforward concepts or simple procedural knowledge. Teacher design research grew out of a National Science Foundation CAREER project to address the problem of teachers' progression toward two significant challenges: (a) to develop scientific literacy among young children, and by (b) integrating reading comprehension strategies into, scientific thinking (National Research Council, 2000; Snow et al., 2005). Researchers have called for studies of teachers' views, beliefs, the implementation of inquiry processes, and how these processes may intersect with appropriate reading strategies for scientific subject matter (Keys, 1999; Keys & Bryan, 2001; Palincsar & Magnusson, 2000). Part of the problem lies in the fact that inquiry processes are defined and implemented differently by teachers and researchers in both reading and science (Anderson, 2002; Haury, 1993). A further complication was that suitable instructional materials were difficult to locate, and theories of intervention were underdeveloped.

Teacher Design Research Should be Applied when Teachers' Traditional Professional Development Appears Unequal to the Task

This tenet follows from the first one. The instructional and learning problems should be of a magnitude and complexity not likely to be addressed by brief training sessions for teachers. Instead, TDR draws on the current ideas of theorists about professional development for teachers who recommend:

- Immersing teachers in an intensive experience that focuses on deep learning of the content and processes by challenging them at their level of competence (Loucks-Horsley et al., 1998).
- Having teachers learn by constructing their own meaning from current experiences using previous knowledge (Loucks-Horsley et. al., 1998).
- Supporting teachers to understand more fully the processes of learning through active inquiry (Loucks-Horsley et al., 1998).

- Promoting learning about practice in practice (Hammerness et al., 2005b).
- Focusing teachers on how students learn new content and processes (Loucks-Horsley et al., 1998; Joyce & Showers, 1995).
- Building learning in professional communities with shared goals among teachers (Hawley & Valli, 1999) that includes peer coaching (Joyce & Showers, 1995).
- Helping teachers develop a sense of self-efficacy in their ability to impact students (Fullan, 1991) through a shared understanding of the purposes, rationale, and processes involved in the innovation (Hawley & Valli, 1999).
- Modeling new strategies and helping teachers practice them (Joyce & Showers, 1995).
- Moving from deficit-based to competency-based approaches (Smylie & Conyers, 1991).

Teachers' Professional Development Can be Fostered Through Their Direct Involvement in Multiple Teacher Design Research Cycles

In a TDR experience, teachers participate directly in such activities as:

1 Needs assessment or needs analysis processes.
2 A collaborative review of the literature.
3 A contextual analysis of their school, school district, and state culture and environment.
4 Data collection and analysis of their own and their colleagues', students' and experts' learning.
5 An audience analysis and the construction of "personas" to direct design.
6 A conceptual design direction based on data analyses.
7 Design and prototyping.
8 Cycles of evaluation of the prototype.
9 Data collection and analyses of students' learning processes in relation to design ideas and prototyping.
10 Presentation of the designs' prototype to clients and interested parties.

Teacher Design Research grows out of an instructional system design model that has been developed over time in an extended immersive experience (Bannan-Ritland, 2001). The focus of TDR is on meaningful classroom problems that are selected by and negotiated among the teacher design researchers. The problems are investigated by them with the aim of making explicit their current and transforming practical knowledge about the teaching and learning goal. The design process promotes the articulation of teachers' beliefs and practices. This encourages them to reconsider their own practice in relation to others' approaches and through that impetus to create an optimal design innovation that will extend beyond their own classroom. Teachers share related theory and research, as well as participate in multiple cycles of data collection and analysis about students' and teachers' learning. These cycles prompt design ideas that are grounded in theory, research findings, and the teachers' own practice. The teachers participate fully in decisions about the design, along with the research team and other interested parties, and about using the innovations in their own and their colleagues' classrooms. In this manner, the research phase promotes investment and ownership in the outcome of the design, front-loading the diffusion process as the teachers become engaged in the creativity of innovation. The characteristics of TDR can be described as follows:

- Intensive involvement in multiple cycles of integrated design and research during a long-term initiative (e.g., an academic year).
- Collaborative problem solving and decision making during the design phase between the teachers and researchers.
- Intensive, inquiry-based experience.
- A focus on meaningful and significant learning problems generated by the teachers.
- Direct involvement of the teachers and their full participation in the creative decision making entailed in design research.
- Involvement of students, teacher-colleagues, and experts as resources for design research, but the teacher's practical knowledge remains paramount as a basis for decision making.
- Guidance and support provided by the research team, programmer, and graphic artist who also learn about teachers' learning and perspectives on innovation in the classroom.
- Teachers' reconsideration of their own practices as they design an innovation for their students as well as for other teachers and other children.
- Grounding in the literature of cognitive theory and current research on students' learning as well as teachers' practical knowledge of students' learning.
- Understanding that innovation, change, and reform are long-term, ongoing processes with multiple cycles.
- Teachers are treated as design researchers actively involved in contributing to a conceptual design, and the power of the context of their classrooms is recognized as fundamental to design and research activities.
- Teachers focus on contributing to the design and development of standards-based instruction, fostering students' conceptual learning, and addressing students' misconceptions, through applied design, where possible.

Teacher Design Research is Similar to but Distinct from Other Professional Development Approaches Influenced by Design and Research Activities

Different approaches embodying design and research activities are beginning to emerge in the literature about professional development for teachers. Involving teachers in design has a recent history, which includes such initiatives as teachers-as-designers (Jonassen & Reeves, 1996), teachers' design of curricula (Parke & Coble, 1997), participatory design of science curricula (Shrader et al., 2001), and more direct applications of design research principles (e.g., Clements, this volume; Zawojewski, Chamberlin, Hjalmarson, & Lewis, this volume). Many of these initiatives consisted of short-term, workshop-like experiences for teachers conducted during the summer outside their job context, but other endeavors are moving beyond these bounds.

Other professional enhancement efforts have shown promise in the development of teacher-generated innovations through curricula design, reflection, and reconceptualization of practice. Lewis et al. (2006: 3) advocate employing the Japanese lesson study approach in a manner that considers the "development of a descriptive knowledge base; explication of an innovation's mechanism; and iterative cycles of improvement research." In other work, Zawojewski, Chamberlin, Hjalmarson, and Lewis (this volume) attempt to promote mathematics teachers' professional development through short-term, classroom-based cycles of design research that strive "to produce generalizable theory about the interpretive systems that teachers use to teach." Penuel (2006) presented an experience of a long-term codesign of innovations in which the teachers, researchers, and developers collaborate on the design and evaluation of a prototype. Perhaps the last two examples come closest to the concept of TDR; however, they do not seem to address prominently *integrated* design and research cycles in which the teachers are full participants in data-driven decision making about the design, helping to steer the direction of the conceptual design and ground it in their practice. TDR also seems to differ from some of these other constructs in that there is a deliberate aim to extend the innovation systemically: (a) beyond the teachers' classroom by involving teachers directly in the contextual analysis of local, state, and national issues, (b) through consideration and integration of the multitiered perspectives of the research community, scientists, and teacher-colleagues, and (c) through students' perspectives about the learning issue identified in the design research procedures. Details of the experiences of a group of teachers in this type of TDR activity are given in a later section of this chapter.

Teacher Design Research is Viewed Through a Frame of Diffusion of Innovations

As noted before, TDR does not promote a view of teachers' professional development as a training problem; rather, it views teachers' professional development as a problem in the diffusion of innovations (Rogers, 2003). Zaritsky et al. (2003) describe the diffusion of an innovation as a social process, associating the rate of adoption of the innovation as being determined by: (a) the type of innovation decision, (b) the nature of the communication channels diffusing the innovation at various stages in the innovation's decision process, (c) the nature of the social system, and (d) the extent of the change agents' efforts in diffusing the innovation.

The goal of TDR is to encourage teachers to adapt cognitively their current practice, over time, to more complex and innovative, but still compatible, ideas and practices. The process of adoption takes considerable time. Rogers (2003) claims that the adoption of an innovation involves five distinct processes, which are handled socially:

1   *Knowledge:* coming to learn the existence and function of the innovation.
2   *Persuasion:* being persuaded about the value of the innovation.
3   *Decision:* committing to adopting the innovation.
4   *Implementation:* using the innovation for an extended period of time.
5   *Confirmation:* ultimately accepting or rejecting the innovation.

TDR places the adopter (the teacher) centrally in the diffusion process as a designer and a researcher. The teacher is a part of the team that generates the existence and function of the innovation. The teacher is a part of the persuasion process for himself or herself and for others. The decision to commit is based on the teacher's observation of what Rogers (2003) calls "observability" and "trialability" processes, except that the teacher (as an adopter) is involved actively in the redesign, based on these processes. Further, the teacher is not implementing an outsider's product or process; rather, he or she is putting into effect his or her own theories about an intervention as expressed in the (co)designed intervention and is implementing the intervention across a number of generation-and-testing cycles. The teacher's cumulative decision to accept or reject the innovation is based on multiple design cycles. One of the hopes of TDR's exponents is that innovations that survive to adoption by the designing teacher(s) are more likely to be adopted by other teachers in similar contexts than innovations that are developed by outside experts.

Teacher Design Research Requires a Long-Term, Intensive Commitment to Teachers' Learning

The TDR process does not come without costs, commitment, and effort. Changing teachers' conceptual beliefs and practices is a long-term, intensive process that requires acceptance by teachers. However, analysis of our data suggests that involving teachers in examining their own practices for the purpose of design research over a long period with appropriate resources promotes a high level of engagement and ownership in the development and use of the innovation (Bannan-Ritland et al., 2006). There is also preliminary qualitative evidence that six teachers who participated in TDR reported a shift in their beliefs about teaching and learning. If further research bears this out, TDR and other codesign approaches may hold promise for addressing the perpetual problems inherent in sustaining reform-based innovations in education contexts (see Fishman et al., 2004). However, as Penuel (2006) importantly pointed out, issues of defined roles, accountability, design decision making, time, and expense need to be considered in these forms of complex professional development.

The benefits may outweigh the costs, however, if TDR can promote quality professional development for teachers and can improve the design and fit of classroom-based innovations in which the teachers have ownership and promote in their local contexts. Teacher design research, then, can address Rogers' (2003) factors of relative advantage, compatibility, complexity, "trialability," and "observability" through the direct involvement of teachers in the conceptualization, creation, and testing of prototypes that address problems identified in the classroom. Through multiple cycles of data collection, analysis, and design, the teachers become invested in the innovation and promote its testing in their classrooms and its use through their social networks. These natural cycles that take place in design research provoke a necessary, bottom-up approach to innovation and scaling that also may have the capacity to promote learning and change by teachers.

An Illustration and the Preliminary Results of a Teacher Design Research Experience

An initial foray into TDR involved six teachers in the conceptual design of a technology-based prototype that intersected scientific inquiry processes with reading comprehension at the fourth-grade level. This experience was structured deliberately so that it would engage the teachers in inquiry through their participation in an inquiry-based, design research project investigating how students and teachers learn. The teachers and the research team were asked to identify an area in science and to design learning activities pertinent to national and state standards that incorporated iterative integrated cycles of data collection and analysis and the design of a web-based technology system. Some design decisions were a direct result of the teachers' data analyses; other design decisions were made based on the integration of multiple factors such as teachers' insight and practical knowledge, as well as pragmatic factors (for a discussion of the process of design research decision-making, see Bannan-Ritland and Baek, this volume). The teachers were supported in their conceptual design activities by the project investigator, who is a professor in instructional design, a team of four graduate research assistants, who included a computer programmer and a graphic artist, and a science consultant.

The remainder of this chapter recounts parts of a comprehensive qualitative investigation into the teachers' perceptions of the TDR experience and identifies shifts in the teachers' beliefs and intentions about scientific inquiry during the experience.[1] The context of the study is reported, along with some illustrative data from one teacher's participation. These preliminary results are being analyzed further, together with data from the other five teachers, in a comprehensive, cross-case analysis. Follow-up studies are planned for the purpose of collecting additional video observation data from the classrooms of the participating teachers. These new data will be reviewed against baseline classroom video data collected during the first year of the teachers' involvement in this project (2003–2004) in order to determine any long-term impact on their practice after they took part in TDR.

Participants

Six teachers from four schools in a small school district situated in an urban-suburban area in the mid-Atlantic region of the United States participated in this research. The TDR project consisted of two, nine-credit courses during an academic year that entailed weekly, face-to-face sessions that involved teachers directly in research and design activities and were supplemented by online discussions. The teachers were recruited with the help of the school districts' science supervisor. Tuition for the courses was funded by the National Science Foundation grant. Five of the participants were elementary school teachers who served in various roles: three as fourth-grade classroom teachers, one as a mathematics-special education resource teacher, and one as a science resource teacher for her school. The sixth teacher was a middle-school reading specialist. The rest of this chapter reports the analysis of data from the experience of one teacher (the science resource teacher) during the academic year of her involvement in TDR. Portions of the data analysis and of interviews with this particular teacher are presented as part of a case study to illustrate the potential of TDR for further research (Glaser & Strauss, 1967; Yin, 2003).

The Teacher Design Research Experience

Generally, the TDR experience followed an emerging process model that attempts to intersect systematic, instructional design processes with rigorous research investigation of cognitively-based theories about teaching and learning and with other perspectives on the design and diffusion of innovations entitled the Integrative Learning Design Framework (see Bannan-Ritland, 2003). As noted earlier, the six teachers described above were involved in two, nine-credit, instructional design courses during the 2004–2005 academic year (August through May) that were designed specifically to investigate teaching and learning issues related to science inquiry and reading comprehension in order to inform the design of a technology system that integrated these processes and concepts at the fourth-grade level. The teachers were involved intimately in the needs assessment process, selecting an area of study (e.g., landform change in geoscience), aligning the direction of the design with state and national standards, reviewing current research in science inquiry, earth science, geological reasoning and reading in science. The year-long experience culminated in the teachers presenting their ideas for the design of a technology-based prototype to the funding agency's advisory board.

During their TDR experience, the teachers were instructed specifically to consider their prior knowledge, synthesize current research literature, and collectively translate and integrate their practical knowledge, theoretical constructs, earth science content, and research findings into a conceptual design of a technology-based prototype. During the first semester, the teachers were guided initially through a contextual analysis of their approaches to teaching science, school culture, and obstacles for the integration of science and literacy in the classroom. After much discussion and an interview with a representative from the American Association for the Advancement of Science, learning about the processes of erosion and landform change in earth science was targeted as an area of curricular need that aligned with local, state, and national standards. To gain an informed perspective on this content area, the teachers worked with a geomorphologist who led them through a condensed learning experience about geomorphology that encompassed more than 20 hours of formal instruction and a field learning experience in a nature center next to one of the teacher's schools. During the second semester, the teachers participated in data collection and analysis of their students' prior knowledge and reading abilities in earth science, employing a think-aloud procedure, and interviewed colleagues about their perspectives on inquiry science teaching, which informed subsequent design ideas. Toward the latter half of the second semester, the teachers synthesized their learning and practice into a theoretically-based idea for a conceptual design for teaching the processes of erosion that combined an inquiry-based approach to science with reading comprehension skills.

Research Aims

In this exploratory, single-case study, there was a particular interest in seeing how the science resource teacher's understanding of inquiry, geoscience content, and the intersection of reading and science might change during her TDR experience. There also was considerable curiosity about how she perceived and engaged in the TDR project, her learning through it, and if she found TDR valuable professional development. The theoretical propositions on entering into this study were:

- Participation in a long-term, design research undertaking will give teachers time and space to articulate collaboratively and individually their practical knowledge, beliefs, and understanding about inquiry science; about connecting inquiry science, reading, and students' learning; and the obstacles to success in this endeavor.
- The teachers' involvement in design research will result in changes in their perceptions of scientific inquiry and in their perceptions of their level of knowledge of geoscience content, and an increased awareness of the linkages between science and literacy.

The initial assumptions were that, in a rare collaborative context, the teachers' involvement in design and the design research process might prompt their reflection on, and explicit articulation about, integrated beliefs and classroom practices. It was conjectured that focusing on integrated design and research tasks to produce a conceptual design collaboratively might have the potential to prompt the teachers to reconsider their own practices, practical knowledge, and knowledge of pedagogical content. Although it was thought that the TDR experience would elicit some changes in the teachers, it was unclear what they would be, both individually and collectively. Essentially, these teachers were attempting to generate an inquiry-based learning environment based on the integration of their practical knowledge, research, and collaborative insight while engaged in a challenging, inquiry-based learning context of TDR. In this complex, multitiered, collaborative experience, it was not known what to expect as an outcome.

Data Sources

The data included: (a) many interviews with the teachers, (b) video-recordings from weekly class sessions (four hours across two, 16-week sessions, for a total of 128 hours of video data), (c) online discussions, (d) online journal reflections, (e) individual, teacher-produced artifacts (individual concept maps, transcripts of interviews with colleagues, data analyses, students' think-aloud protocols, transcriptions, and analyses), (f) collaborative, teacher-produced artifacts (concept maps from brain-storming about design), and (g) research team's memorandums and multiple surveys related to teachers' practice, content knowledge, and design knowledge. Individual interviews were conducted with the teachers approximately one month into the nine-month experience, during the fourth month, and at the conclusion of the experience.

Case Study: Jennifer

To explore the potential of TDR for further research, a case study of Jennifer's experience is presented here. Sections of the interviews with Jennifer at the beginning, mid-point, and conclusion of her TDR experience are highlighted to illustrate how TDR may address the desired characteristics of teachers' professional development. The interview data are presented to draw attention to these characteristics and, it is hoped, to spark interest among educational researchers to investigate further the impact of TDR efforts on teachers' professional development.

Jennifer was an elementary science teacher and also provided professional development for teachers in her school. What was notable in Jennifer's case study (as well as informed the preliminary analyses of the case studies of the other teachers), was the shift in her perspective of inquiry-based science from the beginning to the middle to the end of her TDR experience. She articulated her initial and reconceptualized understanding of scientific inquiry as well as her shifting view of the intersection of reading and science to provide some evidence for the viability of TDR to address the necessary components of teachers' professional development.

Jennifer's Changing Perspective of Scientific Inquiry: Teachers as Active Learners who go Beyond their Existing Orientations to Adapt to New Situations

Putnam and Borko (1997: 1281) advocate that the context for teachers' professional development "must take into account and address teacher knowledge and beliefs" because "what teachers know and believe will influence their interpretation and enactment of any new ideas for teaching." The TDR experience begins with a collaborative investigation and an explicit articulation of teachers' current practice and beliefs related to the teaching and learning issue identified. Investigating scientific inquiry and its intersections with reading comprehension were posed as the teaching and learning issues for Jennifer and the group of teachers involved in this TDR experience. During her participation, Jennifer's beliefs and practical knowledge about inquiry seemed to change.

Initially, Jennifer's view of scientific inquiry could be described as conflicted. She attempted to integrate her definition of inquiry, which she described as "coming up with different results and taking different paths" in science, contrasted with a traditional, structured, step-by-step version of the scientific method, which she regarded as being promoted by the curricular materials and her colleagues. In defining inquiry,

Jennifer placed significant emphasis on student's questions and aligned her perspective with her school's philosophy of a constructivist-based, "hands-on, minds-on" approach. Jennifer said that she advocated teaching inquiry with her colleagues with a clear sense of the steps to follow in the scientific method. In her existing mental model of inquiry, the idea of hypothesis testing was paramount. Paradoxically, the focus on the algorithmic nature of this method served to constrain both Jennifer's view of scientific inquiry and her desire to allow for different paths for students traversing inquiry-based experiences in science lessons. This created tensions between the "hands-on" perspective, which supported following set procedures, and a "minds-on" perspective, which permitted students to follow their interests and curiosity, both of which were prominent in her initially articulated knowledge and beliefs about science inquiry.

In the TDR cycles, Jennifer was required to face these tensions directly. At the midpoint after four months, her understanding and representation of inquiry seemed to shift from following algorithms and testing hypotheses to a greater emphasis on process skills such as observing, analyzing data, and writing descriptions. Now, Jennifer saw the usefulness of students' questions, not for their own sake but for the purpose of promoting the students' "ownership" of the scientific process. At the middle of her TDR experience, Jennifer said she had a greater appreciation of science as a collaborative, nonlinear process. Her view of classroom inquiry had expanded to incorporate different ways of investigating scientific phenomena.

By the end of her nine-month TDR cycles and experience, Jennifer had moved away from a view of classroom science inquiry as "recipe following" for hypothesis testing toward a flexible rich representation of the scientific inquiry process, both for herself and for her students. She believed now that science involved experiential learning that can prompt questions that are not always stated as formal hypotheses. Jennifer reconceptualized her understanding of the scientific inquiry process and expanded her definition beyond mere experimentation to include observation and other forms of inquiry. Her emphasis on students' questioning had changed as well because she saw now the role of questioning as an ongoing cyclical process in scientific inquiry, not as a means to an end in the classroom. At the conclusion of her participation, Jennifer seemed to express the desire to adapt her practice to place additional emphasis on using resources beyond the classroom to inform scientific questioning and investigations such as books, the internet, experts, and other resources of the scientific community such as the U.S. Geological Survey and the American Association for the Advancement of Science. After the TDR experience, Jennifer seemed to grasp the idea of science inquiry as a community phenomenon incorporating many different resources, rather than as a simplistic procedural process. Jennifer's new definition of scientific inquiry was:

> I see that a lot of times it begins with an experience, and a question is raised. I've also, and this has changed for me, always felt that you had to make a hypothesis, and I still want kids to make predictions and hypotheses, but I also know that you could be wondering and you don't always have, and scientists don't always have an exact hypothesis. So I may be being a little more flexible in that. I see that they can find the answers to their questions not only by setting up an experiment, but by asking experts, looking on the internet, looking in books. I see the importance of community in inquiry and running your ideas by others, talking about them as you work, and up here I had the importance of presenting and sharing. And it doesn't always have to be a formal presentation, it could be just in your little group, you know, share or have a jigsaw—one person share with another. I also see that it's ongoing, that as you're sharing, you come up with more questions, and as you're

investigating, you come up with more questions. I think the challenge might be that you don't just get really off track. [laughter] So that's my definition of inquiry.

During her TDR experience, Jennifer's knowledge and beliefs about scientific inquiry seemed to change dramatically from her initial stance. Through her participation in TDR, she was forced to adapt to new situations as a teacher-design-researcher involved in data collection, analysis, and design, which demanded that she confront new ideas about scientific inquiry. This provided a context where she had to grapple with her own understanding of pedagogy in science along with other perspectives from her peers, researchers, and the literature. She had to integrate her everyday, action-oriented, person- and context-bound, practical knowledge with the more formal, scientific knowledge that she explored through experts and other resources. Interestingly, Jennifer's expanded view of inquiry seemed to be a result of her inquiry-based activities in design research. Jennifer's TDR experience permitted her to examine her own beliefs, knowledge, efficacy, and efficiency in teaching science in an inquiry-based manner in order to contribute to designing new approaches for the fourth-grade classroom. Along the way, she reconceptualized her beliefs, moving beyond the often articulated perspective that scientific inquiry relies on "hands-on and minds-on," scientific methods-based, procedural directives.

At the end of the TDR experience, Jennifer was able to stand back and analyze her own progression and teaching as they related to scientific inquiry in this way:

> I think that, I didn't really know what inquiry was. I mean, I hear, I say inquiry-based, and I think of it as doing hands-on. I thought that was inquiry. And from this, that has changed. Yes, a lot of it is hands-on, but it's more a way of thinking and it's also that the whole ongoing process has changed. As I said earlier though, I haven't implemented as successfully as I would like to.

Jennifer's Reconsideration of How She Teaches Science: Expanding the Frames and Questioning her Practice

Jennifer's expanded understanding of the strategies, skills, and reasoning involved in scientific inquiry after her involvement in TDR allowed her to see more possibilities in her teaching practice. However, she was frustrated by not being able to enact all that she was learning at that time. Despite this frustration, she was able to integrate her experiences with those of her peers and the scientist, the formal research, and theory-based information with her everyday teaching knowledge. This integration was rooted firmly in, and represented by, her classroom practice. This gives credence to Cochran-Smith and Lytle's (1993) approach to the development of teachers' knowledge in a TDR context as including the development of knowledge for practice, in practice, and of practice. This is evidenced by Jennifer's significant reflection on, and reconsideration of, her teaching practice in science that occurred during her participation in TDR. While planning her next science lesson, she remarked:

> When I was planning it, I thought I'm trying to convey the content, but am I just trying to fill them up and doing some experiments or am I letting them ask questions? And I thought, if I'm only going to have this much time with them, how much time can I let them have to explore their questions? I think it [the TDR experience] has made me question whether I am a good teacher or not, and if I am teaching in the best way.

Cochran-Smith and Lytle (ibid.) state that "the knowledge teachers need to teach well emanates from systematic inquiries about teaching, learners and learning, curriculum, schools and schooling. This knowledge is constructed collectively within local and broader communities" (p. 274). The TDR experience required Jennifer and her colleagues to explore scientific inquiry processes systematically through integrated research and design cycles, which seemed to result in expanded frames for their teaching practices, although not without some cognitive dissonance and struggle. Jennifer continually mapped others' perspectives that were articulated in the design research process back to her own, and her participation in the design of the classroom innovation seemed to prompt a natural process of questioning her own practices.

Jennifer's Perception of Learning in Teacher Design Research: Gaining Vision, Understanding, Dispositions, Practices, and Tools

The TDR experience maps to Hammerness et al.'s (2005a: 385) framework for teacher's learning in communities that includes: (a) developing a vision for their practice, (b) a set of understandings about teaching, learning, and children, (c) dispositions about how to use this knowledge, (d) practices that allow them to act on their intentions and beliefs, and (e) tools that support their efforts. Jennifer's developing vision of scientific inquiry meshed with her teaching practice. Her understanding of children's geoscience reasoning and the collaborative process in TDR informed her knowledge about teaching, learning, and children. The juxtaposition of scientists' and teachers' dispositions, practices, and tools promoted in TDR created the space for Jennifer to progress and act on her own understandings, intentions, and beliefs about scientific inquiry during her TDR experience. By observing and examining the tools and processes of a geoscientist, Jennifer was able to gain a solid foundation in the earth science content of erosion processes, as well as to transfer her understandings of these tools and processes into the classroom to benefit her students.

Jennifer's perception of her professional development was centered on her personal learning processes, which evidenced some transformation in her thinking about her teaching as well as in her appreciation for the TDR approach in promoting teachers' learning. During the TDR experience, she felt that she learned a significant amount of earth science content and the general importance of teachers' foundational knowledge for teaching, learning, and design. Another important insight for Jennifer was that she felt that after experiencing a TDR process, any type of curriculum design project should integrate or address learning theory. By this statement, she implied that many efforts in this area do not address directly students' and/or teachers' cognition, which she felt was crucial and catalytic to the TDR experience. In general, Jennifer described her participation in TDR as "a tremendous learning experience" that was "excellent," "positive," "valuable," and "invigorating." While participating in TDR, Jennifer described herself as highly motivated and said she felt that "the experience was perfectly designed for me." The inquiry-based, generative, creative, but ambiguous nature of uncovering and exploring significant teaching and learning issues seemed to map well to Jennifer's learning style, but, more importantly, promoted her own constructed understanding and knowledge of scientific inquiry and her strong intention to incorporate them into her practice.

Theorists involved in the professional development of teachers speak to the importance of engaging with subject matter in new ways by wrestling with pedagogical problems, issues of students' learning, and a deep understanding of the subject matter content (Putnam & Borko, 1997: 1226). The notion of adaptive expertise also aligns with Jennifer's engagement with new scientific content and processes integrated with the problems and potential she dealt with in the classroom everyday to hold her students' attention successfully. At the end of her TDR experience, Jennifer's expertise about students' learning in geoscience was informed greatly by intersecting research-based knowledge with a geoscientist's modeled practice and a teacher's applied practice. She was able to integrate all of this information successfully to design and create new lessons for her students, thereby promoting her adaptive expertise by adding continually to her knowledge and skills in this area. As evidence of the progression of her adaptive expertise in the area of geoscience, she offered the following from her online journal at the conclusion of the TDR experience:

> After I received Randy's e-mail I decided I should go to Great Falls and do some firsthand research myself (o.k. it was a nice day and I needed a break from my PowerPoint). I talked to a ranger, Miguel Robinson, while I was at Outlook No. 2 at the Falls. He could not answer all my questions. I left my card with him, and he said he would have the park geologist call me. We hiked along the River Walk trail. The potholes are fascinating. I think our students would really get into the force of water in a whirlpool-like action creating these holes in the rocks. You can readily see the evidence that water once shaped the land at this location that is now high above the river.

Jennifer's content knowledge in geoscience and her questions challenged a park ranger's expertise, and the above excerpt demonstrates her formal knowledge in this area integrated with the applied practice of how she might translate that knowledge for the students in her classroom. If Schwartz et al. (2005) are correct, then the two dimensions of expertise in teaching, innovation and efficiency, may be supported by a TDR approach for professional development. Through her experiences in TDR, Jennifer's knowledge of geoscience content became accessible and efficient and promoted her ability to participate in a design innovation for the project, with positive residual effects in her classroom.

Teachers' knowledge and professional development seem to be promoted by their involvement in design research. Cycles of integrated design and research in a specific content area moved Jennifer out of her former understanding of scientific inquiry and caused her to reconceptualize her teaching practice. The collaborative nature of TDR provided a safe, trusting, and supportive environment for creative innovation and change to occur. Hammerness et al. (2005a: 361) stated it this way:

> Lifelong learning along the innovation dimension typically involves moving beyond existing routines and often requires people to rethink key ideas, practices and even values in order to change what they are doing. These kinds of activities can be highly emotionally charged and the capacity to consider change without feeling threatened is an important ability.

This type of change requires professional development experiences beyond the typical training made available to teachers. TDR experiences may provide the context for teachers' adaptive expertise, efficiency, and innovation to flourish and motivate them to engage, re-engage, and transform their practice.

Conclusions

Involving teachers in the ambiguous and complex environment of design prototyping and research cycles places them in situations of fostering their own "adaptive expertise," where they are required to articulate their practical knowledge, integrate and generate new ideas about teaching, and go beyond their current practices to add continuously to their knowledge and skills (Darling-Hammond & Bransford, 2005; Hatano & Oura, 2003).

Engaging teachers in cycles of data collection and analysis that inform prototyping and design decision making promotes a leveling of the field in building trust and collaboration. The researcher must be willing to share power to promote mutual trust and learning among all concerned in order to generate new ideas and facilitate change in the classroom. Generally, teachers' practical knowledge is not valued in many research contexts, but if it is placed in a position of ultimate importance for change and the diffusion of innovations to occur, then reform becomes possible. Teachers also need to be open to new ideas and new ways of doing things, but they are intimately involved in creating those ideas. The teachers participating in these studies took very seriously their role of building something that other teachers and students would use. Fundamentally, TDR provides the context to learn and to make design research decisions with those who will be responsible ultimately for making change happen in the classroom.

Many levels and directions of learning are being explored in the TDR model. Researchers learn about teaching, teachers learn about research, and everyone learns what might and might not work in the classroom, as they proceed through numerous cycles of data-driven, design decision making, prototyping, and streaming of ideas. The collective process of integrating multiple sources of information to improve design research promotes the honoring of all sources of information from both research and practice.

In educational reform efforts, we typically are asking teachers to adopt new practices that researchers create, perceive, and demonstrate as valuable and effective. Asking teachers to replace their current practices in which they are invested and adopt new ways of doing things seems a difficult path. Teachers engage directly in the conceptualization of integrated design and research and carrying out such cycles with their students and their colleagues. This brings to light a broader view of their challenges while providing collaborative support in decision making about teaching practice and innovation. The TDR process naturally provokes the articulation and reconsideration of beliefs about teaching practice when attempting to generate collaboratively a new practice or design. The TDR context may provide an extended timeframe to integrate teachers' practical knowledge with research-based practices and to generate innovative design ideas that will improve learning. This long-term process also may promote the ownership and commitment necessary for teachers to consider changing their long-held beliefs and practices, as well as to work toward the local diffusion of new approaches through teachers' social networks.

Although much more work needs to be done in the research and development of TDR, it potentially could be applied to many different instructional issues. Bringing teachers, researchers, subject matter experts, graduate students, and developers together sparks rich investigations and discussions of teaching and learning that have the capacity to promote change at local levels. Software development and publishing firms that produce teaching and learning materials also may benefit from a TDR approach through improved products. Ideally, participation in these interdisciplinary teams may improve research as well because much information is lost in the design process (e.g., in interviewing learners and other interested parties about teaching and learning issues or testing different approaches to the design of software); if it were captured in more formal ways, it could inform research directly.

The potential benefits of TDR are many, including multitiered, multidirectional learning by researchers, teachers, and students as well as the generation of improved processes and products that embody innovations that can diffuse from the local level through teachers' social networks. Perhaps it is time to revisit the top-down, didactic, traditional models of teachers' professional development and move toward engaging them in challenging, creative, generative, design research processes that may foster their learning and change. If we advocate learning contexts for students that focus on:

- strategic and flexible use of knowledge
- mediating learning as it is constructed
- taking on the role of active constructor of meaningful cognitive networks that are used during problem solving
- defining and representing problems; transforming existing knowledge into one of many possible solutions
- presenting conditions in which failure is accepted as part of learning
- valuing highly self-regulation or cognition
- other students being viewed as resources for learning

Then why would we not want to construct these types of learning environments for teachers, too (Putnam & Borko, 1997)? Despite its challenges and costs, TDR offers a viable new approach to professional development that has the potential to provide teachers with these important features for their learning so that they can serve our children in the best possible manner.

Acknowledgments

This research was supported by funding from a National Science Foundation Career Award (Award No. 0238129). The perspectives presented in this chapter are solely the author's and do not reflect necessarily the positions of the Foundation.

Note

1   This chapter describes a case study in a larger body of work by Brenda Bannan-Ritland, John Baek, Erin Peters, Patricia Martinez, Jolin Qutub, and Qing Xia, some of which was presented at the conference of the American Educational Research Association in 2006 under the title "Teachers as Collaborators in Design-Based Research: Designing a Technology System Integrating Inquiry-Based Science and Reading Comprehension Strategies."

References

Anderson, R. D. (2002). Reforming science teaching: What research says about inquiry. *Journal of Science Teacher Education, 13*, 1–12.

Bannan-Ritland, B. (2001). An action learning framework for teaching instructional design. *Performance Improvement Quarterly, 14*(2), 37–51.

Bannan-Ritland, B. (2003). The role of design in research: The integrative learning design framework. *Educational Researcher, 32*(1), 21–24.

Bannan-Ritland, B., Baek, J. Y., Peters, E. E., Martinez, P., Qutub, J. & Xia, Q. (2006). Teachers as collaborators in design-based research: Designing a technology system integrating inquiry-based science and reading comprehension strategies. Paper presented at the annual meeting of the American Educational Research Association, San Francisco, CA, April.

Borko, H. (2004). Professional development and teacher learning: Mapping the terrain. *Educational Researcher*, *33*(8), 3–15.

Cochran-Smith, M. & Lytle, S. L. (1993). *Inside/outside teacher research and knowledge*. New York: Teachers College Press.

Collinson, V. (1996). What is in a name? The transition from workshops to staff development for sustained school improvement. Unpublished manuscript.

Darling-Hammond, L. & Bransford J. (eds) (with LePage, L., Hammerness, K. & Duffy, H.) (2005). *Preparing teachers for a changing world: What teachers should learn and be able to do*. San Francisco, CA: Jossey-Bass.

Fishman, B., Marx, R. W., Blumenfeld, P., Krajcik, J. & Soloway, E. (2004). Creating a framework for research on systematic technology innovations. *Journal of the Learning Sciences*, *13*, 43–76.

Fullan, M. (with Stiegelbauer, S. M.) (1991). *The new meaning of educational change* (2nd ed.). New York: Teachers College Press.

Glaser, B. G. & Strauss, A. L. (1967). *The discovery of grounded theory: Strategies for qualitative research*. New York: Aldine.

Hammerness, K., Darling-Hammond, L., Bransford, J., Berliner, D., Cochran-Smith, M., McDonald, M., et al. (2005a). How teachers learn and develop. In L. Darling-Hammond & J. Bransford (with LePage, P. Hammerness, K. & Duffy, H.) (eds), *Preparing teachers for a changing world: What teachers should learn and be able to do* (pp. 358–389). San Francisco, CA: Jossey-Bass.

Hammerness, K., Darling-Hammond, L., Grossman, P., Rust, F. & Shulman, L. (2005b). The design of teacher education programs. In L. Darling-Hammond & J. Bransford (with LePage, P. Hammerness, K. & Duffy, H.) (eds), *Preparing teachers for a changing world: What teachers should learn and be able to do* (pp. 390–441). San Francisco, CA: Jossey-Bass.

Hatano, G. & Oura, Y. (2003). Commentary: Reconceptualizing school learning using insight from expertise research. *Educational Researcher*, *32*(8), 26–29.

Haury, D. (1993). *Teaching science through inquiry*. Washington, DC: Office of Educational Research and Improvement (Eric Document Reproduction Service No. ED359048).

Hawley, W. D. & Valli, L. (1999). The essentials of effective professional development: A new consensus. In L. Darling-Hammond & G. Sykes (eds), *Teaching as the learning profession: Handbook of policy and practice* (pp. 127–150). San Francisco, CA: Jossey-Bass.

Jonassen, D. H. & Reeves, T. C. (1996). Learning with technology: Using computers as cognitive tools. In D. H. Jonassen (ed.), *Handbook of Research for Educational Communications and Technology* (pp. 693–719). New York: Macmillan Library Reference USA.

Joyce, B. R. & Showers, B. (1995). *Student achievement through staff development: Fundamentals of school renewal* (2nd ed.). New York: Longman.

Kelly, A. E. (2003). Research as design. *Educational Researcher*, *32*(1), 3–4.

Kelly, A. E. (2004). Design research in education: Yes, but is it methodological? *Journal of the Learning Sciences*, *13*, 115–128.

Keys, C. W. (1999). Revitalizing instruction in scientific genres: Connecting knowledge production with writing to learn in science. *Science Education*, *83*, 115–130.

Keys, C. W. & Bryan, L. A. (2001). Co-constructing inquiry-based science with teachers: Essential research for lasting reform. *Journal of Research in Science Teaching*, *38*, 631–645.

Lewis, C., Perry, R. & Murata, A. (2006). How should research contribute to instructional improvement? A case of lesson study. *Educational Researcher*, *35*(3), 3–14.

Loucks-Horsley, S., Love, N., Stiles, K. E., Mundry, S. & Hewson, P. W. (1998). *Designing professional development for teachers of science and mathematics*. Thousand Oaks, CA: Sage.

National Research Council (2000). *Inquiry and the national science education standards: A guide for teaching and learning*. Washington, DC: National Academy of Sciences.

Palincsar, A. S. & Magnusson, S. J. (2000). *The interplay of firsthand and text-based investigations in science education*. Ann Arbor, MI: Center for the Improvement of Early

Reading Achievement, Resources in Education (ERIC Document Reproduction Service No. ED439928).

Parke, H. M. & Coble, C. R. (1997). Teachers designing curriculum as professional development: A model for transformational science teaching. *Journal of Research in Science Teaching, 34,* 773–789.

Penuel, W. R. (2006). *Report on professional development plans and materials for the TIDES Project.* Menlo Park, CA: SRI International.

Putnam, R. T. & Borko, H. (1997). Teacher learning: Implications of new views of cognition. In B. J. Biddle, T. L. Good & I. F. Goodson (eds), *The international handbook of teachers and teaching* Volume II, (pp. 1223–1296). Dordrecht, The Netherlands: Kluwer.

Rogers, E. M. (2003). *Diffusion of innovations* (5th ed.). New York: Free Press.

Schwartz, D. L., Bransford, J. & Sears, D. (2005). Efficiency and innovation in transfer. In J. P. Mestre (ed.), *Transfer of learning from a modern multidisciplinary perspective* (pp. 1–52). Greenwich, CT: Information Age.

Shrader, G., Williams, K., Lachance-Whitcomb, J., Finn, L.-E. & Gomez, L. (2001). Participatory design of science curricula: The case for research for practice. Paper presented at the annual meeting of the American Educational Research Association, Seattle, WA.

Smylie, M. A. & Conyers, J. G. (1991). Changing conceptions of teaching influence the future of staff development. *Journal of Staff Development, 12*(1), 12–16.

Snow, C. E., Griffin, P. & Burns, M. S. (2005). *Knowledge to support the teaching of reading: Preparing teachers for a changing world.* San Francisco, CA: Jossey-Bass.

Sparks, D. (1995). Focusing staff development on improving student learning. In G. Cawelti (ed.), *Handbook of research on improving student achievement* (pp. 163–169). Arlington, VA: Educational Research Service.

Sparks, D. & Loucks-Horsley, S. (1989). Five models of staff development for teachers. *Journal of Staff Development, 10*(4), 40–57.

Yin, R. K. (2003). *Case study research: Design and methods* (3rd ed.). Thousand Oaks, CA: Sage.

Zaritsky, R., Kelly, A. E., Flowers, W., Rogers, E. & O'Neill, P. (2003). Clinical design sciences: A view from sister design efforts. *Educational Researcher, 32*(1), 32–34.

Part 5

Modeling Stakeholder Commitments Using Design Research

13 Toward Assessment of Teachers' Receptivity to Change in Singapore

A Case Study

Jeanne Wolf
Centre for Research in Pedagogy and Practice

Mani Le Vasan
Universiti Brunei Darussalam

Introduction

As a nation without natural resources, Singapore believes that the impact of global political and economic change is redressed best through change in education practices (Gopinathan, 2001). However, there is a dearth of international benchmarks (Luke et al., 2005). Toward this end, the National Institute of Education established the Centre for Research in Pedagogy and Practice (CRPP) in 2003, with a S$47 million commitment over a five-year period to enhance pedagogical innovation and classroom practice, build the national research infrastructure, and train a new generation of educational researchers (ibid.). As new interventions are initiated in schools, there is a need to gather information about the factors that enhance or inhibit educational change in Singapore's context, create a common pool of knowledge among decision-makers about the characteristics of successful change, and develop tools for evaluating the impact of change.

However, change is a process filled with ambiguity, uncertainty, and risk (Fullan, 1991); consequently, fostering change can be difficult. Not surprisingly, explanations abound about the disappointing results of efforts to reform schools (Hopkins & Reynolds, 2001; Rogers, 1995; Waugh & Godfrey, 1995). In fact, pedagogy has proven quite resistant to change (Desimone, 2002). Since the late 1970s, researchers have argued that schools often respond to pressures in the institutional environment by merely making symbolic changes in structure and procedures while decoupling these changes from actual classroom practice and buffering the classroom from environmental pressures (Meyer & Wong, 1998). This suggests that the institutional environment has little influence on teachers' work in the classroom and provides an explanation for the legion of studies that have recounted the failure of school reform efforts to reach classroom practice (Cohen & Ball 1990; Cuban, 1998; Elmore, 1997; Sarason, 1990). Teachers often have a way of shutting their classroom doors to unwanted pressures and priorities.

Our study reports an exploratory attempt to develop a tool to assess the receptivity of Singaporean teachers to change. We develop this tool by examining the available literature, surveying CRPP staff to get an in-depth understanding of their perspectives, assessing their experiences in schools, and then conducting qualitative data analysis to make sense of their experiences doing research in Singapore's schools. The draft tool will assist in negotiations with teachers and school leaders about potential intervention sites. It also will enable us to make sense of the conditions that enhance and inhibit teachers' receptivity to change throughout the life of an intervention.

We anticipate that the instrument will evolve over the course of educational interventions. This is important because the instrument potentially has multiple uses in the change process, among them diagnostic, enabling, and evaluative applications, and may offer one method to assess the viability and sustainability of the innovation introduced at a particular school. Nevertheless, the perceived benefits of this tool will be realized only through empirical evidence once it has been pilot-tested, validated, and used in Singaporean schools over time.

Singapore's Educational Context

Singapore provides a unique venue for a case study. With the recent suite of innovations, it is moving away from a tightly coupled, state education model to a looser one, thus opening up the system. In addition, Singapore's education system is at the top on many international comparative measures of conventional educational achievement (Luke et al., 2005). For example, Singapore was ranked number one and number two in the world for mathematics and science, respectively, in the Third International Mathematics and Science Study and first in Quality Mathematics and Science Education in the Global Competitiveness Report 2002–2003 (Kelly et al., 2000; Mullis et al., 2000). There is consensus that the system is a success and there is sustained governmental funding (Sharpe & Gopinathan, 2002). Teachers, too, are comfortable and experienced in the current system. However, moving such a "successful" environment to the next level has unique challenges.

The tradition in Singapore has been top-down educational planning. Two decades ago, a number of reforms were launched to diversify educational provisions (Luke et al., 2005). Recent major initiatives include Thinking Schools, Learning Nation (Goh, 1997) (this is the name of the initiative and the reference is the title of the speech from which this initiative was derived) and the Master Plan for Information Technology in Education (Ministry of Education, 1997) to increase the tools and resources available, augment instructional flexibility, and produce more autonomous, independent learners. Innovation and Enterprise (Ministry of Education, 2003) is another recent initiative launched at the annual workplan seminar to emphasize further the spirit of questioning, risk-taking, and tenacity that students need to respond to a fast-changing, global landscape. Another important reform was launched in 2004—the Teach Less Learn More (TLLM) (Ministry of Education, 2002) initiative whereby schools are expected to reduce the syllabus and develop local curricula and pedagogical strategies and teachers are encouraged to act as facilitators rather than authoritative dispensers of knowledge.[1] Furthermore, this package of initiatives includes the allocation of more teachers to schools and the provision of teacher-assistants to help with administrative work in the classroom. Nonetheless, the mandate for TLLM is reverberating both optimism and worry among school leadership, teacher-trainers, and the teaching fraternity.

There is a feeling that there have been too many initiatives within a short span of time with the assumption that once policies are executed, real changes will take place (Tan & Tan, 2001). Teachers do not have the time and space to understand the innovations well enough for genuine acceptance, therefore they tend not to take risks (Tan, 2002). These latest initiatives open up more space and possibilities for the teacher to do less teacher-led, content-driven work, but they also create a need for teachers to move into a more independent and proactive educational context.

Other factors may contribute to an aversion to change. Singapore uses an annual public ranking of school performance on the grounds that it promotes competition and provides information for parents. Schools are judged by how much "value added" has been achieved through their performance on these standardized examinations (Mortimore et al., 2000). Critical examinations make both parents and teachers nervous about innovative pedagogy because of uncertainties about outcomes, the final standardized measure of success, and the perceived need for top grades for future life pathways. Additionally, there is an aging teaching force, with 31 percent of primary school teachers and 22.8 percent of secondary school teachers aged 50 years and above (Ministry of Education, 2001).

The rate, pace, and intensity of innovations in Singapore have been relentless. Yet the Singaporean government, although zealous in its curricula initiatives (Gopinathan, 2001; Nathan, 2001), has not been very flexible in modifying the end measure of educational success. Teachers complain of little time to plan and develop an initiative before the next one gets started. Anecdotal accounts through informal discussions indicate that the heavy workload and the "voice" of teachers are often neglected. Rosenblatt's (2004) cross-country study showed that teachers tended to use their skills when they had more of a role in the change, rather than receiving it top-down from management. In implementing school wide reform, the corpus of available research (which identifies a substantial number of failures and only a few successes) points to the need to stage interventions carefully to avoid resistance and to promote teachers' acceptance and successful outcomes.

This need to ensure the success and sustainability of educational reforms is the concern and preoccupation of educators and policy-makers elsewhere, not only in Singapore. Education systems around the world are grappling with reforms and with the notion that the more things change, the more they remain the same. The rhetoric of reform often focuses on the role of the teacher in holding the key to change—that teachers matter if we want to realize the intended changes effectively. Singapore is no exception to this rhetoric. Teachers' responses to change led us to develop a tool to assess the conditions contributing to pedagogical change in Singapore. Teachers' receptivity to change is explored further in our study.

Teachers' Receptivity to Change

Many studies have looked at the ways in which teachers implement new ideas. Some highlight the importance of teacher willingness/ability to change (Shulman, 1987), the resistance of teachers to changing their beliefs (Brown & Edelson, 2003; Cohen & Ball, 1990; Spillane, 1999), the adequacies of professional development (Putnam & Borko, 2000), and school culture (Chauvin & Ellett, 1993; Corbett et al., 1984; Fullan, 2001; Hargreaves, 1994). Other seminal works focus on the organizational arrangements and features that enable schools to get their work done and the core principles necessary to deepen reform and create learning organizations (Fullan, 2001; Senge, 1990). Still others provide a comprehensive analysis of the factors of change involved in restructuring, including, but not limited to, teachers' instructional practices, professional activities and their environment, and the influence of outside agencies (Newmann et al., 2000). However, missing from most of these studies is a distinct focus on teachers' receptivity to change.

Nevertheless, there is a small but growing body of literature that studies receptivity to change. One approach (Parsons, 2002) uses "force analyses to estimate the level and strength of forces for and against desired change." In contrast, microlevel studies explore a large number of diverse variables such as individual sense of competence, values, past experiences, feelings of fear, tendency to distort information, and attitudinal changes, along with groups, organizations, and leadership (Chauvin & Ellett,

1993). Alternatively, school-based ethnographies (Lasley et al., 1998; Mellencamp, 1992; Tunks, 1997) provide thick descriptions of change-ready and change-resistant teachers and their receptivity to specific curricula changes.

Other sets of studies examine receptivity to change using a range of instruments. Some, such as West Ed's School Reform Readiness Assessment Matrix (West Ed, n.d.) and Newmann and Associates (1995), use one instrument, whereas others use multiple instruments. For example, Soodak et al. (1998) used the Response Inclusion Survey, Teacher Efficacy Scale, Differentiated Teaching Survey, and School Climate Survey to understand teachers' response to inclusion, but Chauvin and Ellett (1993) used four different instruments (the Receptivity to Change Inventory, Attitudes of Professional Autonomy Scale, Bureaucratic Orientation Scale, and Change Facilitator Style Questionnaire) in their study of the relationship of principal facilitation styles and role orientations to teachers' receptivity to change. Hall and Hord (2001) developed three diagnostic tools to probe change and the attitudinal dispositions of those who are involved in the design and implementation of school programs.

A final body of literature focuses predominantly on methodological issues, such as instrument validation. These include the Appalachian Education Laboratory (AEL) School Capacity for Improvement and AEL School Capacity Assessment (Howley & Riffle, 2002) and models that assess teachers' receptivity to system-wide change during the implementation stage in Australia (Waugh, 2000; Waugh & Godfrey, 1995; Waugh & Punch, 1985, 1987). Studies in the United Kingdom (Jephcote & Williams, 1994), the United States (Fleming, 1992), and Hong Kong (Lee, 2000) have modified and used the Waugh and Godfrey (1995) questionnaire to examine receptivity to change.

Instruments to measure teachers' receptivity to change have different emphases, areas of concern, and measures. Indeed, it is important to note that few, if any, of these instruments have been used in process-driven, collaborative, multilayered, and theory-driven interventions such as design experiments (Brown & Edelson, 2003; Cobb et al., 2003), and few measure teachers' receptivity over the course of an innovation. To our knowledge, teachers' receptivity to change has never been assessed in Singapore. Our study is the first of its kind.

Receptivity to Change Tool: The Development Process

Our literature review supports conceptualizing receptivity to change in terms of three broad categories—educational, organizational, and individual—along with a bridging factor to link the organization with the individual. We now apply this parsimonious framework, shown in Figure 13.1, to our study.

Educational policy in Singapore includes a tide of newly created initiatives to foster creativity and innovation and to enhance economic competitiveness, which teachers are implementing (Tan, 2003). In Singapore, according to Minister of Education, Shanmugaratnam Tharman (2004), there is a strong, robust, education system in which teachers, parents, and students take education seriously and set aspirations for themselves. In tandem with the rate of innovation is the process of linking policies to practice and changing the ways in which teachers work and students learn.

But receptivity is also intervention-specific (Anyon, 1997; Lasley et al., 1998; Mellencamp, 1992; Newmann et al., 2000) and teachers struggle with the extent to which it is doable, practical, and manageable and fits into their current practice (Collins & Waugh, 1998; Rogers, 1995; Waugh, 2000). Over time, they construct meaning from the characteristics of the task and the practicality of accomplishing it in the classroom (Berg, 2002; Waugh, 2000). These factors influence how they deal with inevitable

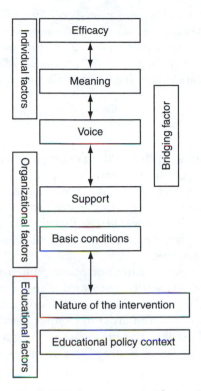

Figure 13.1 Receptivity to Change Framework (adapted from Mellencamp, 1992).

ambiguities (Busik & Inos, 1992), their willingness to take risks (Meister, 2000), and the efforts that they will expend during implementation (Sarason, 1982).

Another key component of this process is the conduciveness of the school climate and the organizational culture to change. In congruent schools, change is greeted; supported by school leaders, colleagues, and community members; and given enough resources to realize the educational aims (Harris & Hopkins, 1999; Newmann & Wehlage, 1995; Purkey & Smith, 1983). Basic conditions, such as mechanisms that align school objectives to the innovation, exert a potent influence on teachers' receptivity to change (Busick & Inos, 1992; Chauvin & Ellett, 1993; Berg, 2002). According to Corbett et al. (1984), one of the most critical resources for successful implementation is time. Fullan (1991) adds "three Rs" for the evaluation of change: relevance, readiness, and resources.

The final salient component in this process consists of the individuals who are faced with innovation, their sense of self and their professional identities (Louis et al., 1999). A substantial body of literature indicates how teachers' enthusiasm is not only tempered by the task but also related to their individual beliefs, expectations about students (Berg, 2002), professional identity, and overall judgment of the efficacy of the intervention (Bandura, 1977). Alteration of beliefs, feelings of uncertainty, and personal theories help explain how they participate and their perceptions (Collins & Waugh, 1998; Hall & Hord, 1987). As indicated earlier, efficacy, or knowing that change makes a difference in the lives of students, is another critical aspect of teachers' receptivity to change (Mellencamp, 1992).

Finally, change is a negotiated process (Meister, 2000). When teachers feel that they have an authentic voice in real change and feel a fit with themselves, their colleagues, and their students, they move beyond the structural and organizational considerations to negotiate personal meaning (Meister, 2000; Mellencamp, 1992). Communication, including the interchange of information and their treatment as respected professionals, not only energizes teachers to initiate change (Hargreaves, 1994; Mellencamp, 1992), but also leads to corresponding physical and cultural changes (Ng, 2004). We turn now to our study of these relationships.

Methodology

A key feature of our design is the underlying assumption that understanding teachers' receptivity to change involves multiple levels of interpretation. Thus, we used a mixed-mode methodology to develop the instruments. To reiterate briefly, items were extracted through the synthesis of previous research, the review of existing instruments, key informant interviews, and informal network input. To ensure further that the survey was grounded in practice, we reviewed our school intervention database and school profiles and spoke to contacts at potential innovation sites.

Initially, we drafted two instruments: (a) one to administer to principal investigators, and (b) a second to administer to school superintendents. Attitudes toward change were measured with a five-part Likert scale and several open-ended questions. Using feedback from reviewers, we decided to survey CRPP staff first in order to identify specific variables for receptivity to change in Singapore. To collect this information, the questionnaire's format was changed from a long list of social desirability statements to open-ended questions, as follows:

- When thinking about your project or Singapore's schools in general, what factors contributed to the success of the adaptation and diffusion of innovative pedagogy?
- When thinking about your present CRPP projects, what factors may inhibit the adaptation and diffusion of innovative pedagogy?
- Would any additional resources at the school have helped you in carrying out your research?

These questions were not set out using unidimensional scales, and theory did not inform their development. A detailed attachment listed a priori categories related to receptivity to change to help participants reconstruct their experiences. Project-specific information was collected as well.

Our sample was purposive, drawn to capture the views of all CRPP research staff. Over 85 percent of the CRPP staff responded. We also e-mailed questionnaires to all teachers and policy-makers who were seconded from the Ministry of Education to the National Institute of Education. Despite prompting with a follow-up e-mail, the response rate from ministry officials remained at less than 5 percent. Consequently, separate analyses were not conducted.

Data Analysis

Our study used a qualitative, semi-inductive process to analyze the responses. Initially, we coded into two overarching factors: enablers and inhibitors. Then, subcategories were established and triangulated across a range of multidisciplinary works in order to maximize local and institutional contexts. Disconfirming evidence was sought, too. Not surprisingly, most of the findings were consistent with the literature, as well as with the Mellencamp (1992) framework.

Findings and Discussion

Of those who responded, over 90 percent were involved in a school-based innovation. Across school types, grade levels, and subject areas, respondents highlighted the complexity of real change. They detailed numerous qualitative indicators and captured school-level conditions that enhance or impede teachers' receptivity to change.

In sum, the findings suggest that innovations must fit within the educational, policy-making context, but they also must fit within the school culture and the organizational structure and become compatible with the individual teachers. Forty percent of the respondents highlighted organizational factors, such as competent leadership, as critical for success. They suggested numerous ways in which organizational configurations have a salient influence on receptivity to change. Elements viewed consistently as central included: (a) leaders', parental, and community support, (b) school structures (e.g., workload, intensification, and examinations), (c) time, and (d) students. Moreover, they commented repeatedly on both the positive and negative effects of staff and leadership support, the availability of resources, and perceptions of the innovations' cohesiveness, practicality, efficacy, and benefits. In contrast, the context of Singapore's educational policy was interwoven across the responses. Individual variables, such as teachers' instructional practices and intentions, were mentioned by roughly 15 percent of the staff; whereas the impact of the innovations and subject-specific variables were mentioned by less than 10 percent of the respondents. In the sections that follow, we discuss these potential enablers and barriers.

Potential Enablers

Educational Factors

Perhaps the most common theme was that teachers become favorably disposed toward change when they perceive congruency between the innovation and the benefits to themselves and their students, but they need time to find out that it works. They also want to know that there is a clear and convincing rationale for change and that the particular innovative pedagogy meets the goals of the Singaporean educational system. Respondents reported a link between sustained outside support, such as a letter from Ministry of Education officials supporting the innovation, and receptivity to change.

Organizational Factors

Various organizational factors related to receptivity to change were cited. The first factor was the importance of all the participants in the educational system—teachers, leaders, students, parents, and teachers' aides—to help move innovation forward. The second was the need for structural variables to be in place to enhance receptivity. Among the microlevel variables, time was far and away the resource seen as most essential. Other dimensions included equipment, materials, and incentives to adopt innovative pedagogy, along with space to innovate and opportunities for further professional development. Resources are important, but it is also important to create an outlet where teachers, as a group, can show off what they have tried. A final dimension was the provision of incentives to encourage teachers to learn new skills and try new methods, along with venues for ongoing collaboration.

The micro, macro, and contextual roles of school leaders (defined broadly as principals, vice principals, and heads of departments) exert a powerful influence on teachers' receptivity to change. Not only did respondents stress the power of transformational leadership to shape a compelling vision that challenges teachers to rethink and build their skills, but also they were clear about the need to build consensus for how and why the project fits with school priorities. Facilitative school leaders were seen as stretching themselves over the organization, helping to procure vital resources, promoting public recognition of school achievement, and keeping teachers informed of progress. A theme uniting these comments was that receptivity also goes hand in hand with leaders who promote a learning organization.

Teachers

Ultimately, teachers are the innovators and reformers. However, researchers only partially captured teachers' receptivity to change and their social world. Respondents did note that support, time, and resources help them prepare to handle change. Additionally, teachers feel empowered to take risks and to try new methods when they perceive benefit for their students and their school. At the same time, teachers seek explicit support or permission to proceed from their principal and their colleagues.

Researchers

Researchers explored their own cognitive and affective roles in school innovation. They noted that teachers must be willing to deal with their presence in the classroom, along with the introduction of new methods and materials. Teachers not only pay attention to researchers' expertise, but also they value other characteristics of researchers—their cultural sensitivity, people skills, and knowledge of the unique nature of the school community. At times, change requires the researcher to support the teacher in order to increase the teacher's confidence. According to one researcher, during the ups and downs of implementation, a sense of fun also heightens receptivity to change.

Potential Inhibitors

Educational and Policy Context

Even in Singapore, where explicit reform initiatives are introduced routinely, teachers tend to be fearful of change. Constraints arise from haste to complete the syllabus, dense workloads, and reduction of the teacher's time to prepare and to learn. Innovations take considerable time from standard classroom practices. Ignoring these transaction costs can have a detrimental impact. Although some teachers will put in extra time, most of them need a reduced workload, relief of their duties, or ongoing new ways of being positioned into innovations. Without incentives, support, and structural adjustment, change is less likely to become institutionalized.

Coupled with innovation is the continuing demand of assessment requirements for ever-improving examination scores and higher school rankings (Tan, 2003). Another issue raised was that the results of critical examinations remain the criterion for assessing school performance. According to one respondent, if degrees of freedom are not addressed, significant barriers to change will persist. We note that this variable may or may not be subject to manipulation.

Organizational Factors

Over half of the respondents articulated ways in which organizational factors decrease receptivity to change. Paradoxically, although teachers may be thrown new ideas every year, their school culture remains focused on time-tested, pedagogical practices that may not align with innovations. These contradictions require delicate balancing acts.

Singaporean teachers are provided with the resources and the environment to do their job well. Yet, organizational structures and resources vary from site to site. This situation was recognized by the respondents who observed that teachers in schools with insufficient computers and network connections, technical support, and space were less favorably disposed to change.

Additional factors hampering receptivity to change were noted. Inconsistencies, such as cases where principals do not tolerate possible failure, noise, or differentiated results, overemphasize output, and do not impede teachers' receptivity to change. One respondent cited an experience where low receptivity to change was attributed to the principal showcasing the highest performing students to enhance their status and community image, rather than the benefit of the innovation for all the students. Without a shared sense of purpose, teachers' receptivity to change is likely to be low.

Parents

Concerns about parents focused on their opposition to innovative pedagogy (even as they complain about existing pedagogy) when they are uncertain about outcomes. Singaporean teachers face growing demands from parents and managing their expectations is no easy task (Khang, 2001). Despite these demands, many innovations promoting students' achievement are limited in scope and leave other parts of a school unaltered. Receptivity to change can be enhanced when schools think in terms of systemwide change, with classroom projects as one tool available to add value to schools, teachers, and the public.

Teachers

Taken together, the educational context and school culture exert a powerful influence on receptivity to change. But change occurs as a result of the interplay of those factors with teachers' beliefs and professional dispositions, along with interactions with staff and other myriad relations (Ng, 2004). Respondents noted cases in which teachers were not invited to participate or be involved in planning innovations. Consequently, they questioned whether the costs of change outweigh the benefits at the initiation stage. Similarly, when innovations were handed top-down to teachers by individuals with different personal, professional, and cultural views, the teachers hesitated to take risks.

Respondents highlighted the immense emotional labor required by change processes. Specifically, older teachers struggled to teach students in ways that they themselves did not know. Slightly more than 10 percent of the respondents noted that a lack of fit between professional identity and the design of the innovation or complex innovations involving huge changes can decrease teachers' receptivity to change. Teachers facing competing demands tend to retreat to their old ways.

Additional obstacles exist to modifying classroom practices and beliefs about change. For example, teachers feel uncertainty regarding innovations seen as complex and theoretically based. Lack of fit causes them to assert their authority and impose rigid structures over time or to be less inclined to take risks. In the longer term, when coupled with iterative research cycles, receptivity to change may diminish.

Conclusions

Volumes have been written about the three major findings that were identified in our study:

- The importance of numerous organizational, contextual, and individual variables in receptivity to change, including, but not limited to, the enhancement of internal capacity, support for teachers' personal and professional growth, and a climate that supports risk and change.
- The dynamic multidimensional nature of teachers' receptivity to change.
- The complexity of this negotiated process.

Moreover, change is inherently a political process (Hargreaves, 1994) and must address ways that teachers cope with assessment procedures and students' and parental expectations. Although this logic is clear, a key problem for educators is how to learn from these findings.

Thus, in the Appendix, we propose a three-part instrument to assess Singaporean teachers' receptivity to change. This instrument-in-progress builds upon the researchers' perception survey and the voices of outsiders who are often omitted from the receptivity dialogue and shifts now to the voices of insiders, teachers, and principals. To capture the complex interactions among individuals, innovation, and change, it focuses on:

- perceptions of efficacy
- expectations, along with opportunities to be heard and to participate in decision making
- opportunities to learn and feel supported by principals and colleagues
- opportunities to seek assistance
- expectations about students' performance, enhancement of learning, and outcomes.

Part One solicits perception data. Part Two looks beyond the human impact of change and examines potential, site-specific, contextual, educational, and organizational roadblocks to receptivity to change. Part Three asks open-ended questions.

Data Limitations

In reporting these findings, we want to emphasize that this work is exploratory, and several limitations exist. The first limitation is the scope of the self-reported data. Using researchers' data provides an understandably incomplete picture of teachers' receptivity to change. The second is definitional. The literature defines the essential features of teachers' receptivity to change, but it does not help to distinguish the salient features of those who are ready to change from those who are not or what combinations of factors, if any, exert a greater influence on receptivity to change over the course of innovations. The third limitation involves research-related factors. For example, because of the low response rate from the educators who were seconded from the Ministry of Education, we did not analyze their responses. Additionally, psychometric processes were not tested. Finally, there are inherent limitations in using surveys to explore the complexities of teachers' receptivity to change.

New Areas for Future Research

Understanding teachers' receptivity to change suggests new research directions. Further attention to the processes of implementation and scalability is merited. We also need to continue to ask probing questions about the extent to which individual cognitive, affective, and emotional factors can be assessed over time and the interactive and interdependent relationships of the structural, cultural, political, and individual aspects of the school intervention to receptivity to change (Van der Berg, 2002). Further exploration of what counts as evidence of enhanced receptivity, over the stages of an innovation, is needed also. On a broader level, our study suggests the need for attention to the national educational agenda and even the inclusion of policy-makers' voices.

Another issue worthy of further investigation, one that is not addressed at this time, is whether all innovative pedagogies can include policy design. In regard to policy design, this was not an area that we addressed in our literature review; it is beyond the scope of our study. Simple answers are unwelcome; it is crucial to gather empirical evidence and learn how to take into account what we know already in order to support receptivity to change.

Other Factors Affecting Teachers' Receptivity to Change

Educational change does not operate in a vacuum. Teachers' readiness to change is intertwined with the context of educational policy. In Singapore, the remarkable range and depth of reforms and their impact on teachers' receptivity to change also must be factored into the receptivity-to-change equation continually. When coupled with the very nature of change and other competing demands, ongoing new efforts to work with and learn from these interactions are needed. Ultimately, pedagogical change is achieved by adopting organizational arrangements and changing teachers' beliefs, knowledge, and understandings that underpin pedagogy (Harris, 2003; Murphy, 1993). Encouraging teachers to confront their beliefs and voice their concerns as well as creating a community to address them are important too. Thus, we offer a tool, albeit a partial one, to assess how teachers and schools will embrace change and to spot potential barriers and enablers. Although many of the difficulties identified can be addressed through new resources, professional development, and incentives for teachers to implement new curricula and instructional techniques, other systemic variables may not be so amenable to change. By being proactive and providing institutional resources and support for teachers in classrooms, we can not only enhance teachers' receptivity to change but also address professional development and ongoing organizational learning. We also hope to stimulate additional debate in order to reap the benefits of enhancing teachers' receptivity to change and learning from these assessments.

Note

1 See http://www.moe.gov.sg/speeches/2004/sp20040929.htm

References

Anyon, J. (1997). *Ghetto schooling: A political economy of urban educational reform.* New York: Teachers College Press.

Bandura, A. (1977). Self efficacy: Toward a unifying theory of behavioral change. *Psychological Review, 84,* 191–215.

Berg, R. van den (2002). Teachers' meanings regarding educational practice. *Review of Educational Research, 72,* 577–625.

Brown, M. & Edelson, D. C. (2003). *Teaching as design: Can we better understand the ways in which teachers use materials so we can better design materials to support their change in practices?* LETUS Report Series US: Centre for Learning Technologies in Urban Schools.

Busick, K. U. & Inos, R. H. (1992). *Synthesis of research on educational change.* Honolulu, HI: Pacific Regional Educational Laboratory.

Chauvin, S. W. & Ellett, C. D. (1993). *Teacher receptivity to change: An empirical examination of construct validity using the results of large-scale factor analyses.* Paper presented at the annual meeting of the American Educational Research Association. Atlanta, Georgia (ERIC Document Reproduction Service No. ED361379).

Cobb, P., Confrey, J., diSessa, A., Lehrer, R. & Schauble, L. (2003). Design experiments in educational research. *Educational Researcher, 32*(1), 9–13.

Cohen, D. K. & Ball, D. L. (1990). Policy and practice: An overview. *Educational Evaluation and Policy Analysis, 12,* 347–353.

Collins, P. R. & Waugh R. F. (1998). Teachers' receptivity to a proposed system-wide educational change. *Journal of Educational Administration, 36,* 183–199.

Corbett, H. D., Dawson, J. A. & Firestone, W. A. (1984). *School context and school change: Implications for effective planning.* New York: Teachers College Press.

Cuban, L. (1998). A fundamental puzzle of school reform. *Phi Delta Kappan, 69,* 341–344.

Desimone, L. (2002). How can comprehensive school reform models be successfully implemented? *Review of Educational Research, 72,* 433–480.

Elmore, R. F. (1997). The politics of education reform. *Issues in Science and Technology Online,* at: http://bob.nap.edu/issues/14.1/elmore.htm.

Fleming, M. (1992). Teachers' receptivity to teacher models. *Dissertation Abstracts International, 53*(04), 1129 (UMI No. 9225169).

Fullan, M. G. (1991). *Professional development of educators.* New York: Teachers College Press.

Fullan, M. G. (2001). *The new meaning of educational change* (3rd ed.). New York: Teachers College Press.

Goh, C. T. (1997). *Shaping our future: "Thinking schools" and a "learning nation."* Speeches (pp. 12–20). Singapore: Ministry of Information and the Arts.

Gopinathan, S. (2001). Globalisation, the state and education policy in Singapore. In J. Tan, S. Gopinathan & W. K. Ho (eds), *Challenges facing the Singapore education system today* (pp. 3–18). Singapore: Prentice Hall.

Hall, G. E. & Hord, S. M. (1987). *Change in schools: Facilitating the process.* Albany, NY: State University of New York Press.

Hall, G. E. & Hord, S. M. (2001). *Implementing change patterns, principles and potholes.* Boston: Allyn & Bacon.

Hargreaves, A. (1994). *Changing teachers, changing times: Teachers' work and culture in the postmodern age.* New York: Teachers College Press.

Harris, A. (2003). Teacher leadership as distributed leadership: Heresy, fantasy or possibility? *School Leadership and Management, 23,* 313–324.

Harris, A. & Hopkins, D. (1999). Teaching and learning and the challenge of educational reform. *School Effectiveness and School Improvement: An International Journal of Research, Policy and Practice, 10,* 257–267.

Hopkins, D. & Reynolds, D. (2001). The past, present and future of school improvement: Towards the third age. *British Educational Research Journal, 27,* 459–475.

Howley, C. & Riffle, M. J. S. (2002). *A pilot test of AEL's school capacity assessment.* Charleston, WV: Appalachian Education Laboratory.

Jephcote, M. & Williams, M. (1994). Teacher receptivity to the introduction to economic and industrial understanding. *Economics and Business Education, 2,* 163–167.

Kelly, D. L., Mullis, I. V. S. & Martin, M. O. (2000). *Profiles of student achievement in mathematics at the TIMSS International Benchmarks: U.S. performance and standards in an international context.* Chestnut Hill, MA: Boston College.

Khang, L.Y. L. (2001). Effective parenting and the role of the family in education mediation in Singapore. In J. Tan, S. Gopinathan & W. K. Ho (eds), *Challenges facing the Singapore education system today* (pp. 158–175). Singapore: Prentice Hall.

Lasley, T. J., Matczynski, T. J. & Benz, C. R. (1998). Science teachers as change-ready and change-resistant agents. *Educational Forum*, *62*, 120–130.

Lee, J. C.-K. (2000). Teacher receptivity to curriculum change in the implementation stage: The case of environmental education in Hong Kong. *Journal of Curriculum Studies*, *32*, 95–115.

Louis, K. S., Toole, J. & Hargreaves, A. (1999). Rethinking school improvement. In J. Murphy & K. S. Louis (eds), *Handbook of research on educational administration* (2nd ed., pp. 251–276). San Francisco, CA: Jossey-Bass.

Luke, A., Freebody, P., Shun, L. & Gopinathan, S. (2005). Towards research-based innovation and reform: Singapore schooling in transition. *Asia Pacific Journal of Education*, *25*, 5–27.

Meister, D. G. (2000). *Teachers and change: Examining the literature*. Paper presented at the annual meeting of the American Educational Research Association, New Orleans, Louisiana, April. (ERIC Document Reproduction Service No. ED440968).

Mellencamp, A. V. (1992). *Making connections through voice: Teacher receptivity to change*. Burlington, VT: Vermont University (ERIC Document Reproduction Service No. ED365030).

Meyer, S. J. & Wong, K. K. (1998). Title 1 schoolwide programs: A synthesis of findings from recent evaluations. *Educational Evaluation and Policy Analysis*, *20*, 115–136.

Ministry of Education (1997). *Master plan for information technology in education*. Singapore: Author.

Ministry of Education (2001). *Education statistics digest 2000*. Singapore: Author.

Ministry of Education (2002). *Teach less learn more*. Singapore: Author.

Ministry of Education (2003). *Innovation and enterprise*. Singapore: Author.

Mortimore, P., Gopinathan, S., Leo, E., Myers, K., Sharpe, L., Stoll, L., et al. (2000). *The culture of change: Case studies of improving schools in Singapore and London*. London: Institute of Education, University of London.

Mullis, I., Martin, M., Gonzalez, E., Gregory, K., Garden, R., O'Connor, K., et al. (2000). *TIMSS 1999 international mathematics report: Findings from IEA's repeat of the third international mathematics and science study at the eighth grade*. Chestnut Hill, MA: Boston College.

Murphy, J. (1993). Restructuring: In search of a movement. In J. Murphy & P. Hallinger (eds), *Restructuring schools: Learning from ongoing efforts* (pp. 1–31). Newbury Park, CA: Corwin.

Nathan, J. M. (2001). Making "thinking schools" meaningful: Creating thinking cultures. In J. Tan, S. Gopinathan & W. K. Ho (eds), *Challenges facing the Singapore education system today* (pp. 35–50). Singapore: Prentice Hall.

Newmann, F. & Associates (1995). *Authentic achievement: Restructuring schools for intellectual quality*. San Francisco, CA: Jossey-Bass.

Newmann, F., King, B. & Young, P. (2000). Professional development that addresses school capacity: Lessons from urban elementary schools. *American Journal of Education*, *108*, 259–299.

Newmann, F. & Wehlage, G. G. (1995). *Successful school restructuring: A report to the public and educators*. Madison, WI: Center on Organization and Restructuring of Schools (ERIC Document Reproduction Service No. ED387925).

Ng, D. F. O. (2004). *Change leadership: Communicating, continuing and consolidating change*. Singapore: Pearson Prentice Hall.

Parsons, B. A. (2002). *Evaluative inquiry using evaluation to promote student success*. Thousand Oaks, CA: Corwin.

Purkey, S. C. & Smith, M. S. (1983). Effective schools: A review. *Elementary School Journal*, *83*, 427–452.

Putnam, R. T. & Borko, H. (2000). What do new views of knowledge and thinking have to say about research on teacher learning? *Educational Researcher*, *29*(1), 4–15.

Rogers, E. (1995). *Diffusion of innovations* (4th ed.). New York: Free Press.

Rosenblatt, Z. (2004). Skill flexibility and school change: A multinational study. *Journal of Educational Change*, *5*, 1–30.

Sarason, S. B. (1982). *The culture of the school and the problem of change.* Boston: Allyn & Bacon.

Sarason, S. B. (1990). *The predictable failure of education reform: Can we change course before it's too late?* San Francisco, CA: Jossey-Bass.

Senge, P. (1990). *The fifth discipline: The art and practice of a learning organization.* New York: Doubleday.

Sharpe, L. & Gopinathan, S. (2002). After effectiveness: New directions in the Singapore education system. *Journal of Educational Policy, 17,* 151–166.

Shulman, L. (1987). Knowledge and teaching: Foundations in the new reform. *Harvard Educational Review, 57,* 1–22.

Soodak, L. C., Podell, D. M. & Lehman, L. R. (1998). Teacher, student, and school attributes as predictors of teachers' responses to inclusion. *Journal of Special Education, 32,* 480–497.

Spillane, J. P. (1999). External reform initiatives and teachers' efforts to reconstruct their practice: The mediating role of teachers' zones of enactment. *Journal of Curriculum Studies, 31,* 143–175.

Tan, J. (2002). Education in the early 21st century: Challenges and dilemmas. In D. D. Cunha (ed.), *Singapore in the new millennium* (pp. 154–186). Singapore: Institute of Southeast Asian Studies.

Tan, J. (2003). Reflections on Singapore's education policies in an age of globalization. In K. Mok & A. Welch (eds), *Globalization and educational restructuring in the Asia Pacific region* (pp. 32–57). New York: Palgrave Macmillan.

Tan, S. & Tan, H. (2001). Managing change within the physical education curriculum: Issues, opportunities and challenges. In J. Tan, S. Gopinathan & W. K. Ho (eds), *Challenges facing the Singapore education system today* (pp. 50–71). Singapore: Prentice Hall.

Tharman, S. (2004). *To light a fire: Enabling teachers, nurturing students,* at: http://www.moe.gov.sg/speeches/2004/sp20040929.htm.

Tunks, J. L. (1997). *From isolation to integration: The change process in an elementary school. The teachers' perspective.* Paper presented at the annual meeting of the American Educational Research Association. Chicago, ILL, March (ERIC Document Reproduction Service No. ED408251).

Waugh, R. F. (2000). Towards a model of teacher receptivity to planned system-wide educational change in a centrally controlled system. *Journal of Educational Administration, 38,* 350–367.

Waugh, R. F. & Godfrey, J. (1995). Understanding teachers' receptivity to system-wide educational change. *Journal of Educational Administration, 33,* 38–54.

Waugh, R. F. & Punch, K.F. (1985). Teacher receptivity to system-wide change. *British Educational Research Journal, 11,* 113–121.

Waugh, R. & Punch, K.F. (1987). Teacher receptivity to system-wide change in the implementation stage. *Review of Educational Research, 57,* 237–254.

West Ed (n.d.). *A guide to school wide improvement.* Region XI North California Comprehensive Assistance Center, at: http://www.wested.org/csrd/guidebook/pdf/foundation.pdf.

Appendix

The purpose of this survey is to gather information about various aspects of your work and the CRPP-"X" school innovation.

These questions cover many different areas and they are all important. Please read them carefully and please give honest answers. Most of the questions can be answered by placing an "x" in the appropriate circle.

If you have any questions about how to respond to a particular question, do not hesitate to ask for assistance.

Thank you for your cooperation.

Teacher's Background

How many years have you taught in Singapore? _____

How many years have you taught at this school? _____

Part One: School Year Teaching and Professional Life

Please indicate the extent of your concern with the following statements:

	Irrelevant	Not true	Somewhat true	Very true	Do not know
Context					
1 I am worried that there are already too many innovations.	○	○	○	○	○
Overall characteristics					
2 I have been told how my teaching will change with this innovation.	○	○	○	○	○

3	I have been given information about the time and energy commitments required by this innovation.	○	○	○	○	○
4	I am not worried about this innovation.	○	○	○	○	○
5	I need more time to learn about the change and how best to adapt it to the class.	○	○	○	○	○
6	I feel unprepared because I have limited knowledge of the innovation.	○	○	○	○	○
7	I am concerned about how this innovation affects my students.	○	○	○	○	○
8	I would like to know more about how this innovation is better than our current programme.	○	○	○	○	○

Innovation

9	I will need training to implement this innovation.	○	○	○	○	○

Culture

10	I can ask for advice from others in my school if I have problems with the innovation.	○	○	○	○	○
11	The principal has provided good incentives to participate in this project.	○	○	○	○	○
12	I think decision making in my school is a collaborative process.	○	○	○	○	○

Managing the change at school

13	I will be able to raise concerns about the innovation in school.	○	○	○	○	○
14	I have the principal's support for my contribution to this innovation.	○	○	○	○	○

Innovation

15	This innovation fits with our school's goals and vision.	○	○	○	○	○

Indicate the adequacy of the following statements:
VI = Very inadequate   SI = Somewhat inadequate
A = Adequate   VA = Very adequate   DNK = Do not know

		VI	SI	A	VA	DNK

Decision making

		VI	SI	A	VA	DNK
16	How adequate are the opportunities to participate in decisions about the innovation and implementation?	○	○	○	○	○
17	Based on your understanding of this project, how adequate are the planned professional development programs?	○	○	○	○	○

Indicate the accuracy of the following statements:
NVA = Not very accurate   SA = Somewhat accurate
A = Accurate   VA = Very accurate   DNK = Do not know

		NVA	SA	A	VA	DNK
18	Teachers will receive the help that they require when problems arise.	○	○	○	○	○
19	Teachers and administrators will work well together as a team during this innovation.	○	○	○	○	○
20	Parents are likely to support the planned innovation.	○	○	○	○	○

Part Two: Potential Roadblocks

In this section, we are interested in potential roadblocks to change. Please answer the following questions regarding your school.

1 How were you selected to participate in this innovation?

    ○ Volunteered   ○ Selected to participate   ○ Other: _____

2 Indicate the months in which you do not want to be involved in this innovation. Check all that apply.

○ January	○ February	○ March	○ April	○ May	○ June
○ July	○ August	○ September	○ October	○ November	○ December

3 During a typical week, on average, how much time do you spend in total: teaching, planning lessons, meeting students, supervising CCA, meeting with other teachers to collaborate and get advice, attending meetings, grading students' work and examinations, meeting parents, participating in professional development activities, and/or doing administrative work?

	Monday	Tuesday	Wednesday	Thursday	Friday	Saturday
Hours						

4 What type of incentives would help you to implement this innovation? Check all that apply:

    ○ Professional development credit   ○ Reduction in teaching load
    ○ Do not know   ○ Additional resources
    ○ Change in assessment policies   ○ Other: _____

5 Estimate the number of innovative strategies currently planned and/or implemented:

    ____ in your school   ____ in your classroom(s):   ____ in your department

6 Over the last year, the time that you have spent on testing and test preparation has:

    ○ Increased a great deal   ○ Moderately increased   ○ Stayed about the same
    ○ Moderately decreased   ○ Decreased a great deal

7 In the following matrix, indicate the extent to which any of the following resources pose a problem for you.

Resource	Very often	Often	Occasionally	Seldom or never	Not applicable
Workspace	○	○	○	○	○

Instructional materials	○	○	○	○	○
Reporting systems	○	○	○	○	○
Functioning computers	○	○	○	○	○
Internet access	○	○	○	○	○
Photocopiers	○	○	○	○	○
Administrative support	○	○	○	○	○

8 For each resource that might pose a problem, indicate if there are plans to deal with it. If so, by when?

	Is there is a plan to deal with the problem?			
Resource	Yes	No	Do not know	If there is a plan, when will it be implemented?
Workspace	○	○	○	_____
Instructional materials	○	○	○	_____
Reporting systems	○	○	○	_____
Functioning computers	○	○	○	_____
Internet access	○	○	○	_____
Photocopiers	○	○	○	_____
Administrative support	○	○	○	_____
Other: _____	○	○	○	_____

9 If this innovation were to start in your school tomorrow, which of the following might pose a significant challenge? For each challenge, indicate if it is amenable to input from a research team.

	Is it a significant challenge?		Is it amenable to change?	
	Yes	No	Yes	No
Parent relationships	○	○	○	○
Improvement of instruction	○	○	○	○
Alignment of innovation with school culture	○	○	○	○
Student expectations	○	○	○	○
Student progress	○	○	○	○
Student ability	○	○	○	○
Grading, testing, and tracking	○	○	○	○
Recognition and rewards	○	○	○	○
Time management	○	○	○	○
Other: _____	○	○	○	○

10 To what extent is the vision of this innovation shared and supported by:

	Not at all	*To some extent*	*Moderate extent*	*Great extent*	*Do not know*
You	○	○	○	○	○
Department	○	○	○	○	○
Colleagues	○	○	○	○	○
Other colleagues	○	○	○	○	○
Head of department	○	○	○	○	○
Principal	○	○	○	○	○

Part Three: Open-Ended Questions

1 What other concerns, if any, do you have at this time?

_____

_____

_____

2 What will be the most significant barrier to the implementation of this innovation? Describe one only.

_____

_____

_____

3 What type of assistance do you want from CRPP to help you to implement this innovation effectively?

_____

_____

_____

4 Your assistance in completing this survey is very much appreciated. If there is anything else that you would like to tell us about this survey, please do so in the space provided below.

_____

_____

_____

Thank you for taking the time to participate in this survey.

14 A Design Research Approach to Investigating Educational Decision Making

S. David Brazer
George Mason University

L. Robin Keller
University of California, Irvine

Introduction

Two hundred parents, a few students, and a handful of science teachers settled as comfortably as they could in the high-school band room, waiting for the meeting to begin. The issues were how to create the right combination of entry-level, college preparatory, honors, and advanced placement (AP) science courses to serve the needs of this diverse high school. Two weeks before the meeting, the principal and the science department chair sent letters to every household explaining the purpose of the meeting, laying out their preferred science curriculum, and urging all interested parents to attend the meeting to provide feedback on the courses offered. Despite their attempts to bring in parents with a wide range of views, the band room contained nearly exclusively parents most concerned about honors and AP, with a few parents interested in establishing stimulating courses for college preparatory students. Only the school's staff thought about the needs of students with low skills, learning disabilities, or limited proficiency in English.

Several constituent groups had specific objectives that they hoped to achieve through the decisions made at the meeting. The department chair and the principal were concerned primarily with providing a set of course offerings that would meet a wide range of student needs. Nearly as important was the administration's desire to make this the first and last meeting to settle some long-standing science curriculum issues. The principal and the department chair also shared one of the primary objectives of the science teachers—keeping course preparations to a minimum. Many parents came to the meeting prepared to advocate for the inclusion of specific courses that they wanted to see in the curriculum. These compatible and conflicting objectives were promoted that evening.

The predictable outcome of the meeting is that the principal and the department chair made some modifications to their original curriculum proposal that addressed the objectives of parents concerned about honors and AP. They thought they got the kind of final agreement they sought. All of the signs looked good for satisfying the major interested parties. Unfortunately, the principal and the department chair misread the situation to some degree. After they publicized a final decision that resulted from the meeting, the principal was subjected to intense private lobbying by parents of students in the middle, who ultimately prevailed on him to put back one course that was cut from the original proposal. This small change upset the delicate balance achieved with the teachers and led to a chain of reactions that eroded some of the agreements made about the course of study in life science. Many people who had been satisfied became dissatisfied. The end result was that the administration felt compelled to conduct similar meetings and to tinker with the science curriculum in each of the next two years.

The above scenario could be seen as a simple case of poor decision making—the original public agreement should never have been adjusted. Unfortunately, life in schools is not so simple, particularly because school leaders are expected to be responsive to the needs and desires of their school communities (Bolman & Deal, 2003; Lambert, 1995; Schlechty, 2001). When many constituents are involved in decision making, decisions made at one point can be adjusted, unmade, or ignored at a later point. Parents often disagree with one another as they advocate for what is best for their own children. Principals and teachers, if not at odds with one another, frequently have goals that compete or conflict with those of parents. Typically, decisions have been treated as one-time events with specific consequences, but the science curriculum scenario helps to reveal more of an evolutionary, drawn-out process.

To understand and aid decision making in educational contexts requires a research method that captures decision-making processes over time, allows for ambiguity and variation, and permits the researcher to study decision making as it happens. The purpose of this chapter is to demonstrate how a model that incorporates the multiple objectives of multiple interested parties can be used as a design research tool to describe, intervene in, and improve decision processes. Following a brief analysis of the gaps in current educational leadership literature, we describe a model we have developed in order to explain decision making more completely. Then, we use an example research site to explain how a methodology combined with a design research approach would test and allow for modification of our model. In conclusion, we review the above scenario to explain how the principal, with assistance from researchers, could factor the multiple objectives of the many constituents into his decision-making process.

Current Treatment of Decision Making

Three books used widely in educational leadership courses represent current thinking about how schools and school districts should be led. All three books are written by giants in the leadership field and all three contain a great deal of wisdom and insight. They also share a common problem, however. These books neither provide an explanation of how decisions are made nor do they prescribe how decisions ought to be made. This seems surprising in light of the fact that making decisions is a frequent leadership behavior.

The primary goal of *Leading in a Culture of Change* (Fullan, 2001) is to develop a prescriptive theory that, if followed, will cause " 'more good things to happen' and 'fewer bad things to happen' " (p. 10). Fullan focuses on the kinds of things that educational leaders should know and how they should behave generally. For example, leaders must act in a manner consistent with the moral purpose they espouse and they should build relationships throughout the organization. There is no doubt that this is sound advice. But Fullan is silent about the kind of process that effective leaders engage in when they sit down with others to decide how the school or school district should change to improve itself. Fullan leaves the reader with the impression that if leaders start with the right mind-set, build strong relationships with many interested parties, and communicate well, education will improve. Ambiguity is the great spoiler here, however. If it is not clear what kinds of changes should be made, honorable people will disagree, causing conflict. How a leader should make decisions under conflicted circumstances Fullan does not tell us.

Sergiovanni (2001) dwells largely in the same realm as Fullan, advocating for ways in which principals ought to perceive their roles in schools. He touches briefly on decision making by emphasizing that, in making choices, principals create opportunities for themselves and their schools to improve. Creating more decision opportunities is a hallmark of good leadership. How these decisions are made, or how they should be made, is never discussed. The rest of *The Principalship: A Reflective Practice Perspective* describes Sergiovanni's "New Theory for the Principalship" that emphasizes the development of a positive school culture, strong relationships in a community of practice, and responsiveness to the needs of students and their families. Similar to Fullan, what is missing from Sergiovanni's theory is any treatment of how principals make decisions, especially when there is disagreement in the community.

Fullan claims to speak to educators and non-educators, whereas Sergiovanni obviously is focused on principals. In *Reframing Organizations: Artistry, Choice, and Leadership*, Bolman and Deal (2003) speak primarily to the private sector, but they do generalize somewhat to schools and school districts with their use of a few education sector examples. The main mission of the book, as the title suggests, is to help leaders understand that there are multiple perspectives, or frames, which reveal how organizations work. Consistent with Fullan and Sergiovanni, Bolman and Deal provide a great deal of information about how leaders ought to think about organizations and to treat the people in them, but they are essentially silent about how the decision-making process works or how leaders ought to involve others.

Through their analysis of the organization theory literature and its application to schools and other settings, Fullan, Sergiovanni, and Bolman and Deal provide important insights into the structure of school districts and schools and how leaders might manipulate that structure for better results. By not providing a comprehensive treatment of decision-making processes, however, these authors leave educational leaders with no systematic way to think about how decisions are made and how decisions might be improved. This is not to say, however, that there is no literature on decision making.

The books discussed above are based in part on the past 100 years of a wide range of thinking about how organizations work and decisions are made, ranging from the superrational (Scott, 1998) to the rational within limits (Allison & Zelikow, 1999; March & Simon,1993; Simon, 1993) to the completely non-rational (Cohen et al., 1972; March, 1994; Weick, 2001). Most of this literature is theoretical, with the empirical being entirely retrospective (Allison & Zelikow, 1999; Rogers, 1995; Weick, 2001). Our model is intended to facilitate the study of decision making prospectively, rather than retrospectively, and to help fill in gaps in the literature typically used in thinking about educational leadership. This model and the field-based research that stems from it deliberately adopt a middle position on the issue of rationality. Consistent with Rogers (1995), we see many major decisions as deliberate and forward-looking. At the same time, we recognize significant nonrational aspects of decision making that must be understood by leaders if they are to work with multiple constituencies with any degree of success.

Discovering How Decisions are Made

It is not obvious immediately why the hard-won decision worked out that night in the band room did not hold. Why were parents of students in the middle in such a small minority? Why did the principal cave in to pressure in a meeting-after-the-meeting? To understand this commonplace kind of educational decision making requires methods that are interactive between the research participants and the researchers. A conceptual foundation for examining the influence of many people with many objectives in a decision scenario such as the high-school science curriculum described above is established clearly (Brazer & Keller, 2006; Keeney & Raiffa, 1976; Keeney et al., 1987; von Winterfeldt & Edwards, 1986; Winn & Keller, 1999, 2001). We build on this foundation and bring in concepts that create a more dynamic model intended to capture features of decision making in educational contexts.

A Conceptual Framework for Educational Decision Making[1]

Many decisions involve multiple constituents who bring multiple objectives into decision making (Allison & Zelikow, 1999; Cohen et al., 1972; March, 1994). Winn and Keller (1999, 2001) present a model of multistakeholder multi-objective decision making based on the retroactive examination of decisions made in business contexts that reveal how influence from different sources is brought to bear on decision making. Those with interests in a specific decision will display varying degrees of power, legitimacy, and urgency as they seek to influence the ultimate outcome. Power derives from position, relationships, and access to resources, or a combination of all three (Pfeffer, 1982), and manifests as an individual's or a group's ability to compel others to do as they wish (Bolman & Deal, 2003). Legitimacy refers to constituents' rights to involve themselves in a particular decision. Urgency conveys the time pressure that they will perceive with regard to making a decision. Those with moderate to high levels of power, legitimacy, and/or urgency are considered most salient to a problem and the ultimate decisions stemming from it (Winn & Keller, 2001).

The multistakeholder multi-objective approach applied by Winn and Keller (1999, 2001) has evolved from studies in both educational and business contexts. Our conceptual framework is more multidimensional and dynamic than the Winn and Keller (1999, 2001) model. To illustrate, we describe one way in which the flow of decision making might occur. A word of caution, however; simplifying decision making for the sake of explanation makes it appear far more linear and ordered than we believe it to be. The model helps researchers know where to look for decision-making dynamics, but the specifics of how they play out will vary from site to site and from decision to decision.

For the sake of simplicity, we assume a traditional hierarchy of decision making that begins with the school board identifying a policy-level issue. Formally and/or informally, the board informs the superintendent that change needs to occur to resolve the issue. Newly motivated to make change, the superintendent has just been influenced by one major interested group—the school board members.

As the superintendent considers what to do to meet the interests of the school board, he or she weighs input from central office employees. Each set of central office constituents, such as those in the professional development or curriculum and instruction departments, tries to persuade the superintendent to pursue his or her favored solution. Similar to the board and the superintendent, each of these interested parties has his or her own power, legitimacy, and urgency with regard to the issue, as well as a set of objectives with varying degrees of importance (an objectives hierarchy) that drives individual decisions about what to present to the superintendent.

This unfolding process of deciding to change is both rational and nonrational (Rogers, 1995). The decision is rational in the sense that the board, the superintendent, and other school district officials will engage in a process of articulating a teaching or learning problem as clearly as possible, based on evidence that specific goals are not being met. For example, if elementary reading scores do not meet state standards, experts in the school district may determine that insufficient time during the school day is spent in reading instruction. But knowing how much time should be spent and what the time should be used for is not clear. In the face of ambiguity, constituents may promote pet solutions based on their objectives hierarchies and promoted with varying degrees of power, legitimacy, and urgency. The give-and-take that follows influences how the decision to change takes shape. Some objectives will promote better reading instruction, but others will not.

Implementing Change

After arriving at a decision to change, the superintendent must decide how to present it to those who will lead implementation of the change, namely, principals. Presumably, the superintendent is strategic about obtaining commitment from principals in what she or he assumes to be the most effective manner. Choices for the superintendent include mandating implementation of the change decision, working with principals to obtain their commitment (or "buy-in") to the change decision, or inviting principals to help refine the change decision before implementing it.

Principals are the agents of the superintendent and the school board in the sense that they work with their teachers to carry out decisions made at the upper echelon of school district leadership. Yet, simultaneously, principals have direct and indirect influence over the decisions that they are expected to carry out. Therefore, superintendents will communicate about a particular decision based on how principals have influenced them and their assumptions about how principals function as agents. There is substantial uncertainty about how decisions will be implemented because principals have their own objectives hierarchies that may drive them in different directions from those that the superintendent intends. Allison and Zelikow (1999) refer to this as the principal–agent problem (in this case, meaning that the superintendent initiates something as the "principal" figure and the school principals carry it out as agents of the superintendent). How consistently principals put into place the wishes of their superintendents is based in part on how tightly coupled school sites are to the central office (Weick, 1976); that is, the degree to which a superintendent's directive will be carried out as intended.

In their own schools, principals face choices similar to those of the superintendent as they work toward implementation. They must decide how they will respond to the decision to change that the superintendent communicated and how they will get teachers and students to implement it. Their power, legitimacy, and urgency with regard to the issue combine with their objectives hierarchies to influence the choices they make. In turn, teachers decide how they will implement the decision to change based on how the principal approaches them; their perceptions of the principal's power, legitimacy, and urgency; and their own objectives hierarchies. With so many different choices made by a multitude of people, it is easy to see how implementation might deviate from the original conceptions of what the change should look like.

Board members, superintendents, principals, and teachers do not make decisions in isolation. Starting from their objectives hierarchies and self-perceptions of power, legitimacy, and urgency, they take into account the influences of the interested parties around them and outside the organization. Any individual choice made by the constituents involved in a decision could influence reactions that, in turn, will affect decisions at a later time. Therefore, the entire process is not so much linear as it is reciprocal and/or cyclical, and it is always iterative. For example, school board members may observe how teachers react to the change that the superintendent decided upon based on the original directive from the board and conclude that the benefits they anticipated are not worth the resulting negative consequences. In such a case, board members may indicate to the superintendent one way or another that they are not as strongly interested in the change as they once were. Alternatively, other members of the organization—principals, teachers, or parents—could initiate just as easily the process of articulating the problem that leads to a decision to change.

To test the usefulness of our conceptual framework requires fieldwork tools that will reveal the influences that shape all of the relevant players' thinking and actions about a particular set of decisions. Such a need suggests the kind of interactive approach between researchers and participants that is embedded in design research.

Constructing a Methodology

The prescriptive focus of decision analysis, the field on which our multistakeholder multi-objective approach is based, is consistent with design research that is aimed at improving practice (of educational decision making, teaching, etc.). Design research is concerned primarily with linking research and practice by examining how theory is applied in instructional settings, how it should be adapted given practical results, and how learning takes place in the school as an organization (Cobb et al., 2003; Design-Based Research Collective, 2003). Although design research is a helpful point of view that encourages hypothesis testing, interaction, and adaptation as research evolves, it is not a methodology in and of itself (Kelly, 2004).

The methodology we employ in conjunction with design research begins with description to verify that the educational, decision-making landscape is understood. After describing how decisions are made, prescription can follow as a result of the trial–analysis–retrial process embedded in design research. Ultimately, normative research findings may follow description and prescription. See Table 14.1 for an explanation of descriptive, prescriptive, and normative foci for both research and practice.

Table 14.1 Three Foci for Multi-objective Multistakeholder Educational Decision-Making in Research and Practice

Educational decision-making research and practice	Focus		
	Descriptive	*Prescriptive*	*Normative*
Research aim	*Describe* how decisions are made by empirical observations, surveys, and interviews; experiments and statistical analysis may follow later	*Prescribe* how people should make decisions, given limitations and complexities (as in design research)	Identify *ideal* decision making based on data analysis from multiple sites or from logical analysis of (often very simplified) stylized examples
Link with practice (training, consulting, etc.)	Study the evolution of specific decisions as they are happening in field locations, not attempting to change the process or the outcomes	Guide/aid decision making, for one decision at a time; make generalizable tools and observations to improve future practice (as in design research)	

Our multistakeholder multi-objective model of educational decision making represents a hypothesis to be tested in two ways: as a description of what happens and as a prescription for what should happen. The model has not been developed yet to fulfill the second function because it is only beginning to be field-tested. We believe that it is sufficiently well developed to facilitate field-based data collection and analysis describing how decisions happen, but until it is used as an intervention in decision making, we will not know how well it functions prescriptively. Through the modification required by field testing in multiple sites with varied decisions and contexts, the model will evolve into a normative framework that explains the ideal means of engaging in educational decision making involving many constituents who have many objectives.

Descriptive Focus

Most of the descriptive studies of multiple influences on decision making have been conducted retrospectively. Although greatly helpful for fleshing out decision-making processes, retrospectives are limited by the memories of participants that may have eroded substantially or be false by the time researchers interview them. Furthermore, decision making nearly always involves an element of serendipity that is filtered out over time as those involved in the decision making rationalize their decisions (Rogers, 1995) or explain decisions in order to make sense of the actions that preceded them (Weick, 2001).

A decision is more of a process than an event because constituents and leaders continue to influence one another from the initial change decision through implementation. As decisions evolve, the interested parties come and go, attention waxes and wanes, and problems and solutions get redefined (Cohen et al., 1972). Who participates in the decision making is often a vital piece of information for understanding how a decision gets made in a particular way (March, 1994). Decision-makers and their organizations allow certain individuals or groups to have access to them during the process while denying such access to others (Allison & Zelikow, 1999). Yet, among those who have access, there will be variations in influence.

Our model and the methodology that accompanies it are intended to capture the unpredictable comings and goings of decision participants, problems, solutions, and circumstances. The methodology presented here investigates decision making as it happens, in order to yield more accurate and detailed results. One of our research sites helps to illustrate the advantages of studying decision making from a contemporary perspective.

Salmon Run[2] is a small, kindergarten-through-grade eight school district located in northern California. The superintendent has been there for five years. Just before his arrival, the school board approved a narrowly drawn retention policy: any student not meeting state and local standards at a particular grade level would be retained. The superintendent has explained to our research team that he wants to engage the school board and school community members (predominantly teachers and administrators) in a "data-driven," decision-making process to determine if the retention policy is meeting its original goals and what, if anything, should be done about it. As of this writing, the school district is engaged in fact-finding about the policy.

The rational aspects of the decision to change the retention policy (or not) are relatively clear at this point. The superintendent has brought together key constituents in the school district, including two school board members, two school site administrators, and ten teachers, with each of the district's schools represented. Working with a consultant from a university in the region, this group has divided into subcommittees to study, through the school district's student data and surveys, how the current retention policy is being implemented and the teachers' and parents' perceptions of the effects and effectiveness of the policy.

The superintendent's process seems likely to yield one of four recommendations to the school board: (a) preserve the current retention policy as it exists, (b) modify the current policy, (c) replace the current policy with a new one, or (d) remove the current policy and do not replace it with a new one. These prospects are listed as possible change decisions and are laid out in Table 14.2, along with related possible implementation decisions.

As obvious as it may seem to choose among the four alternatives listed in Table 14.2, looking at the implementation decisions brings nonrational factors into the picture. How is it possible that the implementation choices remain the same for all four policy alternatives? In an organizational context such as a school district, implementers are often different from decision-makers (Rogers, 1995). They have their own objectives hierarchies that may or may not be consistent with those of the decision-makers. Two examples from Table 14.2 illustrate the point. If the board decides to preserve the current policy, it is possible that some teachers have been so dissatisfied with it that they will find ways to modify the current implementation, such as by identifying more students for special education or Section 504 eligibility, thereby exempting them from the retention policy. At the other extreme, if the board removes the policy and does not replace it, teachers and principals could continue to retain students just as they have for the past five years because "that's the way we've always done it."

Table 14.2 lists the likely sets of choices for the change decision, but without observing the decision process and talking with those involved, it would be very difficult to determine why a particular choice was made. We know that key Salmon Run constituents are involved somehow in making the ultimate decision because we know that the superintendent has brought them into the consultations deliberately. But we do not know what influence, if any, a given individual or group has and it is difficult to determine this based only on the final outcome. To reconstruct the influence of the various interested parties after the decision has been made, we would have to rely on retrospective accounts from individuals who would be motivated to "make sense" of the decision made and who might have difficulty remembering their thought processes at the time of the decision.

Table 14.2 Possible Outcomes from Retention Policy Choices

Change decision	Implementation decisions
Preserve the current policy	Continue the current implementation Modify the current implementation Replace the current implementation
Modify the current policy	Continue the current implementation Modify the current implementation Replace the current implementation
Replace the current policy	Continue the current implementation Modify the current implementation Replace the current implementation
Remove the current policy	Continue the current implementation Modify the current implementation Replace the current implementation

The nonrational, serendipitous, or unpredictable aspects of change and implementation decision making require researchers to be present while decisions are being made in order to document how they happened. Our method begins with surveying the participants in the superintendent's decision-making group and the teachers throughout the school district to learn their perceptions of the district's orientation to change and the power, legitimacy, and urgency of the different parties interested in the retention policy decision. Combining survey results with interviews of participants to discover their objectives hierarchies and to discern their power, legitimacy, and urgency with regard to the decision enables researchers to map out potential patterns of influence. Observing the interactions among those involved helps to verify or draw new maps based on the actions of individuals and groups. Perhaps most important, observation allows for the capture of serendipitous events without having them filtered through participants' retrospection.

The concepts embedded in our model of educational decision making provide the groundwork for coding interview and observation data. In addition to searching for other factors that influence how change and implementation decisions evolve, the model requires finding evidence of the exercise of power, legitimacy, and urgency; explaining which objectives are most important and why; and how perceptions of loose or tight coupling influence communication choices and implementation decisions.

Prescriptive Focus

The multistakeholder, multi-objective, decision-making model employed in the field work referred to above is a working hypothesis for how decisions happen. It is also potentially more than that. We envision our model serving as the basis for educational leaders' professional development, which would be a specific intervention consistent with design research. At this point, we present Salmon Run school district as a hypothetical example of how professional development could aid future decision making because, thus far, the district has declined to engage in professional development centered on decision making. The kind of interaction between researchers and participants that we describe below is similar to the design research model proposed by Bannan-Ritland (2003).

Having demonstrated to Salmon Run officials how our model helps to explain their decision-making processes, we would work collaboratively with school and school district leaders to improve their decision making by using a multistakeholder multi-objective perspective. Professional development could include learning how to identify the key constituents and their objectives; how to assess the power, legitimacy, and urgency of the various involved groups: how to analyze the degree to which organizational entities are coupled loosely or tightly to one another; how to be strategic in the implementation phase; and what to do with feedback that occurs throughout the process.

Using the model in professional development and practice will surface weaknesses. For example, principals know that power in educational settings may be exercised by not doing something, rather than by getting others to engage in an activity. This stems from teachers' relatively high degree of autonomy. This kind of thinking would lead to a new conception of power that entails both accomplishment and inaction. The consequences for implementation from this reconceptualization seem substantial. By explaining their experience of power, educational leaders help to improve the model by exposing its shortcomings to researchers.

Under ideal circumstances, researchers would work side by side with administrators to observe how the model functions in practice, to coach administrators on the use of the model, and to make modifications to the model that enhance its prescriptive legitimacy. If school and school district leaders are able to use the model well, researchers would examine the quality of their decisions in terms of measures such as consensus or stability or adopt a decision quality framework such as Matheson and Matheson (1998) provide. If leaders use this model with a high degree of fidelity, but decision processes or outcomes are poor quality based on some objective measure, then practitioners would engage with researchers to determine what is invalid or missing from the model, make modifications, and try again. If the model is used well and helps to develop higher quality decisions, it would make sense to try it in different contexts to see if the validity and quality hold.

By co-designing professional development focused on decision making and testing jointly the hypotheses implicit in professional development activities, both researchers and practitioners will learn more about educational decision making. This partnership uses the model as a design research tool, marrying together the perspectives of research and practice. Collaboration on professional development would allow us to test what we believe about educational decision-making processes and would strengthen the explanatory and predictive value of our model.

Normative Focus

In the normative phase of model development, descriptive and prescriptive results from Salmon Run and a wide variety of other school districts would be synthesized to produce a more generalized model that describes productive, decision-making processes for a broad range of issues and educational contexts. The value of such a grounded theoretical model is that it would serve as a set of guidelines to improve decision making in schools and school districts with the hope that students, families, and society would benefit from enhanced educational quality.

To know on a more general level the degree to which our model helps to improve decision making, we would look for the following kinds of evidence in school districts: greater consensus, fewer reversals of decisions, transferring process tools (software, survey forms, and process steps) to new domains, repeated budget allocations for decision analysis interventions, etc. Matheson and Matheson (1998) have developed a specific decision quality spider diagram for decision analysis in practice. The diagram is a six-pointed star that displays graphically scores on six dimensions of the quality of a decision: the appropriate frame of the decision; creative doable alternatives; meaningful reliable information; clear values and trade-offs; logically correct reasoning; and a commitment to action.[3] Whatever measures are used, to identify ideal decision making requires establishing criteria and standards against which decisions deriving from the process described in our model can be measured.

The normative phase methodology likely would involve comparative case studies that employ both qualitative and quantitative measures. It can be achieved only after a sufficient body of experience at the descriptive and prescriptive stages has been amassed and understood.

Methodology Summary

To describe educational decision-making processes, prescribe what works, and establish decision-making norms requires collecting and analyzing data about both the rational and the nonrational aspects of decisions, from the initial choice to make a change through implementation of the change. On the rational side, the specific aspects of a problem and the choices available to address the problem will be known and agreed upon by the key constituents. On the nonrational side, the constituents' objectives hierarchies contain objectives that are self-serving, peripheral to, and/or at odds with, decisions to change. Sorting through the objectives hierarchies and how the interested parties promote their own goals through the use of their power, legitimacy, and urgency is central to understanding the multiple influences in decision-making processes.

With the notable exception of Allison and Zelikow (1999), the few studies that examine decisions focus on the decision itself, not the process. Furthermore, the decisions investigated are typically change decisions and not implementation decisions. There is little follow-through in the literature from first conception to ultimate implementation, and virtually nothing about the evolution of decisions in educational contexts. In this type of uncharted water, it is more appropriate to begin with exploration and informing practice (Kelly, 2004). But as case studies are developed, we are optimistic about recasting our model in prescriptive and normative forms.

The Science Curriculum Revisited

Had the principal and the department head been working from the multistakeholder multi-objective model, they might have seen and reacted differently to the evening in the band room and been able to anticipate problems from a missing interest group. They needed to recognize their failure to involve all those who had moderate power, high legitimacy, and high urgency when they conducted their meeting.

The principal's most serious mistake may have been to assume that a decision could be made soon after the meeting in the band room. Had he anticipated that typically underrepresented constituencies would not attend the meeting, but that they would care about its outcome, he could have set up other avenues for parents to express their views about the curriculum. Doing so would have dispelled the false impression that "all parents" agreed on what the curriculum should look like and he would have been able to understand more parents' objectives hierarchies.

Thinking from a multistakeholder multi-objective approach, the principal might have seen that the following main objectives were at work for the parents interested in honors and AP courses: (a) getting their children into the best colleges and universities, (b) preparing their children to take SAT subject and AP examinations, (c) getting their children into the best high-school situations possible, and (d) keeping their children away from unmotivated and/or "bad influence" students. Understanding that the first objective is probably the most heavily weighted in the objectives hierarchy for this group and, perhaps in a somewhat modified form, for all the other parent groups, the principal would have seen potential common ground among those parents who appeared to disagree with one another.

Finding common ground would not be sufficient, however, because to offer one class means that another likely would be cut; one group wins while another loses. This is the reason the principal was lobbied so hard to restore a college preparatory course that had been cut as a result of the meeting. Therefore, it is necessary for the principal to assess the power, legitimacy, and urgency of all the constituencies with which he is working. The principal reacted to his perception of the power of the parents concerned about honors and AP courses by making the modifications in his proposal that they requested. But he was subjected later to the power of the parents of college preparatory students and made a change. It might have worked better for the principal to recognize that parental power stemmed from the ability of parents to influence school board members, the superintendent, and/or central office administrators in this small school district, suggesting that the principal should have known what these other interested parties would support before he modified the curriculum. It is easier to stand firm on a decision arrived at collectively when the principal knows that superiors will not intervene to overturn it.

Principals' abilities and time are stretched to engage in this kind of analysis in the midst of busy schedules and multiple demands. For this reason, a design research approach is very attractive. Instead of principals being expected to engage in the above kind of thinking alone, it seems more feasible to have a partner, perhaps an academic, who can engage in the analysis with them and serve as a professional coach. By providing description and prescription, the researcher can help principals through difficult passages. By testing recommended strategies against predetermined criteria for the quality of decision outcomes, both researchers and principals will learn how to engage in collaborative decision making more effectively.

By partnering with practitioners, researchers using our model and method are more likely to be able to describe for leaders the entire perspective and the important details of decisions simultaneously. With this kind of knowledge, principals and superintendents may be more capable of making decisions that serve their intentions better and are less prone to be weakened through the implementation process. If so, leadership is enhanced because the fundamental act of leaders in all contexts is decision making.

Notes

1 This section is a much abbreviated description of our conceptual framework that is described in Brazer and Keller (2006).
2 Salmon Run is a pseudonym used to protect the identity of the school district and the research participants.
3 At the middle of the star is the worst performance level on each dimension (0 percent achievement); the outer ends of the six points are the best, 100 percent level. A large symmetric star would signify excellent scores on all six dimensions. In an educational decision context, the quality of the decision could be tracked over time for one school site and compared between school sites.

References

Allison, G. & Zelikow, P. (1999). *Essence of decision: Explaining the Cuban missile crisis*. New York: Longman.

Bannan-Ritland, B. (2003). The role of design in research: The integrative learning design framework. *Educational Researcher*, 32(1), 21–24.

Bolman, L. G. & Deal, T. E. (2003). *Reframing organizations: Artistry, choice, and leadership*. San Francisco, CA: Jossey-Bass.

Brazer, S. D. & Keller, L. R. (2006). *A conceptual framework for multiple stakeholder educational decision making*. International Journal of Education Policy and Leadership, 1(3), at: http://www.ijepl.org.

Cobb, P., Confrey, J., diSessa, A., Lehrer, R. & Schauble, L. (2003). Design experiments in educational research. *Educational Researcher*, 32(1), 9–13.

Cohen, M. D., March, J. G. & Olsen, J. P. (1972). A garbage can model of organizational choice. *Administrative Science Quarterly*, 17, 1–25.

Design-Based Research Collective (2003). Design-based research: An emerging paradigm for educational inquiry. *Educational Researcher*, 32(1), 5–8.

Fullan, M. (2001). *Leading in a culture of change*. San Francisco, CA: Jossey-Bass.

Keeney, R. & Raiffa, H. (1976). *Decisions with multiple objectives: Preferences and value tradeoffs*. New York: Wiley.

Keeney, R., Renn, O. & von Winterfeldt, D. (1987). Structuring Germany's energy objectives. *Energy Policy, 15,* 352–362.

Kelly, A. E. (2004). Design research in education: Yes, but is it methodological? *Journal of the Learning Sciences, 13,* 115–128.

Lambert, L. (1995). *The constructivist leader.* New York: Teachers College Press.

March, J. G. (1994). *A primer on decision making.* New York: Free Press.

March, J. G. & Simon, H. (1993). *Organizations* (2nd ed.). Cambridge, MA: Blackwell.

Matheson, D. & Matheson, J. (1998). *The smart organization.* Boston: Harvard Business School Press.

Pfeffer, J. (1982). *Organizations and organization theory.* Boston, MA: Pitman.

Rogers, E. (1995). *Diffusion of innovations* (4th ed.). New York: Free Press.

Schlechty, P. C. (2001). *Shaking up the schoolhouse.* San Francisco, CA: Jossey-Bass.

Scott, W. R. (1998). *Organizations: Rational, natural, and open systems.* Upper Saddle River, NJ: Prentice Hall.

Sergiovanni, T. J. (2001). *The principalship: A reflective practice perspective.* Boston: Allyn & Bacon.

Simon, H. (1993). Decision making: Rational, nonrational, and irrational. *Educational Administration Quarterly, 29,* 392–411.

Weick, K. E. (1976). Educational organizations as loosely-coupled systems. *Administrative Science Quarterly, 21,* 1–19.

Weick, K. E. (2001). *Making sense of the organization.* Malden, MA: Blackwell.

Winn, M. I. & Keller, L. R. (1999). Harnessing complexity, idiosyncrasy and time: A modeling methodology for corporate multi-stakeholder decisions. In D. J. Wood & D. Windsor (eds), *International Association for Business and Society 1999 Proceedings* (pp. 482–487). Paper presented at the tenth annual conference, Paris, France, June.

Winn, M. I. & Keller, L. R. (2001). A modeling methodology for multi-objective multi-stakeholder decisions: Implications for research. *Journal of Management Inquiry, 10,* 166–181.

Winterfeldt, D. von & Edwards, W. (1986). *Decision analysis and behavioral research.* New York: Cambridge University Press.

Part 6

Reflecting on Design Research at the Project Level

15 Investigating the Act of Design in Design Research
The Road Taken

Brenda Bannan-Ritland
George Mason University

John Y. Baek
Center for Advancement of Informal Science Education

Design Research is a Complex, Practical, and "Wicked" Journey

This chapter investigates the roads taken and not taken in the LiteracyAccess Online (LAO) design research case (see Bannan-Ritland, 2003). LAO was designed to help adults help children with reading difficulties. This project revealed the complex and practical aspects of design in balancing constraints, trading off one set of requirements with another, and dealing with ambiguity and heuristics where design details often emerge only after narrowing down the design alternatives (Preece et al., 2002; Spillers & Newsome, 1993). The continual redefinition of constraints and the generation of new goals in the design phase highlight how pragmatic, dynamic, and generative processes are integrated in design research.

The acts of design in the LAO project detailed an attempt to balance the tensions of the theoretical and the practical. Nelson and Stolterman (2003: 49) discuss this tension by distinguishing between reactive and proactive stances in design by ". . . 'finding meaning' in things that happen and 'making meaning' by causing things to happen." It is clear from the decision making and judgments made in the LAO design research case that the theoretical and practical issues of design are intertwined and interdependent.

Linking the theoretical and practical aspects of design research to the required complexity of problem solving aligns this form of inquiry with Rittel and Webber's (1973) description of "wicked" problems. Nelson and Stolterman (2003) interpret Rittel and Webber's description of "wicked" problems for design as: (a) not being formulated exhaustively in systematic terms, (b) addressing them as statements of a solution, (c) not being true or false and not possessing an exhaustive list of functions, (d) containing many explanations, (e) requiring unique, effective, single solutions that have no immediate or ultimate test, and (f) demanding that the problem-solver not make a mistake and avoid significant problems that could occur.

Designing and testing school and classroom-based interventions, like LAO, certainly reflect the described characteristics of a "wicked" problem in attempting to generate, address, and diagnose teaching and learning issues and solutions. Many of the learning issues embedded in LAO cannot be articulated fully, involved multiple variables, and potentially could be explained by many possible factors. The challenge in design research seems to be how to provide a warrant for the selection of the intertwined design and research decisions, all of which are not made purely on a theoretical or an empirical basis. Indeed, employing design research to address the complexity of teaching and learning environments can never address exhaustively all of the theoretical or empirical possibilities and typically involves a unique, highly contextual problem that is difficult to evaluate and even more difficult to generalize. Most importantly, because all the related issues of a particular social problem in education cannot be dealt with, design research involves instances of practical, political, and other types of decision making and selective judgments to reduce the complexity of the issue to address manageably the acts of design and research (Nelson & Stolterman, 2003). The design decision making made in LAO highlighted the many directions that were possible and demonstrated the selective judgment used to deal with this "wicked" and complex problem. Multiple factors as described below, not only theoretically- or empirically-based decisions, influenced the selective judgments in this case, suggesting that increased attention to and consideration of the nature and process of design may help to shed light on the formation of explicit procedures and processes for design research.

Introduction

The current state of design research in the field of education has been characterized as possessing a significant lack of agreement on the processes and procedures of this emerging form of inquiry (Kelly, 2004; O'Donnell, 2004). Agreement does exist among design researchers that uncovering and testing theoretically-based propositions are crucial in the design and development of educational innovations; however, there is no clear articulation about how many of these theoretical and empirical decisions are made in the context of design. O'Donnell (2004) raised significant issues about how research questions emerge in design research as well as how the researcher knows which question, of the many possible, to focus on and why. Similar questions were raised in the same article concerning the implementation of theoretical constructs in design, such as which design features were selected for the implementation of a theory, again from the many possible, which were not, and why. These questions point to the possibility that other factors may be involved in clarifying the procedures of design research. We will re-examine the role and emergence of theory in justifying decision making during the process of design research.

Design research inherently involves the act of design. The process of design research subsumes many of the characteristics and processes representative of the nature of design as described by Lawson (2004), including locating relevant information, structuring a problem, exercising creative insight, proposing a solution, and evaluating that solution. If design research subsumes the act of design, then those involved in this work may benefit from using the lens of the design process to uncover the decisions and complex judgments made in design research.

In this chapter, we propose to accomplish four goals:

1   Reveal the complexity of the decisions and judgments made during acts of design in design research.
2   Uncover how the process of design research unfolds; specifically, which design roads are taken and which are not, as well as which research questions and methods fall from this work and at what points.
3   Illuminate factors in design research that may contribute to, influence, and propel the process forward.
4   Highlight the broad themes related to the nature of design that were uncovered in this analysis.

We will accomplish these goals by expanding upon a previously presented example of design research, LiteracyAccess Online (LAO), a web-based technology system that provides support for teachers, tutors, and parents (literacy facilitators) by addressing one of the most important goals for all children—developing literacy skills—with particular focus on those with disabilities (see http://literacyaccessonline.org). The goal of the intervention is not to teach literacy skills in a didactic fashion. It is to offer a technology-based environment that supports both helping literacy facilitators and children as dyad.

The LiteracyAccess Online research project is described through the phases of the Integrative Learning Design Framework (ILDF). The ILDF presents a multidisciplinary and complementary blending of perspectives on design and research (see Bannan-Ritland, 2003) and provides a structure within which to position design problems, selected methods, and design moves at different points in the design research process (see Figure 15.1). Previously presented descriptions of LAO as a case example of design research were constrained by the space requirements of the academic journals in which the articles appeared; therefore, in this chapter, we relate much more of how the decisions and judgments were made and their impact on the emergent theory. Significant focus is placed on how the LAO design research team interpreted and framed design problems through progressive research questions and methods. These and other factors prompted design moves that revealed different design problems. By employing a design process lens, this examination of the road taken and those not taken illuminates the many factors, decisions, and judgments that may prompt and influence the process of design research.

In our examination of the LAO design research process, the following four broad themes emerged, which will be addressed more fully in the discussion section of the chapter. Design research:

- Encompasses a complex, practical, and "wicked" journey.
- Involves multiple decision–evaluation spaces that are manifested in problem states, design moves, and the framing of the design problem.
- Is an interpretive, social and multidimensional process.
- Involves many factors that prompt acts of design and reinterpretation of theory.

The emergence of the research questions and the selection of the methods in design research are intertwined inexorably with the act of design. Examining the inherent acts of design and what prompts these acts in this case example may shed light on and clarify further theoretical and research decision making—or the complexity of the road taken in design research.

Research Questions and Methods

The Informed Exploration Phase

The goals of the informed exploration phase in the ILDF are: (a) to identify, describe, and analyze the state of the problem or phenomenon, (b) to generate initial theoretical perspectives about how people learn and perform, and (c) to identify the corresponding design directions. Although not necessarily a linear process, we have attempted to delineate a rough sequence of the design actions that we engaged in throughout this phase. In this initial phase, the team was charged with the broad, general, social goal of how to provide literacy support for children, particularly those with disabilities. An early research question that evolved from the design team's collaborative interaction was: "What are the best practices in basic literacy acquisition for fourth- through

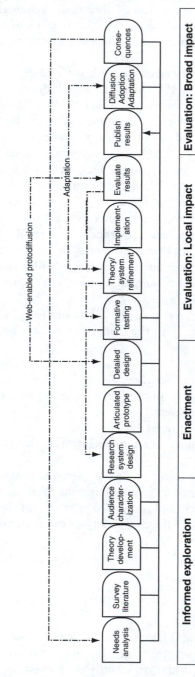

Figure 15.1 Questions and Methods for Design Research by ILDF Phase.

eighth-grade students with or without disabilities and what opportunities exist to provide technology-enhanced literacy support for this population?" To address this question, the team borrowed from and integrated methods employed in product design, performance or needs assessment, and usage-centered design, as well as traditional literature review techniques. These methods were particularly useful for the primary phases of design research: namely, to locate the problem; to integrate practice, theory, and research perspectives in literacy and technology-supported learning; and to work toward the generation of initial models to enact in design.

Needs Analysis

Gap or needs analysis is a traditional technique used to begin instructional design; it involves identification and documentation of the current state and the proposed ideal solution. Typically, this type of analysis is conducted from a problem-solving orientation that starts by articulating the problem and solution clearly; however, in education, this process does not traditionally involve market analysis or benchmarking techniques. Benchmarking is an evaluation method that involves gathering information about other companies' or organizations' best practices to inform one's own practice (Barksdale & Lund, 2001). Given the proliferation of software tools that address the reading and writing processes, the team elected to capitalize on marketing and benchmarking techniques to examine many examples of the literacy software then available. Practical decision making drove this investigation in the team's desire not to "reinvent the wheel." Therefore, early in the life cycle of the project, existing literacy software programs were reviewed and analyzed in order to identify instructional gaps in the marketplace and to provide benchmarking of competitive products as a rich source of ideas for potential designs that would have utility beyond their publication in research papers. This effort resulted in a broader understanding of the landscape of literacy software design and identified gaps or needs that existed in the marketplace.

Following this exploration, design ideas related to variations on tutorial-based support of children's reading processes that seemed more prevalent in the marketplace were investigated initially. Unexpectedly, an important team member, who was also a parent with a child with a disability, argued for the importance of providing support for the literacy facilitator (as well as the child) in the collaborative reading process. She emphasized her practice of reading with her child, rather than children reading solely on their own, and her desire for resources to improve her interaction with her child. Her insight prompted a major turning point in the team's design direction. This resulted in a design move or decision away from child-centered, tutorial-based, literacy practices to supporting both the facilitator or tutor and the child in a collaborative literacy process. This design move was based primarily upon the interests of someone involved in the project and upon a parent's insights and needs related to her reading practice with her own child. These initial insights were affirmed by interviews with other parents and experts, which suggested a gap or need that had not been addressed yet by commercial software developers or research involving technology support. This design move was made for both political and pragmatic reasons to fill an identified need. This decision changed fundamentally and defined further our design problem state and goals. The decision also restricted the type of research questions and methods that we could now ask because a goal had been established to design for collaborative literacy exchanges. This design move, or "road taken," placed new constraints on the emergent theory and design and eliminated other design research directions such as investigating individual, tutorial-based, literacy support and nontechnology or whole classroom-based, literacy support.

Survey Literature

Once the need for collaborative support of the literacy process had been identified and established, the next step was to conduct a review of the literature to clarify the learning processes, skills, and techniques employed by both literacy facilitators and children while they were reading. At this stage, our questions were focused on what information could be gleaned from the data or literature that provided insights into the tutoring or facilitation processes and what reading strategies for children with or without special needs could be located in previous research. Sources included the National Assessments of Educational Progress' reading achievement levels for the United States, a comprehensive study detailing the demographics and skills of Literacy Volunteers of America, best practices in reading and tutoring strategies, and studies related to the needs of students with physical, emotional, sensory, or cognitive deficits in the reading process, among others (e.g., Gambrell, 1999; Grossen, 1998; Mastropieri & Scruggs, 1997; National Assessments of Educational Progress, 1998; Simmons & Kameenui, 1998). Synthesizing these resources informed our efforts and allowed for integrating our theoretical approaches with the practical theories espoused by parents on the team, as well as expanding our notion of the collaborative process of reading and tutoring, which would continue to evolve as the design research progressed. The resulting design move was to integrate some established collaborative reading practices into the technology environment and to generate others. These decisions further solidified the convergent processes of design that shifted the design problem space toward determining more specifically how to support collaborative literacy exchanges.

After reviewing the market demand and research literature related to the collaborative reading process between facilitators and children with or without disabilities, the research team was ready to examine specific learners' (represented by a facilitator and a child) needs more closely. In line with needs assessment and performance analysis procedures recommended by Rossett (1999), focus group interviews were conducted with the parents of four struggling readers. Essentially, the first cycle of focus groups was conducted to answer the question: What are the baseline skills, experiences, and perceptions of novice (or untrained) and expert literacy facilitators? The results were scrutinized for reading activities that parents undertook with their children, specific reading strategies used, feelings of efficacy about assisting their child in the reading process, and current partnerships that exist for facilitating reading, both inside and outside the school environment. In addition, surveys were used to solicit information from literacy and special education experts on effective literacy activities and strategies, what to avoid in one-to-one reading sessions, and their perspectives on the characteristics of good literacy facilitators. These methods of gathering and analyzing data provided a more elaborated understanding and definition of the design problem, as well as the targeted audience members, their experiences, the knowledge level of both the child and the facilitator, and how they worked together. This in-depth, qualitative exploration provided a solid foundation for the team's subsequent design moves to address collaborative literacy and assistive technology support from the strong position of having observed the phenomena directly.

Audience Characterization

The above analysis also expanded dramatically our notion of the "context" of the collaborative reading process and determined that we needed to address much more than simply a parent reading with a child. The informed exploration phase emphasizes the investigation of contextual factors of influence that may impact the emergent theoretical model situated in a specific environment and the consideration of factors that may impact the eventual diffusion and adoption of the design. The question for the LAO project now was: "What were the social, cultural, and organizational influences on the literacy facilitators who were attempting to support children with or without disabilities in the reading process?" It was at this stage that the inherent complexity of the instructional problem involving multiple target audiences was first revealed. As an initial step (which was incorporated in later cycles also), the team identified and interviewed representatives of many target audiences such as parents, children in the fourth through eighth grades with or without disabilities, teachers, reading specialists, special education personnel, and literacy tutors in order to create audience profiles. This analysis focused specifically on the collaborative reading process between children and literacy facilitators identified earlier, and it revealed a broad range of experience levels and disabilities as well as the inherent complexity of designing for the necessary interaction between the multiple combinations of facilitator and child. The applied methods used in this analysis included role modeling, as part of a usage-centered design process (Constantine & Lockwood, 1999), and the development of personas (Cooper, 1999), based on direct experiences with the target audience members. Role models or personas are similar to the creation of vignettes that strive to capture the substance of a setting, person, or event to communicate a central theme of the data but do not represent real life directly (Graue & Walsh, 1998). Profiles generalize audience analysis information from multiple interviews and observations. They became the focus for targeted design concepts. In this case, profiles described struggling readers.

Analyzing the interview data and crafting personas brought to light a new design problem. It was paramount to think carefully about furnishing a consistent supportive environment for children who at different times may read with parents, siblings, teachers, reading specialists, and tutors, as well as accommodating a broad range of reading levels and disabilities. Consideration of the social, cultural, and organizational contexts (such as the intersection of school and home environments) led the team to define further the theoretical design concept or direction as one that provided simultaneous assistance to facilitators with varied levels of experience and access to the child's progress by multiple facilitators in order to support the child's needs better. These design moves resulted not from preconceived theory but from direct experience with individual and combinations of target audience members, analysis of the context of performance, and close investigation of the potential intersections of collaborative exchange among the participants. The integration of existing theory, research, applied practice, and contextual information about the task did generate a unique theoretical position for promoting high-level, collaborative literacy experiences incorporating reading strategies and assistive technology, which are detailed in the next section.

The Enactment Phase

In the enactment phase, researchers operationalize what has been learned in the informed exploration phase into an intervention or a design that articulates the theoretical model, allowing for feedback and iterative revision of the emerging model and design. Although this process is depicted linearly, in reality it is much more ill-structured, chaotic, and heavily reliant on social negotiation. Participatory design methodologies were used in the LAO research to clarify and communicate the conceptual design and research direction to all team members and, at times, to different teams. This phase occurred through progressive intensive brain-storming and planning sessions. These sessions required the participation of: (a) members of the design research team at various levels and at different times, (b) involved funding agency representatives; (c) project investigators, (d) content experts, (e) graduate research assistants, (f) parents, (g) teachers, (h) children, and (i) other school support personnel. Although intense and conflictual at times, this collaboration was crucial to the design research and to the collective learning of all who participated to progress LAO forward.

Research/System Design

After identifying the general direction of providing simultaneous support for various combinations of literacy facilitator–child dyads in reading strategies and assistive technology in the informed exploration phase, the design research team was ready to attempt to solidify better the emergent theoretical grounding or framework by establishing initial theoretical conjectures. A theoretical conjecture is a theory-based inference based on related practical experience, literature, and previous studies that expresses the content and pedagogical dimensions or focus of the designed intervention (Confrey & Lachance, 2000). Documenting inferences for learning processes requires moving from the creative, implicit, generative design process to the explicit, systematic, and often reductionistic process of presenting the suppositions or assumptions in writing in order to communicate them clearly to others. The LAO research team did not articulate these assumptions formally until later in the design research cycle. Our assumptions were embedded implicitly in the evolving prototype and were discussed frequently; however, it was not until later cycles of the design that we were able to articulate them fully.

We elected to ground our theoretical conjectures or design assumptions in a sociocultural perspective of learning that ultimately would inform the design and development of the technology system. This pedagogical perspective was assumed in our selection of later methods and tools, and it seemed to align well with the design direction of supporting the complex interaction between parents, teachers, tutors, and children with and without disabilities in the multiple contexts present in the collaborative reading process. It is important to note that this pedagogical orientation was not formed before determining the design direction; rather, it was selected after the informed exploration phase as a good fit to complement and expand our theoretical notions of collaborative literacy exchange.

Selecting a sociocultural perspective on learning prompted us to think about the alignment of our conjectures about learning with this orientation. Initially, these assumptions were implicit; gradually they became explicit and usable. Eventually, they were combined and stated in this primary conjecture: by providing a consistent environment, access to assistive technology, and reading support strategies for both members of the dyad, the facilitator and child will engage collaboratively in higher level literacy processes. Although this theoretical conjecture provided some initial direction for our design, it was not specific enough to inform our detailed design. Over time, the team was able to transform this broad statement into more well-defined learning or performance targets with some established criteria, while attempting to adhere still to the established assumptions and theoretical orientation (McMillan & Schumacher, 2001; Nitko, 2004). Ultimately, the following learning targets were articulated:

- Literacy facilitators (represented by parents, teachers, or others) will acknowledge the importance of and demonstrate their ability to implement research-based reading strategies when provided with technology-based support in a collaborative reading session with a child.

- Children with or without disabilities will demonstrate their abilities to access information, activities, and assistive technology support related to reading as well as to interact with literacy facilitators in a collaborative reading session.
- The facilitator–child dyad will be able to explore and select appropriate assistive technology integrated with internet-based supports that can facilitate performance in reading and writing.
- Children, regardless of their disability, will be able to capitalize on technology-based supports and a collaborative process to improve their literacy skills.

These evolving learning targets directed the system design and integrated research process of the LAO project and provided a basis for assessment and evaluation. Many design sessions would take place before we were able to identify a framework that could move our integrated research and design efforts forward substantially.

Articulated Prototype

In line with Dabbagh and Bannan-Ritland (2005), the team aligned the design research conjectures or learning targets with existing pedagogical models, where possible, in order to ensure a grounded design. Similarly, Bell et al. (2004) describe identifying design principles that can be interpreted to inform instructional activities or guide empirically- or theoretically-based design. Rather than generating a totally new design framework or principles, the team looked first to pedagogical models that seemed to provide a good fit and alignment with the existing theoretical design directions. We took advantage of the fact that one of the team members was an expert in activity theory, which guided our analysis of instructional and performance tasks.

The task analysis technique based in activity theory was applied to the LAO project to elaborate the types of instructional tasks and supports that might be incorporated into the theoretical design (Jonassen et al., 1999). The original conjectures, identified learning targets, and revised elements for evaluation were in alignment (see Figure 15.2). The task analysis of the learning targets isolated and explicated the interaction among the components: (a) *a subject*, the facilitator–child dyad, (b) *an object*, the LAO system, (c) *the tools*, literacy strategies, assistive technologies, (d) *the division of labor*, the division of tasks between the facilitator and the child in the reading process, (e) *the community*, facilitator–child dyads are members of school, home, and tutoring communities, and (f) *the rules*, the social norms, relationships or constraints that guide the collaborative literacy process. The identification of, and interaction among, these elements shaped the resulting evaluation procedures, as well as informed the theoretical model of collaborative literacy that was embedded subsequently in the instructional innovation.

Detailed Design

Clarifying the cognitive and performance processes or tasks inherent in the design is crucial for creating and testing a theoretically-based innovation. We found that activity theory captured the interactions between the facilitator–child dyad across context more richly than traditional, hierarchical, task analysis. In the LAO design study, the design problem and our questions at this point were exactly how we should operationalize the cognitive and performance tasks identified in the task analysis related to web-based technology in order to promote rich, higher-level interaction between the literacy facilitator and the child when they are reading together. We elected to generate a design

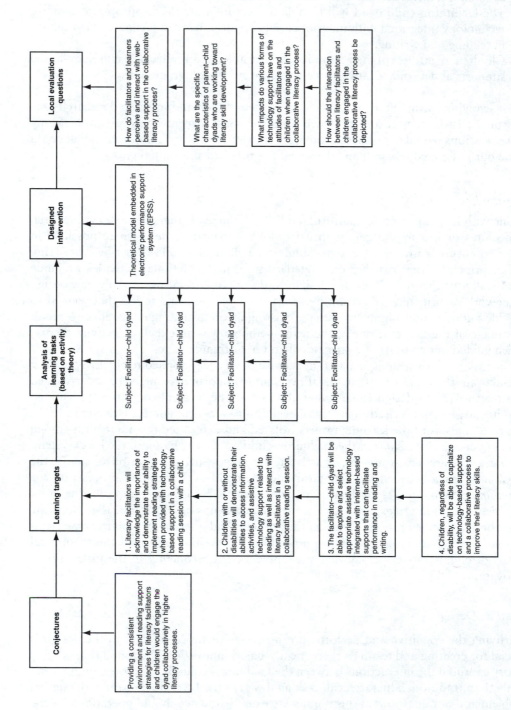

Figure 15.2 Progressive Formulation of Conjectures to Local Evaluation Questions for the LAO Project.

structure that aligned with elements of activity theory using a usage-centered design process (Constantine & Lockwood, 1999) that would assist the enactment of our emerging model of collaborative literacy processes.

To address the problem of explicating features and functions, we identified some prescriptive design models that structured the many levels of users and complexity in our theoretical model. The team decided that the challenge of constructing a technology-based environment that improved both the literacy facilitator's guidance and the children's reading aligned well with an electronic performance support systems (EPSSs) design approach (Bannan-Ritland et al., 2000). Originally, EPSSs were conceived as integrated electronic environments that are immediately accessible to learners and provide for dynamic communication akin to the productive exchange between a master and an apprentice (Gery, 1991). In addition, an EPSS design could embed the theoretical assumptions of a sociocultural perspective on learning and activity theory by focusing on the creation of a technology-based object incorporating various tools to support the performance of and exchange between facilitators and children while they are engaged in the "work" of reading. The synergy between the EPSS design approach and activity theory also permitted investigation of the multiple social and contextual issues (or the intersection between the subject, object, tools, division of labor, community, and/or rules), providing an important alignment between our theoretical stance, design principles, and evaluation efforts (see Figure 15.2). Much of this alignment was not apparent and explicit immediately; only upon retrospective analysis does the clear alignment of the theory, the design, and the evaluation reveal itself fully. This level of clarity about the cognitive and performance processes was reached after many sessions where ideas ebbed and flowed—and stalled many times—during four years of design and revision cycles and problem-solution states.

The design problem revealed in this phase was how to embed into the theoretical model the features and functions that would comprise the interface that would allow for cycles of evaluation or testing of the theory. Providing opportunities to evaluate, or give feedback on, the expression of the theory in the design seems crucial to the validity of the research. Therefore, we used flexible techniques that allowed the team to provide feedback many times and in many ways on the expression of the theoretical model and our corresponding assumptions of support of, and collaboration in, the reading process embedded in our design. Opportunities for feedback on the initial designs were facilitated through a usage-centered design process by the creation of use cases, task models, and content models, culminating in the development of a prototype. Paper-based prototypes allowed for flexibility in making conceptual changes and permitted a modeling process that allowed the interested parties to document, validate, and communicate about theory. Through participatory design practices, various members of the team were engaged in what Schön (1983) referred to as a shaping process where the current design state "talks back" to the team and each major design move or combination of moves contributes to reframing the design problem.

In the LAO project, use cases, task models, and content models were generated and revised to develop technology-based performance support for the literacy facilitator to have immediate access to research-based, reading strategy information while reading with the child. Training and information on assistive technology modifications (text-to-speech, enlarged text, etc.) were provided to the facilitator as additional support for the struggling reader with disabilities, based on the results from multiple cycles of design and feedback on the abstract prototypes. Ultimately, the team operationalized the cognitive and performance processes of supporting the reader and the facilitator in a collaborative guided approach to reading through the provision of interactive, online reading activities, with feedback for the child and progress reports shared by multiple facilitators. Experts and representative learners alike reviewed learning targets, task analyses, initial design concepts, system-level architecture, and detailed design templates at several points during a single cycle. Data from these reviews ranged from determining to what extent the design embodied the theoretical model to, more commonly, general reactions to the interface, look, and feel of the features presented.

The challenge of the participatory design process should not be understated because it involves social discourse processes in an environment where both innovation and efficiency are being encouraged simultaneously. Modeling the interface using the flexible methods of usage-centered design encompassed many prototypes as well as many microlevel design problems and moves, which translated our theoretical assumptions about learning into a pragmatic design. Such documentation supports designers at all levels.

The Local Impact Evaluation Phase

In the evaluation phase, decisions at the local level are only as good as the focused planning and forethought of what exactly to evaluate. The LAO project progressed through multiple cycles of evaluation, focusing first on the usability and validity of the intervention designed for the users and later on evaluating its impact on learning. Some of these evaluations were informal, whereas others encompassed more formalized studies; however, the cycles of evaluation and revision built upon one another to improve the theoretical model embedded in the design.

Formative Testing

Design-based research is characterized by iterative cycles of design, enactment, and detailed study that have been represented as ministudies or microcycles (Bell et al., 2004). These microcycles take place throughout the design research process but are essential in the evaluation phases for uncovering the local validity of the enacted theoretical model or design and the usability or fit of the innovation for the context. During this phase in the LAO project, the research questions were centered on how to ensure that the design was usable and effective and that the enacted theory of design had internal validity or relevance to the potential target audience and context. In this time-intensive phase, the research team employed methods based primarily on usability testing and formative evaluation processes (Rubin, 1994; Tessmer, 1993).

The LAO project progressed through several iterative microcycles of development, usability, and formative evaluation testing. Each microcycle could be characterized as a problem state and a subsequent design move. In this project too many microcycles occurred to describe them all adequately here. The overall purpose of these multiple microcycles of testing usability and other factors was to reveal major and minor weaknesses in navigation and in the interface, prompting data-driven changes in format and functionality. In addition, a series of expert reviews and one-to-one, small group, and field-testing were implemented in progressively more authentic settings. Qualitative studies characterized the target audience's interaction with the enacted theoretical model in relation to the learning targets. Specifically, the team was interested in how the facilitators and the learners perceived and interacted with the web-based support in the collaborative literacy process (which included both reading and writing tasks). Initially, a pilot study comprising five dyads of mostly parent facilitators and one sibling facilitator was conducted that simulated some of the tasks in LAO and provided feedback on the emerging site. The methods included collecting data through semistructured interviews and observations of parent–child interactions with the prototype and the complementary assistive technologies (e.g., text-to-speech, etc.) that promoted reading and writing activities.

Theory/System Refinement

The preliminary study revealed that the children were motivated to complete reading and writing activities on the web and that the facilitators developed awareness for implementing reading activities in a collaborative process but desired additional support for the children's disabilities. Although the web-based activities and supports for the reading process were useful for providing more authentic and self-initiated reading and writing activities, the research also revealed that interactions between the parent and child dyads during these activities often created tensions that were not present when the children were working with nonfamily members. Revisions to the use of behavioral prompts directed toward the parent–child dyad to release tension (such as prompts to take a break, positive reinforcement techniques, etc.) when engaged in collaborative reading and writing tasks and additional reading strategy supports and activities.

A follow-up qualitative study was conducted with eight parent–child dyads who represented a variety of skill levels and disabilities (Jeffs, 2000). The goals of the study were: (a) to identify the characteristics of the parent–child dyads working together, especially in literacy skill development, (b) to depict the interactions of the dyad, and (c) to investigate the impact of various forms of technology (internet, EPSS, and any assistive technology) on the attitudes of the participants. The participants included parents and children with various disabilities in grades four through six who were reading at least two grades below their expected level and who tended to avoid reading and writing tasks before they joined the study. The study revealed that the parents recognized the importance of immediate feedback and the assistive technology features in the tools provided. Other results showed that, with the support of their parents, children can select appropriate technologies and that with integrated use of the internet and assistive technologies, children's writing samples improved in both quantity and quality. As a result LAO was revised to include text-to-speech capabilities and reading selections reflecting varying abilities and areas of interest.

At this point, traditional research and design processes diverge somewhat in that the analyzed results are not an end in and of themselves but are used for data-driven decision making or problem solving to build upon or revise the theoretical assumptions and improve the design. Often, based on testing results, we would need to throw out previous prototype features and totally redesign, revise, or add new features. The team's informed design judgment and collaborative social negotiation were keys to this decision making.

Evaluate Results

Testing the intervention in progressively more realistic settings provides valuable information to inform theoretical assumptions related to the design and also to begin to identify variables that might be tested further empirically. Conducting additional research to investigate further the collaborative process promoted by the technological environment as well as to isolate the effects of the multiple reading supports and assistive technologies afforded by the prototype remains an important objective.

Although LAO's funding cycle has ceased, in order to progress from local effects to more externally generalizable effects, additional testing cycles are needed to isolate and test particular variables using multiple sites, diverse participants, and settings progressively limiting the researcher–participant interaction. With more funding, additional data collection is necessary using selected measurements, online surveys, and interviews with parents and children in homeschool environments, preservice teachers, and in-service teachers in several geographic locations where there are interactions with children with a range of disabilities. These data would provide additional evidence for the effectiveness of both the theoretical assumptions embodied in the collaborative reading and literacy process, as well as the prototype at its highest fidelity in the full context of the intended use.

The Broader Impact Evaluation Phase

Traditionally, academic publishing of research results was the final product of many isolated studies. The difficulty of addressing directly the systemic scalability and sustainability of educational interventions or innovations represents a current challenge for design research (Fishman et al., 2004).

Diffusion, Adoption, Adaptation

Although, at this point, we can only speculate what variables or factors might influence the problems of design diffusion, adoption, and adaptation, Rogers' (2003) work on the diffusion of innovations provides an excellent starting point for what might be termed a "metadesign" move. Earlier phases of design research and the problem states-design moves associated with those phases can provide valuable insights into issues of relative advantage, compatibility, complexity, trialability, and observability (Rogers, 2003). In turn, this knowledge can be used to inform research questions and methods in the final phase of broader impact in many ways, such as using data collected from interviews with audience members in the exploration phase to suggest how the innovation might be perceived by users or participants as better than the current situation and thus promote adoption (relative advantage).

Attempting to identify attributes of the intervention related to diffusion and adoption in the early stages of design research may avoid issues of incompatibility, such as an intervention that does not align with school district policies or one that induces nonactor-oriented views of the transfer of learning (Fishman et al., 2004; Lobato, 2003). At the metalevel, design moves that attempt to engineer the receptivity of target audience members comprise the next frontier and challenge of articulating design research clearly.

Web-Enabled Proto-Diffusion

In the LAO project, the research team has scratched only the surface of the issues of scalability and sustainability. However, promising directions for diffusion and adoption are based on the collection of preliminary data from early participants engaged with the prototype intervention. For example, the LAO project consists of an open, database-driven site that allows the continual tracking of users who interact with the EPSS, forming a sophisticated method of identifying early adopters and their needs. The site assembles profiles of all its users and contains multiple structured and open feedback forms that collect data on the early adopters who locate and use it. Having an "open" site across all the phases of design and development potentially gathers information about many of Rogers' (1995) attributes from a worldwide community, which may lead to insights into the theoretical model and design revisions, as well as factors related to the adoption and diffusion of this educational product.

Plans are in progress for implementing more complex, data-gathering methods that track in detail the literacy facilitators' and children's interactions with LAO through data-mining techniques. This initiative will be similar to current research efforts that trace students' actions (e.g., clicks, navigation paths, etc.) and responses, as well as participants' reactions or journaling in an electronically collected "log file" for extensive analysis (Buckley et al., 2002). As the number of sites and users of LAO expand and direct observational research activities become more difficult, a methodology that relies on an automatic, online, detailed collection of users' activities can produce interesting results for both theoretical model testing and diffusion purposes. The research team anticipates that these methods will answer questions such as: How do the members of the learning dyad progress through the web-based innovation over time and what components do they use? How do potential users discover the LAO system and how does it diffuse through identified social networks and communities such as schools, parent groups, homeschooling organizations, etc.? What factors are important to potential and actual participants when they consider adopting the system? How do the facilitators and the children use, adopt, or adapt LAO for their own needs? Massive quantities of data could be collected from the children and the literacy facilitators as they interact with the features and strategies embedded in LAO. These data, combined with the user profile information and quantitative and qualitative feedback, make it possible to search for significant patterns of use correlated with particular users. Based on multivariate adaptive regression and correlational statistics, data-mining provides the opportunity to identify associations and anticipate behavior patterns and trends. The exciting implications of this type of research are that it can provide unprecedented amounts of data and detailed information for analysis to inform the continual revision and diffusion of the educational innovation or to warn of unanticipated problem states requiring corresponding design moves.

Consequences

Most design researchers may aspire to the goal of systemic change, but remain rooted in the microcontext of individual classrooms, teachers, and schools. Fishman et al. (2004) attempt to bridge this gap by advocating studies that employ system-level variables such as adoption, sustainability, or spread and that focus on schools and school systems as the unit of analysis. Systemic change is the most challenging of educational objectives. At the very least, a thorough analysis and understanding of system-level policies and culture are crucial for informed design and evaluation. As an innovation matures progressively through multiple design research cycles, information about the school's or organization's culture, capabilities, policies, and management can be gathered to guide both the design and the later diffusion and innovation studies (Blumenfeld et al., 2000). For example, Rossett (1999: 30) advocates a systemic approach assessing performance or learning in the context of a performance system that ". . . comprises standards, feedback, knowledge, incentives, recognition, information, management, sponsorship, technology, tools, processes and more." These factors can be analyzed in the early phases and then re-examined later to determine if the enacted design meets the learning targets and aligns with the established policy and cultural norms of the target system(s).

In the LAO project, the informed exploration phase revealed multiple target audience members in different contexts of use. Each of these contexts of use presents a different social and cultural system with its own inherent policies and norms that may be examined for the potential adoption, adaptation, or diffusion of LAO. Potential questions related to this final phase of LAO may include: What are the perceptions of the target audience members (in different contexts of use) of the "fit" of LAO or its alignment with specific cultural, policy, and organizational structures? What drivers and barriers exist for the adoption and diffusion of LAO in each context of use (school, home, tutoring environment, etc.)? How do current practical, cultural, or organizational relationships contribute to the use or nonuse of LAO? Does use of the LAO system change current practical, cultural, or organizational relationships? What broad systemic factors concerning the scalability and sustainability of LAO can be identified to inform other design research?

Some of these results may be mapped to the assessment of this information in earlier phases to determine if there have been any changes in perception or emergent problems related to the use, adoption, or unanticipated adaptation of LAO. Methods such as logging computer activity, multisite interviews, surveys, observations, and data-mining techniques may provide ways to examine the interrelationships and complexity of the factors involved in the diffusion and adoption of an educational innovation both within and across individual contexts. Employing methods that can illuminate systemic-level questions and identify factors influencing educational changes constitutes the "meta" problem state, resulting design move, and the next major challenge for design researchers.

Discussion

Our retrospective analysis of the acts entailed in the design of LAO revealed that the decisions, judgments, or turning points that propelled this case of design research forward involved other factors in addition to the theoretical conjectures such as:

- practical considerations
- serendipity
- applied design techniques
- implicit, pretheoretical learning assumptions
- divergent and convergent research questions
- simplifying design options
- judgments of adequacy
- the design team's prior experience
- prototyping and modeling methods that externalize understanding
- collaborative questioning and evaluation
- budgetary factors.

These factors prompted many important decisions and evaluations that spurred the design research forward or, in some cases, restricted or constrained the design efforts. Examining these factors also disclosed what was involved in the emergence and selection of the theoretical components, research questions, methods, and features for the design of LAO. The complexity of this journey is evident in the narrative of the LAO example and presents some broad themes related to the nature of the design process, which are discussed in the next section.

Decision–Evaluation Spaces, Problem States, and Design Moves

Our analysis of the design decision making, or the road taken, in the LAO design research highlights the cascade of judgments and decisions and provides a useful metaphor for examining more closely the many potential acts of design that embody theory. MacLean, Young et al. (1989: 247) speak to the selection of options and to providing a design rationale for their work in interface design in this manner: "To understand why a system design is the way it is, we also need to understand how it could be different, and why the choices which were made are appropriate." These authors describe their consideration of the many alternative options in design as the "decision space" and the generation of explicit reasons for selecting a particular option from many possible options as the "evaluation space." Viewing the design research process as involving emergent progressive decisions, spaces, or states provides a way to analyze when, where, and how multiple design ideas emerge and may provide the means to examine the selection and justification of those choices.

Similarly, Doblin (1987) characterized the design process as consisting of a current beginning state, followed by a design process that contains analysis, genesis, and synthesis activities, culminating in a different state. These states change and evolve dynamically as decisions are made and design paths are selected, and they may require different forms of analysis, decision making, and evaluation at different points in the process. These states can be described as different problem states that engender interpretive, evaluative, or analytical processes and then prompt corresponding design moves. Viewing design research through this conceptualization of the design process promotes a new way of examining design research as continually evolving problem states that incorporate multiple decision–evaluation cycles and result in specific design moves. Each design move impacts the ensuing problem state significantly.

Examining the decision making in the LAO design research revealed an overall pattern of analysis of problem states, decision–evaluation cycles, and corresponding design moves that resulted in the creation of a new design problem space, prompting the cycle to repeat itself once again and continuously throughout this four-year program of research. Knowledge of the decision making that occurred at different points in defining the problem state, evaluating the design options, and enacting a particular design move rather than the alternative promoted clarification of and necessary boundaries around what type of phenomena (e.g., collaborative processes of literacy) could be investigated logically. Revealing this complex decision making in design research provides greater insight into how the problem is understood, framed, and reframed, perhaps the most challenging and important determination in more general processes of design as well as in design research.

Design is an Interpretive, Social, and Multidimensional Process

If the most difficult part of design is to locate, frame, and describe the design problem fully, then it is complicated further by involving a team of people. As Coyne (2005: 5) states: ". . . problem setting is a contingent, fraught, and sometimes consensual process for which there is no authoritative set of rules, criteria, or methods." Framing a problem and other acts of design rely heavily on interpretation and social negotiation. How we choose to see the problem, how we analyze or evaluate it, and what features are selected ultimately for a particular design embody interpretations or judgments of what pragmatic factors and aspects of theory are considered. Collectively, in team-based design settings, these judgments or interpretations need to be negotiated amid the different interests and personal concerns that may be present in the design process. When negoti-ated successfully, design activity resulting from participation in team-based design can become the catalyst for a shared learning process that ". . . educates individuals and shapes the evolving choices simultaneously" (Liedtka, 2004: 14).

In the LAO design research, perspectives from the research team members, interested parties, and potential audience members were all brought to bear on the decision mak-ing that took place or the judgments that were made. Every iteration of the LAO design became an interpretation, and each design team member progressed further toward a more fluid, adaptive expertise or understanding of the collaborative literacy process as he or she participated in creating the evolving design (Winograd & Flores, 1986). This participatory design research experience represents a multidimensional process where a group of individuals are engaged in the individual interpretation and collective negoti-ation of framing a continually changing design problem as well as determining decision –evaluation cycles and negotiating design moves. Kelly and Lesh (2000) described a similar multilevel approach to research in their multitiered teaching experiment. How-ever, additional layers of complexity are also evident in the design research process if we consider the many ways in which we might interpret and frame individually and collect-ively the dynamic problem states and many factors discussed in this chapter that may prompt the decision making or judgments at different points in a design process. Given this, the act of design in design research becomes a much more complex activity, with many layers of decision making and perspectives that may influence theory and design.

Many Factors Prompt Acts of Design and Continual Reinterpretation of Theory

Analysis of the LAO research revealed many factors that prompted acts of design, among them the pragmatic, theoretical, and applied influences on decision making. Some of these factors converged in the decision–evaluation cycles or the team diverged from existing information or approaches to attempt to promote new directions for research and design. This iterative process of convergence and divergence evident in the LAO design research and its influence on emergent theory present a final broad theme in this analysis. As an example of the convergent–divergent process, the formulation and selection of the initial research questions in LAO were based on merging existing, theoretical, and applied perspectives on collaborative literacy and then diverging from more typical, child-centered, tutorial-based approaches. The exploration of multiple options converging in a particular direction and departing from the traditional forms of design present in the stages of the LAO research created the foundation for the next cycle of design research activity and influenced future cycles heavily.

Other examples of the convergent–divergent process in the LAO design research included the convergence of a sociocultural pedagogical orientation and the applied design principle of EPSS design. Additionally, when a more detailed design direction was needed, the team members found that they were dissatisfied with the existing applied methods of task analysis and selected an alternative method based on one team member's familiarity or prior experience with activity theory. With the selection of this alternative analytical tool, the team diverged from existing traditional approaches to task analysis to generate new features and functions of online literacy support that maintained alignment with our theoretical direction. Dym et al. (2005) refer to this process as alternating between convergent thinking that promotes deep reasoning and more creative, divergent thinking where the designer (or design researcher) attempts to diverge from the known information in order to generate unknown directions. The progression of research questions posed in LAO and our emergent theoretical under-standing of collaborative literacy were prompted by this continual, iterative, convergent–divergent process.

Important influences on the emergence, selection, and reconsideration of the theor-etical components embodied in the design of LAO were the prioritizing and pruning of the many design ideas put forth by the team. Evident in any design activity, this reductionist task began with defining learning targets in the enactment phase and con-tinued iteratively through the local evaluation phase as multiple design ideas were generated, then evaluated, and ultimately implemented, discarded, or adapted in some way. Decisions and judgments were made about the adequacy of design ideas in order to select particular aspects of a theory, design options, and research methods from the many possible alternatives at multiple points in the design path. Some simplification or reduction of information was necessary in the design because ". . . to deal realistically with the complexity and complication of large amounts of information, within a rea-sonable amount of time, it is necessary to find ways to simplify. This means ignoring or leaving out things that cannot easily be characterized" (Nelson & Stolterman, 2003: 187). Some theoretical constructs may be difficult to express in a design, so constructs that translate more easily to the classroom or technology environment may be more prevalent in design research. Because design is an interpretive act, theoretical constructs embedded in LAO were selected, reinterpreted, and refined continually as design ideas were generated, adapted, implemented, or discarded.

Conclusions

What is clear from investigating the act of design in design research is that the process is more complex than considered previously. By acknowledging the fluid, dynamic, evolving nature of design in design research, as well as the many layers of decisions and judgments required in design, we conclude that multiple factors may influence empirical and design decision making. These factors can include pragmatic, political, and applied methodological influences, among others, and provoke design researchers to consider other factors involved in design research beyond a sole focus on theoretical conjectures. Investigating the acts of design inherent in design research by analyzing the multiple cycles of problem states, decision–evaluation processes, and design moves can help to clarify and illuminate important decision making. Tracing this decision making in the LAO example revealed that the generation and refinement of theory and the selection of research questions, methods, and design features were intertwined inexorably with the more pragmatic processes of design.

There are many possible paths in design research, and knowledge of the design road taken as well as the one not taken can inform empirical decisions. Employing the lens of the design process can assist design researchers in generating and examining the pro-gression of their decision making and judgments based on multiple factors and may shed light on important contextual issues that promote the selection of specific research questions and design features (O'Donnell, 2004). Acknowledging fully the act of design in design research may move us closer to articulating the processes and procedures explicitly and provide improved information on how researchers determine which aspects of theory, research questions, and design features to address in this complex endeavor.

References

Bannan-Ritland, B. (2003). The role of design in research: The integrative learning design framework. *Educational Researcher, 32*(1), 21–24.

Bannan-Ritland, B., Egerton, E., Page, J. & Behrmann, M. (2000). Literacy explorer: A support tool for novice reading facilitators. *Performance Improvement Journal, 39*, 47–54.

Barksdale, S. & Lund, T. (2001). *Rapid evaluation.* Alexandria, VA: American Society for Training and Development.

Bell, P., Hoadley, C. M. & Linn, M. C. (2004). Design-based research in education. In M. C. Linn, E. A. Davis & P. Bell (eds), *Internet environments for science education* (pp. 73–85). Mahwah, NJ: Lawrence Erlbaum Associates.

Blumenfeld, P., Fishman, B., Krajcik, J. S., Marx, R. W. & Soloway, E. (2000). Creating usable innovations in systemic reform: Scaling-up technology-embedded project-based science in urban schools. *Educational Psychologist, 35*, 149–164.

Buckley, B. C., Gobert, J. D. & Christie, M. T. (2002). Model-based teaching and learning with hypermodels: What do they learn? How do they learn? How do we know? Paper presented at the annual conference of the American Educational Research Association, New Orleans, LA, April.

Confrey, J. & Lachance, A. (2000). Transformative reading experiments through conjecture-driven research design. In A. E. Kelly & R. A. Lesh (eds), *Handbook of research design in mathematics and science education* (pp. 231–266). Mahwah, NJ: Lawrence Erlbaum Associates.

Constantine, L. L. & Lockwood, L. A. (1999). *Software for use: A practical guide to the models and methods of usage-centered design.* Reading, MA: Addison-Wesley.

Cooper, A. (1999). *The inmates are running the asylum: Why high-tech products drive us crazy and how to restore the sanity.* Indianapolis, IN: Sams.

Coyne, R. (2005). Wicked problems revisited. *Design Studies, 26*, 5–17.

Dabbagh, N. & Bannan-Ritland, B. (2005). *Online learning: Concepts, strategies and application.* Upper Saddle River, NJ: Pearson Merrill Prentice Hall.

Doblin, J. (1987). A short, grandiose theory of design. *STA Design Journal, Analysis and Intuition*, 6–16.

Dym, C. L., Agogino, A. L., Eris, O., Frey, D. D. & Leifer, L. J. (2005). Engineering design thinking, teaching and learning. *Journal of Engineering Education, 94*, 103–120.

Fishman, B., Marx, R. W., Blumenfeld, P., Krajcik, J. & Soloway, E. (2004). Creating a framework for research on systemic technology innovations. *Journal of the Learning Sciences, 13*, 43–76.

Gambrell, L. B. (1999). *Best practices in literacy instruction.* New York: Guilford Press.

Gery, G. J. (1991). *Electronic performance support systems: How and why to remake the workplace through the strategic application of technology.* Boston, MA: Weingarten.

Graue, M. E. & Walsh, D. (with Ceglowski, D.) (eds) (1998). *Studying children in context: Theories, methods, and ethics.* Thousand Oaks, CA: Sage.

Grossen, B. (1998). *30 years of research: What we know about how children learn to read*, at: http://cftl.org/30years/30years.html.

Jeffs, T. (2000). Characteristics, interactions and attitudes of parent/child dyads and their use of assistive technology in a literacy experience on the Internet. *Dissertation Abstracts International, 61*(09), 3526 (UMI No. 9987987).

Jonassen, D. H., Tessmer, M. & Hannum, W. H. (1999). *Task analysis methods for instructional design.* Mahwah, NJ: Lawrence Erlbaum Associates.

Kelly, A. E. (2004). Design research in education: Yes, but is it methodological? *Journal of the Learning Sciences, 13*, 115–128.

Kelly, A. E. & Lesh, R. A. (eds) (2000). *Handbook of research design in mathematics and science education.* Mahwah, NJ: Lawrence Erlbaum Associates.

Lawson, B. R. (2004). Schemata, gambits and precedent: Some factors in design expertise Design Studies, *25*(5), 443–457.

Liedtka, J. (2004). Strategy as design. *Rotman Management, Winter*, 12–15.

Lobato, J. (2003). How design experiments can inform a rethinking of transfer and vice versa. *Educational Researcher, 32*(1), 17–20.

MacLean, A., Young, R. M. & Moran, T. P. (1989). Design rationale: The argument behind the artifact. In K. Bice & C. Lewis (eds), *Proceedings of the SIGCHI conference on Human factors in computing systems: Wings for the mind* (pp. 247–252) New York: ACM Press.

Mastropieri, M. & Scruggs, T. (1997). Best practices in promoting reading comprehension in students with learning disabilities: 1976–1996. *Remedial and Special Education, 18,* 197–213.

McMillan, J. H. & Schumacher, S. (2001). *Research in education: A conceptual introduction* (5th ed.). New York: Longman.

National Assessments of Educational Progress (1998). *Reading assessment: Report card for the nation.* National Center for Education Statistics, at: http://nces.ed.gov/nationsreportcard/pubs/main1998/1999459.pdf.

Nelson, H. G. & Stolterman, E. (2003). *The design way: Intentional change in an unpredictable world: Foundations and fundamentals of design competence.* Englewood Cliffs, NJ: Educational Technology Publications.

Nitko, A. J. (2004). *Educational assessment of students* (4th ed.). Upper Saddle River, NJ: Pearson Merrill Prentice Hall.

O'Donnell, A. (2004). A commentary on design research. *Educational Psychologist, 39,* 255–260.

Preece, J., Rogers, Y. & Sharp, H. (2002). *Interaction design.* New York: Wiley.

Rittel, H. W. & Webber, M. M. (1973). Dilemmas in a general theory of planning. *Policy Sciences, 4,* 155–169.

Rogers, E. M. (2003). *Diffusion of innovations* (5th ed.). New York: Free Press.

Rossett, A. (1999). *First things fast: A handbook for performance analysis.* San Francisco, CA: Jossey-Bass/Pfeiffer.

Rubin, J. (1994). *Handbook of usability testing: How to plan, design, and conduct effective tests.* New York: Wiley.

Sandoval, W. (2004). Developing learning theory by refining conjectures embodied in educational designs. *Educational Psychologist, 39,* 213–223.

Schön, D. A. (1983). *The reflective practitioner.* New York: Basic Books.

Simmons, D. C. & Kameenui, E. J. (1998). *What reading research tells us about children with diverse needs: Bases and basics.* Mahwah, NJ: Lawrence Erlbaum Associates.

Spillers, W. R. & Newsome, S. L. (1993). Engineering design, conceptual design and design theory: A report. In M. J. de Vries, N. Cross & D. P. Grant (eds), *Design methodology and relationships with science* (pp. 103–120). Dordrecht, The Netherlands: Kluwer Academic.

Tessmer, M. (1993). *Planning and conducting formative evaluations.* London: Kogan-Page.

Winograd, T. & Flores, F. (eds) (1986). *Understanding computers and cognition: A new foundation for design.* Norwood, NJ: Ablex.

16 Illuminating the Braids of Change in a Web-Supported Community

A Design Experiment by Another Name

Sasha A. Barab
Indiana University

Eun-Ok Baek
California State University, San Bernardino

Steve Schatz
University of Hartford

Rebecca Scheckler
Radford University

Julie Moore
University of Georgia

Design-Based Research

The methodological paradigm of "design experiments" is traced back to 1992 when Alan Collins (1992) and Ann Brown (1992) advocated a new methodological approach that would guide them as they carried out research and design work in the context of real-life settings. What began as a reaction to traditional experimentation and its focus on controls, laboratory settings, and replicable results has emerged into a growing field that can be grouped under the label of DESIGN-BASED RESEARCH METHODS. In communicating the activity and the need, Brown (1992: 141) stated:

> As a design scientist in my field, I attempt to engineer innovative educational environments and simultaneously conduct experimental studies of those innovations. This involves orchestrating all aspects of a period of daily life in classrooms, a research activity for which I was not trained.

Design-based research involves introducing innovations into the booming, buzzing confusion of real-world practice (as opposed to constrained laboratory contexts) and examining the impact of those designs on the learning process. Specifically, this type of research involves examining the design team, interactions among the designers and the members of the communities being researched, and the everyday practices of the users of the innovation as they use the current iteration of the design. Then, the implications of the findings are cycled into the next iteration of the design innovation in order to build evidence of the particular theories being researched. Because design experiments develop theory in practice, they have the potential to lead to interventions that are trustworthy, credible, transferable, and ecologically valid (Barab et al., 2001a; Brown, 1992; Kelly, 2003; Roth, 1998).

Collins (1999) suggested seven major differences between traditional psychological methods and the design experiment methodology (see Table 16.1 for an abbreviated list). Central to this distinction is the emphasis in design-based research on understanding the messiness of real-world practice, with context being a central part of the story and not an extraneous variable to be minimized. On a related note, design-based research involves flexible revision of the design, multiple dependent variables, and capturing social interaction. Further, participants are not "subjects" assigned treatments but, instead, are recognized as coparticipants in the design and analysis, contributing their expertise and in-depth understanding to the research. Lastly, given the focus on characterizing situations (as opposed to controlling variables), the outcome of design-based research concentrates on developing a profile that characterizes the design in practice (as opposed to testing a hypothesis).

The importance of characterizing the design process more generally is that, in design research, the focus is on developing a design and generating new theory simultaneously. At one level, the design work occurs in the service of theory generation with evidence of

Table 16.1 Comparing Psychological Experimentation and Design-Based Research Methods

Category	Psychological experimentation	Design-based research
Location of research	Conducted in laboratory settings	Occurs in the buzzing, blooming confusion of real-life settings where most learning occurs
Complexity of variables	Frequently involves a single or a couple of dependent variable(s)	Involves multiple dependent variables, including climate variables (e.g., collaboration among learners, available resources); outcome variables (e.g., learning of content, transfer); and system variables (e.g., dissemination, sustainability)
Focus of research	Focuses on identifying a few variables and holding them constant	Focuses on characterizing the situation in all its complexity, much of which is not known beforehand
Unfolding of procedures	Uses fixed procedures	Involves flexible design revision in which there is a tentative initial set that is revised depending on its success in practice
Amount of social interaction	Isolates learners to control interaction	Frequently involves complex social interactions, with participants sharing ideas, distracting each other, etc.
Characterizing the findings	Focuses on testing a hypothesis	Involves looking at multiple aspects of the design and developing a profile that characterizes the design in practice
Role of participants	Treats participants as subjects	Involves different participants in the design in order to bring their differing expertise into producing and analyzing the design

Source: From Collins, A. (1999). The changing infrastructure of education research. In E. C. Lagemann & L. S. Shulman (eds), *Issues in education research: Problems and possibilities* (pp. 289–298). San Francisco, CA: Jossey-Bass. Adapted with permission.

its effectiveness being a precursor to theory development. Barab and Squire (2004: 5–6) state:

> Although providing credible evidence for local gains as a result of a particular design may be necessary, it is not sufficient. Design-based research requires more than simply showing a particular design works but demands that the researcher [move beyond a particular design exemplar to] generate evidence-based claims about learning that address contemporary theoretical issues and further the theoretical knowledge of the field.

Although one can use traditional validation schemes as evidence for the effectiveness of a design, a central challenge for design-based researchers is to determine how to characterize and share their local experiences in ways that will advance and make useful theoretical claims; in other words, how can they package their local stories in a manner that will prove useful to others (Geertz, 1976)? For such ends, it is our belief that an effective, design-based research program must include the following information:

- The designed product.
- The context within which the design was implemented.
- Warrants for evidence of the local impact.
- The theoretical assertions and their relations to the design work.
- The conditions through which the theoretical assertions were generated.
- Warrants for evidence of the theoretical assertions.

This all needs to be carried out in ways that are useful to others engaged in similar work (Barab & Squire, 2004). Furthermore, as evidenced in our six criteria listed above, for the work to be useful, there must be reasonable warrants with respect to both the design work and the theoretical assertions being advanced. In this chapter, rather than restating methods used traditionally to assess the worth of a product or program (see, for example: qualitative methods [Stake, 1983]; quantitative methods [Isaac & Michael, 1990]; mixed method [Greene & Caracelli, 1997]) or methods used to justify the methodological warrants of one's research, the goal is to provide a specific example of one methodological process-design narrative—for sharing design trajectories and accompanying theoretical assertions in ways that will be credible, trustworthy, and useful to others. In providing a specific example of a method for sharing design trajectories, it is necessary to touch on these other aspects in order to justify to the reader that the design and the design story are worthwhile; that is, we are not saying a lot about nothing.

A Design Narrative

A challenging part of doing educational research on design-based interventions is to characterize the complexity, fragility, messiness, and eventual solidity of the design so that others may benefit from it. One of the central ideas in the scientific paradigm is replicability; however, because design-based researchers cannot (and may not want to) manipulate cultural context, it becomes difficult to replicate others' findings (Hoadley, 2002). Therefore, in helping others to determine the generalizability of the theoretical assertions derived, the goals are to lay open and express as a problem the completed design in ways that provide insight into the construction of the design (Latour, 1987). This involves not only sharing the designed artifact but also providing rich descriptions of the context, the guiding and emerging theory, the design features of the intervention, and the impact of these features on participation and learning. Hoadley (2002) argues that design-based researchers must meet the challenge of replicability by describing the research adequately in a form that he suggests should be a design narrative. Narrative?one way of making sense of a particular design trajectory—is a historical method that involves conveying a series of related plots and describing the unfolding of the design over time (Abbott, 1984, 1992; Mink et al., 1987).

In describing the process of building narratives, Abbott suggests that the first step of narrative analysis is to delimit the case itself, or what historiographers refer to as the "central subject problem" (Hull, 1975). The crucial difficulty lies in "drawing boundaries around the central subject given the continuous character of the social manifold" (Abbott, 1992: 63). However, these boundaries are fuzzy because the properties have case-specific meanings and the cases pass through transformation over time. In fact, in design studies, the focus of the research is on understanding these transformations and on highlighting the conditions that led to particular transformations. It is *the unpacking* of these transformations or the describing what the case endures that philosophers refer to as the "colligation" problem (see Abbott [1984] for an extended discussion on this topic).

All too often, designers merely report the ready-made structures, thereby concealing the trajectories through which design decisions are made. This is problematic in that much of the theory generation process necessary to move from design work to design-based research occurs through an examination of these processes. However, uncovering these processes and sharing them in ways that allow others to understand the conditions that gave rise to the theoretical assertions presented is a complex business. According to historians, the important and somewhat disheartening point with respect to the colligation problem is the awareness that each event is complex, enduring multiple transformations, having multiple antecedents, and resulting in myriad consequences (Isaac, 1997). Abbott (1992) discusses the coming of an event as a sequence of major turning points (kernels) and sets of situational consequences flowing from these kernels. As such, a fundamental challenge in presenting design narratives lies in uncovering these events so that the reader understands their complexity but doing so in a way that will give global meaning to other work while simultaneously capturing meaningfully the dynamic unfolding of the phenomena.

It is important to note that we do not see the sharing of design trajectories as a theory-forming methodology after which we can strip out contextual variables and run "true experiments." For some theoretical issues, we believe that the design narrative provides the minimal meaningful methodology for understanding the theoretical issue at hand. This is especially true when examining something as complex as community. From the proliferation of work about researching and designing online communities (e.g., Collison et al., 2000; Hakken, 1999; Jones, 1999; Kim, 2000; Preece, 2000; Smith & Kollock, 1999), we can assume correctly an urgent interest in online communities, even those with the specific focus of supporting learning (Barab et al., 2004; Renninger & Shumar, 2004). However, it is one thing to theorize or proselytize about the importance of such communities and the structures they might employ, and it is another thing to design an online space that a community and its associated members will use to support their learning.

Even if a group can design something resembling a community online, it is an even greater challenge to share these experiences in a manner that will be useful to others engaged in similar design efforts. It is these types of messy complex contexts and her realization that much of the phenomena of interest to learning scientists occur as parts of these contexts that led Ann Brown (1992) to introduce the design experiment methodology initially. Therefore, although some theory can be tested by isolating variables and randomly assigning participants theoretically distinct treatments, much of the theoretical assertions of interest to learning scientists and educators more generally require understanding the phenomena of interest in rich contexts—online community is one of these types of variables that it may be impractical to study and generate theory about in laboratory-based contexts. In this chapter, as an attempt to illuminate the challenges of designing for a community online, we use a design narrative methodology to share the process of making a web-based community—the Inquiry Learning Forum (ILF)—highlighting the design challenges and successes and advancing some theoretical assertions in the hope that others may carry out their own design work more fruitfully.

Context of this Study

Theoretical Grounding

The term community has a long and rich tradition. It is used in sociology, anthropology, psychology, philosophy, advertising, business, popular culture, and education, among others (Barab & Duffy, 2000; Bellah et al., 1985; Brown, 2001; Grossman et al., 2001; Kim, 2000; Preece, 2000; Rogoff, 1994; Smith & Kollock, 1999; Weedman, 1999; Wenger, 1998; Westheimer, 1998). In its many different uses, the term community has become so varied and omnipresent that we must be cautious about its continued usefulness as a descriptor of specific societal relations. For example, "intentional community" is used to describe the people who form joint housing projects where they share common space, recreational facilities, and common goals and values in the way they choose to live and negotiate together on a daily and continuing basis. Compare this account to talking about a "community of accountants" who share a common way of making a living but have never met the vast majority of their fellow community members.

Many authors note the variability of the notion of community and struggle with its use in their research (Riel & Polin, 2004). Bellah et al. (1985: 333) stated that a community is "a group of people who are socially interdependent, who participate together in discussion and decision making, and who share certain practices that both define the community and are nurtured by it." Jenny Preece (2000), who researches computer-mediated communities, defined community as a collection of people who interact socially with a shared purpose, guiding policies, and supportive computer systems. Carolyn Shields and Patricia Seltzer (Shields, 1997) struggled for a robust definition of community in highly diverse and bilingual school communities on Indian reservations. After deciding that community is too variable to be encompassed by one term, they proposed three separate concepts of community: a moral community, a community of difference, and a community of dialogue.

Lave and Wenger (1991) advanced the term community of practice to capture the importance of activity in fusing individuals to communities and of communities in legitimizing individual practices. In the context of communities of practice, learning is conceived as a trajectory in which learners move from legitimate peripheral participants to core participants. Based on a review of the literature, Barab et al. (2003: 23) define online community as "a persistent, sustained socio-technical network of individuals who share and develop an overlapping knowledge base, set of beliefs, values, history and experiences focused on a common practice and/or mutual enterprise." Communities of practice have histories, cultural identities, interdependence among members, and mechanisms for reproduction (Lave & Wenger, 1991). The important point is not whether another researcher can add or delete specific indicators, or produce a different definition, but the acknowledgment that communities are more than a temporary coming together of individuals around a particular goal, for a workshop, or for a course (see Riel & Polin, 2004). Much like a living organism, they are self-organizing and do not emerge designed at their first appearance. They grow, evolve, and change dynamically, transcending any particular member and outliving any particular task.

In spite of the challenges of building something like community online, we are seeing numerous examples of designed communities that exist primarily online.[1] Notwithstanding the fact that community has become an obligatory appendage attached liberally to almost any website, or that "community member" is a label applied to anyone who visits a website and pays a fee or types in a password, building online community is an important and viable opportunity for supporting learning that educators need to understand better. Building and maintaining online communities involves the design and manipulation of technologies in ways that foster human connection (Grossman et al., 2001; Kim, 2000; Preece, 2000; Schlager & Fusco, 2004). Indeed, online communities face all the challenges of copresent communities, with the additional challenges caused by the technologies and by the physical distancing that these technologies allow. In this chapter, we focus on the design decisions that we have made in attempting to support the development of an online community of practice for mathematics and science teachers.

Design Context

The Inquiry Learning Forum was developed over three years as a National Science Foundation-funded project, and it had a design/research team of five graduate assistants, five faculty professors, a programmer, a project manager, and a postdoctoral fellow (see Barab et al., 2001b, 2003, for more discussion). It was designed to support a virtual community of in-service and preservice mathematics and science teachers sharing, improving, and creating inquiry-based, pedagogical practices (register or take a tour at: http://ilf.crlt.indiana.edu/) (see Figure 16.1). Founded in our previous research and consistent with our pedagogical commitment (Barab & Duffy, 2000; Chaney-Cullen & Duffy, 1998), the ILF was designed with the belief that teachers need to be full participants in and owners of their virtual space. Specifically, although our conceptualization of the ILF has evolved over time, four principles guided its original design and are still powerful elements in the current iteration of the project:

1 *Foster ownership and participation.* We believe that a truly effective professional development environment must include a community of professional practitioners with varied experiences and skills who accept responsibility for building and maintaining their environment.
2 *Focus on inquiry.* Our goal is to foster inquiry, both in terms of inquiry pedagogy in the classroom and teachers' inquiry into their own practices.
3 *Visit the classroom.* A central strategy in the design and implementation of our knowledge network is the use of video streaming and web-based technologies to situate participants in the social context of other community members' teaching practice.
4 *Support communities of practice.* Initially, we focused on the more general notion of communities of practice; however, over time, we adopted the more constrained focus of a common purpose. We focused on bringing together and supporting groups of teachers organized around a collective experience and/or a curricular interest.

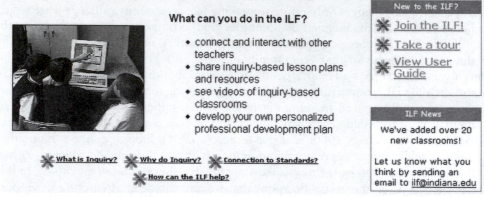

Figure 16.1　The Inquiry Learning Forum (ILF) Home Screen. The "Take a Tour" Option Links to Visit Classrooms, ILF Office, Collaboratory, Lounge, Library, Auditorium, and My Desk.

The hallmark of this environment is that teachers and students with a broad range of experiences and expertise come together in a virtual space to observe, discuss, and reflect upon pedagogical theory and practice anchored to video-based teaching vignettes (see Figure 16.2). When the antecedent to this chapter was written in 2000, there were over 1,500 registered ILF members, among them university faculty and preservice and in-service teachers.

The ILF encompasses a large and complex website, called the e-ILF (electronic ILF) in this chapter, and a large group of people as users and designers who transact with the e-ILF and each other. We have come to view the ILF not merely as a website but more as a sociotechnical interaction network (STIN) that includes technical structures, people, and the interactions among them (Barab et al., 2003; Kling et al., 2002). All these people come to the project with their unique, sometimes overlapping, and sometimes conflicting historical cultural settings. As a result, the project's trajectory, including the social, technological, and pedagogical elements, was complex, transactive, and dynamic. It is our understanding that this will be the case almost always when the design work is not geared toward producing a particular artifact that will be "boxed" and disseminated but, instead, is participatory and is focused on social interaction or even targeted toward the development of a community with a reform agenda. This is because the creation of a design is a much more complex, situated, and problematic process than is represented frequently in the straightforward reporting of the "ready-made," final, blackbox product (Latour, 1987).

Methodological Process

Data Collection

Our research can be described best as naturalistic inquiry, with interpretations based on qualitative data (Guba & Lincoln, 1983; Stake, 1983). Although some interpretations

| ✳ ILF Home | Classrooms | ILF Office | My Desk | Lounge | Library | Inquiry Lab | Collaboratory |

The video will appear in this window. Please use the following controls to view it.

Volume
Play/Pause　　Menu
Status Bar　　Scan
Review

◄ ▌► ○ ◄◎ ►

Tony H's Biology Class
⦿ Modem　○ High Speed　○ Full Screen

On the first day of class, Tony introduces his students to himself and the scientific process with a unique exercise in which the students must determine how the "Volume Exchanger" works.

1. Introduction (6.0 min)
2. The Volume Exchanger (3.5 min)
3. Making Journal Observations (6.5 min)
4. Observations vs. Inferences (4.0 min)

5. Making Models (11.5 min)
6. Model Discussions (15.5 min)
7. Testing Predictions (8.5 min)
8. The Scientific Process (3.3 min)

ILF 🖉 | PUBLIC Discussion | Tony's Reflections | Overview | Lesson Plan | Student Work | Standards | Resources | Help

Lesson Overview

Lesson Description　This activity is designed to engage students in scientific problem solving on the very first day of class. A variation on a "Black Box" type problem is presented and a variety of science process skills are used to attempt to solve the problem.

Figure 16.2　Current Iteration of a Specific Inquiry Learning Forum Classroom, Including Links to an Overview of the Lesson, Reflective Commentary, Descriptions of Teaching Activity, Lesson Plans, Students' Examples, and Connections with Both State and National Standards.

were based on ILF team members ("insiders") writing about their experiences and their perspectives about events in which they participated directly, other interpretations were developed by two researchers ("outsiders") who were hired to observe the ILF *team* as it developed and researched the ILF. In addition to attending meetings and taking field notes, this research team conducted structured and semistructured interviews with both the member-participants and the designers. The structured interviews consisted of over 20 questions that covered a wide range of project design issues and individual perceptions. The questions were derived from the conversations with team members and an analysis of the literature on knowledge networks, and they evolved continually through group meetings. The interviews typically lasted 60 to 90 minutes.

In addition to these sources of data, interpretations were triangulated using field notes, interviews, document analysis, and member checks (Lincoln & Guba, 1985). Some of these data were collected as the events occurred and other data were based on retrospective recall through interviews and examinations of traces. For example, the authors reviewed shared e-mail, early iterations of documents, and project notebooks, with the goal of using these multiple sources of data to build a story about the making of the ILF. These collection efforts resulted in a large corpus of data, such as field notes, interview transcripts, design artifacts at various stages in the project, record-keeping, meeting notes, e-mail interactions, ethnographic observation of the online space, ethnographic observation of members in their classes, and interviews with the research and design team as well as with teacher users of the e-ILF. Comments on the manuscript also were received from eight ILF teachers, who, as members of the ILF's Participant Advisory Board, provided feedback and were co-designers of many ILF features.

Data Analysis

In analyzing the data, we began by having each of the authors examine the data, their personal notes, and e-mail, and reflecting on their firsthand experiences in order to develop a timeline that communicated the core design episodes of the ILF history. Each episode consisted of four components: (a) a definable and bounded set of preconditions, (b) a change in our thinking, (c) design intervention, and (d) impact. The preconditions of the design intervention were envisioned as those nested occurrences that gave rise to the particular design intervention, which could have been a technical interface change or a change in our practice (e.g., conducting face-to-face workshops to introduce the e-ILF).

Design interventions usually came about as a result of a change in our thinking, which was triggered by a single event or a cluster of related events, such as design team meetings, comments by the research and participant advisory boards, interviews with teachers, visits to classrooms, focus groups, or other activities. The impact involved writing a description of what happened after we implemented the change in design. Our goal with this four-step analysis was to identify the events and their constituent features with the intention of developing what historians refer to as a "loose causal order" of the design trajectory. Each of the six authors compiled a timeline of episodes from his or her perspective and shared it with the other members. Based on this list, we produced a representation and the design episode trajectory discussion described in The Nature of the Design section later in this chapter.

Although we found this linear episode trajectory useful for gaining a coarse picture of the design trajectory, it was incomplete. As we began to fill out the specifics of each design episode, we found the portrayal illuminative but somewhat artificial and not representative of the actual complexity. More specifically, drawing boundaries around the episode was problematic given the continuous, dynamic, and complex character of the process and the product. As such, we grew uncomfortable with, and had difficulty characterizing, the phenomena using discrete events as starting points or as ending points, in part because many of the changes we made involved complex social interactions occurring over extended timeframes. We also were concerned with the usefulness of the timeline-of-episodes approach for characterizing our work in ways that would be useful to others. We started with a conception of design episodes as points in time, like stones placed in a river, changing the direction of the flow. However, we came to understand design decisions in terms of tensions that boiled over periodically and, in time, yielded substantive social and technological changes in the ILF. As we pushed the discussion toward more detail, we further came to appreciate that bracketing change in terms of a point, even when conceived as a chaotic attractor (Prigogine, 1984), did not capture adequately the unfolding trajectories of life. In our observations, we witnessed multiple social, technological, economic, and emotional forces all transacting to form extended plots in ways that gave rise to (or transacted with) emergent design interventions.

As we struggled to reconceptualize the design episodes identified into something more representative of the complexity of the process, we realized two things. First, each episode by itself was not critical enough to stand alone as the primary cause for a change in design. The episodes were the confluence of many prior happenings and experiences and the realization of the change was distributed across an extended trajectory in time. Second, each one of the changes was interconnected. It is almost impossible to talk about changes in one area without referring to changes in another. We struggled with how to convey the complexity of the interconnected episodes and finally decided to treat and represent our experiences as "braids of change." Each experience can be talked about independently, yet, by weaving them together, one gets a better sense of the design of the whole.

In understanding the braids, we used the timeline to identify core issues or major turning points, including the sets of situational consequences flowing toward and away from these points. Similar to the constant-comparison method (Glaser & Strauss, 1967; Strauss & Corbin, 1997), we looked across the multiple episodes identified, collapsed them into major categories of the ILF experience, and then highlighted those that were most significant to the project and that would be most useful to others. Our goal was to capture and present the identified braids as theoretical constructs that potentially would prove useful to others engaged in similar design work. As such, it was our challenge and, we would argue, a challenge of design-based research more generally, that the braids be both methodologically sound and theoretically useful. The former is dependent on our ability to convince others that our methods were credible and trustworthy, whereas the latter caveat (theoretically useful) is based in part on our ability to connect the derived assertions to the literature; however, it is also important that we justify the usefulness of the assertions for ourselves while showing their relevance to others.

This process resulted in the identification of four braids that are presented in the Braids of Change section: (a) Evolving an Identity; (b) Supporting Bounded Participation; (c) Moving Beyond the Technical Dimensions; and (d) Designing for Sociability. It is our intention that these braids have both local resonance with the data, as well as global significance in that they serve as theoretical assertions with respect to the challenges of designing for something like online community. We come to understand the boundaries and how a particular braid endures over time. This led us to re-examine the data and our participant observer experience in order to determine the contingencies that pushed a state along a particular path. We viewed each design braid as being engaged in a perpetual dialogue with its environment, a dialogue of action and constraint that historians refer to as "plot" (Abbott, 1992). The plot of a particular braid is complex, with each weave of the braid having "many immediate antecedents, each of which has many immediate antecedents, and conversely a given event has many consequents, each of which has many consequents" (ibid.: 66). As such, the issue of a braid having a beginning, a middle, and an end (what historians call periodization) is a major problem that required us to make boundary commitments in terms of what events constitute a particular braid.

The Nature of the Design

Before exploring the instantiation of the braids in the ILF project, readers may find it useful to have some background to the project. Figure 16.3 provides a graphic timeline to illustrate the following points. The ILF was conceived during the spring of 1999 in a graduate seminar composed of faculty and students from various curricular areas and interests (Reynolds et al., 2001). Class members interviewed teachers, built and tested prototypes, and studied the literature and latest thinking about online communities. During this period, some of the faculty codified the thinking of the seminar into a grant proposal that could be submitted to the National Science Foundation (NSF). Hoping to bring a broad perspective to the project, co-principal investigators included faculty in instructional systems technology, math education, educational psychology, and library and information science. By the end of the semester, three prototypes had been developed and the grant request had been submitted. One group of students continued to work after the semester had ended, developing one prototype further.

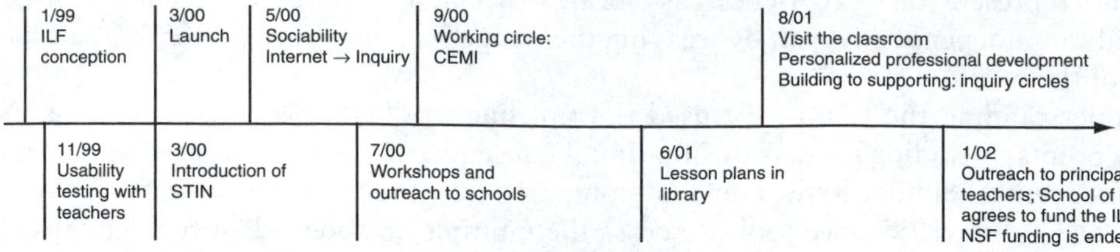

1/99 ILF conception	3/00 Launch	5/00 Sociability Internet → Inquiry	9/00 Working circle: CEMI	8/01 Visit the classroom Personalized professional development Building to supporting: inquiry circles
11/99 Usability testing with teachers	3/00 Introduction of STIN	7/00 Workshops and outreach to schools	6/01 Lesson plans in library	1/02 Outreach to principals and teachers; School of Education agrees to fund the ILF after NSF funding is ended

Figure 16.3 Timeline of Design Episodes in the Inquiry Learning Forum. For Space Reasons, Some Information is Placed Above and Below the Line, But There is No Meaningful Difference to the Different Placements.
CEMI = Collaboration to Enhance Mathematics Instruction. ILF = Inquiry Learning Forum. NSF = National Science Foundation. STIN = Sociotechnical Interaction Network.

During the summer of 1999, NSF sent notice that the grant would be funded, so work on the prototype continued. Throughout the fall of 1999, project team members were hired, and work began on the development of the website. Testing with teachers in November 1999 led to fundamental changes in the user interface. In addition, the teachers brought in to provide input became ongoing members of the Participant Advisory Board (PAB), a group that met every few months throughout the project to provide insight and feedback from the perspective of the in-service teachers who were using inquiry in their classes. The site went online in March 2000, with seven virtual classrooms complete with streaming videos of teachers doing inquiry in their classes, lesson plans, teachers' reflections, examples of students' work, and more. Mathematics or science teachers in grades six through twelve in Indiana were welcome to join. Members were sent a password and were invited to explore the classes. Discussion areas encouraged members to reflect on the practice they saw and on their own practice. The site used an interface that resembled a simple map of a school, with rooms branching out from a central space. The central space was Visit Classrooms. The adjoining rooms included the Lounge, a space to connect to discussions, and the Auditorium, where developers envisioned posting videos of guest lectures. Although there were other spaces, our focus was to push teachers toward the classrooms and discussions as opposed to their using the ILF only to download lesson plans, for example.

About three months after the site was online, the introductions of new theoretical perspectives and philosophies were reshaping the ways in which the research and development teams viewed the ILF. This resulted in changes in the design of the website and the instigation of other activities. For example, the idea that a project such as the ILF might be portrayed more accurately as transactions among people, technology, resources, and populations, and not merely as the electronic artifact (the website), led to changes in the project. The project team began to view the website as one part of the entire sociotechnical interaction network (STIN; Kling et al., 2002). The website began to be called the e-ILF (electronic ILF) internally, to emphasize that it was a part of the entire ILF project. More emphasis was placed on face-to-face interactions through outreach activities and workshops. Development team members became more active participants in online discussion forums. The overriding emphasis on "online" community was lessened, with the belief that online interactions were only one of many different interactions possible in the STIN. The most visible change on the website was the new name of the project. No longer the Internet Learning Forum, the site and the project became known as the Inquiry Learning Forum, highlighting the new emphasis on all of the parts of the project above and beyond the website.

A second complementary theory circulated throughout the development team in the spring of 2000. It involved focusing on sociability instead of usability in the design of communities. Moving away from the focus of the development team on such technical questions as "Can we build the site?" and "Can people navigate through the site?" the new focus became, "How can we support people talking and working together?" and "How can we support more meaningful and richer dialogue?" Throughout the spring and summer of 2000, development continued, with small alterations to the site. More classrooms were added. The technology was improved to make the site work better. The PAB met and discussed adding features, including lesson plans. A rubric to be used by ILF community members to evaluate videos was developed. In fall 2000, a new functionality that would have great impact was introduced. One of the co-principal investigators received a grant to support a group of in-service teachers, university faculty, and practitioners in the collaborative iterative design of mathematics lessons. This group could use the e-ILF, but they needed some extra tools, and, more importantly, they needed their own online space. Although not available to the general ILF community, the ability to create these spaces, which came to be known as Inquiry Circles, and the tool set necessary to support the tasks were developed in collaboration with this group and brought online in October 2000.

Another important development during this time was the beginning of onsite training sessions in inquiry. In January 2001, membership hit 500. Although a significant number, it was not the thousands of enrollments hoped for in our grant proposal. There were never explicit goals for enrollments or numbers of postings, but, clearly, the website was not meeting our expectations. This problem grew to be all-consuming throughout the winter and spring of 2001. Outreach efforts were not being very successful. A presentation at a science association for Indiana teachers was sparsely attended. Workshops were not generating many postings. Membership requirements were relaxed to allow all educators in Indiana, some educators in other states, and administrators to participate. An area was added to the front page that provided the date, new events, hot topics, and links to new classrooms. The belief was that this would make the front end more dynamic, indicating that the site was active and interesting.

Even with this change, comments about tumbleweeds blowing through the streets of the ILF became common at development team meetings. It was obvious that the postings were neither numerous nor particularly rich. Teachers on the site were posting mostly "I like . . ." types of messages. It was becoming clear that critical reflection on another teacher's practice was not a part of school culture and that neither inclination nor training supported this type of collaborative critical practice. In one teacher's words, "We don't usually sit around the water cooler and critique each other's teaching . . . it's just not what happens." To expect that this type of critical dialogue would begin naturally because there was an online space for it was naïve. In March 2001, a student doing a usage study found that fewer than ten people who were not members of the development team logged on for longer than five minutes. During March and April 2001, there was a growing realization that something revolutionary had to be done. Although it had been planned that this second year of the grant would involve little design and development work, switching instead to a research focus, that was not possible. There was not enough going on to study. There was an interesting contradiction between what potential users said in usability tests or during the needs analysis and what they did. At demonstrations, the responses were overwhelmingly positive. Teachers and other educators loved the e-ILF and loved the idea of an online space for teachers. However, they did not use it, not even those teachers participating directly in the design process. As a result, the development team realized in spring 2001 that it was necessary to revisit the core design decisions and consider a fundamental redesign of the site.

During this time, three parts of the sociotechnical interaction network of the ILF were fostering change. The first change involved partitioning off private areas of the ILF. The tool set developed for the mathematics collaborative lesson plan project was being used to good result. The feedback from the group using it led to several changes, with the resultant online area proving useful to this project. Another researcher, peripherally connected to the project, expressed an interest in creating an Inquiry Circle (as they were being called) for a project involving teachers working on a water quality curriculum. The second change was the first use of the ILF in a preservice teaching methods course. Students who were training to be teachers were able to see teachers engaging in the practice of teaching and discuss it not only among themselves, but also with the teachers who were featured on the video. Although there were some problems with the class usage, the overall response was positive, and plans were made to use the ILF in more methods classes. The final change was in personnel. The lead programmer, who had spearheaded a drive to freeze the feature set of the e-ILF while undertaking to rewrite the original underlying code for the site, left (amicably) in March 2001. Programmers often have very different styles. The new lead programmer did not feel that rewriting the code was an essential task and did not mind continuing to support the evolution and change of the technical side of the project. As a result, suggesting and implementing changes became much easier, and, so, a much more common practice.

During the late spring and throughout the summer of 2001, an intense re-evaluation of the basic design tenets of the entire project resulted in several dramatic changes. Perhaps the most obvious was setting aside the key metaphor of "visit the classroom." Instead of its key position both on the website and in the stories used to explain the ILF, visiting the classroom became merely one of the online tools used to support inquiry. In addition, the focus for support and promotion of the ILF turned to bounded groups or Inquiry Circles. This meant that instead of trying to attract members from the general population of mathematics and science teachers, the development team solicited pre-existing groups, offering the ILF as a tool set and web space and for online and offline community support. We offered other universities the opportunity to use the ILF as a resource for preservice teacher education. Lastly, instead of being merely a space to support member-directed activities, we developed a set of explicit, professional development activities that involved a more directive, top-down approach.

The visual representation of the ILF in 2001 used a new map in which inquiry was the central focus; the Classrooms were at the periphery of the map and the other participant structures were represented at the same level as the Classrooms. Figure 16.4 included two iterations of the front page, illuminating the theoretical and design changes of our thinking over the life of the project. Because the site had become more complex and diverse, a bookmarking function was added to allow users to tag an Inquiry Circle or a discussion. These tagged discussions showed up in a member's My Desk area, allowing an easy way to keep abreast of new postings in areas of interest. There were now organizing documents for those visiting the site. The central area of the front page once filled by the link to the classrooms now contained four brief explanations under the tag What is Inquiry? Those four links provided brief guides to what inquiry is, why one might want to do inquiry, how to link inquiry to standards, and how the ILF may help. This indicated a shift from a commitment to discovery ("We shouldn't provide a definition, they should decide for themselves what constitutes inquiry") to trying to make the site more explicit, more guided, and potentially more useful. Providing even more guidance was an Inquiry Lab area in which teachers could access modules that provide

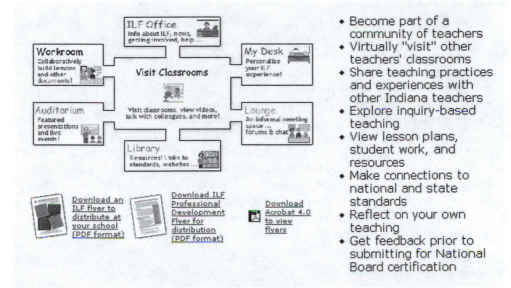

- Become part of a community of teachers
- Virtually "visit" other teachers' classrooms
- Share teaching practices and experiences with other Indiana teachers
- Explore inquiry-based teaching
- View lesson plans, student work, and resources
- Make connections to national and state standards
- Reflect on your own teaching
- Get feedback prior to submitting for National Board certification

Figure 16.4   Iteration of an Inquiry Learning Forum (ILF) Inquiry Circle (Water Ecology). The Sections in an Inquiry Circle Include Announcements, Highlighted Documents, External Resources, ILF Resources (with Activities), ILF Classrooms, ILF Discussion Forums, and the Private Discussion Forums.

concrete ways to use the ILF for professional development. These laboratories introduced ways to use the ILF to bring inquiry teaching into one's practice. They can be used individually or as part of a group.

A new area, the Collaboratory, allowed access to and creation of the Inquiry Circles. As of this writing in the fall 2001 there were 49 of these circles, with some open to all members who asked for entry, and some with restrictions. More were being started on a regular basis. The Lounge area linked to the (at the time of this writing) 21 discussions not specifically part of an Inquiry Circle or a classroom. An ongoing debate among the members of the development team about whether or not to include teaching resources such as lesson plans was resolved by establishing a virtual library. Lessons in the library supported inquiry and had discussions linked to each resource. Members were encouraged to share their experiences and lessons learned, using each lesson as an opportunity to reflect on practice. The Classrooms were still a major part of the site, allowing inservice and preservice teachers to see inquiry on site, to read these teachers' reflections on their experience, to view the actual lesson and students' work, to make connections to standards, and to engage in reflections with the teacher in the video and with other teachers about inquiry in their own practice.

Having put the story of the ILF in context, we can explicate the braids of change that occurred throughout the development cycle. We believe that this will add texture and focus to the understanding of what happened and why during this project. Whereas the above discussion provides a general historical narrative, each braid provides a more indepth perspective into the challenges we faced in the design of a web-based community in the service of learning. The discussion of braids is followed by a brief review of participation and value warrants.

Braids of Change[2]

In examining the braids of change, we touched on four dimensions that focused our discussions and that we believe provide the minimal context for characterizing a braid. First, we focus on the *sociohistorical and cultural context* through which the braid emerged and operates. Second, we discuss *guiding theory* and how it evolved in relation to the particular braid being presented. Third is the actual *practice*, including both technical design changes as well as social interventions. Fourth, we review the *impact* of the particular outcome being considered. In addition, we highlight tensions that we faced in the design process (e.g., usability and sociability; designing with and designing for; online and face-to-face; supporting needs and facilitating reform). With this framework, we now discuss the four braids that emerged as pertinent to our analysis: Evolving an Identity, Supporting Bounded Participation, Moving Beyond the Technical Dimensions, and Designing for Sociability. Beyond providing an organizing structure for the sharing of our experience, the braids serve as theoretical reflection points for others engaged in similar design work.

Evolving an Identity

Over the course of the three years that the ILF community had been active at the time of writing this paper, groups involved in the ILF collaboratively evolved an identity for the project; which involved changes in people, assumptions, and commitments, as well as the e-ILF. This evolving identity influenced our theoretical vision of what the ILF should be and how that vision should be represented in the multiple technical structures. This identity also influenced the design of the e-ILF in three main areas: changing the name of the site, changing our visual representation of the site, and changing the rules about who should be allowed to participate.

A name is an instantiation of identity. As noted earlier, in June 2000, after three months online, the ILF changed its name from *Internet* Learning Forum to *Inquiry* Learning Forum. This change reflected an evolution in the perception of the ILF by those involved. Initially, the ILF was regarded as primarily an internet-centered, professional development project that sought to develop online community. In time, this vision grew to become a vision of the ILF as a project that is centered on supporting student and teacher inquiry, with participation on the website, in person, through workshops, and more. This change was evident in our tagline on the opening page of the website. Our earlier tagline, "Building a community of Indiana math and science teachers," was changed to "Supporting student learning and teacher growth through inquiry." These changes paralleled our shift in focus from building an online community of practice to supporting existing groups in developing and implementing inquiry in the classroom. These changes were prompted by conversations with our Research Advisory Board (RAB), our PAB, and informal conversations with teachers who concentrated our thinking on their everyday needs and not on the more theoretical notions of building community. The tension between our reform agenda and the practical needs of the participants created a design challenge that we balanced continually throughout the project.

It was our intention to have the core activity be observing classroom videos. Each classroom became a narrative case study, developed collaboratively by the video production team and the featured teachers. A help page was added to guide interactions between the participants and the video, and, later on, featured teachers were asked to provide opening questions for discussions in an attempt to structure participation.

"Should I have been more specific when asking them to order or classify the galaxy pictures? Were my instructions too vague?" are examples of a featured teacher's questions that fostered many responses and modeled self-reflection for other teachers.

The website's central focus on the classroom videos developed into a tension between the ILF developers and the ILF participants. The ILF developers attempted to push classroom videos as the central focus of the site and as a model for the critical reflection of practice. However, the ILF teacher-participants were more interested in obtaining resources such as lesson plans, lesson ideas, and materials. Many had no time to view videos or lacked the practice or inclination to engage in critical reflection in a semipublic forum. A PAB member gave us this candid feedback at a focus group on inquiry and science that was a part of the PAB meeting in February 2001:

> But let me share a perspective with you. I must admit I don't come very often to the site simply because I'm so darn busy that just, I mean, when I get a chance at school, I'll peek in, but not a lot. I will be honest.

At the same time, a suite of tools was developed to support collaborations among university faculty in the School of Education, faculty in the College of Arts and Sciences, in-service teachers, and preservice teachers to study and develop lessons collaboratively. This tool suite was one of a series of new technical structures that led to a radical shift in focus from having the classrooms as the central point of the site to treating the classrooms as merely one of several resources to support inquiry (see Figure 16.4 above). This tool suite also led to a dramatic decrease in the development time spent on classroom video production.

Two new areas of the site were added to the map: the Collaboratory, which included all of the Inquiry Circles, and the Inquiry Labs, which offered structured, professional development modules that showed and used the ILF to support inquiry teaching. In addition to changing the visual appearance of the front end, a definition of inquiry was added to the front end page. We were spurred on to make these changes by the feedback from several RAB members at the RAB meeting in May 2001. One wrote these reflections at the end of the meeting:

> I think there needs to be a commonality of purpose reflected in the ILF, the state standards, and the teacher-participants. I am troubled by the duality between teacher needs and ILF objectives as separate. I encourage us to find ways to satisfy teacher needs for curriculum and activities or lesson plans and at the same time to encourage methods of inquiry which help meet teacher standards.

Another wrote:

> You need a mission statement. The ILF needs to have a stronger, more obvious focus. It needs a theme and that theme needs to speak to teacher needs. You've got to stand for something more than online learning community. For example, it could be sold as a resource for teachers who are trying to use inquiry teaching to meet state standards. A theme based on a problem that teachers have and know they have—this can be the subterfuge for pulling in customers.

This reflected a theoretical shift from a view of the ILF in which definitions would emerge from community participation to a view of the ILF in which the designers collaborated with teachers to provide more structure for participation.

Supporting Bounded Participation

The creation of the suite of tools that would support bounded groups or Inquiry Circles led to changes in epistemological and ontological commitments. The initial assumption of the site was that if a critical mass of teachers came to the site and discussed the classroom videos, a community of teachers would emerge. The very strong commitment to developing community and the belief that allowing private work groups would discourage the development of community was challenged about twelve months after the ILF launched, when the numbers of postings and registrations were still minimal. It led the ILF team to re-examine the design approaches it took.

Pressured by one principal investigator's critique of low usage and confirmed by the RAB and PAB, there was an extreme epistemological shift from designing the ILF community of practice to supporting multiple pre-existing communities. The PI saw this mandate coming from the requirements of the NSF, which wished to see its monetary investment yield positive results and not be another boutique project. The PI also had a social relationship with participants in a number of different organizations and projects (e.g., the Indiana Mathematics Initiative project) and saw their needs of private space as congruent with the NSF's needs to see more action in the ILF. This excerpt from an e-mail that was part of an exchange between a PI and a doctoral student on the project demonstrates the PI's view on private spaces, here called bounded groups:

> The bounded groups finesse this problem by "off-loading" trust formation and group development to the real-life groups . . . so when CEMI [one of the Inquiry Circle groups] uses the e-ILF facilities, their communications can be more open than perhaps among e-ILF newbies in other parts of the site because they have developed some level of trust elsewhere and bring their preexisting relationships online.

After the fall 2000 PAB meeting, the design team decided that teachers were unlikely to take the risk of critiquing other teachers whom they do not know unless they felt safe to speak freely, thus recognizing that such trust building is difficult within such a large social space. The reconceptualization of the ILF mandate was aided by the initiation of regular PI meetings, with the PIs taking a more active role in decision making, whereas, previously, there had been a loose, consensus-building venture at research meetings.

The first venture to provide social structures that could nurture teachers' collaborations and deep reflections was to design a space for the new federally-funded project entitled Collaboration to Enhance Mathematics Instruction (CEMI) in the fall of 2000. The CEMI project is modeled on the Japanese Lesson Study Groups that bring together kindergarten-through-grade-twelve teachers, university educators, and preservice teachers who collaboratively develop, teach, critique, and redesign lessons in their respective areas of expertise (Lewis & Tsuchida, 1997; Stevenson & Stigler, 1992). The CEMI project met in face-to-face settings but wished also to have an online space to facilitate the collaborative construction of lesson critiques, lesson plans, and unit plans during times when they could not meet face-to-face. They needed a collaborative editing tool and private discussion forums. The ILF design team created a space called the Working Circle, in which small groups could construct their own private areas. In the Working Circle, CEMI created a bounded group that brought together several in-service and preservice teachers, mathematics educators, and mathematicians to develop and revise mathematics lesson plans through implementing them in kindergarten-through-grade-twelve classrooms. The design of the CEMI approach was different from the design of other public areas on the ILF in that the circle was initiated by a group who shared a similar interest area and was tailored to the group's specific needs. Beginning with supporting existing or already connected groups, this concept expanded gradually to include initiating new groups and seeking to support courses for preservice teachers. It is this feature that prompted the Indiana University's School of Education to fund the continuation of the ILF for three years.

The endeavor inspired other small-group activities. By the spring of 2001, there was general consensus that the ILF needed to support already existing community groups with bounded groups of Inquiry Circles, but that there also needed to be a major redesign of the ILF to support this change. The programmer on the project began a very deliberate and prolonged redesign of the e-ILF. This effort bogged down quickly from lack of coordination and lack of interest in such a tedious task of redesigning for such a deferred goal of change. However, the programmer left the project voluntarily and was replaced by a colleague who was willing to tinker with the program to make it support bounded groups, rather than requiring a totally new system. The result was that, by the end of the summer of 2001, the concept of bounded groups was actualized as the ILF Collaboratory, with groups of members referred to as Inquiry Circle members. These spaces became populated quickly because they were used both in preservice classes and by existing professional development groups looking to expand their collaboration beyond face-to-face meetings.

In fall 2001, there were 49 Inquiry Circles in the ILF Collaboratory that ranged in emphasis from elementary science methods classes from four different universities, a group of middle-and high-school science teachers who participated in a summer workshop on teaching science through inquiry, to teachers who use water ecology and water quality as a focus in their classes. The important point was that the group shared a common purpose, whether it be a class focus, a workshop focus, or a topic focus. It was in this way that our emphasis shifted from an interest in supporting a community of practice to supporting groups with a common purpose. However, rather than predefining the practice and the purpose discussed in the space, our emphasis was on networking with groups of teachers who needed collaboration tools to support their own goals. Each Inquiry Circle space enabled teachers to: (a) organize the ILF classrooms and resources and create discussion forums of interest to this group, (b) share announcements, ideas, weblinks, and electronic documents, (c) create and edit documents collaboratively, and (d) organize the efforts and interests of this group as they used this space as a way to keep in touch (see Figure 16.5).

Along with these bounded groups (Inquiry Circles), another level of bounded activities was being implemented; for example, discussions that go on for only a certain time period and time-focused events. Also, the inquiry modules discussed briefly above provided a bounded sequence of activities that members could use as a guide to structure their ILF participation. The bounded group opportunities revitalized the ILF and contributed to a change in the basic notion of the ILF from building communities of practice to supporting groups. Members of the Working Circles have participated steadily in the discussion, especially preservice teachers using the Collaboratory as part of a university course. Moreover, a few teachers in the PAB created Inquiry Circles and moderated their groups, which exemplified the transfer of ownership from the designers to the teacher-participants. In fact, it was these Inquiry Circles that were the most prolific in terms of postings. (Note the rise in postings in September 2001 in Figure 16.5, one month after the space supporting Inquiry Circles was implemented.)

Many Inquiry Circles applied strategies to create groups that included both online and multiple, face-to-face meeting options, with an informal, web-based, professional development approach being written into future grants and grants already funded. A

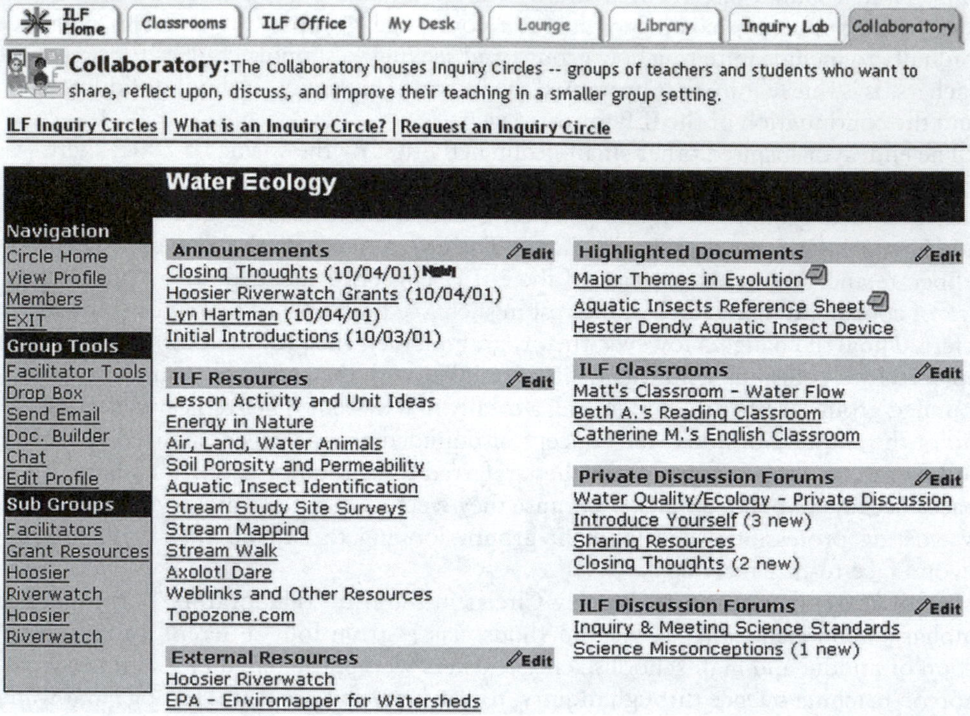

Figure 16.5 Current Iteration of an Inquiry Learning Forum (ILF) Inquiry Circle (Water Ecology). The Sections in an Inquiry Circle Include Announcements, Highlighted Documents, External Resources, ILF Resources, ILF Classrooms, ILF Discussion Forums, Private Discussion Forums, and Activities.

major goal of an ILF designers' and researchers' retreat in August of 2001 was to provide a structure of copresent meetings and goal-setting for the Inquiry Circles. This approach involved an initial face-to-face meeting in which a pedagogical skill (e.g., open inquiry, anchored instruction) or a tool (e.g., graphing calculators, innovative software) was introduced and a lesson or a unit was developed by each member, followed by an implementation period in which Inquiry Circle participants used the ILF to share lessons and reflections about implementing their lessons. Then, the group was expected to reconvene for a second face-to-face meeting in which they shared what they had learned, developed relations and built trust further, learned about new skills and tools, and planned another inquiry-based lesson or unit. This was to be followed by another round of implementation and online reflection and sharing, with a last face-to-face meeting for final reflections and closure. Multiple groups have adopted this model already, writing the ILF and this participatory framework into funded grants. However, for the most part, we have not been able to sustain this consistency of activity across Inquiry Circles. This is partly a function of the large number of Inquiry Circles and partly a function of our philosophy that supports the needs of teachers rather than imposing values on them.

Moving Beyond the Technical Dimensions

An important question that we wrestled with was that in spite of the positive perceptions and although teachers communicate and demonstrate continually to us the value of the ILF, why was it so hard to monitor participation? One simple, but important, response is time. Time is perhaps the scarcest commodity of in-service teachers. Another is that the practice of inquiry-based teaching is not necessarily compatible with preparing students for standardized tests and the necessary factual retention. Another more complex response is related to the culture of teachers, a culture in which collaboration and critique of each other's practice are not the norms (Grossman et al., 2001). Exacerbating this problem is the challenge of situating this activity in an online space where any critique is permanent, where the people involved may not know each other, and where this delicate act of critiquing each other involves adding an online comment (a posting) that is available for the public scrutiny of over 1,500 members.

The initial proposal for the ILF included face-to-face elements, but, as the project got under way, we focused mainly on the development of the technical space. When the site launched in March 2000, we had forgotten principally the face-to-face aspects of our original proposal, looking instead for the development of a community almost exclusively through the online environment. We hired a person in the role of teacher liaison, for the first year of the project. Primarily, the teacher liaison communicated with teachers being video-taped as a part of the video production process. We had hoped that the classroom videos would create a source for encouraging posting, but we learned that, for in-service teachers, they wanted to interact with teachers they knew. As one member commented during a face-to-face meeting with other teachers, including those who were featured in the ILF Classroom area:

> I have not spent a lot of time in anybody's video. Okay? But now that I've met these people, I'll go home and do it. What's missing is I don't want to look at home movies if I don't know the people.

This comment suggested to us that we need to spend more time focusing on face-to-face relations. Given this awareness, coupled with shift from project development to project impact and use, we began to concentrate more on outreach and professional development options as means to get teachers involved in the ILF. In essence, we found ourselves falling back on the traditional avenues of workshops and conference sessions to promote this "new" model of professional development through the online community that the ILF offered.

In the spring of 2000, we developed a three-tiered outreach plan. First, we were available for demonstrations and hands-on workshops about the ILF free of charge to anyone in the State of Indiana. Second, we developed a two-day workshop called "Why Ask Why? Inquiry Based Teaching in Math and Science," which was conducted four times at the Indiana University campus and was offered (but never conducted) on-site at schools. There was a minimal cost for this two-day workshop, charged primarily to provide a level of commitment on behalf of the participant or school. Although both of the first two strategies were valuable, they did not reflect either our values or what the research literature says is the importance of long-term, sustained professional development (Grossman et al., 2001; Guskey & Huberman, 1995; Heaton & Lampert, 1993; Westheimer, 1998). Our third outreach option involved co-designing a long-term partnership with a school or schools to design professional development options that met their specific needs and goals. Two such relationships have been developed, one during the spring 2001 semester and one in fall 2002. Although we certainly were able to generate activity in the ILF during the face-to-face sessions, this did not translate necessarily into long-term, active participation in the ILF community.

This last outreach may prove to be our most important strategy because preservice teachers in mathematics methods, science methods, and educational psychology courses have found the ability to "see" lessons and connect with real-world teachers incredibly valuable. Some of the impetus to support preservice teachers came from the enthusiastic response of these students, as shown in this posting from one of our discussion forums:

> I really enjoyed getting to see her lesson because it allows students like us who want to be teachers to go over what she is teaching and look at how things went. It is almost as if we are in there observing her and it is nice because we can watch her while at home. I thought the students were using inquiry because she was prompting them to give out information and open-ended questions allowed students to reply. I really like watching the examples.

Two forces combined in the summer of 2001 to compel a reconsideration of our outreach activities. First, we were concerned that the pedagogical focus of the original workshops and outreach activities was too broad to create any real sense of community for or commitment by other participants. Second, as stated above, the project's emphasis shifted from creating community to supporting existing communities. Thus, during the 2001–2002 year, we changed our outreach focus in three major ways, leading to an increase in member participation; note the resultant peak in activity in the fall of 2001 in Figure 16.5. First, we developed curricular-based workshops that brought teachers together around a particular curricular topic (axolotls or water ecology). Although this would not work necessarily as a long-term or scalable strategy (with limited curricular expertise on our staff), it did provide an opportunity to see how the ILF might be used to support other such efforts. Our second new outreach focus evolved from our shift toward supporting existing communities by reaching out to existing professional development efforts. We began to work with state professional organizations in Indiana and the State of Indiana's Department of Education to support professional development efforts in the state. Third, we began to promote and use the ILF with preservice classes at Indiana University and other institutions.

Additionally, our hope is that as these students move into classroom positions, they will take their experience in the ILF with them into their schools. Coinciding with this rethinking of our outreach program was the development of the online group workspace. Thus, not only did we shift the nature of our outreach, but also the online environment now provided rich tools for group identification, organization, and work. In the last year of the project, the teacher liaison role focused on professional development, connecting ILF members, and promoting the project, with video organization responsibilities going to another staff member. Overall, the evolution of ILF's outreach can be seen as moving toward a mixed-modal model, evolving hand-in-hand with the change in the project's focus and identity from an "online" community to a "web-based" community.

Designing for Sociability

Once the initial design and implementation of the e-ILF coalesced into a functional and potentially meaningful entity (March 2000), we began to understand that merely having a usable structure would not foster social collaboration necessarily. We began to view the ILF not only as an electronic structure, the e-ILF, but also as a sociotechnical structure (Barab et al., 2003). This new conception had important implications for the continued design of the electronic structures as well as the nontechnical ones, and it was our belief that the ILF writ large consisted of both. It was in the second year that we began to concentrate on issues of sociability, meaning those social policies and technical structures that support the community's shared purpose and the social interactions among group members (Barab et al., 2001b; Preece, 2000).

The core sociability challenge was to increase connectedness and active collaboration among members. Reported in previous work (Barab et al., 2001b), our examination of meeting notes, e-mails, usability documents, and relevant literature highlighted three, core, sociability themes:

- The need to develop participant structures to support group collaboration and work.
- The need to provide structured tasks for using the e-ILF and for engaging the ILF community.
- The need to provide more visible connections to people, conversations, and artifacts of interest.

In addressing these needs, a number of design steps and participant structures were implemented, with the broad focus of fostering increased opportunities for collaboration and a greater sense of connectedness among the ILF community.

In fostering sociability, we recognized that a feeling of trust was a necessary prerequisite for teachers to feel comfortable reflecting on their own and other teachers' practice. Teachers usually have a lot of autonomy in their classrooms. There, they are able to shut the door and concentrate on the needs of their students in a self-contained space. This individualism in classroom culture, this type of isolation, is very different from the atmosphere of collaboration, openness, and self-reflection that we were trying to foster in the ILF. Postings tended to be few and lacking in critical reflection. An example of the many very agreeable postings follows:

> It was interesting to see this lesson in action. I thought that the students appeared engaged in the activity, and the examples of student work were impressive. I wonder, was there any aspect of the lesson that you felt needed to be tailored to needs and concerns of the students?

In the second PAB meeting, in the spring of the second year, we heard from several members that face-to-face, social connection was necessary before participation would be comfortable. Often, the need for a social connection was compared to the experience of the PAB members who had gotten to know each other in their copresent meetings and then used the online interactions to continue that relationship.

This need for connection with people they knew relates to a core misconception dating back to the development of the original prototype in which the designers believed that any inquiry-based classroom placed on the website would be of interest to in-service teachers. Teachers interviewed during the development process identified seeing another teacher teach as their overriding desire for improved professional development. The ILF was constructed to allow teachers to "visit classrooms" and view teachers. However, over time and through interviews and observations, we have come to narrow our understanding of what teachers wanted. They wanted to view *specific* teachers that they knew. Similarly, they wanted to reflect on practice with teachers they knew, not merely anyone who happened to be in an online space. One teacher said during a focus group:

> It's a developed collegiality that can only be established truly, authentically when

you are warm bodies in a room, and there's immediate feedback. Not, "Let's wait and see if they've posted and responded," which is effective to a point, but I think that there's probably more of a willingness to share and be truthful with each other about our videos when we can understand the personalities and what makes, you know, good feedback for you without hurting your feelings or you know, making you feel like, "Yeah. Okay. I'm going to try some more."

It is these types of comments that led us to view and develop multilayered interventions that treated the ILF as a web-supported community and not as an online community.

In 2000, we also were struggling with what we considered a lack of sufficient involvement in the discussion forums. There would be a surge of activity to post after a workshop or class assignment, followed by a quick leveling-off in postings. We implemented a number of design changes in order to address what we perceived as insufficient interaction in the e-ILF. The teacher liaison and other ILF staffers made a point of getting online and modeling critical dialogue. We instituted user profiles with self-description and pictures as an option for all members. Our PAB suggested, and we implemented, a procedure whereby each teacher who had produced a video also would provide a series of questions meant to foster critical dialogue in the discussion forums in their classrooms.

We encouraged teachers to facilitate discussion forums on topics of their chosen interests, reasoning that this would give more ownership to our members. Indeed, some of most active discussion forums turned out to be the ones designed and facilitated by in-service teachers. It is in these discussion forums that we saw some of the most useful and productive debates, with teachers arguing and pushing their understandings about what counts as good practice. For example, "Useless Math," "Science Misconceptions," and "Technology: How much is too much?" are examples of teacher-initiated and -facilitated forums that have been popular with both preservice and in-service teachers. The extended example below is a thread from "Technology: How much is too much?" where teachers questioned the "accepted" place of technology in teaching as well as exchanged information in a meaningful way.

Teacher 1:   Using technology in my classroom has opened doors for my students as well as myself. My students can find organisms or specimens under a microscope, capture them with a flexible camera and software, and save them for their computerized lab portfolio. They have the ability to produce a cool pond water lab, the stages of mitosis, or chart the progression of their lab dissections. With just a little technology, I have turned some "boring" labs into really cool activities! It really can be a great tool when used as a stepping stone instead of a crutch!

Teacher 2:   Hi. I enjoyed reading how you are using technology. What grade(s) do you teach? I am interested to hear what you have your students do for the pond lab. We are doing a water ecology unit this fall and using a similar camera setup might work really well for some things I have in mind.

Teacher 3:   I agree with using technology as an additional aide in biology, yet it cannot be the only way to teach. I am a preservice teacher in a school district whose technology coordinator wants all labs to be computerized; this came from the head of the science department. As she states, and I agree, nothing takes the place of hands-on lab time. There are some things you just can't teach with a computer.

Teacher 4:   I would agree with that, although I am a math teacher, so I can't really speak or the topic of teaching or running a science lab. I do remember how

> much I loved science labs; the hands-on stuff was great. What is your opinion on graphing and charting data? Would you have the students do that by hand as well, or would you allow them to use a spreadsheet program to analyze and chart data?

This is just one example of the engaged types of comments that took place in these forums.

One of the most significant design changes that occurred during the summer between project years two and three (one year post-implementation) was the institution of bounded groups—smaller, more intimate areas on the website that could have restricted access, created to support interest groups, workshops, and preservice classes. Initially, we resisted making this change from a single web space open to all members to a larger space that also allows many smaller, restricted spaces. We resisted for a philosophical reason. We thought that fostering a community of practice online required as many interactions as possible among members. Finally, we accepted that affective issues of trust and intimacy were crucial to engaging in dialogue. Teachers would not participate in the larger space, so we moved to a model of both bounded private spaces organized by interest and the larger space as well (see the section on Supporting Bounded Participation for more details).

Less dramatic changes made to encourage sociability included rethinking participants' roles and enlisting more teachers to be facilitators and "critical friends." In some cases, we paid teachers to take on this role. The Inquiry Lab and its focus on specific tasks in the ILF, with the consequent reward of earning continuing education units, was another attempt to enhance sociability, although also a part of our new professional development model. One example of a directed professional development laboratory is:

> Visit Tony's Earth Science Class. View Clip 3: "Preparing the Class for Groupwork" and read Tony's reflection about using "talking chips." Why does Tony use them? How effective is this strategy?

Lastly, we made a policy change to house a library of curricular materials, with the caveat that each one would have a discussion forum attached to it. We had resisted being a repository for curricular materials because many other websites met this need already and because we wanted to encourage the reflective use of materials, not be a "download and go" repository. We finally saw a role for a library of curricular materials as a carrot to get teachers to enter, be comfortable, and form social bonds before engaging in the difficult processes of self-reflection and reform. Not all of our attempts at fostering sociability have been successful. For example, although every library resource includes a discussion forum, these forums have had virtually no postings except the initial ones that are required when the item is added to the library. This area of increasing sociability continues to evolve. We have found it best to follow Harry Truman's advice—"Try something . . . if that doesn't work, we'll try something else." The important point is that this trying of something else is not haphazard but is based on reviews of the literature, needs analyses, and observations of teachers using the space in their everyday lives.

Participation and Value Warrants

In December 2001, there were 1,489 registrants,[3] suggesting that the e-ILF as a product was adopted and used. During that month, new levels of use were set with 16,817 site hits, including 2,233 hits from teachers, 12,921 hits from preservice teachers, and 1,424 hits from university faculty. Teachers logged 198 sessions, with an average visit lasting ten minutes. Preservice teachers logged 791 sessions, with an average length of 23.8 minutes. There were 598 new postings during December 2001 and 1,600 the previous month in the discussion forums (see Figure 16.6). The site was being used extensively. In addition, face-to-face outreach rose, with members of the research and development teams spending much more time in schools talking with teachers about how they were using or might use the ILF. Presentations at a science educators conference were full, in stark contrast to the empty room of a year before.

We have investigated not only usage, but also the value and impact of participation for teachers. In trying to understand the value of the ILF for preservice teachers, MaKinster (2002) compared the reflections and carried out interviews with preservice teachers who were assigned conditions in which they either reflected on their student-teaching placements in a private journal, in a collaborative discussion forum with other preservice teachers, or in a public discussion forum in the ILF Lounge area. The Private Journal group wrote more complete initial reflections, but they saw the experience as merely another assignment and attached little meaning or value to the exercise. The students in the Private Discussion Forum considered their teaching both through their initial reflections and the responses that they posted to the reflections of their peers. Their perceptions of the assignment were mixed and several students found little value in the experience. Finally, the students in the ILF Lounge Discussion Forum also reviewed their experiences both through their initial reflections and the responses that they posted to the reflections of their peers, but these students found significant value in the assignment, the interactions they had with their peers, the interactions with the ILF in-service teachers, and the idea of thinking about one's teaching as a means for personal and collaborative professional development. During a post-interview, one student stated:

> It was being able to think back about what I had done, what had gone well and what hadn't gone so well. That I could kind of make note of that and maybe the next time around I teach this [differently]. . . . The more minds that are looking over what you are doing and being able to positively critique you, I think the better off you are. You know, if you are able to take criticism, which I would hope most teachers would take that to help better their instruction and their curriculum . . .

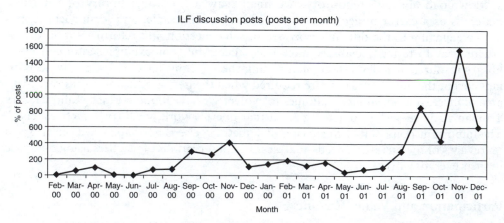

Figure 16.6 Inquiry Learning Forum (ILF) Number of Postings Per Month from its Release in February 2000 through December 2001.

The results of this study pointed to the value of using web-based, community-integrated discussion forums as a means to foster meaningful and engaged reflection.

In another study, Barab et al. (2001b) interviewed teachers who reported their ILF experiences as highly beneficial. The following teachers' comments are not unique perspectives:

> Doing this [participating in the ILF] makes me do a couple of things. It makes me assess my lesson more than I normally do . . . spend a little bit more time thinking about what questions I'm going to ask, thinking about the follow-up questions, thinking about introducing the lesson in an interesting and meaningful way. And all the things that it'd be nice if every lesson I taught met those qualifications. . . . Assessing my teaching. By viewing and making notes and having those little discussions and being asked some good questions that normally I wouldn't ask myself. So yeah, that's why I like this.

Or:

> Well, I've always emphasized in my teaching what I call the nature of science and inquiry is part of that. And I probably haven't put the right emphasis on inquiry until I got more active and I wouldn't say that I'm still putting as much emphasis on inquiry as I should but at least I know what I need to do now and can work toward it. . . . Yeah, I see myself as I continue to be involved in this forum to be bringing more inquiry-style instruction into my classroom.

We have carried out dozens of interviews and multiple case studies with teachers both to understand their thoughts and observe their actions, with the goal of understanding better how through ILF participation teachers' understanding and the practice of inquiry-based teaching improve over time.

Examination of the content of online discussions provides further evidence of the value of participation, with there being numerous postings in which teachers reflected deeply on their own practice and that of their peers.

> In my methods class, we are learning a lot about teaching through inquiry; it certainly has its benefits. However, we realize that you cannot teach everything through inquiry. . . . If your students are struggling with open or guided inquiry, go back and try something more concrete. By the way, this topic relates well to a concern Alex [Alsmith] was having concerning his student teaching experience in Barton's [a different discussion forum in the ILF] discussion.

Finally, as teachers participated online and in face-to-face meetings, we have observed the forming of meaningful relations, with some teachers collaborating on lessons, others merely providing each other a voice of support, and still others developing friendships that go beyond professional interactions. An example of an experienced teacher being a voice of support can be seen in the following:

New Teacher: I am a first-year teacher and I am having trouble getting started. I will be teaching biology this fall. I don't know where to start. It all seems so overwhelming. Any pointers on where to begin?

Experienced Teacher: I always start with a nature of science unit and even though it can be done within biology content, I don't restrict myself to biology content.

The experienced teacher eventually decided to contribute a video of his classroom that shows the first day of his three-week, nature of science unit. More generally, the value of the ILF has been expressed by various interested parties. For example, although funding from the original grant ended in July 2002, the School of Education at Indiana University agreed to fund continued operation of the project for the next year. This expenditure underscores the perceived worth for preservice teachers that the project has offered and can continue to offer. In spite of the observed and perceived value of the ILF, maintaining participation has not been a straightforward task; we have examples of teachers coming once to the site or participating in a workshop, never to return, and other examples of sustained participation.

Theoretical Assertions

Online communities face hurdles that are similar to—but more challenging than—the issues in copresent communities (Wellman, 1999). The absence of visual bodies or any kinds of visual cues makes for greater difficulties in establishing trust among participants. Members cannot see to whom they are speaking and thus cannot gauge their reactions, emotional state, or interest in the conversations. Verbal explanations, emotive icons (emoticons), and textual smiles are used to fill this emotional void, with only limited success. In fact, one might argue that online communities are best at supporting the needs of already existing copresent communities rather than being the site of new community development (Barab et al., 2003). However, the potential of supporting learning anytime, anywhere, and the pedagogical as well as social appeal of a community model have led to current interest in designing for online communities in the service of learning (Barab et al., 2004).

This work suggests that there are not only technological issues of establishing online communities, but also social issues that are important in establishing functional communities. Further, in spite of the challenges of building online communities, our work provides evidence that designers can facilitate successfully the emergence of online spaces that support active member interactions, even those with the goal of supporting learning. In understanding the sociotechnical challenges and lessons learned, four issues were identified and presented as braids of change using a design narrative methodology (Abbott, 1992). Beginning with Evolving an Identity, our commitment to change our conceptions continually and the resultant design allowed the e-ILF to evolve in ways that met the everyday needs and interests of the site users. For example, terms like internet and community were too broad and general to engage members. Although teachers' professional development and reform were our focuses, these goals could be achieved best by providing teachers with materials that they could use immediately and then supporting discussions of professional development through the implementation of their practical needs. With respect to Moving Beyond the Technical Dimensions, we found that internet-only participation structures did not offer sustained levels of activity. Our best successes involved a mixed-mode approach that used the ILF as an extension of face-to-face professional development activities.

Related to the Supporting Bounded Participation braid was an appreciation that outreach efforts were improved by taking a more focused approach to supporting specific topic areas and connecting with pre-existing groups, rather than inviting all visitors to the website to discuss inquiry in an open (semipublic) forum. On a related note, although the internet allows for professional development anytime, anywhere, our participants wanted bounded time chunks with a clear beginning and for which they could experience closure. Although initially we concentrated on human–computer interactions and developing a usable structure, in the Designing for Sociability braid, we discussed the importance of supporting member–member interactions and in thinking through the challenges of fostering meaningful online discussions. For example, supporting critical dialogue is more of a social challenge than it is a usability one, even though developing the Inquiry Circle feature facilitated such dialogue.

Although much design-based research has focused historically on human–computer interactions, in many current design efforts, the emphasis is on designing structures to support social interactions, especially those that are web-based or targeted toward building virtual communities. In these design efforts, the issues shift from human–computer interactions to human–human interactions as mediated by the technology. As such, one needs to move beyond issues of usability and address also issues of sociability. In response to this challenge, our research dealt with sociotechnical issues and the design efforts that relate to understanding local contexts and norms as much as they relate to designing a technical product. Techniques such as recognizing the contributions of members, identifying members in profiles, establishing guides or mentors for newcomers, celebrating events, and meeting face-to-face all tend to build connections and trust (Kim, 2000; Preece, 2000). Also, establishing bounded groups with a common purpose and limited membership further helps establish and maintain trust in an online community. Additionally, our more successful interventions involved a combination of face-to-face meetings and online activities, using the e-ILF to support what teachers are doing already, as opposed to being a space in which all the activities, relationship building, and outcomes occurred. Working with this complexity is a central design challenge that community-focused, design-based researchers must grapple with and understand.

Although participatory design is an important commitment in theory, it is much more challenging in practice, especially when one has a reform agenda in which a core goal is to change practice (Schwen & Hara, 2004). Issues of ownership, codeveloping intentions, and respecting local practices while simultaneously fostering change become problematic, with power, agency, and ownership all coming into play. In our case, our development involved "metadesign," in which we developed structures that afforded others the opportunity to design for themselves. This feature was an essential aspect of the successful Collaboratory and supported the Inquiry Circles. It was also evident in the fact that all the most successful discussion groups were created and moderated by teachers. On a related note, designing for online community in the service of learning requires a deep understanding not only of design, but also of the context in which the design will be used. Although our commitment to building community and supporting open inquiry might have been laudable theoretically; in practice, it did not meet the everyday needs of the teachers. In part, this is because most of our design work, even though involving numerous teachers, took place in a university context. We can only speculate how teachers' recommendations might have been different if we had done more design work in their everyday environment, surrounded by their everyday pressures. In fact, the Collaboratory, one of the most successful participant structures in the e-ILF, was a space and a suite of tools that were designed with teachers in the kindergarten-through-grade-twelve schools. Participatory design with a reform agenda faces complex challenges that complicate design work in ways that make it personal, social, and cultural, not only technical. It requires leaving commitments at the door, or at least in the shadows, first understanding local culture and then bringing in the voice of reform opportunistically.

Implications

Design narratives are especially useful for characterizing design work focused on supporting the emergence of complex contexts in which multiple members and technologies transact, as is the case when using technology to support the emergence of something like an online community. In these cases, assigning participants randomly to conditions or isolating specific variables, although possible for some research questions, results in an impoverished design condition for understanding many of the complex dynamics that are critical for designing for the emergence of online communities (Barab et al., 2003). Given the importance of voice, agency, power, trust, and other sociopolitical issues, it becomes challenging to take the designed outcome, examine it, reproduce it, and implement it successfully with another group of participants in a manner that community will emerge. One needs to understand the sociotechnical dynamics through which the design decisions were made and the solutions were implemented so that one can navigate more intelligently the struggles in one's own design work.

In presenting the design narrative of the ILF, we had to make a number of decisions. For example, we could have encompassed our interests by using discrete events as starting points of discussions or as ending points of discussions. However, we found ourselves being unable to have our discussion of design changes bracketed by both starting points and ending points. This was because, for the most part, the changes we experienced were not discrete and linear; thus, the issue of causation was complicated, if not impossible, to untangle. Also, it would have been inappropriate if we described changes in ILF usage as a direct effect of a design change when, as we have explained already, the ILF was more than the e-ILF. Many of the changes we made involved complex social interactions, sometimes instantiated as planning and design sessions where many people voiced opinions and were heard and heeded differently. Power, social rank, and eloquence of speech—as well as the confidence of the speaker—all played roles in determining the outcome of these meetings.

For these reasons, we searched for an appropriate metaphor to explain the reasons and the consequences of a multitude of design changes over the three years of the NSF-funded part of the project. We started with the notion of being able to locate specific changes on a timeline and then used the linearity of time to look at the causes and the results of these specific and well-defined changes. This notion of discrete change gave way quickly to recognizing the need to encompass a larger time span and, thus, the notion of design episodes because we realized that very few of our substantive design changes were rolled out instantaneously. We began to see the emotional aspects of our work and started talking about the tensions that grew and boiled over periodically to yield substantive social and technological changes in the ILF. We then examined the metaphor of braided or knotted changes where many social, technological, economic, and emotional forces coalesced to provoke movement and change in our very dynamic system. It is in this last metaphor that we have attempted to communicate our experience in this research project.

Although we frequently present the outcomes of our designs in terms of completed, ready-made artifacts, what may be more useful to others is to highlight the making of our designs (Latour, 1987). Toward this end, we attempted to highlight the ebbs and flows, characterizing our design-based research in terms of four core design trajectories that we refer to as braids of change. It is through understanding and balancing the interplay within and among these braids that designers can inform and evolve their own and others' design efforts. The challenges are to illuminate these local braids in ways that will have local meaning but, at the same time, to present them in ways that have relevance to others in other contexts with different goals (Geertz, 1976). Doing this well requires attending to the local issues while concurrently having a deep appreciation for the global issues, situating design in the hermeneutic dialectic that has become so common in qualitative research.

Methods associated traditionally with program evaluation can be used to determine local impact, but we are still learning what methods will provide warrants for advancing credible, trustworthy, and useful theoretical assertions. At one level, we can use methods employed already for conducting rigorous research, such as providing evidence of the reliability and validity (or credibility and trustworthiness) of interpretations. However, in sharing design-based research it is our belief that usefulness to others is a necessary warrant that is not discussed usually in design-based research circles (Barab & Squire, 2004). We have attempted to present this discussion in a manner that will allow other designers to identify readily patterns that occur in their own designs and to navigate intelligently the challenges they face in their design process. This is because it is our belief that, for many complex processes, such as designing for online communities in the service of learning, it becomes meaningless to attempt to research these issues irrespective of the rich contexts in which they exist and are given meaning.

Here, we had to make decisions about the methodological processes that would prove most useful for illuminating the design, the theoretical assertions, and the conditions through which both operate. When reading a design narrative, one must question to what extent such theoretical claims are generalizable beyond the instantiation through which the initial narrative was built. Merely telling a local story, no matter how credible and trustworthy is one's account, does not mean that the story will have meaning or prove useful to others. We would not want policy-makers to make decisions with tax dollars based on a case of one, no matter how convincing the case. At the same time, to consider the only "true" research to be that which takes place in laboratory contexts or with randomized trials would prove incomplete also. Clearly, both approaches are useful. However, if the generalizability of design narratives is to extend beyond a particular case, it is necessary that the designs and theoretical assertions be presented in ways that provide others insight into: (a) the designed product, (b) the context in which the design was implemented, (c) the theoretical assertions and their relations to the design work, and (d) those conditions through which the theoretical assertions were generated.

Additionally, the researchers need to provide warrants for the evidence of local impacts and for the theoretical assertions being advanced. In our research, this involved presenting the design trajectory in ways that illuminated the conditions through which our assertions were derived and would allow others to determine whether the theoretical assertions seemed justified. Ultimately, a line of study would examine other trajectories to determine the extent to which similar assertions revealed themselves. In this way, and consistent with the generation of grounded theory as discussed by Glaser and Strauss (1967), over time, the theoretical assertions might become saturated and suggest theoretical generalizability. However, another form of generalizability that may be relevant to design narratives is the notion of "petite generalization"; that is, when others use the case to identify more readily patterns that exist in their own work and to navigate the challenges they face there more intelligently (Stake, 1995). It is in supporting the generation of theoretical claims from which others can make petite generalizations that we view design narratives as most useful. We look forward to hearing about other design efforts, comparing the braids identified, and compiling the lessons learned, so that as a field, we can have the greatest impact on those the design work is meant to serve.

Acknowledgments

This material is based upon work supported by the National Science Foundation under Grant No. 9980081. However, any opinions, findings, conclusions, or recommendations expressed in this material are those of the authors and do not necessarily reflect the views of the Foundation.

Notes

1 Some widely used, online communities include those targeted toward, for example, e-commerce (e.g., http://yahoo.com; http://www.talkcity.com/), social interactions (http://www.aa-intergroup.org/; http://www.ca.org/), adventure gaming (e.g., http://asheronscall.com; http://www.everquest.com; http://www.ultimaonline.com), kindergarten-through-grade-twelve students learning disciplinary content (e.g., http://forum.swarthmore.edu/; http://onesky.engin.umich.edu), and teachers' professional development (e.g., http://www.tappedin.sri.com/; http://ei.cornell.edu), among others.

2 In this chapter we have drawn on a variety of data sources, including minutes from weekly research meetings, various advisory board meetings, outside observers' reflections on these meetings, focus groups with teachers, individual interviews with teachers, usability studies, and discourse from the online discussions occurring in the e-ILF. Given the diversity of the data and to maintain the fluidity of the chapter we have integrated these data and contextualized them in terms of the source by using textual descriptions in the body of the chapter rather than formalized, field-note references.

3 At the writing of this chapter in December 2003, there were over 4,000 registered members, with an average of over 5,000 hits (each unique page visited is considered a hit) per day for the period from December 2002–December 2003.

References

Abbott, A. (1984). Event sequence and event duration: Colligation and measurement. *Historical Methods*, 17, 192–204.

Abbott, A. (1992). What do cases do? Some notes on activity in sociological analysis. In C. C. Ragin & H. S. Becker (eds), *What is a case? Exploring the foundation of social inquiry* (pp. 53–82). Cambridge, MA: Cambridge University Press.

Barab, S. A. & Duffy, T. (2000). From practice fields to communities of practice. In D. Jonassen & S. M. Land (eds), *Theoretical foundations of learning environments* (pp. 25–56). Mahwah, NJ: Lawrence Erlbaum Associates.

Barab, S. A. & Squire, K. D. (2004). Design-based research: Putting our stake in the ground. *Journal of the Learning Sciences*, 13, 1–14.

Barab, S. A., Hay, K. E., Barnett, M. G. & Squire, K. (2001a). Constructing virtual worlds: Tracing the historical development of learner practices/understandings. *Cognition and Instruction*, 19, 47–94.

Barab, S. A., Kling, R. & Gray, J. (2004). Introduction: Coming to terms with community. In S. A. Barab, R. Kling & J. Gray (eds), *Designing virtual communities in the service of learning*. New York: Cambridge University Press.

Barab, S. A., MaKinster, J., Moore, J., Cunningham, D. & the ILF Design Team (2001b). Designing and building an on-line community: The struggle to support sociability in the Inquiry Learning Forum. *Educational Technology Research and Development*, 49, 71–96.

Barab, S. A., MaKinster, J. & Scheckler, R. (2003). Designing system dualities: Characterizing a web-supported teacher professional development community. *Information Society*, 19, 237–256.

Bellah, R. N., Madson, N., Sullivan, W. M., Swidler, A. & Tipton, S. M. (1985). *Habits of the heart: Individualism and commitment in American life*. Berkeley: University of California Press.

Brown, A. L. (1992). Design experiments: Theoretical and methodological challenges in creating complex interventions in classroom settings. *Journal of the Learning Sciences*, 2, 141–178.

Brown, R. E. (2001). The process of a community-building in distance learning classes. *Journal of Asqachronous learning Networks*, 5(2), 18–35.

Chaney-Cullen, T. & Duffy, T. (1998). Strategic teaching frameworks: Multimedia to support teacher change. *Journal of the Learning Sciences*, 8, 1–40.

Collins, A. (1992). Toward a design science of education. In E. Scanlon & T. O'Shea (eds), *New directions in educational technology* (pp. 15–22). New York: Springer-Verlag.

Collins, A. (1999). The changing infrastructure of education research. In E. C. Lagemann & L. S. Shulman (eds), *Issues in education research: Problems and possibilities* (pp. 289–298). San Francisco, CA: Jossey-Bass.

Collison, G., Elbaum, B., Haavind, S. & Tinker, R. (2000). *Facilitating online learning: Effective strategies for moderators*. Madison, WI: Atwood.

Geertz, C. (1976). *The religion of Java*. Chicago: University of Chicago Press.

Glaser, B. G. & Strauss, A. L. (1967). *The discovery of grounded theory: Strategies for qualitative research*. New York: Aldine.

Greene, J. C. & Caracelli, V. J. (eds) (1997). Advances in mixed-method evaluation: The challenges and benefits of integrating diverse paradigms. *New Directions for Evaluation*, 74.

Grossman, P., Wineburg, S. & Woolworth, S. (2001). Toward a theory of teacher community. *Teachers College Record*, 103, 942–1012.

Guba, E. G. & Lincoln, Y. S. (1983). Competing paradigms in qualitative research. In G. F. Madaus, M. S. Scriven & D. L. Stufflebeam (eds), *Evaluation models: Viewpoints on educational and human services evaluation* (pp. 195–220). Boston, MA: Kluwer-Nijhoff.

Guskey, T. R. & Huberman, M. (eds) (1995). *Professional development in education: New paradigms and practices*. New York: Teachers College Press.

Hakken, D. (1999). *Cyborgs@cyberspace: An ethnographer looks to the future*. New York: Routledge.

Heaton, R. & Lampert, M. (1993). Learning to hear voices: Inventing a new pedagogy of teacher education. In M. W. McLaughlin, J. E. Talbert & D. K. Cohen (eds), *Teaching for understanding: Challenges for practice, research, and policy* (pp. 207–239). San Francisco, CA: Jossey-Bass.

Hoadley, C. P. (2002). Creating context: Design-based research in creating and understanding CSCL. *The Proceedings of Computer Support for Cooperative Learning*. Boulder, CO: Lawrence Erlbaum Associates.

Hull, D. L. (1975). Central subjects and historical narratives. *History and Theory*, 14, 253–274.

Isaac, L. W. (1997). Transforming localities: Reflections on time, causality, and narrative in contemporary historical sociology. *Historical Methods*, 30, 4–12.

Isaac, S. & Michael, W. B. (1990). *Handbook in research and evaluation: For education and the social sciences*. San Diego, CA: Edits.

Jones, S. (ed.) (1999). *Doing Internet research*. Thousand Oaks, CA: Sage.

Kelly, A. E. (2003). Research as design: The role of design in educational research. *Educational Researcher*, 32(1), 3–4.

Kim, A. J. (2000). *Community building: Secret strategies for successful online communities on the web*. Berkeley, CA: Peachpit Press.

Kling, R., McKim, G., Fortuna, J. & King, A. (2002). A bit more to IT: Scholarly communication forums as socio-technical interaction networks. *Journal of the American Society for Information Science and Technology*, 54(1), 47–67.

Latour, B. (1987). *Science in action: How to follow scientists and engineers through society*. Cambridge, MA: Harvard University Press.

Lave, J. & Wenger, E. (1991). *Situated learning: Legitimate peripheral participation*. New York: Cambridge University Press.

Lewis, C. & Tsuchida, I. (1997). Planned educational change in Japan: The shift to student-centered elementary science. *Journal of Educational Policy*, 12, 313–331.

Lincoln, Y. S. & Guba, E. G. (1985). *Naturalistic inquiry*. Beverly Hills, CA: Sage.

MaKinster, J. G. (2002). The effect of social context on the reflective practice of pre-service science teachers: Leveraging a web-supported community of teachers. *Dissertation Abstracts International, 63*(05), 1772 (UMI No. 3054451).

Mink, L. O., Fay, B., Golob, E. O. & Vann, R. T. (1987). *Historical understanding*. Ithaca, NY: Cornell University Press.

Preece, J. (2000). *Online communities: Designing usability, supporting sociability*. Chichester: Wiley.

Prigogine, I. (1984). *Order out of chaos: Man's dialogue with nature*. New York: Bantam.

Renninger, K. A. & Shumar, W. (eds) (2004). *Building virtual communities: Learning and change in cyberspace*. New York: Cambridge University Press.

Reynolds, E., Treahy, D., Chao, C.-C. & Barab, S. A. (2001). The Internet Learning Forum: Developing a community prototype for teachers of the 21st century. *Computers in the Schools, 3*(4), 107–126.

Riel, M. & Polin, L. (2004). Models of community learning and online learning in communities. In S. A. Barab, R. Kling & J. Gray (eds), *Designing virtual communities in the service of learning* (pp. 16–52). New York: Cambridge University Press.

Rogoff, B. (1994). Developing understanding of the idea of communities of learners. *Mind, Culture, and Activity, 4*, 209–229.

Roth, W.-M. (1998). *Designing communities*. Dordrecht, The Netherlands: Kluwer.

Schlager, M. S. & Fusco, J. (2004). Teacher professional development, technology, and communities of practice: Are we putting the cart before the horse? In S. A. Barab, R. Kling & J. H. Gray (eds), *Designing for virtual communities in the service of learning* (pp. 120–153). New York: Cambridge University Press.

Schwen, T. & Hara, N. (2004). Communities of practice: A metaphor for online design. In S. A. Barab, R. Kling & J. H. Gray (eds), *Designing for virtual communities in the service of learning* (pp. 154–180). New York: Cambridge University Press.

Shields, C. M. & Seltzer, P. A. (1997). Complexities and paradoxes of community: Toward a more useful conceptualization of community. *Educational Administration Quarterly, 33*, 413–439.

Smith, M. A. & Kollock, P. (eds) (1999). *Communities in cyberspace*. New York: Routledge.

Stake, R. E. (1983). Program evaluation, particularly responsive evaluation. In G. F. Madaus, M. S. Scriven & D. L. Stufflebeam (eds), *Evaluation models: Viewpoints on educational and human services evaluation* (pp. 287–310). Boston, MA: Kluwer-Nijhoff.

Stake, R. E. (1995). *The art of case study research*. Thousand Oaks, CA: Sage.

Stevenson, H. W. & Stigler, J. W. (1992). *The learning gap*. New York: Summit Books.

Strauss, A. & Corbin, J. (eds) (1997). *Grounded theory in practice*. Thousand Oaks, CA: Sage.

Weedman, J. (1999). Conversation and community: The potential of electronic conferences for creating intellectual proximity in distributed learning environments. Journal of the American Society for Information Science, *50*, 907–928.

Wellman, B. (1999). *Networks in the global village: Life in contemporary communities*. Boulder, CO: Westview Press.

Wenger, E. (1998). *Communities of practice: Learning, meaning, and identity*. Cambridge: Cambridge University Press.

Westheimer, J. (1998). *Among school teachers: Community, autonomy, and ideology in teachers' work*. New York: Teachers College Press.

17 Design Methods for Educational Media to Communicate

When We Cannot Predict What Will Work, Find What Will Not Work

Raul A. Zaritsky
Construction Management Association of America

Introduction

In the last decade, innovations in mathematics and science education have been accomplished through convergences between fields such as artificial intelligence, cognitive science, and teaching methods. Increasing accessibility through visualizations, often with computationally enhanced tools for science students, lead to changes in curricula and pedagogical transformations of the culture and practice in the classroom. Communication of these innovations is still largely through text-based journals that focus on theoretical issues. This is in contrast to the known communication variables required to change the adoption rates of such innovations. One part of the solution for disseminating these new measures is to turn to case study methods constructed from situated video-recordings. Using video cases helps ground teachers' understanding of learning theories in the actual clinical details of a change in classroom procedures.

This chapter reports on the design research and testing of a case-based video resource that uses DVD technology and is intended to serve as a teachers' resource that can support the diffusion of innovations in mathematics education and their adoption. This DVD exemplar is the commercially available companion to the *Children's Math Worlds* mathematics curricula for students from kindergarten through grade five. DVD technology was selected for this companion resource because it uses broadcast, television-image-quality resolution to present classroom detail, and because, as a technology, it has become ubiquitous in many homes and most classrooms. Although benchmark testing showed that several promising affordances and construction methods of this resource failed to function with the target audience, these failures are often unreported. However, they were extremely formative and predictive of the changes needed throughout the development of this medium. Therefore, this chapter argues for the reporting of malfunctioning features as a significant component of all empirical and design methodologies. Although the research methods used do not offer the means to predict final market adoptions, they do identify significant, ineffective, media constructions. Certainly, if these features were to remain in this project's "workshop-in-a-box" format, they surely would predict poor performance of the DVD in the real marketplace.

The Children's Math Worlds Project

Many voices have been calling for significant improvements in mathematics education, especially for students from impoverished backgrounds. The Children's Math Worlds project (CMW; Fuson, 2003) developed ways to build on students' understandings. For over a decade, researchers at the CMW project have worked intensively with classroom teachers to study how children think in mathematical situations. During this time, these researchers and teachers have devised informal and formal learning activities based on how children think and have generated ambitious, world-class curricula that can support high levels of mathematical understanding by all students. These curricula were formulated in classrooms in diverse urban and suburban communities in five states and involved 200 teachers and 4,000 students in kindergarten through grade five.

One important goal of the CMW curricula is the creation of a classroom culture of conversation and activities that will enable children to understand the use of formal mathematical notation and methods. Over the course of the project, various kinds of conceptual supports were developed to help students link their informal ways of thinking to formal mathematics. In 1993, the research team began to work in English-speaking and Spanish-speaking urban classrooms; then, research was extended to suburban classrooms. Year after year, all the curricula and training were revised based on what the CMW researchers learned in classrooms and from teachers. This design process was empirically based and iterative. In general, lessons about what worked and what did not work for teachers and students were reflected in the next iteration.

To communicate the complex details of the CMW curricula and promote their adoption, a six-hour video resource, a sort of workshop-in-a-box, was created. DVD technology was selected both for image resolution and image size and also to build on the widespread adoption of this technology in the home. The design of this DVD was grounded in principles from learning theory and the literature on case construction. The research method used an iterative design that tested both the effectiveness of various designs and, specifically, the opportunities offered by DVD-based technology in each of the multiple versions developed over a four-year period. One of the objectives was to produce a workshop-in-a-box that is widely effective in the marketplace. Interestingly, the practical nature of the design process resulted in a final design that varied significantly from the initial, theoretically-formulated designs. The new DVD technology did not function as theorized in the grant application. For example, because DVD technology offers multiple audio and video channels, several audio tracks to provide teachers' commentaries on their classes and an audio channel to provide expert commentary on the classroom pedagogy were incorporated. Several video channels allowed the teachers to switch between views of the classroom and the new media grammars of construction, which were included to focus attention. Media grammars include all of the normal forms of changes in the film frame and the editing that we know how to read in TV and mainstream film. These included the dissolve (a transition between the picture of one place to another place to indicate a change in location or time) and the dip (a transition to all white or black or to a brief title sequence to indicate that the program is moving onto the next topic).

As a practical matter, designing effective media for mathematics education is likely to result in disconnects between theory and practice. These gaps are rarely the focus of researchers nor are they reported in journal articles; however, they can illuminate methodology and suggest areas of research in which the predictive components of various theoretical formulations can be tested. Although usability issues may account for some problems with any facet of technology, a general concern of design based on learning theory is that there is an assumption that most design variables that support effective use have common predictive value. This chapter hopes to make a contribution by detailing those features of design that are not equally effective in media for mathematics education. Therefore, the research focus turns now to early benchmarks for discovering these ineffective design features.

The realization that design and knowledge do not have a continuous landscape but, rather, are multidimensional and have a separate epistemological basis is an essential twentieth-century philosophical understanding made clear by Ludwig Wittgenstein. Wittgenstein explored the highly complex, multidimensional character of knowledge in his *Philosophical Investigations* (2001). Some readers may misunderstand the complex epistemological contribution made in this book and its implications for psychology and learning theory. The persuasiveness of the summary metaphor of knowledge as a landscape may be partially to blame. One can misunderstand this statement to mean that knowledge is like a simple landscape. This chapter describes the author's journey in creating the commercial version of a new media form on DVD with sufficient empirical benchmark testing to ensure that, at a minimum, the components and technology that had malfunctioned were removed, even though there is considerable literature about their promising benefits.

Developing an Educational Research Visualization for Mathematics Innovations

The final DVD has three major parts: the first one is explanatory; the second one is devoted to the main classroom components that demonstrate the major engines of the CMW innovations; and the third one contains on-camera interviews with teachers about these classroom components.

Demonstrating complex systems is the focus of the field of scientific visualizations where modeling systems serve both to predict and to integrate research and theory. Complex societal problems have required science to respond with complex models that provide both explanations and predictions. Today, in most scientific efforts, new models contain accurate and predictive visualizations that inform both the community of researchers and the community of practitioners. In the same manner, the classroom video cases and the other features of this new DVD resource provide not raw data but an authentic representation. Thus, one way this media form can be approached is as the educational version of a scientific visualization—in other words, an educational research visualization (ERV).

The DVD needed to present complex details of real-world situations through word problems in the curricula and those generated by students. The students were in grades one through five and came from four public schools that used the CMW curricula. Three of the schools were located in high-poverty, urban areas; the fourth was a suburban school that contained immigrants from many countries. The selected examples represented teachers and students who were at various points along the path to a collaborative classroom where the students demonstrated high levels of explanations about mathematical thinking.

The CMW project developed some inexpensive manipulatives to help students make more sense of the content. Later in the project, large, dry-erase MathBoards™ with conceptual supports were created to enable students to make mathematical drawings, or "proof pictures," which they can share with the rest of the class. These mathematical drawings are central to the project. As a visualization of knowledge, they enable students to integrate their mathematical understanding with formal solution methods and notations, thus providing a bridge from concrete to more abstract thinking. After some time, students no longer make drawings, but they can still use mental visual images from their drawings to explain and make sense of their formal numerical methods.

These important aspects of the project that enabled students to find meaning in their mathematical experiences are shown and discussed in the main segments of the DVD. For example, a typical CMW curriculum always began with a new mathematics topic, with students making their own mathematical drawings. Then, it introduced the kinds of drawings that have been powerful in classroom research. For multidigit numbers, these are drawings of hundreds, tens, and ones. For word problems, there are mathematical tools that show the structure of the real-world situation described in the word problem. For multidigit multiplication, there are area models of rectangles. For fractions, length models using unit fractions are shown.

Some of these methods or algorithms for solutions are unfamiliar to teachers. During focus groups teachers reported the need for more domain knowledge, so almost an hour of new mathematics knowledge was added. Interviews with the CMW teachers were filmed at the end of each school day, but it was not until later in the development of the ERV that it was found that, by making these interviews available on the DVD, they would be highly persuasive in explaining how the CMW innovations could be adopted and used in the classroom. So, again, a new section of the DVD was created, containing both long, largely unedited versions of the interviews and shorter, single-point, summary segments. Providing both short and long versions of these interviews reinforces the attempt to represent authentically what was discovered in the classrooms.

The CMW research shows clearly that more "accessible algorithms" are available than the more complex methods commonly taught. In fact, these accessible algorithms can be used with any curriculum, as can the mathematical drawings used by CMW students and shown in the classroom segments on the DVD. Also, we believe that the best way of communicating these accessible methods is through the complete clinical detail that can only be provided in high-resolution video.

The Look and Feel of Educational Research Visualization

Given the limitations of written descriptions of live media, the reader will understand that only an overview of the DVD is provided here. However, the following figures represent the feel of the final ERV and will give the reader a sense of this new form.

The still from the video reproduced in Figure 17.1 is from one of the main segments and shows several features of the curriculum (which includes students using graphical visualization methods) and the DVD-based, educational research visualization. Ethnographic film-makers working in the classrooms were able to film close up by using two video cameras and two, high-resolution, still cameras to follow specific students' work and questions as well as teacher–student interactions. Segments of the DVD demonstrate the pedagogy and mathematics and how these new algorithms are used effectively by students. What the reader can take from the images in Figures 17.1 and 17.2 is a perception of how the ERV essentially created "existence proofs" for teachers. In many grades, with many students and teachers, this ERV shows how these more accessible mathematics algorithms, developed by Fuson (2003), are used easily by a broad range of students to solve and explain mathematical problems.

When sections of mathematics domain knowledge were added to the DVD, simple computer graphic animations of the mathematical solutions were combined with the classroom footage (this builds on a film form created by the ethnographic film-maker Timothy Asch; Asch & Chagnon, 1975). Figure 17.2 is an example of the simple graphics style used in the explanatory sections of the ERV on the DVD. The new algorithm shown in Figure 17.2 is called the "new groups below" method; the CMW research had shown that these accessible algorithms improved students' work. Although each new accessible algorithm represents a significant research result that needs to be diffused, each one also needs to be presented to teachers in the context of situated pedagogy supporting students in talking about mathematics, which is another significant component of

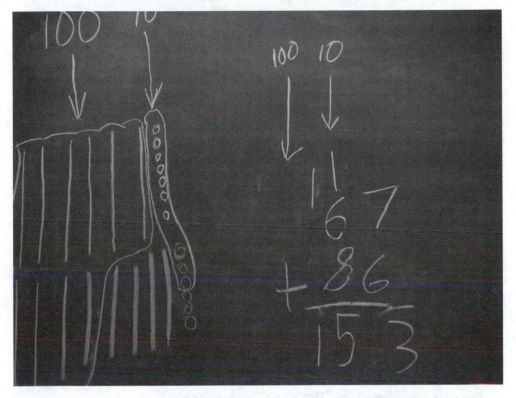

Figure 17.1 A Still from the Educational Research Visualization Video Showing a Student Using Multiple Methods to Explain her Work.

the CMW innovation. An example of the explanation section in the DVD is given below. In it, the mathematical processes are animated while the steps are narrated and the advantages are explained to students of placing the new ten on the equals line, rather than putting it above the tens column.

The animation gives complete explanations of the use of this accessible algorithm called "new groups below." In Figure 17.2, two-digit numbers (58 + 36 =) are being added together. However, the extra ten created in adding 6 and 8 is placed on the equals line, rather than above the tens column, as in the typical algorithm. Fuson's research (2003) has shown that such transformations in the graphical visualization of the problem and the mathematics representation combine to make the solutions easier for students. The new ten is more visible to students on the equals line. Also, graphical proof drawings, as seen in the student's work in Figure 17.1, are obvious examples of the principle of making meaning through scientific visualizations, which informed the Children's Math Worlds research.

To continue with the explanation of the student's solution using this method, Figure 17.1 shows how eight ones are combined with two more ones from the six to make one additional ten. Four ones are left; thus, four is the answer in the ones column to the problem of 8 plus 6. The additional ten is written graphically by students on the equals line, rather than above the tens column, as is more familiar. In the final segments, only simple graphics, such as a circle, as seen in Figure 17.1, are used to highlight for viewers and teachers that the additional ten has been placed on the equals line.

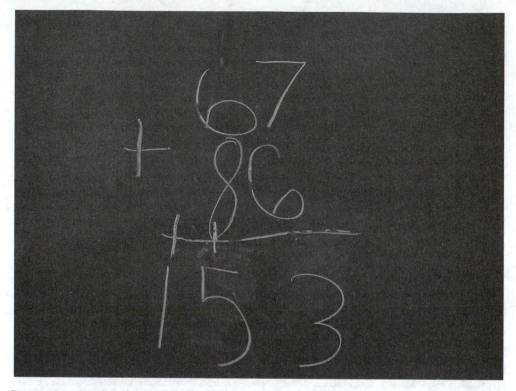

Figure 17.2 Graphic Showing the "New Groups Below" Method.

Components of Educational Research Visualization

The main segments of the ERV were edited to provide focused presentations of the significant research results at each grade level. Additional, largely unedited, video segments of longer duration were constructed so that audiences would have a less processed and more natural set of representations from real classrooms that conveyed the students' and teachers' mathematical conversations. Brief and in-depth interviews with the CMW teachers were included too. The completed ERV contains:

1 Segments of mathematics domain explanations in which graphics are used to animate the students' work; while the narration by Fuson (2003) provides the details for understanding the mechanisms of representation that create a more accessible algorithm.

2 Long and largely unedited segments from each grade level, in which the students' use of these new algorithms is presented as it happened in the classroom.

3 Interviews with teachers that focus on some of the main features of the CMW innovations. These interviews are presented both in a shorter edited form and at length, so that the ERV user can select the amount of detail desired. Teachers explaining how they developed these innovative curricula in their classrooms are highly effective communicators of the details of the variables that improve the prospects for adoption of the new curricula.

Testing late in the project confirmed that teachers respond well to information communicated to them through interviews with the CMW teachers; therefore, such interviews were included as an additional, 40-minute component of the final ERV. The total DVD package can be almost six hours long because of the large recording capabilities of a single, 9-gigabyte DVD. In 2006, the new, 30 and 50-gigabyte DVD systems became available; so shown in standard definition rather than for HDTV, up to 50 hours of standard definition video could be recorded on a single disc.

To summarize the scientific and design issues of validation and redesign, many features could not be tested during the design phase, so final scientific validation has to await release and distribution of the commercial product. Market testing is needed for a complete empirical validation of this ERV medium. Until such market results are added to the research results, effectiveness cannot be claimed. Although the features were maximized and benchmarked to ensure their functional use, the expectation is that, as a package, all of the segments will coalesce into an effective visualization that will be useful for a large, clinical-style innovation. This video form will be used differently by different audiences. However, the question remains whether the sum of such a large database of highly constructed segments combined with explanations and longer, less-edited segments will be persuasive in changing the current classroom behavior in mathematics pedagogy of those considering adoption of the CMW curricula. The benchmark testing was formative in its goals, rather than attempting to support theoretical constructions primarily. In other words, the ERV has formative empirical validation from benchmark testing of its offerings by users in the real-world market.

Standard Methods Versus Design Engineering Methods

Earlier papers (McCormick et al., 1987; Zaritsky, 2006; Zaritsky et al., 2003) discussed the emerging importance of using video cases in education and teacher preparation and summarized the difficulty of being able to generalize formative design principles from one project to another. Focus groups containing teachers, mathematics educators, and college professors tested each version of this ERV. In 2003, some results demonstrated that certain constructions and learning opportunities seemed to malfunction, were used ineffectively, or were not used. Although this should not have come as a surprise because such designs cannot be developed from untested theory, what was especially surprising was that these malfunctions did not fall along any distinct theoretical lines such as case length, the use of close ups, or application of the new mathematical algorithms. Instead, the malfunctions ranged from complaints that some of the teachers filmed were too attractive, confusion about how to use the additional audio channels, and unfamiliarity with the new mathematics of the CMW algorithms demonstrated in the classroom video. Thus, a primary finding is that the design of a visualization method for education needs formative benchmark testing across the range of its educational opportunities and media constructions with innovative media grammars and DVD navigational forms.

The sister field of design engineering also reports that, in the early stages, one should expect to find many malfunctioning components or even malfunctions of whole designs. One implication is that projects designing similar, video, case-based materials may need a greater focus on empirical methods in order to determine the malfunctioning elements.

Rapid, design-based benchmarking provided a successful set of methods that the ERV project borrowed from the sister field of design engineering (Ulrich & Eppinger, 2000). Flowers (Zaritsky et al., 2003) of the design engineering program at the Massachusetts Institute of Technology, has written that design-based creations must rely on a willingness to learn and change paths, with each phase being based on the recognition of malfunctioning goals or construction methods:

Effective design is, of course, not a random process; however, it does change direction, sometimes dramatically. Throughout the process, when a path is recognized as non-optimal (e.g., using data drawn from prototyping, focus groups, benchmarking, and market research), a different path is considered and chosen. Further, though stages of the design may be treated independently, the combined effort must amount to more than the sum of its parts and result in a robust solution.

(Zaritsky et al., 2003: 32)

In the ERV project, focus groups and individual testing with oral recordings made by the users were the methods employed to gather data for the benchmark tests. This process of formative benchmarking differs from a statistical form of laboratory research in many ways; for example, the number of subjects differs, the discovery of patterns of malfunctions differs, and the understanding of the mechanisms of broken components varies with the clarity of the reports. The ERV project's goal was not the discovery of how the human brain functions when using multimedia but the limited goal of developing a design that would work in the real world to diffuse and support the adoption of the CMW curricula in tens of thousands of classrooms. Therefore, the validation methods used were largely formative and far from comprehensive; thus, they do not support accepted general principles. However, benchmark testing throughout the project's cycles did ensure that such formative methods were effective in validating the goals in advance of obtaining the results of actual, market-based data.

The original grant from the National Science Foundation for this project was for researching the use of new technologies, such as multiple video and audio channels on DVD platforms. After three years' work, it was found that too many channels created undue complexity and, thus, were likely to be a problem for many teachers when a commercial version was published. The reader who buys or rents DVDs will know that these channels are features common to theatrical DVD releases; consequently, there are market forces at work supporting their use. However, it is hoped that two years of DVD use of multiple channels will not produce the same complexity for most teachers. Because early testing resulted in the discovery of several problems, features such as the navigation tool had to be redesigned, resulting in the size of the final DVD package nearly doubling in order to provide a complete presentation of the mathematical knowledge required by teachers. Focus groups and individuals reported that required components were missing.

During the development stage, the number of reports required to convince the researchers of the presence of nonfunctioning components changed, but, for the most part, the nonfunctional components could be identified from the first five or ten accounts. When individual reports were similar in their descriptions of broken features and broken mechanisms, redesign began. When a significant new component of domain knowledge was created late in the project, only the mathematics knowledge segments were tested by a small number of the project's staff and mathematics education experts. Such formative testing is the recommended method in a design engineering project. However, a research method such as a randomized controlled trial, which would force significant quantitative results, would not have produced more scientific results than these formative methods.

A somewhat easier way to state the project designers' research goals is to suggest a simple thought experiment. For example, given a radically new bicycle design project, how many subjects need to fall off the bicycle before another design approach is considered? In the later phases of the ERV project, fewer reports of malfunctions were needed to prompt a redesign. In an earlier article written with Professor Flowers and others (Zaritsky et al., 2003), iterative design and phase-appropriate testing as they are used in the field of design engineering were summarized in this way:

> The value and relevance of qualitative or quantitative methods in product design vary as a function of the design stage. When designers "solidify" designs, they do so only in accordance with proven merit using the appropriate metrics for data collected by the appropriate method at the appropriate stage within a context with known (or assumed) limited resources.
>
> (p. 33)

Standard statistical forms were less appropriate approaches during the formative stage of the ERV project. Instead, the model of iterative design, as detailed in design experiments (Collins, 2004; Kelly, 2006), was used as a research foundation and method. Design experiments are essentially formative efforts, often research conducted in classrooms, in which the team continues to improve the research innovations, the curriculum, the science tools, or the cognitive approaches of the learners by means of iterations of the research design. Journal reports contribute narrative and other ethnographic details that provide warrants for the innovation's claims and support the foundational theory. In the ERV project, through iterative phases, it became clear that the ERV media needed to be redesigned to eliminate malfunctions. The ERV project also needed to ask intended audiences what they found was missing and what was needed for the DVD to function on its own. As noted above, it was more appropriate for this iterative design project to use formative benchmarking methods, rather than standard, statistically validated, empirical methods.

Education Needs Empirical Results on Video Case Construction

The literature on case-based video has yet to develop criteria for the construction of appropriate video cases and for appropriate clinical skills for the recording teams. The literature does not suggest methods for determining the appropriate length of cases for various goals; it does not explain the views needed for the cameras; and it does not offer solutions when a project requires close-ups of the work of students. These are the reasons we have been explicit in describing our recording methods. The case literature has yet to specify testing methods that will ensure sound construction with effective repetition of individual case examples in order to build up a family of examples that stretches across students and classrooms. Although numerous theories and research projects informed the construction of the ERV project, in practice, the theories were only generally useful or suggestive. "Generally useful" is far less useful than "prescriptive," for example, in describing how text-based cases should be constructed (Shulman, 1992). I do not disagree with these goals for text-based cases, but they are far more diffuse and less specific than what is needed to guide the construction of video-based cases.

The research and writings in educational psychology informing case-based projects include the theory of cognitive flexibility, which attempts to explain how individual cases, when added together, provide an understanding of the family of features that are required in order to comprehend science. In general, this theory says that, in messy domains, one needs to present a large population of cases so that learners can determine the common features of the family. In this manner, learners will be enlightened by the deeper nature of the processes demonstrated by the features that form the family. In designing this project, a large database of video cases of the CMW innovation was included, rather than only a few specific cases. Although cognitive flexibility theory (Spiro et al., 1987, 1988) was helpful as a guiding notion for building a large database of cases in the ERV, it provided little or no guidance or specifications for individual cases. For example, how many and what type of video-recordings constitute the most effective family of cases? As pointed out in this chapter, in moving from general goals or theories developed from retrospective empirical work to specific, predictive, prescriptive visualization construction methods, suggestions are required.

Many theories do not inform practice; rather, they suggest explanations. A partial reason for this disconnect, as seen with cognitive flexibility theory and other cognitive theories, is that they have been constructed retrospectively and have not been validated with predictive experiments. Although based on scientifically sound studies, developing theories based on retrospective analysis without also testing these theories on predictive experiments means that we often turn to theory that has yet to be validated as to its predictive ability. In public health and other related fields, this lack of a full scientific attack on questions would be far more problematic. The author's prescriptive questions are: Which visualizations will work effectively for which audiences? Why did they work? These questions still await research. Here, the reader should note the difference between scientific visualizations—which include predictive claims for practical applications to pressing social issues, for example predictive outcomes to problems such as the risk of an avian flu pandemic—and educational visualizations. Theories in education serve a different function—consolidating research into a compacted explanation—rather than provide the sort of systemic model seen in a scientific visualization that clarifies and predicts the likely results of a scenario proposed as a solution to a problem.

Benchmark testing of the ERV asked questions similar to those in other studies, but they were used formatively. We explored how best to fit together in a case detailed narrations and their accompanying images. The need for an empirical test of the use of narrations arose when focus groups of teachers reported trouble repeating the points made in the short narrative introductions to some of the five, major, classroom segments. Narratives are used in each of the five segments and are presented by voice-over. These narratives are fairly brief and attempt to provide the viewer with some background and a focal point for looking at the segments that present the major engines of the mathematics innovations. Initially, these explanatory narrations were constructed over live video shots of the classrooms. The narrations were about four minutes' long and at the beginning of an approximately 14-minute, edited segment.

A series of benchmark studies were developed in which an introductory narration over live video was compared to introductions using simple pans and scans of still photographs—a standard method used in history documentaries. The solution selected uses a small step that eliminates complex, eye-tracking demands placed on the viewer by live video details. This is the most common solution used in media grammars for minimizing disruptions when hearing a narration and watching a picture simultaneously. With pan-and-scan, postprocessing software, the live video was replaced with a visually authentic view of work in the classroom, but one that is less distracting than a live video created from high-resolution, still images taken at the same time as the video. The still images were animated and turned into video by panning and zooming in the high-resolution frame—a technique used frequently in history documentaries broadcast on public television. The animation of still photographs is an old technique, one that is "tried and true" in the craft of film-making. Benchmark results showed that teachers were more able to repeat the summary points of the narrations when the postprocessed, pan-and-scan background was used as video, compared to the segments in which live video was used as background with the same narration. Clearly, in sections containing more complex narration, less busy classroom detail on the screen improved attention to, and retention of, the information presented. However, it still left a visual focus on the classroom.

While narrations are being played, the ERV uses zooms and slow pans across a digital photograph of the classroom, rather than live footage, to minimize the viewer's problem of eye-tracking. Mayer and his colleagues (Mayer & Moreno, 2003) do not measure eye-tracking in their experiments, so it is impossible to know whether film craft solutions or cognitive theories of overloading the human mind have been proven experimentally as the best way to hear narration in media. These factors may interact, but the ERV results suggest that any further laboratory studies must include the earlier traditions of film editing if they are to make important discoveries of all of the variables that affect narration. In general, the ERV used the tradition from film editing; this use accords with scientific methods in which the ERV researchers were guided by the most parsimonious explanations. Given that media construction is based on 100 years of simple explanations by film editors, testing explanations early in a project is warranted.

Further, research in multimedia forms is investigating media that are different in character, image size, resolution, and delivery from the ERV made for this project, which is a convergence of scientific visualization methods and ethnographic methods. Providing an exemplar from promising theory and laboratory experiments was an initial goal of the project; however, a few validated new grammars and advanced features were included in the final DVD. Rather than suggested grammars, the literature of film was the source of the ERV's media grammars. The results suggest that, with each specific media creation and technology, education researchers must use an empirical, design-based process with increasingly demanding benchmarks that focus on both the learning design and on those aspects of the design that contribute to malfunctions.

Benchmark Testing for Commercial Release

Some of the results of, and the approaches used in, the ERV benchmark tests and the iterative design of the final commercial version are summarized below:

1 *Media grammars.* In general, complex media grammars decreased the teachers' abilities to say where they were in the DVD cases, to identify the grade level, or to recount what they were seeing, even though they had been given this information by narration, graphics, and video effects. Complex media grammars were replaced throughout with standard film grammars. Silent-film-era inter-titles (of the kind used in silent film between the action to present the text of the dialogue) were used in graphics to indicate the grade level, and slow, pan-and-scan images were used when providing detailed information in narrations (as in history documentaries). Unexpectedly, although many promising ideas suggested by colleagues were tried, no advanced grammatical innovations were validated; therefore, none were used in the final commercial version.

2 *Innovative video graphics.* Computer graphics images helped to explain a mathematics domain. In the explanations section of the mathematics domain, where teachers are given the detailed steps of the new algorithms developed for students, enhanced video with zooms, complex graphics created with new digital tools such as Rotoscoping and 3-D software, and other, complex, graphical enhancements of the students' chalkboard work were tried. Benchmark testing showed that they distracted teachers and, equally important for this project, these new media solutions concerned mathematics educators because the results looked unlike actual

blackboard work. Simple recreations of images from a blackboard made by off-the-shelf, image-editing packages were used instead.

3   *Multiple angles.* Some DVD features, such as a switch between two cameras giving alternative points of view, were unknown to most of the teachers. When such features were built into the menu, complications ensued. However, when an image contained both camera views, experienced DVD owners were able to switch between the camera angles. Nonetheless, this feature was not used in the final version because it was still too complex.

4   *Multiple audio commentary tracks.* In addition to the synchronous sound used in the classroom cases, two, additional, audio commentary channels were created. One featured teachers discussing their goals and classroom management issues while the DVD showed their classrooms. In the other one, mathematics educators discussed the domain-specific features of the new curricula. However, DVD production is time-consuming. Because so many video versions containing significant changes to all of the final major segments had been created, it was unclear when the audio commentary should be rerecorded. Moreover, because only those teachers who owned DVDs knew how to use this feature, it was excluded from the final product, although it remains a highly promising feature. Perhaps later, when switching between audio channels is made simpler by the hardware manufacturers and by personal computers' DVD software and when more viewers are familiar with its potential, this option could be tried again.

Validation must use phase-appropriate benchmarks that test likely, real-world, audience adoption of domain and pedagogical innovations. Also, the goal of large-scale distribution required a shift from promising designs to those with clear empirical validation. Thus, in creating diffusion media, the possibilities offered should be limited mainly to tested theoretical formulations that produce positive, empirical, benchmarking results for learning, effectiveness, and usability, thereby providing empirical support for their inclusion in a package of media features.

Scientific visualizations owe their increasing warrants not only to their ability to support or refute theory, but also to the increasing number of experts who can gain traction on real-world phenomena by predicting the effect of possible scenarios or researchers who can suggest more productive areas for further study. In the education field, there is concern about the disconnect between theory and practice. Scientific visualization systems provide predictive outcomes for the sciences that they support, whether it is hurricane prediction or theories about the spread of epidemics. Central to the application of theories, in most fields, is that they must lead to increased understanding of the relative ability of various features to contribute to the probability of predicting outcomes. In medicine, health research, and public education, for example, researchers have to fit together the relative risks of various elements (family history, lifestyle, drug interactions, compliance, etc.) that are derived from biological theories but are based on large-scale, empirical results. At-scale solutions require multiple approaches, including real-world validation of the variables that support the outcomes; namely, communication of the innovations through wide-scale diffusion and through the variables that can be predictive of the adoption of these innovations. Although the results discussed in this chapter are pertinent primarily to this CMW innovation and to the ERV exemplar, in practice, the project's researchers found that theory exists, as Wittgenstein predicted, not on a common landscape, but in a complex, fractured, and discontinuous manner. Thus, only by using formative benchmarks to guide design and development could the project's researchers feel assured of having improved the design over the project's life cycle. Throughout the chapter, attention has been called to problems unique to the ERV and the need for help in creating appropriate new benchmarks for learning effectiveness in time to predict and guide design.

Conclusions

The educational research visualization model was created for the Children's Math Worlds project to meet the goal of communicating an effective set of new warrants for the CMW's innovations. Results from this media format and from testing provided an initial finding that the design of a visualization method for education needs iterative, formative, benchmark testing across the range of its possibilities and media construction forms. Further, given that such constructions are design efforts, evidence of the usability and nonusability of the features appears early in the process and is one of the primary results of testing. Thus, a clear conclusion from the tests is that benchmarks must be developed in order to discover malfunctions. This should be a focus of all such research and design efforts.

Although the results support the broad application of visualization techniques to education research projects and argue for a subdiscipline in educational visualization methods, they do not contribute to generalizations about the theoretical value and predictive potential of the various possibilities. However, in the ERV project, an attempt has been made to provide an example of how removing malfunctions early in the design process is essential in the construction of video, case-based, media materials.

Acknowledgments

This research was supported by funding from a National Science Foundation Career Award (Award No. 0107008). The perspectives presented in this chapter are solely the author's and do not reflect necessarily the positions of the Foundation.

References

Asch, T. (Director) & Chagnon, N. (Director) (1975). *The Ax Fight* [Motion picture]. Available from Documentary Educational Resources, 101 Morse Street, Watertown, MA 02472.

Collins, A., Joseph, D. & Bielaczye, K. (2004). Design research: Theoretical and methodological issues. Journal of the Learning Sciences, *13* (1), 15–42.

Fuson, K. C. (2003). Developing mathematical power in whole number operations. In W. Kilpatrick, G. Martin & D. Schifter (eds), *A research companion to principles and standards for school mathematics*, Volume 1 (pp. 68–94). Reston, VA: National Council of Teachers of Mathematics.

Kelly, A. E. (2006). Quality criteria for design research: Evidence and commitments. In J. van den Akker, K. Gravemeijer, S. McKenney & N. Nieveen (eds), *Educational design research* (pp. 166–184). London: Routledge.

Mayer, R. E. & Moreno, R. (2003). Nine ways to reduce cognitive load in multimedia learning. *Educational Psychologist, 38*, 43–52.

McCormick, B. H., DeFanti, T. A. & Brown, M. D. (eds) (1987). Visualization in scientific computing [Special issue]. *ACM SIGGRAPH Computer Graphics*, 21(6), 1–14.

Shulman, J. H. (1992). *Case methods in teacher education*. New York: Teachers College Press.

Spiro, R. J., Coulson, R. L., Feltovich, P. J. & Anderson, D. K. (1988). Cognitive flexibility theory: Advanced knowledge acquisition in ill-structured domains. *Proceedings of the tenth annual conference of the cognitive science society* (pp. 375–383). Hillsdale, NJ: Lawrence Erlbaum Associates.

Spiro, R. J., Vispoel, W., Schmitz, J., Samarapungavan, A. & Boerger, A. (1987). Knowledge acquisition for application: Cognitive flexibility and transfer in complex content domains. In B. K. Britton & S. M. Glynn (eds), *Executive control processes* (177–200). Hillsdale, NJ: Lawrence Erlbaum Associates.

Ulrich, K. T. & Eppinger, S. D. (2000). *Product design and development* (2nd ed.). Boston, MA: Irwin/McGraw-Hill.

Wittgenstein, L. (2001). *Philosophical investigations: The German text, with a revised English translation* (G. E. M. Anscombe, Trans., 3rd ed.). Oxford: Blackwell.

Zaritsky, R. (2006). Creating an educational research visualization: Using visualizations as scientific warrants in the earlier research phases. In R. Goldman, R. Pea, B. Barron & S. J. Derry (eds), *Video research in the learning sciences*. Mahwah, NJ: Lawrence Erlbaum Associates.

Zaritsky, R., Kelly, A. E., Flowers, W., Rogers, E. & O'Neill, P. (2003). Clinical design sciences: A view from sister design efforts. *Educational Researcher, 32*(1), 32–34.

Part 7

Reflecting on Design Research at the Program Level

18 Getting to Scale with Innovations that Deeply Restructure How Students Come to Know Mathematics

Jeremy Roschelle
SRI International

Deborah Tatar
Virginia Tech University

Jim Kaput
Deceased

Introduction

Most people enter the field of educational research with good intentions of improving education and the lives of children. Countless good ideas, however, remain in university halls. Curricular and pedagogical innovations rise and fall in schools because there is insufficient understanding of how the innovation can and will be used. At the same time, technological innovations in schools are becoming more and more politically contentious. People, reasonably, want to know that we are giving their children "proven" curricular materials. To Congress, this means that evaluators should engage in "scientifically based research" ("No Child Left Behind Act" 2001). Not willing to cede the definition of scientific methodology to lawmakers, educational researchers have begun their own vigorous debate. Fundamentally, they ask (and this book asks), what should count as a scientific warrant that evidence supports a claim?

Partisans of two important educational research perspectives have made strong progress towards defining and defending their answers. Taking the perspective of program evaluation and educational psychology, some researchers ask *"What works?"* (Shavelson & Towne, 2002). The objects of their inquiry are selected from available materials or programs and the measures are closely related to today's high stakes test. Although researchers in this group acknowledge the utility of multiple research methods, they make their strongest case for the virtues of experimentation, preferably with randomized, controlled designs (Cook, 2000; Torgerson, 2001).

Taking the perspective that builds on cognitive science insights and aims for the design of new materials, technologies, or practices, another group (Design-Based Research Collaborative, 2003) asks: *"What could work?"* Their object of inquiry is the design of materials for students to learn important yet vexingly difficult mathematics and science concepts. Proposals often argue that existing materials do not meet this challenge and therefore research must be tightly coupled with design. Although researchers in this group acknowledge the utility of multiple methods, they make the strongest case for design research methods. Research methods that reveal students' deep progress on difficult concepts and that yield theoretical insight into the "active ingredients" of innovations are especially valued (Cobb et al., 2002; Edelson, 2002).

In this chapter, we highlight a third perspective. Like the design researchers, the third perspective attends to *innovation*. And like the program evaluators, this perspective is also fundamentally concerned with *what works*. Linking these two concerns is a drive towards scale. We ask: *"What could scale up?"*

Getting to scale is an increasingly important mandate for educational research (Fullan, 2000), but the history of educational change is largely the history of failure, either failure to be sustained or a failure to reach what Elmore (1996) calls the "core"—what happens in classrooms on a daily basis. Innovations, particularly those involving technology, have often been cited as having high potential to address our largest learning challenges (President's Committee of Advisors on Science and Technology, 1997). However, vociferous critics point out the long history of failures of innovations to solve real problems in schools at scale, particular those involving technology (Cuban, 2003).

In mathematics education, technology has already achieved impressive scale in the form of the graphing calculator. Evidence from the National Assessment of Educational Progress (NAEP) shows that "eighth-graders whose teachers reported that calculators were used almost every day scored highest" (National Center for Education Statistics, 2001: 144). This evidence is correlational and thus does not constitute proof that technology causes high scores (perhaps smart students are more likely to use calculators). The link between technology use and high test scores on NAEP does suggest that careful research about the effects of scaling-up technology in mathematics education could address questions of great interest to parents and policy-makers.

We affiliate with a group of researchers who believe that this failure or success of innovations in education is not the result of an intrinsic match or mismatch between technological innovations and educational problems, but rather a failure of past research to address the problems of scaling-up innovations (Blumenfeld et al., 2000). Research on scaling-up innovation, we argue, is different from research on "what works?" or "what could work?" Like "what could work?" research, scaling-up research is concerned with the potential of new innovations that may achieve ends not measured in established tests. Like "what works?" research, scaling-up research is concerned with the presence of a systematic effect despite environmental variability. Thus, scaling-up research can be concerned with showing that an outcome is reproducible and measurable at scale despite the fact that the outcome (a) does not already have an established benchmark, and (b) may occur infrequently in current conditions.

Research on scaling-up innovation is not merely a matter of extending interventions to a larger number of subjects (Cobern, 2002). In addition to extending the number of subjects ("*n*"), research on scaling up involves an intellectual agenda, with new foci, methods, and warrants coming into play over time. The research explicitly seeks to move from a concept to a scalable intervention. This research starts before an innovation is well specified (and thus long before conclusive evaluation research can begin). Researchers must resolve a large set of design details before research at scale can sensibly begin, while at the same time they must build evidence that makes a convincing provisional case that the research program is promising and deserving of continued support. This process takes a long time, spanning multiple two–four-year funding cycles.

By using a case study, we seek to clarify issues at the heart of research programs concerned with scaling-up innovation. We will analyze the case at two levels. First, we use the case to draw out characteristics of research programs that incorporate a drive to scale. The case will reveal how a program of scaling-up research is different from a program of basic research or evaluation research. Second, we highlight three driving questions that lie at the transition of projects from design research to implementation research. We consider what sorts of warrants are appropriate to link evidence to claims in the context of these driving questions.

The case study presents the research trajectory of SimCalc, an innovation that supports learning the mathematics of change and variation. By presenting this case, we aim to ground our arguments in details about the evolution of a research program over time. We synoptically describe SimCalc research as occurring in six phases, each moving successively closer towards scale. We roughly group the six phases into two larger parts containing three phases each. The first part of the case is about research in the context of design. The second part of the case is about research in the context of implementation. We begin each section with a brief presentation of a theoretical framework that helps to organize the case.

Part 1: Research in the Context of Design

International comparisons (Schmidt et al., 2001), as well as national tests (National Center for Education Statistics, 2001), have highlighted the gap between (a) the Americans' aspiration to provide world-class mathematics and science education, and (b) the middling, inequitable outcomes of the current K–12 educational system. To close these gaps, leaders and policy-makers call for an increased role for research in determining how to scale up new approaches to improving mathematics and science education (National Science Foundation, 2004; President's Committee of Advisors on Science and Technology, 1997).

Technology is often featured in discussions of opportunities to improve math and science education (e.g., Bransford et al., 2000). Prior literature particularly draws out the importance of leveraging the unique representational affordances of technology (Kaput, 1986; Roschelle et al., 2000b). By 1990, basic cognitive research on the use of representation in learning difficult mathematics and science concepts had largely concluded that the application of technology must be domain-specific (Kaput, 1992). This leads to a central design problem—the problem of designing *representations* particular to subject matter that unlock cognitive potential for learning.

This design problem is at the heart of the first part of the SimCalc case. As we shall see, the SimCalc team was deeply concerned with using cognitive (and later social cognitive) perspectives to improve mathematics education. Team members sought to employ the innovative potential of technology and they sought warrants at the level of mathematical cognition to relate evidence to claims.

In the first few years of the SimCalc project, the researchers articulated a framework, called "Restructuring Knowing" (RK) to express the coherence across varied design challenges. This framework may be visualized as a Venn diagram of three interlocking circles. The circles signify overlapping perspectives. The challenge of designing for restructuring knowing is to find overlaps that unite all three perspectives (Figure 18.1).

The three intertwined perspectives of the RK design framework are:

1   *Learner strengths.* RK designs build on a developmental analysis of well-established cognitive, kinesthetic, and linguistic strengths and interests (as well as misconceptions) that learners can bring to mathematics, rather than merely their level of mastery of the current curriculum's prerequisite structure.
2   *Representational technology.* RK designs emphasize the novel capability of technology to represent important domain concepts dynamically, in ways that generate insights among learners.

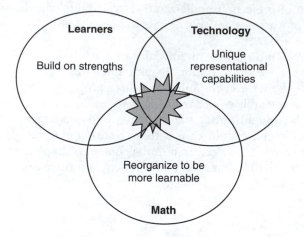

Figure 18.1 Three Perspectives of the Restructuring Knowing Framework.

3 *Reorganized curriculum.* RK designs reorganize the curricular sequence to be more learnable and efficient, drawing on deep analysis of the historical precedents and the conceptual structure of mathematical ideas.

Each of these perspectives has a strong base in educational and cognitive theory. The perspective of learner strengths is intrinsic to constructivism: if students are to construct knowledge, they must construct it from prior knowledge. The alternative (but less sound) view is that we could simply eliminate bad knowledge ("misconceptions") and then start with a *tabula rosa* (see Smith et al., [1993] for a critique of this view). The perspective that technology provides novel representational capabilities also has a long-standing and distinguished theoretical pedigree (Roschelle et al., 2000b). Finally, investigators have noted that our present curricular structure is in many ways an arti-fact of the media available for representing concepts (Kaput et al., 2002). We are not making the problematic argument that media alone affect the quality of learning (Clarke, 1983); rather we argue that media enable and constrain curricular possibilities, and new media can give rise to radically reorganized curriculum (Kaput, 1994, 1997). Thus, the cardinal principle of RK design is:

> Identify design elements that elegantly draw upon and unite the perspectives of learner strengths, representational technology, and reorganizing the curriculum and its underlying epistemology.

One reason that design research is time-consuming is the difficulty of finding design elements that work from all three perspectives. Table 18.1 describes the findings of SimCalc research using the tripartite RK principle. We will refer to this table throughout the case study. We do not provide detailed descriptions of SimCalc's technology and curriculum here but they are available in related publications (Kaput & Roschelle, 1998; Roschelle & Kaput, 1996; Roschelle et al., 2000a).

Phase 1: Early Planning (Pre-1994)

The path to large-scale adoption of an innovation begins with definition of a problem and an approach. The problem should be enduring, because it will likely take a long

Table 18.1 SimCalc's Approach to Uniting Three Perspectives

SimCalc's approach	Three perspectives		
	Learner strengths	Representational technology	Reorganized curriculum
Foregrounding the relation of mathematical representations to phenomenological motion	Perceiving, describing, and reasoning about motion in the concrete	Linked animation and mathematical notations make tangible the connection between formalism and common sense	Emphasizes phenomena as a tool for building understanding
Formalisms are introduced to help consolidate and extend knowledge previously established	Natural progression from case-based specific learning to more integrative, general understanding	Unites and reifies mathematical formalism and more intuitive expressive notations in one medium	Provides substantial informal learning opportunities before introducing formal concepts
Piecewise functions	Reasoning about intervals, can leverage arithmetic and simple geometric skills to compute quantitative aspects	Can visually represent and allow purposeful manipulation of piecewise-defined motions	Uses piecewise functions as an essential building block for all calculus concepts
Emphasizing reasoning across rate (velocity) and accumulation (position) descriptions	Build on ability to think about "same" object in "different" views	Dynamic links among different representational views of the mathematical object	Focuses on rate-accumulation relationships expressed qualitatively and arithmetically
Primary focus on graph-based and linguistic reasoning	Making sense of and guiding action within graphical, visual forms	Supports visual presentation and direct editing of graphical forms in newly expressive ways	Shifts the emphasis from symbol manipulation to more democratically accessible forms of expression
Inquiry cycle of plan, construct, experience, reflect	Ability to understand a challenge, hypothesize possible solutions, and distinguish success from failure	Computational apparatus allows for many, quick, iterative feedback cycles	A more playful, expressive microworlds approach to mathematics.

time to arrive at a scalable implementation. The approach should draw upon at least one mechanism that plausibly has the potential to affect change at scale.

In the case of SimCalc, Kaput (1994) articulated the core goal as "democratizing access to the mathematics of change and variation." The essence of the SimCalc approach proposed by Kaput was to integrate new curriculum with new dynamic representational capabilities made possible by computer technology. The arguments for this problem and approach were made using historical, curricular, and literature synthesis methods. By using historical analysis, Kaput argued that changing representations play a fundamental role in determining what and how we think mathematically (Kaput, 1987a, 1987b, 1991). Further, he recognized that reasoning about motion situations was central in the emergence of calculus (Kaput, 1994), but that calculus is taught today with only weak reference to motion phenomena. He noted that the dynamic representational features of technology (visual animation and simulation, in particular, linked to more conventional mathematical representations of functions and graphs) could bring motion phenomena back to the center of calculus education.

But Kaput (1994) did not want to merely improve the standard calculus course (indeed, a parallel but different calculus reform movement was simultaneously occurring). He argued that we are in the midst of a long-term trend requiring more students to gain access to more complex mathematical ideas. For example, whereas only a small percentage of students were expected to learn algebra a century ago, today we expect algebra for all students in eighth or ninth grade. Thus, he anticipated a need for a bigger and more diverse population of students to gain access to calculus earlier (Kaput, 1997). A curricular analysis revealed that the target concepts had been sequestered in a particular layer but could be unpacked into a strand that would begin in middle school (Kaput & Nemirovsky, 1995).

Finally, Kaput's literature review and synthesis (1992) suggested that dynamic representation was emerging as a powerful force for educational change. Further, it was clear that the technology to support dynamic representation in school was becoming cheaper and more readily available and could eventually become ubiquitous. Indeed, in the period from 1990 through 1997, graphing calculators—a dynamic representational appliance costing $100 or less—went to scale. Likewise, over a similar time span, another dynamic representational tool, the Geometer's Sketchpad (Jackiw, 1997), progressed from research prototype to the most used computer software in mathematics classrooms in the United States (Becker & Anderson, 1998). Hence, using technology for its dynamic representation capabilities has turned out to be popular among mathematics teachers.

In the planning phase of the SimCalc project, Kaput formulated the above argument, created a movie to depict his concept, and brought together a team of consultants to help him plan a first research effort. The concept at this time was largely limited to linking motion phenomena to mathematical formalisms (see the first row in Table 18.1). This idea, present in the video, is still foundational for the SimCalc program 12 years later. However, no other significant design features depicted in the video remain; later research phases discovered stronger alternatives.

Phase 2: Designing Representations for Difficult Math (1994–1997)

In the second phase (1994–1997), the National Science Foundation (NSF) funded a three-year SimCalc project. The team's objectives were of the "what could work?" variety—how to design representations for key concepts in the mathematics of change and variation that could help students learn. Thus, the research methods focused on microanalyses of very small numbers of students as they tried to learn these topics with preliminary materials and software. The team consisted of a mathematician, a cognitive/computer scientist, and a developmental psychologist/educational researcher. The technology used cost at least $10,000 per student to build, as the team used it with only tens of students.

In the first year, the team explored a number of ideas to realize the vision of the original movie. These were presented as video games, a design element that has largely dropped out of the SimCalc program, as none of these games proved compelling in small-scale trials with students. Indeed, small-scale explorations suggested that extensive game narrative and reliance of gaming goals stood in tension with the deep learning that the team sought. Neither large-scale research nor a sophisticated methodology was needed to rule out innovations with little potential.

A defining transition came when the team realized the powerful synergies represented in the third row of Table 18.1, which occurred sometime in our second year of research. Through micro-analytic developmental studies, Nemirovsky and colleagues (Monk & Nemirovsky, 1994; Nemirovsky, 1996) found that students naturally reason about motion sequences by breaking the complex motion into intervals. Interval-based analysis is more natural to them than continuous function-based analysis. Roschelle, in technological explorations influenced by his cognitive science training, found that computers made "direct manipulation" (Shneiderman, 1982; Smith et al., 1982) of piecewise-defined functions easy to represent; potentially, students could "drag" the shape of a piecewise velocity or position graph to a desired shape and see the consequences as a simulation. The project lead, Kaput, saw the opportunity to create a more learnable curricular sequence by exploring inversions of the normal prerequisites. For example, in the normal sequence, position graphs are taught before velocity graphs, symbolic algebra is taught before integration or differentiation, and continuous functions are taught before piecewise functions. Through the use of directly manipulable piecewise functions, all these normal prerequisites could be eliminated, along with the traditional stumbling block at the onset of a calculus course, the definitions of continuity and limit processes.

At the end of this phase, the team was able to build on this insight (and the related ones in Table 18.1) to develop a fairly complete software tool, called SimCalc MathWorlds, in about a year. Kaput's slogan at the time was "software without new curriculum is not worth the silicon it's written in." Much parallel exploration sought to identify curricular structures that could build off these newly recognized learner strengths, representational capabilities, and curricular starting points. The SimCalc team carried out these explorations in locally available classrooms with Kaput and other project staff teaching the courses, as the team did not yet have time to define suitable teacher professional development resources. The researchers gathered much video and field-note data, which provided a compelling demonstration that students were learning. Pretest/post-test data showed strong gains. But a rigorous randomized experimental trial would have been very hard to plan and execute: What conditions would the team try? What would make an appropriate control? Too many variables were still in flux, and the research group was not yet sure of what were the most important ideas of the innovation. Importantly, we had not yet defined a stable innovation package (materials, teacher professional development, curriculum, assessment) that could be tested in a normal classroom setting. Phase 2 was deeply a design experiment deliberately probing new territory.

Phase 3: Designing a Technology-Rich Curriculum (1997–2000)

In a third phase (1997–2000), with a second round of funding, the group began to tackle additional issues of teacher preparation, curriculum integration with core curricular sequences and newly important state and national standards, an assessment framework, and more modular software. The research now began to focus on replicated classroom design experiments, each with defined but varied curriculum and teacher professional development. The group was not seeking to show that one package worked across all settings but to understand the variance in settings and also the range of curricular approaches and teacher training that might work. Consequently, we expanded the team to involve researchers at Rutgers-Newark (New Jersey), Syracuse University (New York State), and San Diego State University (California), and to engage teachers and schools in Boston and the southeastern Massachusetts region. Under the theme of democratization of access to important ideas, the target schools and populations were those where students were least likely to have access to calculus in their academic futures, which in turn meant that students at the (largely urban) sites typically had low or very low SES status. The explicit assumption was that "if we can make it work here, it can be made to work anywhere."

The research team now included teacher educators, master teachers, and more frequent interaction with commercial publishers of similar innovations. We redesigned our software to be more flexible, to run on as wide a hardware base as possible, and to the extent it was technologically possible, to continue to allow low-cost quick prototyping of an ever widening range of uses. In our design experiments, we deliberately included studies with varied technology, including motion detectors, devices that translated graphs into physic motion, and machines that enabled the exploration of chaotic motion. Versions were eventually built for desktop computers, both Mac OS and Windows, as well as handhelds, the Palm OS, and the world's most popular platform for school mathematics, the "TI-83 Plus" graphing calculator. These technological investigations embodied the adaptability of SimCalc's representational features to varied, inexpensive, and readily available platforms, a prerequisite for scale.

One key accomplishment of this phase was independent replication of the value of SimCalc; independent researchers tried it in varied settings and reported their video, field-note, and pretest/post-test data. Importantly, however, these were not "replications" in the traditional sense of replicating an experiment. The core SimCalc curricular insights and technologies were used in each case, but in localized packages of software-based lessons, curricula, teacher professional development, and assessment. The implementation "package" was not yet standardized or replicated. Further, since the content could be addressed at levels from middle school to university calculus, parallel implementations were less important than implementations that explored the wider curricular range of the innovations. In this way, the team was learning about the variability of settings, implementers' preferences, opportunities and constraints, and alternative ways of packaging the materials, in preparation for putting its best foot forward.

Another important accomplishment was detailed analysis and experimentation with how SimCalc materials could connect into, enrich, and render more learnable core content in the standard curriculum. This is a critical issue for scale, as an innovation that is too distant from curricular reality will not be adopted widely. The team defined and elaborated a strategy of both improving learning on important but conceptually difficult topics already in the curriculum and simultaneously adding new opportunities to learn the mathematics of change.

In this phase we worked on the conceptual challenges presented in the latter three rows of Table 18.1. For example, we came to understand that a key aspect of SimCalc across all implementation was how the materials emphasized, problematicized, and worked through the relationships among rate and accumulation representations. From the developmental theory and learner strengths perspective, Walter Stroup joined the team and brought a Piagetian focus to the question of how children come to understand the difference between "how much?" and "how fast?" as the core developmental dilemma SimCalc addresses (Stroup, in press). Technologically, we related this to one of the most cited benefits of technology in the cognitive science literature: the use of multiple representations (Goldenberg, 1995; Kozma et al., 1996). But whereas "multiple representation" is quite a generic term in that literature, for SimCalc it came to emphasize the ability of students to think fluidly with and between both position and velocity graph representations. During this time, we explored many other representations but rejected them as more problematic, less powerful, or too difficult to fit into school mathematics within existing constraints, e.g., phase–space descriptions of motion or related quantities. On the curricular side, the SimCalc group came to understand that a key powerful functionality of SimCalc was "snap to grid"—a technological ability that could be used to limit graphical adjustments of functions to whole number values. This has the curricular benefit of producing a calculus in which computations can be guided geometrically and executed within the arithmetic of whole numbers and simple fractions, instead of algebraically.

Thus, by the end of this phase, the team was increasing its warrant for belief that the underlying concept was strong and adaptable to a wide variety of settings. We had a good understanding of which things among the many that varied across settings were essential to success in all settings, and which of the many ways to align the learner, technological, and curricular possibilities brought the most benefit within existing school constraints (e.g., technological, curricular, and, to a lesser extent, teacher capacity). Such understanding is critical to the issue of what to try to scale up among the many variations of materials that are invented and tried.

Part 2: Research in the Context of Implementation

Toward the end of Phase 3, the concept of "scaling up" was in the air. The internet was beginning its exponential explosion in availability and use. Commercial learning tools specific to mathematics, such as the Geometer's Sketchpad and the TI-83 graphing calculator, were showing market success. Further, researchers and policy-makers in the community funded by the National Science Foundation were beginning to ask questions about how innovative research materials and practices could go to scale.

The SimCalc team had always been driven by a vision of "democratizing access to the mathematics of change and variation"—a vision that implies scale, especially to include disadvantaged populations. Two strategies were developed to move towards scale. One, strongly encouraged by the funders and led by Kaput, was to make SimCalc commercially available—a move towards sustainability of the effort required to keep materials available and up-to-date. The other strategy, led by Roschelle, sought to engage in research relating to scale. Early on, the team recognized it was not ready to directly engage in large-scale research and thus sought and won a planning grant, followed by a Phase I grant and a Phase II grant, all under the Interagency Educational Research Initiative.

Although the RK framework had served well to date, scaling up exposed new design challenges, and a new framework was needed. The team turned to the work of Cohen and Ball (1999), who had formulated a simple, elegant theory of scaling-up classroom innovations (also see Cohen et al., 2003). Their theory called attention to the trade-off between the degree of ambition in an innovation and its degree of elaboration (or careful specification). Innovations that are not ambitious are close to current classroom practice and thus need little specification. Ambitious innovations like SimCalc that deal with deep changes in representational infrastructure, on the other hand, require a great deal of specification. Coupled with the growing need to articulate our innovations to varied audiences, particularly teachers, this work helped us realize that our innovation was not yet sufficiently specified.

Further, the Cohen and Ball (1999) framework is classroom-centric: it emphasizes features of classroom learning in a school environment. In essence, Cohen and Ball call attention to education as an interaction among teachers, students, and resources (i.e., textbooks, software) in an environment (Figure 18.2). Relative to this triangle, Phases 1 and 2 had dwelt mostly on the student-to-resource relationship and had completely bracketed the environment. Phase 3 began to explore the teacher-to-resource relationship through design experiments in preservice and in-service teacher professional development. Elements of the environment such as curricula, assessments, and teacher professional development were beginning to come weakly into focus. Arguably, the environmental features we understood best at the end of Phase 3 were the nature of available technical platforms that could support widespread dissemination and use, and to a slightly lesser extent, the curricular constraints at work across the country, constraints that increased in salience during Phase 3 due to the rapid rise in accountability systems across many states.

We now continue the case study through three somewhat shorter phases, using the Cohen and Ball (1999) framework to organize the details.

Phase 4: Planning for Scale Up (2000–2002)

In a fourth phase, starting in 2000, the SimCalc team began to work intensively on the issue of scale. We began our planning effort with a substantially expanded team, supplemented by expert advisors. The two new additions to the team were an experimental psychologist and an assessment development expert. The experimental psychologist brought discipline to the process of developing a research question and experimental design. The assessment development expert helped us formulate an assessment blueprint. Through discussion with our expanded team, reading the literature, and meeting with our advisors, we became aware of the many dimensions of the scaling-up challenge.

This phase consisted entirely of planning and preparation—no new empirical research was performed. In the course of planning, the team sought to address:

- Broadening our team and grounding in scale-up literature.
- Specifying the innovation.
- Refining our experimental design.
- Choosing an implementation partner.

We discuss each point in turn. A key message of this phase is the huge number of decisions required for a transition from design research to experimental implementation research. It takes a substantial planning effort to work through these decisions.

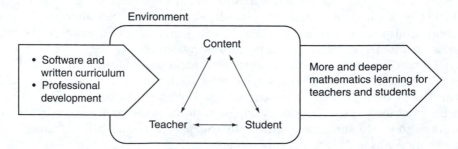

Figure 18.2 Framework for Classroom Learning (adapted from Cohen et al., 2003).

Curriculum

Curriculum is a dominant factor in what teachers teach and what students learn. At scale, we either have the choice of integrating with the variety of textbooks in use or writing one of our own. Textbook authors and publishers, we found, were not interested in working with us to deeply integrate our materials. They perceived their existing constraints as barely manageable and were reluctant to take on new ones, especially ones that involved technology and that might add yet another barrier to adoption. Writing a whole new textbook would be very expensive and time consuming.

Teacher Professional Development

Teachers require significant support to learn to use ambitious materials like SimCalc. The literature suggested that a major trade-off exists between short-term, relatively isolated support for teachers and long-term support that is highly-integrated with school structures and communities. The latter is clearly better, but would introduce major expense and place the measurement of results far into the future.

Systemic Reform

NSF had made a major investment in systemic reform as well as standards-based curriculum development. Many researchers held the belief that it only made sense to test an innovation in the context of systemic reform. However, this would clearly limit the generality of findings since only a small fraction of schools engage in systemic reform and subject our relatively simple experiment to the uncertain results of a larger, more complex experiment.

Standards

Also during this time, decision making at the district and school level was increasingly influenced by national and state standards. SimCalc had not been initially developed to address a specific standard but rather to address a conceptual strand that spanned many years of development, the mathematics of change and variation. We could adapt our innovation more narrowly to particular state standards but potentially move the innovation away from its "sweet spot," or we could connect only weakly to standards but potentially face major problems in recruiting districts and schools.

Assessment

The most reputable assessments are those used for high stakes testing by states, comparisons among states, and comparisons among countries. Yet, assessments tend to be very conservative in the content they cover. We could find very few items on standardized tests that cover SimCalc's topic directly, the mathematics of change and variation. Thus, we could take the risk of using an established test with poor alignment to our innovation or a less established test (that we would have to construct ourselves) that was well aligned.

Grade Level

SimCalc materials had been developed and tested primarily for use in mathematics classes in grades seven to eleven, although they had been used with students as early as the elementary grades and as late as university calculus. Optimally, the creators envisioned the program as longitudinal, with students revisiting and deepening their understanding of an important strand of mathematics across many grade levels. But a multiyear, longitudinal experiment seemed overly risky because we would have to commit to so many details without feedback at the beginning. Furthermore, even one round of testing would exceed the likely available budget. Thus we had to choose a particular grade level.

An experiment consists of many features that are not central to the hypothesis, but nonetheless need to be implemented satisfactorily. A methods professor might call the process of getting these details right the "art of experimentation." In part because of these factors, one wants to aim for simplicity, supplemented with replication and extension of the crucial points. Because of the desire for simplicity, specifying the innovation was harder than it might seem. After six years of research, the team knew a lot about the adaptability of SimCalc to many different student populations, teacher styles, textbooks, state standards, etc. We needed to winnow the innovation down to a core, testable intervention. The team asked itself: "What is the potentially implementable essence of SimCalc, and what is worth subjecting to a rigorous test?"

The "essence" of SimCalc was a serious question because by this time we had software running on the Mac OS, in Java, on graphing calculators, and on the Palm OS, each with different feature subsets. We had many versions of curricular and teacher professional development material covering topics ranging from the idea of rate in middle school to the fundamental theorem of calculus in university calculus. We had a very large collection of assessment items that we had tried over time. If we defined SimCalc overly simplistically, as a particular software version and curriculum materials version, then our results might not generalize to the most important version of software, materials, teacher professional development, and assessment items. In the end, we did not start by specifying the innovation; rather, we addressed all the other points first. With these constraints in place, specifying the details of the innovation became much easier. (The case study will return to the issue of specifying the innovation in Phase 5.)

Our planning came to focus on "what was worth subjecting to a rigorous test?" Three possibilities came to mind:

1   A test parallel to the Force Concept Inventory (Hestenes et al., 1992).
2   A full-year curriculum in eighth grade.
3   A replacement unit strategy in multiple grades.

Our reading of the work of Cohen and Hill (2001) suggested the last alternative—a replacement unit strategy. Professional development centered on replacement units had been somewhat successful at a large scale in mathematics reform in California. We were particularly attracted to the idea that replacement units offered good opportunities for both teacher learning and student learning. Further, SimCalc had developed some materials at each grade level, but not enough materials to cover an entire grade level course. A replacement unit strategy could allow us to test a carefully targeted subset of our materials at each grade level, consistent with SimCalc's multigrade, strand orientation.

Several additional considerations brought us to the conclusion that replacement unit strategy was our best choice. First, while a longer intervention promised more significant benefits than a shorter one, we doubted that we could persuade a wide variety of teachers to try something unknown, which potentially departed significantly from existing standards and which required substantial use of scarce computing resources. Second, a long intervention meant that we would have to put tremendous up-front emphasis on material development. Third, a long intervention would mean more difficult implementation metrics; that is, it would be harder to monitor whether and how teachers complied with the condition. Fourth, a longer implementation would mean that teachers would need more ongoing support, exceeding our likely budget. Our feeling was that if SimCalc was successful under experimental conditions, then we would be positioned later to ask questions about how much support was required for successful long-term adoption.

Within this context, it was finally possible to pose a specific research question. We had already shown positive pretest/post-test results for students in many different settings. Most of these settings were economically disadvantaged, but one was quite affluent. As we considered how to pursue the question of student learning across settings, we began to focus on teachers. In most of the prior work, we worked with "convenience samples" of teachers—teachers who were, if not enthusiastic, certainly interested in our approaches, located near a major research institution, and supported throughout the year by researchers or their staff (who were, on occasion, more experienced SimCalc teachers). As the Cohen and Ball triangle highlighted (Figure 18.2), a focus on student-to-materials interactions was only one leg of the classroom learning process. We knew the materials to be ambitious and at more risk of failure than materials closer to existing teaching practice. We thus identified an important uncertainty about "what could scale up" relating to teacher-level variables. A critique we often heard also influenced our increasing emphasis on teachers, a critique we paraphrase as: "Sure it works with your boutique teachers, but it won't work with the teachers in my school." We concluded it would be an important step towards scale to show that SimCalc could work with a wide variety of teachers.

The focus on teachers necessitated further refinement of our expectations. Although our major hypothesis was to predict a main effect for SimCalc compared to no SimCalc across a wide variety of teachers, we had to ask whether we expected all teachers truly to benefit. Two factors conditioned our expectations: one was the belief that students with the "strongest" teachers and sites would be able to make the best use of the intervention; the other was the belief that students with the "weakest" teachers and sites would benefit the most from the clarity of the interface and the depth of the student experience. "Strong" here means high SES, well-prepared students, low percentage LEP students, teacher with experience and a positive attitude, a functional school, and so forth. "Weak," at the extreme, means the opposite on all criteria.

Three alternative models deriving from these factors were that: (a) the strong gain more, (b) the weak gain more, and (c) that the very strong and the very weak gain more than the middle. Our democratization prediction, and our hope, was that students of all kinds of teachers would gain with SimCalc, but that students of weak teachers would narrow the performance gap.

Following from the selection of a replacement unit strategy and a wide variety of teachers, it became clear that we would need to build our own assessment. Nonetheless, to increase validity, the team vowed to use items from validated tests to the greatest extent possible. An assessment blueprint was developed that specified how we would seek to measure outcomes. It also became clear that we would have to explore a relatively limited teacher professional development strategy rather than the longer-term strategy most often recommended; it would not make sense to scale up a three-week replacement unit that required three years of teacher professional development. We decided we would need an implementation partner with existing outreach to a wide variety of teachers and a track record of success with shorter-term professional development.

At this point, we discovered that the Dana Center at the University of Texas, Austin, was leading mathematics teacher professional development (TPD) for the state of Texas. Teachers and administrators appeared to trust the Dana Center and Dana Center personnel had long histories of teaching mathematics and working with mathematics teachers. In the 2000–2001 school year, 21,000 mathematics teachers attended professional development workshops designed by the Dana Center. Further, the lead of the Dana Center had a long-standing interest in the strand of mathematics leading to Advanced Placement Calculus and had performed much work to align Texas standards across grades to support the goal of democratizing access to AP Calculus. Thus, it would be easier to align SimCalc to Texas standards than in some other states. The data from this census are made public. We met with Dana Center leadership, and they became interested in joining forces for a scale-up research project. The only downside was that they wanted us to focus first in seventh grade because an eighth-grade intervention was too close to the highly charged eighth-grade state test. We perceived seventh as less promising than eighth grade for showing SimCalc's impact, but we agreed to start with seventh grade and expand longitudinally to eighth.

Thus, after nearly two years of planning, we came to a set of compromises and decisions that enabled us to plan our first scaling-up research project. Our deliberations had resulted in a lower risk plan with regard to curriculum (a replacement unit), grade levels (only slightly longitudinal), alignment to standards, and a research question (focusing on an important mediating variable, the teacher), but a high risk plan elsewhere. Providing only short-term, relatively bounded teacher professional development, developing our own assessment, targeting seventh grade and not attempting systemic change all seemed to lower the odds of finding a systematic effect in a controlled experiment. With these decisions in place, the team set out to test them and our organization via a pilot experiment.

Phase 5: Preparation and Pilot of an Experiment (2002–2004)

Preparing and piloting an experiment was a complex process requiring another two years. In this process, we had to return to the problem of specifying the innovation and solve it. Further, the details of the experimental design required definition; a particularly thorny problem was defining the control group. Next, the team had to identify and/or create measures for all variables of interest. As will become clear, we needed to either find or create instruments to measure each aspect of the Cohen and Ball (1999) framework. Last, but hardly least, we had to recruit teachers to participate in our pilot. We discuss each aspect of the process below.

Given the decisions of Phase 4, the team knew it needed a replacement unit for seventh grade with accompanying teacher professional development. The selection of the specific topic was made by examining Texas state standards. Rate and proportionality were highlighted in the standards: "Within a well-balanced mathematics curriculum, the primary focal points at Grade 7 are using proportional relationships. . . . Students use algebraic thinking to describe how a change in one quantity in a relationship results in a change in the other; and they connect verbal, numeric, graphic, and symbolic representations of relationships." We should point out that the curricular choice, constrained as it was by state standards, methodological needs, and time and resource limits, left out a large amount of previously developed and tested content and technological capacity. We avoided velocity functions, velocity-position connections, and their generalization across other, non-motion quantity-types, algebraic notations, and, indeed, most of the mathematics of change.

A middle-school math curriculum designer with extensive experience in teacher professional development, Jennifer Knudsen, joined the team. She reviewed existing SimCalc materials, whose coverage of the target topics was not in the form of a self-contained unit, did not contain the needed teacher-support material, and lacked the requisite production quality. Hence, Knudsen wrote a new workbook and Kaput's team adjusted the software to match. The materials were designed to be explicit about both the teachers' and students' tasks. The materials were also designed to be easy to comprehend in a short amount of time, using text sparingly for example. We note that while we were still *designing* in this phase, there was no design research. Rather, the team trusted in the accumulated wisdom from past phases of research to guide the specification of the innovation.

Equally important to specifying the innovation in an experiment is specifying the control condition. Choosing an inappropriate control could render the experiment meaningless. Thus the distinction between a "what works?" question and a "what could scale up?" question becomes critical. The former tends to lead to control conditions that provide an existing benchmark for student gains against which the treatment could be shown to lead to stronger gains. The latter, however, may not have an existing, established benchmark for student gains, as reflected in the word "could."

The SimCalc project was interested in showing that students could learn more complex and conceptually difficult mathematics than is typically measured. Moreover, we had narrowed down this extra learning to a particular context: a replacement unit on rate and proportionality. The question of "what could scale up?" had turned into the demonstration that a suitable effect size could be obtained in the presence of significant, randomly distributed, context variation. The control condition would serve to guarantee that the observed effect was due to intervention, and not due to, for example, merely taking the same test again three weeks later.

A consequence of this decision was that there would be many "what works?" questions that remained unanswered by the design. For example, the design would not show that technology works better than no technology, because we did not insist that teachers in the control use no technology. We also could not assert on the basis of this experiment that SimCalc is the "best" approach to teaching seventh-grade rate and proportionality or that we have the best approach to teacher professional development for using technology in seventh-grade mathematics.

The best control for this interpretation of our study, then, might have appeared to be providing no intervention for teachers in the control group, and just measuring any student gains across two administrations of the same test. However, in designing an experiment, one has to consider the Hawthorne effect: the idea that just knowing one is in an experimental condition produces beneficial results. Thus, we had to create a control condition in which the control teachers would similarly feel that they were engaged in meaningful professional development. We could then argue, using standard experimental logic, that any differences between the control and experimental groups were due to our intervention.

Happily, the Dana Center had developed a highly regarded workshop for middle-school teachers on teaching rate and proportionality. The force of the workshop was to encourage the teachers to take a $y = kx$, or rate-based, approach to proportionality. This approach was complementary to our own. To ensure that we were treating the groups equitably, we therefore decided to teach this workshop to both experimental and control teachers. The nature of our control condition was also influenced by the idea that, just as in medicine, few people want to be in the control condition. Therefore, we decided to give the experiment a "delayed treatment" structure in which we promised to give all teachers the SimCalc treatment condition in the second year. Thus, all participating teachers eventually receive all the benefits of participating in the experiment, with the delayed teachers waiting a year for the SimCalc materials.

With this design in hand, the team's next step was to identify existing measures wherever possible and design new measures only where necessary. We sought measures for each aspect of the Cohen and Ball (1999) framework (Figure 18.2). First, consider the vertices of the triangle. We decided to measure student gains (our major outcome variable) using a paper-and-pencil test. We likewise decided to measure teachers' growth in content understanding, a secondary outcome variable and possible predictor of student learning. The quality of the materials was "measured" by vetting them with experts from the SimCalc team, teaching experts from within Texas, and an experienced editor of mathematics textbooks.

Next, considering the three sides of the framework (Figure 18.2), we decided to observe student interaction with the materials by collecting the complete workbooks at the end of the unit. We observed teachers' interaction with the materials by collecting a daily log in which teachers were asked to record what they did with the materials each day. We captured teachers' interactions with students using an observation protocol based on Schorr's protocol (Schorr et al., 2003) and through video-tape analysis (Schorr was an advisor to the project). Each of these three connecting lines represents a potentially significant mediating variable in implementations (i.e., inappropriate teacher–student interaction could explain a failure to produce student gains). Finally, we sought to measure many elements of variation in the environment. Given our hypothesis, we first wanted to measure how teachers varied—in their background, their attitudes, and their school setting. We collected background data using an application form, the existing Teaching, Learning and Computing Survey (Becker & Anderson, 1998) and school-setting information from Texas Education Authority data sets, and our own more specific attitude scale.

Each of these measures required a significant effort to select or develop. A discussion of the process for developing some of the intermediate and outcome measures appears elsewhere (Shechtman et al., 2005). Finally, with a well-specified intervention, an experimental design, and measures all in place, the final step was to recruit participants and run a pilot of the experimental design. The results of our pilot phase have been reported elsewhere (Roschelle et al., 2005); the important point for the present context is that the findings were both positive enough and raised enough interesting questions to warrant a scale-up study.

Before closing this phase of the case presentation, we call attention to the issue of building trust within a multi-institutional team. Executing research on scaling up requires a large, cohesive team. It would be too easy to see the story of Phase 5 only in terms of a rational research design process. It was also a story of identifying and working through tensions and conflicts. Although it is somewhat of an oversimplification to present it this way, each of the three partner institutions brought a different main interest to the study. The University of Massachusetts had the strongest interest in the integrity of its innovation. The Dana Center had the strongest interest in serving Texas teachers. The SRI International team (including Tatar at Virginia Tech) had the strongest interest in clean research methodology. These interests were often in tension and sometimes in conflict. For example, to obtain sufficient power required treating teachers as individuals across varying school contexts, but best practices of professional development would work with teachers in teams, and SimCalc had most often worked with teachers in schools undergoing systemic reform. Project members also met with Texas regional education leaders and further developed mutual understandings regarding the nature of districts across Texas and the kinds of constraints and practices in place across the various groups of districts. A very important component of working through a pilot experiment together is building the relationships needed to form a cohesive team.

Phase 6: First Scale-Up Experiment (2005–2008)

Phase 6 is carrying out SimCalc's first scale-up experiment, starting 12 years after the first research began. The design for the scale-up experiment involves 120–140 seventh-grade teachers and 70–80 eighth-grade teachers. At this scale, any mistake is extremely costly. Consequently, the agility of the Phase 1 and Phase 2 design processes, in which anything could be tried quickly and cheaply, was replaced by very careful, deliberate, slow processes. In Phase 6, SimCalc added two advisory boards to check each step of the process. The first advisory board is reviewing each significant feature of the experimental design. The second advisory board is reviewing the mathematical content.

There are relatively few changes from Phase 5 to Phase 6, except in recruitment. Whereas the pilot drew teachers randomly from across the state, the full experiment will recruit teachers through Educational Services Centers (ESCs) in particular regions. By concentrating in a few regions, we maintain significant diversity but avoid skimming only the best teachers from across the state.

With regard to experimental design, a statistician joined the team. Hierarchical linear modeling will be employed more systematically through the design, sampling, and analysis processes. In addition to the experimental contrasts, an education researcher whose area of study is focused on teachers joined the team and will conduct case studies embedded within the main experiment to examine questions that are not immediately amenable to experimental treatment.

In the course of the editorial process for this chapter, the first results from the experiment have become available (Roschelle et al., 2007). The statistically significant results show that the SimCalc approach was effective in a wide variety of seventh-grade Texas classrooms, that teachers successfully used these materials with a modest investment in training, and that student learning gains were robust across variations in gender, poverty, ethnicity and prior achievement. More in-depth reporting of these results, as well as results from the second year of the seventh- and eighth-grade studies will be available in forthcoming publications.

What We Are *Not* Doing in this First Experiment

We call this the "first scale-up experiment for SimCalc" because there is so much left to do. This experiment is occurring in one state at a few grade levels. It does not consider longitudinal impacts on students. It does not consider the implications of extending dynamic representation technology across the curriculum, for example to data analysis and geometry. It tests only a small subset of SimCalc's curricular scope. It does not consider the relationship between this innovation and systemic reform. It does not consider how gains or losses on proportionality topics interact with gains or losses in other seventh-grade topics. It does not test the usefulness of technology compared to no technology but similar curricular materials. It does not test how much teacher professional development is required for the benefits to accrue. It does not test whether teachers who resist participation are still able to work with the innovation because participation is voluntary.

We term this the "first scale-up experiment" for another reason, as well. This one experiment cannot determine whether the core innovation—building on students' cognitive strengths using dynamic representation integrated with a restructured curriculum—is "what works" or is a failure. It could be that the experiment will fail, but for reasons of not scaling up correctly rather than the weaknesses of the underlying innovation. For example, a replacement unit strategy may be an incompatible way to scale up the SimCalc approach. On the other hand, if we get results, as in all experimentation, replication and extension will be required for confirmation. After all, perhaps our teacher professional development or materials themselves will not scale up. Furthermore, while we have approached what we consider the most tractable, practical, and meaningful questions in this experiment, it may turn out that publishers and policy-makers want other kinds of questions answered before adopting this innovation. Indeed, SimCalc cannot scale significantly without publishers willing to produce and/or integrate SimCalc curriculum.

Finally, the technology and the larger educational environment (political and economic dimensions, especially) continue to evolve so that optimizing to current conditions is not likely to serve the longer run without corresponding updates to account for the continuing evolution. For example, wireless classroom networks linking students' handhelds and a teacher's workstation have become a major technological factor in ongoing SimCalc work, but they are not part of the current experiment because neither the technologies nor the curricula are sufficiently mature to support the level of precision sought in the current experiment.

Case Summary

Many trends can be observed in this case study. First, it is long, covering more than ten years and five different funded "projects." Within this long timeline, the overall drive to scale can been seen in the case study in many dimensions. We note a gradual expansion of the research focus from students' interactions with novel presentations of content to include teachers' interactions with materials and teachers' interactions with students. Over time, more factors in the environment come into focus and under control or measurement: curricular integration, teacher professional development, assessment, state standards, regional teacher service centers, etc. Further, the number of students expands by orders of magnitude, from small numbers of students, to small numbers of teachers, to schools to statewide regions. In parallel, an effort was made to constantly reduce costs and increase access to the technological prerequisites. The team expanded over the years to include more disciplines, eventually including people with over ten different kinds of disciplinary expertise and high-profile advisory boards.

In concert with these changes over time, the intellectual agenda and methods evolved. Work in Phase 1 had no empirical methodology; the basics of the design relied on historical, curricular, and literature analyses. Phase 2 used primarily micro-analysis of a small number of students. Phase 3 involved design experiments, with pretest/post-test measures. Phase 4 was a planning phase and not particularly methodological. Phases 5 and 6 focused on an experimental design but include embedded case study analyses. At each phase, there are still a huge number of design questions to resolve, more than can be resolved using only "gold standard" methods. Research on scaling-up innovation is a complex enterprise.

A particularly important and difficult transition occurred during Phase 4, when the team finally had to confront the question: "What is the essence of SimCalc and what is worth subjecting to a rigorous test?" We suspect this transition was difficult because of the lack of overlap between design researchers and experimental implementation researchers. Thus although copious effort in the first three phases of SimCalc had addressed questions of scale, too little effort had been devoted to the eventual demands of scale-up research. In retrospect, we would have put more effort earlier into firming up measures and instruments and better documenting potential recruitment difficulties.

We also wish to emphasize that carrying an innovation through this level of growth and transition requires leadership and vision. The project mission never varied from "democratizing access to the mathematics of change and variation" (although the specifics of how the vision was addressed did change: although "rate" was an early focus, "proportionality" per se was not). Throughout, the team sought to re-affirm that it was addressing important mathematics, both in terms of present assessments and in terms of future needs. It also consistently sought evidence that the technology works in traditionally underserved settings. Finally, the role of technology and the basic form of the SimCalc representational system and the commitment to integrate technology with textual curriculum have remained unchanged since 1995.

Generality and Limits of the Case

We suspect that the long time and multiproject nature of scaling-up educational innovation is typical. Indeed it is common to think of five–seven year school adoption cycles, and some educational reforms take multiple decades to implement (Schoenfeld, 2002). Similar innovations, like the Geometer's Sketchpad, also took a long time to reach scale, even with a more direct route from research to commercialization (Scher, 2000). Perhaps the most successful educational technology product, the graphing calculator, took about seven years to transition from initial product to large-scale use—not counting the development of the research base on which it rests (Ferrio, 2004). Long timelines, requiring spanning multiple two-to-four year project cycles, are more likely to be the rule than the exception. We note that without the earlier, less structured exploration, the later concern with scaling would have nothing to bring to scale!

We expect that the two frameworks we used to describe the case are quite general. Cohen and Ball's (1999) framework is fairly simple and has a straightforward ring of truth to it. Our own restructuring knowing framework is purposely specific to the style of technical innovation we were pursuing, but we would include in this class the many software products that emphasize the computer as a tool for making visual, manipulable representations available in the mathematics classroom.

In addition, many elements of the case fit a third framework. Rogers (2003) has organized and summarized a multidisciplinary body of work on the diffusion of innovations. One can view this case as a series of moves to increase the potential rate of adoption of SimCalc. Rogers argues that five factors influence the rate of adoption:

1   SimCalc has always been strong in *observability*. After a short demonstration of the software, most teachers express the feeling that their students could learn more easily with the graphic and animated representations that SimCalc provides.

2   But SimCalc has been weak in *compatibility* Indeed, SimCalc's early aim was a strand of the curriculum, the mathematics of change and variation, which is not currently important to the average mathematics educator. Starting in Phase 3 and continuing through Phase 5, the team worked hard to connect SimCalc more closely with the mathematics topics, standards, and curriculum considered important by most mathematics educators.

3   Further, SimCalc has been somewhat difficult for teachers in terms of *complexity*, requiring the extensive use of technology that is often unfamiliar to them. Some of this complexity is irreducible—the technology is essential—so efforts focused on

making the curricular materials and training workshops as clear and simple as possible.

4   A related effort, especially in Phases 4 and 5, was to increase the *trialability* of SimCalc by defining a trial-use unit of implementation. We found that a replacement unit with a very clear scope and place in the standard curriculum made it easier to recruit teachers to try the software for our studies.

5   Finally, one can read the trajectory of the case study as a continuous effort to develop research-based messages that strongly communicate the *relative advantage* of SimCalc.

In Part 1, we communicated the relative advantage through case studies and the restructuring knowing framework. The team was able to show ordinary students learning more complex mathematics and was able to articulate the potential advantage of using new representational capabilities to draw upon learners' strengths and re-organize the curricular content to be more learnable. In Part 2, the team wished to make causal claims about SimCalc's relative advantage and to support generalization: hence the methodological shift to controlled experiments and more carefully defined outcome measures. An additional resonance with the Rogers' framework is the alliance of *change agents* and *opinion leaders* we formed for the work in Part 2. Our alliance coupled Kaput, an external change agent who has sought to influence the use of innovations in local schools with Hopkins and the Texas Educational Service Centers who have been opinion leaders in the adoption of innovations in mathematics education in Texas. Finally, from Phase 2 onwards, SimCalc has been designed to be highly adaptable by users to specific settings, a capability Rogers terms *re-invention*. Re-invention increases adoption by allowing users to make an innovation fit their local needs. In Phases 4 and 5, we "re-invented" SimCalc to fit the needs of the seventh-grade curriculum in Texas (while still drawing upon the essential innovation). Without being conscious of this framework, it appears that the SimCalc team made a series of moves that fit well-documented patterns in the diffusion of innovation.

Despite the apparent applicability of these frameworks to related innovations, it would be a mistake to overgeneralize from this case; the field needs to consider cases of scaling-up innovation beyond our own before reaching firm conclusions. Although it is likely that many scale-up projects will require increasingly multidisciplinary teams, projects that start with experimental psychologists might take different paths than projects that start with a mathematician. Further, the funding climate and research policy is always changing. Most likely, if this effort had started today instead of 12 years ago, the team would have taken a shorter path to estimating effect sizes, for instance. Finally, because we did not have the luxury of outside observers, this case study was written by core members of the team. An objective observer might have produced a different account.

Discussion of Research Questions and Warrants

The case of SimCalc makes it clear that multiple kinds of research questions are asked in a scaling-up project over time and that multiple methods are employed to answer them. Yet, this case potentially has a stronger message than merely that multiple methods are acceptable as long as they match the questions asked. Indeed, the major impact of this case may be to clarify what kinds of questions *are asked* in an innovation project. These are not just "what is happening?" or "is a systematic effect present?" Nor are the questions asked just "what could work?" or theory-development questions. We suggest that the many specific research questions boil down to three categories, described below. In covering each category, we discuss the form of warrants that might be appropriate in supporting answers.

Question 1: Is the Candidate Innovation Well-Specified?

Researchers studying scale up of an ambitious innovation must ask: "Is the candidate innovation well specified?" This question is important because, as Cohen and Ball (1999) argue, ambitious innovations must be well specified if they are to be implemented with any degree of fidelity. Further, a strong answer to this question increases *trialability* and reduces the *complexity* factors in Rogers (2003) framework, thus contributing to a higher potential rate of adoption. As a project progresses to scale, different levels of warrant provide reasonable assurance. Initially, SimCalc benefited by showing its materials to panels of experts. Their reaction was sufficient evidence that the prototype curricular materials were not ready. The panel-of-experts approach to obtaining a scientific warrant continues through our use of advisory boards to review our experimental design and expert panels to examine the construct validity of our assessment. Another level of warrant is obtained by design experiments: if a few, hand-picked teachers cannot implement an innovation, there is no chance that many teachers will implement it at scale. Replication of design experiments in multiple sites with multiple investigators (as occurred in Phase 3) strengthens the case that the innovation is reasonably well specified. The strongest warrant we pursued to date was in the pilot study (Phase 5): a wide range of teachers were given materials and a measured amount of professional development and then asked to implement a SimCalc replacement unit in the context of an experimental design. Their ability to do so, as measured by daily teaching logs, interviews, their own improvement in mathematics content knowledge, and the differential gains of their students (versus a control group) on an assessment yields compelling evidence that the innovation is well-specified. Hence, we suggest that a range of methods are scientifically warranted for addressing this question.

Question 2: Is the Candidate Innovation Adaptable to a Wide Variety of Circumstances?

Researchers studying an innovation must ask: "Is the candidate innovation adaptable to a wide variety of circumstances?" Adaptability is important because, given the variety in American schools, some degree of curricular adaptation almost always occurs (Porter, 2002). Further, an innovation is more likely to reach scale if it fits a variety of both circumstances and curricular scope than if it is a "point solution" (fitting only a small topic in restricted settings). Rogers (2003) uses the similar concept of "re-invention" to highlight the need for adaptability.

In the case study we presented, empirical evidence for adaptability came primarily from design experiments. The team tried using SimCalc software at many grade levels, with many different student populations, and in many different school settings. In most cases, pretest/post-test measures were used to ascertain that the design resulted in students making the expected learning gains. Pretest/post-test design can provide a fairly strong warrant in some cases, particularly when researchers seek to justify that the design provided students with an "opportunity to learn" content that very few students at their grade level have the opportunity to learn. For example, students in eighth grade rarely learn to relate velocity graphs to position graphs (an aspect of the fundamental theorem of calculus). Further, base rates for success at this task are established for AP

Calculus and the concept is known to be hard for university students—after all, its initial development required the best minds of western civilization. Thus pretest/post-test results provide a pretty convincing warrant when they show that students in the eighth grade make substantial gains on this kind of task. A control group would allow a stronger warrant, but it would be extraordinarily expensive to explore the full range of adaptation of a tool like SimCalc or the Geometer's Sketchpad through formal, ran-domized control experimentation. We expect the norm to be that investigators justify adaptability through case studies and will choose one, fairly constrained use of the innovation to rigorously establish cause–effect relationships.

Question 3: How Do the Effects of the Innovation Vary Within a Variable Environment?

Researchers must ask: "How do the effects of the innovation vary within a variable environment?" This type of question is important because scale implies lack of control over the environment, which varies significantly from teacher to teacher, school to school, district to district, and state to state. In Rogers' (2003) framework, research-based claims about effects can produce strong messages about the *relative advantage* of an innovation. Further, because our specific question involved variable teachers and settings, research also examines the *compatibility* of the innovation with variations in setting. In our case, a question of this type (i.e., how do student gains vary with a wide variety of teachers?) will be addressed using a randomized, controlled design and analy-sis via hierarchical linear modeling. This research method produces a strong warrant by allowing the research to establish a cause–effect relationship between the treatment and the outcomes and to model the contribution of various mediating environmental vari-ables (in our case, teacher and teaching-context variation) on the outcomes. We do not see viable alternative methods to answer this sort of research question.

Diagramming the Tensions

The tensions among these three questions, along with the need for a long-term innov-ation program to have a vision, can be represented in a spider diagram (Figure 18.3). In this sort of diagram, progress over time is visualized as increasing area. Increases in area occur as the research grows strong along multiple vectors. We place a far-reaching vision and a model of how effects vary with the environment at opposite poles, because a more ambitious vision makes measurement more difficult. Measurement is more dif-ficult because current tests are less likely to probe desired outcomes, and because it is harder to get a large population to agree to test an innovation that has a long-term focus. Similarly, adaptability and specification are in tension; it is difficult for an innovation to be both adaptable and tightly specified.

The spider diagram shows that SimCalc began with a strong vision, but little by way of specification, adaptability, or documented effects—for good reason: the innov-ations needed to be designed in the first place. Five years into the project, the team was emphasizing adaptability, with a smaller degree of effort directed at documenting effects and refining the specification. The last two phases of the case study suggest a contraction in adaptability (the scope of the project narrowed to replacement units in two grade levels) but dramatic expansion of efforts to address the degree to which the innovation was well specified and to model how effects varied with the environment. In general, one might expect efforts that emphasize the vision and adaptability dimensions to use warrants from historical and curricular analyses, literature reviews, and design

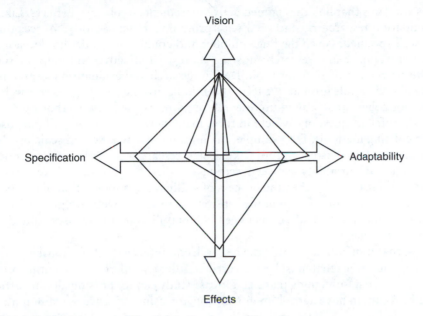

Figure 18.3 Spider Diagram of SimCalc's Coverage of Four Concerns.

experiments, whereas efforts that emphasize a well-specified innovation and modeling effects would use warrants from advisory boards and statistical analyses of controlled experiments. Some scaling-up innovation efforts, like SimCalc, might start high on innovative vision. Others might begin with great strength in specification and demonstrating experimental effects but with little evidence regarding adaptability to varying school contexts. On the path to scaling up an innovation, we conjecture that researchers must expand the area along all four vectors so that a variety of means for obtaining a scientific warrant for claims will be required.

Conclusions

In the present political climate, innovations in mathematics and science education are both strongly needed (to address national goals) and suspect (because of a history of repeated failures to scale up innovations and a conservative mindset towards educational innovation). Increasingly, stakeholders in our educational system look to research to overcome this tension by identifying innovations that work at scale. Research can only live up to this task with additional attention to methodology, and in particular, attention to the question: What should count as a scientific warrant that evidence supports a claim? Currently, debate among educational researchers and research policy-makers has begun to shore up answers for two kinds of research: small-scale innovation and large-scale evaluation research.

By using the case of SimCalc, we have argued for the need to define and defend warrants for a third kind of research: research concerned with getting a serious, foundational innovation to scale. The case suggests that research concerned with getting to scale is different. Design research has the goal of finding out "what could work?" by developing theories of how children or teachers learn, how school-based communities can be productively supported, and so on. Initial evidence that an innovation could work is very valuable to scaling up. The kind of theory development particularly needed in scaling-up research is a theory of the active ingredients in an innovation, a theory that provides warrants that link the claimed active ingredients to observed effects. Likewise, most evaluation research is concerned with programs, practices, or resources that are already well specified. Given the huge number and complexity of design decisions that face an innovation team, research must be more cost-effective and agile to support formative refinement of an innovation. Design research and evaluation research need a well-articulated middle ground. We term this middle ground "scaling-up research."

We do not believe that scaling-up research requires its own new methods per se, but it does ask different questions which, in turn, make new demands on and purposefully integrate existing methods. For example, the question of "what could scale up?" combines elements of an existence proof (like design research) with elements of modeling how randomized variability between settings mediates effect sizes (like large-scale experimental research). Further, the process of scaling up an innovation places particularly strong demands on managing the tensions both (a) between program vision and what can be measured, and (b) between adaptability to many uses and detailed specification for one use.

We hope that future dialog within the research community firmly establishes warrants for the many questions that must be answered in order to undertake a scientific program of scale-up research, something that a single case study cannot possibly do. In particular, it would be useful to have agreed-upon warrants for using evidence to claim that:

- An innovation, when fully realized, could result in large-scale benefits to the public.
- An innovation is sufficiently well-specified to be tested at scale.
- An innovation is adaptable to and attractive for a sufficiently wide range of uses to be worthy of scaling up.
- The experimental model for scaling up the innovation and measuring the results is valid.

We suspect that these warrants will need to relate claims to evidence gathered via a mix of design, expert panel, and experimental methods.

Acknowledgments

This material is based upon work supported by the National Science Foundation, most specifically under Grant No. 0228515. Any opinions, findings, conclusions, or recommendations expressed in this material are those of the authors and do not necessarily reflect the views of the Foundation.

References

Becker, H. J. & Anderson, R. E. (1998). *Teacher's survey: Combined version 1–4.* Center for Research on Information Technology and Organizations, University of California, Irvine.

Blumenfeld, P., Fishman, B., Krajcik, J. & Marx, R. W. (2000). Creating useable innovations in systemic reform: Scaling up technology-embedded project-based science in urban schools. *Educational Psychologist, 35,* 149–164.

Bransford, J., Brophy, S. & Williams, S. (2000). When computer technologies meet the learning sciences: Issues and opportunities. *Journal of Applied Developmental Psychology, 21,* 59–84.

Clarke, R. (1983). Reconsidering research on learning from media. *Review of Educational Research, 53,* 445–459.

Cobb, P., Confrey, J., diSessa, A., Lehrer, R. & Schauble, L. (2002). Design experiments in educational research. *Educational Researcher, 32*(1), 9–13.

Cobern, C. E. (2002). Rethinking scale: Moving beyond numbers to deep and lasting change. *Educational Researcher, 32*(6), 3–12.

Cohen, D. K. & Ball, D. L. (1999). *Instruction, capacity, and improvement* (No. CPRE Research Report No. RR-043). Philadelphia, PA: University of Pennsylvania, Consortium for Policy Research in Education.

Cohen, D. K. & Hill, H. (2001). *Learning policy: When state education reform works*. New Haven, CT: Yale University Press.

Cohen, D. K., Raudenbush, S. & Ball, D. L. (2003). Resources, instruction, and research. *Educational Evaluation and Policy Analysis, 25*(2), 1–24.

Cook, T. D. (2000). *Reappraising the arguments against randomized experiments in education: An analysis of the culture of evaluation in American schools of education*, at: http://www.sri.com/policy/designkt/cokfinal.doc.

Cuban, L. (2003). *Oversold and underused: Computers in the classroom*. Cambridge, MA: Harvard University Press.

Design-Based Research Collaborative (2003). Design-based research: An emerging paradigm for educational inquiry. *Educational Researcher, 32*(1), 5–8.

Edelson, D. C. (2002). What we learn when we engage in design. *Journal of the Learning Sciences, 11*, 105–121.

Elmore, R. F. (1996). Getting to scale with good educational practice. *Harvard Educational Review, 66*, 1–26.

Ferrio, T. (2004). What year did the graphing calculator get to scale? (e-mail correspondence).

Fullan, M. (2000). The return of large scale reform. *Journal of Educational Change, 1*, 5–27.

Goldenberg, P. (1995). Multiple representations: A vehicle for understanding understandings. In D. N. Perkins, J. L. Schwartz, M. M. West & M. S. Wiske (eds), *Software goes to school* (pp. 155–171). New York: Oxford University Press.

Hestenes, D., Wells, M. & Swackhamer, G. (1992). Force Concept Inventory. *Physics Teacher, 30*, 141–158.

Jackiw, N. (1997). *The Geometer's Sketchpad* (various versions). Berkeley, CA: Key Curriculum Press.

Kaput, J. (1986). Information technology and mathematics: Opening new representational windows. *Journal of Mathematics Behavior, 5*, 187–207.

Kaput, J. (1987a). Representation and mathematics. In C. Janvier (ed.), *Problems of representation in the learning of mathematics* (pp. 19–26). Hillsdale, NJ: Lawrence Erlbaum Associates.

Kaput, J. (1987b). Toward a theory of mathematical symbol use. In C. Janvier (ed.), *Problems of representation in the learning of mathematics* (pp. 159–196). Hillsdale, NJ: Lawrence Erlbaum Associates.

Kaput, J. (1991). Notations and representations as mediators of constructive processes. In E. von Glaserfeld (ed.), *Constructivism and mathematics education* (pp. 53–74). Boston, MA: Reidel.

Kaput, J. (1992). Technology and mathematics education. In D. Grouws (ed.), *A handbook of research on mathematics teaching and learning* (pp. 515–556). New York: Macmillan.

Kaput, J. (1994). Democratizing access to calculus: New routes using old roots. In A. Schoenfeld (ed.), *Mathematical thinking and problem solving* (pp. 77–155). Hillsdale, NJ: Lawrence Erlbaum Associates.

Kaput, J. (1997). Rethinking calculus: learning and thinking. *American Mathematical Monthly, 104*, 731–737.

Kaput, J. & Nemirovsky, R. (1995). Moving to the next level: A mathematics of change theme throughout the K–16 curriculum. *UME Trends, 6*(6), 20–21.

Kaput, J. & Roschelle, J. (1998). The mathematics of change and variation from a millennial perspective: New content, new context. In C. Hoyles, C. Morgan, & G. Woodhouse (eds), *Rethinking the mathematics curriculum*. London: Falmer Press.

Kaput, J., Noss, R. & Hoyles, C. (2002). Developing new notations for a learnable mathematics in the computational era. In L. D. English (ed.), *Handbook of international research on mathematics education* (pp. 51–75). Mahwah, NJ: Lawrence Earlbaum Associates.

Kozma, R. B., Russell, J., Jones, T., Marx, N. & Davis, J. (1996). The use of multiple, linked representations to facilitate science understanding. In S. Vosniadou, E. De Corte, R. Glaser & H. Mandl (eds), *International perspectives on the design of technology-supported learning environments* (pp. 41–60). Mahwah, NJ: Lawrence Erlbaum Associates.

Monk, S. & Nemirovsky, R. (1994). The case of Dan: Student construction of a functional situation through visual attributes. In E. Dubinsky, J. Kaput & A. H. Schoenfeld (eds), *Research in collegiate mathematics education*, Volume 4 (pp. 139–168). Providence, RI: American Mathematics Society.

National Center for Education Statistics (2001). *The nation's report card: Mathematics 2000* (No. NCES 2001–571). Washington, DC: U.S. Department of Education.

National Science Foundation (2004). *Interagency education research initiative (IERI): Program solicitation* (No. NSF 04–553). Washington, DC: National Science Foundation.

Nemirovsky, R. (1996) Mathematical narratives. In N. Bednarz, C. Kieran & L. Lee (eds), *Approaches to algebra: Perspectives for research and teaching* (pp. 197–223). Dordrecht, The Netherlands: Kluwer Academic. United States Congress (2001). No Child Left Behind Act.

Porter, A. C. (2002). Measuring the content of instruction: Uses in research and practice. *Educational Researcher*, *31*(7), 3–14.

President's Committee of Advisors on Science and Technology (1997). *Report to the President on the use of technology to strengthen K–12 education in the United States*. Washington, DC: President's Committee of Advisors on Science and Technology (PCAST).

Rogers, E. M. (2003). *Diffusion of innovations* (5th ed.). New York: Free Press.

Roschelle, J. & Kaput, J. (1996). SimCalc MathWorlds for the mathematics of change. *Communications of the ACM*, *39*(8), 97–99.

Roschelle, J., DeLaura, R. & Kaput, J. (1996). Scriptable applications: Implementing open architectures in learning technology. In P. Carlson & F. Makedon (eds), *Proceedings of Ed-Media 96: World conference on educational multimedia and hypermedia* (pp. 599–604). Charlottesville, VA: American Association of Computers in Education.

Roschelle, J., Kaput, J. & Stroup, W. (2000a). SimCalc: Accelerating student engagement with the mathematics of change. In M. J. Jacobsen & R. B. Kozma (eds), *Learning the sciences of the 21st century: Research, design, and implementing advanced technology learning environments* (pp. 47–75). Hillsdale, NJ: Lawrence Erlbaum Associates.

Roschelle, J., Pea, R., Hoadley, C., Gordin, D. & Means, B. (2000b). Changing how and what children learn in school with computer-based technologies. *The Future of Children*, *10*(2), 76–101.

Roschelle, J., Shechtman, N., Knudsen, J., Tatar, D., Kaput, J. & Hopkins, B. (2005). Scaling up innovative technology-based math with a wide variety of 7th grade teachers. Paper presented at the annual meeting of the National Council of Teachers of Mathematics, Anaheim, CA, April.

Roschelle, J., Tatar, D., Shechtman, N., Hegedus, S., Hopkins, B., Knudsen, J., et al. (2007). *Can a technology enhanced curriculum improve student learning of important mathematics? Scaling up SimCalc project*. Technical Report Series, Report #1. Menlo Park, CA: SRI International.

Scher, D. (2000). Lifting the curtain: The evolution of the Geometer's Sketchpad. *Mathematics Educator*, *10*(2), 42–48.

Schmidt, W. H., McKnight, C. C., Houang, R. T., Wang, H. C., Wiley, D. E., Cogan, L. S., et al. (2001). *Why schools matter: A cross-national comparison of curriculum and learning*. San Francisco, CA: Jossey-Bass.

Schoenfeld, A. H. (2002). Making mathematics work for all children: Issues of standards, testing, and equity. *Educational Researcher*, *21*(1), 13–25.

Schorr, R. Y., Firestone, W. & Monfils, L. A. (2003). State testing and mathematics teaching in New Jersey: The effects of a test without other supports. *Journal for Research in Mathematics Education*, *34*, 373–405.

Shavelson, R. J. & Towne, L. (eds) (2002). *Scientific research in education*. Washington, DC: National Academies Press.

Shechtman, N., Roschelle, J., Haertel, G., Knudsen, J. & Tatar, D. (2005). Measuring student learning gains in conceptual mathematics when scaling a technological intervention for middle school mathematics. Paper presented at the annual meeting of the American Educational Research Association, Montreal, Canada, April.

Shneiderman, B. (1982). The future of interactive systems and the emergence of direct manipulation. *Behaviour and Information Technology, 1*, 237–256.

Smith, D. C., Irby, C., Kimball, R. & Verplank, B. (1982). Designing the Star user interface. *Byte, 7*(4), 242–282.

Smith, J. P., diSessa, A. A. & Roschelle, J. (1993). Misconceptions reconceived: A constructivist analysis of knowledge in transition. *Journal of the Learning Sciences, 3*, 115–163.

Stroup, W. M. (in press). Understanding qualitative calculus: A structural synthesis of learning research. *International Journal of Computers for Mathematical Learning, 7*, 167–215

Torgerson, C. (2001). The need for randomised controlled trials in educational research. *British Journal of Educational Studies, 49*, 316–328.

19 Music Training and Mathematics Achievement
A Multiyear Iterative Project Designed to Enhance Students' Learning

Michael E. Martinez
University of California, Irvine

*Matthew Peterson, Mark Bodner,
Andrew Coulson, Sydni Vuong,
Wenjie Hu, and Tina Earl*
Mind Research Institute

Gordon L. Shaw
Deceased

Introduction

In a seminal study of the Mozart effect, college students who listened to the first ten minutes of Mozart's Sonata for Two Pianos in D Major (K. 448) experienced a short-term enhancement of spatial–temporal (ST) reasoning (Rauscher et al., 1993, 1995). Findings from this study were reported widely in the popular media.

The community of research psychologists took a more critical view of the study and its implications than the general public did. Indeed, among psychologists and educational researchers, the Mozart effect has been highly controversial. A claimed connection between listening to Mozart and becoming smarter as a result seemed scarcely believable, more akin to magic than to a cognitive effect. Moreover, the results of the original study, when replicated, sometimes seemed explainable by factors not originally accounted for, including arousal or musical preference.

Over time, the original claims of the Mozart effect have broadened to de-emphasize short-term improvement of cognitive functioning. At the same time, empirical studies and theoretical developments have lent credibility and coherence to claims about associations between musical experience and certain forms of cognition. This nexus takes the form of neuronal circuitry common to: (a) listening to music and playing a musical instrument, (b) mathematical cognition, and (c) spatial–temporal reasoning. In relation to this nexus, Schellenberg (2004) showed significant increases in measured intelligence quotient with music instruction. These associations, sometimes called the Generalized Mozart Effect (Shaw, 2000), are detectable on multiple measures: behavioral and neurophysiological data, functional magnetic resonance imaging (Bodner et al., 2001), treatment of epilepsy patients (Hughes et al., 1998, 1999), electroencephalogram (Sarnthein et al., 1997), animal models (Rauscher et al., 1998), music training studies (Graziano et al., 1999; Rauscher et al., 1997; Schellenberg,

2004), computational/theoretical models (Bodner & Shaw, 2001; Leng & Shaw, 1991), and meta-analyses (Hetland, 2000).

During the past six years, a research and development team at the MIND Institute in Costa Mesa, California, has tested the possibility that a combination of musical and spatial–temporal training can promote mathematics learning among elementary school students. The pedagogical approach was conceptualized to be distinct from standard ways of teaching mathematics. Typically, mathematics instruction relies heavily on symbolic notation in the form of numerals, operations, and equations. Often, and more fundamentally, these formalisms express patterns that can be represented as images or transformations of images. Whereas the formalisms of symbolic mathematics are ultimately conventions, the underlying patterns of mathematics are expressions of the natural or experienced world. In our research program, the ability to make sense of patterns is assumed to be an inherent human capacity. The human brain has an innate ability to find and manipulate patterns. This pattern-finding capacity, experienced largely as subjective imagery, is a natural, near-universal propensity of the human mind and its underlying neural circuitry. Self-reports of many eminent scientists clarify that their most creative notions often arise from ideas experienced as visual mental images. Hawking, Feynman, Einstein, and other luminaries have reported that their intellectual breakthroughs were experienced at least sometimes as dynamic mental images. Only later are these intuitions reduced to the precise language of equations.

In the research reported here, certain experiences with music are believed to evoke activation of brain circuitry common also to spatial–temporal reasoning. Huttenlocher (2002: 161) noted that "spatial tasks and music are both represented in the same general cortical region, the non-dominant parietal cortex posterior to the postcentral gyrus." Huttenlocher raised the possibility that brain activity associated with one task (e.g., music interpretation) might "prime" the performance of another cognitive task whose associated brain activity is anatomically proximal (e.g., spatial–temporal reasoning). Data from brain imaging documents reveal correspondences between the two. For more than a decade now, numerous brain-imaging studies have evidenced robust anatomical correspondences between brain areas activated by certain musical forms and by tasks that require spatial–temporal reasoning. Listening to the Mozart sonata mentioned earlier (K. 448), for example, has been demonstrated in imaging studies to activate a brain network that includes:

- The dorsolateral prefrontal cortex (Brodmann areas 9 and 46).
- Specific areas of the occipital lobe (Brodmann areas 17, 18, and 19) whose activation has been implicated in visual representation.
- The cerebellum, implicated in the manipulation of visual representations (e.g., rotation).

These same areas become activated when subjects engage in spatial–temporal tasks, such as the Stanford-Binet paper-folding task (Muftuler et al., 2004). Specific areas activated such as the dorsolateral prefrontal cortex are known to be important in coordinating complex tasks in working memory (Bodner et al., 1996; Fuster et al., 2000). These areas were not always activated when listeners experienced other musical compositions, such as Beethoven's *Für Elise*. Intersubject variability greatly complicates the task of identifying specific cognitive functions to particular brain circuits. The brain activation patterns described here were notable for their cross-subject consistency.

The fact of common neural circuitry supporting spatial–temporal cognition and the experience of particular musical forms led to the conjecture that music could enhance spatial–temporal cognition. There was empirical support for this priming function. In one study, preschool children who received piano keyboard training for six months made substantial gains on a spatial–temporal reasoning task (ST; Rauscher et al., 1997). Contrasting control groups did not improve significantly on the ST task. If music could enhance ST cognition, a second conjecture was that the same music also might enhance mathematics learning—if mathematics were taught and learned in a spatial–temporal mode. Specifically, the experience of some musical forms could prime brain circuitry that would support learning mathematical patterns depicted as the transformation of images.

This chapter traces the MIND Institute's project, called M + M (Math+Music), during the academic years 1998 through 2005. Our intent is, first, to describe the intervention and its effects. A second goal is to show how the M + M project evolved through feedback over the course of its implementation. Recursive cycles of development, intervention, and redesign of the intervention illustrate one example of the research genre called design experiments. Design experiments have been defined as "extended (iterative), interventionist (innovative and design-based), and theory-oriented enterprises whose 'theories' do real work in practical educational contexts" (Cobb et al., 2003: 13; also see Cobb & Gravemeijer, in this volume). In turn, real-life educational contexts are settings for experimental tests of the intervention. In path-breaking work on the design experiment methodology, Brown (1992: 141) attempted to "engineer innovative educational environments and simultaneously conduct studies of those innovations." The M + M project satisfies these criteria in that the intervention proceeds from and informs a general theoretical model. Like all design experiments, it is highly contextualized in real-world settings (mostly, classrooms), is implemented over several years, and is iterative in using feedback from one intervention, "draft n," to inform the design of draft "$n + 1$." During the course of this project, many aspects of it evolved simultaneously. These included the intervention proper, but also the nature and range of feedback, the length of the feedback cycle, and the underlying local and general theories motivating and guiding the project.

Our general conclusion is that elementary school students trained in the piano keyboard and spatial–temporal reasoning outperformed significantly control group students on standardized measures of mathematical achievement. These data support hypotheses about cognitive and neurological associations between music and spatial–temporal reasoning and affirm their combined ability to enhance learning mathematics. Our own experiences also illuminate how the efforts of a group of researchers, over several years of sustained effort, can produce revisions and refinements to a guiding theory and can result in progressively more effective experiences for learners.

Method

Students

M + M has been tested on students from kindergarten through grade four, but, in this chapter, we focus mainly on second-graders. M + M was developed originally for second-grade students, and the project staff has the most complete data from them. Most participating second-graders were primarily from low socioeconomic backgrounds. We further concentrate on data from schools in which some second-graders did not participate in the M + M program. Both participating and control classes exhibited a range of academic achievement and did not differ systematically in their demographic composition.

Instructional Components

Keyboard Training

The music component of M + M was designed to teach students some basic musical concepts and skills necessary for playing the piano keyboard. One reason for selecting the piano keyboard for teaching musical skills is that a keyboard allows the user to see the entire instrument while performing—all the keys are in plain view and correlated spatially to the musical staff. The keyboard also avoids the need for excessively technical manual dexterity as is required for many string instruments. It is possible for a beginning keyboard player to sound clear notes and simple melodies almost from the start of instruction.

Normally, students received two lessons per week in keyboard instruction. A typical, 45-minute lesson consisted of an initial segment of activities such as clapping note values, reading musical notation, learning about composers, and listening to the first movement of the Mozart Sonata (K. 448). During keyboard practice, children sometimes worked independently and at other times in groups to learn a repertoire of progressively more difficult pieces. By the end of the second grade, participating children had developed skill in a variety of musical activities. These included the manipulation of note values as small as sixteenths, knowledge of basic musical symbols, and recognition of the basic sonata form in listening examples. All students mastered approximately 15 pieces that employed parallel and contrary motion between the hands, as well as textures involving right-hand melody with left-hand accompaniment.

STAR Software

A second component of M + M is training in mathematical concepts through spatial–temporal reasoning. This training was accomplished by a series of computer-based experiences using software named STAR (spatial–temporal animated reasoning; MIND Institute, 2003). STAR software was designed to develop skill in transforming mental images and so, presumably, to enhance spatial–temporal abilities generally. The transformations involve symmetry operations applied to two-dimensional figures: folding and unfolding around multiple axes in the x–y plane of the computer screen, rotations around the z axis perpendicular to the screen, 180-degree flips around the x and y axes, and translations in the x–y plane.

Other activities challenge children to apply their spatial–temporal skills to solve mathematics problems in particular problems involving fractions, proportions, and symmetries. These are the kinds of mathematical operations that are difficult to teach using the language-analytic approach, which relies heavily on words and symbols. They are more amenable to visual image representations.

The STAR software presents a series of games for each mathematics topic. Each game computes a current score to indicate a student's progress. Students are required to display mastery of a level before progressing to a more difficult level in a game. The software tracked all the actions taken by the learner as well as the scores attained.

Mathematics Achievement

We report Stanford 9 and California Achievement Test 6 mathematics scores as indicators of general mathematics achievement. We also report program effects by results on the California Standards Test, a criterion-reference test that indexes students' success in mastering prescribed content standards. These tests were used as standardized instruments of accountability in the state of California's public schools. In addition to these broad measures of mathematics achievement, the project staff sometimes used their own tests designed to measure specific aspects of mathematics learning.

Results

In this section, findings are reported year by year, starting with pilot work in 1997. We note the findings for each year and the effect of those findings on the subsequent redesign of our intervention.

Preliminary Work: 1997–1998

Starting in 1997, preliminary work involved two studies, a pilot study and a main study (Graziano et al., 1999). In the pilot study, second-grade students engaged in computer-based exercises designed to enhance their ST skill. The experimental design involved three groups: Group One ($n = 19$) engaged the ST computer game exercises, Group Two ($n = 20$) used a computer game that taught English language skills; and Group Three ($n = 62$) received no extra instruction. Group comparisons showed that Group One students scored significantly higher in ST mathematics reasoning in contrast with both Groups Two and Three.

The main study, also involving second-graders, tested the effects of piano keyboard training paired with the ST computer games on spatial–temporal reasoning. The main experimental group (Piano-ST, $n = 26$) was contrasted with a second group (English-ST, $n = 29$), who received computer-based instruction in English language skills. A third group (No Lesson, $n = 28$) received no additional instruction. On a computer-administered post-test of such mathematical concepts as fractions and proportionality, the Piano-ST group showed significantly higher outcomes ($p < 0.05$) than the other two comparison groups.

1998–1999

In the first year of implementation, the M + M intervention was tested in a single, urban, elementary school. The centerpiece of the intervention was a version of the computer game software used in pilot work to enhance ST reasoning. Students who engaged in the computer exercises improved their performance on the Stanford 9 mathematics subtest. On the Stanford 9 test, M + M second-graders' ($n = 18$) average performance was at the 65th national percentile. A comparison group of second-graders ($n = 36$) averaged at the 36th percentile.

1999–2000

Starting in the fall of 1999, the project expanded from one elementary school to four. One lesson learned from earlier versions of M + M is that a desirable design feature of the software—concentrating on visual, image-based representations—probably was taken too far. To be clear, the studied attempt to avoid mathematical notation and language completely was a miscalculation. The project staff realized that children needed to use both verbal and mathematical/symbolic language to express their mathematical ideas. In response, the project introduced a new, teacher-led component. This new element, called "math integration," bridged students' experience of the computer game software (and their resulting ST learning) to standard, language-analytic expressions of mathematics, including numerals and symbolic notation for operations.

To some degree, the addition of a "math integration" component was a concession to the known requirements of tests—that assessment of mathematical achievement inevitably requires a student to use conventional symbols and language. Although students demonstrated mathematical competence in the symmetry and proportionality operations required by the software games, they were less competent at translating their ST representations into the symbolic notation and forms required on standardized tests.

Other insights were gained during this year. Not all of these insights can be tied to strictly controlled research designs and to reliable measurement of valid learning constructs. For example, the research team became aware that the transfer of training was a problem. As psychologists and educators have learned and relearned through the decades, beginning with E. L. Thorndike (1924), it is very easy to overestimate the applicability of learned skills to new problem contexts. Many skills that students ostensibly performed competently did not transfer to other tasks that required essentially the same skill set. Rather, students needed much more direct assistance to accomplish this transfer. The response was to train students more directly to transfer their newly acquired concepts and skills to new tasks. Particularly beguiling was students' use of mathematical language. The use of the right words suggested that students understood the relevant concept, but this often was not the case. Frequently, a lack of understanding was revealed by students' difficulty in crossing between language-analytic representations and spatial–temporal problems. It was not uncommon for a student to show competence in one modality but be unable to translate that competence to another expressive form.

Another rather basic lesson that had to be learned and relearned was that *showing* students was not enough to ensure understanding. It was necessary to ask them to *do* something. A compelling visual illustration showing that a triangle's area was exactly half of its extension to a parallelogram did not translate directly to the formula for computing the area of a triangle: half the base multiplied by the height. Such are the simple lessons, or rather fundamental assumptions, of constructivism. Yet, through hard experience, design experiment research can bring us back to foundational ideas.

2000–2001

In the third year of implementation, three elementary schools had both participating and nonparticipating students. The summative comparisons of participating and control students showed an advantage for the M + M experience. Students in the M + M intervention had a higher mean score on the Stanford 9 Mathematics Test ($M = 55$, $SD = 11.2$, $N = 102$) than nonparticipating, control-group students ($M = 40.2$, $SD = 17.8$, $N = 77$). In each of the schools, M + M students outperformed control-group students on the Stanford 9 Mathematics Test ($p < 00.2$) but not to a degree that was statistically significant by the most common criteria. In this year also, the project staff appreciated more deeply the connections between language and measures of assessment. The language integration portion of the M + M program continued to be important.

M + M made regular attempts to send information to teachers about the progress of individual students. The form of this feedback shifted over time in accord with changing technologies, project team expertise, and experience with what was effective. During this project year, class- and student-level feedback was sent to teachers by conventional mail. Many teachers did not have e-mail at this time, so the low-technology option was chosen even with its obvious disadvantage of the time lag.

2001–2002

During this academic year, M + M spread to seven schools that had both participating and nonparticipating students. A contrast of treatment and control groups on the Stanford 9 Mathematics Test showed a significant advantage of M + M students ($M = 63.7$, $SD = 21$, $N = 514$) over control-group students ($M = 48.8$, $SD = 21$, $N = 285$). This difference was statistically significant ($p < 0.0001$). The size of the overall effect of the intervention was impressive—approximately 0.75.

On another metric of the program's effectiveness, the number of children who scored in the top quartile in national performance was about 40 or 50 percent. This percentage was remarkable given that the project schools were largely poor, minority-serving institutions whose baseline performance on standardized tests was unremarkable to poor. During this time also, longitudinal tracking of students showed a cumulative effect through multiple years' exposure to M + M. Some teachers became more comfortable and skilled with the approach because they had many years of experience.

During this year, M + M activity sequences were altered, again to conform more satisfactorily to students' experience in schools. The initial ordering had a cognitive justification: exercises in ST reasoning were administered first to give students a basis for learning mathematics in this modality; instruction in mathematics concepts proper followed. A second change was that the order of the games was rearranged to conform to typical teaching sequences. These changes were wrought partly because of teachers' feedback. In classroom lessons, teachers wanted to be able to make connections to what students were learning in the M + M games. Moreover, during this time, there was some sifting of the games; new ones were introduced and others were pulled.

2002–2003

By September 2002, M + M had spread to 16 schools that had both participating ($N = 4,173$) and nonparticipating ($N = 1,546$) students. The improvement of the math integration component was a major change to M + M. Structurally, math integration was being incorporated into the software, rather than being conveyed through a weekly lesson by a teacher. An advantage was greater assurance that each student was getting practice with math integration concepts—in particular, linking the ST representation with more standard, language-analytic approaches. The desire was not to circumvent the teacher, but there was a clear realization that students' exposure to the classroom math integration lessons was spotty. Some teachers and schools were dependable in providing this crucial component, but others did not do so or taught math integration only irregularly.

In California, the state's accountability test shifted to the CAT 6. Again, the M + M participants exhibited higher overall mathematics learning. On the CAT 6, M + M students had considerably higher average scores ($M = 54.5$, $SD = 7.2$, $N = 1,680$) in comparison to nonparticipating students ($M = 30.0$, $SD = 10.8$, $N = 382$). This difference was statistically significant, $p < 0.001$. Considering only classes that completed 40 percent more of the M + M program, the CAT 6 Mathematics mean was higher still ($M = 59.2$, $SD = 6.9$, $N = 1,009$). Below that threshold, the achievement distributions were identical to nonparticipating students. Translating this latter advantage into standard deviation equivalents, the overall impact of the program on standardized test scores was approximately two sigma, historically considered the maximum effect achievable by an educational intervention (Bloom, 1984). Similar results favoring the M + M group were found at the third- and fourth-grade levels (MIND Institute, 2004).

During this year, the California Standards Test became much more significant in the state's accountability. The number of students who tested at a proficient or higher level was significantly greater for M + M students than for nonparticipants. Differences among groups were more pronounced when participating students were separated into those who completed less than 50 percent of the treatment and those who completed more than 50 percent. Those students who completed less than 50 percent were regarded by the research team as not truly experiencing the intervention. Among full participants in grades two, three, and four, those who completed at least 50 percent of the activities, about 60 percent of the students were ranked as being "advanced" or "proficient" (ibid.). Among nonparticipating classes and those students completing less than 50 percent of the activities, only about 40 percent of the students were either "advanced" or "proficient." Also, at the second-, third-, and fourth-grade levels, the number of students at "far below basic" was almost nonexistent among participants (ibid.). In other words, among M + M students, the entire distribution—the mean and both tails—shifted to higher levels. Intraschool comparisons, which contrast similar students more clearly, also show substantial achievement differences favoring students who engaged in at least 50 percent of M + M activities at grades two, three, and four (ibid.).

2003–2004

During the 2003–2004 academic year, M + M was implemented in approximately 40 elementary schools. A shrinking percentage of project schools, only nine, had both participating and nonparticipating students. By this time in the project, most schools wanted to implement M + M gradewide. Presumably, this shift reflected, in part, a greater confidence that M + M offered benefits to all students and that the approach was workable for most teachers. During this year also, more concepts were covered to reach a progressively wider swath of the accepted mathematics curriculum. The project team understood, especially as state-level accountability systems were rising to full implementation, that the M + M curriculum needed to span the expected state content to be relevant and acceptable.

In March through May of 2004, individual student's records were analyzed to seek patterns of learning progress. Data-mining techniques showed that these learning curves clustered into four distinct types. Three of the generic learning curves showed students reaching an impasse at particular points (Hu et al., 2004). Eventually, a culprit was identified. It became apparent that features of the software intended to elicit and maintain students' interest were having the opposite effect. Some of the software animation, sound effects, background texturing, and extra "fun" activities were undermining students' focus on the intended content and skills. Rather than co-opting students' interests to ST learning, the design elements proved to be a distraction. For example, one game incorporated a walkway used by the main character, Jiji. Second by second, the walkway shrank, such that, eventually, Jiji could not make it across. Interestingly, a histogram showing the frequencies of the students' game scores revealed an impasse at 130 points (see Figure 19.1) that corresponded to the shrinking walkway feature. Many students could not proceed beyond this rather incidental software feature. Such features were reduced or eliminated.

Feedback to teachers at this point was provided by e-mail and over the web. The

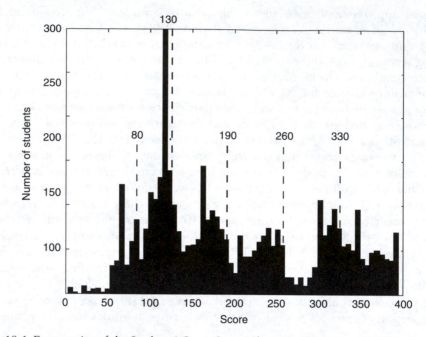

Figure 19.1 Frequencies of the Students' Game Scores Showing an Impasse at 130 Points.

curriculum also expanded to include more grade levels. During this year, the fourth-grade curriculum was introduced, and work began on kindergarten to grade-one software. School staff—teachers and principals—conveyed the distinct desire to have even younger primary students begin their experience with ST concepts. For example, they wanted entering second-graders to be proficient in working with proportions.

2004–2005

Preliminary data indicate a performance advantage on mathematics achievement for M + M students. A separation was made subsequently in recognizing high participants ($Y > 50$) as those who completed at least 50 percent of the prescribed M + M curriculum for a given grade level. Low participants complete less than 50 percent. A third group of nonparticipants (NP) did not experience M + M. On the California Standards Test of mathematics, a higher percentage of high participants was judged "proficient" or "advanced" than was the case among nonparticipants. This pattern held at the three grade levels examined: second grade ($Y > 50$: 54%; NP: 41%), third grade ($Y > 50$: 63%; NP: 40%), and fourth grade ($Y > 50$: 44%; NP: 30%).

In approximately January 2005, the project staff realized that there was an unworkable time lag between the feedback cycles from the results of the standardized tests to the redesign of the software. Results from standardized testing associated with accountability testing were reportable approximately one year after students were assessed. That meant that a full two years were needed from the time of program redesign and implementation to the reporting of results from standardized tests. If changes were made in response to assessment results, these, too, required time. Yet another year of implementation was followed by a one-year lag as schools waited for test results. Piecing these phases together, the total design/implementation/outcome cycle extended over three years. Of course, these phases were not followed in strict serial fashion;

curriculum redesign was ongoing, as was field testing. Still, the true feedback cycle for any particular design plus implementation stretched over several years. The lag on the feedback cycle impeded the redesign and development of the software.

At this point, and partly in response to these suboptimal development models, the MIND Institute initiated a different development process. Named after the penguin mascot of the Institute, a subdivision called Jiji Labs began to develop new modules on such topics as place value, decimals, and elapsed time. Unit-based pre- and post-tests were modeled after questions on standardized tests. Staff members tested the modules rapidly through a succession of pretests, focused games, and post-tests. This allowed field testing to be completed within weeks. The development cycle was compressed thereby from three years to about one month. For example, in teaching place value to first-graders, students engage initially in the spatial–temporal problems alone. Pre- and post-tests showed no gains on the standard, language-analytic understanding of place value. A short additional experience with the language and notation of place value resulted in significant gains on a second comparable post-test (see Figures 19.2 and 19.3).

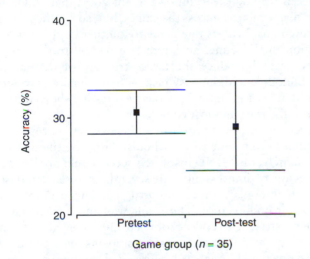

Figure 19.2 Accuracy in Pre- and Post-Tests of the Place Value Spatial Games.

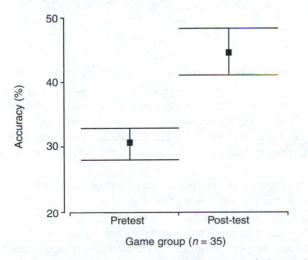

Figure 19.3 Accuracy in Pre- and Post-Tests of Place Value Language Integration.

During the previous year, the research team noted that students performed differently when taking quizzes online rather than on paper. Children treated computer-based tests like computer games, sometimes making arbitrary choices or skipping sections. The electronic versions of quizzes were not taken seriously, as if the ephemeral quality of electrons made them trivial in comparison to pencil lead. In response, during this year the project used paper-based tests.

Other changes were made in the design of games. Besides instituting a more rapid development/feedback cycle, the games were redesigned for greater consistency of format. Previously, each game had its own rules. This meant that teachers had to teach rules for each new mathematical topic. To do this, they often had to refer to a manual to acquaint themselves with the rules of the game so that they could provide explanations to the children. This requirement added considerably to the time and effort overhead needed of participating teachers. The research team was not at all confident that every teacher introduced the rules of each game; probably some did, but others did not.

The redesign of the games this year was based on a common and very simple goal—to get Jiji the penguin across the screen from left to right. We might guess that children would become bored quickly with this regularity across the games, but, so far, they seem to enjoy this consistency. The known goal bridges one game to another easily. Rather than relying on external instruction in the game, an interactive demonstration or a tutorial was built into each module to introduce the basic structure of the game. Another change was to begin each module with an easy task—often trivially easy—to ensure that students were successful at least initially. Previous field testing showed that some students experienced failure at the start and lost confidence.

During this year, feedback to teachers was sent entirely over the internet. Since 2000, the scale of implementation expanded from four to 60 schools. Also, the number of games implemented increased. Ultimately, the MIND Institute's server could not handle the volume of data and the necessity of interfacing with several, remote, database applications. Data gathered from the schools were often corrupted. This prompted a switch to an industry-standard server architecture. The result was an efficient data-gathering process, ending a long-term struggle to collect complete and timely data from the participating schools. Now, even with 13,000 participating students, data could be collected. In turn, classroom-level data could be analyzed, aggregated, summarized, and plotted—and then returned to teachers in real time by a web portal to guide their instruction planning decisions.

2005–2006

Starting in the fall of 2005, the curriculum expanded to include 98 percent of the mathematical standards. Consequently, the M + M curriculum comprised a larger percentage of the content assessed on standardized tests. In other ways, too, the software intervention was substantially revised. Improvements to some specific games have been substantial. In addition, language integration has expanded to include more than half of the software. Feedback systems, from the schools and back to the schools, are now being made in real time.

Another program change was a response to feedback from teachers. Many teachers wanted quizzes to be incorporated into the software. These quizzes were constructed and incorporated into M + M. One problem with this system was that the quizzes did not provide reliable information about the students' learning. Some students treated quizzes in a fashion similar to the less important games. They felt free to experiment, skip screens, and even try making errors intentionally to see what would happen. In other words, the mindset that functioned well in the regular M + M activities did not transfer effectively to the online quizzes. These were eliminated during the 2005–2006 school year.

Discussion

M + M Effects

Our data show that the M + M intervention produced substantial gains in mathematics achievement among participating second-grade students in comparison to control group students. During the school years for which we have robust data, M + M students displayed a mathematics achievement advantage of at least 14 percentile points over control students. That advantage grew each year even as the intervention spread to larger numbers of sites. The effects were manifest on standardized measures of broad mathematics achievement, the Stanford 9 and the CAT 6. Advantages were evident also in the achievement of proficiency on the California Mathematics Standards tests.

Our data affirm that a spatial–temporal approach to learning mathematical concepts, allied with music instruction, can produce gains in proficiency with mathematics concepts and skills among children. Music instruction can be allied profitably with spatial–temporal mathematics instruction to produce increases in broad mathematics learning. Even so, it is hard to parcel the effects of the program on mathematics achievement precisely. Much of the benefit of M + M appears not to be attributable directly to the music component. Instead, most of the boost in mathematics learning is attributable to the spatial–temporal approach of teaching mathematics concepts. We estimate that about 80 percent of the M + M effect is associated with our adoption of a spatial–temporal approach, and the remaining 20 percent can be linked to the music component. Admittedly, these are rough estimates and are somewhat speculative. Relatedly, we do not have a definitive answer yet to the question: Would there be an enhancement to mathematics achievement based on music instruction alone?

The cumulative findings of this multiyear research project imply that a large segment of students, perhaps most, could benefit from an approach to learning mathematics that appropriates ST reasoning along with music training. The use of ST reasoning and representations might hold special promise with English language learners because of its relative de-emphasis of language—specifically, mathematical terms expressed in English.

The Design Experiment Approach

The research project presented here illustrates how an educational model can co-evolve with an educational product. This is the core logic of a design experiment: New stages in the evolution of an educational intervention are shaped by data from previous stages. Still, there are aspects of our experience that are not always considered in the literature on design experiments. Our experience with M + M permits us to make the following observations on this multiyear iterative project:

- Precise and reliable measurement using formal instruments functioned largely to tell interested parties that the basic intervention was effective. Achievement tests assured teachers, school administrators, parents, sponsors, and the research team that our program was working and, therefore, worthwhile. Their function was significantly motivational, and partly political, in that good results from tests sustained the will to continue. Traditional instrumentation was less important in informing decisions about alterations to the design of the intervention.

- Alterations in the design of the M + M intervention were informed sometimes by more detailed examination of performance on home-grown instruments (which led, for example, to a realization that students also needed a language integration component) and by tracking students' progress through the software (on which data-mining techniques led eventually to the identification of impasses in learning curves).

- Data that informed design decisions were often informal, contextual, and personal. Teachers frequently had specific ideas about which functions worked well and which needed alteration. This told us that even when reliable instrumentation is included in the design of an experiment, it can be other, more ideographic, and detailed sources of information that have practical influence on decisions about the design of the program. We suspect that this pattern is typical of other multiyear iterative projects. Whether it is inevitable or not is unclear.

- In the course of this project's evolution, there was a drift away from controlled research designs with more-or-less clear demarcations between treatment and control groups. This drift coincided with the expansion of the project to larger numbers of participating schools and with a growing confidence that the intervention was essentially effective. Motivational and political functions served by data from standardized tests became less important. As before, design improvements were often motivated by other, less formal, information sources. Inevitably, this weakened inferences from the data to generalizable conclusions, but it did not slow down the development cycle or dampen the effectiveness or expansion of the program. These changes might be natural or typical concomitants of scaling up.

In aggregate, the M + M project demonstrates the viability of the design experiment approach to educational interventions for advancing students' learning and the theories on which effective interventions are based. In our experience, though, the program drifted from the rigorous design ideals of pure experiments. Reliable standardized instrumentation became less important over time. This is partly because more formal designs and instruments functioned initially to convince researchers, teachers, parents, and others that the M + M program was worthwhile. More specific design decisions were informed instead by detailed analysis of homegrown (and less reliable) instrumentation, data from performance on the computer-based games, and feedback from teachers. All things considered, the logic of the design experiment, with some variation, proved to be vital to the ongoing improvement of the design, scope, and effectiveness of the project.

Acknowledgments

The authors thank Jill S. Hansen for contributions to the early stages of this research program.

References

Bloom, B. S. (1984). The 2 sigma problem: The search for methods of group instruction as effective as one-on-one tutoring. *Educational Researcher*, 13(6), 4–16.

Bodner, M. & Shaw, G. L. (2001). Symmetry operations in the brain: Music and reasoning. In Y. Saint-Aubin & L. Vinet (eds), *Algebraic methods in physics* (pp. 17–35). New York: Springer.

Bodner, M., Kroger, J. & Fuster, J. M. (1996). Auditory memory cells in dorsolateral prefrontal cortex. *Neuroreport, 7*, 1905–1908.

Bodner, M., Muftuler, L., Nalcioglu, O. & Shaw, G. L. (2001). FMRI study relevant to the Mozart effect: Areas involved in spatial–temporal reasoning. *Neurological Research, 23*, 683–690.

Brown, A. L. (1992). Design experiments: Theoretical and methodological challenges in creating complex interventions in classroom settings. *Journal of the Learning Sciences, 2*, 141–178.

Cobb, P., Confrey, J., diSessa, A., Lehrer, R. & Schauble, L. (2003). Design experiments in educational research. *Educational Researcher, 32*(1), 9–13.

Fuster, J. M., Bodner, M. & Kroger, J. (2000). Cross-modal and cross-temporal association in neurons of frontal cortex. *Nature, 405*, 347–351.

Graziano, A. B., Peterson, M. & Shaw, G. L. (1999). Enhanced learning of proportional math through music training and spatial–temporal training. *Neurological Research, 21*, 139–152.

Hetland, L. (2000). Listening to music enhances spatial–temporal reasoning: Evidence for the "Mozart Effect." *Journal of Aesthetic Education, 34*, 105–148.

Hu, W., Bodner, M., Jones, E. G., Peterson, M. R. & Shaw, G. L. (2004). Dynamics of innate spatial–temporal learning process: Data driven education results identify universal barriers to learning. Paper presented at the International Conference on Complex Systems. Boston, MA, May.

Hughes, J. R., Daaboul, Y., Fino, J. J. & Shaw, G. L., (1998). The "Mozart Effect" in epileptiform activity. *Clinical Electroencephalography, 29*, 109–119.

Hughes, J. R., Fino, J. J. & Melyn, M. A. (1999). Is there a chronic change of the "Mozart Effect" on epileptiform activity? A case study. *Clinical Electroencephalography, 30*, 44–45.

Huttenlocher, P. R. (2002). *Neural plasticity: The effects of environment on the development of the cerebral cortex.* Cambridge, MA: Harvard University Press.

Leng, X. & Shaw, G. L. (1991). Toward a neural theory of higher brain function using music as a window. *Concepts in Neuroscience, 2*, 229–258.

MIND Institute (2003) *STAR software* [Computer software]. University of California, Irvine.

MIND Institute (2004). *STAR treatment effect on mathematics performance levels of 2nd, 3rd, and 4th grade students measured using the California Advanced Test Form 6 and the California Standards Test, 2002/3.* Unpublished research bulletin available at: http://www.mindinstitute.net

Muftuler, T., Bodner, M., Shaw, G. L. & Nalcioglu, O. (2004). fMRI study to investigate spatial correlates of music listening and spatial–temporal reasoning [Abstract]. *Proceedings of the 12th annual meeting of the International Society of Magnetic Resonance in Medicine*, Kyoto, Japan, May.

Rauscher, F. H., Robinson, K. D. & Jens, J. J. (1998). Improved maze learning through early music exposure in rats. *Neurological Research, 20*, 427–432.

Rauscher, F. H., Shaw, G. L. & Ky, K. N. (1993). Music and spatial task performance. *Nature, 365*, 611.

Rauscher, F. H., Shaw, G. L. & Ky, K. N. (1995). Listening to Mozart enhances spatial–temporal reasoning: Towards a neurophysiological basis. *Neuroscience Letters, 185*, 44–47.

Rauscher, F. H., Shaw, G. L., Levine, L. J., Wright, E. L., Dennis, W. R. & Newcomb, R. L. (1997). Music training causes long-term enhancement of preschool children's reasoning. *Neurological Research, 19*, 2–8.

Sarnthein, J., von Stein, A., Rappelsberger, P., Petsche, H., Rauscher, F. H. & Shaw, G. L. (1997). Persistent patterns of brain activity: An EEG coherence study of the positive effect of music on spatial–temporal reasoning. *Neurological Research, 19*, 107–116.

Schellenberg, E. G. (2004). Music lessons enhance IQ. *Psychological Science, 15*, 511–514.

Shaw, G. L. (2000). *Keeping Mozart in mind.* San Diego, CA: Academic Press.

Thorndike, E. L. (1924). Mental discipline in high school studies. *Journal of Educational Psychology, 15*, 1–22.

20 Design Experiments and Curriculum Research

Douglas H. Clements
University at Buffalo, State University of New York

Introduction

Building curriculum is a complex problem of creative engineering. At first blush, design experiments could appear to be the most appropriate strategy for connecting curriculum development to research. In this chapter, I argue that design experiments should play an important role, but also that a complete research program requires the inclusion of additional, complementary, research methods.

Curriculum development is not always connected to research, with unfortunate consequences for students and for the field (Battista & Clements, 2000; Clements & Battista, 2000). Ideally, curriculum development is a design science (Brown, 1992; Simon, H. A., 1969; Wittmann, 1995) with the goals of engineering a learning process and developing local instructional theories (Cobb et al., 2003). As a science, knowledge created during curriculum development should be generated and published within a scientific community. Because scientific advances are achieved ultimately by the self-regulating norms of a scientific community over time, the goal cannot be to develop a single ideal curriculum but, rather, dynamic problem solving, progress, and advancement beyond the present limits of competence (Dewey, 1929; Tyler, 1949). Science cannot tell you what your goals are (Hiebert, 1999); neither can it generate an ideal approach (James, 1958).

On the other hand, another implication is that curricula *should* be based on research, albeit using a complete framework as proposed here. The reason is that, contrary to a popular notion, research is not conducted by objective detached scientists. All research is social/political (Latour, 1987), with researchers attempting to gather support for their perspectives, research issues, methodologies, and interpretations. Particularly when financial gain is involved, such biases affect curriculum development and research; therefore, the checks and balances of science are essential to support progress and full disclosure.

What goals should we hold for a complete program of research on curriculum development? What methods should be used? When should they be used?

Goals and Research Activities for Scientifically-Based Curricula

A complete, scientific, curriculum development program should address two types of questions—about effects and conditions—in three domains: policy, practice, and theory (Clements, 2007). In the domain of policy, we ask whether the curriculum goals are important, what the effects are on teachers, and what the size of the effect is for different populations. Questions of conditions include the support requirements for various topics and variations in the effects and the sizes of the effects for different populations.

In the domain of practice, we need to know if a curriculum is effective in helping children achieve specific learning goals and to identify both its intended and unintended consequences. Conditions under which it is effective must be identified. Theoretical questions include why the curriculum is effective, what theoretical bases were used, to what degree they were explanatory, what cognitive changes occurred, and what processes were responsible. Conditional questions include why certain sets of conditions decrease or increase the curriculum's effectiveness, how specific strategies produce previously unattained results, and why?

To answer these questions, we contend that writers and scientists must conduct four related types of research and development activities. Researchers do the following: (a) draw implications from existing research so that what is known can be applied to the anticipated curriculum, (b) develop curricular components in accordance with models of children's thinking and learning in a domain, (c) conduct formative evaluations of research and refine the curriculum in a series of progressively expanding social contexts, and (d) perform summative evaluations, also in expanding contexts, to provide warranted evidence for claims of effectiveness.

The Role of Design Experiments

Design experiments play a significant role in research and development activities in a scientifically-based curriculum development program, but they are not sufficient in themselves. Design experiments were developed as formative research tools, to test and refine educational designs based on principles derived from previous research (Brown, 1992; Cobb et al., 2003; Design-Based Research Collective, 2003). Thus, they provide a useful set of tools for several phases of a complete research and development program (Clements, 2007). However, their unique focus confines their contribution to only some phases of such a curriculum research program, for at least four reasons. First, design experiments are often limited to pilot-testing (Fishman et al., 2004; NRC Committee, 2004: 75). Second, they tend to place less emphasis on the development of a curriculum itself and more on the development of local theories (or more abstract principles). Third, they do not address adequately the full range of questions or methods of the proposed framework (but see Bannan-Ritland, 2003). Fourth, they can be swept awash by too much data and too many interacting variables and possibilities, with too little theoretically-determined constraints. Fortunately, design experiments and other established methods, such as research reviews, teaching experiments, and formative and summative curriculum evaluation, complement each other. A comprehensive framework integrating all these methods is described in the following section.

A Curriculum Research Framework

The Curriculum Research Framework (CRF) consists of ten phases of the development research process that warrant claiming that a curriculum is based on research (this section summarizes and thus draws heavily upon the full description of the CRF in Clements, 2007). These ten phases are classified into four categories reflecting the types of questions asked to meet the previously described goals. The following sections describe the CRF's cyclic phases.

A Priori Foundations

Activities in the first category establish the a priori foundations for the curriculum. A main activity is generating, or applying, extant, scientific research reviews to curriculum questions. These help to achieve the policy goal of establishing the importance of the curriculum's educational objectives, the practice goal of credible documentation of the a priori research indicating the efficacy of the approach, and the theory goal of determining why the curriculum is effective and the validity of its theoretical bases. This category contains three interrelated phases. These phases could be, but are not always, used in design research projects.

Subject Matter A Priori Foundation

Establishing educational goals involves multiple considerations that include, but also go beyond, science. Socially determined values and goals are important determinants of any curriculum (Hiebert, 1999; Schwandt, 2002; Tyler, 1949). Thus, determining goals requires a dialectical process among all the legitimate, direct, and indirect interested parties (van Oers, 2003). This is consistent with the approaches of the reconceptualists and the poststructuralists (Pinar et al., 1995; Walker, 2003). In contrast to their position, I acknowledge that scientific approaches have limitations, but maintain that they make critical contributions, even in determining curricular goals. This research phase contributes to the process by identifying the subject-matter content that is valid within the discipline and makes a substantive contribution to the mathematical development of students in the target population (cf. Tyler, 1949). In other words, concepts and procedures of the domain that are being considered for inclusion in the curriculum should play a central role in the subject-matter domain itself (Tyler, 1949). They should build from the students' past and current experiences (Dewey, 1902/1976). Finally, they should be generative in students' development of future understanding (for an explication and examples, see Clements et al., 2004). In mathematics, documents from the National Council of Teachers of Mathematics (NCTM; 2000, 2006) were created by a dialectical process among many legitimate interested parties, and thus serve as a valuable starting point, as are comparisons to other successful curricula and reviews of research. These research-oriented strategies constitute parts of comprehensive content analyses (cf. NRC Committee, 2004).

Other types of inquiry may be needed to complement scientific research, from perspectives such as historical (Darling-Hammond & Snyder, 1992), literary criticism (Papert, 1987), narrative (Bruner, 1986), aesthetic (Eisner, 1998), phenomenological (Pinar et al., 1995), or humanistic (Schwandt, 2002). Of course, no single scientific finding or set of findings should dictate pedagogy:

> No conclusion of scientific research can be converted into an immediate rule of educational art. For there is no educational practice whatever which is not highly complex; that is to say, which does not contain many other conditions and factors than are included in the scientific finding. Nevertheless, scientific findings are of practical utility, and the situation is wrongly interpreted when it is used to disparage the value of science in the art of education. What it militates against is the transformation of scientific findings into rules of action.
>
> (Dewey, 1929: 19)

One final note applies to this and all the other phases. Ideally, one member of the research team is responsible for taking a perspective of "standing outside," observing and documenting the curriculum development and research team's activities, decisions, and the reasons for their decisions (a "triarchic" design, see Lesh & Kelly, 2000).

General A Priori Foundation

Broad philosophies, theories, and empirical results on teaching and general curriculum issues are reviewed. Curriculum theory and research are studies for guidelines on students' and teachers' experiences with curricula, as well as on school and society, all of which helps to establish general education goals and directions (Pinar et al., 1995).

Pedagogical A Priori Foundation

Empirical findings on making specific types of activities educationally effective, that is, both motivating to students and effective in supporting students' learning, are summarized to create general guidelines for the generation of instructional designs and activities. Intuition and creative work complement scientific information (Dewey, 1929; Hiebert, 1999; James, 1958).

Learning Model

The second category involves the determination and development of learning models. This phase addresses mainly the theory goal of identifying the cognitive changes that occurred and the processes, including the specific curricular components and features that are responsible for the changes. Here, it becomes clear that, although the CRF can be discussed in general, applied research and development are based in specific, subject-matter content, which cannot be added effectively to a general structure.

Structure According to Specific Learning Models

In this phase, the curriculum's activities are structured to be consistent with domain-specific models of children's thinking and learning. This may involve two strategies. First, activities might be designed to be consistent with empirically-based models of children's thinking and learning, which can affect curriculum design substantially by focusing it on teaching and learning (Tamir, 1988; Walker, 1992). For example, research indicates that young children can invent their own solutions to simple arithmetic problems (Baroody, 1987; Carpenter & Moser, 1984; Ginsburg, 1977; Kamii & Housman, 1999; Steffe & Cobb, 1988) and that this benefits them more than direct instruction on prescriptive procedures (Hiebert et al., 1997; Kamii & Dominick, 1998; Steffe, 1994). Based on these findings, some curricula pose problems and ask children to figure out how to solve the problems and explain their solutions (Baroody, with Coslick, 1998; Fuson et al., 2000; Hiebert, 1999; Kamii & Housman, 1999).

Initial cognitive models may be available for a particular domain a priori. However, when models do not exist or do not give sufficient detail developers might use grounded theory methods (Strauss & Corbin, 1990) or clinical interviews to examine students' knowledge of the content domain. Once a model has been developed, it can be tested and extended with teaching experiments, to build models of children's thinking and learning that also suggest guidelines for instructional activities (Steffe & Thompson, 2000).

In the second strategy of this phase, sets of activities are developed and sequenced to complete *learning trajectories* (Simon, M. A. 1995)—paths of learning and teaching the concepts and skills of the goal domain (Clements, 2002; Cobb & McClain, 2002; Gravemeijer, 1999). Such learning trajectories have been based on the historical development of mathematics and observations of children's informal solution strategies (Gravemeijer, 1994b) and on emergent mathematical practices (Cobb & McClain, 2002). The CRF's learning trajectories build directly upon the previously discussed cognitive models; that is, upon developmental progressions identified in empirically-based models of children's thinking and learning (Carpenter & Moser, 1984; Case, 1982; Griffin & Case, 1997; Steffe & Cobb, 1988). Such learning trajectories are:

> ... descriptions of children's thinking and learning in a specific mathematical domain, and a related, conjectured route through a set of instructional tasks designed to engender those mental processes or actions hypothesized to move children through a developmental progression of levels of thinking, created with the intent of supporting children's achievement of specific goals in that mathematical domain.
>
> (Clements & Sarama, 2004: 83)

This detailed theoretical structure permits researchers to test theories by testing curricula (Clements & Battista, 2000). Such testing frequently involves teaching experiments and design experiments. Design experiments are preferred, as they emphasize a greater variety of types of interventions developed to support specific types of learning (with the latter emphasizing intervening to support particular forms of learning [Cobb et al., 2003]). As a science, these experiments include conceptual analyses and theories that "do real design work in generating, selecting and validating design alternatives at the level at which they are consequential for learning" (diSessa & Cobb, 2004: 77).

Design experiments are, therefore, a prime method of this; a critical phase of curriculum development. The CRF requires that all a priori foundation phases are conducted before and/or alongside design experiments and, most critically, that theoretically-based learning trajectories underlie the design experiments themselves.

Evaluation (Formative)

The next four phases, in the third category of evaluation, involve collecting specific empirical evidence in marketing and formative evaluations. The first of these, market research, addresses the policy goal of establishing the importance of the curriculum's objectives and, to a limited extent, the theory goal of explaining why the curriculum is effective.

Market Research

Market research is about what customers want. Traditional market research is the most common type of research in commercial curriculum writing. It involves surveying state standards, guidelines, and curricula and tests, especially of the key adoption states, as well as widely-administered standardized tests. Prototype materials are prepared and presented to focus groups. Traditional market research fails to meet the standards for scientific research, but eschewing it as mere commercialism, as researchers often do, is unwise. In the United States especially, the products of those who ignore the concerns of publishers and teachers are not widely adopted (Tushnet et al., 2000). To meet the needs of research and marketability, researchers and developers should conduct studies that are grounded in the disciplines and reported fully (Jaeger, 1988). This has the additional advantage of connecting the scientific curriculum research to information with which publishers are comfortable, helping to bridge the gap between developers and publishers that is especially problematic for innovative curricula (Tushnet et al., 2000). Such market research might be conducted as a component of the a priori foundation phases through the last phase of planning for diffusion (Rogers, 2003).

The following three phases are types of formative evaluation. They address the practice goal of determining where the curriculum is and is not effective in helping children achieve specific learning goals and the theoretical goal of identifying cognitive changes and the responsible environmental attributes and processes. In addition, they begin to address conditions: *for policy*, what the support requirements are; *for practice*, under what conditions the curriculum is effective; and *for theory*, why certain sets of conditions decrease or increase the curriculum's effectiveness and how specific strategies produce previously unattained results and why. These phases often involve repeated cycles of design, enactment, analysis, and revision (Clements & Battista, 2000), with increasing sizes of the populations and the research variables.

Formative Research: Small Group

In this phase, developers conduct pilot testing with individuals or small groups, evaluating particular curricular components, such as an activity, game, software environment, or longer section of the curriculum. Early interpretive work evaluates components using a mix of model- (or hypothesis-) testing and model-generation strategies. Therefore, design experiments play a major role, but methods also might include grounded theory, microgenetic, microethnographic, and phenomenological approaches (Pinar et al., 1995; Spradley, 1979; Steffe et al., 2000; Strauss & Corbin, 1990). The objective is understanding the meaning that students give to the curriculum objects and tasks and to alter these as necessary to better assist children in moving along the learning trajectory (Lincoln, 1992; Pinar et al., 1995).

Emphasis is placed on determining the accuracy of the learning trajectory, realized in practice. Such checking distinguishes this and subsequent phases from traditional formative and summative evaluations, which do not typically maintain connections to theory or create new theories (cf. Barab & Squire, 2004). The developer creates more refined models of the thinking of particular groups of students and describes what elements of the teaching and learning environment are observed as having contributed to students' learning (Walker, 1992). Such connections help describe the knowledge and abilities that are expected of the teacher, laying the foundation for generating teacher support materials in the final curriculum.

This phase includes repeated, close, cycles of evaluation and redesign, sometimes within twenty-four hours (Burkhardt et al., 1990; Clements & Sarama, 1995; Cobb et al., 2003). Design experiments may be conducted in multiple classrooms, allowing revised lessons to be tested in a classroom staggered to be one to five days behind in implementing the curriculum (Flagg, 1990). Extensive documentation, such as field notes and audio-tapes or video-tapes, allows researchers to relate the findings to specific components and characteristics of the curriculum and specifically evaluate components of the design that were based on intuition and subconscious beliefs.

Formative Research: Single Classroom

Although, ideally, teachers are involved in *all* of the phases, the emphasis in this phase is the process of curricular enactment (Ball & Cohen, 1996). First, classroom-based, teaching experiments are used to track and evaluate students' learning, with the goal of making sense of the curricular activities as they are experienced by individual students (Gravemeijer, 1994a; Pinar et al., 1995).

Second, the class is observed to evaluate the usability and effectiveness of the curriculum. Ethnographic participant observation is used heavily to examine the teacher and students as they interact to establish a classroom culture (Spradley, 1980). Such observation is important because events and properties cannot always be predicted or understood solely from analyses of the components, but emerge within a complex system (Davis & Simmt, 2003). Focus is on how teachers use materials and guide students through activities, what classroom processes are prominent and how these processes connect to intended and unintended outcomes. In this phase, the learning trajectory per se remains the focus of the formative evaluation; therefore, teachers who can enact the curriculum in reasonable harmony with the developers' vision—often the developers or teachers working closely with them—implement the curriculum.

Formative Research: Multiple Classrooms

In contrast to the previous phase, several classrooms involving teachers not closely connected to the developers are observed to learn about the effectiveness and usability of the curriculum. The emphasis turns to the curriculum's usability, conditions that influence the curriculum's effectiveness, and how it might be revised to serve all teachers and students better. Innovative materials, including those created in research and development projects, many times provide less support than the traditional materials with which teachers are familiar (Burkhardt et al., 1990), increasing the need for ecologically-valid studies for such materials. Understanding how and why the curriculum works in various contexts aids researchers in developing theory and practitioners in implementing the curriculum in local settings. Ethnographic research (Spradley, 1979, 1980) is useful, especially as teachers may appear to agree with a curriculum's goals and approach, but their implementation may be inconsistent with the developers' intention (Sarama et al., 1998).

Evaluation (Summative)

The final two phases are forms of summative evaluation. They address the policy goal of establishing the size of the effect for teachers and for students, the practice goal of documenting whether the curriculum is effective in helping children achieve learning goals, and the theory goal of identifying why the curriculum is effective. In addition, they address the conditions: *in policy*, the support requirements for various contexts; *in practice*, the conditions under which the curriculum is effective; and *in theory*, explanations as to why certain sets of conditions decrease or increase the curriculum's effectiveness and how and why specific strategies produce previously unattained results.

Summative Research: Small Scale

In this phase, researchers evaluate what can be achieved with typical teachers under realistic circumstances (Burkhardt et al., 1990; Rogers, 2003). In four to ten classrooms, pre- and post-test, randomized, experimental designs using measures of learning are used. Those on the forefront of innovative research and curriculum development often eschew such experiment; however, they are the most efficient and least biased designs to determine causal relationships, and criticisms often confuse limitations of the design with misapplications of it (Cook, 2002). Further, innovators may reject logical positivism, noting that theories cannot be tested definitively and that curriculum development and research are social in nature. However, this does not imply that experiments cannot contribute to evidence on causal claims. It does imply that experiments should be carefully designed to have greater explanatory power, by connecting specific processes and contexts to outcomes so that moderating and mediating variables are identified (ibid.).

In the CRF, experiments are conducted in conjunction with methods described previously. These methods, including qualitative work, are actually stronger if conducted within the context of a randomized experiment. For example, neither quantitative nor qualitative techniques alone will discriminate easily between the effects of an intervention and the teachers' dispositions and knowledge that led to their decision to volunteer for a quasi-experimental study. Experimental designs require that the intervention is described fully and explicitly and can be implemented with fidelity, according to the definition adopted. The curriculum used in the comparison classrooms should be selected on a principled basis and described completely. In addition, the quantity and quality of mathematics instruction must be measured in all participating classrooms with common measures. In addition, a combination of survey and interpretive information helps determine whether teachers view the extant supports as adequate and whether the intervention has altered their teaching practices.

Such summative research extends traditional summative evaluations. In the CRF, theoretical frameworks are a sine qua non. Comparison of the scores outside a framework is inadequate. In addition, connecting specific attributes of the curriculum, its enactment, and outcomes provides an adequate basis for contributing to theories of learning and teaching in complex settings and advising future curriculum development, as well as for implementing the curriculum in diverse contexts.

Summative Research: Large Scale

Increased attention has been given to the unique problem of scaling up a curriculum or other innovation that has proven successful in small-scale evaluations (Berends et al., 2001; Cuban, 2001; Elmore, 1996; Tyack & Tobin, 1992). With any curriculum, but particularly innovative curricula, researchers conduct evaluations to address this problem directly. Issues include the curriculum's effects in contexts where implementation is usually expected to vary widely (Cook, 2002) and the critical variables, including the contextual variables—settings, such as urban/suburban/rural; type of program; class size; teachers' characteristics; students'/families' characteristics—and the implementation variables—engagement in professional development opportunities; fidelity of implementation; leadership and support; peer relations; and incentives used (Berends et al., 2001; Cohen, 1996; Elmore, 1996; Mohrman & Lawler III, 1996; Sarama et al., 1998; Weiss, 2002). A randomized experiment provides an assessment of the average impact of exposure to a curriculum and a series of analyses such as hierarchical linear modeling provides correct estimates of the effects and standard errors when the data are collected at several levels. Because no set of experimental variables is complete or appropriate for each situation, qualitative methods supplement these analyses to ascertain the significant meanings, relationships, and critical variables that affect implementation and effectiveness (Lincoln & Guba, 1985) and thereby link meaningfully implementation processes to learning outcomes.

To complete this phase, the curriculum must be sustained and evaluated in multiple sites for more than two years (Berends et al., 2001; Fishman et al., 2004) and evaluations must be confirmed by researchers unrelated to the developers of the curriculum (Darling-Hammond & Snyder, 1992), considering issues of adoption and diffusion of the curriculum (Fishman et al., 2004; Rogers, 2003).

Conclusions

Design experiments are an important component of curriculum research and development activity within the proposed Curriculum Research Framework (CRF). However, this framework shows that other research and development strategies are necessary to meet the goals of a complete curriculum research and development program. Design experiments cannot control the many variables in their complex settings; the large amount of data collected rarely can be analyzed fully before the next cycle of revision, enactment, and analysis takes place (Collins et al., 2004); and different participants may have different data and perspectives, so that the ultimate paths and products may be arbitrary to an extent and generalization may be difficult (Kelly, 2004). Experiments (randomized trial designs) provide some of what design experiments cannot. In addition, the use of phases in the A Priori Foundations and Learning Model categories of the CRF provide useful constraints and theoretical groundings for design experiments.

Conversely, design experiences, as well as other methods such as teaching experiments and classroom-based teaching experiments, can help accomplish what randomized trials cannot. In the CRF context, these methods include conceptual and relational, or semantic, analysis, and thus are theoretically grounded. As such, they allow researchers to build models of the child's mathematics, of mental actions on objects, of learning, and of teaching interactions (L. Steffe, personal communication, July 18, 2005). Because it includes a coherent complement of methods, the CRF has built-in checks and balances that address the limitations of each method, with concentration on the learning model especially useful for maintaining theoretical and scientific foci.

In summary, embedding design experiments within the CRF encourages the conduct of a comprehensive research and development program. Such a program is theoretically sound and scientifically defensible. Further, it addresses the full range of curriculum research questions, about effects and conditions in the three domains of policy, practice, and theory (Clements, 2007). CRF-based programs thus contribute to both the research field and produce a curriculum that is a contribution to practice.

Acknowledgments

This chapter was supported in part by the National Science Foundation under Grant No. ESI-9730804, and by the Institute of Educational Sciences under Grant No. R305K05157. Any opinions, findings, conclusions, or recommendations expressed in this chapter are those of the author and do not reflect necessarily the views of the National Science Foundation or the Institute of Educational Sciences.

References

Ball, D. L. & Cohen, D. K. (1996). Reform by the book: What is—or might be—the role of curriculum materials in teacher learning and instructional reform? *Educational Researcher*, 16(2), 6–8, 14.

Bannan-Ritland, B. (2003). The role of design in research: The integrative learning design framework. *Educational Researcher*, 32(1), 21–24.

Barab, S. & Squire, K. (2004). Design-based research: Putting a stake in the ground. *Journal of the Learning Sciences*, 13, 1–14.

Baroody, A. J. (1987). *Children's mathematical thinking*. New York: Teachers College.

Baroody, A. J. (with Coslick, R. T.) (1998). *Fostering children's mathematical power: An investigative approach to K–8 mathematics instruction*. Mahwah, NJ: Lawrence Erlbaum Associates.

Battista, M. T. & Clements, D. H. (2000). Mathematics curriculum development as a scientific endeavor. In A. E. Kelly & R. A. Lesh (eds), *Handbook of research design in mathematics and science education* (pp. 737–760). Mahwah, NJ: Lawrence Erlbaum Associates.

Berends, M., Kirby, S. N., Naftel, S. & McKelvey, C. (2001). *Implementation and performance in New American Schools: Three years into scale-up*. Santa Monica, CA: Rand Education.

Brown, A. L. (1992). Design experiments: Theoretical and methodological challenges in evaluating complex interventions in classroom settings. *Journal of the Learning Sciences*, 2, 141–178.

Bruner, J. (1986). *Actual minds, possible worlds*. Cambridge, MA: Harvard University Press.

Burkhardt, H., Fraser, R. & Ridgway, J. (1990). The dynamics of curriculum change. In I. Wirszup & R. Streit (eds), *Developments in school mathematics around the world*, Volume 2 (pp. 3–30). Reston, VA: National Council of Teachers of Mathematics.

Carpenter, T. P. & Moser, J. M. (1984). The acquisition of addition and subtraction concepts in grades one through three. *Journal for Research in Mathematics Education*, 15, 179–202.

Case, R. (1982). General developmental influences on the acquisition of elementary concepts and algorithms in arithmetic. In T. P. Carpenter, J. M. Moser & T. A. Romberg (eds), *Addition and subtraction: A cognitive perspective* (pp. 156–170). Hillsdale, NJ: Lawrence Erlbaum Associates.

Clements, D. H. (2002). Linking research and curriculum development. In L. D. English (ed.), *Handbook of international research in mathematics education* (pp. 599–636). Mahwah, NJ: Lawrence Erlbaum Associates.

Clements, D. H. (2007). Curriculum research: Toward a framework for "research-based curricula." *Journal for Research in Mathematics Education*, 38, 35–70.

Clements, D. H. & Battista, M. T. (2000). Designing effective software. In A. E. Kelly & R. A. Lesh (eds), *Handbook of research design in mathematics and science education* (pp. 761–776). Mahwah, NJ: Lawrence Erlbaum Associates.

Clements, D. H. & Sarama, J. (1995). Design of a Logo environment for elementary geometry. *Journal of Mathematical Behavior*, 14, 381–398.

Clements, D. H. & Sarama, J. (2004). Learning trajectories in mathematics education. *Mathematical Thinking and Learning*, 6, 81–89.

Clements, D. H., Sarama, J. & DiBiase, A.-M. (2004). *Engaging young children in mathematics: Standards for early childhood mathematics education*. Mahwah, NJ: Lawrence Erlbaum Associates.

Cobb, P. & McClain, K. (2002). Supporting students' learning of significant mathematical ideas. In G. Wells & G. Claxton (eds), *Learning for life in the 21st century: Sociocultural perspectives on the future of education* (pp. 154–166). Oxford: Blackwell.

Cobb, P., Confrey, J., diSessa, A., Lehrer, R. & Schauble, L. (2003). Design experiments in educational research. *Educational Researcher*, 32(1), 9–13.

Cohen, D. K. (1996). Rewarding teachers for student performance. In S. H. Fuhrman & J. A. O'Day (eds), *Rewards and reforms: Creating educational incentives that work*. San Francisco, CA: Jossey-Bass.

Collins, A., Joseph, D. & Bielaczyc, K. (2004). Design research: Theoretical and methodological issues. *Journal of the Learning Sciences*, 13(1), 15–42.

Cook, T. D. (2002). Randomized experiments in educational policy research: A critical examination of the reasons the educational evaluation community has offered for not doing them. *Educational Evaluation and Policy Analysis, 24,* 175–199.

Cuban, L. (2001). *Oversold and underused.* Cambridge, MA: Harvard University Press.

Darling-Hammond, L. & Snyder, J. (1992). Curriculum studies and the traditions of inquiry: The scientific tradition. In P. W. Jackson (ed.), *Handbook of research on curriculum* (pp. 41–78). New York: Macmillan.

Davis, B. & Simmt, E. (2003). Understanding learning systems: Mathematics education and complexity science. *Journal for Research in Mathematics Education, 34,* 137–167.

Design-Based Research Collective (2003). Design-based research: An emerging paradigm for educational inquiry. *Educational Researcher, 32*(1), 5–8.

Dewey, J. (1902/1976). The child and the curriculum. In J. A. Boydston (ed.), *John Dewey: The middle works, 1899–1924. Volume 2: 1902–1903* (pp. 273–291). Carbondale: Southern Illinois University Press.

Dewey, J. (1929). *The sources of a science of education.* New York: Liveright Publishing Corp.

diSessa, A. A. & Cobb, P. (2004). Ontological innovation and the role of theory in design experiments. *Journal of the Learning Sciences, 13,* 77–103.

Eisner, E. W. (1998). The primacy of experience and the politics of method. *Educational Researcher, 17*(5), 15–20.

Elmore, R. F. (1996). Getting to scale with good educational practices. *Harvard Educational Review, 66,* 1–25.

Fishman, B., Marx, R. W., Blumenfeld, P. C., Krajcik, J. S. & Soloway, E. (2004). Creating a framework for research on systemic technology innovations. *Journal of the Learning Sciences, 13,* 43–76.

Flagg, B. (1990). *Formative evaluation for educational technology.* Hillsdale, NJ: Lawrence Erlbaum Associates.

Fuson, K. C., Carroll, W. M. & Drueck, J. V. (2000). Achievement results for second and third graders using the *Standards*-based curriculum *Everyday Mathematics. Journal for Research in Mathematics Education, 31,* 277–295.

Ginsburg, H. P. (1977). *Children's arithmetic.* Austin, TX: Pro-ed.

Gravemeijer, K. P. E. (1994a). *Developing realistic mathematics instruction.* Utrecht, The Netherlands: Freudenthal Institute.

Gravemeijer, K. P. E. (1994b). Educational development and developmental research in mathematics education. *Journal for Research in Mathematics Education, 25,* 443–471.

Gravemeijer, K. P. E. (1999). How emergent models may foster the constitution of formal mathematics. *Mathematical Thinking and Learning, 1,* 155–177.

Griffin, S. & Case, R. (1997). Re-thinking the primary school math curriculum: An approach based on cognitive science. *Issues in Education, 3*(1), 1–49.

Hiebert, J. C. (1999). Relationships between research and the NCTM Standards. *Journal for Research in Mathematics Education, 30,* 3–19.

Hiebert, J. C., Carpenter, T., Fennema, E. H., Fuson, K. C., Wearne, D., Murray, H. G., et al. (1997). *Making sense: Teaching and learning mathematics with understanding.* Portsmouth, NH: Heinemann.

Jaeger, R. M. (1988). Survey research methods in education. In R. M. Jaeger (ed.), *Complementary methods for research in education* (pp. 303–340). Washington, DC: American Educational Research Association.

James, W. (1958). *Talks to teachers on psychology: And to students on some of life's ideas.* New York: Norton.

Kamii, C. & Dominick, A. (1998). The harmful effects of algorithms in grades 1–4. In L. J. Morrow & M. J. Kenney (eds), *The teaching and learning of algorithms in school mathematics* (pp. 130–140). Reston, VA: National Council of Teachers of Mathematics.

Kamii, C. & Housman, L. B. (1999). *Young children reinvent arithmetic: Implications of Piaget's theory* (2nd ed.). New York: Teachers College Press.

Kelly, A. E. (2004). Design research in education: Yes, but is it methodological? *Journal of the Learning Sciences*, *13*, 115–128.

Latour, B. (1987). *Science in action*. Cambridge, MA: Harvard University Press.

Lesh, R. A. & Kelly, A. E. (2000). Multitiered teaching experiments. In A. E. Kelly & R. A. Lesh (eds), *Handbook of research design in mathematics and science education* (pp. 197–230). Mahwah, NJ: Lawrence Erlbaum Associates.

Lincoln, Y. S. (1992). Curriculum studies and the traditions of inquiry: The humanistic tradition. In P. W. Jackson (ed.), *Handbook of research on curriculum* (pp. 79–97). New York: Macmillan.

Lincoln, Y. S. & Guba, E. G. (1985). *Naturalistic inquiry*. Newbury Park, CA: Sage.

Mohrman, S. A. & Lawler III, E. E. (1996). Motivation for school reform. In S. H. Fuhrman & J. A. O'Day (eds), *Rewards and reform: Creating educational incentives that work* (pp. 115–143). San Francisco, CA: Jossey-Bass.

NCTM (2000). *Principles and standards for school mathematics*. Reston, VA: National Council of Teachers of Mathematics.

NCTM (2006). *Curriculum focal points for prekindergarten through grade 8 mathematics: A quest for coherence*. Reston, VA: National Council of Teachers of Mathematics.

NRC Committee (2004). *On evaluating curricular effectiveness: Judging the quality of K–12 mathematics evaluations*. Washington, DC: Mathematical Sciences Education Board, Center for Education, Division of Behavioral and Social Sciences and Education, National Academies Press.

Papert, S. (1987). Computer criticism vs. technocentric thinking. *Educational Researcher*, *16*(1), 22–30.

Pinar, W. F., Reynolds, W. M., Slattery, P. & Taubman, P. M. (1995). *Understanding curriculum: An introduction to the study of historical and contemporary curriculum discourses*. New York: Peter Lang.

Rogers, E. M. (2003). *Diffusion of innovations* (4th ed.). New York: Free Press.

Sarama, J., Clements, D. H. & Henry, J. J. (1998). Network of influences in an implementation of a mathematics curriculum innovation. *International Journal of Computers for Mathematical Learning*, *3*, 113–148.

Schwandt, T. A. (2002). *Evaluation practice reconsidered*. New York: Peter Lang.

Simon, H. A. (1969). *The sciences of the artificial*. Cambridge, MA: MIT Press.

Simon, M. A. (1995). Reconstructing mathematics pedagogy from a constructivist perspective. *Journal for Research in Mathematics Education*, *26*, 114–145.

Spradley, J. P. (1979). *The ethnographic interview*. New York: Holt, Rhinehart & Winston.

Spradley, J. P. (1980). *Participant observation*. New York: Holt, Rhinehart & Winston.

Steffe, L. P. (1994). Children's multiplying schemes. In G. Harel & J. Confrey (eds), *The development of multiplicative reasoning in the learning of mathematics* (pp. 3–39). Albany, NY: SUNY Press.

Steffe, L. P. & Cobb, P. (1988). *Construction of arithmetical meanings and strategies*. New York: Springer-Verlag.

Steffe, L. P. & Thompson, P. W. (with Glasersfeld, von E.) (2000). Teaching experiment methodology: Underlying principles and essential elements. In A. E. Kelly & R. A. Lesh (eds), *Handbook of research design in mathematics and science education* (pp. 267–306). Mahwah, NJ: Lawrence Erlbaum Associates.

Strauss, A. & Corbin, J. (1990). *Basics of qualitative research: Grounded theory procedures and techniques*. Newbury Park, CA: Sage.

Tamir, P. (1988). The role of pre-planning curriculum evaluation in science education. *Journal of Curriculum Studies*, *20*, 257–262.

Tushnet, N. C., Millsap, M. A., Abdullah-Welsh, N., Brigham, N., Cooley, E., Elliot, J., et al. (2000). *Final report on the evaluation of the National Science Foundation's Instructional Materials Development program*. Arlington, VA: National Science Foundation.

Tyack, D. & Tobin, W. (1992). The "grammar" of schooling: Why has it been so hard to change? *American Educational Research Journal*, *31*, 453–479.

Tyler, R. W. (1949). *Basic principles of curriculum and instruction.* Chicago: University of Chicago Press.

van Oers, B. (2003). Learning resources in the context of play: Promoting effective learning in early childhood. *European Early Childhood Education Research Journal, 11,* 7–25.

Walker, D. F. (1992). Methodological issues in curriculum research. In P. W. Jackson (ed.), *Handbook of research on curriculum* (pp. 98–118). New York: Macmillan.

Walker, D. F. (2003). *Fundamentals of curriculum: Passion and professionalism* (2nd ed.). Mahwah, NJ: Lawrence Erlbaum Associates.

Weiss, I. R. (2002). Systemic reform in mathematics education: What have we learned? Research presession of the 80th annual meeting of the National Council of Teachers of Mathematics.

Wittmann, E. C. (1995). Mathematics education as a "design science." *Educational Studies in Mathematics, 29,* 355–374.

21 The Design Principles Database as a Means for Promoting Design-Based Research

Yael Kali
Technion-Israel Institute of Technology

Introduction

From its early stages, design-based research (DBR) has had the vision of developing into a design science of education (Collins, 1992), in which critical elements in learning environments are explored systematically in terms of their effect on learning. Herbert Simon (1969) identified various professions, such as architecture, engineering, computer science, medicine, and education, with the sciences of the artificial, which Collins et al., (2004) refer to as design sciences. One of the approaches adopted by these fields is to gather and abstract designers' experiences and research by creating collections of design principles or design patterns that synthesize each of these fields and can guide new designs. Some examples are from the areas of architecture (Alexander et al., 1977), information science (Tufte, 1983), and computer science (Gamma et al., 1995).

The Design Principles Database, described below (and accessible at http://design-principles.org), was developed in this spirit to coalesce and synthesize emerging design knowledge about the use of technologies for education. Kali (2006) illustrates how the Design Principles Database can serve as a collaborative, knowledge-building endeavor for the community of the learning sciences. This chapter focuses on the utility of the database to fill a missing niche in DBR. The chapter commences with a short review of the literature about the methodological challenges in DBR. Then, an approach for conducting DBR is introduced, which uses the Design Principles Database as a means for warranting and generalizing DBR outcomes. A three-phase analysis of the ways in which researchers used the database, an example of a DBR study about peer evaluation, is provided to demonstrate this approach. Finally, the potential of the Design Principles Database to promote DBR is discussed.

Methodological Challenges in Design-Based Research

In order to explore how curricular innovations affect learning in naturalistic settings, more and more researchers are adopting the emerging paradigm of DBR. The notion of DBR is very much in vogue in the learning sciences community, but it faces obstacles in the broader research community (Collins et al., 2004). Recently, three major journals have dedicated special issues to illuminating the added value of this methodological niche and to discussing still unsolved challenges (Barab & Squire, 2004b; Dede, 2005b; Kelly, 2003).

Collins et al. (2004: 21) describe "design experiments" (one of the labels referring to the early stages of DBR) in the following manner:

> Design experiments bring together two critical pieces in order to guide us to better

educational refinement: a design focus and assessment of critical design elements. Ethnography provides qualitative methods for looking carefully at how a design plays out in practice, and how social and contextual variables interact with cognitive variables. Large-scale studies provide quantitative methods for evaluating the effects of independent variables on the dependent variables. Design experiments are contextualized in educational settings, but with a focus on generalizing from those settings to guide the design process. They fill a niche in the array of experimental methods that is needed to improve educational practices.

However, DBR is still in its infancy (Barab & Squire, 2004a; Dede, 2005a; Design-Based Research Collective, 2003), and its methodologies are still being challenged (e.g., Kelly, 2004; Shavelson et al., 2003). Questions that doubt DBR methodologies focus on issues of generalization in a field that is contextual in its nature. For instance, Kelly (2004: 120), in his remarks in the special issue of the *Journal of the Learning Sciences* about DBR, asks: "When one foregoes experimental controls, how can one generalize to other settings regardless of how rich are the local descriptions?" Similarly, Shavelson et al. (2003: 27) ask: "To what extent would the tool developed in one intensively engineered setting generalize to another setting?"

In order to answer such questions, it is clear that more positivist-reductionist methodologies are required. To be able to generalize that learning, or any other behavior, is caused by the interaction of students with a technology, and not by any of the vast number of other potential factors involved in naturalistic settings, one is required to reduce all of these factors and design a more controlled study. One approach to bridge between these two methodological polarities, and to earn both the insights gained in naturalistic methods and the generalizability acquired with more quantitative methods, is to sequence them. As Collins et al. (2004) suggest, DBR can include both formative and summative strategies. The formative strategies are used to describe lessons learned in successive implementations of an innovation in particular settings; the summative strategies seek to derive more general conclusions. For example, they state that

> ... if we wanted to compare how effective the Waterford and Peabody reading programs are, we would need to carry out comparative analyses in a variety of different settings, such as urban, suburban, and rural schools, and perhaps even homes, workplaces, and military settings. In such studies there must be a fixed experimental procedure, unlike the flexible design revision we recommend for formative evaluation.
>
> (Collins et al., 2004: 39)

The current study, by using the Design Principles Database, suggests an alternative to the sequencing approach described above for providing warrants for lessons learned by DBR.

The Design Principles Approach

Successful curricular materials depend on a process of iterative refinement to respond to the complex system that impacts classroom learning. DBR methods suggest ways to capture this process and describe how research teams gather evidence to make decisions about refinements (e.g., Bell et al., 2004; Linn et al., 2004). However, it is difficult to use the design knowledge residing in traditional forms of publication for creating new designs. To make this knowledge more useful, new approaches for its organization and synthesis are needed. Linn et al. (2004) suggested using design principles as an organizational unit. According to this approach, design principles that cut across a variety of designs are synthesized and abstracted based on various DBR projects. Bell et al. (2004: 83) refer to such design principles as:

> . . . an intermediate step between scientific findings, which must be generalized and replicable, and local experiences or examples that come up in practice. Because of the need to interpret design principles, they are not as readily falsifiable as scientific laws. The principles are generated inductively from prior examples of success and are subject to refinement over time as others try to adapt them to their own experiences. In this sense, they are falsifiable; if they do not yield purchase in the design process, they will be debated, altered, and eventually dropped.

Thus, the warrants for design principles are provided in this approach by the empirical studies that explore their application in new designs and contexts and are based on the cumulative design knowledge of the community.

This chapter focuses on the potential of the Design Principles Database to provide an alternative type of warranting for DBR outcomes, based on the design principles approach described above. The type of corroboration supported by the database is based on a community endeavor, in which researchers build on each others' knowledge of design, articulated as principles for design, to create new designs. They explore the application of these principles in new contexts and bring their findings back to the database. In this manner, knowledge about design grows in the community, and the principles are debated, refined, or warranted with additional, field-based evidence.

The Design Principles Database

Evolution of the Project

The Design Principles Database has emerged from meetings, conversations, and collaborative activities that occurred between 2001 and 2004. The design principles project started as a grassroots movement and grew gradually to involve a substantial number of educational software designers who contributed to the development of the current form of the database. The project was initiated at a conference of the Center for Innovative Learning Technologies (CILT) in 2000. Participants in a visualization and modeling workshop requested a set of guidelines that would synthesize the knowledge in the field and enable designers to create innovative, technology-based, learning environments that are founded on principled design knowledge (Kali, 2002). This call resulted in a CILT, seed-grant project, in which a series of invited, face-to-face, and online workshops were organized subsequently that led to the development of the Design Principles Database. The database was intended to guide conversations in the workshops and interactive poster sessions; to capture the library of features of technology-enhanced, learning environments; to link features, empirical evidence, and theoretical underpinnings of this work; and to synthesize design knowledge at multiple levels of analysis. Today, through the NSF-funded Technology Enhanced Learning in Science (TELS) Center, we continue to develop the Design Principles Database and use it as a core framework to capture, synthesize, discuss, and disseminate the research-based design ideas of TELS technology software innovations.

Design Vocabulary

The design principles project has stimulated the development of an emergent vocabulary to communicate design ideas. Terms used in this chapter follow:

- *Feature* is used to refer to any design effort to use technology to advance learning. In particular, we use feature to describe designed artifacts, or parts of artifacts, such as modeling tools (e.g., Buckley et al., 2004; Wu et al., 2001), visualizations (e.g., Dori & Belcher, 2005; Kali & Orion, 1997), collaboration tools (e.g., Guzdial et al., 2001; Ronen et al., 2006), games (e.g., Barab et al., 2005; Shaffer, 2005), and assessment tools (e.g., Birenbaum et al., 2006). The term also is used for activities designed to support the use of any of these tools.
- *Learning environment* is defined as a system that incorporates a set of features along with a navigation system and curricular materials.
- *Design principle* is used to refer to an abstraction that connects a feature to a form of rationale. Design principles are described at several levels of specificity, which are articulated below.

Structure of the Design Principles Database

The Design Principles Database is a set of interconnected features and principles. Each feature is linked with a principle and principles are linked between themselves in a hierarchical manner. Principles in the database are described in three levels of generalization:

- *Specific principles* describe the rationale behind the design of a single feature or a single research investigation. Because of their direct relation to one feature, specific principles in the database are embedded in the features.
- *Pragmatic principles* connect several specific principles (or several features).
- *Meta-principles* capture abstract ideas represented in a cluster of pragmatic principles.

Figure 21.1 illustrates these multiple connections schematically and provides examples of software features and principles in the three hierarchical levels.

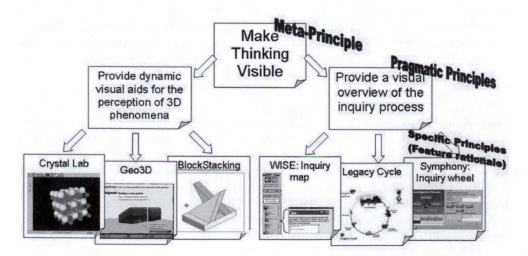

Figure 21.1 Schematic Representation of the Structure of the Design Principles Database.

The database includes two main modes of interaction: a *Contribute* mode and a *Search/Browse* mode. The *Contribute* mode enables designers to submit new features and principles to the database. To publish features in the database, authors are required to provide the following pieces of information: (a) a detailed description of the functionality of the feature, (b) the rationale behind the design (i.e., the specific principle), (c) the context in which the feature was used, and (d) the category, or several categories, that describe the feature (e.g., visualization tools, inquiry tools, communication tools, ubiquitous computing, etc.). Finally, it is required that every feature be connected to a pragmatic principle. Once a feature is connected to a pragmatic principle, the author of the feature can edit any part of the pragmatic principle, which usually is authored by another contributor, using Wiki technology (e.g., Nicol et al., 2005). The Wiki tools enable multiple authoring while keeping track of the principle's history to ensure the retrieval of old documentation, if needed. In order to contribute a pragmatic principle, authors are required to provide a detailed description of the principle, its theoretical background, and tips for designers, including the limitations, trade-offs, and pitfalls for designing with the principle. Authors also are required to connect pragmatic principles to meta-principles. There are four meta-principles, which are built into the database and which originate from the Scaffolded Knowledge Integration framework (Linn et al., 2004). The *Contribute* mode thus enables the database to grow while maintaining connectedness between features and principles and between principles in the different levels. It also enables the community to refine pragmatic principles continually. About 120 features, with their specific principles, have been contributed already to the Design Principles Database from several disciplines (mainly the physical, life, and earth sciences, but also mathematics, humanities, and others). About 80 of these features are in the public area; the others are in areas designated for groups, such as workshops and graduate courses, or are at draft stages.

The *Search/Browse* mode enables users (researchers, teachers, and students in the learning sciences) to search for features and principles using filters, which include any of the pieces of information described above. The database is navigated through the connections between the features and the three levels of principles. For instance, one might start a browsing path by using filters, to find all the features in chemistry that are based on inquiry learning for the tenth grade. After choosing one of these features to review the details, the user might want to link to a pragmatic principle connected to the feature in order to understand the overarching rationale better and to read the theoretical background. Finally, the user can review other features connected to this pragmatic principle and see how it is applied in other learning environments in various contexts.

Promoting Design-Based Research Through the Design Principles Database: A Three-Phase Study Example

The potential of the Design Principles Database for advancing the field of design is illustrated here by the analysis of a particular DBR project about a peer evaluation activity in an undergraduate-level course on the philosophy of education (Kali & Ronen, 2005). The analysis of this particular study demonstrates how the researchers used the database in three stages to build on the existing body of knowledge for designing a new peer evaluation activity and how this use led eventually to the generation of new design knowledge that was shared with the community, which strengthened the original claims. The description of the study below is followed by an analysis of the three phases in which the researchers used the Design Principles Database.

The peer evaluation study, which is analyzed here to demonstrate the researchers' use of the database, took place in a philosophy of education course for undergraduates at the Technion-Israel Institute of Technology, taught by the author of this chapter. The main goal of the course was to help students develop their own perceptions about fundamental issues in education and schooling (e.g., What is the goal of schooling? What contents should be taught in school? What should be the role of the teacher?). A main theme in the course was the "ideal school" project, in which groups of three-to-four students constructed a conceptual model of a school that met their evolving educational perceptions. Toward the end of the semester, each group gave a short presentation describing one day in their ideal school. For this purpose, most of the students used PowerPoint, but other, less conventional means such as drama performances, were used also. The presentations took place in three class meetings, with three or four presentations in each session. One challenge the instructor faced during these presentations was how to ensure that students made the most out of these meetings. Prior teaching experience in similar contexts had revealed that students tended to focus on accomplishing the course's requirements (their own presentations in this case) and are less interested in their peers' projects.

This challenge was addressed by designing a peer evaluation activity, in which students were involved in the assessment of their peers' ideal school presentations. The rationale for engaging students in this activity was to: (a) ensure their involvement in their peers' projects, (b) create a framework for them to learn from each other's projects, (c) help them develop evaluation skills that they would need as future educators, and (d) reinforce criteria for designing their projects. The analysis of this peer evaluation activity by the instructor involved the integration of hundreds of assessments (35 students times ten groups times about four criteria). To help facilitate the analysis, a computerized system was used, which enabled gathering, presenting, and analyzing these assessments in a productive manner. The activity was performed online with Collaborative e-Learning Structures (CeLS) (accessible at http://www.mycels.net), a novel system that allows the instructor to create and conduct a variety of online, structured, collaborative activities (Ronen et al., 2006). The sections below illustrate how this particular DBR was supported by the Design Principles Database.

Methodological Approach

The current study is designed as a metastudy; it analyzes the process by which the peer evaluation DBR study described above shaped the design knowledge represented in the Design Principles Database. To do this, three main phases in the researchers' use of the database in the peer evaluation study were defined: Phase One: Articulating design principles; Phase Two: Design–enactment–refinement iterations; and Phase Three: Revising pragmatic principles. The metastudy used descriptive analysis to characterize the researchers' use of the database in these three phases. The peer evaluation study used DBR methodologies, which are described below.

It is important to note that the current metastudy is carried out by one of the researchers who conducted the DBR analyzed in the metastudy. In this sense, the metastudy is a reflective description of using the Design Principles Database to support the DBR studied. However, it is assumed that the involvement of the researcher in the DBR does not constrain the analysis. Rather, it helps in describing the details required to illustrate the potential of the database for supporting other DBR studies and for synthesizing the cumulative knowledge in the field.

Phase One: Articulating Design Principles

Because the Design Principles Database is still in its beginning stages, no design principles were articulated for peer evaluation when the study was conducted. Therefore, it was necessary to abstract design principles from existing empirical studies in this field and to design the first version of the peer evaluation activity based on these principles. The literature reviewed for articulating the pragmatic and specific principles included: Cuddy and Oki (2001); Davies (2000); Dominick et al. (1997); Falchikov (2003); Falchikov and Goldfinch (2000); Mann (1999); McConnell (2002); Miller (2003); Ronen and Langley (2004); Suthers et al. (1997); Topping (1998); and Zariski (1996). At the end of this phase, one pragmatic principle (Figure 21.2) linked with three specific principles (embedded in features) were added to the database as follows (more details for each principle and feature are available in the database):

- *Pragmatic Principle:* Enable students to give feedback to their peers.
- *Specific Principle One:* Involve students in developing the evaluation criteria for the peer evaluation.
- *Specific Principle Two:* Ensure anonymity to avoid bias in evaluating peers.
- *Specific Principle Three:* Make the synthesis of the peer evaluation results visible for learners.

It is important to note that the rich body of knowledge concerning peer evaluation can be translated into many more design principles. For the purpose of this study, only ideas that seemed useful for designing the peer evaluation activity were articulated as design principles and contributed to the database.

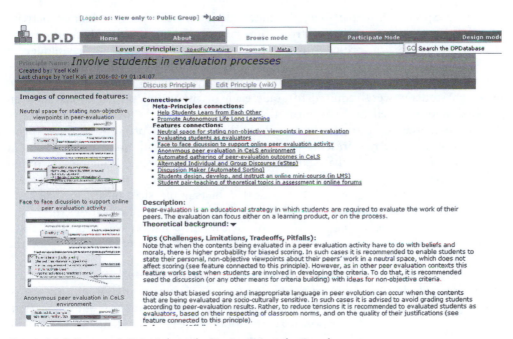

Figure 21.2 Pragmatic Principle in the Design Principles Database.

Phase Two: Design–Enactment–Refinement Iterations

Methods in the Peer Evaluation Study

In order to explore the challenges of peer evaluation in the specific context, the study was organized around three design–enactment–refinement iterations. These took place in three successive semesters, with a total of 144 students participating (Iteration One: Fall 2003, with 80 students in two groups; Iteration Two: spring 2004, with 29 students; Iteration Three: fall 2004, with 35 students). Each iteration was followed by an analysis of the data and refinements to the design of the online, peer evaluation activity. Data sources included:

- Peer evaluation data (numeric grades and textual justifications) gathered in the CeLS environment.
- Artifacts created by each group (PowerPoint slides of the ideal school project and online discussions used by each of the groups for developing the conceptions for their project).
- Students' responses to an attitude questionnaire administered at the end of the course.
- Students' spontaneous online discussions in a virtual "coffee corner" at the course's site.
- Instructor's reflective journal, including remarks about the events that took place during class.

First Iteration: Initial Design

Following Specific Principle One, the initial design of the peer evaluation activity included criteria that were derived from students' suggestions in a classroom discussion that occurred before the presentations and included the following: (a) Is the uniqueness of the school apparent? (b) Is the rationale for the activities clear? (c) Are the activities that take place in the school demonstrated clearly? The activity included an online form in which students were required to grade each of the group presentations between 1 (poor) and 7 (excellent). The form also included text fields for students to justify their grading according to the three criteria. Students used printout of these forms to take notes during the presentations and entered their grades and justifications at the online environment in the next few days. Following Specific Principles Two and Three, at the end of the activity, all of the students were able to view: (a) a histogram of the scores for each group, (b) statistical data (sample size, mean, median, and standard deviation), and (c) the individual scores and the justifications for them (presented anonymously) (Figure 21.3). All of this information was generated automatically by the CeLS environment without requiring any extra work from the instructor.

In order to assess the validity of the students' scoring, the set of mean scores that were given by the students for each of the ten presentations was compared with the set of scores given by the instructor for these presentations. The analysis indicated that, although there was a moderate positive correlation between the students' scores and the instructor's scores ($r = 0.43$), it was not significant ($p = 0.10$). A detailed examination of the qualitative data enabled the cases in which large discrepancies were found between the students' and the instructor's scoring to be identified. Such discrepancies were especially apparent in presentations that introduced educational perceptions that were

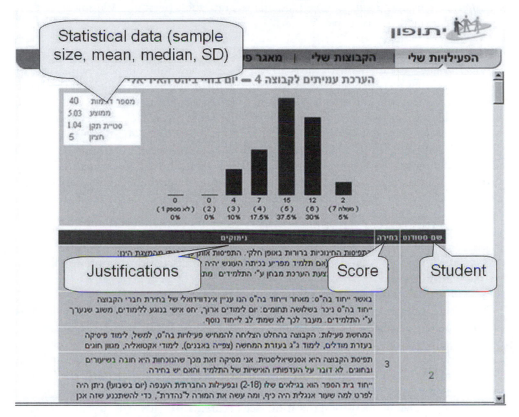

Figure 21.3 Interface of the Peer Evaluation Activity in the Collaborative e-Learning Structures Environment.

relatively "extreme," according to views held by many students. Although the students were instructed specifically to try to ignore personal viewpoints in their grading, it seems that they found it difficult to do so. The issue of differentiating between objective criteria and personal stands was taken as a focus for the second iteration. It is important to note that this study assumed that purely objective criteria do not exist because we are all somewhat subject to our personal viewpoints. However, an essential aspect of peer evaluation is to find those criteria that will provide equitable measures that will minimize biases.

Second Iteration: Differentiating Between Objective Criteria and
Personal Stands

Based on the outcomes of the first iteration and in order to foster objectivity, it was decided to refine the design of the online, peer evaluation activity so that it would provide students with a way to differentiate between objective aspects of the presentation and their personal nonobjective viewpoints. The rationale was that if students were given a chance to express these views in a neutral area, which does not affect the score, they would be more aware of their personal values and emotional stands and, thus, provide a more objective score. Therefore, the following specific principle, to explore in this iteration, was defined:

- *Specific Principle Four:* Enable students to state their personal nonobjective viewpoints about their peers' work.

As in the first iteration, a class discussion about evaluation criteria preceded the activity. To engage students with the issue of personal viewpoints in peer evaluation, the class discussion was seeded with ideas for criteria, including a criterion about the degree to which a student is in agreement with views introduced during the presentation. After the class discussion, four text fields for justifying scores were defined. The first three were similar to those defined in the first iteration (referring to the uniqueness of the school, the rationale for it, and a demonstration of its activities), but a fourth text field was added, named "My personal opinion about this school." As suggested by the students, the ideas expressed in this field did not affect the scoring. Rather, this component of the peer review was intended to provide general feedback for the presenters about the degree of acceptance of their ideas by the other students. Another specific principle was defined for further exploration, namely:

- *Specific Principle Five:* Design features to foster discussion about nonobjective evaluation criteria.

Outcomes indicated that the refined design, which enabled the students to express their personal viewpoints, assisted them in differentiating better between objective criteria and personal stands. This was evident from a higher correlation between the set of scores provided by the instructor for each of the groups and those provided by the students ($r = 0.62$, $p = 0.03$), compared to the first iteration. Furthermore, the learning gains from the peer evaluation activity, as indicated by the attitude questionnaire, seemed to be higher in the second iteration (see Figure 21.4). However, it was found that because the contents that are being evaluated involved cultural and political values, tensions in class discussions between students were aroused, and they infiltrated as biased scoring and inappropriate language, even affecting justifications in the peer evaluation activity (Kali & Ronen, 2005). Therefore, the issue of respecting classroom norms was decided as a main focus for exploration and design in the third iteration.

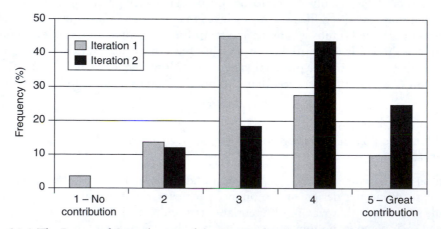

Figure 21.4 The Degree of Contribution of the Peer Evaluation Activity to Students' Learning in the First Two Iterations, as Indicated by the Attitude Questionnaire.

Third Iteration: Evaluating Students as Evaluators

Based on the findings of the second iteration and in order to foster further objectivity, classroom norms, and tolerance, a third iteration of the activity was designed according to the following principle:

- *Specific Principle Six:* When the contents being evaluated are socially or culturally sensitive, avoid grading students according to peer evaluation results. Rather, evaluate students as evaluators.

According to this principle, 15 percent of the students' scores in the fall semester of 2004 were derived from the peer evaluation activity and indicated how well they had served as evaluators. The score was comprised of: (a) the number of evaluations provided, (b) the respect shown for predefined classroom norms, (c) the quality of the justifications, and (d) the degree of correlation with the instructor's score. The outcomes indicated that implementation of the redesigned activity enabled students to exploit better the vast advantages of peer evaluation, tensions were decreased (Kali & Ronen, 2005), and a higher correlation with the instructor's score ($r = 0.7$, $p = 0.02$) was found. Furthermore, learning gains and students' satisfaction, as indicated from the attitude questionnaire, stayed high.

Phase Three: Revising Pragmatic Principles

After the new specific principles were added to the database, together with the example features that were explored in Phase Two, the researchers of the peer evaluation study were able to enrich the original pragmatic principle ("Enable students to give feedback to their peers"), which connects these features, with lessons learned through the cycles of the DBR. An important way to enrich a pragmatic principle in the database is to add emerging design knowledge to the section entitled "Tips (Challenges, Limitations, Trade-offs, Pitfalls)." Because the knowledge gained through the particular DBR related to a very specific context, it was decided to articulate this knowledge as limitations of the pragmatic design principle. These limitations were stated in the database as follows:

- Note that when the contents being evaluated in a peer evaluation activity relate to beliefs and morals, there is a higher probability for biased scoring. In such cases, it is recommended that students be enabled to state their personal nonobjective viewpoints about their peers' work in a neutral space, which does not affect scoring. As in other peer evaluation contexts, this feature works best when students are involved in developing the criteria. To do that, it is recommended that the discussion be seeded (or other means be used for criteria building) with ideas for nonobjective criteria.
- Note also that biased scoring and inappropriate language in peer evaluation can occur when the contents being evaluated are socioculturally sensitive. In such cases, it is advised to avoid grading students according to peer evaluation results. Rather, to reduce tensions, it is recommended that students be evaluated as evaluators, based on their respect for classroom norms and on the quality of their justifications.

Another revision to the original pragmatic principle was done automatically by the system. The new features (and specific principles) that were explored in this study became parts of the pragmatic principle in the form of links that exemplify the use of the principle and provide additional evidence and further warranting for the principle.

Discussion

The three-phase study described above illustrates a process in which design knowledge, abstracted from the existing body of knowledge about peer evaluation and contributed to the Design Principles Database, was explored in a new context. The design knowledge was strengthened by this exploration; the pragmatic principle "Enable students to give feedback to their peers" was applied successfully in the philosophy of education course and thus was connected with additional empirical outcomes. Furthermore, new theoretical knowledge about issues of bias and objectivity in peer evaluation was created, brought back to the database, and synthesized with the existing knowledge. The development of this theoretical knowledge was articulated as practical design knowledge; namely as tips for designing peer evaluation activities in which the contents being evaluated relate to morals, values, or sensitive issues.

Ideally, researchers who refine pragmatic principles based on their outcomes are not those who are the original contributors of the principles, as in the case of this research. A design study that uses the Design Principles Database could start when a researcher or a research group articulates a pragmatic design principle that summarizes outcomes from a DBR study in a certain area. The researchers provide the theoretical background and connect the pragmatic principle with one or more features, which provide field-based evidence and illustrate how the principle was applied in their specific context (this corresponds to Phase One in the current study, with the exception that the pragmatic principle was abstracted from the literature). Then, another research group uses the information provided in the pragmatic principle to design new features and explore them in new contexts (this corresponds to Phase Two in the current research). Up to this stage, this is quite similar to the common process in which researchers build on knowledge published by the traditional means of publication.

The added value of the Design Principles Database is particularly evident in the next stage (which corresponds to Phase Three), in which new contributions to theory are brought back to the database and synthesized with the existing knowledge. This can be performed in several ways: (a) empirical outcomes from the design iterations are translated explicitly into new features and specific principles and connected to the original pragmatic principle, (b) additional, practical, design knowledge based on the research, such as limits, trade-offs, and pitfalls, is added to a pragmatic principle, and (c) the pragmatic principle is refined, using the Wiki capabilities of the database, to capture the new design knowledge gained in the research.

Conclusions

The analysis above indicates that the Design Principles Database can contribute to the development of theory, on the one hand, and to design practice, on the other. Theory is developed through the continuous empirical re-examination, negotiation, and refinement of pragmatic design principles by the community. At the same time, these principles become more useful for designers (and thus deserve their name better) when they are connected with a variety of features and specific principles, which exemplify how they can be applied to different contexts.

At the beginning of this chapter, methodological challenges in design-based research, expressed by several researchers such as Kelly (2004) and Shavelson et al. (2003), were stated. These authors were concerned that because of the contextual nature of DBR, methodologies usually refrain from experimental controls. Therefore, they questioned the ability of DBR methodologies to generalize findings and to warrant claims. The current study suggests that the process of synthesizing design knowledge through the use of the Design Principles Database can move DBR toward meeting these challenges. This process maintains the naturalistic methodologies required in order to gain a deep understanding about the effect of technology on various aspects of learning. Yet, it also enables re-examination of the outcomes, articulated as design principles, by different researchers in other settings. It is argued here that this process, supported by the Design Principles Database, can serve as a productive approach for advancing DBR.

Nonetheless, the Design Principles Database is still in its initial stages, and its framework is open for public negotiation and refinement. Other research teams have suggested frameworks for connecting elements of design and generalized design guidelines. One important endeavor in this direction is the Scaffolding Design Framework for designing educational software suggested by a group from the University of Michigan and Northwestern University (Quintana et al., 2004). Another important venture in this direction is the Design Patterns trajectory (Linn & Eylon, 2006), which seeks to identify common factors in promising sequences of activities and define them as patterns that can guide designers of learning environments. Advances to merge efforts between these projects are taking place.

Additionally, in order to attain the full potential of the Design Principles Database, a critical mass of contents needs to be contributed and negotiated by the community. As Collins et al. (2004: 33) state:

> Our approach to design research requires much more effort than any one human can carry out. We put forward these ideas not because we expect each and every design experiment to embody them, but to give an overview of all the things the design research community is responsible for. In our ideal world, design research will move in the direction of embodying many of the practices we outline here. But it will take teams of researchers and accessible archives documenting design experiments . . . to make these dreams at all possible.

We envision this dream coming true when the Design Principles Database is populated with hundreds of features and specific principles, connected to pragmatic principles, which evolve continuously through the negotiation of a dynamic, knowledge-building community. To meet this challenge, the TELS (Technology Enhanced Learning in Science) Center continues to organize workshops and graduate courses that support researchers in contributing features and principles to the database. Additionally, we encourage readers who are involved in DBR to take part in this endeavor and share their design knowledge with the community associated with the Design Principles Database.

Acknowledgments

The Design Principles Database is supported by the National Science Foundation as a part of the Technology Enhanced Learning in Science (TELS) Center (Grant No: ESI/CLT 0334199). I would like to thank Marcia Linn, the TELS Principal Investigator, for her enormous inspiration, support, and contribution to the Design Principles Database project. I also would like to thank the postdoctoral scholars and principal investigators at the Center for Innovative Learning Technologies who supported and encouraged the design principles project in its early stages.

Many thanks to Miky Ronen, at the Holon Academic Institute of Technology, for providing the Collaborative e-Learning Structures environment and helping with the peer evaluation analysis; to Orit Parnafes, at the University of California, Berkeley; and to the design group graduate students at the Technion-Israel Institute of Technology, for their very thoughtful comments on drafts of this chapter.

Finally, thanks to all of the people who helped shape the framework of, and contributed features and principles to, the Design Principles Database.

References

Alexander, C., Ishikawa, S. & Silverstein, M. (1977). *A pattern language: Towns, buildings, and construction*. New York: Oxford University Press.

Barab, S. A. & Squire, K. D. (2004a). Design-based research: Putting our stake in the ground. *Journal of the Learning Sciences, 13*, 1–14.

Barab, S. A. & Squire, K. D. (eds) (2004b). Design-based research: Clarifying the terms [Special issue]. *Journal of the Learning Sciences, 13*(1).

Barab, S. A., Thomas, M., Dodge, T., Carteaux, R. & Tuzun, H. (2005). Making learning fun: Quest Atlantis, a game without guns. *Educational Technology Research and Development, 53*, 86–107.

Bell. P., Hoadley, C. M. & Linn, M. C. (2004). Design-based research in education. In M. C. Linn, E. A. Davis & P. Bell (eds), *Internet environments for science education* (pp. 73–85). Mahwah, NJ: Lawrence Erlbaum Associates.

Birenbaum, M., Breuer, K., Cascallar, E., Dochy, F., Dori, Y. J., Ridgway J., et al. (2006). A learning integrated assessment system. In EARLI Series of Position Papers, R. Wiesemes & G. Nickmans (eds). *Educational Research Review, 1*(1), 61–69.

Buckley, B. C., Gobert, J. D., Kindfield, A., Horwitz, P., Tinker, R., Gerlits, B., et al. (2004). Model-based teaching and learning with BioLogica™: What do they learn? How do they learn? How do we know? *Journal of Science Education and Technology, 13*, 23–41.

Collins, A. (1992). Toward a design science of education. In E. Scanlon & T. O'Shea (eds), *New directions in educational technology* (pp. 15–22). Berlin: Springer-Verlag.

Collins, A., Joseph, D. & Bielaczyc, K. (2004). Design research: Theoretical and methodological issues. *Journal of the Learning Sciences, 13*, 15–42.

Cuddy, P. J. & Oki, J. (2001). Online peer-evaluation in basic pharmacology. *Academic Medicine, 76*, 532–533.

Davies, P. (2000). Computerized peer assessment. *Innovations in Education & Training International, 37*, 346–355.

Dede, C. (2005a). Why design-based research is both important and difficult. *Educational Technology, 45*, 5–8.

Dede, C. (ed.) (2005b). Advances in design based research [Special issue]. *Educational Technology, 45*(1).

Design-Based Research Collective (2003). Design-based research: An emerging paradigm for educational inquiry. *Educational Researcher, 32*(1), 5–8.

Dominick, P. G., Reilly, R. R. & McGourty, J. (1997). The effects of peer feedback on team member behavior. *Group and Organization Management, 22*, 508–520.

Dori, Y. J. & Belcher, J. W. (2005). How does technology-enabled active learning affect students' understanding of scientific concepts? *Journal of the Learning Sciences, 14*, 243–279.

Falchikov, N. (2003). Involving students in assessment. *Psychology, Learning and Teaching, 3*, 102–108.

Falchikov, N. & Goldfinch, J. (2000). Student peer assessment in higher education: A meta-analysis comparing peer and teacher marks. *Review of Educational Research, 70*, 287–322.

Gamma, E., Helm, R., Johnson, R. & Vlissides, J. (1995). *Design patterns: Elements of reusable object-oriented software*. Reading, MA: Addison-Wesley Longman.

Guzdial, M., Rick, J. & Kehoe, C. (2001). Beyond adoption to invention: Teacher-created collaborative activities in higher education. *Journal of the Learning Sciences, 10*, 265–279.

Kali, Y. (2002). CILT2000: Visualization and modeling. *Journal of Science Education and Technology, 11*, 305–310.

Kali, Y. (2006). Collaborative knowledge-building using the Design Principles Database. *International Journal of Computer Support for Collaborative Learning, 1*(2), 187–201.

Kali, Y. & Orion, N. (1997). Software for assisting high school students in the spatial perception of geological structures. *Journal of Geoscience Education, 45*, 10–21.

Kali, Y. & Ronen, M. (2005). Design principles for online peer-evaluation: Fostering objectivity. Proceedings of CSCL 2005, Taipei, Taiwan. In T. Koschmann, D. D. Suthers & T. W. Chan (eds), *Computer support for collaborative learning: The next 10 years!* (pp. 347–251). Mahwah, NJ: Lawrence Erlbaum Associates.

Kelly, A. E. (ed.) (2003). The role of design in educational research [Special issue]. *Educational Researcher, 32*(1).

Kelly, A. E. (2004). Design research in education: Yes, but is it methodological? *Journal of the Learning Sciences, 13*, 115–128.

Linn, M. C. & Eylon, B.-S. (2006). Science education: Integrating views of learning and instruction. In P. A. Alexander & P. H. Winne (eds), *Handbook of Educational Psychology* (2nd ed., pp. 511–544). Mahwah, NJ: Lawrence Erlbaum Associates.

Linn, M. C., Bell, P. & Davis, E. A. (2004). Specific design principles: Elaborating the scaffolded knowledge integration framework. In M. C. Linn, E. A. Davis & P. Bell (eds), *Internet environments for science education* (pp. 315–339). Mahwah, NJ: Lawrence Erlbaum Associates.

Mann, B. (1999). Web course management "Post and vote": Peer assessment using generic Web tools. *Australian Educational Computing, 14*(1), 15–20.

McConnell, D. (2002). Collaborative assessment as a learning event in eLearning environments. Proceedings of CSCL 2002, Boulder, CO. In G. Stahl (ed.), *Computer support for collaborative learning: Foundations for a CSCL community*. Hillsdale, NJ: Lawrence Erlbaum Associates.

Miller, P. J. (2003). The effect of scoring criteria specificity on peer and self-assessment. *Assessment & Evaluation in Higher Education, 28*, 383–394.

Nicol, D., Littlejohn, A. & Grierson, H. (2005). The importance of structuring information and resources within shared workspaces during collaborative design learning. *Open Learning, 20*, 31–49.

Quintana, C., Reiser, B. J., Davis, E. A., Krajcik, J., Fretz, E., Golan-Duncan R., et al. (2004). A scaffolding design framework for software to support science inquiry. *Journal of the Learning Sciences, 13*, 337–386.

Ronen, M. & Langley, D. (2004). Scaffolding complex tasks by open online submission: Emerging patterns and profiles. *Journal of Asynchronous Learning Networks, 8*, 39–61.

Ronen, M., Kohen-Vacs, D. & Raz-Fogel, N. (2006). Adopt and adapt: Structuring, sharing and reusing asynchronous collaborative pedagogy. Proceedings of ICLS 2006, Bloomington, IN. In S. A. Barab, K. E. Hay & D. T. Hickey (eds), *International conference of the learning sciences: Making a difference* (pp. 599–605). Mahwah, NJ: Lawrence Erlbaum Associates.

Shaffer, D. W. (2005). Epistemic games. *Innovate, 1*(6), at: http://www.innovateonline.info/index.php?view = article&id = 79.

Shavelson, R. J., Phillips, D. C., Towne, L. & Feuer, M. J. (2003). On the science of education design studies. *Educational Researcher, 32*(1), 25–28.

Simon, H. A. (1969). *The sciences of the artificial*. Cambridge, MA: MIT Press.

Suthers, D. D., Toth, E. E. & Weiner, A. (1997). An integrated approach to implementing collaborative inquiry in the classroom. Proceedings of CSCL 1997, Toronto, Ontario, Canada. In R. Hall, N. Miyake & N. Enydey (eds), *The second international conference on computer support for collaborative learning* (pp. 272–279). Mahwah, NJ: Lawrence Erlbaum Associates.

Topping, K. (1998). Peer assessment between students in colleges and universities. *Review of Educational Research, 68*, 249–276.

Tufte, E. R. (1983). *The visual display of quantitative information*. Cheshire, CT: Graphics Press.

Wu, H. K., Krajcik, J. & Soloway, E. (2001). Promoting understanding of chemical representations: Students' use of a visualization tool in the classroom. *Journal of Research in Science Teaching, 38*, 821–842.

Zariski, A. (1996). Student peer assessment in tertiary education: Promise, perils and practice. Proceedings of the 5th annual Teaching Learning Forum. In J. Abbott & L. Willcoxson (eds), *Teaching and learning within and across disciplines* (pp. 189–200). Perth, Australia: Murdoch.

Part 8

Extending Design Research Methodologically

22 Design Research and the Study of Change

Conceptualizing Individual Growth in Designed Settings

Finbarr C. Sloane
Arizona State University

Anthony E. Kelly
George Mason University

Introduction

All educational research involves design choices. For design researchers, the nature of the choice is most explicitly about the character of the designed artifact (e.g., software or learning environment) or about the students' navigation of some content terrain (Cobb et al., 2003). Less obvious, and perhaps unconscious, are the education researcher's beliefs about the nature of change. These beliefs affect the researcher's choice of theoretical frame, choice of measure, and choice of analytic tool. These choices interact one with another and critically affect the way inferences are drawn (either qualitatively or quantitatively). The goal of this chapter is to highlight some of the defining features of change implicit in education research to guide design researchers as they move to quantify student growth over time. We note that the challenges posed to design researchers in modeling change afflict, equally, the modeling of change even by those with mastery of current statistical modeling formalisms. Models of change over time intersect with and are grounded in larger construct validity issues facing all education researchers that are not resolved (but at least made more explicit) by quantitative techniques.

Assessing Change in Designed Settings

In some areas of social science research such as those in developmental psychology (e.g., Slater & Bremner, 2003), the concept and assessment of change is explicitly the focus of study. In much design research, the concept of change over time is less explicit but no less fundamental. For example, the Design-Based Research Collective (2003) focused on the design of technological artifacts that support and change student learning, while Cobb et al. (2003) focused explicitly on changes of student learning of content with less emphasis placed on the "designed intervention." In both cases, change over time is fundamental. Accordingly, it is important that design researchers possess a good grasp of the basic but often ignored issues relating to its conceptualization and measurement.

Standard Pre-Post Testing Models

The standard model for measuring change in educational research is the pre-post testing model. Generally, pre-post testing models are two time-point models and are found

in general studies of learning (Shadish et al., 2004; Singer & Willett, 2003; Willett, 1989), and in design research studies (e.g., Fishman et al., 2004). Data from such a design are analyzed by some two-wave analytic technique such as computing a difference (or change) score, a residual change score, or a regression estimate of true change.

Technical Concerns

The ubiquity of two-wave analytic techniques in applied educational research would suggest that these techniques are uncontroversial. Actually, the difference score has been criticized on technical and substantive grounds. The difference score frequently has negative correlation with initial status (i.e., the change score is often negatively correlated with the pretest score). Its relatively low reliability (Bereiter, 1963; Cronbach & Furby, 1970; Linn & Slinde, 1977) is related to a number of factors including measurement error. For a more complete treatment, including cases in which difference scores can be viewed as unbiased estimates of change over time, see Rogosa and Willett (1985). The lesson for design researchers is that unreliability of measurement (and consequently its validity) poses problems even for quantitative researchers with sophisticated instruments. The measures used by design researchers (sometimes using a very small number of items or subjective judgments based on observations of complex classroom processes) cannot be assumed to be either reliable or valid. This clouds the quality of the claims that emerge at each time point, and the change (or learning) that occurs over time.

Substantive Issues

Two time-point designs generate problems because these data provide no precise information on intra-individual change over time. As Willett (1989: 347) noted, it is a:

> . . . conceptualization that views individual learning, not as a process of continuous development over time, but as a quantized acquisition of skills, attitudes, and beliefs. It is as though the individual is delivered a quantum of learning in the time period that intervenes between the pretest measure and the posttest measure, and that our only concern should be with the size of the acquired chunk.

Because many design researchers use two time-point studies few non-content oriented design researchers detail their work in this manner.

Framed analytically, with only two snapshots, individual growth curves cannot be characterized with certainty (Bryk & Weisberg, 1977). The simplest approach is to assume that any growth from time 1 to time 2 is linear (thus allowing the difference score calculation). Mathematically, however, an infinite number of curves could pass through two points. Yet, some design researchers may find reasons to challenge the simple linear model by demonstrating changes over time in terms of apparent mastery by students of increasingly difficult content (e.g., hypothetical learning trajectories [Cobb et al., 2003]).

Considering More Than Two Time-Points

Multiwave (three or more time-points) repeated measurement within a longitudinal design allows for the possibility of better mapping to intra-individual change as it unfolds (Raudenbush & Bryk, 2002; Singer & Willett, 2003). However, the majority of published methodological work in this area is highly technical, requiring quantitative methodological expertise and valid reliable quantitative measures of learning, which typically are not available given the prospective and the iterative character of design research. To bridge the gap between these statistical advances and design research in substantive areas we present a non-technical presentation of several fundamental questions concerning the conceptualization and analysis of change over time.

Fundamental Questions Regarding the Understanding of Change

An adequate methodology for building and assessing a theory of change can be evaluated in terms of the extent to which the theory and commensurate methodology can address the following problems, which are derived from discussions in Collins (1991), Golembiewski et al. (1976), Nesselroade (1991), and Pellegrino et al. (2001).

Problem 1

Do researchers assume the measure of change to be systematic or random? Change can refer to interpretable systematic differences or random fluctuation. As educational and design researchers, we are almost always substantively interested in interpretable systematic change (as opposed to making sense of random fluctuation). However, most, if not all, measuring instruments used in educational research have measurement error. That is, they are not perfectly reliable or valid and as such there are many discrepancies between the constructs and the measures used to operationalize them. As we noted, the difficulty of establishing high reliability in measures can create difficulties for the field in conceptualizing an adequate model of change. An adequate change assessment methodology should account for measurement error and allow observed variance to be partitioned into true construct variance, nonrandom (systematic) error variance, and random error variance.

When the same student or set of students is measured, repeatedly, then time-specific and time-related errors have to be considered carefully. When consecutive measurements, or measurement occasions, are closely spaced, as in teaching experiments, measurement errors will also be correlated. This is especially true when the same measurement tool, or set of items, is used by the researcher. We need to be cognizant of these possible dilemmas and ways to deal with them in our analyses. Where sound quantitative measures are available, autocorrelated error regression models can be used to address this problem (Hedeker & Gibbons, 1997). The solution for mixed method or design research studies is not yet clear. Researchers in each methodological tradition will likely find unique, but somewhat different, answers.

Problem 2

Do researchers consider the change to be reversible? This assumption or realization has important implications for the functional form of the growth curves to be modeled. While it is simple to assume that the growth trajectory may be monotonically increasing or decreasing (e.g., linear), perhaps most psychological interest resides in U-shaped or inverted U-shaped learning curves. These curves may show growth–decline–growth, or decline–growth–decline, respectively. Learning scientists are also interested in curves with plateaus (e.g., stages in growth), or curves that display cubic growth (growth–plateau–further growth). Additionally, an adequate change assessment methodology should allow two things. First, the researcher should be able to specify a priori one or more functional forms. Second, the researcher should be able to assess the goodness-of-fit of each form and the incremental fit of one form over another. The learning theory helps the researcher specify the anticipated functional form of the learning to be measured and modeled. Moreover, such a theory also helps the researcher specify an adequate number of measurement occasions, and the spacing of such measurements.

Problem 3

Change may be assumed to be proceeding in a fixed pathway between sampled time-points. Multiple paths may also occur as students proceed from one time-point to another. For example, some students may follow a linear trajectory, while others followed a quadratic trajectory. An adequate theory of learning should be able to identify and describe why certain subgroups of students follow different paths. In parallel, an adequate assessment methodology should also be able to identify these subgroups, and when data should be optimally collected for each group. Qualitative studies bring these concerns to our attention. Design research studies that purposefully (re)intervene to effect changes in learning can be assumed to promote multi-pathway growth, adding complexity to the statistical and theoretical modeling problems.

Problem 4

Do researchers view change: (a) to be continuous and gradual, (b) to have large magnitude shifts on quantitative variable(s), or (c) to progress through a series of qualitatively distinct stages? Gradual or large shifts can be captured by multi-point analyses. Where there are sharp qualitative shifts in the conceptualization of the phenomenon being measured between time-points (as may be expected with researcher-induced interventions), continuous metric models may be inadequate. One candidate approach to handling such eventualities is Wilson's *Saltus* model (for Piagetian and other stage dependent developmental theory). This model will allow for the detection of stages when these stages have been built into the careful writing and testing of the item pool (Wilson, 1989).[1] A theory for such discrete changes would need to be developed (see Case, 1985) and articulated before the measurement items can be developed, piloted, and tested. But even here the discrete shifts are embedded as an extra parameter in the Rasch model: a psychometric model that forces continuity for fit to the psychometric assumptions of the model to occur (Rasch, 1980).

Sharp, qualitative, and substantive changes in the assumed measurement construct pose significant problems for quantitative modeling. Under certain conditions, not discussed here, growth models can be used to analyze change in non-continuous outcomes such as counts, dichotomies (whether a student persists in a content area or not), and ordinal outcomes. These models are decidedly more sophisticated and draw on the statistical theory of generalized linear models (McCullagh & Nelder, 1989). Only recently, have these statistical models been extended to allow for the analysis of nested data structures (Raudenbush & Bryk, 2002; Singer & Willett, 2003).

Problem 5

Is student growth occurring in what Golembiewski et al. (1976) would consider as *alpha, beta*, and *gamma* change? Alpha change is assumed to be measured against a reasonably constant knowledge base—one that is reliably and validly measured. Measurement invariance across time exists when the numerical values across time are on the same measurement scale (Drasgow, 1984, 1987). Alpha change refers to changes in absolute differences given a constant conceptual domain and a constant measuring instrument (much like data gathered in the Longitudinal Study of American Youth [Miller et al., 2000]).

Beta change refers to changes in the measuring instruments given a constant conceptual domain. Beta change occurs when there is recalibration of the measurement scale. That is, in beta change the observed change results from an alteration in the respondent's subjective metric rather than from actual change in the construct of interest. When beta change occurs there is a stretching or shrinking of the measurement scale, making direct pretest/post-test comparisons problematic.

Gamma change refers to changes in the conceptual domain, e.g., those involving dramatic qualitative shifts in understanding by the students. Lord (1963) highlights this problem in the context of multiplication: "he argued that a multiplication test may be a valid measure of a mathematical skill for young children, but it becomes a measure of memory among teenagers" (Singer & Willett, 2003: 14). Gamma change can take a variety of forms. For example, in the context of factor analysis, the number of factors assessed by a given set of measures may change from one point in time to another. Alternatively, the number of factors may remain constant across time, but a differentiation process may occur so that the factor inter-correlations vary over time. When there is gamma or beta change over time, it is unlikely that a simple growth model will provide usable insight.

Problem 6

Do researchers consider the change to be a shared characteristic of a group of individuals over time, what occurs within individuals overtime, or both (Lave & Wenger, 1990)? This question originally derives from Allport's (1937) distinction between the nomothetic research orientation, which focuses on lawful relations that apply across individuals, and the idiographic research orientation, which focuses on uniqueness of individuals. In design research, this issue of coordinating analyses at the individual and group levels poses significant methodological challenges, particularly when it is difficult to characterize contingent versus the necessary processes affecting learning (Kelly, 2004).

Problem 7

Do researchers assume that there are systematic inter-individual differences in the values of the individual growth parameters (e.g., initial status, and rate of change) that define the individual trajectory (Huttenlocher, et al., 1991), assuming that all individuals have trajectories of the same functional form (e.g., linear, quadratic, etc.)? If so, how can we predict and increase our understanding of these inter-individual differences? The rate of change is a critical individual growth parameter that has been, until recently, neglected in the conceptualization and measurement of inter-individual differences. In many content domains of design research (e.g., learning in mathematics and science), the rate of change is of theoretical and practical importance, and is in need of further study. Moreover, as was demonstrated by Sloane, Helding, and Kelly (this volume) and Sloane (this volume), these rates can now be measured, carefully planned for, and analyzed.

Problem 8

Do researchers assume that there are cross-domain relationships (e.g., issues between content, content knowledge for teaching, and teacher instructional performance) in change over time? Is the relationship between inter-individual differences in intra-individual change over time and the predictors of those differences invariant across domains? These questions can only be addressed statistically with a multivariate, multi-level type analytic tool (see Thum, 1997).

Problem 9

Finally, in order to draw differential claims, the models of change assumed in a group of students under scrutiny may need to be compared to the behavior and learning of students in some other group (e.g., matched comparison students or students in a randomized cohort). The question of interest is whether a specific change pattern found in one group is equal to or differs from (in either magnitude or form) the change pattern found in the comparison group. The drawbacks of non-randomized controls or even matched groups have been documented elsewhere in advocacy pieces for randomized clinical trials in education, but the focus in design research represents a new challenge, methodologically, given the desire to recursively change instruction or artifact design in response to student changes.

Conclusions

If the parameters of growth models are to be valuable for researchers (e.g., educational and design researchers), the actual trajectories being modeled must make conceptual and theoretical sense from the perspective of the researcher and be consistent with a particular learning theory (e.g., the construction of Vergnaud's [1988] theory of additive and multiplicative changes in students' understanding of mathematical constructs). Moreover, the measures must map to the goals of the study. Longitudinal analysis imposes three additional conditions because the metric, validity and precision of the measured outcome must be preserved across the time period under study. The conditions include: (a) the outcome scores must be equitable across time, (b) the outcomes must be equally valid across occasions, and (c) the precision of the measure should also be preserved across time. Meeting these working conditions in educational research, however, is non-trivial, and generates a major challenge for future research.

Given their propensity to actively adapt instructional interventions, to change artifact design repeatedly in response to student learning, to involve subjects (both teacher and students) in iterative design cycles, and to adapt measures and concepts over time, design researchers pose significant challenges to methodologists and psychometricians. In keeping with the creative commissive space of design research (Kelly, 2006), we suggest cooperation across the fields of applied research and methodology in order to provide design researchers with the tools they need, rather than simply fault them for not comporting with models of change in education that are often simplistic or chosen primarily for their mathematical tractability.

Acknowledgments

The first author would like to thank Dan Battey (Mary Lou Fulton College of Education, Arizona State University) for his comments on an earlier draft of this chapter.

Additionally, the first author acknowledges funding from the National Science Foundation, NSF 0634103 (Moving from Arithmetic to Algebra) and NSF 0412537 (i.e., MSP: Project Pathways). Opinions expressed here are those of the author and not necessarily those of the Foundation.

Note

1 Wilson (1989) designed the Saltus model as a developmental extension of the Rasch (1980) model to measure discontinuous stage changes in persons. Saltus is the Latin word for leap. The Saltus model measures state changes using multiple tasks at each of the various developmental levels. Wilson (1989) described the Saltus model in terms of distinctions between first-order and second-order discontinuities. First-order discontinuities are sudden or abrupt changes in a single ability, whereas second-order discontinuities, or shifts, are sudden or abrupt changes in at least two dimensions. The Rasch model is used for the first-order discontinuities, and the Saltus model, which estimates parameters for persons, dimensions, and levels, is used for the second-order discontinuities.

References

Allport, G. W. (1937). *Personality*. New York: Holt.

Bereiter, C. (1963). Some persisting dilemmas in the measurement of change. In C. W. Harris (ed.), *Problems in the measurement of change* (pp. 21–39). Madison: University of Wisconsin Press.

Bryk, A. S. & Weisberg, H. I. (1977). Use of non-equivalent control group design when subjects are growing. *Psychological Bulletin, 104*, 396–404.

Case, R. (1985). *Intellectual development: Birth to adulthood*. New York: Academic Press.

Cobb, P., Confrey, J., diSessa, A., Lehrer, R. & Schauble, L. (2003). Design experiments in educational research. *Educational Researcher, 32*(1), 9–13.

Collins. L. M. (1991). Measurement in longitudinal research. In L. M. Collins & J. L. Horn (eds), *Best methods for the analysis of change* (pp. 137–148). Washington, DC: American Psychological Association.

Cronbach, L. J. & Furby, L. (1970). How should we measure "change"—or should we? *Psychological Bulletin, 74*, 68–70.

Design-Based Research Collective (2003). Design based research: An emerging paradigm for educational inquiry. *Educational Researcher, 32*(1), 5–8.

Drasgow, F. (1984). Scrutinizing psychological tests: Measurement equivalence and equivalent relations with external variables are central issues. *Psychological Bulletin, 95*, 134–135.

Drasgow, F. (1987). Study of measurement bias of two standardized psychological tests. *Journal of Applied Psychology, 72*, 19–29.

Fishman, B., Marx, R., Blumenfeld, P., Krjcik, J. & Soloway, E. (2004). Creating a framework for research on systemic technology innovations. *Journal of the Learning Sciences, 13*, 43–76.

Golembiewski, R. T., Billingsley, K. & Yeager, S. (1976). Measuring change and persistence in human affairs: Types of change generated by OD designs. *Journal of Applied Behavioral Science, 12*, 133–157.

Hedeker, D. & Gibbons, R. (1997). Applications of random effects pattern mixture models for missing data in social sciences. *Psychological Methods, 2*, 64–78.

Huttenlocher, J., Haight, W., Bryk, A., Seltzer, M. & Lyons, T. (1991). Early vocabulary growth: relation to language input and gender. *Developmental Psychology, 27*, 236–248.

Kelly, A. E. (2004). Design research in education: Yes, but is it methodological? *Journal of the Learning Sciences, 13*, 115–128.

Kelly, A. E. (2006). Quality criteria for design research: Evidence and commitments. In J. van den Akker, K. Gravemeijer, S. McKenney & N. Nieveen (eds), *Educational design research* (pp. 166–184). London: Routledge.

Lave, J. & Wenger, E. (1991). *Situated learning: Legitimate peripheral participation*. Cambridge: Cambridge University Press.

Linn, R. L. & Slinde, J. A. (1977). The determination of the significance of change between pre- and posttesting periods. *Review of Educational Research, 47*, 121–150.

Lord, F. (1963). Elementary models for measuring change. In C. W. Harris (ed.), *Problems in the measurement of change* (pp. 21–39). Madison: University of Wisconsin Press.

McCullagh, P. & Nelder, J. A. (1989). *Generalized linear models* (2nd ed.). London: Chapman and Hall.

Miller, J. D., Kimmel, L. Hoffer, T. B. & Nelson, C. (2000). *Longitudinal study of American youth: User's manual*. Chicago: International Center for the Advancement of Scientific Literacy, Northwestern University.

Nesselroade, J. R. (1991). Interindividual differences in intra-individual change. In L. M. Collins & J. L. Horn (eds), *Best methods for the analysis of change* (pp. 92–105). Washington, DC: American Psychological Association.

Pellegrino, J. W., Chudowsky, N. & Glaser R. (2001). *Knowing what students know: The science and design of educational assessment*. Washington, DC: National Academy Press.

Rasch, G. (1980). *Probabilistic models for some intelligence and attainment tests* (expanded edition). Chicago: University of Chicago Press.

Raudenbush, S. W. & Bryk, A. S. (2002). *Hierarchical linear models* (2nd ed.). Thousand Oaks, CA: Sage.

Rogosa, D. R. & Willett J. B. (1985). Understanding correlates of change by modeling individual differences in growth. *Psychometrika, 50*, 203–228.

Shadish, W., Cook, T. & Campbell, D. (2002). *Experimental and quasi-experimental designs for generalized causal inference*. New York: Houghton Mifflin.

Singer, J. & Willett, J. B. (2003). *Applied longitudinal data analysis: Modeling change and event occurrence*. Oxford: Oxford University Press.

Slater, A. & Bremner, G. (2003). Introduction to developmental psychology. Malden, MA: Blackwell.

Thum, Y. M. (1997). Hierarchical linear models for multivariate behavioral data. *Journal of Educational and Behavioral Statistics, 22*, 77–108.

Vergnaud, G. (1988). Multiplicative structures. In J. Hiebert & M. Behr (eds). *Number concepts and operations in the middle grades* (pp. 141–161). Reston, VA: National Council of Teachers of Mathematics.

Willett, J. B. (1989). Some results on reliability for the longitudinal measurement of change: Implications for the design of studies of individual growth. *Educational and Psychological Measurement, 49*, 587–602.

Wilson, M. (1989). Saltus: A psychometric model of discontinuity in cognitive development. *Psychological Bulletin, 105*, 276–289.

23 Longitudinal Analysis and Interrupted Time Series Designs

Opportunities for the Practice of Design Research

Finbarr C. Sloane and Brandon Helding
Arizona State University

Anthony E. Kelly
George Mason University

Introduction

Design researchers are interested in devising and iterating innovative interventions to support student (and teacher) learning, particularly in situations where the extant research provides little guidance. In the practice of design research, many students and teachers participate in multiple forms or iterates of the designed artifact or emerging practice. Multiple iterates make it difficult to know which version of the artifact, or changed practice, caused the observed change, or learning, on the part of the participants. Logically, there is no counterfactual (e.g., control condition). From the perspective of data modeling and analysis, one option is to treat students as their own control. That is, researchers can look at student trajectories over time and ask whether the growth trajectory changes significantly with parallel changes that are occurring in the artifact or practice (that is being re-designed). Taking a longitudinal perspective can provide design researchers with insight and sources of evidence to support causal claims they could not otherwise entertain. This chapter will describe the use of an "interrupted time series research design" as a plan for the conduct of design research. This type of design offers strength and direction regarding the number of subjects and the spacing of time-points needed to buttress the design researchers' efforts to warrant their claims for the effectiveness of their design interventions.

We begin by describing a simplified design research study and suggest how its argumentative grammar could be structured by re-conceptualizing it, methodologically. Next, we outline recent changes in the analysis of longitudinal data. Then, we describe a research design framework for such analysis: the interrupted time series design, and show that this framework maps nicely to needs of design researchers. In sum, we show that it is possible to marry the many advances in statistical modeling and quantitative research methods to the emerging procedures, practices, and goals of design research.

The Simulation

Here, we simulate a design research study in which we envisage a researcher who is interested in understanding how students' comprehension of ideas in mathematics (in an area with little prior research) can be advanced by the design and re-design of some artifact (e.g., instructional software, curricular intervention, or pedagogical technique). The goal of the researcher is to determine the extent to which it is possible to advance the students' comprehension as measured by a disciplinary description of the content, and, simultaneously learn from and provide feedback to the teacher:

1   The researcher should establish a baseline of competence or mastery in the domain for the students. This step requires one or more measures, which should be reliable and valid. These tests may be given once, or a number of times in order to establish the character of the trend in understanding.
2   The design researcher then intervenes with an early version of the artifact and determines the impact of this "perturbation" on the classroom system (i.e., how do the students and teacher respond?). This intervention is video-taped and otherwise documented.
3   As in Cobb et al. (2003), the design researcher then retrospectively analyzes the learning events with the teacher and other researchers. He or she may administer an additional test or other form of assessment. On the basis of this analysis, the design researcher then decides what changes, if any, to make to the artifact.[1]
4   The design researcher may intervene with a modification to the artifact. The study then advances, repeating Steps 2 and 3 (with the evolving artifact) until some stopping rule is triggered (e.g., end of semester, unit, and resource limitations).

In Figure 23.1 we describe the general process associated with the simulation. First, we see that the testing of student knowledge without intervention shows little by way of student development. Next, we see the effects of the first designed iteration across four measurements. Finally, we see the effects of the second major design iterate. In the context of learning rational numbers, we might consider phases B and C as mapping to Vergnaud's (1988) conceptualization of student understanding of additive and multiplicative mathematical structures. Explicitly, the goal of the design intervention might be: (a) to improve student knowledge of additive structure, and (b) to develop multiplicative insight and models on the part of students as they learn rational numbers. Design iterate number II, which occurs during measurement phase C, serves to develop a qualitative change in student understanding of rational numbers. It is clear that not all students will follow this idealized trajectory. However, the figure serves to highlight the explicit goals of the design researcher in terms of student learning of mathematics.

The products of the design research include documentation of the changes in student learning from the baseline, changes in teacher learning or behaviors, early and later versions of the artifact, some humble theorizing about learning and teaching this

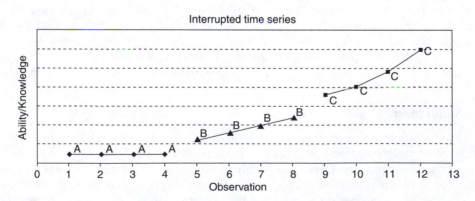

Figure 23.1 The Simulation from an Interrupted Time Series Perspective.

content (e.g., a local instructional theory, Cobb et al., 2003), and an argument for implications that the study may have in larger or other contexts.

Modeling Change: Recent Advances

Over the past 25 years, longitudinal modeling has become increasingly popular in the social sciences (Raudenbush & Bryk, 2002) because the tools to support these analyses have improved significantly (Hedecker, 2004). For example, the hierarchical linear model, a tool described by Sloane (this volume), allows for irregularly spaced measurements across time, time-varying and time-invariant covariates, accommodations of person specific deviations from the average time trend, and the estimation of population variance associated with these individual effects (Bryk & Raudenbush, 1992). However, longitudinal data analysis requires the researcher to be explicit about the outcomes of the designed intervention and how they will be measured. Sloane and Kelly address this issue of measurement in design research (this volume). We do not take up this issue in this chapter other than to note the need for high quality measurement tools that work well at single and multiple time-points (for greater specificity, see Singer and Willett, 2003).

In longitudinal models, subjects are measured on a number of occasions (three or more), and the researcher is interested in the shape of the learner's development (or growth) over time and what predicts differences across learners in their respective growth curves. Specifically, the researcher is interested in answers to two separate, but entwined questions (Singer & Willett, 2003): (a) how does the measured outcome change over time for individuals (or groups), and (b) can we predict or model the character of these differences that occur over time? These two questions are central to design researchers who iteratively build artifacts to positively affect student learning. Moreover, they sit at the core of every study of change. The first question is descriptive in its nature, asking us to characterize each subject's pattern of change over time. Is the change linear or non-linear? Is the pattern of change consistent or not? In our simulation this question asks if students improve their capacity to function as mathematical learners moving from additive to multiplicative insight with respect to their knowledge of rational numbers. The second question is relational and predictive. Here we focus attention on the association between independent variables and patterns of change in the sampled data. Does participation in the design study change one's pattern of learning? Following our simulation, we use the baseline data to simulate what learning could have been without the designed intervention. We can now examine the data patterns to see if a significant change in the learning trajectory has occurred for students who participated in the design innovation. Additionally, we can ask if all subjects experience the same pattern of change. For example, do males and females share the same pattern of change?

The first question requires the formulation of a within-person model (the intra-individual growth model); the second question requires a between-person model (the inter-individual model). These questions are also important for design researchers. However, they are framed as what changes occur within, or during, a design iterate, and what predicts differences between these changes across design iterates (see Cobb et al., 2003; Design-Based Research Collective, 2003; Fishman et al., 2004).

In an effort to deal with these questions, the statistical modeling of change has improved significantly in the past 25 years (Hedecker, 2004). These relatively new modeling tools have not influenced the conduct of design research, perhaps because they are quite technical in nature. Whatever the reason, this result is unfortunate as the iterative structure of design research leads itself nicely to the study of student growth over time. The design researcher can pose the following set of questions: what growth occurs in student learning during a design iterate of an intervention? Is this growth the same for all participants? Is the growth due to the innovation? Does the growth trajectory change for participants who stay in the study during design iterate two? Following our simulation, we ask if students draw on multiplicative models when responding to items used to measure rational number knowledge. Does the trajectory of learning increase or decrease as a consequence of changes in the learning artifact? Again, are the growth trajectories the same across groups of participants?

Clearly, the designed artifact changes carefully with each design iteration and many of the research questions will themselves recur in parallel with the number of artifact iterations. Consequently, we argue for a one-to-one correspondence between the style of analysis, and the design research paradigm as presented by members of that research community (Cobb et al., 2003; Design Based Research Collective, 2003; Fishman et al., 2004).

Longitudinal or Multiwave Analysis

We define longitudinal studies as studies where subjects are measured repeatedly, and where the research interest focuses on characterizing subject growth across time. Traditional analysis of variance methods for such repeated measures models are described by Bock (1975). These traditional methods are of limited use to design researchers because of restrictive assumptions concerning missing data across time, and the variance-covariance structure of the repeated measures. The univariate "mixed-model" analysis of variance assumes that the variances and covariances of the dependent variable are equal across time. This is rarely sustainable in practice. The multivariate analysis of variance for repeated measures is also quite restrictive. Models of this variety force the researcher to omit from the analysis subjects without complete data across all time-points. In general, these two procedures focus our attention on the estimation of group trends across time and provide little by way of assistance to our understanding of specific individual's change over time. For these reasons, hierarchical linear models (HLMs; Bryk & Raudenbush, 1992) have become the method of choice for quantitative growth modeling of longitudinal data.

Several features make HLMs especially useful to the longitudinal researcher. First, subjects are not assumed to be measured on, or at, the same number of time-points. Consequently, subjects with incomplete data across time are included in the analysis. The ability to include subjects with incomplete data across time is an important advantage relative to procedures that require complete data for all children across all time-points because we can include all the collected data, increasing the statistical power of the analysis. Further, complete case analysis suffers from biases to the extent that children with complete data are not representative of the larger population of children. That is, many children miss days during the school year—this is particularly true of lower SES children—and when we exclude these children from our analysis our results reflect only those students who happened to always attend when data were collected. This bias would reflect very unrealistic school and design research settings. Second, because time is treated as a continuous variable in HLMs, individuals do not have to be measured at the same time-points. In general, this is useful for analysis of longitudinal studies in which follow-up times are not uniform across all participants. This is particularly useful to design researchers as it is unlikely that student interviews or testing for example will occur on the same day for all children. Third, time-invariant and time-varying covariates can be included in the longitudinal model, providing a conceptually rich framework for analysis, a framework that better maps to the realities of schools and classrooms. Put simply, changes in student learning may be due to characteristics of the individual that are stable over time (e.g., student gender) as well as characteristics that change across time (e.g., individual interactions with the design innovation). Finally, whereas traditional approaches estimate average change in a population (across time), HLMs can also estimate individual change for each subject. These estimates of individual change are particularly useful when proportions (or groups) of students exhibit change that differs from the average trend. That is, HLMs afford richer insight when we expect different groups of students to grow at differing rates because these differences can be modeled. The HLM modeling technique affords the longitudinal researcher the opportunity to (Bryk & Raudenbush, 1992):

- Specify the structure of the mean growth trajectory.
- Model the extent and character of individual variation around the mean growth.
- Estimate the reliability of the measures for studying both status and growth.
- Estimate the correlation between entry status and growth rate.
- Model correlates of both status and growth.

In the next section we describe the general structure of the hierarchical linear model when used to investigate change. It should come as no surprise that its features parallel the two basic questions we have posed about change, the former descriptive and the latter predictive.

A General Two-Level Growth Model

Many individual change phenomena can be represented through a two-level HLM. At Level 1, each subject's development is represented by an individual growth trajectory that depends on a unique set of parameters and some error. As a set, these individual parameters become the outcome variables at Level 2, where their variability can (possibly) be accounted for by a set of between-person characteristics. Formally, the repeated measures on each subject are considered nested within each individual. As a consequence, this model is less restrictive than the multivariate repeated measures model, allowing for uneven spacing of measures and missing data in the Level 1 model.

We assume the Y_{it}, the observed status at time t for individual i, is a function of a systematic growth trajectory (or growth curve) plus random error. It is convenient to assume that systematic growth over time can be represented as a polynomial of degree P. Then, the Level 1 model is:

$$Y_{it} \text{ (Subject i's response at time t)} = f \text{ (Growth parameters + error)} \qquad (1)$$

In the Level 2 model, we ask if these growth parameters vary across subjects. We represent this parameter variation in the between-subject model:

$$\text{Growth curve of subject} = f \text{ (Subjects' background characteristics + error)} \qquad (2)$$

We use these two equations to structure our longitudinal investigations. The first equation forms the basis for our descriptive questions. The second equation supports our predictive explorations of the variation that occurs across individuals in the first equation. Consequently, the two models map in one-to-one correspondence with the two questions posed earlier: (a) how does the measured outcome change over time, and (b) can we predict differences in these changes? The shape of the growth curve is central to our understanding, and estimation, of the designed innovation.

In sum, modeling techniques for longitudinal data have changed dramatically over the past 25 years, affording the educational design researcher more opportunity to map to the practical (and often) critical realities of classrooms and schools. These advances afford design researchers access to a set of analytic tools they normally do not use but which are now robust to the daily life of the learning settings in which design researchers work.

A Research Design for Design Research: The Interrupted Time Series Model

To properly discuss interrupted time series designs (ITSDs), it is first necessary to define them in some functional way. According to Cook and Campbell (1979), ITSDs involve multiple observations over time on the same units (e.g., particular individuals) or on different, but similar, individuals (e.g., same community or worksite); and require knowing when an intervention took place in order to compare before and after treatment. We draw on this definition and address each element of the definition separately. The elements include: methodological variations of interrupted time series designs, and considerations that need to be met when using ITSDs and its variants.

Observations

A crucial element of ITSDs is the number of time-points over which data are collected. The number of time-points needed varies based on the type of inferences and analyses intended. Time-points typically consist of observations on some measurement device (e.g. interview, assessment, or test) that occur, on a number of occasions before, during and after the treatment or design iterate. Whatever measure is used at each time-point, validity of the measuring tool is a required condition. Because validity is a very broad topic, it is not included in this discussion (see Nitko & Brookhart, 2007). Likewise, reliability of whatever measure is employed is critically important to the ITSD; although it, too, is not discussed in depth here (see Brennan, 2001).

The frequency and quantity of observations is largely based on other design characteristics, including analytic design features, expected main effects, and a desired model (Shadish et al., 2002). Classic statistical analyses (e.g., t- or F-tests) require that data at one time point be independent of data collected at any other time point. But, because ITSDs, much like design research, use multiple observations over the same or similar participants, its observations are necessarily autocorrelated. When traditional techniques are used to estimate the size of an autocorrelation, the task is laborious and large samples of time-points are needed (Box et al., 1994; Shadish et al., 2002; Velicer & Harrop, 1983). However, hierarchical or multilevel modeling tools allow one to adjust for autocorrelated errors without the need for this additional data collection—sometimes in the hundreds. In fact, one can get by with as few as three measures per design iterate (Hedeker, 2004). Additional design features can be integrated into an ITSD to reduce the number of observations needed, but trade-offs between the quality of inferences desired and the number of observations are inevitable. The combination of the ITSD with modern multilevel statistical tools offers the design researcher a flexible analytic environment in which to work.

Same or Similar Units

Interrupted time series designs include multiple observations over time on the same or similar units. These "units" are embodied in the social sciences as people or groups of people. For the learning scientist, these units include individuals, dyads, groups, and classrooms of learners. One requirement of ITSDs is that the same units be employed over time. This requirement is not problematic as many design researchers use the same students over many cycles of the design process. And, fortunately, this is an advantage from the ITSD perspective.

Knowledge and Timing of the Intervention

Interrupted time series designs can provide a reasonably strong "causal" frame even in quasi-experimental settings. Consequently, this discussion will focus on ITSDs when randomized control-treatment groups are not possible and multiple observations are used as the quasi-experimental alternative. One of the primary distinguishing elements of the ITSD, apart from more general time series designs, is knowledge of the intervention.

The onus of the intervention is yoked to the researchers or those implementing the research. This feature is again advantageous from a design research perspective. This is especially true when changes in the intervention itself are held constant during different intervals (or cycles) of the time series, the fidelity and similarity of each treatment (within cycle) is then vital to comprehensible results. Given that design researchers develop the innovation, this feature of ITSD aligns nicely with the design researcher's intent.

The three design elements—multiple observations, timeliness of intervention, and similar units of analysis—work in concert to provide for strong inferential possibilities. Interrupted time series designs, like all quasi-experimental designs, are fraught with plausible alternative causes, but accurate knowledge of intervention with multiple observations across similar units serve as design elements that can be optimized to reduce the likelihood that alternative hypotheses come into play, and in doing so they increase the resulting accuracy of the final inferences.

Methodological Variations

To address threats to internal validity listed by Shadish et al. (2002), we suggest possible alterations to the ITSD. Variations on the ITSD include adding a control group, observing multiple variables, removing treatment, lapsed treatment, and switching control and treatment groups (ibid.). We discuss a number of these alternatives that we think may be appropriate to the design researcher.

Including a Control Group

The classic variation on ITSDs includes a no-treatment control group (Shadish et al., 2002). Randomization to the conditions is preferable because it increases the internal validity of the study, but is often not possible. In many design studies no control group is included, and as noted earlier, ITSD allows the individual students to serve as their own control as long as good baseline data are available. The inclusion of a different group that is not randomly selected and not given an intervention allows for comparison over time with a treatment group and strengthens resulting inferences. Because the comparison group is not randomly selected, trade-offs between inferential ability and experimental design are inevitable. Systematic differences between groups confound inferences, but insofar as the groups are similar, and systematic differences do not exist, the effect demonstrated through observation is the result of the designed artifacts (rather than latent or unknown causes).

Observing Multiple Variables

Shadish et al. (2002) also suggest adding measures that focus on another variable that is conceptually related to the primary dependent variable and that is equally sensitive to threats of internal validity. Consequently, any documented change in the main dependent variable that does not occur in the secondary dependent variable is unlikely to be caused by a threat to validity that both variables share and increases the internal validity of the study.

Removing the Learning Artifact

Another concession to the threats of internal validity is adding a treatment over some number of intervals, and then removing the treatment. The ITSD constitutes, in this case, essentially two interrupted time series experiments, one that tests the addition of the treatment, and one that tests its removal (Shadish et al., 2002). Problems associated with plausible alternatives still exist, especially when a treatment's effect is long-lasting or permanent. For instance, if a treatment's effects are permanent, removing that treatment will not yield any new results. Furthermore, given the sensitivity of children as research subjects, it is not always ethical to remove a treatment that proves effective. As such, removing a treatment in ITSDs is not always possible in practice, but can, and does, strengthen the inferential space when this level of control is available and appropriately used by design researchers.

Considerations

We believe that the interrupted time series research design, aligned with improvements in the statistical modeling of longitudinal data, provides the design researcher with a quantitative methodology to investigate the effect of design-based innovations. However, this belief is not without caveat. Assumed throughout this discussion of ITSDs and previously mentioned, is the a priori requirement of a reliable and valid measure at each observation. This point should be emphasized. Without a reliable measure each observation may produce slightly different results and mimic a successful treatment. Moreover, effective results can also be missed due to lack of reliable measurement. These are not trivial insights and the issues of measurement in design research are deserving of further investigation (Sloane & Kelly, this volume, address some of these concerns and highlight others). Additionally, without a valid measure each observation may not reflect the intended phenomenon and produce spurious or falsely negative results. A reliable and valid measure is critical to effectively implement an ITSD in a design research setting.

   All treatments do not behave equally. Some treatments are slow acting. That is, they take time to diffuse sufficiently throughout the sample to produce results (Shadish et al., 2002). Step functions are one way of analytically negotiating slow-acting treatments (Holder & Wagenaar, 1994; Shadish et al., 2002). Other treatments have delayed effects that, without long observational periods, can be missed. Some treatments may be more abrupt than expected. Innovations lasting longer than necessary can produce unintended consequences that can overshadow the effect of one properly timed. The operative point is that treatments can have unpredictable effects over time based on idiosyncrasies within samples (and the treatment itself), and we need to exercise due caution in our inferences. In sum, the interrupted time series research design offers the potential strong warrant when properly implemented and analyzed.

Some Lessons for Design Researchers

Design researchers are invariably interested in student learning. They spend their research careers devising and iterating innovative ways of supporting student learning. Whether framed explicitly or implicitly, fundamental questions in design research center upon issues of individual and group learning. If we are to improve educational practice in our schools by way of improved instruction, or by the deployment of innovative technologies, then the accurate measurement of individual learning can provide one yardstick by which the effectiveness of pedagogy and the effectiveness of innovation can be judged. Similarly, valid and reliable statistical tools are required for the measurement and modeling student learning in designed settings. Design researchers employ iterative design as a central tenet of their work. Moreover, much design research is conducted with students in what might be considered a case setting. As such, many students participate in multiple forms or iterates of the designed artifact. This makes it difficult to know which version of the artifact caused the wanted change or learning on the part of the participants. One way to work around this lack of control is to treat students as their own control. That is, researchers can look at student trajectories over time and ask whether the growth trajectory changes significantly with parallel changes that are occurring simultaneously in the artifact under study. Taking a longitudinal perspective can provide design researchers in education insight they could not otherwise entertain.

The ITSD is a mode of investigation that allows us to explicitly consider change over time when the intervention is well understood, or in development (but held constant within a design iterate), when multiple observations are possible during the testing of a design iterate, and when the same or similar units of analysis can be measured at each observation. Having access to a control group can yield an experimental design that adheres both to traditional control treatment and interrupted time series research designs. We believe that the interrupted time series design, when aligned with appropriate analytic techniques (e.g., HLMs or other multilevel modeling techniques) provide the design researcher with a stronger arsenal of research tools that go beyond case study methods. The employment of this new tool kit will impose measurement precision on the design researcher.

Conclusions

In this short chapter, we sought to indicate by use of a simulated example how it is possible to marry the many advances in statistical and research methods to the emerging procedures, practices, and goals of design research. We hope that this work can serve to inspire conversations among different genres of research to the mutual benefit of all in the service of advancing educational research methods and the tenor of our scientific claims, generally. We hope that this chapter has helped increase the awareness and understanding of longitudinal methods and longitudinal designs and their potential for analyzing the learning outcomes inherent in design-based research.

Acknowledgments

The first author would like to thank Dan Battey (Mary Lou Fulton College of Education, Arizona State University) for his having to listen to the many drafts of this paper that occurred orally. Additionally, the first author acknowledges funding from the National Science Foundation, NSF 0634103 (Moving from Arithmetic to Algebra) and NSF 0412537 (i.e., MSP: Project Pathways). Opinions expressed here are those of the author and not necessarily those of the Foundation.

Note

1 We suggest that the design researcher collect measures on multiple occasions within a design iterate. Here, we define a design iterate as a period where the innovation is reasonably stable. That is, it is a period where the researcher (and his or her team) is involved in thinking about changes to the design but has not as yet enacted those changes. The length of this "period" is not fixed across iterations.

References

Bock, R. D. (1975). *Multivariate statistical methods in behavioral research*. New York: McGraw-Hill.

Box, G. E. P., Jenkins, G. M. & Reinsel, G. C. (1994). *Time series analysis: Forecasting and control* (3rd ed.). Englewood Cliffs, NJ: Prentice Hall.

Brennan, R. L. (2001). An essay on the history and future of reliability from the perspective of replications. *Journal of Educational Measurement, 38*, 295–317.

Bryk, A. S. & Raudenbush, S. W. (1992). *Hierarchical linear models: applications and data analysis methods*. Newbury Park, CA: Sage.

Cobb, P., Confrey, J., diSessa, A., Lehrer, R. & Schauble, L. (2003). Design experiments in educational research. *Educational Researcher, 32*(1), 9–13.

Cook, T. D. & Campbell, D. T. (1979). *Quasi-experimentation: Design and analysis issues for field settings*. Chicago, IL: Rand-McNally.

Design-Based Research Collective (2003). Design based research: An emerging paradigm for educational inquiry. *Educational Researcher, 32*(1), 5–8.

Fishman, B., Marx, R., Blumenfeld, P., Krajcik, J. & Soloway, E. (2004). Creating a framework for research on systemic technology innovations. *Journal of the Learning Sciences, 13*, 43–76.

Hedeker, D. (2004). An introduction to growth modeling. In D. Kaplan (ed.), *The Sage handbook of quantitative methodology for the social sciences* (pp. 215–234). Thousand Oaks, CA: Sage.

Holder, H. D. & Wagenaar, A. C. (1994). Mandated server training and reduced alcohol-involved traffic crashes: A time series analysis of the Oregon experience. *Accident Analysis and Prevention, 26*, 89–97.

Nitko, A. J. & Brookhart, S. M. (2007). *Educational assessment of students* (5th ed.). Upper Saddle River, NJ: Prentice Hall.

Raudenbush, S. W. & Bryk, A. S. (2002). *Hierarchical linear models* (2nd ed.). Thousand Oaks, CA: Sage.

Shadish, W. R., Cook, T. D. & Campbell, D. T. (2002). *Experimental and quasi-experimental designs for generalized causal inference*. Boston, MA: Houghton Mifflin.

Singer, J. & Willett, J. (2003). *Applied longitudinal data analysis: Modeling change and event occurrence*. Oxford: Oxford University Press.

Velicer, W. F. & Harrop, J. (1983). The reliability and accuracy of time series model identification. *Evaluation Review, 7*, 551–560.

Vergnaud, G. (1988). Multiplicative structures. In J. Hiebert & M. Behr (eds), *Number concepts and operations in the middle grades* (pp. 141–161). Reston, VA: National Council of Teachers of Mathematics.

24 Multilevel Models in Design Research

A Case from Mathematics Education

Finbarr C. Sloane
Arizona State University

Introduction

Because of the inherently hierarchical nature of many learning environments, data collected in these environments are nested in structure. More specifically, students work in dyads or groups. These groups are nested in classrooms, classrooms in schools, and schools in local cultures and school districts. Design researchers working in field settings build theory and design products to support learning in such environments. Consequently, design researchers must deal constantly with data structures of the type described here. Although much design research is qualitative in nature, this chapter takes a quantitative perspective and describes how quantitative researchers have begun to deal with nested data structures and the complexities of building theory and drawing inferences when data have this nested structure. In this chapter, the hierarchical linear model (HLM) is described and it is shown how this model provides a conceptual and statistical mechanism for investigating simultaneously how phenomena at different levels interact with each other. In so doing, the aggregation concerns raised by Saari (this volume) are addressed.

In his insightful chapter in this volume, Saari raises a number of issues that mathematics education researchers (in particular) and design researchers (in general) need to be wary of as they study data that have a nested or hierarchical structure. Of central concern in Saari's discussion is the issue of data aggregation. One purpose of this chapter is to demonstrate a particular resolution for the aggregation problem in hierarchically-ordered data structures known as HLMs. This chapter will show why these models are important for design researchers as they try to build theories with data from individual students and the environments in which they learn. In taking this quantitative approach, design researchers can construct and test stronger, more theoretically valid, inferences that are free from the aggregation and ecological issues raised by Saari.

In schools, classrooms, and other learning environments (e.g., after-school settings), students are often placed in groups for the purposes of play and learning (whether the groups are dyads or larger learning groups). How to investigate these hierarchically-ordered structures, where students are nested in learning environments, has been a concern for educational, psychological and sociological researchers since the middle of the twentieth century (Robinson, 1950). The study of hierarchy has been of intellectual interest in a number of disciplines for quite some time. For example, researchers in sociology (Mason et al., 1983), economics (e.g., Hanushek, 1974), education (e.g., Bryk & Raudenbush, 1992; Burstein, 1980; Murchan & Sloane; 1994), biology (e.g., Laird & Ware, 1982), and statistics (e.g., Longford, 1989, 1993), have all discussed the issues and solutions to problems generated when data are drawn from hierarchically-ordered systems. From a design science perspective, two themes have dominated these discussions: (a) issues about the aggregation of data, and (b) how to investigate relationships between variables residing at different hierarchical levels (see Saari, this volume).

With regard to aggregation, discussions have focused on whether it is appropriate to aggregate data and on the types of inferences that can be made from aggregated data (see Burstein, 1978; Firebaugh, 1978; Hannan & Burstein, 1974; Robinson, 1950). These discussions, as they relate to theory building, can be found in the learning science literature (see Barab & Kirshner, 2001), and in statistics (Goldstein, 1995; Hannan & Burstein 1974; Raudenbush & Bryk, 2002) have examined the theoretical and statistical issues associated with the use of aggregate measures to draw inferences about higher-level units.

Although aggregation issues are certainly an important aspect of design research, they are not the focus here. The aim in this chapter is to address the second major theme: namely, how to investigate relationships between variables located at different levels of a learning hierarchy (see Bryk & Raudenbush, 1992) while avoiding the issues attendant to aggregation (for example, ecological fallacies; Robinson, 1950). These inferential fallacies occur, as Saari (in this volume) hints, when the researcher observes a relationship at one level of analysis, say the group, and infers incorrectly that the relationship will hold in the same way at another level of analysis, say the individual student (Murchan & Sloane, 1994).

Relationships that Cross Hierarchical Levels

Given the structure of learning environments, it is clear that variables at one hierarchical level (e.g., the group) can and do influence variables at another hierarchical level (e.g., individuals). Numerous theoretical discussions and empirical investigations have identified relationships between variables that reside at different levels. For example, Cobb and Yackel's (1996) work on the development of sociomathematical norms looks at these relationships from the other direction—from the bottom up. Sloane (2005) has argued the need for a multilevel theory in educational research that goes beyond single-level perspectives and blends both psychological and sociological theoretical lenses with the mutual goals of improved theory and increased capacity to scale designed interventions in real-world settings. In other words, in the scaling of educational interventions in mathematics we need a multilevel theory of implementation that accounts for and maps better to the learning settings in which students find themselves (Fishman et al., 2004).

Hierarchical Data: Three Possible Options

Following on the theoretical work of Yackel and Cobb (1996), Sloane (2005) argued that researchers in education need to investigate variables that span multiple levels of analysis. Thus, to study individual behavior in learning environments, one must measure and integrate individual attributes of students and also salient aspects of the environment in which they are performing (Lave & Wenger, 1991). Similarly, in order to investigate the structure of learning environments as a whole, one needs to measure the attributes of the learning settings as well as the organizational environments that support them. For example, we need to investigate students' learning both in groups and in classrooms that support such group learning. In either case, the resulting data will include variables that reside at different levels of analysis (i.e., variables describing the lower level units as well as the higher-level contexts). Typically, researchers are interested in investigating both lower-level and higher-level influences on a lower-level outcome variable. This type of investigation has been referred to as cross-level in nature (Sloane, 2005).

In cases where variables exist at more than one level of analysis (e.g., a lower-level outcome and both lower-level and higher-level predictors), there are three main options for data analysis. First, one can disaggregate the group level data such that each lower-level unit is assigned a score representing the higher-level unit within which it is nested. The data analysis for this option, therefore, would be based on the total number of lower-level units included in the study and represents a traditional psychological approach with an emphasis on individual differences. For example, all individuals might receive a score representing their classroom's sociomathematical norms, with the investigation centered on the relationship between such norms and individual students' beliefs about mathematics. The problem with this solution is that multiple individuals are in the same learning group and, as a result, are exposed to similar stimuli in the group. Thus, one cannot satisfy the independence of observations assumption that underlies traditional statistical approaches (Raudenbush & Bryk, 2002). Even when two students share the same classroom we should not infer that each has equal access to the same instructional resources as would be implied in this psychological model setting. In addition to violating this assumption, the disaggregation approach results in another problem. Statistical tests involving the variable at the higher-level unit are based on the total number of lower-level units (e.g., the effect of the group's cohesion is assessed based on the number of individuals, and not the number of groups). This practice underestimates the standard errors and raises questions about the associated statistical inferences (Bryk & Raudenbush, 1992).

The second major approach is to aggregate the lower-level units and investigate the relationships at the aggregate level of analysis. This we consider a traditional sociological perspective. For example, one could investigate the relationship between group characteristics and individual outcomes by aggregating the individual outcomes to the group level. This parallels the process followed by McClain and her colleagues in their qualitative studies of developmental research in mathematics education (McClain et al., 1996). From a statistical perspective, the disadvantage of this approach is that potentially meaningful individual-level variance in the outcome measure is ignored. Theoretically, one is limited to conceptualizations of the group structure only; that is, no cross-level inferences can be drawn. Sensibly, McClain and her colleagues infer correctly to group characteristics only. However, interactions (rich or otherwise) across levels are not evaluated in this research tradition. In summary, the traditional choice has been between a disaggregated model that violates statistical assumptions and assesses the impact of higher-level units based on the number of lower-level units, or an aggregated model that discards potentially meaningful, lower-level variance. Neither of these two options, the simple psychological approach or the solely sociological approach, is fully satisfactory.

HLMs represent the third major approach to dealing with hierarchically-nested data structures. Statistically, these models are designed specifically to overcome the weakness of the disaggregated and aggregated approaches discussed above. First, these models recognize explicitly that individuals in a particular group may be more similar to one another than individuals in other groups and, therefore, may not provide independent observations. These multilevel statistical approaches explicitly model both individual and group residuals, thus recognizing the partial interdependence of individuals in the same group (this is in contrast to ordinary least-squares [OLS] regression approaches where individual and group residuals are not estimated separately). Second, these statistical models allow one to investigate both lower-level unit and higher-level unit variance in the outcome measure while maintaining the appropriate level of analysis for the independent variables. Therefore, one can model both individual and group variance in individual outcomes while using individual predictors at the individual level and group predictors at the group level. Thus, HLMs overcome the disadvantages of the two previous approaches because one can explicitly model both within- and between-group variance, as well as investigate the influence of higher-level units on lower-level outcomes, all the while maintaining the appropriate level of analysis. This top-down model contrasts significantly with the bottom-up, or emergent models in which some qualitative design researchers engage.[1]

Hierarchical Linear Models

A Framing

As noted above, one of the primary advantages of HLMs is that they allow one to investigate simultaneously relationships within a particular hierarchical level, as well as relationships between or across hierarchical levels. In order to model both the within-level and between-level relationships, the researcher needs to estimate two models simultaneously: one that models relationships within each of the lower-level units and another to model how these relationships within units vary between units. This type of two-level, modeling approach defines HLMs (Bryk & Raudenbush, 1992).

Conceptually, HLMs are relatively straightforward. For clarity, we refer to the two levels here as individuals and groups; however, the methods apply to any situation in which there are lower-level units nested within higher-level units. These models adopt the following two-level approach to cross-level investigations where the level-one model is estimated separately for each group. Typically, this takes the form of a regression-based model such as:

$$\text{Level 1: } Y_{ij} = B_{0j} + B_{1j}X_{ij} + e_{ij} \tag{1}$$

where:

Y_{ij} = the outcome measure for individual i in group j
X_{ij} = the value of the predictor for individual i in group j
B_{0j} and B_{1j} = intercepts and slopes estimated separately for each group (as noted by the subscript j)
e_{ij} = the residual

An example consisting of several different groups will illustrate the nature of these equations. When separate regression equations are estimated for each group, four different patterns can emerge. Figures 24.1(a), (b), (c), and (d) present these four possible options. In Figure 24.1(a), each of the groups in the sample has identical regression lines. Therefore, each group has identical intercepts and slopes. In Figure 24.1(b), the groups still have identical slope terms; now, the intercept terms vary significantly across the groups. Thus, even though the relationship between X_{ij} and Y_{ij} is equivalent across the groups, the initial "location" (i.e., the intercept) of this relationship varies across the groups. In Figure 24.1(c), the groups have similar intercept terms, but the relationship between X_{ij} and Y_{ij} varies significantly across the groups. In Figure 24.1(d), both the

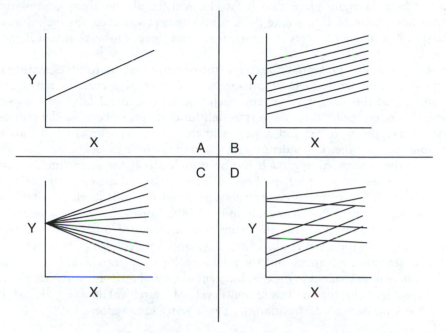

Figure 24.1 Four Possible Patterns for Intercepts and Slopes when the Level 1 Model is Estimated Separately for Each Group. (This figure was adapted from the National Research Council's report: *Knowing what students know* (2001.)

initial location and the relationship between X_{ij} and Y_{ij} vary significantly across the groups (i.e., both the intercepts and the slopes vary across the groups).

Three of these figures display systematic patterns or differences across the groups (i.e., Figures 24.1(b), (c) and (d)). These differences raise the question of whether there are group-level variables associated with the variation across the groups. For example, group-level variables may be associated with varying intercepts in Figures 24.1(b) and (d) and varying slopes in Figures 24.1(c) and (d). This is precisely the question that the Level 2 analysis in HLMs answers. The Level 2 analysis uses the intercepts and slopes from the Level 1 analysis as dependent variables. For example, a typical, Level 2 model may take the following form:

Level 2a: $B_{0j} = \gamma_{00} + \gamma_{01}Z_j + U_{0j}$ (2)

Level 2b: $B_{1j} = \gamma_{10} + \gamma_{11}Z_j + U_1$ (3)

where:

Z_j = a group-level variable
γ_{00} and γ_{10} the second-level intercept terms
γ_{01} and γ_{11} = the slopes relating Z_j (the group level variables) to the intercept and slope terms from the Level 1 equation
U_{0j} and U_{1j} = the Level 2 residuals

Depending on the pattern of variance in the Level 1 intercepts and slopes, different Level 2 models would be required. For example, in situations such as Figure 24.1(b), where there is no variance in the slope parameter, the inclusion of Z_j in Equation 3 would not be meaningful given that B_{1j} is identical for all the groups. Similarly, in situations like Figure 24.1(c), where there is no intercept variance, the inclusion of Z_j in Equation 2 would not be very meaningful because there is no variance in B_{0j} across the groups.

The three equations presented above are not new approaches to investigating relationships occurring across hierarchical levels. A quarter of a century ago, Burstein (1980) discussed this same type of approach under the general label of "slopes-as-outcomes." Conceptually, this is a very insightful description because the regression parameters (i.e., the intercepts and slopes) estimated for each group at Level 1 are used as outcome measures (i.e., dependent variables) in the Level 2 model.

Although the conceptual approach has been understood for some time, statistical concerns about the adequacy of the Level 1 intercept and slope estimates as well as the estimation of the variance components hindered the full development of these models (Burstein et al., 1989). Throughout the 1980s, however, several, separate, statistical advances improved greatly the estimation strategy for intercepts- and slopes-as-outcomes models (Burstein et al., 1989). Bryk and Raudenbush (1992) enumerated the specific statistical advances and their relationship to hierarchical linear models. These advances have resulted in the development of several different software packages designed specifically for the analysis of multilevel or hierarchical data (e.g., HLM; Bryk et al., 1994; Mln; Rasbash & Woodhouse, 1995; VARCL; Longford, 1990).

Estimating the Effects

In estimating the Level 1 and Level 2 models discussed above, a distinction is made between fixed effects, random coefficients, and variance components. Fixed effects are parameter estimates that do not vary across groups, for example the γs from Equations 2 and 3. Alternatively, random coefficients are parameter estimates that are allowed to vary across groups such as the Level 1 regression coefficients (e.g., β_{0j} and β_{1j}). In addition to these Level 1 and Level 2 regression coefficients, the HLM software also includes estimates of the variance components, which include: (a) the variance in the Level 1 residual (i.e., e_{ij} referred to as σ^2), (b) the variance in the Level 2 residuals (i.e., U_{0j} and U_{ij}), and (c) the covariance of the Level 2 residuals [i.e., $cov(U_{0j}$ and $U_{ij})$]. The variance–covariance matrix of the Level 2 residuals is referred to in the hierarchical linear modeling literature as the τ matrix. The element τ_{00} represents the variance in U_{0j}, element τ_{11} represents the variance in U_{ij}, and element τ_{12} represents the covariance between U_{0j} and U_{ij}. Obviously, the number of elements in the τ matrix will depend on the number of Level 2 equations estimated, the number of Level 1 predictors that vary and are modeled.

The Fixed Effects

The predictor weights (γ) in Equations 2 and 3 represent fixed effects in HLMs. Although these Level 2 regression weights could be estimated using an OLS regression approach, this is not appropriate given that the precision of the Level 1 parameters will vary across the groups (as the groups are not required to be of equal size). Given this variation in precision, an OLS approach is not appropriate because of the violation of the homoscedasticity assumption. HLMs use a generalized least-squares (GLS) estimate for the Level 2 parameters, this generates a weighted Level 2 regression. The groups with more precise Level 1 estimates receive more weight in the Level 2 regression equation.

The Variance–Covariance Components

The variance–covariance components in HLMs represent the variance of the Level 1 residuals (i.e., the variance in the e_{ij}) and the variance–covariance of the Level 2 residuals (i.e., the variance–covariance of U_{0j} and U_{1j}). These variance components are estimated using maximum likelihood estimation and the EM algorithm (Raudenbush & Bryk, 2002).

Level 1 Random Coefficients

Frequently, especially in the context of education research, a researcher is interested in obtaining the best estimate of a particular, Level 1 random coefficient (Raudenbush, 1988). In the design context, this might be when a researcher is interested in estimating the effectiveness of a particular learning environment where effectiveness is conveyed by the design and significance of the Level 1 slope coefficient. For example, a learning environment may be defined as being most effective when it reduces the effect of socioeconomic status within groups on mathematics performance—a classic condition for the study of equity in mathematics performance. One of the simplest ways to estimate the Level 1 coefficient for a particular group or school is to compute an OLS regression equation for that particular unit (e.g., Equation 1). Assuming large sample sizes in each group, this analysis should provide relatively precise estimates. In practice, however, group size can be small (and certainly unequal); fortunately, HLMs deal with this possibility explicitly. When groups are smaller, these estimates will not be stable (Burstein, 1980). Inspection of Level 2 equations (i.e., Equations 2 and 3) reveals that there are two estimates of the Level 1 intercepts and slopes. The first estimate comes from an OLS regression equation estimated for a particular unit (i.e., Equation 1), whereas the second estimate comes from the Level 2 regression model (i.e., the predicted values of B_{0j} and B_{1j} from Equations 2 and 3). In other words, for any particular unit, two predicted, intercept and slope values can be estimated: the first from the Level 1 regression equation and the second from the Level 2 regression model. Therefore, the question becomes which of these estimates provides a more accurate assessment of the population intercept and slope parameters for that particular unit. Alternatively, we can ask how the two sets of estimates might be weighted optimally.

Instead of forcing a choice between these two estimates, HLMs (and the HLM software program; Bryk & Raudenbush, 1992) compute an optimally-weighted combination of the two estimates using an empirical Bayes estimation strategy (Raudenbush & Bryk, 2002). In other words, the HLM software program computes an empirical Bayes estimate of the Level 1 intercepts and slopes for each unit, which optimally weights the OLS, Level 1 estimates (Equation 1) and the Level 2 predicted values for these same estimates (Equations 2 and 3). These empirical Bayes estimates are contained in the residual file generated by the HLM software. Raudenbush (1988) provides proofs demonstrating that this composite estimate produces a smaller mean square error term than either the Level 1 estimate or the Level 2 predicted value. Thus, when one is interested in obtaining the best estimate of the Level 1 coefficient for a particular unit, the empirical Bayes estimate will meet this criterion. Of course, this assumes that both the Level 1 and Level 2 models are specified correctly.

The empirical Bayes estimates are a weighted composite of the two estimates discussed above where the weight is based on the reliability of the OLS estimate. The HLM software program provides an estimate of the "reliability" of the OLS Level 1 regression coefficients. First, the software partitions the variance in the OLS regression parameters for each group into its estimated true parameter variance and error variance (e.g., variance in B_{0j} = true variance in B_{0j} + error variance in B_{0j}). This parallels the classical test theory model. Then, after obtaining these estimates, one can use the software to compute a "reliability coefficient" for each group's OLS parameters as the ratio of the true parameter variance to the total parameter variance (i.e., reliability = true variance/total variance). The HLM software reports the reliability of each Level 1 random coefficient averaged across the groups. This reported reliability can be interpreted as the amount of systematic variance in the parameter across the groups (i.e., the variance that is available to be modeled by between-group variables).

Possible Statistical Tests

The HLM software contains several statistical tests for hypothesis testing. Specifically, there are *t*-tests for all of the fixed effects (i.e., the second-level regression parameters), which test whether these parameter estimates depart significantly from zero. Chi-square tests are provided for the Level 2 residual variance (e.g., variance in the Us; for instance, $[\tau_{00}$ and $\tau_{11}]$, indicating whether the residual variance departs significantly from zero). Other more complicated tests are available but we do not discuss them here. For the majority of HLMs, these basic tests should suffice.

In the above introduction we reviewed the background, logic, rationale, and estimation approach of HLMs. In the next section we explore how these models can be applied to answer questions relevant to design researchers in general and design researchers in mathematics education in particular. To illustrate the hierarchical linear modeling approach further, a hypothetical set of research questions is presented first. This deliberation is followed by a discussion of the sequence of the models that would be used to investigate these questions.

Investigating the Effects of Group Sociomathematical Norms on Individual Performance in Mathematics

Hierarchical linear models are valuable in the design process at two end points: at the end of each design iteration (see Cobb et al., 2003; Design-Based Research Collective, 2003) to examine a theory (and its possible effect), and then at the end of the design process. In each case, the HLM analysis provides the qualitative design researcher with a quantitative mechanism for checking if the designed product is having the anticipated learning effects.

Suppose that a mathematics education design researcher is interested in predicting mathematics performance at the individual level. Suppose also that the researcher has identified beliefs about mathematics (an individual-level variable) and sociomathematical norms (a group-level variable) as potential predictors of this mathematics performance. Then, the summative analyses proposed an outlined here are likely candidates that a design researcher could employ at the end of the design process. This makes sense when the goal of the researcher is to verify or check the size and direction of these multilevel relationships. Further, comparable analyses could be conducted at the end of the design iterate.

Historically, there has been a dichotomy of views about mathematical learning that distinguish the individual cognitive perspective of constructivism (von Glasersfeld, 1995) from the sociocultural perspective based on symbolic interactionism (Blumer, 1969). The emergent perspective represents the possibility of coordinating the two views, with the underlying assumption that mathematical learning can be characterized "as both a process of active individual construction and as a process of mathematical enculturation" (Cobb, 1994: 35). Cobb and his colleagues (e.g., Bauersfeld, 1995; Cobb & Bauersfeld, 1995; Yackel & Cobb, 1996) have made significant contributions through their articulation of an interpretive framework that coordinates both the psychological and sociocultural (cognitive) perspectives on students' learning (see Table 24.1). Table 24.2 provides an adaptation from Cobb and Yackel (1996) to frame this multilevel example.

The goals of framing the theory and analysis from a multilevel perspective allow us to ascertain the strength of these relationships and to investigate whether the shared perspective affects students' performance in mathematics. This latter goal, the impact of group norms on student performance, is assumed in the Cobb model but never investigated because his theoretical focus is on the emergent production of group-level sociomathematical norms.

Table 24.1 specifies three, rather straightforward, hypotheses about the relationship between mathematics performance, beliefs about mathematics, and group sociomathematical norms. In order for these hypotheses to be supported, several conditions must be met. These conditions are listed in the bottom half of Table 24.1.

Table 24.1 Working Hypotheses and their Assumed Conditions: Mathematical Performance, Beliefs About Mathematics, and Sociomathematical Norms (Within Groups)

Working hypotheses	Assumed conditions
Belief about mathematics is related positively to performance in mathematics.	Systematic within- and between-group variance in mathematics performance.
Sociomathematical norms are related positively to performance in mathematics after controlling for beliefs about mathematics (i.e., on average, individuals learning in environments with positive sociomathematical norms are more likely to have positive beliefs about mathematics; in other words, such individuals will show a group-level main effect for sociomathematical norms after controlling for mathematical beliefs).	Significant variance in the Level 1 intercept. Significant variance in the Level 1 slope. Variance in the intercept is predicted significantly by sociomathematical norms of group members. Variance in the slope is predicted significantly by the sociomathematical norms of group members.
Sociomathematical norms moderate the beliefs about mathematics–mathematics performance relationship (i.e., the relationship between beliefs about mathematics and mathematics performance is stronger in situations where group members are in closer sociomathematical norms to one another).	

Table 24.2 Framework for Interpreting Individual and Social Activity in Learning

Psychological perspective	Social perspective
Individual student belief about his or her own role, the roles of others, and the general nature of mathematical activity.	Social norms in the classroom.
A student's specific mathematical beliefs and values.	Sociomathematical norms in the classroom.
A student's conceptions and activities in mathematics.	Mathematical practices in the classroom.

Source: Adapted from Cobb and Yackel (1996).

Hypotheses 1 and 2 suggest that mathematics performance will be related significantly to both an individual-level variable (i.e., beliefs about mathematics), and a group-level variable (i.e., sociomathematical norms). Thus, one should expect meaningful within- and between-group variance in mathematics performance (Condition 1). Hypothesis 2 proposes that, after controlling for beliefs about mathematics, mathematics performance will be associated significantly with sociomathematical norms. In this example of an HLM, the variance in the Level 1 intercept term represents the between-group variance in mathematics performance after controlling for beliefs about mathematics. Thus, for Hypothesis 2 to be supported, there needs to be significant variance in the intercept term (Condition 2), and this variance needs to be related significantly to the sociomathematical norms of group members (Condition 4 and Hypothesis 2). Hypothesis 3 proposes that the relationship between beliefs about mathematics and mathematics performance will vary as a function of the sociomathematical norms of group members. Therefore, for this hypothesis to be supported, there would need to be significant variance in the Level 1 slope coefficient across the groups (i.e., the relationship between beliefs about mathematics and mathematics performance; Condition 3), and this variance would have to be related significantly to the sociomathematical norms of group members (Condition 5 and Hypothesis 3). In the following section we outline a typical sequence of models that would allow the design researcher the opportunity to assess (and statistically test) the viability of each of these necessary conditions as well as the three hypotheses listed in Table 24.1.

One-way Analysis of Variance

The first condition specifies systematic within- and between-group variance in mathematics performance. The investigation of within- and between-group variance suggests that the variance in mathematics performance needs to be partitioned into each component separately. To accomplish the variance partitioning in HLMs, the following set of equations is estimated:

Level 1: Mathematics performance$_{ij}$ = B_{0j} + e$_{ij}$ $\hspace{2cm}$ (4)

Level 2: B_{0j} = γ_{00} + U$_{0j}$ $\hspace{3cm}$ (5)

where:

B_{0j} = mean mathematics performance for group j
γ_{00} = grand mean mathematics performance (across all groups)
Variance (e$_{ij}$) = [σ^2] = within-group variance in mathematics performance
Variance (U$_{0j}$) = [τ_{00j}] = between-group variance in mathematics performance

In Equations 4 and 5, the Level 1 equation (4) includes no predictors. Therefore, the regression equation includes only an intercept estimate. In order to compute intercept terms in regression, the analysis includes a unit vector as a predictor in the equation. The parameter associated with this unit vector represents the intercept term in the final regression equation. When a researcher specifies no predictors in a Level 1 or Level 2 equation, the variance in the outcome measure is regressed implicitly onto a unit vector producing a regression-based intercept estimate. In the Level 1 equation above (4), mathematics performance is regressed onto a constant unit vector, which is implied when one chooses no predictors. Because there are no additional predictors in the model, the B_{0j} parameter will be equal to that group's mean level of mathematics performance (i.e., if a variable is regressed only onto a constant unit vector, the resulting parameter is equal to the mean).

The Level 2 model (Equation 5) regresses each group's mean mathematics performance onto a constant; that is, B_{0j} is regressed onto a unit vector, resulting in a γ_{00} parameter equal to the grand mean of mathematics performance (i.e., the mean of the group means, B_{0j}—dyad by dyad, group by group, or classroom by classroom). Given that each of the respective dependent variables is regressed onto a constant, it follows that any within-group variance in mathematics performance is forced into the Level 1 residual (i.e., e_{ij}) and any between-group variance in mathematics performance is forced into the Level 2 residual (i.e., U_{0j}).

Although hierarchical linear modeling does not provide a significance test for the within-group variance component, it does provide a significance test for the between-group variance (i.e., τ_{00}). In addition, the ratio of the between-group variance to the total variance is presented as an intraclass correlation (ICC). In the model above (Equations 4 and 5), the total variance in mathematics performance has been decomposed into its within- and between-group components [i.e., Variance (mathematics performance$_{ij}$) = Variance $(U_{0j} + e_{ij}) = (\tau_{00} + \sigma^2)$]. Therefore, an intraclass correlation can be computed by investigating the following ratio: ICC = $[(\tau_{00})/(\tau_{00} + \sigma^2)]$. This intraclass correlation represents a ratio of the between-group variance in mathematics performance to the total variance in mathematics performance (i.e., the percentage of variance in mathematics performance that resides between groups).

In summary, the one-way analysis of variance provides the following information about the mathematics performance measure: (a) the amount of variance residing within groups, (b) the amount of variance residing between groups, and (c) the intraclass correlation specifying the percentage of the total variance residing between groups.

The Random Coefficient Model

After assessing the degree of within- and between-group variance in mathematics performance, one can investigate now whether there is significant variance in the intercepts and slopes across groups (Conditions 2 and 3). In other words, for Hypothesis 2 to be supported there needs to be significant variance across groups in the intercepts. For Hypothesis 3 to be supported, there needs to be significant variance across groups in the slopes. In addition to providing evidence in support of Conditions 2 and 3, this model also will test Hypothesis 1 directly. The random coefficient regression model takes on the following form:

Level 1: Math performance$_{ij}$ = B_{0j} + B_{1j} (Beliefs about math$_{ij}$) + e_{ij} (6)

Level 2a: B_{0j} = γ_{00} + U_{0j} (7)

Level 2b: B_{1j} = γ_{10} + U_{1j} (8)

where:

γ_{00} = mean of the intercepts across groups
γ_{10} = mean of the slopes across groups (a check of Hypothesis 1)
Variance (e_{ij}) = Level 1 residual variance
Variance (U_{0j}) = $[\tau_{00}]$ = variance in intercepts
Variance (U_{1j}) = $[\tau_{11}]$ = variance in slopes

Because there are no Level 2 predictors of either B_{0j} or B_{1j}, the Level 2 regression equations (7 and 8) are equal to an intercept term and a residual. In this form, the γ_{00} and the γ_{10} parameters represent the Level 1 coefficients averaged across groups (i.e., they represent the pooled B_{0j} and B_{1j} parameters). Similarly, given that B_{0j} and B_{1j} are regressed onto constants, the variance of the Level 2 residual terms (i.e., U_{0j} and U_{ij}) represents the between-group variance in the Level 1 parameters.

Hierarchical linear modeling provides a *t*-test related to the γ_{00} and γ_{10} parameters, where a significant *t*-value indicates that the parameter departs significantly from zero. In the case of the γ_{10} parameter, this *t*-test provides a direct test of Hypothesis 1. In other words, this tests whether beliefs about mathematics are related significantly to mathematics performance. This test assesses whether the pooled Level 1 slope between beliefs about mathematics and mathematics performance differs significantly from zero. Thus, this test investigates whether, on average, the relationship between beliefs about mathematics and mathematics performance is significant.

Hierarchical linear modeling also provides a chi-square test for the two residual variances (i.e., τ_{00} and τ_{11}). These chi-square tests indicate whether the variance components differ significantly from zero and afford a direct test of Conditions 2 and 3. In other words, these tests determine whether the variance in the intercepts and slopes across groups is significantly different from zero. Thus, the random regression model furnishes two primary pieces of information: (a) it tests the significance of the pooled Level 1 slopes, which are used to test Level 1 hypotheses, and (b) it evaluates whether there is significant variance surrounding the pooled Level 2 intercepts and slopes. In other words, the random regression model provides a significance test for the mean of the Level 1 regression coefficients, as well as a significance test for the amount of variance in each of the Level 1 regression coefficients.

In addition to estimating the fixed (γ) and random (τ) effects, hierarchical linear modeling also estimates the Level 1 residual variance (i.e., the variance in e_{ij} or σ^2). Recall that in the one-way analysis of variance model (Equation 4), σ^2 was equal to the within-group variance in mathematics performance. Because the random regression model adds a Level 1 predictor (Equation 5), σ^2 is now equal to the Level 1 residual variance. Therefore, comparing these two values of σ^2 provides an estimate of the Level 1 variance in mathematics performance accounted for by beliefs about mathematics. More specifically, the R^2 (i.e., the variance accounted for) in mathematics performance can be obtained by computing the following ratio:

$$R^2 \text{ for Level 1 model} = \frac{(\sigma^2 \text{ one-way ANOVA}) - (\sigma^2 \text{ random regression})}{(\sigma^2 \text{ one-way ANOVA})}.$$

This ratio represents the percentage of the Level 1 variance in mathematics performance accounted for by beliefs about mathematics.

The Intercepts-As-Outcomes Model

Assuming that Condition 2 was satisfied in the random regression model (i.e., there was significant variance in the intercept term), the intercepts-as-outcomes model assesses whether this variance is related significantly to the sociomathematical norms of group members. This model tests Condition 4, which is also a test of Hypothesis 2.

The HLM would take the following form:

Level 1: Math performance$_{ij}$ = B_{0j} + B_{1j} (Beliefs about math$_{ij}$) + e_{ij} (9)

Level 2a: $B_{0j} = \gamma_{00} + \gamma_{01}$ (Sociomathematical norms$_j$) + U_{0j} (10)

Level 2b: $B_{1j} = \gamma_{10} + U_{1j}$ (11)

where:

γ_{00} = the intercept for Level 2
γ_{01} = the slope for Level 2 (a test of Hypothesis 2)
γ_{10} = mean (pooled) slopes
Variance (e_{ij}) = $[\sigma^2]$ = residual variance for Level 1
Variance (U_{0j}) = $[\tau_{00}]$ = residual intercept variance Level 2a
Variance (U_{1j}) = $[\tau_{11}]$ = variance in slopes Level 2b

This model is similar to the random regression model discussed above, with the addition of the variable "sociomathematical norms" as a Level 2 predictor of B_{0j}. Therefore, the t-test associated with the γ_{01} parameter provides a direct test of Hypothesis 2; that is, the relationship between sociomathematical norms and mathematics performance after controlling for individual beliefs about mathematics. Given that the Level 2 equation for B_{0j} now includes a predictor (i.e., sociomathematical norms), the variance in the U_{0j} parameter (i.e., τ_{00}) represents the residual variance in B_{0j} across groups. If the chi-square test for this parameter is significant, it indicates that there remains systematic Level 2 variance that could be modeled by other theoretically valid Level 2 predictors. If the chi-square test of this residual variance is not significant, the researcher may use an option in hierarchical linear modeling to fix this variance component to zero (i.e., implying that all of the systematic, between-group variance in B_{0j} has been accounted for by sociomathematical norms). All other parameters take on the same meaning as they did under the estimation of the random regression model (i.e., the chi-square for τ_{11} provides an assessment of Condition 3).

To obtain information about the percentage of variance accounted for by inclusion of the predictor variable "sociomathematical norms" in the Level 2 model, the same type of procedure described above is invoked. In the random regression model, τ_{00} was equal to the between-group variance in the intercept term (i.e., B_{0j}). In this intercepts-as-outcomes model, a Level 2 predictor (sociomathematical norms) has been added to the equation, rendering τ_{00} equal to the residual or between-group variance in the intercept term. Thus, by comparing these two variance estimates, one can obtain the R^2 for sociomathematical norms. The R^2 is computed as follows:

R^2 for Level 2 intercept model = ([τ_{00}-random regression] − [τ_{00}-intercepts-as-outcomes]) / (τ_{00}-random regression).

Once again, this ratio compares the amount of variance across the intercept terms accounted for by sociomathematical norms.

Slopes-As-Outcomes Model

Assuming that Condition 3 was supported in the intercepts-as-outcomes model, one can now investigate whether the variance in the slope across groups is related significantly to the sociomathematical norms of group members. Therefore, the slopes-as-outcomes model provides a direct test of Condition 5, which is also a test of Hypothesis 3.

The HLM would take the following form:

Level 1: [Math performance$_{ij}$] = B_{0j} + B_{1j} (Beliefs about math$_{ij}$) + e$_{ij}$ (12)

Level 2a: B_{0j} = γ_{00} + γ_{01} (Sociomathematical norms$_j$) + U$_{0j}$ (13)

Level 2b: B_{1j} = γ_{10} + γ_{11} (Sociomathematical norms$_j$) + U$_{1j}$ (14)

where:

γ_{00} = the intercept at Level 2a
γ_{01} = the slope at Level 2 (a test of Hypothesis 2)
γ_{10} = the intercept at Level 2b
γ_{11} = the slope at Level 2b (a test of Hypothesis 3)
Variance (e$_{ij}$) = [σ^2] = Level 1 residual variance
Variance (U$_{0j}$) = [τ_{00}] = residual intercept variance
Variance (U$_{1j}$) = [τ_{11}] = residual slope variance

The differences between this model and the intercepts-as-outcomes model above are that the variable sociomathematical norms is included as a predictor of the B_{1j} parameter, and, as a result, the U$_{1j}$ variance is now the residual variance in the B_{1j} parameter across groups, as opposed to, or instead of, the total variance across groups. Once again, if the chi-square test associated with this parameter variance is significant, it indicates that there remains systematic variance in the B_{1j} parameter that could be modeled by additional Level 2 predictors. In addition, the t-test associated with the γ_{11} parameter provides a direct test of Hypothesis 3. This hypothesis repre-sents a cross-level interaction because a group-level variable is hypothesized to mod-erate the relationship between two, individual-level variables (the intercept itself and the estimated effect of the beliefs variable). As Saari notes (this volume), making inferences across levels requires appropriate analytic tools and the HLM is one such tool.

We now compute the R^2 for sociomathematical norms as a Level 2 moderator of the relationship between individual-level beliefs about mathematics and mathematics per-formance using the value of τ_{ll} from the intercepts-as-outcomes model (i.e., the total, between-group variance in B_{ij} and the value of τ_{11} from the slopes-as-outcomes model). We obtain an estimate of the R^2 as follows:

R^2 for Level 2 slope model = (τ_{11}-intercepts-as-outcomes − τ_{11}-slopes-as-outcomes)/ (τ_{11}-intercepts-as-outcomes).

This ratio compares the percentage of variance accounted for by sociomathematical norms to the total variance in the belief performance behavior slope across groups.

The preceding sequence of models provides a general introduction to HLMs and the HLM software. The extension of these models to include more Level 1 and Level 2 predictors is relatively straightforward. The purpose of this overview is to provide a general introduction to the ways in which researchers might ask and answer multilevel questions in the hierarchical modeling framework. Additional details about more com-plex estimation strategies and the statistical intricacies of HLMs can be found in Bryk and Raudenbush (1992), Goldstein (1995), and Longford (1993).

Additional Comments

Before concluding, several additional issues are worth mentioning: the application of HLMs to longitudinal data, centering issues, and expanding the models to include more levels.

A Longitudinal Formulation

Although it might not be apparent, virtually all longitudinal investigations conducted by design researchers are hierarchical in nature (Raudenbush & Bryk, 2002). The nested nature of these data would include multiple observations within a unit and a sample of multiple units. Thus, one would have a within-unit, Level 1 model and a between-unit Level 2 model. From a theoretical perspective, one is investigating inter-unit differences in intra-unit change (Nesselroade, 1991).[2] The resulting data structure is one where a time series of data is nested within a larger number of students, thus allowing for an investigation of inter-student differences in change or growth. Sloane, Helding, and Kelly (this volume) highlight the value associated with this possibility in the context of design research and interrupted time-series analysis.

Centering the Intercepts: The Need for Theory

Because HLMs use the Level 1 regression parameters (i.e., intercepts and slopes) as outcome variables to be predicted by the Level 2 equation(s), it is imperative that researchers understand fully the specific interpretation of these parameters. As noted in basic regression texts (e.g., Cohen et al., 2003), the slope parameter represents the expected increase in the outcome variable for a unit increase in the predictor variable, whereas the intercept parameter represents the expected value of the outcome measure when all the predictors are zero. In the ongoing example used in this chapter, the slope merely represents the predicted increase in mathematics performance given a unit increase in belief. The intercept term represents the predicted level of mathematics performance for a person with zero belief about mathematics. However, an obvious question about the meaning of the intercept comes to mind: "How can someone have zero beliefs?"

   Like the belief example above, a value of zero is not particularly meaningful for many of the constructs studied in design research (e.g., the following standard equity variables: ethnicity, gender, and socio-economic status). For the Level 2 model we can, and should, ask: what does it mean for a learning environment to have zero norms? To make intercepts more interpretable level by level, a number of researchers have discussed different ways in which to rescale the Level 1 predictors. "Centering" describes the rescaling of the Level 1 predictors, for which three primary options are now available:

1   A raw metric approach, where no centering takes place and the Level 1 predictors retain their original metric—as in the example above.
2   A grand mean centering, where the grand mean is subtracted from each individual's score on the predictor (e.g., $[\text{belief}_{ij}]-[\text{belief}_{\text{grand mean}}]$).
3   A group mean centering, where the group mean is subtracted from each individual's score on the predictor (e.g., $[\text{belief}_{ij}]-[\text{belief}_{\text{group mean}}]$).

   With grand mean centering, the intercept represents the expected level of the outcome for a person with an "average" level on the predictor. In the current case, it would be the expected mathematics performance for a person with average belief. With group mean centering, the intercept represents the expected mathematics performance for a student with his or her group's average beliefs about mathematics. In both cases, the intercept is theoretically more substantive, and more interpretable than the raw metric alternative. However, centering issues do not begin and end with intercept interpretation.

Recently, several researchers have discussed how the various centering options can change the estimation and meaning of the HLM as a whole (Longford, 1989; Raudenbush & Bryk, 2002). The choice of centering options goes well beyond the interpretation of the intercept term. A researcher must consider the overarching theoretical paradigm primarily and, from that, discern what centering option represents the paradigm best.

Dealing With More Complexity: Adding More Levels

So far the discussion has focused on two-level models, but it is quite obvious that learning settings can represent more than two hierarchical levels. The extension of the two-level model to higher-level models is relatively straightforward but adds theoretical difficulty. For example, in the current example, if individuals were sampled across different learning groups within classrooms, a three-level model could be estimated, where the Level 1 model would describe individuals within groups, the Level 2 model would be groups within classrooms, and the Level 3 model would be a between-classrooms model. The HLM software is available for up to three levels, and a revised version of the Mln (Rasbash & Woodhouse, 1995) software program allows the researcher to work with as many as 15 levels of hierarchy (or nesting). One should keep in mind, however, that very large numbers of levels put more demands on the researcher's capacity to theorize sensibly, not to mention the overt need for additional data resources.

Conclusions

As the call for developing multilevel theories in education and design research continues (Sloane, 2005), it is important to acknowledge and use methodological advances from other disciplines to begin testing hypothesized relationships across levels. Although HLMs have been discussed for several years in the methodological literature in education and in other disciplines, they have yet to gain much attention in the design sciences. HLMs represent an avenue by which more complex theories of learning and the environments that support such learning can be investigated, tested, and understood (Barab & Kirshner, 2001). Moreover, they are built to address the aggregation issued raised by Saari (this volume). HLMs are far from perfect but they represent a great technical leap forward and provide a mechanism for testing the relationships between variables that cross multiple nested levels. The continuing thrust for the integration of macro and micro concepts into design theories, coupled with these technical advances, should lead to a better understanding of how to design learning environments while honoring their complexity.

Acknowledgments

The author would like to thank Anthony E. Kelly (George Mason University) and Daniel Battey (Mary Lou Fulton College of Education, Arizona State University) for their helpful comments on an earlier draft. The author acknowledges funding from the

National Science Foundation, NSF 0634103 (Moving from Arithmetic to Algebra) and NSF 0412537 (i.e., MSP: Project Pathways). Opinions expressed here are those of the author and not necessarily those of the Foundation.

Notes

1 In Chapter 23, Sloane, Helding, and Kelly describe how the framework of HLM can be employed to model longitudinal data.
2 This idea is elaborated by Sloane, Helding, and Kelly (this volume). The elaboration is important for design researchers given that iterations over the same group of students will require some form of time-series analytic tools for estimates to adjust for the autocorrelated error structure of the data. From a design perspective, the fact that some, if not all, students use various versions of the design tool to improve their learning has to be considered before any statement can be made about the efficacy of the designed product. This can be ameliorated by using different groups of students across the various design cycles.

References

Barab, S. A. & Kirshner, D. (eds) (2001). Rethinking methodology in the learning sciences [Special issue]. *Journal of the Learning Sciences, 10*(1&2).

Bauersfeld, H. (1995). The structuring of structures: Development and function of mathematizing as a social practice. In L. P. Steffe & J. Gale (eds), *Constructivism in education* (pp. 137–159). Mahwah, NJ: Lawrence Erlbaum Associates.

Blumer, H. (1969). *Symbolic interactionism: Perspectives and method*. Englewood Cliffs, NJ: Prentice Hall.

Bryk, A. S. & Raudenbush, S. W. (1992). *Hierarchical linear models*. Newbury Park, CA: Sage.

Bryk, A. S., Raudenbush, S. W. & Congdon, R. J. (1994). *Hierarchical linear modeling with the HLM/2L and HLM/3L programs*. Chicago, IL: Scientific Software International.

Burstein, L. (1978). Assessing differences between grouped and individual-level regression coefficients. *Sociological Methods and Research, 7*, 5–28.

Burstein, L. (1980). The role of levels of analysis in the specification of education effects. In R. Dreeben & J. A. Thomas (eds), *The analysis of educational productivity, Volume 1, Issues in microanalysis* (pp. 119–190). Cambridge, MA: Ballinger.

Burstein, L., Kim, K. S. & Delandshere, G. (1989). Multilevel investigations of systematically varying slopes: Issues, alternatives, and consequences. In R. D. Bock (ed.), *Multilevel analysis of educational data* (pp. 235–276). New York: Academic Press.

Cobb, P. (1994). Where is the mind? Constructivist and sociocultural perspectives on mathematical development. *Educational Researcher, 23*(7), 13–20.

Cobb, P. & Bauersfeld, H. (1995). Introduction: The coordination of psychological and sociological perspectives in mathematics education. In P. Cobb & H. Bauersfeld (eds), *Emergence of mathematical meaning: Interaction in classroom cultures* (pp. 1–16). Mahwah, NJ: Lawrence Erlbaum Associates.

Cobb, P. & Yackel, E. (1996). Constructivist, emergent, and sociocultural perspectives in the context of developmental research. *Educational Psychologist, 31*, 175–190.

Cobb, P., Confrey, J., diSessa, A., Lehrer, R. & Schauble, L. (2003). Design experiments in educational research. *Educational Researcher, 32*(1), 9–13.

Cohen, J., Cohen, P., West, S. & Aiken, L. (2003). *Applied multiple regression/correlation analysis for the behavioral sciences* (3rd ed.). Mahwah, NJ: Lawrence Erlbaum Associates.

Design-Based Research Collective (2003). Design based research: An emerging paradigm for educational inquiry. *Educational Researcher, 32*(1), 5–8.

Firebaugh, G. (1978). A rule for inferring individual-level relationships from aggregate data. *American Sociological Review, 43*, 557–572.

Fishman, B., Marx, R., Blumenfeld, P., Krajcik, J. & Soloway, E. (2004). Creating a framework for research on systemic technology innovations. *Journal of the Learning Sciences, 13*, 43–76.

Goldstein, H. (1995). *Multilevel statistical models*. London: Edward Arnold.

Hannan, M. T. & Burstein, L. (1974). Estimation from grouped observations. *American Sociological Review, 39*, 374–392.

Hanushek, E. A. (1974). Efficient estimators for regressing regression coefficients. *American Statistician, 28*(2), 66–67.

Laird, N. M. & Ware, H. (1982). Random-effects models for longitudinal data. *Biometrics, 38*, 963–974.

Lave, J. & Wenger, E. (1991). *Situated learning: Legitimate peripheral participation*. Cambridge: Cambridge University Press.

Longford, N. (1989). To center or not to center? *Multilevel Modeling Newsletter, 1*(2), 7, 8, 11.

Longford, N. (1990). *VARCL: Software for variance component analysis of data with nested random effects (maximum likelihood)*. Princeton, NJ: Educational Testing Service.

Longford, N. (1993). *Random coefficient models*. Oxford: Clarendon.

Mason, W. M., Wong, G. M. & Entwistle, B. (1983). Contextual analysis through the multilevel linear model. In S. Leinhardt (ed.), *Sociological methodology* (pp. 72–103). San Francisco, CA: Jossey-Bass.

McClain, K., Cobb, P. & Bowers, J. (1996). A contextual investigation of three-digit addition and subtraction. In E. Jakubowski, D. Watkins & H. Biske (eds), *Proceedings of the 18th annual meeting of the North American chapter of the international group for the psychology of mathematics education*, Volume I (pp. 125–129). Columbus, OH: ERIC Clearinghouse for Science, Mathematics, and Environmental Education.

Murchan, D. P. & Sloane, F. C. (1994). Conceptual and statistical problems in the study of school and classroom effects: An introduction to multilevel modeling techniques. In I. Westbury, C. Ethington, L. Sosniak & D. Baker (eds), *In search of more effective mathematics education* (pp. 247–272). Norwood, NJ: Ablex.

Nesselroade, J. R. (1991). Interindividual differences in intraindividual change. In L. M. Collins & J. L. Horn (eds), *Best methods for the analysis of change: Recent advances, unanswered questions, future directions* (pp. 92–105). Washington, DC: American Psychological Association.

Rasbash, J. & Woodhouse, G. (1995). *Mln command reference*. London: University of London, Institute of Education.

Raudenbush, S. W. (1988). Educational applications of hierarchical linear models: A review. *Journal of Educational Statistics, 13*, 85–116.

Raudenbush, S. W. & Bryk, A. S. (2002). *Hierarchical linear models* (2nd ed.). Thousand Oaks, CA: Sage.

Robinson, W. S. (1950). Ecological correlations and the behavior of individuals. *American Sociological Review, 15*, 351–357.

Sloane, F. C. (2005). The scaling of educational interventions: Multilevel insight. *Reading Research Quarterly, 40*, 361–366.

von Glasersfeld, E. (1995). An introduction to radical constructivism. In P. Watzlawick (ed.), *The invented reality* (pp. 17–40). New York: Norton.

Yackel, E. & Cobb, P. (1996). Sociomathematical norms, argumentation, and autonomy in mathematics. *Journal for Research in Mathematics Education, 27*, 458–477.

25 Modeling Complexity in Mathematics Education

Donald Saari
University of California, Irvine

What is Needed?

There is no debate; the fundamental issues confronting mathematics education are so complex that significant help is needed when trying to model them. The underlying complexity of this area probably is what motivated some experts both at the workshop on The Modeling of the Modeling of Mathematics Education, held in Santa Fe, New Mexico in December 2001, and elsewhere to wonder whether help, advice, or at least insight might be found in the formal studies of complexity such as chaos, dynamical systems, fractals, and other forms of mathematics. As discussed here, maybe.

The nature of the general questions about mathematics education means that finding answers probably will require using some form of system thinking. The challenge is to find a way to capture the associated complexities. This is a necessary step whether a preferred research approach involves the theoretical, an assessment, or a statistical analysis. For instance, as we have learned from economics and other social sciences, data without theory is just data. Namely, a data analysis in the absence of a testable, carefully designed, and considered theory has limited value; rather than being informative, even replicated outcomes can be misleading and counterproductive. But although modeling and theory are crucial, it is not clear how to model the complexities central to education.

With this reality in mind, it is reasonable to explore whether modeling and theoretical insight for mathematics education can be gained by examining the source of the different forms of mathematical complexity that arise within systems. This is reasonable, so I describe new ways to address this approach. But let me caution against expecting help to come from the technical aspects of these mathematical advances. It will not happen. This is because modeling in mathematics education—actually, for most issues in most social sciences—is at such an early stage that it is premature to use these technically precise tools. So, while outlining how the conceptual aspects of these mathematical developments might offer help in structuring thought and analysis, I indicate briefly why those commonly heard terms such as *sensitivity with respect to initial conditions, self-symmetry, and fractals* are of minimal to zero value for modeling in this area—at least for now.

To be specific, motivated by the concerns that were raised and discussed actively during the above-mentioned workshop in Santa Fe in December 2001, I will discuss four themes:

1 *Complexity.* Conceptual help in handling the "system complexity" inherent in this area of mathematics education can come from chaos. This is not obvious, so to show that it is possible to transfer notions from dynamics to non-dynamic settings,

I use voting paradoxes to simplify the exposition and illustrate the ideas. I also raise doubts about currently used assessment procedures.

2   *Parts–whole*. A source of the complexity in mathematics education is the constant confrontation with "parts–whole" interactions; for example, a mathematics curriculum is divided into units—the parts—designed so that, it is hoped, all the students understand the material—the whole. Conversely, a large research project—the whole—may be divided into units—the parts—that are addressed by different groups. Central to modeling, then, is to understand "parts–whole" connections. The discussion here indicates, in a general way, what to emphasize; what to examine; and how to identify opportunities, pitfalls, and, maybe, new directions for mathematics education. One message is that beyond "the whole can be greater than the sum of the parts" adage, it can be that the "whole" is qualitatively and radically different from each part and the sum.

3   *Social norms*. A perplexing problem is to understand how to change the system—the "social norms." Education is full of discouraging stories where, after investing considerable effort to introduce innovation and reform, the prevailing social norms defeat the lofty objectives and beat us back into a "much-the-same" environment. How can we model and address these pressing concerns? How can progress be made? I have no answers, but I can indicate ways to address these concerns. Some conclusions are discouraging, while others may provide insight into what needs to be done.

4   *Social movement*. Closely related to social norms is the pragmatic issue of whether educational reform can be promoted through a social movement. To make this a personal issue for the reader, restate it in terms of the modeling of mathematics education or another personal professional objective. How can you motivate researchers, teachers, and the community to sign on to your goals? Although I cannot answer this monumental concern, I can identify research that indicates what might be needed. This literature does provide some lessons.

Fractals

Mandelbrot sets and related pictures of fractals are powerful technical tools for understanding subtle aspects of dynamics; they also form intriguing art forms that can be displayed proudly. But other than serving as valued lessons in a mathematics classroom, it is doubtful whether they tell us anything about mathematics education. On the other hand, this topic does add excitement to the classroom.

To explain, let me describe a fractal in terms of the Chaos game (see Barnsley, 1988; Devaney, 1992).[1] All you need is a die and an equilateral triangle, such as the one on the left in Figure 25.1, where the vertices are labeled A, B, C. To play the game, select an

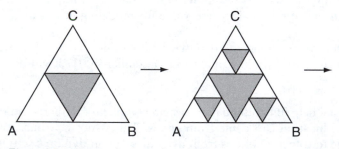

Figure 25.1 Sierpinski Triangle.

initial point in the interior of the triangle; it does not matter where. Rolling the die determines how to move from a current position to the next point according to the following rules; the game continues forever:

- If a 1 or 2 comes up, move halfway from the current point toward vertex A.
- If a 3 or 4 comes up, move halfway toward vertex B.
- If a 5 or 6 comes up, move halfway toward vertex C.

Playing this game displays a fascinating phenomenon, the iterates rapidly start tracing out the Sierpinski triangle, whose construction is depicted in Figure 25.1. To understand this figure, divide the original equilateral triangle into the four smaller equilateral triangles as shown on the left side of Figure 25.1. Throw out the interior of the center triangle—the large shaded region in the first large triangle. Next, divide each of the remaining three unshaded smaller triangles in an identical manner. So, as shown in the second large triangle of Figure 25.1, each of the three remaining smaller triangles is divided into four even smaller equilateral triangles where the center (shaded) portion is dropped. Continue this process—forever. The boundary of what remains is the attractor of this dynamic; namely, the location of the points from the game move ever closer to the figure. Self-symmetry arises from the construction of dividing continually whatever equilateral triangle remains; it reflects a symmetry of this particular dynamic (going halfway toward one vertex or another).

How should this weird object, which clearly is more than one-dimensional, be classified? The final figure is too holey to be two-dimensional. A two-dimensional region, for instance, should contain the complete interior of at least one open ball, even if it is very small. But if this holey triangle contained such a ball, eventually the interior of the ball would be invaded by a triangle where the middle portion will be removed, making the ball incomplete. So, if the figure is not one- or two-dimensional, what is it? To describe these kinds of objects, mathematicians invented fractional dimensions: the so-called fractals. For instance, the fractal dimension of the Sierpinski triangle is $\ln(3)/\ln(2) \approx 1.58$ ... (e.g., Devaney, 1992). Fractals play such an important role in mathematical considerations that I encourage using them in the classroom (see Devaney, 1999). But, they play no natural role in understanding issues of mathematics education, so we can dismiss them safely from here on.

Chaotic Behavior

Whenever I ask a general audience for their sense of "chaos," the typical response is "sensitivity with respect to initial conditions." This familiar phrase is merely a technical description of a typical consequence of chaotic dynamics; it has nothing to do with the driving force causing complex behavior. On the other hand, this phrase, and the underlying source of the complexity of chaotic dynamics, might offer structure to understand the system complexity that arises in mathematics education.

Start by recalling some personally chaotic event. Typical responses I have received include "Life with my children"; "Being a PhD student, thanks to my advisor's demands"; and even "Family gatherings after Uncle Fred has had too much to drink." Surprisingly, these examples capture more accurately a sense of the force behind mathematical chaos than the sensitivity phrase.

To indicate what makes each example chaotic consider what can happen with children getting up in the morning. A typical story starts with several possible initial events such as, "When Torik and Heili get out of bed, they. . . ." Then, as anyone with children understands readily, each possible event spawns several new possibilities ("Torik didn't want to watch the same video as Heili, so he . . ."), and each of these generates another set of new events, and each of these. . . . The story goes on and on forever, creating a chaos tree of the form depicted in Figure 25.2. The complexity of the situation is manifested by the myriad possible paths with different consequences where it is not clear in advance whether the less traveled one, or something else, will be taken.

The different paths defined by the never-ending tree describe differing consequences of consequences of consequences of. . . . With slight reflection, each of us can identify with this structure: just think of our own life experiences where if we had not been somewhere or done something at a particular time, our life most surely would have assumed a very different path and structure ("If I hadn't met her at that banquet, I most surely would have married someone else, and . . ." or "Standing in an airport line, I happened to overhear Professor So-and-So describing the importance of . . ."). These are the "sensitivity-to-initial-conditions" events; a slight change could cause the dynamic to travel down a completely different chain of events. Examples also come from the classroom, ranging from discipline to insightful learning.

Important to the concerns of the chapters in this book about mathematics education—and, more generally, to the social sciences—is to understand how to analyze such complexity. A natural inclination is to modestly select a particular path and then follow its listing of cascading causes and effects. Be honest; this is precisely what we do in our research when we carve out a particular task. But, as we painfully learn, the analysis can be very difficult and involve a multitude of careful considerations. Such research most surely requires developing the necessary discipline to avoid becoming sidetracked by related issues or by the temptation to examine another path. But, with respect to modeling, emphasizing the particular can mask the appropriate general assumptions.

The surprising counterintuitive claim is that, at times, it may be simpler and more productive to tackle the far more ambitious objective of identifying everything that could possibly occur. Rather than following a single path, the more global perspective is to determine all the possible paths that can occur, along with their cascading consequences, and how the paths relate and interact with each other. This captures the underlying spirit of a technical approach (symbolic dynamics) used to describe chaotic behavior. There is an associated cost, but it may be minimal with respect to the potential gains.

This change in perspective mandates a change in analysis—a change that, by being forced to identify and understand the relationship and interaction among paths, we are required to emphasize general operative assumptions. This change in direction may assist in the modeling of mathematics education. For readers who recall the freshman calculus lesson about using Newton's method to find a zero of a polynomial, see Saari (1995) for a description of this different perspective. In terms of playing a game of pool, an intuitive discussion starts on page 84 of Saari (2001a). Anyone interested in the mathematics of astronomy might be intrigued by the wild chaotic motion reported in Saari and Xia (1995). But to advance my intent of suggesting new ways to address the system complexities in mathematics education, this change in perspective is introduced

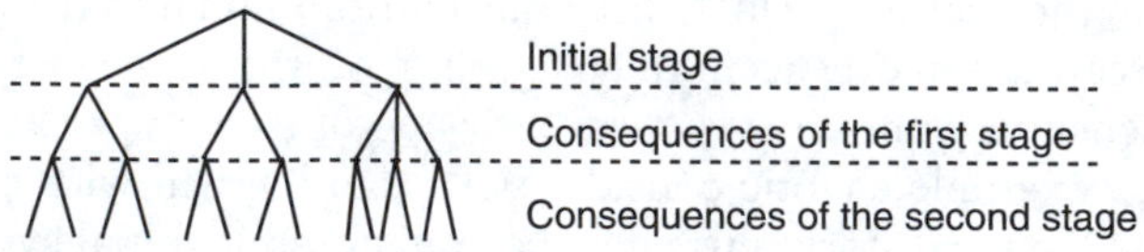

Figure 25.2 Chaos Tree.

with my favorite voting example. Voting is used because the details have been worked out to show how to transfer ideas from dynamics to non-dynamical settings. My hope is that this approach will provide a template to encourage readers to develop similar arguments for the modeling of mathematics education.

Suppose 15 people get together for a drink after a hard day at a conference. To save on cost, they agree to buy one beverage in bulk; to select the beverage of choice, they vote. Six prefer milk to wine to beer, five prefer beer to wine to milk, and four prefer wine to beer to milk. Using our usual voting method ("Let's have a show of hands"), this group prefers milk (six votes) to beer (five votes) to wine (only four votes).

Do these people really prefer milk? By comparing these beverages pairwise, we discover that these voters prefer anything to milk. A landslide proportion of 60 percent prefer wine to milk by a 9 to 6 vote, and 60 percent prefer beer to milk by a 9 to 6 vote. Even more surprising, this same group prefers last place wine to anything; 60 percent prefer wine to milk by 9 to 6; and 66.7 percent of them prefer wine to beer by 10 to 5. So, it is arguable that wine, not milk, is their top choice. Anyone want beer? Beer is the top choice with a runoff, where wine is dropped at the first stage, and beer beats milk in the runoff.

What makes this example disturbing is that it violates long-held beliefs about decision procedures. More troubling, the example demonstrates that the election outcome can reflect more accurately the choice of a procedure, rather than what the information really means. This comment should raise red flags: If voting, which is a particularly simple aggregation procedure, can suffer serious problems, then what should we expect from the more complicated methods typically used in mathematics education? So, before moving on, it is worth reviewing what message this statement implies for, say, assessment procedures and even statistical methods. After all, we are far more comfortable and familiar with these centuries-old voting methods than with assessment and statistical methods. Yet, in spite of our acceptance of voting methods, rather than reflecting the data, we now know that an outcome can reflect which voting method has been adopted. Consequently, some "trusted" outcomes must be misleading and distorted. Similarly, we must worry whether the more complex assessment methods can distort the message in the data. As we are discovering, these fears are well founded.

The next natural question is to go beyond the specific example to determine what else can happen. Quite frankly, progress in this direction had been agonizingly slow. The reason is that, for over two centuries, a main approach used in voting theory required finding particular paradoxical examples of the above type; in our terms, this is equivalent to trying to create an example to establish that part of a particular path on the tree can occur. Notice that this approach is similar to what often is done in mathematics education. What slowed progress in voting theory, and in mathematics education, is that it can be very difficult to discover examples to demonstrate a particular peculiarity. To illustrate the challenge, try, if you can, to create a four-candidate example where the plurality rankings of each of the four triplets reverse the four-candidate plurality ranking, but the six pairwise rankings flip again to agree with the original plurality ranking. (Many examples exist.) That is to say, this standard approach of examining carefully each particular type of election effect is so complex and difficult that it has severely limited progress for this research area. My suspicion is that when a similar approach is used in the modeling of mathematics education, it also will be accompanied by an arduous analysis with limited conclusions. To achieve progress, we must explore how to simplify the analysis while expanding the conclusions.

The goal of the approach I developed, by modifying the conceptual framework of chaos, was to analyze everything that could happen with any possible method. In other words, rather than searching for specific paradoxical examples, my goal was to identify all possible paradoxical effects that could occur with any example and any standard voting method. A big surprise was that this significantly more ambitious goal turned out to be technically easier to achieve! Relevant for this chapter is my suspicion that there are several issues in the modeling of mathematics education that can be addressed in a related manner. Consequently, to encourage exploration, the approach is described in detail.

To illustrate how this was done by using Figure 25.2, my initial stage consisted of all 13 possible election rankings that could occur with the plurality vote; this defines 13 branches. (Six involve strict rankings, six involve one tie, and the last has a complete tie.) The second set of branches, the consequences of the first stage, involved possible rankings of a particular pair, say beer and wine, that could accompany what happens at the first stage. There are three possible rankings (beer is better than wine, wine is better than beer, and a tie); the goal is to understand which election rankings of all three beverages—the 13 branches of the first stage—could be accompanied by which election rankings of the pair. In this analysis, throw away all the complications. If it takes more voters than participants in my Friday night poker club to create an example where a complete milk, wine, beer tie is accompanied by a "wine is preferred to beer" branch, that is perfectly okay. The goal, then, is to determine everything that can happen; refinements are left for later. The third stage of the branches is to understand what rankings of another pair, say milk and wine, can accompany the earlier branches. The fourth stage is to find what paths allow different beer and milk comparisons.

Incidentally, the conclusion is that all $13 \times 3 \times 3 \times 3 = 351$ paths are possible. This means that you can list *any* ranking of the three beverages, *any* ranking for each of the three pairs, and you are assured that an example of voter preferences can be constructed where the specified listing defines the voters' election outcomes for the different subsets of candidates. Notice the trade-off: although the approach allows us to describe everything that could possibly happen, we may not know how to construct an illustrating example for each behavior. (Thanks to subsequent research, I can do this now.)

The value of this approach becomes clear by learning that my approach analyzes what happens with any number of candidates. To make my point, it turns out that, with only five candidates, the number of admissible paths in the tree is far greater than 6×10^{27}—a number that exceeds the number of seconds since the big bang. This astronomical value is mentioned to make it clear that it is impossible to analyze each and every path. Instead, to make progress, indirect approaches must be developed that identify when a barrier to the existence of a branch occurred and when branches can be extended. In doing so, and this is an implied message for mathematics education, the new approach forces us to identify variables and assumptions that are basic for a general analysis, rather than for creating a particular example.

The flavor of this approach (motivated by chaotic dynamics) is given by my pool-playing example from Saari (2001a): the analysis emphasizes what it takes to go from one stage to the next. Suppose we want to strike the cue ball to hit the one-ball to hit the six-ball to. . . . A highly experienced and exceptionally talented player may know exactly where to strike the cue ball; this is equivalent to constructing one of the voting examples. But, instead of trying to understand how to make the precise shot, change the emphasis to determine whether a shot is possible. The new emphasis changes the analysis; we might find first all the ways to hit the cue ball so that the cue ball will hit the one-ball—somewhere. Then, scrutinize the one-ball, six-ball alignment to find all the ways to hit the one-ball so that it would hit the six-ball. A refinement is necessary as we need to determine where to hit the cue ball so that it hits the one-ball—not somewhere, but in a specific region so that the one-ball will hit the six-ball. (This refinement causes the sensitivity-with-respect-to-initial-conditions comment.) Of course, when analyzing possible shots, it may be impossible for the one-ball to hit the six-ball because it is surrounded by others. Similarly in the voting analysis, when using a method known as the Borda Count (this is where 2, 1, 0 points are assigned, respectively, to a voter's first-, second-, and third-ranked candidates), obstructions make it impossible for the Borda Count ranking to be the opposite of the pairwise rankings.

Carrying out this pool-playing illustration in terms of Figure 25.2, suppose we wish to analyze the path down the extreme right-hand side. Instead of a traditional "forward" reasoning of showing how to go from the initial stage to the second stage, then to the third, adopt the iterated, "inverse-function" nature of the pool illustration. That is, instead of looking forward, look backwards: examine what it takes to get somewhere. That is, start with the branch in the second stage and determine all the possible ways to get there from the initial stage. Next, select the specified branch in the third tier; use this same "looking backwards" approach to understand all the possible ways to get there from the second stage. A refinement is needed: we need to characterize all the ways to get from the initial stage not only to the indicated branch in the second stage, but also to those positions that lead to the desired third-stage consequences. While this sounds complicated, I'll show a bit later how simple this can be.

The value of this approach is that it imposes structure upon the total complexity of a system. Rather than emphasizing specifics, this approach requires understanding how different effects are related. Think of this approach as a parts–whole study of examining how all the parts can be connected to create various wholes.

Can this approach be used in the modeling of mathematics education? At a very minimum, the tree format imposes a disciplined yet suggestive structure that will force us to consider the totality of events and to place added emphasis on how the events are related. The approach helps to identify and structure feedback and other notions when branches farther down a tree are constructed. The approach also helps solve the crucial problem in the modeling of mathematics education by identifying what assumptions *should* be made.

It is my sense that, at a minimum, a serious attempt to diagram the cascade of cause-and-effect behaviors will identify previously unexpected behavior and consequences, and it will raise new questions. My optimism is based on the fact that this approach has provided these kinds of rewards in other areas where these techniques have been used. For instance, knowing that we can dismiss a particular path means that a certain effect cannot be combined with others; this can be important information. (In the voting illustration, the fact that it is impossible to have the path where the Borda Count ranking is the opposite of the pairwise rankings is an important feature of this voting procedure.) Another advantage of addressing the totality of a tree structure is that it forces researchers to pose new kinds of questions, develop different methodologies, and, by necessity, worry about potential connections. The rewards could be worth the effort.

The Parts and the Whole

Understanding parts–whole conflicts provides a tool to determine which branches of a tree diagram can or cannot occur. But, before addressing these issues, let me digress by mentioning that my friend Erik is an avid fan of Lakers basketball to the extent that he will give 2:1 odds that the Lakers will beat San Antonio next season. In other words, if the Lakers win, Erik keeps the money you bet with him; should San Antonio win, Erik will return your money and give you $2 for each dollar you bet with him. Anni, another good friend who happens to dislike the Lakers team, is equally as impulsive because she will give 2:1 odds that San Antonio will beat the Lakers. You happen to have $100 designated for household bills. What will you do?

Many people in mathematics education are described best as being "professional basketball-challenged." As such, the usual answer is: "I would pay my bills. Anyway, I don't follow basketball, and I don't gamble." This reasonable reaction reflects the reality that, even for a knowledgeable expert, each gamble carries a financial risk.

But the combination of the parts—the two gambles—creates a whole with a radically different characteristic than either part or even the sum of the parts. To explain, if you bet $50 with Erik and $50 with Anni, you are guaranteed a risk-free, $50 profit. To see why, you will lose $50 to either Erik or Anni, depending on which team wins. But, you will receive $100 from the other person for a profit of $50. The lesson, then, is that the sum of the parts can create an object with distinctly different properties. When stated in terms of our concerns about mathematics education, this lesson becomes a warning to worry, for instance, about the educational consequences resulting from how the parts of a curriculum are assembled. It also identifies opportunities, such as where to improve the educational product.

The main point is that the usual tacit assumptions commonly made about the sum of the parts can be false. Just as mixing the parts of tin and copper could create a mess, or something valuable such as bronze, any hope to describe adequately which "whole" is constructed from the parts requires understanding how the parts are mixed and connected. Indeed, we must expect different ways to combine the parts to define different wholes.[2] To describe what can happen, I borrow an example from my book Saari (2001b) that relates to education, then offer comments about how this parts–whole story speaks to issues of chaos and mathematics education.

In 1999, the state of California instituted an Academic Performance Index (API), "carrot-and-stick" program. The incentives, the "carrots," involve considerable monetary rewards for teachers in those schools where the students in each of the different ethnic groups show substantial improvement. The "stick" is a threatened intervention for those schools that do not meet certain growth targets. The incentives were sufficiently attractive that teachers in one Orange County junior high school celebrated the improvement over the previous year of each of the two main ethnic groups: Whites and Latinos. But, rather than enjoying substantial financial rewards, the school was threatened with intervention because, overall, it did a poorer job. How could this happen!

The manufactured numbers in Table 25.1 demonstrate this paradoxical situation. Suppose that only two groups of students, the blues and the greens, showed improvement from last year to this year.

With both groups showing improvement, it is reasonable to expect that this hypothetical school did better. But, the data in Table 25.2 show why the school's overall performance could decline.

This example is hypothetical, but the phenomenon is real and so robust that it must

Table 25.1 Improved Performance

Group	Meeting standards in	
	1999 (%)	2000 (%)
Blue	33.33	37.50
Green	45.83	50.00

Table 25.2 Overall Decline in Performance

Group	Meeting standards in	
	1999	2000
Blue	20 out of 60	90 out of 240
Green	110 out of 300	120 out of 300
School	130 out of 300	120 out of 300

be anticipated. Indeed, this effect, where the parts suggest improvement while the whole carries the contrary message of deteriorating standards, affected about 70 schools in California during the first (year 2000) API evaluation cycle! (See Saari, 2001b.) Again, my point is that the sum of the parts and the whole can differ significantly, even qualitatively.[3]

The parts–whole tree diagram in Figure 25.3 provides a quick visual way to list all the consequences of the parts where "D" and "I" indicate a decline and an improvement over last year. The eight branches identify the eight potential scenarios; for example, the extreme left path of D, D, D indicates that the greens, the blues, and the whole school declined in performance. The intentional similarity of Figures 25.2 and 25.3 underscores my point that the parts–whole analysis is related closely to study of the totality of what can occur. The goal is to understand which branches are admissible; that is, which paths can occur. With Figure 25.3, the answer is that all of them can; for example, the performance of the full school could agree with, or differ from that of the individual parts. Let me provide a challenge that is related to the discussion of the last section: How would you establish that the D, D, I branch can occur—a situation where even though each part declined in performance, the school as a whole did better—and what are the implications?

To explain what happens, imagine the shudders of any elementary school mathematics teacher watching a student trying to add fractions in the following fashion:

$$\frac{20}{60} + \frac{110}{240} = \frac{(20 + 110)}{(60 + 240)} = \frac{130}{300} \tag{1}$$

But, this is the correct computational approach when computing the fraction of success for the whole school. After all, the two numerators of 20 and 110 are the number of successes for the two groups, whereas the denominators of 60 and 240 indicate the number of students in each group represented in the first column depicting the 1999 data in Table 25.2 Consequently, and more generally, we must anticipate that whenever parts are combined into a whole in unusual ways, the connecting factor can generate a whole that differs radically from the parts.

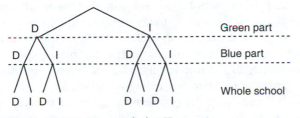

Figure 25.3 A "Part–Whole" Tree.

But, if an example as simple as this one can create surprise and confusion—as it did throughout the state of California—we must anticipate even greater surprises with the far more complex events of mathematical education. This includes parts–whole problems of understanding how our students assimilate and connect the information of the parts from our curricula. These comments suggest the importance of placing as much, or perhaps even more, attention on how the parts are combined and the consequences. As only one illustration, although we design the course material carefully so that the parts coincide with our vision of the whole, we often make the implicit (and probably incorrect) assumption that the parts can and will be assembled in only one manner. Just as the often-told story where a student learning that

$$\lim_{x \to 8} \frac{1}{(x - 8)^2} = \infty \tag{2}$$

mimics the pattern carefully by answering the question $\lim_{x \to 5}(x - 5)^2$ with a 5 lying on its side, there are many unanticipated ways to connect information. The interface, the role of the connections, must be understood better.

Finally, let me use Figure 25.3 and the above to illustrate my earlier comments about the chaos tree diagram in Figure 25.2 A natural way to try to establish that the D, D, I path can occur is to construct an example. Unfortunately, a particular example fails to identify the underlying structure of the parts–whole construction, and it can be difficult to find through the usual trial-and-error approach. Instead, let me demonstrate the pool hall approach by indicating how to find all the examples that support a D, D, I path. To do so, let $G_{I,99}$, $B_{I,99}$ denote, respectively, the numbers of greens and blues that met the standards in 1999; $G_{D,99}$, $B_{D,99}$ describe the numbers that failed to meet the standards. Similarly, $G_{I,00}$, $B_{I,00}$, and $G_{D,00}$, $B_{D,00}$ describe the year 2000 data.

The first step is to establish all the ways in which the first two steps, D, D, of the D, D, I path can occur. This means that the two inequalities:

$$\frac{G_{I,00}}{G_{I,00} + G_{D,00}} < \frac{G_{I,99}}{G_{I,99} + G_{D,99}}, \frac{B_{I,00}}{B_{I,00} + B_{D,00}} < \frac{B_{I,99}}{B_{I,99} + B_{D,99}} \tag{3}$$

must be satisfied. Each inequality imposes no constraint of any kind on the other. Hence, this independence of the variables make this possible.

Now suppose that the full school does better even though each group declined. This performance of the whole requires satisfying the inequality:

$$\frac{G_{I,99} + B_{I,99}}{(G_{I,99} + G_{D,99}) + (B_{I,99} + B_{D,99})} < \frac{G_{I,00} + B_{I,00}}{(G_{I,00} + G_{D,00}) + (B_{I,00} + B_{D,00})} \tag{4}$$

These three inequalities are much easier to solve and analyze than trying to invent an illustrating example. Even more can be accomplished; we can determine all eight branches of Figure 25.3 by keeping, or reversing, the various inequalities. Consequently, a full analysis is achieved merely by replacing each inequality with an equality and determining how these three equations in eight unknowns split up the space. In this manner, we can consider the totality of the tree (along with the missing branches that indicate ties) in a far more complete manner. So, trying to create an illustrating example makes the issue difficult, but analyzing the problem in this more general and ambitious framework, which reduces to three equations in eight unknowns, makes it fairly apparent that anything can happen. Although other mathematical tools often are needed, a similar effect arises with voting and with other places where this approach has been used.

What does this mean about the modeling of mathematics education? It is my sense that moving to the general analysis of part–whole connections will result in a richer theory along with a way to identify the valued and basic assumptions. Just as the above analysis identifies what kinds of interactions cause all possible different consequences, it would be exciting if something similar could be developed for, say, the understanding of mathematical principles.

Social Norms

How are social norms developed? As an illustration, in the United States, we drive on the right-hand side of the road, rather than the left. Why? The obvious response is that this is the way we do things. In other words, in some manner, we adopt particular social norms.

This social norm situation, where the accepted this-is-the-way-we-do-things customs are sufficiently strong to overrule proposed changes, has powerful positive consequences of ensuring orderliness and efficiency. On the other hand and of particular concern to education, is the reality that norms can create a serious drag that can destroy valued reform efforts. Sandy Sharma, one of my Ph.D. students, is studying how social norms from her country, which include bribery and the dowry, inhibit progress. She is trying to understand the nature of the policy changes needed to change these norms.

Can social norms be changed? I observed an example in 1983 when I was in Recife, Brazil, to deliver a series of lectures. Upon arrival, I noticed the peculiarity where, without hesitation, my host would drive through all the red lights. Although I tightened my seat belt, I said nothing until we approached a green light—where he immediately slowed down! In response to my obvious inquiry, he stated, "I had to stop because someone might be driving through the red light in the other direction." It turns out that there was an excellent rationale for this reversed social norm. This region was suffering an unfortunate crime wave where criminals would dash toward cars waiting at a red light to accost the occupants. For fitness' sake, drivers needed to drive through red lights.

In recent years, an actively studied question is to understand how social norms are created and modified. The current tools of preference involve dynamical systems. In keeping with the spirit of this chapter, let me introduce basic notions in an intuitive manner and leave technicalities to references.[4]

Start with what is known as the ultimatum game. Think of this as where you have an opportunity to earn a portion of a certain sum of money, say, $100,000. The rules are as follows: you propose a split of this money to another person. If that person agrees with your division, that is the agreement. But if the person disagrees, neither of you get anything. What division should you propose?

In the United States, the standard response is the "fair," 50–50 outcome; this sense is supported by experimental evidence where large numbers of people reject offers involving sizable amounts of money if the proposed division is viewed as not being fair. A surprise, however, is that this division is not universal. Conducting experiments in a manner to ensure the anonymity of the two players, Heinrich (2000) discovered that the stable division can differ in different societies even to the extreme where the proposer could demand consistently 80 percent of the reward and get it. Why? What is going on?

To understand by using the kind of example considered by Skyrms (1996), suppose that there are two types of individuals. The first are those who demand two-thirds of the proceeds in any setting, and the others demand only one-third. Assume that these individuals meet at random where the conclusion of their encounter determines the "fitness" of each species. If an individual receives something, this type is reinforced in that there will be more individuals of this type. On the other hand, if the encounter ends in nothing, then the discouragement leads to fewer individuals of this type. When assuming large numbers of people, Skyrms found that the dynamic reached an equilibrium where half of the individuals were of one type and the other half of the other type. Another illustration of the fitness dynamic is the driver in Recife going through a red light; when comparing the consequences of an unlikely traffic ticket to a robbery, fitness supported those who drove through the red light. Here, unanimity in ignoring the red lights characterized the social norm.

Now turn to my student Ms. Sharma's "toy example" that she developed at the start of her studies for the purpose of developing her intuition. It starts with a group of people trying to create a public good; as an illustration, think of this as providing security— say, hiring a doorman or guard—for their private community. In her model, only those who cooperate enjoy the rewards. The problem is that those who cooperate incur a personal expense, and any real payoff of social benefit requires the participation of enough people. After all, if only one or two people participate, they could not afford a guard, and they would abandon their efforts quickly. A sufficiently large group, however, could afford this security easily. Then, beyond the cooperators, there are others who are not interested in contributing to this community benefit if only because of the added personal cost. As a slight but important digression: notice how this description resembles educational reform where the incurred expense involves learning and adapting to the new methods, where only those who sign on to the reform procedure can benefit from their involvement, and where the full community benefits only after enough people are involved. Read on; the similarity is intentional.

In her modeling, technical conditions are imposed to capture how people decide whether to cooperate or not. These conditions are based on how individuals interact randomly with others and determine whether this cooperation is, or is not, to their personal advantage. What Ms. Sharma discovered with her dynamical model is the common finding for this area: a threshold effect of the kind indicated in Figure 25.4.

To describe this figure, the extreme ends represent where "nobody" and "everyone" is involved in the cooperative venture. The key is the bullet that indicates a threshold effect. To explain, suppose that there is only a small initial involvement that locates the starting position (the dagger) of the movement to the left of the threshold. According to the figure, the natural dynamic of interaction, involvement, and discouragement will cause a decline in cooperation, leading to its eventual demise. On the other hand, with a sufficiently massive start that places the initial position to the right of the bullet, the dynamic of encouragement indicates a gradual increase in the level of community cooperation, leading to a situation where cooperation takes over the full society. A key factor in Ms. Sharma's analysis is the location of the threshold; she finds that its location is a combination of the entry costs and the extent of the benefit for the community. For instance, a community benefit that offers more rewards for a smaller cost has a

Figure 25.4 Dynamics of Social Norms.

smaller threshold; it is one that is easier to overcome. But, a higher expense of entry requirements, such as needing to learn a new approach, combined with uncertain benefits, will define a discouraging location for the threshold. Here, it would be unlikely to sustain the change, even with a massive starting bloc.

Will this model explain the problems and adoption of reform procedures? Because Ms. Sharma's model was intended (at this early stage) to provide intuition and guidance, where several accompanying relevant features are ignored, it is too simple. On the other hand, her model does provide insight. (For a more general perspective, see my notes in Saari, 2002). Let me offer a suggestive example before providing a warning.

Ever since the introduction long ago of the Apple IIc computer, the potential value of computers in the classroom had been appreciated and discussed. But, even with the pioneering efforts of several advocates, it took a surprisingly long time for this approach to take hold in our schools. The explanation is easy to understand in terms of Figure 25.4. In the early years, the location of the threshold point reflected the sizable commitment. Relative to today, desktop computers were expensive and learning how to use them effectively was difficult and hindered by poorly written manuals. In other words, the entry expense was relatively high. Moreover, software for the classroom was primitive and scarce, not many families had computers at home that would allow for homework, and the internet with its vast sources of readily available information was yet to be developed. Stated in Ms. Sharma's terms, the personal costs were high and the community benefits were limited, so the threshold (the bullet) was located far to the right. This location indicates the need for a sizable movement to achieve wider acceptance. Thus, it is not surprising that computers were relatively scarce in classrooms and restricted to more affluent communities where both the expense and the community benefit (e.g., the availability of computers at home) were met.

What we had, then, was computer usage restricted to certain communities, as indicated by the dagger in Figure 25.4, but this was only until improved conditions moved the location of the threshold. With corporations donating computers and software, with the cost of computers coming down, with programs becoming more user-friendly, the entry costs and continuing expense came down. Once more software, the internet, and larger numbers of homes with computers became available, the benefits became greater. Accordingly, the social threshold point (the bullet) moved to the left. The model predicts that once the threshold (the bullet) moves to the left of the current practicing standard (the dagger), we should expect a rapid increase in adoption, and that is precisely what we observed. On the other hand, suppose that there were no pockets of acceptance; suppose that the current level of the use of computers still remained to the left of a less imposing threshold; we still would expect a tendency toward extinction.

The message and warnings suggested by this simple model are clear. For instance, expect difficulty in getting a reform approach adopted. Even with an initial success, unless and until some societal threshold is passed, the approach will tend to be ignored. This, of course, has been the fate of several reforms. During the meeting on the modeling of mathematics education in Santa Fe in December 2001, several private conversations debated the wisdom of introducing reform in a small dosage or with a larger approach. Figure 25.4 supports the larger approach, but with the constraint that we have no notion about the location of the threshold point. Consequently, Ms. Sharma's example suggests that a more sophisticated and successful approach toward reform must include understanding how to reduce the cost of getting involved and how to maximize the benefits. Stated in words, we must find ways to reduce entry costs and share the benefits; we need to change the threshold location.

Social Movement

Remember those Friday night beer parties during our college days when a hat was passed around seeking donations to buy a keg of beer and when each person was to contribute an amount of money compatible with the amount of beer that will be consumed. You remember the problem: some paid little and drank much. Surprisingly, ways to resolve this free-rider problem in collegiate beer parties offer insight about how to convert an educational reform movement into a broader social movement. Insight and help come from mathematical economics where a goal of the incentive literature is to find ways to convert the societal and/or organizational structures and reward system so that it now is in the best interest of an individual to cooperate with a specified objective. With the beer party illustration, the goal is to design an approach so that each person feels it is in his or her best interest to contribute an amount of money commensurate with his or her personal beer consumption. Similarly, when worrying about converting educational reform into a social movement, part of the goal must be to find ways to encourage individuals to make it in their personal interest to sign on. Such encouragement must continue until the societal threshold is passed, where the social dynamic of encouraging benefits takes over.

How is this done? Although the technical material involves gradients and game theory, the intuition is clear. If you want me to do something, the rewards and punishments must be expressed and designed to make it compatible with my personal interests. This most surely is the case when trying to involve in a project educators and others who are overworked and have an agenda that already is too full. The incentives must be high, but remember, for educators some rewards may be much stronger than money. As an illustration, professional recognition and research opportunity are important motivating factors in any community of educators and researchers.

I leave the technicalities of the design of incentives to the reader; they are easy to find by checking several of the current, graduate-level books in microeconomics. But, for intuition, consider the task of attempting to enlist teachers to try out a new approach for the teaching of mathematics. If an invitation involves a certain degree of prestige and recognition from fellow teachers and the administration, it is reasonable to anticipate active involvement and participation. However, when it is time to enlist more teachers, resistance can occur. Why? This is a mystery because some of the personal costs of being involved have been eliminated through the efforts of the first group of teachers. So why is the second group not as enthusiastic? The answer is clear: although personal costs have dropped, so have the personal incentives of recognition of participating in a pioneering group. In other words, the incentives for the next wave of teachers must be thought through carefully; they cannot be "more of the same."

This intuition captures a technical lesson that comes from the incentive literature. Namely, do not expect to find a one-size-fits-all incentive; the usual case is that the incentive must be designed for the individual. But, with reflection, this important lesson is natural and instinctive. Let me suggest that readers interested in this topic check the incentive literature from economics.

Conclusions

I started this chapter by acknowledging the underlying complexity of the issues in mathematics education. Of course, I have strong views about these topics. But beyond my personal explorations where I worry about how to stimulate my students to appreciate the power and beauty of mathematics, to explore new ways to convey information efficiently and accurately in a large class, to encourage students to separate concepts from technical details, I have no expertise in this particular area. On the other hand, my research interests include decisions, aggregation, dynamics, and complexity. It is my sense that, if used carefully, general principles from these areas will help address the research concerns of mathematics education.

But just as I want my students in a course on analysis, or dynamical systems, or calculus to separate the concepts and the technicalities, it is worth repeating my warning in the introductory section. Although it is reasonable to seek help from mathematics, be careful. I am skeptical whether anything useful will follow from technical descriptions and conclusions. On the other hand, basic concepts phrased properly often are transferable to other disciplines. Guided by these principles, we can expect to identify better central assumptions for mathematics education and to uncover the sources of complexity.

Acknowledgments

This chapter is a written and slightly revised version of my comments made at a conference on The Modeling of the Modeling of Mathematics Education, which was held in Santa Fe, New Mexico in December 2001. My thanks to my hosts Eamonn Kelly and Richard Lesh. The research described in this chapter was supported by NSF grant 0233798.

Notes

1 Also, I highly recommend checking out R. Devaney's delightful web page: http://math.bu.edu/DYSYS.
2 This parts–whole conflict is the theme of the book *Decisons and elections: explaining the unexpected* (Saari, 2001b). Please see this publication for a detailed discussion.
3 The reader might suspect that the change in numbers in each unit for the two years played a role; as explained in Saari (2001b), this is the case. This migration of different ethnic groups occurred in all the schools affected by the paradox of the state of California's Academic Performance Index.
4 Starting points include Skyrms' (1996) readable book on the development of social norms, Samuelson's (1998) book describing technical tools for economics, and Frank's (1998) book examining social evolution.

References

Barnsley, M. (1988). *Fractals everywhere*. New York: Academic Press.
Devaney, R. (1992). *A first course in chaotic dynamical systems*. Boston, MA: Addison-Wesley.
Devaney, R. (1999). *The dynamical systems and technology project at Boston University*, at http://math.bu.edu/DYSYS.
Heinrich, J. (2000). Does culture matter in economic behavior? Ultimatum game bargaining among the Machiguenga. *American Economic Review*, 90, 973–979.
Saari, D. G. (1995). A chaotic exploration of aggregation paradoxes. *Society for Industrial and Applied Mathematics Review*, 37, 37–52.
Saari, D. G. (2001a). *Chaotic elections! A mathematician looks at voting*. Providence, RI: American Mathematical Society.
Saari, D. G. (2001b). *Decisions and elections: Explaining the unexpected*. New York: Cambridge University Press.

Saari, D. G. (2002). *Mathematical social sciences: An oxymoron?*, at: http://www.pims.math.ca/science/2002/distchair/saari/.

Saari, D. G. & Xia, Z. (1995). Off to infinity in finite time. *Notices of the American Mathematical Society, 42*, 538–546.

Skyrms, B. (1996). *Evolution of the social contract.* New York: Cambridge University Press.

26 Design-Based Research in Physics Education

A Review

Richard R. Hake
Indiana University

Some Physics Education Research is Design-Based Research

In this chapter I argue that some physics education research (PER) is design-based research (DBR). An important DBR-like facet of PER, the pre/post testing movement, has the potential to improve drastically the effectiveness of undergraduate instruction generally, the education of preservice teachers in particular, and, as a net result, the education of the general population.

In their resource letter on physics education research, McDermott and Redish (1999) list about 160 empirical studies, extending over almost three decades that (a) focus on the learning of physics by students, (b) represent systematic research, and (c) give procedures in sufficient detail that they can be reproduced. My own effort in developing, testing, and disseminating Socratic dialogue inducing (SDI) laboratories is rather typical of the work reported by long-established physics education research groups and referenced by McDermott and Redish.

SDI laboratories emphasize hands- and heads-on experience with simple mechanics experiments and facilitate the interactive engagement of students with course material. They are designed to promote students' mental construction of concepts through:

- Interactive engagement of students who are induced to think constructively about simple Newtonian experiments that produce conflict with their commonsense understandings.
- The Socratic method (e.g., Arons, 1997; Hake, 1992, 2002d) of the *historical* Socrates (Vlastos, 1990, 1991), not Plato's alter ego in the *Meno* (as mistakenly assumed by many—even some physicists), utilized by experienced instructors who have a good understanding of the material and are aware of common student preconceptions and failings.
- Considerable interaction between students and instructors and thus a degree of individualized instruction.
- Extensive use of multiple representations (verbal, written, pictorial, diagrammatic, graphical, and mathematical) to model physical systems.
- Real-world situations and kinesthetic sensations (which promote student interest and intensify cognitive conflict when students' direct sensory experience does not conform to their conceptions).
- Cooperative group effort and peer discussions.
- Repeated exposure to the coherent Newtonian explanation in many different contexts.

As described in Hake (1987, 1991, 1992, 2000, 2002d, 2007), Hake and Wakeland

(1997), and Tobias and Hake (1988), SDI laboratories were inspired by the astute empirical observations of Arnold Arons (1973, 1974, 1983, 1986, 1997) who had the uncommon sense to "shut up and listen to what students say" in response to probing Socratic questions.

In numerous publications, I scientifically and iteratively developed (Hake, 1987), explored (Hake, 1991, 1992; Tobias & Hake, 1988), confirmed (Hake, 1998a, 1998b, 2002a, 2002b, 2005, 2006, in preparation), and disseminated (Hake, 2000, 2002b, 2002d, 2007) SDI laboratories. My research and development involved active innovation and intervention in the classrooms of introductory physics classes for prospective elementary teachers (Hake, 1991), premedical students (Hake, 1987, 1992; Hake & Wakeland, 1997), and even nonphysical science professors (Tobias & Hake, 1988). Further, my research and development drew upon models from design and engineering, in that SDI laboratories were designed initially by taking into account my own teaching experience, the advice of the late Arnold Arons, and the physics education and cognitive science literature. Then, trial runs that exposed design failures and successes were carried out in regularly scheduled courses; this phase was followed by exploratory out-of-class research with paid student subjects involving video-tape analysis of SDI laboratory sessions (Hake, 2000) and interviews with students.

Three redesigns, retests, and more exploratory, in- and out-of-class research and development over many cycles of application—all in typical engineering fashion—generated new ideas for physics teaching (Hake, 1987, 1992, 2007; Hake & Wakeland, 1997; Tobias & Hake, 1988) and contributed to the transformation of the traditional recipe laboratory. I sought to understand learning and teaching while I was active as the instructor (Hake, 1987, 1992; Hake & Wakeland, 1997; Tobias & Hake, 1988). As explained in Hake (2002a) (in the section titled "Can educational research be scientific research?"), my research and development were examples of use-inspired, basic scientific research, consistent with the theses of Shavelson and Towne (2002) and Stokes (1997). Such work contributed to the movement of at least some introductory mechanics courses from malfunction to function, as shown by pre/post test results (Hake, 1998a, 1998b; 2002a, 2002b, 2005, 2006, in preparation).

Considering the above two paragraphs, I submit that some PER qualifies as design-based research as characterized by Kelly (2003a). Should not the major concern of education research be K–12, as appears to be the area of activity for most education specialists, psychologists, and cognitive scientists? Not necessarily. The National Science Foundation's report *Shaping the Future* hit the nail squarely on the head (my italics):

> . . . Science, mathematics, engineering, and technology (SME&T) [programs] at the postsecondary level continue to blame the schools for sending underprepared students to them. But, increasingly the higher education community has come to recognize the fact that *teachers and principals in the K–12 system are all people who have been educated at the undergraduate level, mostly in situations in which SME&T programs have not taken seriously enough their vital part of the responsibility for the quality of America's teachers.*
>
> (1996: 35)

In my opinion, the DBR-like, pre/post testing movement, stimulated to some extent by physics education research, has the potential to improve undergraduate science instruction dramatically and thereby upgrade K–12 science education. Currently, prospective K–12 teachers derive little conceptual understanding from traditional, undergraduate, introductory science courses; then they tend to teach as they were taught, with similar negative results. As emphasized by Goodlad (1990: xi–xii):

> Few matters are more important than the quality of the teachers in our nation's schools. Few matters are as neglected. . . . A central thesis of this book is that there is a natural connection between good teachers and good schools and that this connection has been largely ignored. . . . *It is folly to assume that schools can be exemplary when their stewards are ill-prepared.*

Pre/Post Testing in Physics Education Research

The pre/post testing movement in PER was initiated by the landmark work of Halloun and Hestenes (1985a, 1985b). Previously, in "Lessons from the physics education reform effort" (Hake, 2002a) I wrote:

> For over three decades, physics education researchers repeatedly showed that *traditional* (T) introductory physics courses with passive-student lectures, recipe laboratories, and algorithmic problem exams were of limited value in enhancing conceptual understanding of the subject (McDermott & Redish, 1999). Unfortunately, this work was largely ignored by the physics and education communities until Halloun and Hestenes (1985a, 1985b) devised the *Mechanics Diagnostic* (MD) test of conceptual understanding of Newtonian mechanics. Among the virtues of the Mechanics Diagnostic, and the subsequent *Force Concept Inventory* (FCI) tests (Hestenes, Wells, & Swackhamer, 1992) are: (a) the multiple-choice format facilitates relatively easy administration of the tests to thousands of students, and (b) the questions probe for conceptual understanding of basic concepts of Newtonian mechanics in a way that is understandable to the novice who has never taken a physics course (and thus can be given as an introductory-course pretest), while at the same time are rigorous enough for the initiate.

Construction of the Mechanics Diagnostic test involved laborious *qualitative* analysis of extensive interviews with students and the study of prior qualitative and quantitative work on misconceptions (McDermott & Redish, 1999). All this led to a "taxonomy of common sense concepts about motion" (Halloun & Hestenes, 1985b; Hestenes et al., 1992) and finally the formulation of a balanced and valid test that has proven consistently to be highly reliable, as judged by relatively high Kuder-Richardson reliability coefficients KR–20 in the 0.8 to 0.9 range (see, e.g., Hake, 1998a, 1998b; Halloun & Hestenes, 1985b).

Halloun and Hestenes (1985a, 1985b) then used the Mechanics Diagnostic in *quantitative* classroom research involving massive pre/post testing of students in both calculus and noncalculus-based introductory physics courses at Arizona State University. Their conclusions were:

- the student's initial, qualitative, common-sense beliefs about motion and . . . [its] . . . causes have a large effect on performance in physics, but conventional instruction induces only a small change in those beliefs.
- Considering the wide differences in the teaching styles of the four professors . . . [involved in the study] . . . the basic knowledge gain under conventional instruction is essentially independent of the professor.

(Halloun & Hestenes, 1985a: 1048)

Can multiple choice tests gauge higher-level cognitive outcomes such as the conceptual understanding of Newtonian mechanics? Wilson and Bertenthal think so, writing:

> Performance assessment is an approach that offers great potential for assessing complex thinking and learning abilities, but multiple choice items also have their strengths. For example, although many people recognize that multiple-choice items are an efficient and effective way of determining how well students have acquired basic content knowledge, many do not recognize that they can also be used to measure complex cognitive processes. For example, the *Force Concept Inventory* . . . [Hestenes et al., 1992] . . . is an assessment that uses multiple-choice items to tap into higher-level cognitive processes.
>
> (2005: 94)

The Halloun and Hestenes (1985a, 1985b) research results were consistent with the findings of many researchers in physics education (McDermott & Redish, 1999), which suggested that traditional, passive-student, introductory physics courses, even those delivered by the most talented and popular instructors, imparted little conceptual understanding of Newtonian mechanics. But the Halloun and Hestenes research went far beyond earlier work because it offered physics teachers and researchers a valid and consistently reliable test that could be employed to gauge the effectiveness of *traditional* mechanics instruction, then to track continually the merit of the *nontraditional* methods with respect to (a) traditional methods, (b) one another, and (c) various modes of implementation. Thus, it could contribute to a steady, albeit very slow, iterative increase in the effectiveness of introductory mechanics instruction nationwide.

For example, consider the Mechanics Diagnostic/Force Concept Inventory-induced changes in introductory physics courses at pacesetting Harvard University and the Massachusetts Institute of Technology. Harvard University's Mazur wrote:

> When reading this [Halloun & Hestenes, 1985a, 1985b, 1987; Hestenes, 1987] . . . my first reaction was "Not my students . . .!" Intrigued, I decided to test my own students' conceptual understanding, as well as that of physics majors at Harvard . . . the results of the test came as a shock: The students fared hardly better on the Halloun and Hestenes test [1985a] than on their midterm exam. Yet the Halloun and Hestenes test is *simple*, whereas the material covered by the examination (rotational dynamics, moments of inertia) is of far greater difficulty, or so I thought.
>
> (1997: 4)

In Table I of Crouch and Mazur (2001: 972), note:

1   The abrupt increase in the average normalized gain <g> (see below) from 0.25 in 1990 to 0.49 in 1991 when Mazur replaced his passive-student lectures (that netted very positive student evaluations—many administrators erroneously regard student evaluations as valid measures of students' learning!)—with the interactive engagement of peer instruction.
2   The gradual increase in the average normalized gain <g> from 0.49 in 1991 to 0.74 in 1997 as various improvements were made in the implementation of peer instruction.

Belcher, describing his institute's introductory physics course transition from traditional to interactive-engagement, wrote:

What is the motivation for this transition to such a different mode for teaching introductory physics? First, the traditional lecture/recitation format for teaching 8.01 and 8.02 has had a 40–50% attendance rate, even with spectacularly good lecturers (e.g., Professor Walter Lewin), and a 10% or higher failure rate. Second, there has been a range of educational innovations at universities other than MIT over the last few decades that demonstrate that any pedagogy using "interactive-engagement" methods results in higher learning gains as compared to the traditional lecture format (e.g., see Halloun & Hestenes, 1985a, 1985b; Hake, 1998a; Crouch & Mazur, 2001), usually accompanied by lower failure rates. Finally, the mainline introductory physics courses at MIT do not have a laboratory component.

(2003: 8)

The Harvard University and MIT results are consistent with those from hundreds of other introductory physics courses employing either traditional or interactive engagement methods, as evidenced by the meta-analysis discussed below.

Considering the canonical arguments regarding the invalidity of pre/post testing evidence, should not all the results cited above be viewed with grave suspicion? The Coalition for Evidence-Based Policy (2003: 2), in its *Identifying and implementing educational practices supported by rigorous evidence: A user friendly guide* states:

Pre–post study designs often produce erroneous results. . . . A "pre–post" study examines whether participants in an intervention improve or regress during the course of the intervention, and then attributes any such improvement or regression to the intervention. The problem with this type of study is that, without reference to a control group, it cannot answer whether the participants' improvement or decline would have occurred anyway, even without the intervention. This often leads to erroneous conclusions about the effectiveness of the intervention.

In my opinion, the above objection is irrelevant for most of the pre/post testing studies considered here. The reason is that fairly well-matched control groups *have* been used; they are the courses taught by the traditional method. The matching is due to the fact that (a) within any one institution, the test (interactive engagement [IE]) and the control (traditional [T]) groups are drawn from the same, generic, introductory course taken by relatively homogeneous groups of students, and (b) IE- and T-course teachers in all institutions are drawn from the same generic pool of introductory course physics teachers who, judging from the uniformly poor, average, normalized gains $<g>$ (see below) they obtain in teaching traditional courses, do not vary greatly in their ability to enhance students' learning.

Even if one were to maintain unrealistically that the traditional courses and instructors were not at all matched and that the pre/post testing of IE courses had no controls whatsoever, Table 2 of Lipsey and Wilson (1993) shows that, for the data they survey, the mean effect size of one-group pre/post testing studies is 0.76, compared to the control and comparison studies mean of 0.46. But both the difference in these two means and their individual magnitudes are small in comparison with the Cohen effect size of 2.43 (as calculated by comparing average $<g>$s for IE and T courses), or 2.16 (as calculated from the *actual gains* $[<\%_{post}> - <\%_{pre}>$ of IE courses]) that I have reported (see Hake, 2002a). It is interesting that the same Lipsey and Wilson table shows that, for the meta-analyses surveyed by them, the average effect size is 0.46 for random studies and 0.41 for nonrandom studies. Thus, the non-random studies evidently tend to *underestimate* the effectiveness of programs, if we are to accept the Coalition for

Evidence-Based Policy's (2003: 1) dubious pronouncement that randomized controlled trials are the gold standard for gauging the effectiveness of an intervention.

Well-designed and implemented randomized controlled trials are considered the "gold standard" for evaluating an intervention's effectiveness, in fields such as medicine, welfare and employment policy, and psychology. This section discusses what a randomized controlled trial is, and outlines evidence indicating that such trials should play a similar role in education.

Then, too, as discussed in Hake (2005, 2006, in preparation), the anti pre/post testing arguments by the psychometric authorities Lord (1956, 1958) and Cronbach and Furby (1970) that gain scores are unreliable have been called into question by, for example, Rogosa et al. (1982), Zimmerman and Williams (1982), Rogosa and Willett (1983, 1985), Rogosa (1995), Wittmann (1997), Zimmerman (1997), and Zumbo (1999). All this more recent work should serve as an antidote for the emotional, pre/post testing paranoia that grips many educational researchers.

Meta-analysis of Pre/Post Learning Gains

A reservation regarding meta-analysis has been raised by DBR pioneer Carl Bereiter. In *Design research for sustained innovation*, he wrote:

> Rather more successful than [attribute-treatment interactions (ATIs) to discover the optimal matching of persons to treatments (Cronbach, 1975)] has been meta-analysis (Glass, McGaw, & Smith, 1981), in which a number of different studies that are judged to involve the same variable are brought together into a statistically powerful test of the effects of the variable. Educational research journals regularly carry meta-analyses on topics ranging from the effects of computer use to the effects of phonemic awareness training. Meta-analysis, however, takes quantitative research an additional step away from design relevance. In combining results from a large number of experiments in the use of educational games, for instance, all the differences among games and in ways of using them are averaged out, leaving nothing to aid the person who would like to design a more effective educational game.
>
> (2002: 10)

But Bereiter's hypothetical failure of the meta-analysis of the effects of heterogenous computer games does not justify the conclusion that all meta-analyses take "quantitative research an additional step away from design relevance." For example, my own meta-analysis (Hake, 1998a, 1998b, 2002a, 2002b) of pre/post test data for the Mechanics Diagnostic and Force Concept Inventory as used in introductory Newtonian mechanics instruction, shown graphically in Figure 26.1, has proven to be of direct interest to course designers, even though the data were not (and could not have been!) obtained from randomized controlled trial studies.

In Figure 26.1, %<Gain> versus %<Pretest> scores on the conceptual *Mechanics Diagnostic* (MD) or *Force Concept Inventory* (FCI) tests for 62 courses enrolling a total $N = 6542$ students: 14 traditional (T) courses ($n = 2084$), which made little or no use of interactive engagement (IE) methods, and 48 IE courses ($n = 4458$), which made considerable use of IE methods: (a) the average normalized gain <g> is the actual gain ($<\%_{post}> - <\%_{pre}>$) divided by the maximum possible gain ($100\% - <\%_{pre}>$) where the angle brackets indicate the class averages, (b) IE courses are defined *operationally* as those designed, at least in part, to promote conceptual understanding through the

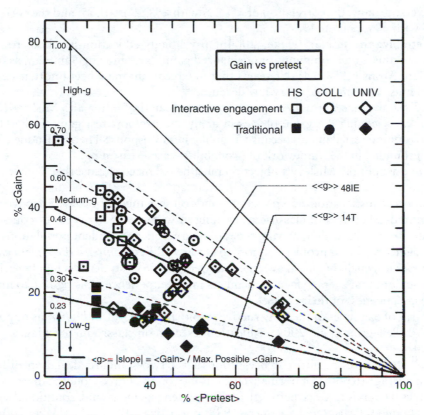

Figure 26.1 %<Gain> Versus %<Pretest> Scores on the Conceptual *Mechanics Diagnostic* (MD) or *Force Concept Inventory* (FCI) Tests for 62 Courses.

From Hake (1998a). © 1998 American Institute of Physics. Reprinted with permission of the author.

interactive engagement of students in heads-on (always) and hands-on (usually) activities that yield immediate feedback through discussion with peers and/or instructors, and (c) T courses are defined *operationally* as those reported by instructors to make little or no use of IE methods, relying primarily on passive-student lectures, recipe laboratories, and algorithmic problem examinations.

Slope lines for the average of the 14 T courses $<<g>>_{14T} = 0.23 \pm 0.04$ (SD) and the 48 IE courses $<<g>>_{48IE} = 0.48 \pm 0.14$ (SD) are shown. The negative-slope straight lines are lines of constant, normalized average gain $<g> = <$Gain$>$/maximum possible $<$Gain$> = (<\%_{post}> - <\%_{pre}>) / (100 - <\%_{pre}>)$. Thus, for example, if a class averaged 40 percent on the pretest and 60 percent on the post-test, then the class-average normalized gain $<g> = (60\% - 40\%)/(100\% - 40\%) = 20\%/60\% = 0.33$. (The random guessing score is 20 percent.)

Regarding the average normalized gain $<g>$, ever since the work of Hovland et al. (1949/1965) it has been known by pre/post testing cognoscenti (which, up until about 1998, was probably less than 100 people worldwide) that $<g>$ *is a much better indicator of the extent to which a treatment is effective than is either gain or post-test* (Cohen et al., 1999; Gery, 1972; Hake, 1998a, 1998b; Meltzer, 2002b). Justification for the use of $<g>$ for the present data set resides in the fact that the correlation of $<g>$ with $<\%_{pre}>$ for the 62 survey courses is a very low +0.02. In contrast, the average post-test score $<\%_{post}>$ and the average gain $<g>$ are less suitable for comparing course effectiveness over diverse groups: the correlation of $<\%_{post}>$ with $<\%_{pre}>$ is +0.55, and the correlation of $<G>$ with $<\%_{pre}>$ is −0.49.

Regrettably, the insular (Hake, 2004b) psychology-education-psychometric community remains largely oblivious of normalized gain. Paraphrasing Shulman, as quoted by the late Arons (1986: 24): "it seems that in education, the wheel (more usually the flat tire) must be reinvented every few decades."

Could the average normalized gain $<g>$ be a "flat tire" after all? Mislevy (2006), while acknowledging the value of $<g>$ in analyzing pre/post test gains Hake (1998a, 1998b), is uninterested in $<g>$ because it, unlike Item Response Theory (Rudner, 2001), is not "grounded in the framework of probability-based reasoning."

But, in my opinion, Mislevy's objection must be balanced against the:

- *Empirical* justification of $<g>$ as an easy-to-use gauge of course effectiveness in hundreds of studies of classroom teaching in widely varying types of courses and institutions with widely varying types of instructors and student populations.
- Evidently unsolved problem of how to employ IRT *to compare the effectiveness of courses* in which the initial average knowledge state of students is highly variable.
- Difficulties that average faculty members might experience in using IRT to improve the effectiveness of their courses.
- Dearth of examples of the constructive employment of IRT in *higher* (as opposed to K–12 [Pellegrino et al., 2001]) education research on classroom teaching.

Figure 26.1 serves as an existence proof that a two-standard deviation difference between average to post-test normalized gains $<g>$ on the Force Concept Inventory and Mechanics Diagnostic tests between interactive engagement and traditional courses *can* be obtained. I calculated a Cohen (1988) effect size "d" of 2.43 (Hake, 2002c), as indicated above, much higher than any found by Lipsey and Wilson (1993) in their meta-meta-analysis of psychological, educational, and behavioral treatments. Seven reasons for the "d disparity" between my survey and other social science research are given in Hake (2002a):

1   *All* courses covered nearly the same material (here, introductory Newtonian mechanics).
2   The material is conceptually difficult and counterintuitive.
3   The *same* test (either Mechanics Diagnostic or Force Concept Inventory) was administered to both IE and T classes.
4   The tests employed are widely recognized for their validity and consistent reliability, have been designed carefully to measure understanding of the key concepts of the material, and are far superior to the plug-in, regurgitation-type tests so commonly used as measures of "achievement."
5   The measurement unit gauges the normalized learning *gain* from start to finish of a course, *not* the "achievement" at the end of a course.
6   The measurement unit $<g>$ is not correlated significantly with students' initial knowledge of the material being tested.
7   The "treatments" are all patterned after those published by education researchers in the discipline being tested.

I should have included in the above list:

8   Possible preferential selection of outstanding IE courses.

In regard to "8," I stated in Hake (1998a):

> As in any scientific investigation, bias in the detector [due to the mode of data collection—voluntary contributions that tend to preselect results that are biased in favor of outstanding courses] can be put to good advantage if appropriate research objectives are established. We do *not* attempt to assess the average effectiveness of introductory mechanics courses. Instead, we seek to answer a question of considerable practical interest to physics teachers [and to physics education researchers]: *can the classroom use of IE methods increase the effectiveness of introductory mechanics courses well beyond that attained by traditional methods?*

For the 48 interactive engagement courses of Figure 26.1, the ranking in terms of number of IE courses using each of the more popular methods follows:[1]

1   *Collaborative Peer Instruction*: 48 (all courses) {CA} (Heller et al., 1992; Johnson et al., 1991, 2000; Slavin, 1995).
2   *Microcomputer-Based Laboratories*: 35 courses {DT} (Thornton, 1995; Thornton & Sokoloff, 1990, 1998).
3   *Concept Tests*: 20 courses {DT} (Crouch & Mazur, 2001; Fagen et al., 2002; Lorenzo et al., 2006; Mazur, 1997; Rosenberg et al., 2006).[2]
4   *Modeling*: 19 courses {DT + CA} (Halloun & Hestenes, 1987; Hestenes, 1987, 1992; Wells et al., 1995).[3]
5   *Active Learning Problem Sets* or *Overview Case Studies*: 17 courses {CA} (Van Heuvelen, 1991a, 1991b, 1995).[4]
6   *Physics Education Research-based Text or No Text*: 13 courses (referenced in Hake, 1998b, Table II).
7   *Socratic Dialogue Inducing Laboratories*: 9 courses {DT + CA} (Hake 1987, 1991, 1992, 2000, 2002d, 2007; Hake & Wakeland, 1997; Tobias & Hake, 1988).[5]

Average normalized gain differences between T and IE courses that are consistent with the work of Hake (1998a, 1998b, 2002a, 2002a) and Figure 26.1 have been reported (Beichner et al., 1999; Belcher, 2003; Bernhard, 2000; Crouch & Mazur, 2001; Cummings et al., 1999; Dori & Belcher, 2005; Fagan et al., 2002; Francis et al., 1998; Heller, 1999; Hoellwarth et al., 2005; Johnson, 2001; Lorenzo et al., 2006; Meltzer, 2002a, 2002b; Meltzer & Manivannan, 2002; Novak et al., 1999; Redish, 1999; Redish & Steinberg, 1999; Redish et al., 1997; Rosenberg et al., 2006; Saul, 1998; Savinainen & Scott, 2002a, 2002b; Steinberg & Donnelly, 2002; Van Domelen & Van Heuvelen, 2002).

This consistency of the results of many investigators in various institutions working with different student populations with the results of Hake (1998a, 1998b, 2002a, 2002b) constitutes the most important single warrant for the validity of conclusion in Hake (1998a: 71) that: "The conceptual and problem-solving test results strongly suggest that the classroom use of IE methods can increase mechanics-course effectiveness well beyond that obtained in traditional practice." Such gradual build-up of an agreed-upon "community map" (Redish, 1999; Ziman, 2000) is characteristic of the progress of traditional science, but it seems to be consistently undervalued in educational research.

Furthermore, that interactive engagement courses would be more effective in enhancing conceptual understanding of counterintuitive Newtonian laws than traditional courses with their passive-student lectures, recipe laboratories, and algorithmic problem sets certainly would be expected from previous physics education research (McDermott & Redish, 1999), including the astute ethnographically-based insights of Arons (1997)—for a discussion, see Hake (2004a).

More exploratory research is required to increase the effectiveness of IE courses. None that I surveyed (Hake, 1998a, 1998b) achieved an average normalized gain <g> greater than 0.69, only fair on an absolute scale. Additional research is needed to ascertain the conditions under which IE courses can be most effective and to test IE courses in a wider variety of environments. In my opinion, what are needed are new meta-analyses of mechanics course results accruing over the past decade and in the future, using new and more secure tests than the Force Concept Inventory or *Force Motion Conceptual Evaluation* (FMCE) of Thornton and Sokoloff (1998).

In addition to enlarging the mechanics pre/post test data bank, PER groups have gone beyond the early survey work. For example, PER groups have shown that there may be significant differences in the effectiveness of various IE methods (Redish, 1999; Saul, 1998). In addition, there may be contributions to the average normalized gain <g> from "hidden variables" such as averages over classes of gender, mathematics proficiency, spatial visualization ability, completion of high-school physics courses, scientific reasoning skills, physics aptitude, personality type, motivation, socioeconomic level, ethnicity, intelligence quotient, scholastic aptitude test, and grade point average. One approach to this question is to investigate the relationship of *individual* student learning gains with such variables for *single courses* (Coletta & Phillips, 2005; Hake, 2002c; Meltzer, 2002b).

PER groups have developed diagnostic tests of students' cognitive and affective states before and after instruction in physics (including areas other than mechanics) and other disciplines (e.g., the listings at North Carolina State University, 2007 and Field-Tested Learning Assessment Guide, National Institute for Science Education, 2007). They also have analyzed multiple-choice conceptual tests that go beyond classical test theory in which only the number of correct answers is considered in the scoring. These more advanced analyses can indicate incorrect models that students form during instruction in a single course or in a series of courses redesigned successively in attempts to improve their effectiveness. Such work has been reported by Bao and Redish (2001) for the Force Concept Inventory, by Thornton (1995) for the *Force Motion Conceptual Evaluation* (FMCE; Thornton & Sokoloff, 1998), and may assist the study of transfer, i.e., the transfer of learning or capability from one area to another; see Bransford et al. (2000, Chapter 3), and also Hake (2004b). Finally, by the intensive study of how physics is learned (Redish, 1994, 1999, 2004), they have gone somewhat beyond the cognitive theories considered by Heller (1999).

Conclusion

The physics education research discussed above qualifies as design-based research as gauged by the Kelly (2003a) criteria. In addition, PER has two attributes that seem to be missing in most DBR, as judged by the articles in Kelly (2003b): concern with under-graduate education—a major influence on the effectiveness of K–12 teaching—and rigorous assessment of the need for, and effects of, reform curricula. It is hoped that the provincialism of current education research (Hake, 2004b) which has hidden PER from DBR and DBR from PER can be reduced in order to make DBR a more interdisciplinary and synergistic effort.

Acknowledgments

This work received partial support from National Science Foundation Grant DUE/ MDR9253965. I thank Anthony E. Kelly for suggesting that I write this article and for his valuable comments.

Notes

1 The notations within the braces {. . .} follow Heller (1999) in associating loosely the methods with learning theories from cognitive science. Here, "DT" stands for "developmental theory," originating with Piaget (Gardner 1985; Inhelder & Piaget, 1958; Inhelder et al., 1987; Phillips & Soltis, 1998); "CA" stands for "cognitive apprenticeship" (Brown et al., 1989; Collins et al., 1989). All the methods recognize the important role of social interactions in learning (Dewey, 1938/1997; Lave & Wenger, 1991; Phillips & Soltis, 1998; Vygotsky, 1978). It should be emphasized that the rankings are by popularity within the survey and have no necessary connection with the effectiveness of the methods relative to one another. In fact, it is quite possible that some of the less popular methods used in some survey courses, as listed by Hake (1998b), could be more effective in terms of promoting students' understanding than any of the popular strategies noted above.
2 Tests available for physics, biology, and chemistry (Galileo, 2007; ILT-BQ Consortium, 2006).
3 A description is on the web at http://modeling.la.asu.edu/.
4 Information on these materials is online at http://www.physics.ohio-state.edu/~physedu/.
5 A description and laboratory manuals are on the web at http://www.physics.indiana.edu/~sdi.

References

Arons, A. B. (1973). Toward wider public understanding of science. *American Journal of Physics, 41*, 769–782.

Arons, A. B. (1974). Toward wider public understanding of science: Addendum. *American Journal of Physics, 42*, 157–58.

Arons, A. B. (1983). Achieving wider scientific literacy. *Daedalus, 2*, 91–122.

Arons, A. B. (1986). Conceptual difficulties in science. In M. R. Rice (ed.), *Undergraduate education in chemistry and physics: Proceedings of the Chicago conferences on liberal education* Volume 1 (pp. 23–32). Chicago: University of Chicago.

Arons, A. B. (1997). *Teaching introductory physics*. New York: Wiley.

Bao, L. & Redish, E. F. (2001). Concentration analysis: A quantitative assessment of student states. *American Journal of Physics, 69*(S1), S45–S53.

Beichner, R. J., Bernold, L., Burniston, E., Dail, P., Felder, R., Gastineau, J., et al. (1999). Case study of the physics component of an integrated curriculum. *American Journal of Physics, 67*(S1), S16–S24.

Belcher, J.W. (2003). Improving student understanding with TEAL [Technology Enhanced Active Learning]. *MIT Faculty Newsletter, XVI*(2), 1, 8–10.

Bereiter, C. (2002). Design research for sustained innovation. *Cognitive studies, Bulletin of the Japanese Cognitive Science Society, 9*, 321–327.

Bernhard, J. (2000). Does active engagement curricula give long-lived conceptual understanding? *Proceedings of GIREP 2000: Physics Teacher Education Beyond 2000*, Barcelona, Spain, at: http://staffwww.itn.liu.se/~jonbe/fou/didaktik/abstracts/girep2000_active.html.

Bransford, J. D, Brown, A. L. & Cocking, R. R. (eds) 2000. *How people learn: Brain, mind, experience, and school*. Washington, DC: National Academy Press.

Brown, J. S., Collins, A. & Dugrid, P. (1989). Situated cognition and the culture of learning. *Educational Researcher, 18*(1), 32–42.

Coalition for Evidence-Based Policy (2003). *Identifying and implementing educational practices supported by rigorous evidence: A user friendly guide*. Washington, DC: U.S. Department of Education.

Cohen, J. (1988). *Statistical power analysis for the behavioral sciences* (2nd ed.). Hillsdale, NJ: Lawrence Erlbaum Associates.

Cohen, P., Cohen, J., Aiken, L. S. & West, S. G. (1999). The problem of units and the circumstance for POMP. *Multivariate Behavioral Research, 34,* 315–346.

Coletta, V. P. & Phillips, J. A. (2005). Interpreting FCI scores: Normalized gain, preinstruction scores, and scientific reasoning ability. *American Journal of Physics, 73,* 1172–1182.

Collins, A., Brown, J. S. & Newman, S. (1989). Cognitive apprenticeship: Teaching students the craft of reading, writing, and mathematics. In L. B. Resnick (ed.), *Knowing, learning, and instruction: Essays in honor of Robert Glaser* (pp. 453–494). Hillsdale, NJ: Lawrence Erlbaum Associates.

Cronbach, L. J. (1975). Beyond the two disciplines of scientific psychology. *American Psychologist, 30,* 116–127.

Cronbach, L. J. & Furby, L. (1970). How we should measure "change"—or should we? *Psychological Bulletin, 74,* 68–80.

Crouch, C. H. & Mazur, E. (2001). Peer instruction: Ten years of experience and results. *American Journal of Physics, 69,* 970–977.

Cummings, K., Marx, J., Thornton, R. & Kuhl, D. (1999). Evaluating innovations in studio physics. *American Journal of Physics, 67*(S1), S38–S44.

Dewey, J. (1997). *Experience and education.* New York: Free Press (original work published 1938).

Dori, Y. J. & Belcher, J. (2005). How does technology-enabled active learning affect undergraduate students' understanding of electromagnetism concepts? *The Journal of the Learning Sciences, 14,* 243–279.

Fagen, A. P., Crouch, C. H. & Mazur, E. (2002). Peer instruction: results from a range of classrooms. *Physics Teacher, 40,* 206–209.

Francis, G. E., Adams, J. P. & Noonan, E. J. (1998). Do they stay fixed? *Physics Teacher, 36,* 488–491.

Galileo (2007). Mazur Group, Harvard University, at: http://galileo.harvard.edu/.

Gardner, H. (1985). *The mind's new science: A history of the cognitive revolution.* New York: Basic Books.

Gery, F. W. (1972). Does mathematics matter? In A. Welch (ed.), *Research papers in economic education* (pp. 142–157). New York: Joint Council on Economic Education.

Glass, G. V., McGaw, B. & Smith, M. L. (1981). *Meta-analysis in social research.* Beverly Hills, CA: Sage.

Goodlad, J. I. (1990). *Teachers for our nation's schools.* San Francisco, CA: Jossey-Bass.

Hake, R. R. (1987). Promoting student crossover to the Newtonian world. *American Journal of Physics, 55,* 878–884.

Hake, R. R. (1991). My conversion to the Arons-advocated method of science education. *Teaching Education, 3,* 109–111.

Hake, R. R. (1992). Socratic pedagogy in the introductory physics lab. *Physics Teacher, 30,* 546–552.

Hake, R. R. (1998a). Interactive-engagement vs traditional methods: A six-thousand-student survey of mechanics test data for introductory physics courses. *American Journal of Physics, 66,* 64–74.

Hake, R. R. (1998b). Interactive-engagement methods in introductory mechanics courses. Unpublished manuscript, at: http://www.physics.indiana.edu/~sdi/IEM-2b.pdf.

Hake, R. R. (2000). Towards paradigm peace in physics education research. Paper presented at the annual meeting of the American Educational Research Association, New Orleans, LA, April.

Hake, R. R. (2002a). Lessons from the physics education reform effort. *Ecology and Society, 5*(2), at: http://www.ecologyandsociety.org/vol5/iss2/art28/.

Hake, R. R. (2002b). *Assessment of physics teaching methods.* Presented at the UNESCO-AsPEN (ASian Physics Education Network) Workshop on Active Learning in Physics, University of Peradeniya, Sri Lanka, December.

Hake, R. R. (2002c). Relationship of individual student normalized learning gains in mechanics with gender, high-school physics, and pretest scores on mathematics and spatial visualization. Paper presented at Physics Education Research Conference, Boise, Idaho, August.

Hake, R. R. (2002d). Socratic dialogue inducing laboratory workshop. Presented at the UNESCO-AsPEN (ASian Physics Education Network) Workshop on Active Learning in Physics, University of Peradeniya, Sri Lanka, December.

Hake, R. R. (2004a). The Arons advocated method. Unpublished manuscript.

Hake, R. R. (2004b). *Design-based research: A primer for physics education researchers*, at: <http://www.physics.indiana.edu/~hake>.

Hake, R. R. (2005). The physics education reform effort: A possible model for higher education, *National Teaching and Learning Forum, 15*(1), 28.

Hake, R. R. (2006). Possible palliatives for the paralyzing pre/post paranoia that plagues some PEPs. *Journal of MultiDisciplinary Evaluation*, 6, at: http://evaluation.wmich.edu/jmde/JMDE_Num006.html.

Hake, R. R. (2007). *Socratic dialogue inducing (SDI) lab website*, at: March 3, 2007 from http://www.physics.indiana.edu/~sdi.

Hake, R. R. (in preparation). Should we measure change? Yes! In R. R. Hake (ed.), *Evaluation of teaching and student learning in higher education*. Fairhaven, MA: American Evaluation Association.

Hake R. R. & Wakeland, R. (1997). What's F? What's m? What's a? A non-circular SDITST-lab treatment of Newton's second law. In J. Wilson (ed.), *Conference on the introductory physics course*, (pp. 277–283). New York: Wiley.

Halloun, I. & Hestenes, D. (1985a). The initial knowledge state of college physics. *American Journal of Physics, 53*, 1043–1055.

Halloun, I. & Hestenes, D. (1985b). Common sense concepts about motion. *American Journal of Physics, 53*, 1056–1065.

Halloun, I. & Hestenes, D. (1987). Modeling instruction in mechanics. *American Journal of Physics, 55*, 455–462.

Heller, K. J. (1999). Introductory physics reform in the traditional format: An intellectual framework. *AIP Forum on Education Newsletter, Summer*, 7–9.

Heller, P., Keith, R. & Anderson, S. (1992). Teaching problem solving through cooperative grouping. Part 1: Group vs. individual problem solving. *American Journal of Physics, 60*, 627–636.

Hestenes, D. (1987). Toward a modeling theory of physics instruction. *American Journal of Physics, 55*, 440–454.

Hestenes, D. (1992). Modeling games in the Newtonian world. *American Journal of Physics, 60*, 732–748.

Hestenes, D., Wells, M. & Swackhamer, G. (1992). Force concept inventory. *Physics Teacher, 30*, 141–158.

Hoellwarth, C., Moelter, M. J. & Knight, R. D. (2005). A direct comparison of conceptual learning and problem solving ability in traditional and studio style classrooms. *American Journal of Physics, 73*, 459–463.

Hovland, C. I., Lumsdaine, A. A. & Sheffield, F. D. (1965). A baseline for measurement of percentage change. In C. I. Hovland, A. A. Lumsdaine & F. D. Sheffield (eds), *Experiments on mass communication* (pp. 284–289). New York: Wiley (original work published 1949).

ILT-BQ Consortium (2006). *Interactive learning toolkit*, Harvard University, at: http://www.deas.harvard.edu/ilt.

Inhelder, B. & Piaget, J. (1958). *Growth of logical thinking from childhood to adolescence: An essay on the construction of formal operational structures* (A. Parsons & S. Milgram, Trans.). London: Basic Books.

Inhelder, B., deCaprona, D. & Cornu-Wells, A. (1987). *Piaget today*. Hove: Erlbaum.

Johnson, M. (2001). Facilitating high quality student practice in introductory physics. *American Journal of Physics, 69*(S1), S2-S11.

Johnson, D. W., Johnson, R. T. & Smith, K. A. (1991). *Cooperative learning: increasing college faculty instructional productivity*. Washington, DC: George Washington University.

Johnson, D. W., Johnson, R. T. & Stanne, M. B. (2000). *Cooperative learning methods: A meta-analysis*, at: <http://www.co-operation.org/pages/cl-methods.html>.

Kelly, A. E. (2003a). Research as design. *Educational Researcher, 32*(1), 3–4.

Kelly, A. E. (ed.) (2003b). The role of design in educational research [Special issue]. *Educational Researcher, 32*(1).

Lave, J. & Wenger, E. (1991). *Situated learning: Legitimate peripheral participation*. Cambridge: Cambridge University Press.

Lipsey, M. W. & Wilson, D. B. (1993). The efficacy of psychological, educational, and behavioral treatment: Confirmation from meta-analysis. *American Psychologist, 48*, 1181–1209.

Lord, F. M. (1956). The measure of growth. *Educational and Psychological Measurement, 16*, 42–437.

Lord, F. M. (1958). Further problems in the measurement of growth. *Educational and Psychological Measurement, 18*, 437–454.

Lorenzo, M., Crouch, C. H. & Mazur, E. (2006). Reducing the gender gap in the physics classroom. *American Journal of Physics, 74*, 118–122.

Mazur, E. (1997). *Peer instruction: A user's manual*. Upper Saddle River, NJ: Prentice Hall.

McDermott, L. C. & Redish, E. F. (1999). RL-PER1: Resource letter on physics education research. *American Journal of Physics, 67*, 755–767.

Meltzer, D. E. (2002a). The relationship between mathematics preparation and conceptual learning gains in physics: A possible "hidden variable" in diagnostic pretest scores. *American Journal of Physics, 70*, 1259–1268.

Meltzer, D. E. (2002b). *Normalized learning gain: A key measure of student learning*, at: http://www.physicseducation.net/docs/Addendum_on_normalized_gain.pdf.

Meltzer, D. E. & Manivannan, K. (2002). Transforming the lecture-hall environment: The fully interactive physics lecture. *American Journal of Physics, 70*, 639–654.

Mislevy, R. (2006). *Correspondence concerning normalized gain scores*, at: http://www.education.umd.edu/EDMS/mislevy/papers/Gain/.

National Institute for Science Education (2007). *Field-tested learning assessment guide (FLAG)*. University of Wisconsin-Madison, at: 2007 from http://www.flaguide.org/.

North Carolina State University (2007). *Assessment instrument information page*. Physics Education R & D Group, at: http://www.ncsu.edu/per/TestInfo.html.

Novak, G. M., Patterson, E. T., Gavrin, A. D. & Christian, W. (1999). *Just-in-time teaching: Blending active learning with web technology*. New York: Prentice Hall.

Pellegrino, J. W., Chudowsky, N. & Glaser, R. (eds) (2001). *Knowing what students know: The science and design of educational assessment*. Washington, DC: National Academy Press.

Phillips, D. C. & Soltis, J. F. (1998). *Perspectives on learning* (3rd ed.). New York: Teachers College Press.

Redish, E. F. (1994). Implications of cognitive studies for teaching physics. *American Journal of Physics, 62*, 796–803.

Redish, E. F. (1999). Millikan lecture 1998: Building a science of teaching physics. *American Journal of Physics, 67*, 562–573.

Redish, E. F. (2004). A theoretical framework for physics education research: Modeling student thinking. In E. F. Redish & M. Vicentini (eds), *Proceedings of the International School of Physics "Enrico Fermi" Course CLVI: Research on Physics Education*, Volume 156, (pp. 1–63). Varenna, Italy: IOS Press.

Redish, E. F. & Steinberg, R. N. (1999). Teaching physics: Figuring out what works. *Physics Today, 52*, 24–30.

Redish, E. F., Saul, J. M. & Steinberg, R. N. (1997). On the effectiveness of active-engagement microcomputer-based laboratories. *American Journal of Physics, 65*, 45–54.

Rogosa, D. R. (1995). Myth and methods: "Myths about longitudinal research" plus supplemental questions. In J. M. Gottman (ed.), *The analysis of change* (pp. 3–66). Mahwah, NJ: Lawrence Erlbaum Associates.

Rogosa, D. R. & Willett, J. B. (1983). Demonstrating the reliability of the difference score in the measurement of change. *Journal of Educational Measurement, 20*, 335–343.

Rogosa, D. R. & Willet, J. B. (1985). Understanding correlates of change by modeling individual differences in growth. *Psychometrika*, 50, 203–228.

Rogosa, D. R., Brandt, D. & Zimowski, M. (1982). A growth curve approach to the measurement of change. *Psychological Bulletin*, 92, 726–748.

Rosenberg, J., Lorenzo, M. & Mazur, E. (2006). Peer instruction: Making science engaging. In J. J. Mintzes & W. H. Leonard (eds), *Handbook of college science teaching* (pp. 77–85). Arlington, VA: NSTA Press.

Rudner, L. M. (2001). *Item response theory*, at: http://edres.org/irt/.

Saul, J. M. (1998). Beyond problem solving: Evaluating introductory physics courses through the hidden curriculum. *Dissertation Abstracts International*, 59(06), 1971 (UMI No. 9836477).

Savinainen A. & Scott, P. (2002a). The force concept inventory: A tool for monitoring student learning. *Physics Education*, 37, 45–52.

Savinainen A. & Scott, P. (2002b). Using the force concept inventory to monitor student learning and to plan teaching. *Physics Education*, 37, 53–58.

Shavelson, R. J. & Towne, L. (2002). *Scientific research in education*. Washington, DC: National Academy Press.

Slavin, R. E. (1995). *Cooperative learning: Theory, research, and practice* (2nd ed.). Boston, MA: Allyn & Bacon.

Steinberg, R. N. & Donnelly, K. (2002). PER-based reform at a multicultural institution. *Physics Teacher*, 40, 108–114.

Stokes, D. E. (1997). *Pasteur's quadrant: Basic science and technological innovation*. Washington, DC: Brookings Institution Press.

Thornton, R. K. (1995). Conceptual dynamics: Changing student views of force and motion. In C. Bernardini, C. Tarsitani & M. Vicentini (eds), *Thinking physics for teaching* (pp. 157–183). London: Plenum.

Thornton, R. K. & Sokoloff, D. R. (1990). Learning motion concepts using real-time microcomputer-based laboratory tools. *American Journal of Physics*, 58, 858–867.

Thornton, R. K. & Sokoloff, D. R. (1998). Assessing student learning of Newton's Laws: The force and motion conceptual evaluation and the evaluation of active learning laboratory and lecture curricula. *American Journal of Physics*, 66, 338–352.

Tobias, S. & Hake, R. R. (1988). Professors as physics students: What can they teach us? *American Journal of Physics*, 56, 786–794.

Van Domelen, D. J. & Van Heuvelen, A. (2002). The effects of a concept-construction lab course on FCI performance. *American Journal of Physics*, 70, 779–780.

Van Heuvelen, A. (1991a). Learning to think like a physicist: A review of research-based instructional strategies. *American Journal of Physics*, 59, 891–897.

Van Heuvelen, A. (1991b). Overview, case study physics. *American Journal of Physics*, 59, 898–907.

Van Heuvelen, A. (1995). Experiment problems for mechanics. *Physics Teacher*, 33, 176–180.

Vlastos, G. (1991). *Socrates, ironist and moral philosopher*. Cambridge: Cambridge University Press.

Vygotsky, L. S. (1978). *Mind in society: The development of higher psychological processes* (M. Cole, V. John-Steiner, S. Scribner & E. Souberman, Eds). Cambridge, MA: Harvard University Press.

Wells, M., Hestenes, D. & Swackhamer, G. (1995). A modeling method for high school physics instruction. *American Journal of Physics*, 63, 606–619.

Wilson, M. R. & Bertenthal, M. W. (eds). (2005). *Systems for state science assessment*. Washington, DC: National Academy Press.

Wittmann, W. W. (1997). The reliability of change scores: Many misinterpretations of Lord and Cronbach by many others. Revisiting some basics for longitudinal research. Paper presented at the conference of Evaluation of Change in Longitudinal Data, Nürnberg, Germany, July.

Ziman, J. (2000). *Real science: What it is, and what it means*. Cambridge: Cambridge University Press.

Zimmerman, D. W. (1997). A geometric interpretation of the validity and reliability of difference scores. *British Journal of Mathematical and Statistical Psychology*, *50*, 73–80.

Zimmerman, D. W. & Williams, R. H. (1982). Gain scores in research can be highly reliable. *Journal of Educational Measurement*, *19*, 149–154.

Zumbo, B. D. (1999). The simple difference score as an inherently poor measure of change: Some reality, much mythology. In B. Thompson (ed.), *Advances in Social Science Methodology*, Volume 5 (pp. 269–304). Greenwich, CT: JAI Press.

Part 9

Tracking the Diffusion of Design Research

27 Design Research and the Diffusion of Innovations

R. Sam Larson
Diffusion Associates

James W. Dearing
Kaiser Permanente of Colorado

Introduction

Dilemmas associated with moving effective curricular and pedagogical practices and programs into broader use among educators have persisted for years. Acknowledgment of these problems, referred to variously as issues of dissemination, knowledge use, scale up, technology transfer, or diffusion, have given rise over the years to organized efforts to reverse gaps between research evidence about effective education on the one hand and what is practiced on the other. For example, the National Science Foundation created Teacher Institutes and used commercial publishers to disseminate curricular innovations beginning in the late 1950s and on through the 1980s. The U.S. Department of Education instituted Project Innovation Packages, the Pilot State Dissemination Project, the Research and Development Utilization program, the National Diffusion Network (Raizen, 1979), and the Educational Resources Information Center Clearinghouse, all in the 1970s. Evaluations and reviews have found some of these efforts unsuccessful (Crandall, 1982; Horst et al., 1975); others were determined to be successful, but expensive or nonsustaining (see Louis & Rosenblum, 1981; Sieber et al., 1972; see also Hutchinson & Huberman [1993] for a review of this set of large-scale efforts at educational change). Most efforts to diffuse innovations are unsuccessful. If graphed in cumulative fashion over time, a no-growth curve in adoption would be evident, as illustrated in Figure 27.1.

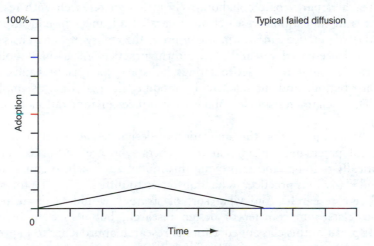

Figure 27.1 Most Purposive Efforts to Spread Innovations Fail. Diffusion is the Exception, Not the Norm, in Social Change.

As the educational system has grown in the United States, so, too, has the research base about students as learners, teachers and teaching, and the joining of the two in classrooms. In particular, the special challenges of science and mathematics education have been studied extensively (Ball et al., 2001; White, 2001), resulting in what some researchers term "scientific teaching" (Handelsman et al., 2004). Yet the translation of evidence into practice—the achievement of broad impact with evidence-based practices, programs, and policies—proves more elusive than ever (National Science Foundation, 2002). This divide is of great concern and an important element of higher education research agendas (Kezar & Eckel, 2000). The gap is exacerbated by the separate tracking of students in training to become researchers and students in training to become teachers, which inhibits the degree to which researchers understand practice and the extent to which teachers understand research (Neumann et al., 1999). And it persists, in part, because information or direction from a distant, outside, change agent is insufficient to affect teachers' practice, which is more the result of locally bounded systems of influences (Fullan, 1985, 1992). Yet, even when changes in practice occur and endure, they do not result often in fundamental reorientation of how teachers think and, thus, construct classroom engagement (Ball, 1990; Cohen, 1990).

It is in this research and application tradition that we assess the diffusion potential of design research. In so doing, it is important to note that design research is not a curricular or pedagogical innovation, but a new method of educational research about practice. Design research is also more than a method. Design research is an approach to the development of theory and method based in the real-time, formative experience of implementing, assessing, and improving classroom practice, classroom research, and classroom learning. It is a combination of quite disparate methods used in certain ways; thus, it is perhaps more an innovation of how one conceptualizes research (commonly referred to as a research design) than of how one collects and analyzes data. We suggest that design research embeds epistemological assumptions about knowledge and knowledge use that more discrete methodologies do not. These somewhat radical characteristics of design research undoubtedly contribute to its attraction to certain educational researchers; these characteristics also will present special challenges to its diffusion among others.

An organizing question for much design research is: "How does the enacted design of a particular classroom experience affect learning outcomes?" Students, teaching assistants, and teachers participate collaboratively in design research with researchers, so that advances in educational research may parallel advances in educational practice and the reality of practice can inform and improve the reality of research as much as we hope that evidence-based research will inform practice. As a methodology, design research is carried out in real practice settings, holistic in the variables and cases studied, causal in attribution, and intended to be modified in real time as implementation proceeds. These characteristics combine to produce an innovation of considerable complexity.

What is the likelihood that the innovation of design research will move beyond the community of practicing educational researchers who are enthusiastically creating, testing, critically refining, and improving this model approach to educational theory, method, and classroom practice? Which obstacles to diffusion can be foreseen reasonably for design research? And what sort of strategy would facilitate not only the classroom-to-classroom transfer of design research, but also a more general and more rapid spread of this class of educational research approaches to improvements in educational research and practice? We address these questions throughout this chapter.

This chapter is rooted in the interdisciplinary literature of the diffusion of innovations.

Many educational innovations, including those of classroom pedagogy, curricula, and instructional technology, have been studied from this theoretical perspective[1] (Ball & Cohen, 1996; Fishman et al., 2004; Hutchinson & Huberman, 1993; Mintrom, 1997; Snyder et al., 1996; Stahl, 1999; Wollons, 2000). Here, like Bannan-Ritland (2003), we apply certain, diffusion-based concepts to the class of innovations known as design research, design experiments, design studies, or, simply, design (Cobb et al., 2003; Kelly, 2003, 2004) for the prospective purpose of overcoming or counteracting perceived uncertainty.

Our purpose in this chapter is to: (a) introduce the diffusion of innovation paradigm and explicate how, in the case of consequential innovations such as design research, diffusion operates, (b) highlight the role of uncertainty in the diffusion process as an obstacle to diffusion, (c) assess the prospects for design research in light of what is known about diffusion and uncertainty, and (d) pose questions that can facilitate a purposive diffusion strategy for accelerating the spread of design research as a new and effective methodology for use by educational researchers.

What is Diffusion?

Rogers (2003: 5) defines "diffusion" as "the process in which an innovation is communicated through certain channels over time among the members of a social system." An *innovation* is anything that potential adopters perceive to be new, inclusive of new ideas and beliefs, explicit and tacit knowledge, processes and protocols, tools and technologies, even value belief systems. Some educational researchers refer to diffusion as scalability (i.e., Fishman et al., 2004); researchers in management use labels such as transfer.

Some innovations spread without apparent effort. These innovations tend to be ideas that do not require much, if anything, in the way of attitude or behavior modification. For example, studies of the diffusion of news document rapid and broad knowledge of events. In such cases, diffusion occurs fast because only a minor amount of attention is necessary for people to know about the event. Other innovations may be complex and expensive, such as new corporate production systems. They spread because of bandwagon effects in which managers or administrators are afraid of lagging behind competitive rivals or because the decision to adopt is decoupled from responsibility for implementation. In both cases, diffusion can be extensive but use of the innovation curtailed.

Diffusion can be a fascinating topic of study because the literature includes many examples of advantageous innovations that do not achieve widespread use, even after many years and even when campaigns are conducted to publicize them. This is so even for highly effective, "best practice" innovations that have demonstrated empirical advantages compared to alternative ways of achieving the same ends, and it is so even when studying diffusion within the same organization, where the rate of adoption might be expected to be more rapid than adoption across separate organizations. Concerning innovation diffusion, what is best and what is used are frequently different. For example, in the field of health promotion, a computer simulation by Stover et al. (2002) found that if proven programs in HIV/AIDS prevention were adopted worldwide, 29 million new infections could be prevented by 2010. In the field of education, Fishman et al. (2004) argue convincingly that effective innovations in the learning sciences have not spread widely into classrooms.

Cases from the diffusion literature do not stop at highlighting effective innovations that do not diffuse; we have cases of innovations with very important implications for the adopters that spread before the communication of any information about their effectiveness, such as in the rapid imitation of strike behavior by eighteenth-century coal miners (Conell & Cohn, 1995). The business literature is rife with stories of corporations adopting workplace and managerial fads and fashions that reflect large investments of money and time. University administrators, too, engage in faddish behavior frequently (Abrahamson, 1991). Further, there are studies demonstrating rapid rates of adoption of ineffective innovations, such as the DARE (Drug Abuse Resistance Education) program (Ennett et al., 1994). Clearly, there are factors other than effectiveness that account for diffusion, such as the alignment between technology-based teaching innovations and organizational conditions such as culture, capabilities, and policies in schools (Fishman et al., 2004). Stated differently, although, typically, effectiveness is related positively to adoption decisions, other factors can be correlated more highly with adoption. Social influence is one of those factors.

So diffusion is a communication process in which information dissemination is necessary but not sufficient to produce change and a process in which the quality of the innovation is merely one among multiple factors that determine adoption behavior. Scholars dating at least to Georg Simmel and Gabriel Tarde 100 years ago theorized about imitative behavior at the level of small groups and in communities and the relation between these microlevel processes to macrolevel social change in which sectors, networks, and cities change. In the 100 years since, researchers have conceptualized diffusion at the macrosociological level of sector, system, national, or state change (Casterline, 2001; Cole, 1998; Garrison, 2001; Grubler, 1996; Viswanath et al., 2000); the social psychological (i.e., communicative) level of local relationships and how those linkages affect adoption patterns (Rogers & Kincaid, 1981; Sen, 1969); or the psychological level of how individuals perceive innovations (Manning et al., 1995).

The paradigm is interdisciplinary, theoretically informed, and practice-based, with empirical studies dating from the 1940s when rural sociologists first sought to understand the reasons for the adoption of hybrid corn in two farming communities in Iowa ("What distinguished earlier from later adopters?" "Why did the rate of adoption change when it did?"). Key publications have highlighted the unique contribution of diffusion as an explanation of social change above and beyond the variance accounted for by economic and structural variables; the importance of social influence by opinion leaders through interpersonal networks; prestige as a motive for adoption; the unintended consequences of adopting and implementing an innovation; the importance of potential adopters' perceptions to their eventual adoption decisions; the low correlation between measures of adoption and implementation when organizations are the unit of adoption; the usefulness of a social network perspective for understanding diffusion; and the rationality of adopters' seemingly irrational decisions (Rogers, 2003). Recent diffusion studies have traced and explained the spread of kindergartens across cultures throughout the world (Wollens, 2000); the spread of schools of choice policies among most of the 50 states (Mintrom, 2000); the diffusion of tobacco control throughout North America (Studlar, 1999); the spread of enterprise zones (Mossberger, 2000); and the adoption and institutionalization of inclusion and participation in community health system planning (Dearing et al., 2001).

Across most of these studies, key variables are found to affect the rate of adoption of innovations. Several of these variables are especially important when considering the adoption and widespread use of design research. One variable is the type of decision made about an innovation associated with design research, a second is the perceived attributes of design research, and a third is the communication channels, specifically, interpersonal communication, necessary to encourage adoption.

Design Research: An Optional and Consequential Adoption Decision

The social and professional structure of higher education affords faculty great latitude in the choice of pedagogy and research practices. Many of the decisions that faculty make about their practice are "optional innovation decisions," where the choice to adopt or reject an innovation is made by the individual independent of the decision of the other members of the social system. Other forms of innovation decisions are authority decisions, where relatively few people in the social system make an adoption decision that impacts many others, and collective innovation decisions, where consensus among members leads to a decision to adopt or reject an innovation. Design research is an optional innovation decision; that is, faculty members in higher education and teachers in kindergarten-through-grade twelve (K–12) systems make their own decisions about whether to engage in design research independent of their colleagues.

Unlike many innovations that require little effort and have minimal impact on the adopters' practice, design research purports to replace routinized practices and has great potential consequences for the adopter. As such, it is a "consequential innovation." Consequential innovations that disrupt or change practice often require considerable information-seeking and advice-seeking, trial-and-error learning, training, and modification to suit an adopter's needs best. Design research has important implications for the adopters' practices and, thus, requires careful consideration.

The more consequential the innovation is for practice, the higher the uncertainty about whether, and how, we should seek more information, gather opinions, and experiment with the innovation. Uncertainty associated with a consequential innovation produces cognitive dissonance in the mind of a potential adopter. Dissonance is an awareness that how we achieve certain objectives might be suboptimal and improved through the use of an alternative (the innovation). Individuals who experience cognitive dissonance often seek additional information to resolve dissonance to a state of cognitive consistency.

When confronted with an innovation perceived to be consequential, potential adopters first experience operational uncertainty about what the innovation is and what it does, often expressed as the innovation's presumed benefits or its operating principles. Potential adopters also experience evaluative uncertainty. They have questions about the costs and outcomes of using the innovation (efficiency and effectiveness), becoming more explicitly evaluative as they approach the point of making a decision about the innovation. Typically, operational uncertainty precedes evaluative uncertainty.

Design research decisions require individuals to gather a great deal of information to reduce the uncertainty associated with this individual and consequential decision. Often, the early operational uncertainty of potential adopters can be reduced or satisfied with packaged impersonal information that identifies clearly what design research is and why it works. Central to reducing this early operational uncertainty is clarity about the innovation's attributes, a point we address later in this chapter. Mass media channels such as websites can transmit effectively information that reduces operational uncertainty.

Evaluative uncertainty associated with the personal advantages and disadvantages of the innovation typically requires a form of interpersonal communication or social influence to assuage the concerns of the potential adopter. Social influence may occur through different channels of communication, although, for consequential innovations, interpersonal communication in the form of word of mouth, personal observation, or social modeling is often considered key to diffusion (Bandura, 1986).

Two dilemmas, then, must be overcome if one wants to accelerate optional and consequential adoption decisions. One dilemma is portraying the innovation so that operational uncertainty is reduced. We can meet this dilemma by focusing on the attributes of an innovation that are found to impact its likely adoption. Typically, this type of portrayal is embedded in information for one-way communication. The second dilemma is the induction of social influence. When an innovation is consequential such that it evokes a high degree of perceived risk or uncertainty (such as a reorientation to the conduct of research), local, informal, opinion leadership is often sought to resolve cognitive dissonance. Triggering social influence based in the existing relations in a social system is the key to intervention-based diffusion.

Operational Uncertainty: Assessing Design Research Attributes

Several recent authors, most of whom are advocates or adherents of design research, have commented on the conceptual, definitional, or operational lack of clarity of design research (Collins et al., 2004; Dede, 2004; Kelly, 2004). A lack of clarity about what design research is does not constitute necessarily a problem for its early adoption. Innovations in an early stage of development are often ill defined in parameter, purpose, outcomes, and language, especially when an innovation is being contributed to and co-developed by loosely coupled networks of participants. However, such conditions usually must be resolved for diffusion to occur. Resolution must occur first among the developers of the innovation, those researchers and educators who are experimenting with design research. Then, once shared agreement and clarity are achieved, the innovation can be communicated to a broader audience of potential adopters. Further change to the innovation is typical, but users change innovations only after they have adopted them initially—and adoption depends, in part, on clarity.

Clarity about the attributes of design research is key because the perceived attributes will determine the information that potential adopters have available to them to decrease the operational uncertainty. Here, we consider design research in terms of codified attributes of innovations. We suggest that attributes function as barriers and catalysts to the diffusion of design research at this point in its development and discuss how demonstrations of design research affect its spread in terms of reducing operational uncertainty. Next, we turn to a consideration of social influence and its role in relation to the dispersion of design research.

How is design research perceived by potential adopters? In lieu of empirical data, we compare perceptions of design research based on publications by and discussions with educational researchers who conduct design research with what is known about the general relationships of the perceived attributes and the rate of adoption of innovations. Relative advantage, compatibility, complexity, trialability, and observability are attributes of innovations shown to explain variance in the rate of adoption. Evidence in the diffusion literature for the first three of these attributes is particularly well established. We use these five attributes as one means to discuss the potential diffusion of design research.

Relative Advantage

This attribute is one of the strongest predictors of an innovation's rate of adoption. Relative advantage can be considered as a ratio of the expected benefits and the expected costs of adoption. The higher an innovation's perceived advantages, the more rapid its adoption. Costs and benefits typically associated with innovations that can be extended logically to design research include social prestige, monetary and nonmonetary costs, immediacy of reward, and a more nuanced and better documented approach to the study of learning.

Higher education has a finely tuned order of merit and prestige among universities and colleges (Becher & Trowler, 1989). The majority of authors of articles about design research work at Carnegie classification "doctoral/research universities: extensive," such as the University of Chicago, Harvard University, and the University of California, Berkeley. Potential adopters often consider high-status individuals and institutions as legitimizing attention to an innovation, meaning that it is normatively congruent to attend to messages about it. Thus, design research should benefit from such byline association and the fact that many of the preliminary studies and formative tests of design research are occurring at these universities. Faculty at institutions of like or lesser prestige than these initial institutions may be motivated to adopt design research as a means to elevate their own social prestige, so social prestige is an aspect of relative advantage that design research has in its favor.

However, other aspects of relative advantage are likely to present challenges to the diffusion of design research. Although the monetary costs of design research are likely modest in that it does not demand the equipment and facilities that new research methods do in physics, biochemistry, and other sciences, in the educational research community, design research is resource-intensive, perhaps extraordinarily so. Design researchers collect large amounts of data of multiple types in order to create a dynamic and contextualized understanding of the learning process and its outcomes. It can take considerable time and specialized knowledge to carry this out, especially as the research team moves into the process of interpreting of results, where divergence and convergence across the findings of different methods must be accounted for and explained. As noted recently, "design experiments tend to be large endeavors with many different participants, all of whose work needs to be coordinated" (Collins et al., 2004: 19). Like other, triangulated, multimethod, research designs that demand additional iterative layers of analysis and interpretation (Jick, 1979; Kidder & Fine, 1987; Morgan, 1998), design research may require much more time and effort than faculty allocate otherwise to studies based on classroom observations, surveys, or personal interviews. Although the knowledge gained may justify the time and energy costs, the costs are very real to faculty and teachers, for whom time is often considered a most important resource.

A second aspect of time that we expect to be salient to potential adopters of design research is the time lag between entering the field and publication of any resultant work (immediacy of reward). Compared to the use of other research methods and designs, design research likely requires a longer time between initiating a research project and submitting research findings to journals or conferences. More methods of data collection are involved; therefore, more interpretation and resolution will be required in analysis. This length of time between engagement with the innovation and reward (publication) is another, potential, negative aspect of relative advantage that it is reasonable to associate with design research. The time lag between entering the field and publication is especially troublesome for junior faculty facing a reward system that continues to value publication quantity more readily than publication quality.

Finally, concerning relative advantage, design research as an innovation holds a lofty promise of bringing together quantitative and qualitative research epistemologies and methods in the pursuit of more sophisticated and better "learning about learning." Few academics, we suggest, will argue with the pursuit of such a promise, other than those most taken with the beliefs of William of Occam. Parsimony in explanation is unlikely to be a strength of design research. But, from the perspective of educational researchers, we expect the promise of design research to be a powerful incentive for potential adopters to attend to messages about it and consider its advantages and disadvantages.

Compatibility

When adoption decisions are voluntary, that is, when the choice to adopt rests with the person or unit who will implement and use the innovation (i.e., "the users are the choosers"), the perceived compatibility of the innovation with the potential adopter's values, past experiences, and needs is of particular importance. The more compatible an innovation is with the ways in which the adopter thinks and behaves already, the more likely adoption is. Aspects of design research such as the inclusion of multiple interested parties and a strong focus on methodology are likely to be perceived as compatible by potential adopters with how they think and behave already and with what they value as scholars. However, design research has been labeled as "under-conceptualized" (Dede, 2004) and lacking in strong theoretical foundations (diSessa & Cobb, 2004). Researchers who hold theoretically derived research and theory-testing as the foundation for their work may not view design research as compatible (yet) with core research values. Design research is compatible with the experiences of many educational researchers and K–12 research faculty because the innovation does not involve necessarily new methods of data collection and analysis but, rather, new combinations of existing methods. We expect that design research may not strike many educational researchers as all that different from what they have been doing until they become well acquainted with it. Then, the difficulties of the process and interactive nature of design research will impress them.

Compatibility also encompasses the extent to which an innovation meets a felt need. The perceived need for design research may be the most troubling aspect associated with compatibility. Are educational researchers and teachers dissatisfied with current research methods and practice? The problem of compatibility may extend beyond researchers and teachers themselves, too. As Dede (2004: 114) put it bluntly, "neither policymakers nor practitioners want what the DBR [design-based research] community is selling right now." And although policy-makers and practitioners may not be the primary adopters—that would be faculty—faculty needs do not occur in a vacuum. If faculty perceive little support from teachers or funding sources for this work, faculty "need" is truncated.

Complexity

An innovation is complex to the degree to which it is perceived as relatively difficult to understand and use. An innovation low in complexity is adopted more rapidly. To those familiar with classroom-based research or practice, design research may not be perceived as an unusually complex innovation in concept, but, in practice, proposed approaches to design research require more effort than any one human can provide (Collins et al., 2004). A team is required, and what it is required to do is inordinately complex. The research design is malleable for the immediate improvement of practice in action; little about design research is intended to be static. Some requirements of design research embed all the indeterminancy of dynamic interactive systems models. The degree of complexity of such modeling is well beyond all widely used educational research methods. The likely perception that it is atypically complex will contribute centrally to perceptions of uncertainty about how design research will work in practice.

Adding to the complexity of design research is a lack of standards to refer to when making decisions about its use. This innovation is being developed still; the standards that make other research methods recognizable, accessible, and teachable to researchers are being contested actively still.

Trialability

The extent to which a potential adopter can experiment with an innovation before an adoption decision is referred to as testability. An innovation that can be used on an explicitly temporary basis without negative repercussion or that can be phased-in gradually or in terms of its component parts will be adopted more rapidly. We expect design research to be perceived as high in testability because the innovation is of low initial monetary cost, meaning a low barrier to entry, and design research's multiple components make it easy for adopting researchers to implement pieces of design research one component at a time. We also expect that because some accessible archives document the design experiment process, their use could serve as a means by which potential adopters engage in trials of design research without having to invest the time to collect their own data from the field.

Observability

If the results of an innovation are visible to potential adopters and providing that the results are positive, the innovation is more likely to be adopted than if the results are not observable. Seeing is believing. In education pedagogy and research, observability is a challenge. School building design tends to work against observing success with an innovation in a colleague's room during the project, thus limiting observation to those teachers who are members of a research project (Zaritsky et al.). How, then, can those engaged in design research increase its observability? Zaritsky et al. (ibid.) indicate the need to go beyond the traditional dissemination models of text and talk to the use of media on DVDs in the form of scientific visualization. Case studies, such as those used by Collins et al. (2004), can help to make design research more observable. And, as we discuss below, observability can be achieved well through exemplary demonstrations.

From an innovation perspective, design research is complex, its relative advantage is unclear, and, although it is likely to be compatible with the values and experiences of potential adopters, the need for it is not well established. Potential adopters can try out components of design research and it is possible to observe it although this may not be easy. Essentially, design research is in a prediffusion stage, still meeting the objectives of establishing proof of concept (efficacy), effectiveness (internal validity), and robustness or generalizability (external validity). Communicating the continuing and uncertain results of a design experiment—akin to rushing the product to market—will not decrease the onlookers' operational or evaluative uncertainty, and it may heighten both. Time is required for an innovation to be developed through a research and development process. We believe that demonstration warrants special attention in thinking about design research in general and in reducing operational uncertainty in particular.

Innovation demonstrations can be of two types. An experimental demonstration is a field test of an innovation carried out at full scale under real-world conditions to test external validity by varying the setting, the participants, resource availability, implementation protocol, and the methods by which outcomes are measured. An example is design research carried out by a team of educational researchers, a teacher, and students in a classroom. The objective might be to learn about the design research process through observed data about an expected (theoretical) model of relationships. This prediffusion activity is key not only for the formative improvement of an innovation, but also more fundamentally for the determination of whether a particular innovation should be diffused. The purpose of an experimental demonstration is both to prove the innovation's worth in practice and to improve it through iterative adjustment. Experimental demonstrations help innovation developers reduce their own operational uncertainty— a necessary precursor to reducing potential adopters' operational uncertainty.

Once external validity (an acceptable degree of robustness) has been established through applying the approach at second-generation sites, a second type of demonstration is warranted. An exemplary demonstration is a persuasive event calculated to influence adoption decisions to increase the likelihood of diffusion. An exemplary demonstration is not staged for the purpose of merely disseminating information; rather, the objective is to showcase an innovation in a convincing manner. Exemplary demonstrations increase the likelihood of diffusion partly by making a costly, worrisome, and complex innovation more understandable, observable, and predictable in outcomes. Table 27.1 illustrates the distinction between experimental and exemplary demonstrations.

Lack of clarity about the purposes of demonstrations is a frequent culprit in the nondiffusion of innovations. A disconfirmed hypothesis that leads to a design improvement is a positive result in an experimental demonstration; in an exemplary demonstration, such an outcome is noise that will lead to perceptions of higher, not lower, uncertainty among potential adopters. Thus, the real-time conduct of design research in a classroom is not the time for showing off what is going on, just as allowing or encouraging others to view and/or use ongoing website information or preliminary results from design research studies is a mistake if the intent is diffusion. If the point is to spread the word, then teachers and researchers should be invited to a classroom or website only when the likelihood of surprises has passed.

When academic researchers who have developed an innovation communicate its process and outcomes to knowledgeable experts (such as other teachers and educational researchers who know firsthand the opportunities and constraints of classroom practice and how it is embedded in school and school district administrative structures), they talk as they were trained to do: with qualification, with questions, with emphasis on what is not known, and by clarifying the limitations of knowledge about the innovation (Dearing et al., 1994). The complexity of design research as a methodology will engender many such remarks. Despite how enthusiastic the developer may feel about design

Table 27.1 Comparison of the Main Attributes of Experimental Demonstrations and Exemplary Demonstrations

Main attributes	*Experimental demonstrations*	*Exemplary demonstrations*
1 Purpose	To test the feasibility of an innovation under operational conditions	To illustrate the utility of the innovation to potential adopters
2 Attitude of demonstration managers toward the innovation	Skepticism	Advocacy
3 Desired visibility of the demonstration	Low	High
4 Control of possible intervening variables	Moderate control for the purpose of modeling the process	High control

research, the impression of the onlooker will be colored by what he or she is told and can see. The image is likely to be a hazy one in which high potential is masked and muted by the reality of difficult implementation and preliminary results. Design researchers should continue with experimental demonstrations, but they need to be careful not to treat them as exemplary demonstrations.

Evaluative Uncertainty: Social Influence and the Use of Design Research

Uncertainty about what the innovation is and what it does (operational uncertainty), as just discussed, often can be reduced through one-way communication or demonstration. Uncertainty associated with the personal advantages and particularly the disadvantages of the innovation (evaluative uncertainty) typically requires a form of interpersonal communication or social influence to persuade someone to adopt it. Communication about the innovation by local, informal, opinion leaders (near peers) who are respected, knowledgeable, trusted, and accessible triggers a positive or negative resolution to cognitive dissonance by others, reducing their uncertainty about the innovation's worth. The nonrandom unequal distribution of social influence in the form of local informal opinion leaders is a strong and reliable filter through which consequential innovations predictably must pass if they are to gain widespread adoption in a social system.

Especially for innovations high in perceived risk (including the extent to which resources may be reduced or threatened) or evaluative uncertainty, diffusion occurs through an interpersonal social process in which pre-existing influence among people or organizations alternately facilitates and impedes the rate and extent of spread. Factors other than interpersonal influence can start and complete diffusion processes (Kerckhoff et al., 1965), but it is interpersonal influence that accelerates rates of diffusion. When consequential innovations spread rapidly, it means that they have been accorded a high degree of approval by influential people within a social network, in which members are connected to each other through patterned flows of face-to-face and mediated interpersonal communication, or in a social sector, in which members do not comprise an interconnected network but do share common demographic, situational, and/or behavioral characteristics (Katz & Lazarsfeld, 1955; Castro et al., 1995; Mayer & Davidson, 2000; Mintrom, 1997; O'Brien et al., 1998; Puska et al., 1985; Stokes-Berry & Flowers, 1999; Weimann, 1994).

Opinion leadership is the reason why diffusion can be such a very efficient process to jump-start: an innovation source or sponsor need only communicate an innovation to a special small subset of all possible adopters for the innovation to spread through the social system. Opinion leaders are individuals who are able to influence informally (as opposed to exercising authority over) other individuals' attitudes and beliefs. Opinion leaders, through communicating or social modeling, do the rest as long as (a) their attitudes are favorable toward the new practice, and (b) others identify the opinion leader positively with the innovation (Valente, 1995). Alternatively, and indeed more commonly, when influential people have a low opinion of an innovation, it is their avoidance of it (passive rejection) and/or their opposition (active rejection) that impedes its spread (Leonard-Barton, 1985).

Strictly speaking, opinion leaders are not peers. The importance accorded to their opinions makes them somewhat heterophilous to others—a near peer. Opinion leaders tend to be accessible and are in direct or observable social distance with followers. They are leaders in an informal and local sense—that of being advice-givers and example-setters for people they know. Opinion leaders take risks on innovations to the extent that the communication networks of which they are members support risk. More often, they are conservative in their orientation toward innovation; their functions are those of maintaining, protecting, and helping the members of their interpersonal network concerning a certain subject such as research about students' learning.

For new ideas generated from outside their interpersonal network, opinion leaders are gatekeepers, allocating attention and then evaluative judgments for the benefit of their network members. They are in a position to know of outside innovations given their greater number of interpersonal and media contacts, especially with sources outside their network. The approval of opinion leaders is crucial for introducing new ideas into communication networks and lending those ideas credibility. The spread of those ideas through peer-to-peer communication follows opinion leaders' approval. Influence spreads through other processes, too, including structural equivalence, in which people of equivalent rank or function in different organizations or systems adopt innovations at the same times because of common patterns of information exposure rather than interpersonal communication (Burt, 1987, 1999); through other channels, namely, specialty and mass media, through which various social effects such as social modeling may operate (Hornik & McAnany, 2001; McAlister, 2000); and through the depiction of problem solving and efficacy. But, as the perception of consequence rises, the reliance on known and trusted interpersonal sources of evaluative judgment (which reduces evaluative uncertainty) rises.

The two-part, social influence question for design research, as for any consequential innovation, is this: Who is associated with the design research, and, more to the point, how are they regarded by educational researchers and teachers who constitute its potential adopters? In the diffusion paradigm typology of innovators (the first 2.5 percent to adopt), early adopters (whose 13.5 percent includes the 3–5 percent of opinion leaders), early majority and late majority (who comprise 68 percent of potential adopters), and laggards (the more cautious 16 percent), where do the current experimenters and demonstrators of design research fall? Are they opinion leaders for others? Or, as we expect on the basis of their current experimentation, are they less norm-bound and more venturesome? Indeed, although those who are modeling the use of design research may be innovators, we expect that many of them would be categorized more accurately as developers—the creators of the innovation—and be even further removed sociometrically from being able to convert a system toward the adoption of an innovation.

The social influence point here is simple. The ability to influence directly through advice-giving or example-setting does not accrue normally to innovators (the first to adopt), let alone to developers (the creators of innovations). Their functional roles in the diffusion of innovations is something other than social influence: developers create the new and the different; they are generative sources of change. Innovators do not so much create as try out eagerly *without regard for what others think about them.* Very often, the use of an innovation by developers and innovators is a sure sign to the majority of potential adopters that the jury is still out, that the innovation is not ready, that the use and outcomes of the innovation are too uncertain. If current users of design research are seen by the majority of educational researchers as developers and innovators, then it is too soon to expect diffusion. Design research will spread when other educational researchers—those who adopt research methodologies and teaching pedagogies early and who are sought out for their opinions on such matters—come on board.

Making the assumption that those who are motivated to contact us and inquire about what we are doing are also those who are socially well positioned to influence others' perceptions is close to folly. Diffusion studies have shown that innovators and early adopters have their own reasons for early adoption, which can be counterproductive to diffusion. Opinion leaders constitute a small proportion of system members (often about 5 percent), so random approaches to recruitment, volunteerism or self-selection, marketing or advertising, or defaulting to positional authority such as a dean will miss the mark in jump-starting diffusion about 19 times out of every 20 attempts. If the early adopters are seen by others as iconoclasts and loners, they may be damaging the innovation's chances for achieving scale.

This critique of design research is by no means unusual. Rarely is thought given beforehand to whom to involve in using an innovation and when to do so for the purpose of encouraging others to follow along. The authors' experience of working with people and organizations who are trying to diffuse innovations shows that an appreciation for this simple idea is widespread, but only subsequently, when it has been pointed out.

To summarize, operational uncertainty is reduced through knowledge or expertise that is gained largely through the one-way communication of information. Evaluative uncertainty requires persuasion that occurs through two-way communication through pre-existing channels of social influence in the form of informal, extant, local, opinion leadership. Social influence plays a critical role in the positive adoption decision to try a new practice. Information alone, in whatever form, is insufficient to move the individual toward a positive decision or even serious contemplation of the costs and benefits of an innovation when the innovation in question is consequential to the potential adopter (Bero et al., 1998; Evans et al., 1986; Jacoby & Clark, 1986; Kanouse & Jacoby, 1988; Lomas, 1991; Lomas et al., 1989; Mittman et al., 1992). Talking is key (Rutenberg & Watkins, 1997). And it is not talking with anyone; it is talking with a person whom potential adopters believe to be expert and trustworthy. If someone other than an opinion leader advocates or serves as a social model for design research, potential adopters are less likely to make positive adoption decisions.

The fact that the few can influence the many is the special promise of diffusion, the so-called "diffusion effect" that produces the nonlinear (logistic) curve that characterizes the pattern of innovation adoption over time; that is, "successful" diffusion as depicted in Figure 27.2.

In some ways, the history of the diffusion of innovation is one of increasing inequities. Those persons with resources and information reap the benefits of innovative programs early relative to others; those most in need of the benefits adopt programs late (Rogers, 2003). Informational and access advantages beget later advantages. In this way, evidence–practice gaps affect people and organizations differentially. Gaps are more pronounced for some than for others, contributing to social and economic disparities that harden inequality in America and elsewhere (Carter-Pokras & Baquet, 2002). Design research is being developed, tested, refined, and written about at a few, relatively elite institutions. Will educational researchers at lower tier and less wealthy institutions adopt design research as a methodology late relative to educational researchers at more elite institutions? We expect so, on the basis of prior studies of diffusion.

Purposive Diffusion of Design Research

Traditionally, the studies that comprise the diffusion of innovation paradigms have been descriptive or explanatory investigations created to answer questions of the sort: To what extent did an innovation diffuse, and which variables account for this result? Diffusion does or does not occur; researchers assess what happened and why. This post

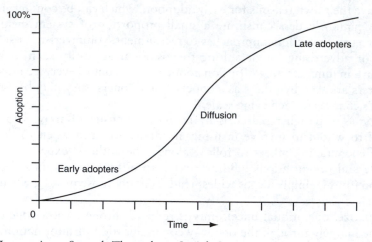

Figure 27.2 Innovations Spread Through a Social System or Social Sector After Positive
Adoption Decisions and/or Social Modeling of the Innovation by Local, Informal,
Opinion Leaders, Who Comprise a Subset of all Early Adopters.

hoc, postdictive orientation to the study of diffusion has aided the inductive reasoning
that has led to our present understanding of the diffusion process.

To use what we know now to diffuse an innovation purposively is an interventionist
form of predictive research. This type of research can be quite dissimilar to the traditional diffusion study. Yet, it is not new. Purposive diffusion has been conducted successfully for several decades, beginning with the purposive diffusion of birth control
in the 1960s (Retherford & Palmore, 1983). Rogers (1973) presented a strategy for
accelerating diffusion based on empirical studies of contraceptive adoption. Scholars
used successfully diffusion concepts such as opinion leadership in field studies and
computer simulations (Abrahamson & Rosenkepf, 1997; Freedman & Takeshita,
1969; Kelly et al., 1997, 1992, 1991; Lomas et al., 1991; Palmore, 1967; Valente &
Davis, 1999). Predictive studies using diffusion attributes have been carried out by
marketing scholars for years, based on the work of Frank Bass (1969) and by him and
his colleagues (Bass et al., 1994, 2000). Tools have been developed for the objective of
using diffusion principles (Dearing & Meyer, 1994). Most purposive diffusion interventions have only operationalized one diffusion principle only, such as opinion leadership
or the attributes of innovations.

A purposive diffusion strategy that integrates and applies multiple validated principles is the most logical way to proceed with developing as intervention because, for
any one innovation type or for any one set of potential adopters, a particular principle
may be especially effective or ineffective, and the enactment of multiple validated principles may function additively to propel adoption decisions. Such a strategy means
identifying and using multiple diffusion principles, each of which is well validated
through empirical study, implementing them in concert, and collecting outcome data
to summarize the effects and to process the data to indicate causes. Several authors have
emphasized this potential of purposive diffusion (Anderson & Jay, 1985; Berwick,
2003; Dearing, 2004, 2005; Lenfant, 2003).

Here, we pose several questions for those involved in creating and refining design
research. Our intent is to encourage consideration at this early stage of what will become
important later if purposive diffusion is used to accelerate the spread of design research
as a new and effective methodology for use among educational researchers and teachers.

Is the Educational Problem that Design Research Addresses of Sufficient Importance to Warrant a Purposive Diffusion Intervention?

If we are to engage in intervention research, we have an obligation to be reasonably certain that the time and attention devoted to the effort is justified, given the costs of not being able to address other, worthy, scholarly topics and applied problems. Tied in to questions of importance is the need of potential adopters. Earlier, we indicated that adoption is tied to the compatibility of an innovation to the potential adopters' values, past experiences, and needs. If adopters do not perceive a need for an innovation, or if they perceive a lack of need by the larger community—including other faculty, K–12 educators, and the funding community—they are unlikely to adopt it. Is design research needed? By whom? And how do we know it is needed?

Is Design Research Ready for Purposive Diffusion?

An analysis of design research using innovation attributes suggests that the innovation is in a prediffusion stage and not ready for widespread diffusion yet. Most appropriate at this time are continued experimental demonstrations, perhaps including selected early adopters who can question aspects of implementation and, along with research teams, suggest modifications that may make adoption more likely. Attempts to diffuse an innovation purposively in a formative stage are likely to increase operational and evaluative uncertainty. If uncertainty leads to negative opinions, it will make the diffusion of design research at a later time even more challenging.

Is the Evidence About the Effectiveness and Efficiency of Design Research Sufficiently Convincing that this Approach to Educational Research and Practice Could be Diffused?

When we have a choice of what to propel into broader use, there is a responsibility to focus on those innovations that have been shown to be most effective and efficient. Effectiveness concerns the internal validity of the design research itself as it is enacted in classrooms: Does it work better than alternatives for research and pedagogical purposes? Efficiency concerns the cost of the innovation in classrooms. Is improvement achieved at advantageous or reasonable cost? This question is central to evaluative uncertainty.

Who are the Potential Adopters of Design Research, and do They Comprise a Social Network or Social Sector for Accessibility?

Educational researchers and communication among them most likely comprise multiple, overlapping, interorganizational, informal networks (invisible colleges) that may be stratified by variables such as institutional prestige, geography, and orientation to practice. Which of these networks should be targeted for the diffusion of design research? The answer(s) to this question can be provided by considering whether the educational researchers in question are accessible in a ready means such as through a professional society or through their ongoing interaction. Information about the existence of a social network (shared interpersonal ties) or shared information sources of people in a social sector (no shared interpersonal ties) is gathered most reliably and validly through the formative administration of questionnaires to network or sector members.

If potential adopters do not communicate already, they do not comprise a social or professional network. Such a set of potential adopters can be considered a social sector; they share common interests, attend to common sources of information, and have common responsibilities. What they do not share is direct and indirect interpersonal communication. When targeting a social sector for the purposive diffusion of design research, the question is how to reach the potential adopters with social influence messages (e.g., Mathematics Association of America sections or American Educational Research Association sections could be used as points of message dissemination) without an interpersonal communication network in place.

When a set of potential adopters constitutes a social network, the task is to conduct formative research to understand the influence structure among the units in the network. Questions designed to determine degree of influence have been posed to probe popularity, advice-giving, communication frequency, as well as asking more directly about influence. These variables are highly correlated. Data about the distribution of influence in a network of educational researchers or teachers could be collected through sociometric roster questionnaires, in which each respondent is given a list of all the other respondents and asked to assign a score for such variables as how often the respondent talks with each person listed and what the nature of those conversations is; open-ended questionnaire items, in which respondents are asked to write in the name of, or an identifier for, those persons or units with whom the respondent communicates; informants, who are asked typically in interviews which others they consider to be most influential; or observation, in cases where the network of people is present in one location and small enough to observe through their interaction and be coded by the observer. The resulting data, analyzed with social network analysis software, identifies which persons are most influential (the opinion leaders) for the given topic. This result is used formatively to contact the opinion leaders and recruit them to assist by learning about the innovations in question and by talking about the innovations with their followers.

Does the Targeted Population Constitute a Socially Responsible Choice?

Left to itself, diffusion often exacerbates societal, economic, and educational inequalities. In passive diffusion processes, early adopters are often the least likely to need the innovation in question but most likely to have the necessary resources to adopt it. Purposive diffusion can turn this around so that we focus on those most in need. For design research approaches, this could mean a focus on researchers who attend to classrooms with high proportions of population groups who are underrepresented in science and mathematics education, including women, ethnic minorities, and low-income students. Such a focus embedded in a purposive strategy has the potential to prompt those educational researchers and practitioners who would be late adopters otherwise into trying design research early, relative to others (see Figure 27.3), and thus accrue the benefits thereof.

Can a Cluster of Innovations be Presented to Potential Adopters?

We postulate a curvilinear relationship between the degree of innovation choice and the likelihood of adoption. When a single innovation is communicated to potential adopters, a negative reaction is likely because of a loss of control born from a lack of choice (Brehm & Brehm, 1981). Given too much choice, potential adopters focus on the costs of adoption instead of considering the benefits (Schwartz, 2004). Offering a delimited choice of effective design research alternatives to potential adopting teachers

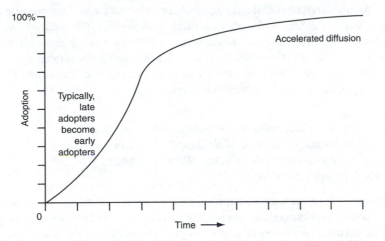

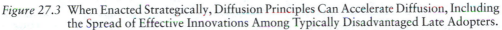

Figure 27.3 When Enacted Strategically, Diffusion Principles Can Accelerate Diffusion, Including the Spread of Effective Innovations Among Typically Disadvantaged Late Adopters.

or researchers heightens the likelihood that they may find an ideal fit between their local circumstances and research and/or teaching needs, on the one hand, and among effective practices in a cluster of design research innovations, on the other.

Clustering can increase both the likelihood of a positive adoption decision being made and of that choice being a most appropriate selection. When graphed over time, adopters of a particular innovation sometimes also adopt other related innovations at about the same time. Clustering has been shown to occur for recycling behavior (Leonard-Barton & Rogers, 1980), consumer information services (LaRose & Atkin, 1992), technologies at the organizational level in the United States (LaRose & Hoag, 1996), ideas, values, and tools at the individual level in Kenya and among Italian and Jewish women in the United States (Rutenberg & Watkins, 1997; Watkins & Danzi, 1994), as well as for other types of innovation.

This body of research concerns a complementary clustering effect, of one positive adoption decision seemingly precipitating several like decisions. Here, we extend the concept of clustering to include "alternative" clusters. An alternative cluster is a set of effective innovations that comprise different means to achieve the same end. For example, a cluster of several proven variants on design research methods, or a cluster of effective educational research methods one of which is design research, can be created and communicated. Piecing together an alternative cluster of effective innovations does not put a sponsor or change agency in the uncomfortable position of promoting one method over another and running the risk of seemingly advocating one intervention or one set of interacting innovations at the expense of solutions developed by others. Rather, potential adopters can choose from among a set, each of which addresses the same problem. Also, an alternative cluster allows potential adopters to engage in direct comparison of effective alternatives in the cluster using common metrics, developed or influenced by the researcher.

Can Design Research be Directed to Intermediaries so that the Broadest Possible Diffusion Effect May Occur?

Intermediaries, when targeted as adopters, in turn create, adopt, and adapt programs for others, such as educators who adopt innovations so that benefits accrue to their students. This approach to social change has been referred to as "intervening upstream" (Singhal & Rogers, 2003: 171). Professional associations (Newell & Swan, 1995), interorganizational networks, and organized centers for teaching excellence on campuses can be fruitful for the identification of potential adopters and their opinion leaders if the formative administration of questionnaires is not conducted to identify sociometrically local, informal, opinion leaders.

Can Design Research Portrayals (the Content and Format of Communication Messages Such as Web-Based, Decision Support Tools) be Developed on the Basis of What We Know About How an Innovation's Attributes are Perceived?

Formative research about how representative potential adopters perceive design research innovations is crucial to develop portrayals that elicit the informational, attitudinal, and behavioral responses that lead to positive adoption decisions. Research into attributes has been conducted to explain adoption decisions and, especially, consumer perception and purchase intention (Agarwal & Prasad, 1997; Manning et al., 1995). Clearly, the potential of the concept of attributes is in its application before diffusion (Rogers, 2003), either as a tool to assess likely reaction on the basis of representative sets of potential adopters during a formative pretesting stage (Dearing & Meyer, 1994) or as a basis for predicting diffusion (Tornatzky & Klein, 1982).

Portrayals of design research with the purpose of informing website visitors about what design research is and how it operates can be assessed for comprehension and perceptions of relative advantage, compatibility, complexity, testability, and observability, then refined. Currently, design research is high in operational uncertainty. When, over time, such uncertainty is reduced and standards are developed, diffusion attributes will provide a well-established framework to use in presenting design research to potential adopters.

Websites are promising media for presenting clusters of innovations because they can be designed to allow for direct comparison among innovations and evaluation under conditions of uncertainty (Hibbard et al., 2002; Tversky & Kahneman, 1982). Testimonials and examples of the innovation in action can be embedded in the site. Websites also are promising media for clarifying to potential adopters the evidence supporting each approach to design research, the causal model that is responsible for the observed effect of using design research and that should not be modified at least in its general terms by adopters, the peripheral components that may have contributed to external validity at second-generation sites, and those complementary assets and capacities at school or work that were present in cases of successful implementation. The objective of such portrayals is to give adopters the information necessary to understand how an innovation and their situation could be made to work well together—what scholars have referred to as a mutual adaptation perspective on implementing an innovation (Fishman et al., 2004; Leonard-Barton, 1988).

Our hope is that answers to these questions can prompt the preliminary exploration of whether to proceed with the purposive diffusion of design research and, if so, how to do it. We submit that the diffusion principles of innovation attributes, social influence, uncertainty reduction through demonstration, and clustering remain the same for design research as they do for many other innovations. What should differ will be the ways in which the principles operate in an intervention.

Note

1 According to the estimate of Everett M. Rogers (2003), the main chronicler of diffusion of innovation studies, there have been over 400 publications about the diffusion of educational innovations since the 1960s.

References

Abrahamson, E. (1991). Managerial fads and fashions: The diffusion and rejection of innovations. *Academy of Management Review, 16,* 586–612.

Abrahamson, E. & Rosenkopf, L. (1997). Social network effects on the extent of innovation diffusion: A computer simulation. *Organization Science, 8,* 289–309.

Agarwal, R. & Prasad, J. (1997). The role of innovation characteristics and perceived voluntariness in the acceptance of information technologies. *Decision Sciences, 28,* 557–582.

Anderson, J. G. & Jay, S. J. (1985). The diffusion of medical technology: Social network analysis and policy research. *Sociological Quarterly, 26,* 49–64.

Ball, D. L. (1990). Reflections and deflections of policy: The case of Carol Turner. *Educational Evaluation and Policy Analysis, 12,* 241–245.

Ball, D. L. & Cohen, D. K. (1996). Reform by the book: What is—or might be—the role of curriculum materials in teacher learning and instructional reform? *Educational Researcher, 25*(9), 6–8.

Ball, D. L., Lubienski, S. T. & Mewborn, D. S. (2001). Research on teaching mathematics: The unsolved problem of teachers' mathematical knowledge. In V. Richardson (ed.), *Handbook of research on teaching* (4th ed., pp. 433–456). Washington, DC: American Educational Research Association.

Bandura, A. (1986). *Social foundations of thought and action: A social cognitive theory.* Englewood Cliffs, NJ: Prentice Hall.

Bannan-Ritland, B. (2003). The role of design in research: The integrative learning design framework. *Educational Researcher, 32*(1), 21–24.

Bass, F. M. (1969). A new product growth model for consumer durables. *Management Science, 13,* 215–227.

Bass, F. M., Jain, D. C. & Krishnan, T. (2000). Modeling the marketing-mix influence in new-product diffusion. In V. Mahajan, E. Muller & Y. Wind (eds), *New-Product Diffusion Models* (pp. 99–122). Dordrecht, The Netherlands: Kluwer.

Bass, F. M., Krishnan, T. & Jain, D. C. (1994). Why the Bass model fits without decision variables. *Marketing Science, 13,* 203–223.

Becher, T. & Trowler, P. (1989). *Academic tribes and territories: Intellectual enquiry and the cultures of disciplines.* Berkshire, UK: Open University Press.

Bero, L.A., Grilli, R., Grimshaw, J. M., Harvey, E., Oxman, A. D. & Thomson, M. A. (1998). Closing the gap between research and practice: An overview of systematic reviews of interventions to promote the implementation of research findings. *British Medical Journal, 317,* 465–468.

Berwick, D. M. (2003). Disseminating innovations in health care. *Journal of the American Medical Association, 289,* 1969–1975.

Brehm, J. W. & Brehm, S. S. (1981). *Psychological reactance: A theory of freedom and control.* San Diego, CA: Academic Press.

Burt, R. S. (1987). Social contagion and innovation, cohesion versus structural equivalence. *American Journal of Sociology, 92,* 1287–1335.

Burt, R. S. (1999). The social capital of opinion leaders. *Annals of the American Academy of Political and Social Science, 566,* 37–54.

Carter-Pokras, O. & Baquet, C. (2002). What is a "health disparity"? *Public Health Reports, 117,* 426–434.

Casterline, J. B. (2001). Diffusion processes and fertility transition: Introduction. In J. B. Casterline (ed.), *Diffusion processes and fertility transition: Selected perspectives* (pp. 1–38).

National Research Council Committee on Population. Division of Behavioral and Social Sciences and Education. Washington, DC: National Academy Press.

Castro, F. G., Elder, J., Coe, K., Tafoya-Barraza, L. M., Moratto, S., Campbell, N. & Talavera, G. (1995). Mobilizing churches for health promotion in Latino communities: Compañeros en la salud. *Journal of the National Cancer Institute Monographs, 18,* 127–135.

Cobb, P., Confrey, J., diSessa, A., Lehrer, R. & Schauble, L. (2003). Design experiments in educational research. *Educational Researcher, 32*(1), 9–13.

Cohen, D. (1990). A revolution in one classroom: The case of Mrs. Oublier. *Educational Evaluation and Policy Analysis, 12,* 311–344.

Cole, R. E. (1998). The macropolitics of organizational change: A comparative analysis of the spread of small-group activities. In J. Van Maanen (ed.), *Qualitative Studies of Organizations* (pp. 95–125). Thousand Oaks, CA: Sage.

Collins, A., Joseph, D. & Bielaczyc, K. (2004). Design research: Theoretical and methodological issues. *Journal of the Learning Sciences, 13,* 15–42.

Conell, C. & Cohn, S. (1995). Learning from other people's actions: Environmental variation and diffusion in French coal mining strikes, 1890–1935. *American Journal of Sociology, 101,* 366–403.

Crandall, D. P. (1982). *A study of dissemination efforts supporting school improvement,* Volumes 3–4. Andover, MA: The NETWORK, Inc.

Dearing, J. W. (2004). Improving the state of health programming by using diffusion theory. *Journal of Health Communication, 9,* 21–36.

Dearing, J. W. (2005). On the gyant's shoulders: Purposive diffusion as an outcome of the diffusion paradigm. In A. Griffen & C. C. Otnes (eds), *16th Paul D. Converse Symposium* (pp. 152–162). Chicago, IL: American Marketing Association.

Dearing, J. W. & Meyer, G. (1994). An exploratory tool for predicting adoption decisions. *Science Communication, 16,* 43–57.

Dearing, J. W., Larson, R. S., Cline, G., Morrison, K., Phillips, C., Brummans, B. H. J. M., et al. (2001). *Cluster evaluation final report and guide for strategic grantmaking with communities.* Final report about the Comprehensive Community Health Models initiative to the W. K. Kellogg Foundation. East Lansing, MI: Health & Risk Communication Center, Michigan State University.

Dearing, J. W., Meyer, G. & Kazmierczak, J. (1994). Portraying the new: Communication between university innovators and potential users. *Science Communication, 16,* 11–42.

Dede, C. (2004). If design-based research is the answer, what is the question? A commentary on Collins, Joseph, and Bielaczyc; diSessa and Cobb; and Fishman, Marx, Blumenthal, Krajcik, and Soloway in the *JLS* special issue on design-based research. *Journal of the Learning Sciences, 13,* 105–114.

diSessa, A. A. & Cobb, P. (2004). Ontological innovation and the role of theory in design experiments. *Journal of the Learning Sciences, 13,* 77–103.

Ennett, S. T., Tobler, N. S., Ringwalt, C. & Flewellin, R. L. (1994). How effective is drug abuse resistance education? A meta-analysis of Project D.A.R.E. outcome evaluations. *American Journal of Public Health, 84,* 1394–1401.

Evans, C. E., Haynes, B. R., Birkett, N. J., Gilbert, J. R., Taylor, D. W., Sackett, D. L., Johnston, M. E. & Hewson, S. A. (1986). Does a mailed continuing education program improve physician performance? *Journal of the American Medical Association, 25,* 501–504.

Fishman, B., Marx, R. W., Blumenfeld, P., Krajcik, J. & Soloway, E. (2004). Creating a framework for research on systematic technology innovations. *Journal of the Learning Sciences, 13,* 43–76.

Freedman, R. & Takeshita, Y. (1969). *Family planning in Taiwan: An experiment in social change.* Princeton, NJ: Princeton University Press.

Fullan, M. (1985). Change process and strategies at the local level. *Elementary School Journal, 84,* 391–420.

Fullan, M. (1992). *Successful school improvement: The implementation perspective and beyond.* Philadelphia, PA: Open University Press.

Garrison, B. (2001). Diffusion of online information technologies in newspaper newsrooms. *Journalism*, 2, 221–239.

Grubler, A. (1996). Time for a change: On the patterns of diffusion of innovation. *Daedalus, 125*, 19–42.

Handelsman, J., Ebert-May, D., Beichner, R., Bruns, P., Chang, A., DeHaan, R., et al. (2004). Scientific teaching. *Science, 304*, 521–522.

Hibbard, J. H., Slovic, P., Peters, E. & Finucane, M. L. (2002). Strategies for reporting health plan performance information to consumers: Evidence from controlled studies. *Health Services Research, 37*, 291–313.

Hornik, R. & McAnany, E. (2001). Mass media and fertility change. In J. B. Casterline (ed.), *Diffusion processes and fertility transition: Selected perspectives* (pp. 207–239). National Research Council Committee on Population, Division of Behavioral and Social Sciences and Education. Washington, DC: National Academy Press.

Horst, D. P. (1975). *Evaluation of the field test of Project Information Packages: Volume II. Recommendations for revisions.* Los Altos, CA: RMC Research Corporation; Menlo Park, CA: Stanford Research Institute.

Hutchinson, J. & Huberman, M. (1993). *Knowledge dissemination and use in science and mathematics education: A literature review* (NSF EHR/RED Report No. 93–75). Arlington, VA: National Science Foundation.

Jacoby, I. & Clark, S. M. (1986). Direct mailing as a means of disseminating NIH consensus statements. *Journal of the American Medical Association, 255*, 1328–1330.

Jick, T. D. (1979). Mixing qualitative and quantitative methods: Triangulation in action. *Administrative Science Quarterly, 24*, 602–611.

Kanouse, D. E. & Jacoby, I. (1988). When does information change practitioners' behavior? *International Journal of Technology Assessment in Health Care, 4*, 27–33.

Katz, E. & Lazarsfeld, P. F. (1955). *Personal influence: The part played by people in the flow of mass communications.* New York: Free Press.

Kelly, A. E. (2003). Research as design. *Educational Researcher, 32*(1), 3–4.

Kelly, A. E. (2004). Design research in education: Yes, but is it methodological? *Journal of the Learning Sciences, 13*, 115–128.

Kelly, J. A., Murphy, D. A., Sikkema, K. J., McAuliffe, T. L., Roffman, R. A., Solomon, et al. (1997). Randomized, controlled community-level HIV prevention intervention for sexual-risk behavior among homosexual men in U.S. cities. *Lancet, 350*, 1500–1505.

Kelly, J. A., St. Lawrence, J. S., Diaz, Y. E., Stevenson, L. Y., Hauth, A. C., Brasfield, T. L., et al. (1991). HIV risk behavior reduction following intervention with key opinion leaders of the population: An experimental analysis. *American Journal of Public Health, 81*, 168–171.

Kelly, J. A., St. Lawrence, J. S., Stevenson, L. Y., Hauth, A. C., Kalichman, S. C. & Murphy, D. A. (1992). Community AIDS/HIV risk reduction: The effects of endorsements by popular people in three cities. *American Journal of Public Health, 82*, 1483–1489.

Kerckhoff, A. C., Back, K. W. & Miller, N. (1965). Sociometric patterns in hysterical contagion. *Sociometry, 28*, 2–15.

Kezar, A. & Eckel, P. (eds) (2000). Moving beyond the gap between research and practice in higher education. *New directions for higher education, 110*. San Francisco: Jossey-Bass.

Kidder, L. H. & Fine, M. (1987). Qualitative and quantitative methods: When stories converge. *New Directions for Program Evaluation, 35*, 57–75.

LaRose, R. & Atkin, C. K. (1992). Audiotext and the re-invention of the telephone as a mass medium. *Journalism Quarterly, 69*, 413–421.

LaRose, R. & Hoag, A. (1996). Organizational adoptions of the Internet and the clustering of innovations. *Telematics and Informatics, 13*, 49–61.

Lenfant, C. (2003). Clinical research to clinical practice—lost in translation? *New England Journal of Medicine, 349*, 868–874.

Leonard-Barton, D. (1985). Experts as negative opinion leaders in the diffusion of a technological innovation. *Journal of Consumer Research, 11*, 914–926.

Leonard-Barton, D. (1988). Implementation as mutual adaptation of technology and organization. *Research Policy*, *17*, 251–267.

Leonard-Barton, D. & Rogers, E. M. (1980). Voluntary simplicity: Precursor or fad? Paper presented at the annual conference of the American Association for the Advancement of Science, San Francisco, CA, January.

Lomas, J. (1991). Words without action? The production, dissemination, and impact of consensus recommendations. *Annual Review of Public Health*, *12*, 41–65.

Lomas, J., Anderson, G. M., Domnick-Pierre, K., Vayda, E., Engin, M. W. & Hannah, W. J. (1989). Do practice guidelines guide practice? The effect of a consensus statement on the practice of physicians. *New England Journal of Medicine*, *321*, 1306–1311.

Lomas, J., Enkin, M., Anderson, G. M., Hannah, W. J., Vayda, E. & Singer, J. (1991). Opinion leaders vs audit and feedback to implement practice guidelines. *Journal of the American Medical Association*, *265*, 2202–2207.

Louis, K. S. & Rosenblum, S. (1981). Designing and managing interorganizational networks. Cambridge, MA: Abt Associates, Inc.

Manning, M. C., Bearden, W. O. & Madden, T. J. (1995). Consumer innovativeness and the adoption process. *Journal of Consumer Psychology*, *4*, 329–345.

Mayer, J. P. & Davidson, W. S. (2000). Dissemination of innovation as social change. In J. Rappaport & E. Seidman (eds), *Handbook of community psychology* (pp. 421–438). New York: Kluwer/Plenum.

McAlister, A. (2000). Action-oriented mass communication. In J. Rappaport & E. Seidman (eds), *Handbook of community psychology* (pp. 379–396). New York: Kluwer/Plenum.

Mintrom, M. (1997). Policy entrepreneurs and the diffusion of innovation. *American Journal of Political Science*, *41*, 914–926.

Mintrom, M. (2000). *Policy entrepreneurs and school choice*. Washington, DC: Georgetown University Press.

Mittman, B. S., Tonesk, X. & Jacobson, P. D. (1992). Implementing clinical practice guidelines: Social influence strategies and practitioner behavior change. *Quality Review Bulletin*, *December*, 413–422.

Morgan, D. L. (1998). Practical strategies for combining qualitative and quantitative methods: Applications to health research. *Qualitative Health Research*, *8*, 362–376.

Mossberger, K. (2000). *The politics of ideas and the spread of enterprise zones*. Washington, DC: Georgetown University Press.

National Science Foundation (2002). *Learning and education: Building knowledge, understanding its implications*. Summary of the panel on issues related to obtaining impact from NSF studies of STEM education. Arlington, VA: National Science Foundation.

Neumann, A., Pallas, A. M. & Peterson, P. L. (1999). Preparing education practitioners to practice education research. In E. C. Lagemann & L. S. Shulman (eds), *Issues in education research* (pp. 247–288). San Francisco, CA: Jossey-Bass.

Newell, S. & Swan, J. (1995). Professional associations as important mediators of the innovation process. *Science Communication*, *16*, 371–387.

O'Brien, D. J., Raedeke, A. & Hassinger, E. W. (1998). The social networks of leaders in more or less viable communities six years later: A research note. *Rural Sociology*, *63*, 109–127.

Palmore, J. A, (1967). The Chicago snowball: A study of the flow of influence and diffusion of family planning information. In D. J. Bogue (ed.), *Sociological contributions to family planning research*. Chicago: Community and Family Study Center, University of Chicago.

Puska, P., Nissinen, A., Tuomilehto, J., Salonen, J. T., Koskela, K., McAlister, A. et al. (1985). The community-based strategy to prevent coronary heart disease: Conclusions from ten years of the North Karelia Project. *Annual Review of Public Health*, *6*, 147–193.

Raizen, S. A. (1979). Dissemination programs at the National Institute of Education. *Knowledge*, *1*, 259–291.

Retherford, R. & Palmore, J. (1983). Diffusion processes affecting fertility regulation. In R. A. Bulatao & R. D. Lee (eds), *Determinants of fertility in developing countries* (pp. 295–339). New York: Academic Press.

Rogers, E. M. (1973). *Communication strategies for family planning*. New York: Free Press.

Rogers, E. M. (2003). *Diffusion of innovations* (5th ed.). New York: Free Press.

Rogers, E. M. & Kincaid, D. L. (1981). *Communication networks: Toward a new paradigm for research*. New York: Free Press.

Rutenberg, N. & Watkins, S. C. (1997). The buzz outside the clinics: Conversations and contraception in Kenya. *Studies in Family Planning, 28*, 290–307.

Schwartz, B. (2004). *The paradox of choice: Why more is less*. New York: HarperCollins.

Sen, L. K. (1969). *Opinion leadership in India: A study of interpersonal communication in eight villages* (Research Report 22). Project on the Diffusion of Innovations in Rural Societies. Hyderabad, India: National Institute of Community Development.

Sieber, S., Louis, K. & Mertzger, L. (1972). *The use of educational knowledge: Evaluation of the Pilot State Dissemination Program*, Volumes 1–2. New York: Columbia University Bureau of Applied Social Research.

Singhal, A. & Rogers, E. M. (2003). *Combating AIDS: Communication strategies in action*. New Delhi, India: Sage.

Snyder, J., Bolin, F. & Zumwalt, K. (1996). Curriculum implementation. In P. W. Jackson (ed.), *Handbook of research on curriculum* (pp. 402–435). New York: Macmillan.

Stahl, S. A. (1999). Why innovations come and go (and mostly go): The case of whole language. *Educational Researcher, 28*(8), 13–22.

Stokes-Berry, F. & Flowers, G. (1999). Public entrepreneurs in the policy process: Performance-based budgeting reform in Florida. *Journal of Public Budgeting, Accounting & Financial Management, 11*, 578–617.

Stover, J., Walker, N., Garnett, G. P., Salomon, J. A., Stanecki, K. A., Ghys, P. D., et al. (2002). Can we reverse the HIV/AIDS pandemic with an expanded response? *Lancet, 360*, 73–77.

Studlar, D. T. (1999). Diffusion of tobacco control in North America. *Annals of the American Academy of Political and Social Science, 566*, 68–79.

Tornatzky, L. G. & Klein, K. J. (1982). Innovation characteristics and adoption-implementation: A meta-analysis of findings. *IEEE Transactions on Engineering Management, EM-29*, 28–45.

Tversky, A. & Kahneman, D. (1982). Causal schemas in judgments under uncertainty. In D. Kahneman, P. Slovic & A. Tversky (eds), *Judgment under uncertainty: Heuristics and biases* (pp. 117–128). Cambridge: Cambridge University Press.

Valente, T. W. (1995). *Network models of the diffusion of innovations*. Cresskill, NJ: Hampton Press.

Valente, T. W. & Davis, R. L. (1999). Accelerating the diffusion of innovations using opinion leaders. *Annals of the American Academy of Political and Social Science, 566*, 55–67.

Viswanath, K., McDonald, D. G. & Lavrakas, P. J. (2000). *Class versus place: Models for diffusion and adoption of new communication technologies*. Paper presented at the conference of the American Association for Public Opinion Research, Portland, OR, May.

Watkins, S. C. & Danzi, A. D. (1994). Women's gossip and social change: Childbirth and fertility control among Italian and Jewish women in the United States, 1920–1940. *Gender and Society, 9*, 469–490.

Weimann, G. (1994). *The influentials: People who influence people*. Albany: State University of New York Press.

White, R. (2001). The revolution in research on science teaching. In V. Richardson (ed.), *Handbook of research on teaching* (4th ed.). Washington, DC: American Educational Research Association.

Wollons, R. (ed.) (2000). *Kindergartens and cultures: The global diffusion of an idea*. New Haven, CT: Yale University Press.

Zaritsky, R., Kelly, A. E., Flowers, W., Rogers, E. & O'Neill, P. (2003). Clinical design sciences: A view from sister design efforts. *Educational Researcher, 32*(1), 32–34.

Index